Praise for

THROUGH WOMEN'S EYES

"With compelling visual sources and imaginatively selected primary documents, Ellen DuBois and Lynn Dumenil draw the reader into the historical moment. On every page, history is tangible, engaging, and real. Beautifully written and cogently argued, *Through Women's Eyes* will stand as the defining text in U.S. women's history for years to come."

— VICKI RUIZ, *University of California, Irvine*

"The visual sources are delightful and the accompanying essays are critical to helping students see how to analyze such material."

— JOHN R. M. WILSON, *Vanguard University*

"I am an enthusiastic admirer of *Through Women's Eyes*. Its many resources allow for the varied learning styles of my community college students."

— MARY C. PRUITT, *Minneapolis Community & Technical College*

"Creation of a readable narrative [in women's history] has been at least thirty-five years in the making."

— SARAH H. GORDON, *Quinnipiac University*

"This text has it all—a lively, coherently organized narrative; coverage of key developments in both national and women's history; a stunning array of primary sources; and a remarkable collection of visual images. Students will be captivated by its engaging style, user-friendly organization, and riveting images, while teachers will find it extremely effective in presenting information and encouraging students to think critically."

—SUSAN HARTMANN, *The Ohio State University*

"Addressing racial, cultural, and ethnic diversity was one of my primary concerns and a reason for selecting *Through Women's Eyes.*"

—LISA MILES BUNKOWSKI, *Park University*

"DuBois and Dumenil have created an excellent textbook. . . . I was very impressed with the variety of primary sources."

—DEBRA MEYERS, *Northern Kentucky University*

"The book reminds students how the points in women's history fit into the bigger picture of U.S. history."

—AMY BIX, *Iowa State University*

"The inclusion of an appendix with important documents related to both women's history and 'traditional' U.S. history makes this book particularly appealing. You could teach women's history on the moon because everything is there for you."

—KAREN MANNERS SMITH, *Emporia State University*

"*Through Women's Eyes* is really excellent, a model for textbooks. It's the best general text in American women's history on the market."

— BARI WATKINS, *Ohio University–Lancaster*

"*Through Women's Eyes* filled a void in the field of women in American history! I love how it works within a historic framework and yet takes care to describe individual women's lives."

— APRIL HEASLIP, *Greenfield Community College*

"I am so delighted with the companion Web site! I know that my class will be better because of the availability of the collection of things on the Web site."

— DANIELLE ALEXANDER, *Napa Valley College*

Second Edition

THROUGH WOMEN'S EYES

An American History

WITH DOCUMENTS

Volume Two: Since 1865

Second Edition

THROUGH WOMEN'S EYES

An American History
WITH DOCUMENTS

Volume Two: Since 1865

Ellen Carol DuBois
UNIVERSITY OF CALIFORNIA,
LOS ANGELES

Lynn Dumenil
OCCIDENTAL COLLEGE

BEDFORD/ST. MARTIN'S
Boston ◆ New York

For Bedford/St. Martin's

Publisher for History: Mary Dougherty
Director of Development for History: Jane Knetzger
Executive Editor for History: William J. Lombardo
Developmental Editor: Kathryn Abbott
Senior Production Editor: Deborah Baker
Senior Production Supervisor: Joe Ford
Executive Marketing Manager: Jenna Bookin Barry
Editorial Assistant: Alix Roy
Copyeditor: Janet Renard
Text Design: Anna Palchik
Indexer: Steve Csipke
Cover Design: Donna Lee Dennison
Cover Art: L to r: Reuters/CORBIS; Library of Congress, Prints and Photographs Division, U.S. News & World Report Magazine Photograph Collection; Time & Life Pictures/Getty Images; Nevada Historical Society; National Portrait Gallery, Smithsonian Institution/Art Resource, NY.
Composition: Pine Tree Composition, Inc.
Cartography: Mapping Specialists Ltd.
Printing and Binding: R.R. Donnelley & Sons Company

President: Joan E. Feinberg
Editorial Director: Denise B. Wydra
Director of Marketing: Karen R. Soeltz
Director of Editing, Design, and Production: Marcia Cohen
Assistant Director of Editing, Design, and Production: Elise S. Kaiser
Managing Editor: Elizabeth M. Schaaf

Library of Congress Control Number: 2008925874

Manufactured in the United States of America.

3 2 1 0 9 8
f e d c b a

For information, write: Bedford/St. Martin's, 75 Arlington Street, Boston, MA 02116 (617-399-4000)

ISBN-10: 0-312-46887-3 (Combined edition)   ISBN-13: 978-0-312-46887-3
          0-312-46888-1 (Volume One)   978-0-312-46888-0
          0-312-46889-X (Volume Two)   978-0-312-46889-7

For Daniel Horowitz

and in memory of Lawrence W. Levine

PREFACE
FOR INSTRUCTORS

WHEN WE CONCEPTUALIZED the first edition of *Through Women's Eyes: An American History with Documents,* we were confident in our vision for an inclusive and diverse U.S. women's history that combined narrative and documents into one text. We have been thoroughly delighted that this book has resonated with instructors and students alike. We are pleased that others share our belief that U.S. women's history is U.S. history and vice versa. In constructing this textbook, we self-consciously followed the lead of Mary Ritter Beard, when she expressed the hope that her book, *America Through Women's Eyes,* first published in 1933, would "illustrate, if in a fragmentary way, the share of women in the development of American Society—their activity, their thought about their labor, and their thought about the history they have helped to make or have observed in the making."[1] In this new edition, we have drawn upon new scholarship published since the appearance of the first edition and have benefited tremendously from the insights of reviewers and adopters of the first edition of *Through Women's Eyes.*

APPROACH AND FORMAT

Through Women's Eyes: An American History with Documents challenges the separation of "women's history" from what students, in our experience, think of as "real history." We treat all central developments of American history, always through women's eyes, so that students may experience the broad sweep of the nation's past from a new and illuminating perspective. *Through Women's Eyes* combines in-depth treatment of well-known aspects of the history of women, such as the experiences of Lowell mill girls and slave women, the cult of true womanhood, and the rise of feminism, with developments in U.S. history not usually considered from the perspective of women, including the conquest of the Americas, the American Revolution, Civil War battlefields, post–World War II anti-communism, the civil rights movement, and the increasingly visible role that women have played in recent politics. Our goal of a full integration of women's history and U.S. history is pragmatic as well as principled. We recognize that the students who read *Through Women's Eyes* may have little background in U.S. history, that they will be learning the nation's history as they follow women through it.

At the same time that we broaden the conception of women's and U.S. history, we offer an inclusive view of the lives of American women. In this edition, we have

[1]Mary Ritter Beard, ed., *America Through Women's Eyes* (New York: Macmillan Co., 1933), 9.

strived to include more coverage of the broad range of classes, ethnicities, religions, and regions that constitute the historical experiences of U.S. women. We continue to decenter the narrative from an emphasis on white privileged women to bring ethnic and racial minorities and wage earning women from the margins to the center of our story. In providing an integrated analysis of the rich variety of women that includes ethnic and racial diversity and class, immigrant status, geographical, and sexual orientation differences, we have also explored the dynamics of relationships between women. Examples of sisterhood emerge from our pages, but so too do the hierarchical relations of class and race and other sources of tensions that erected barriers between women.

Now available in two volumes as well as the combined version.   The format of *Through Women's Eyes* elicited praise from scholars and teachers of U.S. women's history. In response to adopters' enthusiasm for the first edition of *Through Women's Eyes* and their desire to have the text more compatible with their teaching format, this book is now available in separate volumes for courses that do not cover all of women's history: Volume One, To 1900 (Chapters 1–7); and Volume Two, Since 1865 (Chapters 6–12).

In addition, the second edition includes even more written and visual primary sources. Just as many of our students hold preconceived notions of women's history as an intriguing adjunct to "real history," they often equate the historian's finished product with historical "truth." We remain determined to reveal the relationship between secondary and original sources, to show history as a dynamic process of investigation and interpretation rather than a set body of facts and figures. To this end, we divide each of our chapters into narrative text and primary-source essays. Of the essays, 20 center on written documents, providing more than 84 readings ranging from diaries, letters, and memoirs to poems, newspaper accounts, and public testimony. Our 16 visual essays collect over 130 images extending from artifacts, engravings, and portraits to photographs, cartoons, and television screen shots.

Together, the sources reveal to students the wide variety of primary evidence from which history is crafted. Our documentary and visual essays not only allow for focused treatment of many topics — for example, the experience of Native American women before and after European conquest, women on the Civil War battlefields, the Great Migration of African Americans in the World War I era, women's use of public spaces in the early twentieth century, popular culture in the 1950s, the impact of the 1960s and 1970s feminist movement on workplace practices, and the "third wave" feminist revival of the 1990s — but also provide ample guidance for students to analyze historical documents thoughtfully. Each essay offers advice about evaluating the sources presented and poses questions for analysis intended to foster students' ability to think independently and critically. Substantive headnotes to the sources and plentiful cross-references between the narrative and the essays further encourage students to appreciate the relationship between historical sources and historical writing.

NEW TO THIS EDITION

For this new edition, we have built on the strengths of the first edition of *Through Women's Eyes,* while expanding the coverage of a number of topics and offering fresh new document essays and illustrations. By adding new chapters at the beginning and end of the text, we have enhanced its global framework and chronological reach. The second edition provides new material on the experiences of African women, Native American women, and European women in the era before and after the establishment of the first European New World colonies and on the impact of modern globalization on women's work and political activism. In this edition, our treatment of recent history includes more on conservative women in the post–World War II era and on feminism in the late twentieth and early twenty-first centuries. We have also expanded our treatment of key themes such as sexuality and popular culture.

New visual sources essays include "Material Culture in Colonial America," "Depictions of Family in Colonial America," "Alice Austen: Gilded Age Photographer," and "Feminism and the Drive for Equality in the Workforce." Some visual essays from the first edition have also been significantly revised, notably "Women in the World," which devotes more attention to immigration and to women in the military. These essays, plus additional in-text visuals and maps allow for a richer understanding of U.S. women's history.

New primary documents essays include "African Women in the Slave Trade," Elizabeth Cady Stanton's articles in nineteenth-century women's rights magazines, Zitkala-Ša on Indian childhood and boarding schools, "Documents from the Women's Liberation Movement," and "Is a Working Mother a Threat to the Home?" from a 1958 forum published in the *Ladies' Home Journal.*

FEATURES AND PEDAGOGY

We are proud as well of the pedagogical features we provide to help students enter into and absorb the text. Each chapter opens with a *thematic introduction* that starts with a particular person or moment in time chosen to pique students' interest and segues into a clear statement of the central issues and ideas of the chapter. An *illustrated chapter timeline* alerts students to the main events covered in the narrative and relates women's experience to U.S. history by visually linking key developments. At the close of each narrative section, an *analytic conclusion* revisits central themes and provides a bridge to the next chapter.

Beyond the visual sources presented in the essays, *over 95 historical images and 14 maps and graphs* extend and enliven the narrative, accompanied by substantive captions that relate the illustration to the text and help students unlock the image. Also animating the narrative while complementing the documentary essays are *34 primary-source excerpts drawn from classic texts* featuring women such as Anne Hutchinson, Catharine Beecher, Sojourner Truth, Margaret Sanger, and Ella Baker. At the end of each chapter, we provide *plentiful footnotes* and *an annotated bibliography* that gives students a myriad of opportunities for reading and research beyond the boundaries of the textbook.

In addition, we open the book with an *Introduction for Students* that discusses the evolution of women's history as a field and the approach we took in capturing its exciting state today. An *extensive Appendix* includes not only tables and charts focused on U.S. women's experience over time but, in keeping with our mission to integrate women's history and American history, fundamental documents relating to U.S. history: the Declaration of Independence, the U.S. Constitution and its amendments, the Seneca Falls Declaration of Sentiments, a compendium of presidential administrations, and annotated extracts of Supreme Court cases of major relevance to U.S. history "through women's eyes."

ADDITIONAL RESOURCES

Bedford/St. Martin's has published both online and print resources relevant to the women's history course that complements our textbook.

Book Companion Site at bedfordstmartins.com/duboisdumenil   Expanded and revised for this edition, the book companion site provides instructors and students with new and improved resources for teaching and learning U.S. women's history. Resources include a new online instructor's resource guide that includes revised assignment suggestions, term paper suggestions, teaching tips and lecture strategies, multiple-choice questions, and mid-term and final exam suggestions. New features of the book's companion Web site include television and film suggestions, tips on working with visual sources, and content for the classroom using i<clicker. Through Bedford/St. Martin's Make History link, the book companion site integrates maps, selected images, primary documents, links to relevant Web sites, and online research resources. The book's companion Web site also contains new and revised resources for students, including annotated chapter outlines, identification terms, focus questions, and notetaking outlines.

Trade Books   Titles published by sister companies—Farrar, Straus and Giroux; Henry Holt and Company; Hill & Wang; Picador; and St. Martin's Press—are available at a 50 percent discount when packaged with Bedford/St. Martin's textbooks. For more information, visit bedfordstmartins.com/tradeup.

Bedford Series in History and Culture   The more than 80 American history titles in this highly praised series include a number focused on women's history and combine first-rate scholarship, historical narrative, and important primary documents for undergraduate courses. Each book is brief, inexpensive, and focused on a specific topic or period. Package discounts are available.

ACKNOWLEDGMENTS

Textbooks are for learning, and writing this one has taught us a great deal. We have learned from each other and have enjoyed the richness of the collaborative process. But we have also benefited immensely from the opportunity to read and assess the works of literally hundreds of scholars whose research and insights have made this book possible.

We continue to be grateful to friends and colleagues who reviewed the first edition and suggested revisions for the second. For reading this edition's Chapters 1 and 2, we thank Alice Nash of the University of Massachusetts at Amherst. For reading through the entire manuscript, we thank Danielle Alexander, Napa Valley College; Amy Bix, Iowa State University; Lisa Miles Bunkowski, Park University; Mina Carson, Oregon State University; Sarah H. Gordon, Quinnipiac University; April Heaslip, Greenfield Community College; Paula Hinton, Tennessee Technological University; Rebecca Mead, Northern Michigan University; Debra Meyers, Northern Kentucky University; Mary C. Pruitt, Minneapolis Community & Technical College; Linda P. Pitelka, Maryville University; Jennifer Ritterhouse, Utah State University; Karen Manners Smith, Emporia State University; Jean A. Stuntz, Western Texas A&M University; Connie Tripp, College of the Canyons; Bari Watkins, Ohio University-Lancaster; Karol Weaver, Susquehanna University; and John R. M. Wilson, Vanguard University.

Numerous colleagues, former students, researchers, and archivists graciously answered phone and e-mail queries, helping us to find facts, quotations, images, and references. Thanks to Steve Aron, Sharla Fett, Kevin Terraciano, Ann D. Gordon, Kate Flint, Ramón Gutiérrez, Lisa Sousa, Ruth Rosen, and Sheila Tobias. Nicole Rebec provided admirable research assistance and we are also thankful for the assistance of archivists at Tamiment Library, New York University. We both want to thank Rumi Yasutake and her Japan-based team, who are preparing a Japanese-language version of *Through Women's Eyes* and in the process helped us to clarify our own text at crucial points. Lynn thanks Norman S. Cohen for his continued enthusiasm for the project.

We have a great deal of admiration for the people at Bedford/St. Martin's who worked so hard to bring both editions of this book to fruition. Former president Charles H. Christensen and current president Joan E. Feinberg have been warmly enthusiastic, as have editorial director Denise Wydra, publisher Mary Dougherty, director of development Jane Knetzger, senior marketing manager Jenna Bookin Barry, and editorial assistant Alix Roy. We appreciate the enthusiastic engagement of our developmental editor, Kathryn Abbott. Our first editor of *Through Women's Eyes*, Elizabeth Welch, has also continued to be an inspiration. Rose Corbett-Gordon did a superb job researching and clearing photo images; Sandy Schechter and Linda Winters cleared text permissions; Janet Renard copyedited the manuscript; Anna Palchik designed the interior of the book; Donna Dennison designed the cover; and Deborah Baker oversaw the production process.

We viewed the first edition of *Through Women's Eyes* as an exciting new departure, and the wide adoption and warm reception of reviewers and adopters has confirmed our aspirations. The revisions for this new edition benefited significantly from the comments of instructors who have used the textbook in their classes. We also reiterate, as we noted in the first edition, that this book would not have been possible without the dynamic developments and extraordinary output in the field of U.S. women's history since Mary Beard wrote her book. In 1933 Beard acknowledged that the "collection, editing, sifting and cataloguing of sources dealing with women's work and thought in the making of civilization" was ground as yet uncultivated.[2] We have been fortunate to reap a rich harvest from the scholarly literature of the last forty years, a literature that has allowed us to express the diversity of women's lives and to conceive of U.S. history from a gendered perspective.

Finally, we dedicate this edition of *Through Women's Eyes* to Daniel Horowitz, and to the memory of Lawrence W. Levine. They taught us as undergraduates and graduates, inspired us with a great love of U.S. history, provided models for the kind of approach that blossomed into *Through Women's Eyes,* and supported us in all of our efforts.

[2]Ibid.

BRIEF CONTENTS

CONTENTS

CHAPTER 8
Power and Politics: Women in the Progressive Era, 1900–1920
454

CHAPTER 11
Modern Feminism and American Society, 1965–1980
664

CHAPTER 12
U.S. Women in a Global Age, 1980–Present
734

SPECIAL FEATURES

INTRODUCTION
FOR STUDENTS

In reading this textbook, you will encounter a rich array of source materials and a narrative informed by a wealth of scholarship, so you may be surprised to learn that women's history is a comparatively new field. When Mary Ritter Beard, the founding mother of women's history in the United States, assembled *America Through Women's Eyes* in 1933, she argued that an accurate understanding of the nation's past required as much consideration of women's experience as of men's. But so limited were the sources available to her that she had no choice but to present the first women-centered American history as a spotty anthology of primary and secondary writings by a handful of women writers. Not until the 1970s, with the resurgence of feminism that you will read about in Chapter 11, did researchers start to give extensive attention to women's history. In that decade, history, along with other academic disciplines such as literature and sociology, underwent significant change as feminist scholars' desire to analyze as well as to protest women's unequal status fueled an extraordinary surge of investigation into women's experiences. Feminist theorists revived an obscure grammatical term, "gender," to distinguish the meaning that a particular society attaches to differences between men and women from "sex," or the unchanging biological differences between men and women. Because gender meaning varies over time and among societies, gender differences are both socially constructed and subject to change.

The concept of gender and the tools of history go together. If we are to move past the notion that what it means to be a woman never changes, we must look to the varying settings in which people assume female and male roles, with all their attendant expectations. Definitions of femininity and masculinity, family structures, what work is considered properly female or male, understandings of motherhood and of marriage, and women's involvement in public affairs all vary tremendously across time, are subject to large forces like economic development and warfare, and can themselves shape the direction of history. As historian Joan Scott forcefully argues, gender can be used as a tool of historical analysis, to explore not only how societies interpret differences between women and men but also how these distinctions can work to legitimize other hierarchical relations of power.[1]

This textbook draws on the rich theoretical and historical work of the past forty years to present a synthesis of American women's experiences. We begin Volume 1 with a discussion of the many meanings of "America" and end Volume 2 with a set of images that place women in the context of the globalized world of

---

[1]Joan Wallach Scott, "Gender: A Useful Category of Historical Analysis," *American Historical Review* 91, no. 5 (December 1986): 1067.

the twenty-first century. In between we highlight both the broad patterns of change concerning women's political, economic, and family lives and the diversity of American women's experiences.

As its title suggests, however, *Through Women's Eyes: An American History, with Documents* aims for more than an account of U.S. women's history. Beyond weaving together the wealth of scholarship available to U.S. women's historians, we seek to fulfill Mary Beard's vision of a text that covers the total range of the nation's history, placing women—their experiences, contributions, and observations—at the center. We examine major economic developments, such as the emergence of slavery as a labor system, the rise of factories in the early nineteenth century, the growth of an immigrant labor force, and the shift to corporate capitalism. We explore major political themes, from reform movements to political party realignments to the nation's many wars. We look at transformations in family and personal life, the rise of consumer and mass culture, the racial and ethnic heterogeneity of the nation's peoples, and shifting attitudes about sexuality. And we analyze international developments, beginning with the inter-relationship of the Americas, Europe, and Africa in the Atlantic world of the sixteenth and seventeenth centuries and ending with contemporary globalization. But as we do so, we analyze how women experienced these national developments and how they contributed to and shaped them.

THE HISTORY OF WOMEN'S HISTORY: FROM SEPARATE SPHERES TO MULTICULTURALISM

When the field of U.S. women's history began to take off as a scholarly endeavor in the 1970s, one particular form of gender analysis was especially influential. The "separate spheres" paradigm, as historians termed it, focused on the nineteenth-century ideology that divided social life into two mutually exclusive arenas: the private world of home and family, identified with women, and the public world of business and politics, identified with men. In a second phase, as scholarship on women of color increased, the primacy of the separate spheres interpretation gave way to a more nuanced interpretation of the diversity of women's experiences.

Separate Spheres and the Nineteenth-Century Gender System

Women's historians of the 1970s found in the nineteenth-century system of separate spheres the roots of the gender distinctions of their own time. They observed that although ideas about separate spheres had been of enormous importance in the nineteenth century, these ideas had received little to no attention in historical accounts. The approach that women's historians took was to re-vision this nineteenth-century gender system through women's eyes. They found that, although women's lives were tightly constricted by assumptions about their proper place within the family, expectations of female moral influence and a common sense of womanhood allowed women collectively to achieve a surprising degree of social authority.

The separate spheres paradigm proved a valuable approach, but it hid as much as it yielded about women's lives. Early on, historian Gerda Lerner observed that it was no coincidence that the notion of women's exclusive domesticity flourished just as factories were opening up and young women were going to work in them.[2] Because adherence to the ideology of separate spheres helped to distinguish the social standing of middle-class women from their factory-working contemporaries, Lerner urged that class relations and the growth of the female labor force be taken into account in understanding the influence that such ideas held. Subsequent historians have observed that the idealization of women within the domestic sphere coincided exactly with the decline of the economic importance of family production relative to factory production; and that just as class inequality began to challenge the nation's democratic self-understanding, American society came to define itself in terms of the separate spheres of men and women.

Additional problems emerged in the reliance on the separate spheres paradigm as the dominant basis for nineteenth-century U.S. women's history. Historian Nancy Hewitt contends that whatever sense of female community developed among nineteenth-century women rarely crossed class or race lines. On the contrary, hierarchical relationships — slave to mistress, immigrant factory worker to moneyed consumer, nanny to professional woman — have been central to the intricate tapestry of the historical female experience in America.[3] Even among the middle-class wives and mothers who did not work outside the home and whose family-based lives made them the central focus of separate spheres ideology, Linda Kerber urges historians not to confuse rhetoric with reality, ideological values with individual actions.[4] The lasting contribution of the historical exploration of separate spheres ideology is the recognition of the vital impact of gender differentiation on American history; the challenge posed by its critics is to develop a more complex set of portraits of women who lived in, around, and against these notions. As it matures, the field of women's history is able to move from appreciating the centrality of gender systems to accommodating and exploring conflicts and inequalities among women.

Toward a More Inclusive Women's History: Race and Ethnicity

The field of U.S. women's history has struggled to come to terms with the structures of racial inequality so central to the American national experience. As Peggy Pascoe observes, modern scholars have learned to think about race and gender in similar ways, no longer treating either as unchanging biological essences around which history forms but as social constructions that change meaning and content

---

[2] Gerda Lerner, "The Lady and the Mill Girl," *Midcontinent American Studies Journal* 10 (1969): 5–15.
[3] Nancy Hewitt, "Beyond the Search for Sisterhood: American Women's History in the 1990s," in Vicki Ruiz and Ellen Carol DuBois, eds., *Unequal Sisters: A Multicultural Reader in U.S. Women's History*, 3rd ed. (New York: Routledge, 2000), 1–19.
[4] Linda K. Kerber, "Separate Spheres, Female Worlds, Woman's Place: The Rhetoric of Women's History," *Journal of American History* 75, no. 1 (June 1988): 9–39.

over time and place.[5] Building on a century-long scholarly tradition in African American history, black women scholars started in the 1980s to chart new territory as they explored the interactions between systems of racial and gender inequality. Analyzing the implications of the denial to late nineteenth-century black women of the privileges granted white women, Evelyn Brooks Higginbotham observes that "gender identity is inextricably linked to and even determined by racial identity."[6]

Other scholars of color, especially Chicana feminists, advanced this thinking about racial hierarchy and its intersections with the structures of gender. They made it clear that the history of Chicanas could not be understood within the prevailing black-white model of racial interaction. The outlines of a multivocal narrative of U.S. women's history that acknowledge women's diversity in terms of race, class, ethnicity, and sexual orientation are advanced by *Unequal Sisters: A Multicultural Reader in U.S. Women's History,* coedited by Vicki Ruiz and one of the authors of this text, Ellen Carol DuBois. This anthology of pathbreaking research pays particular attention to the historical experiences of Western women, noting that "the confluence of many cultures and races in this region — Native American, Mexican, Asian, Black, and Anglo" — required "grappling with race" from a multicultural perspective.[7] By using her own southwestern experience, Gloria Anzaldúa added the influential metaphor of "borderlands" to this approach to suggest that the division between different communities and personal identities is somewhat arbitrary and sometimes shifting.[8] This new approach took the logic of the historical construction of gender, so important to the beginning of women's history, and pushed it further by emphasizing an even greater fluidity of social positioning.

APPROACHING HISTORY *THROUGH WOMEN'S EYES*

How then to bring together a historical narrative told from such diverse and at times conflicting viewpoints? All written histories rely on unifying themes to organize what is otherwise a chaotic assembly of facts, observations, incidents, and people. Traditionally, American history employed a framework of steady national progress, from the colonial revolt against England to modern times. Starting in the 1960s, the writing of American history emphasized an alternative story line of the struggles of workers, slaves, Indians, and (to some degree) women, to overcome enduring inequalities. Initially, women's history emphasized the rise and fall of the

---

[5]Peggy Pascoe, "Gender," in Richard Wightman Fox and James Kloppenberg, eds., *A Companion to American Thought* (Cambridge, MA: Blackwell, 1995), 273.

[6]Evelyn Brooks Higginbotham, "African American Women's History and the Metalanguage of Race," *Signs* 17, no. 2 (Winter 1992): 254.

[7]Ellen Carol DuBois and Vicki L. Ruiz, eds., *Unequal Sisters: A Multicultural Reader in U.S. Women's History* (New York: Routledge, 1990), xii. This reader has three later editions (1994, 2000, 2008) that include substantially different articles.

[8]Gloria Anzaldúa, *La Frontera/Borderlands: The New Mestiza* (1987; San Francisco: Aunt Lute Books, 1999).

system of separate gender spheres, the limits of which we suggest above. In organizing *Through Women's Eyes,* we employ another framework, one that emphasizes three major themes that shaped the diversity of women's lives in American history—work, politics, and family and personal life.

Work and the Sexual Division of Labor

The theme of women's work reveals both stubborn continuities and dramatic changes. Women have always labored, always contributed to the productive capacity of their communities. Throughout American history, women's work has taken three basic forms—unpaid labor within the home, chattel slavery, and paid labor. The steady growth of paid labor, from the beginning of American industrialization in the 1830s to the present day (women now constitute essentially half of America's workforce), is one of the fundamental developments in this history. As the female labor force grew, its composition changed, by age, race, ethnicity, and class. By the mid-twentieth century, the working mother had taken over where once the working girl had predominated. We have also followed the repeated efforts of wage earning women to organize collectively in order to counter the power of their employers, doing so sometimes in conjunction with male workers and sometimes on their own. Always a small percentage of union members compared to men, women exhibited unanticipated militancy and radicalism in their fight with employers over union recognition and fair wages and hours.

Most societies divide women's work from men's, and America's history has been no exception. Feminist scholars designate this gender distinction as the "sexual division of labor." Yet the content of the sexual division of labor varies from culture to culture, a point made beginning with the discussion of Native American communities in the precolonial and colonial eras and of African women's agricultural labor in their native lands. When women first began to take on paid labor in large numbers, they did so primarily as servants and seamstresses; the nature of their work thus generally followed the household sexual division of labor. The persistence of sex segregation in the workforce has had many sources of support: employers' desire to have a cheap, flexible supply of labor; male workers' control over better jobs and higher wages; and women's own assumptions about their proper place.

The division between male and female work continued, and with it the low wages and limited opportunities on the women's side of the line. This was true even as what counted as women's jobs began to expand, and teaching and secretarial labor, once securely on the male side of the line, crossed over to become "feminized" job categories. American feminism in the late twentieth century has been committed to eroding this long-standing principle that work should be divided into male and female categories. As historian Alice Kessler-Harris puts it, feminists "introduced the language of sex discrimination onto the national stage, casting a new light on seemingly natural patterns of accommodating sex difference."[9] The

---

[9]Alice Kessler-Harris, *In Pursuit of Equity: Women, Men, and the Quest for Economic Citizenship in 20th-Century America* (New York: Oxford University Press, 2001), 245–46.

degree to which the sexual division of labor has been substantially breached— whether it is half achieved or half undone — we leave to our readers, who are part of this process, to determine.

Gender and the Meaning of Politics

The theme of politics in women's historical experience presents a different sort of challenge, for it is the *exclusion* of women from formal politics that is the obvious development in U.S. women's history, at least until 1920 when the Nineteenth Amendment granting woman suffrage was ratified. While the story of women's campaign for the vote plays an important role in our historical account, we have not portrayed the suffrage movement as a monolithic effort. Rather, we have attended to the inequalities of class and race and the strategic and ideological conflicts that ran throughout the movement. We have also stressed the varying political contexts, ranging from Reconstruction in the 1860s to the Populist upsurge in the 1890s to Progressivism in the 1910s, within which women fought for their voting rights. Finally, we have traced the significance of voting in U.S. women's history after the right to it was formally secured, following women's efforts to find their place—as voters and as office holders—in the American political system.

U.S. women's historians have gone beyond the drama surrounding the vote, its denial and its uses, to a more expansive sense of the political dimension of women's historical experience. Feminist scholars have forged a definition of politics that looks beyond the formal electoral arena to other sorts of collective efforts to change society, alter the distribution of power between groups, create and govern important institutions, and shape public policy. Women's historians have given concrete substance to this broad approach to female political involvement by investigating the tremendous social activism and civic engagement that thrived among women, especially through the long period during which they lacked formal political rights. "In order to bring together the history of women and politics," writes Paula Baker, "we need a more inclusive definition of politics . . . to include any action, formal or informal, taken to affect the course or behavior of government or the community."[10]

From this perspective, the importance of women in the realm of politics reaches back to the Iroquois women who elected chiefs and participated in decisions to go to war and the European women colonists who provided the crucial support necessary to sustain pre-Revolutionary boycotts against British goods in the struggle for national independence. Just a small sampling of this rich tradition of women's civic activity through the nineteenth century includes the thousands of New England women who before the Civil War signed petitions against slavery and Indian removal; the campaign begun by Ida B. Wells against the lynching of southern blacks; the ambitious late nineteenth-century national reform agenda of Frances Willard's Woman's Christian Temperance Union; and Jane Addams's lead-

---

[10]Paula Baker, "The Domestication of Politics: Women and American Political Society, 1780–1920," *American Historical Review* 89 (June 1984): 622.

ership in addressing problems of the urban immigrant poor and on behalf of international peace. "Women's organizations pioneered in, accepted and polished modern methods of pressure-group politics," observes historian Nancy Cott.[11]

Indeed, this sort of extra-electoral political activism extended into the twentieth century, incorporating women's challenges to the arms race of the post–World War II era and the civil rights leadership of women such as Ella Baker of the Southern Conference Leadership Conference in the 1950s and Dolores Huerta of the United Farm Workers union in the 1960s. This inclusive sense of what constitutes "politics" has not only enriched our understanding of women's history, but it has generated a more complex understanding of the nature of political power and process within U.S. history in general.

Given the theme of politics as one of the major frames for this book, what is the place of the politics of feminism in the tale we tell? There are many definitions of feminism, but perhaps the clearest is the tradition of organized social change by which women challenge gender inequality. The term "feminism" itself arose just as the woman suffrage movement was nearing victory, but the tradition to which it refers reaches back to the women's rights movements of the nineteenth century. Historical research has unearthed a great deal of breadth and diversity in the many campaigns and protests through which women from different groups, in different times and places, dealing with different challenges, expressed their discontent with the social roles allotted to them and pursued their ambitions for wider options, more individual freedom, and greater social authority.

Feminism and women's history are mutually informing. Feminism is one of the important subjects of women's history, and history is one of feminism's best tools. Knowing what the past has been for women, doing the scholarship that Anne Firor Scott calls "making the invisible woman visible," is a necessary resource in pressing for further change.[12] But feminism is also a method by which historians examine the past in terms of women's efforts to challenge, struggle, make change, and sometimes achieve progress. Like so many of the scholars on whom the authors of this text rely, we have worked from such a perspective, and the passion we have brought to this work has its roots in a feminist commitment to highlighting—and encouraging—women's active social role and contribution to history. For us, however, a women's history informed by feminism is not a simple exercise of celebration, but a continuing and critical examination of what we choose to examine in the past and the methods we use to do so.

The Role of Family and Personal Life

The third integrating category of *Through Women's Eyes* is the theme of family and personal life. In contrast to the categories of labor and politics, which have been recognized in all narratives of the nation's past, women's historians took the

---

[11]Nancy Cott, *The Grounding of American Feminism* (New Haven: Yale University Press, 1987), 95.
[12]Anne Firor Scott, "Making the Invisible Woman Visible: An Essay Review," *Journal of Southern History* 38, no. 4 (November 1972): 629–38.

lead in bringing family and personal life into the mainstream of American history. Indeed, one of the fundamental contributions of feminist scholarship has been to demonstrate that kinship and sexuality have not been static elements of human nature but have their own complex histories. We try to make this clear by discussing the variety of family patterns evident among Native Americans, immigrants, African Americans, white middle-class Americans, and other ethnic groups.

Over the span of American history, family life has gone from the very center of political power and economic production in the seventeenth and eighteenth centuries to a privileged arena of emotional life in the early twenty-first century. As we write this introduction, family life—who can marry whom, what forms of sexuality should be tolerated, who should care for children and how—have become topics of intense public contest and political positioning. Thus concepts and experiences of family and sexual life, once viewed as the essence of women's separate sphere, are increasingly understood as a major connection between private concerns and public issues.

The histories of both motherhood and female sexuality reveal this connection. Motherhood not only has been central to women's individual family lives but also has served larger functions as well. Within slave communities, mothers taught their children how to survive within and fight against their servitude. Among middle-class women in the nineteenth and early twentieth centuries, motherhood became an effective way to claim female public authority. In the 1950s, at the start of the Cold War between the United States and the former Soviet Union, radical women subverted intense anti-Communist interrogations under the cloak of motherhood, thus trumping one of the decade's most dramatic themes with another. The social significance of motherhood has been used for conservative political purposes as well, with claims about the centrality of women's maternal role to social order providing the fuel of the anti-feminist backlash of the 1970s and through it the emergence of a new political right wing.

When it comes to the subject of sexuality, historians have proved particularly innovative in learning to read through the euphemisms and silences that obscure women's sexual lives even more than men's. They have delved into documents left by guardians of sexual propriety about prostitutes and by lascivious masters about slave women, in order to imagine how the objects of these judgments themselves experienced these encounters. When historians set aside modern attitudes toward sexuality and reexamined the lives of seemingly prudish nineteenth-century middle-class women, they found, as Linda Gordon demonstrates, the origins of the American birth control movement and all the radical changes in women's lives that flowed from it.[13] No longer content to portray the history of female sexuality as a simple move from repression to freedom, historians have examined the changing understandings of female sexuality and its shifting purposes in the twentieth century, as it played a major role in advancing new standards of consumerism, and in

---

[13]Linda Gordon, *The Moral Property of Women: A History of Birth Control Politics in America* (1976; Urbana: University of Illinois Press, 2004).

modernizing—though not necessarily making more egalitarian—relations between men and women.

Perhaps historians of women have been most creative in learning to look beyond the heterosexual relations that traditionally have defined sexuality to explore the intimate, romantic, and ambiguously sexual relations among women themselves. Carroll Smith-Rosenberg pioneered in demonstrating how common romantic friendships among women were in the nineteenth century, describing them as "an intriguing and almost alien form of human relation, [which] flourished in a different social structure and amidst different sexual norms."[14] Historical work into what has come to be called "homosociality" has deepened understandings of sexuality overall. Thus, as with the concepts of gender and race, women's history has led us to view sexuality itself as socially constructed, not as biologically prescribed.

Sexuality has been an especially important site for historians to locate the intersections of race and gender. Middle-class white women's historical prominence rested in considerable part on the contrast between their reputed sexual innocence and propriety and the supposedly disreputable (and titillating) sexuality of women of color on the margins, such as black slaves, so-called Indian squaws, and Asian prostitutes. This intersection between sexuality and race has also been investigated from the position of women who found themselves on the other side of the vice-virtue divide. As historian Paula Giddings argues, the rising up of recently freed African American women against their reputations as sexually available and that of African American men as sexually predatory helped to generate the creation of a black middle class and "a distinctive mix which underlined Black women's activism for generations to come."[15]

These and other discoveries in the field of U.S. women's history have made this textbook possible. The rich body of scholarly literature developed over the past decades has also enabled us to achieve our goal of integrating women's history into U.S. history, of showing how material once separated as "women's history" contributes to a broader understanding of the nation's history. In *America Through Women's Eyes,* Mary Beard insisted that women not be rendered as the passive objects of men's actions but as makers of history themselves; and that they not be removed from the historical flow into a separate narrative, but that their history be understood as part and parcel of the full range of national experience. This has been our guiding principle in writing this textbook—and the reason we have titled it an American history "through women's eyes."

---

[14]Carroll Smith-Rosenberg, "The Female World of Love and Ritual," *Signs* 1 (1979): 1–29.
[15]Paula Giddings, *When and Where I Enter: The Impact of Black Women on Race and Sex in America* (New York: William Morrow, 1984), 50.

Second Edition

THROUGH WOMEN'S EYES

An American History

WITH DOCUMENTS

Volume Two: Since 1865

6

Reconstructing Women's Lives North and South

1865–1900

IDA B. WELLS, MARY KENNEY, AND M. CAREY THOMAS were all daughters of the Civil War era. Wells was born in 1862 to Mississippi slaves; Kenney in 1864 to Irish immigrants in Hannibal, Missouri; and Thomas in 1857 to a wealthy Baltimore Quaker family. Despite these great differences in background, the unfolding of each woman's life illustrates the forces that affected American women's history in the years after the Civil War and, in turn, women's capacity to be forces in the making of American history.

Wells (later Wells-Barnett) was shaped by the violent struggles between former slaves seeking to realize their emancipation and white southerners seeking to retain their racial dominance. As a journalist, Wells exposed new, brutal methods of white supremacy, and her work sparked an organized women's movement among African Americans. Kenney (later O'Sullivan) was a lifelong wage earner who recognized that workers needed to act collectively rather than individually to improve their lives. A pathbreaking female labor organizer, she helped form the Women's Trade Union League (WTUL) in 1903 (see pp. 458–59). Thomas, a self-proclaimed tomboy as a child who did not marry as an adult, became a pioneer of higher education for women. She was one of the first women to graduate from Cornell University and to receive a doctorate (in Switzerland), and she was the founding dean of Bryn Mawr College. In the post–Civil War (or postbellum) years, such individuals laid the basis for an era of extraordinary achievement by American women.

"Reconstruction" is the term used to describe the period of American history immediately after the Civil War, the revision of the U.S. Constitution to deal with the consequences of emancipation, the rebuilding of the South after the devastations of war, and the reconstitution of national unity after the trauma of sectional division. The formal period of Reconstruction lasted twelve years. It ended in 1877 when U.S. troops withdrew from the former Confederacy, leaving the South to work out its own troubled racial destiny without federal oversight and the North to concentrate on industrial development and economic growth.

The word "reconstruction" can also be used to cover a longer period, during which the U.S. economy was reconstituted entirely around industrial capitalism. The free labor ethic on which the Republican Party was founded evolved into a commitment to unbridled industrialization. The society's wealth, optimism, and productivity were not shared equally. On the contrary, the gap between rich and poor grew enormously during the postbellum years, producing great tension and violence between owners and workers. With chattel slavery eliminated, industrial society could no longer ignore its internal class divisions, and by the end of the century, conflict between labor and capital overtook the inequalities of race as the most overt challenge to national unity.

Women were reconstructing their lives in these years as well. In the defeated South, women emancipated from slavery grappled with the challenges and dangers of their tentative freedom, while their former mistresses sought to maintain the privileges of white supremacy under new conditions. In the North, a determined group of women sought equal political rights, and the woman suffrage movement came into its own. Industrial capitalism generated both a rapidly expanding female labor force and new leisure and wealth for middle- and upper-class women. Between 1865 and 1900, women's labor, the terms of appropriate womanhood within which women lived, and their scope for public action all expanded. By the end of the nineteenth century, the basis had been laid for an epoch of female assertion and accomplishment unparalleled in American history.

325

GENDER AND THE POSTWAR CONSTITUTIONAL AMENDMENTS

American history's first presidential assassination (Abraham Lincoln), followed quickly by its first presidential impeachment (Andrew Johnson), left the executive branch in shambles and the legislative branch in charge of national Reconstruction. Republicans controlled Congress, and former abolitionists, known as Radicals, controlled the Republican Party. To protect the North's victory and their party's control over Congress, the Radicals were determined to enfranchise the only population on whom the Republicans could depend in the defeated Confederacy—former slaves. In 1866, Radicals proposed an amendment to the U.S. Constitution to establish the citizenship of ex-slaves. The Fourteenth Amendment began with a simple, inclusive sentence: "All persons born or naturalized in the United States, and subject to the jurisdiction thereof, are citizens of the United States and of the State wherein they reside."

Leaders of the women's rights movement hoped to revise the Constitution and reconstruct democracy without distinction of either race *or* gender. Despite their best efforts, however, the ratification of the Fourteenth Amendment in 1868, followed by that of the Fifteenth Amendment in 1870, established black suffrage without reference to woman suffrage. Thwarted in Congress, these women turned to the U.S. Supreme Court to argue that women's political rights were included within the new constitutional definitions of national citizenship and political rights.

Their efforts failed. The only actual enfranchisement of women in the Reconstruction era occurred in the territories of Wyoming (1869) and Utah (1870), where a handful of legislators accorded women the vote in territorial and local elections. Even so, the campaign for women's enfranchisement changed and expanded, drawing new adherents from the Midwest and the Pacific Coast. The old alliance with abolitionists was shattered, and most efforts for women's equality were no longer linked to those for racial equality. The advocates of woman suffrage undertook a campaign that would require an additional half century and another constitutional amendment—the Nineteenth, ratified in 1920—to complete. (See pp. 488–89 and, for the complete text of all amendments to the U.S. Constitution, Appendix pp. A-12–A-17.)

Constitutionalizing Women's Rights

In 1865 and 1866, as Congress was considering how to word the Fourteenth Amendment, women's rights activists called for woman suffrage to be joined with black suffrage in a single constitutional act. Many northern women had fought for the end of slavery, so, in the memorable words of Elizabeth Cady Stanton, "Would it not be advisable, when the constitutional door is open, [for women to] avail ourselves of the strong arm and blue uniform of the black soldier to walk in by his side?"[1] To pursue this goal, Stanton, Anthony and others formed the American Equal Rights Association, dedicated to both black and woman suffrage. "We resolved to make common cause with the colored class—the only other disfranchised class," observed Lucy Stone, "and strike for equal rights for all."[2]

But Radicals in Congress contended that pursuing woman suffrage and black suffrage simultaneously would doom the latter, which was their priority. Accordingly, they wrote the second section of the Fourteenth Amendment, meant to encourage states to grant voting rights to former slaves, to apply only to "male inhabitants . . . twenty-one years of age and citizens of the United States." This was the first reference to gender in the U.S. Constitution. Woman suffragists petitioned Congress to get the wording changed, but abolitionist Wendell Phillips told them, "This hour belongs to the Negro," leaving Stanton to wonder impatiently if "the African race is composed entirely of males."[3]

Two years after the 1868 ratification of the Fourteenth Amendment, congressional Radicals wrote the Fifteenth Amendment to advance black suffrage more forcefully, explicitly forbidding disfranchisement on the grounds of "race, color or previous condition of servitude." Gender was not included, leading Stanton to charge that "all mankind will vote not because of intelligence, patriotism, property or white skin but because it is male, not female."[4]

The American Equal Rights Association collapsed, and in its wake, woman suffragists divided over whether to endorse the Fifteenth Amendment. To reconcile woman suffrage advocacy with the Radical Republican agenda, in 1869 Lucy Stone and her husband, Henry Ward Blackwell, organized the American Woman Suffrage Association. They focused on campaigns for suffrage at the state level and in 1870 inaugurated the *Woman's Journal,* a weekly newspaper published for the next fifty years. Elizabeth Cady Stanton and Susan B. Anthony took a different

◆ **Elizabeth Cady Stanton and Susan B. Anthony**
Taken in 1870, this is the earliest photograph of the most important partnership in the U.S. woman suffrage movement. Stanton and Anthony had already been collaborating for two decades, and would do so for another three. Stanton's rambunctious curls and Anthony's severe bun give some indication of their quite different yet compatible personalities. Despite their bond, there was a hint of inequality between them. Although Anthony was only five years younger, she addressed her friend as "Mrs. Stanton," while Stanton called her "Susan." © *Bettmann/Corbis.*

route. They broke with their former Radical Republican allies and formed the rival National Woman Suffrage Association (NWSA).

Of the two societies, the NWSA pursued the more aggressive, independent path. The organization's newspaper, defiantly named the *Revolution*, lasted only two years. It proclaimed on its masthead: "Women their rights and nothing less; men their rights and nothing more." NWSA gained political autonomy for the suffrage movement but at the cost of an important part of the women's rights legacy: attention to the interrelation of the hierarchies of race and gender. As the larger society left behind the concerns of the ex-slaves and of Radical Reconstruction, much of the woman suffrage movement did, too, envisioning women's emancipation largely in terms of white women.

A New Departure for Woman Suffrage

Once the new constitutional amendments had been ratified, the NWSA proposed an inventive, bold interpretation of them. The argument was both simple and profound: first, women were "persons" whose rights as national citizens were established by the first sentence of the Fourteenth Amendment; second, the right to vote was central to and inherent in national citizenship. Third, and most important, women's right to vote was thus already established and did not require any additional constitutional change.

This argument, which was called the New Departure, brought to prominence one of the most unusual advocates in the history of woman suffrage, Victoria Claflin Woodhull. Born into poverty, Woodhull made her way into the highest ranks of New York society, in large part by cultivating powerful men. Aided by a congressman friend and without the knowledge of other suffragists, in 1871 she presented the case for the New Departure before the Judiciary Committee of the U.S. House of Representatives. Within a year, however, Woodhull had become involved in a scandal over the alleged adultery of Henry Ward Beecher, powerful Brooklyn minister and brother of Catharine Beecher and Harriet Beecher Stowe (see pp. 188–89; 280–81). Under a new federal anti-obscenity law, the Comstock Act (named for Anthony Comstock, the "social purity" crusader who drafted the legislation), Woodhull was jailed for sending accounts of the scandal through the federal mails. Stanton, one of the few suffragists who steadfastly defended Woodhull, insisted, "We have already women enough sacrificed to this sentimental, hypocritical prating about purity. If this present woman be crucified, let men drive the spikes."[5] Woodhull avoided jail but dropped out of public life; she eventually moved to England, where she married a wealthy man, remade her reputation, and lived until 1927.

Independent of Woodhull, suffragists around the country pursued their voting rights on the basis of the New Departure theory that they needed only to take hold of the right to vote, which was already theirs. During the elections of 1871 and 1872, groups of women went to their local polling places, put forth their constitutional understanding to stunned election officials, and stepped forward to submit their votes. In Washington, D.C., the African American journalist Mary Ann Shadd Cary was able to register but not to vote. Susan B. Anthony convinced polling officials in her hometown of Rochester, New York, to let her vote. "Well I have been & gone & done it!!" she wrote exuberantly. "Positively voted the Republican ticket."[6] Two weeks later, she was arrested for violating a federal law meant to disfranchise former Confederates. Her trial was a spectacle from start to finish. The judge ordered the jury to find Anthony guilty, which it did, and the judge's final insult was to refuse to jail Anthony so as to keep her from appealing her verdict (see box, "Not One Is My Peer, All Are My Political Sovereigns").

The U.S. Supreme Court finally considered the suffragists' argument in 1875, in the case of Virginia Minor, of St. Louis, Missouri, who sued the official who

SUSAN B. ANTHONY
Not One Is My Peer, All Are My Political Sovereigns

Soon after voting in the 1872 presidential election, Susan B. Anthony (1820–1906) was arrested for violating federal law. She approached her trial, held in June 1873, as an opportunity to argue the injustice of denying women political equality. For weeks before, she lectured extensively on the constitutional basis of her decision to cast her ballot. At the trial, after being declared guilty, Anthony made a statement that her right to a jury trial was meaningless so long as she was tried by men who did not share her disfranchised condition.

All of my prosecutors, from the 8th ward corner grocery politician, who entered the complaint, to the United States Marshal, Commissioner, District Attorney, District Judge, your honor on the bench, not one is my peer, but each and all are my political sovereigns; . . . [I have been tried] by forms of law all made by men, interpreted by men, administered by men, in favor of men, and against women; . . . But, yesterday, the same man-made forms of law, declared it a crime . . . for you, or me, or any of us, to give a cup of cold water, a crust of bread, or a night's shelter to a panting fugitive as he was tracking his way to Canada. And every man or woman in whose veins coursed a drop of human sympathy violated that wicked law, reckless of consequences, and was justified in so doing. As then, the slaves who got their freedom must take it over, or under, or through the unjust forms of law, precisely so, now, must women, to get their right to a voice in this government, take it; and I have taken mine, and mean to take it at every possible opportunity.

SOURCE: Susan B. Anthony's response to Judge Hunt at her June 1873 trial, "Stanton and Anthony Papers Online Project," Rutgers University, http://ecssba.rutgers.edu/docs/sbatrial.html (accessed June 19, 2004).

had not allowed her to vote. In *Minor v. Happersett*, one of the most important rulings in the history of women's rights (see the Appendix, p. A-25), the Supreme Court ruled unanimously that, while Minor was indeed a citizen, voting was not a right but a privilege bestowed by the federal government as it saw fit. Not only did this decision strike the New Departure theory dead, but it also indicated that the Court was bent on narrowing the meaning of the Fourteenth and Fifteenth Amendments in general. Subsequently, the Court permitted more and more devices to deprive black men of their franchise and constitutional civil rights.

After the *Minor* decision, the NWSA began to advocate a separate constitutional amendment, modeled on the Fifteenth, to bar disfranchisement explicitly "on the grounds of sex." This was the wording that would eventually go into the Nineteenth Amendment (1920), but for the time being, the proposed amendment made little headway. In 1876, NWSA leaders, uninvited, forced their way into the national celebration in Philadelphia of the hundredth anniversary of the Declaration of Independence. "Our faith is firm and unwavering in the broad principles of human rights proclaimed in 1776, not only as abstract truths, but as the corner stones of a republic," they declared. "Yet we cannot forget, even in this glad hour, that while all men of every race, and clime, and condition, have been invested with the full rights of citizenship under our hospitable flag, all women still suffer the degradation of disfranchisement."[7]

WOMEN'S LIVES IN SOUTHERN RECONSTRUCTION AND REDEMPTION

Meanwhile, life in the defeated South was being reconstructed as well. No element of freedom came easily or automatically for the former slaves, and southern whites changed their lives and expectations reluctantly. Black women fought for control over their labor, their children, and their bodies. Elite white women sought new capacities and strengths to accommodate the loss of the labor and wealth that slaveowning had given them. White women from the middle and lower ranks remained poised between loyalties of race and the resentments of class.

By 1870, all the southern states had met the terms Congress mandated for readmission to the Union. After the removal of federal troops in 1877, white southerners, in a process known as Redemption, moved to reclaim political control and to reassert white superiority. The region's economy, still largely agricultural, slowly began to industrialize. The complex result of these post-Reconstruction social, political, and economic changes was known as the New South.

Black Women in the New South

After the defeat of the Confederacy, many freedwomen and freedmen stayed on with their masters for months because they did not know they had been freed or had nowhere to go. Some took to the road to find long-lost spouses and family members. Those who could not travel posted advertisements, such as this one in the *Anglo-African Magazine*: "Martha Ward Wishes information concerning her

◆ The Right to Marry

As disregard of slave marriages had been considered one of the fundamental immoralities of slavery, immediately after the Civil War the Freedmen's Bureau rushed to legalize marriages among freedpeople, who were eager to have their unions recognized. To indicate that slaves had been married in fact if not in law, bureau officials "solemnized" rather than authorized these marriages. In this engraving, an African American Bureau chaplain presides at a ceremony for two former slaves; the husband was serving in the U.S. Army. © *Corbis.*

sister, Rosetta McQuillan, who was sold from Norfolk, Va. About thirty years ago to a Frenchman in Mobile, Ala."[8]

The hard-won family reunions of the freed slaves did not always end happily. Some spouses had formed new unions. Laura Spicer, sold away from a Virginia plantation, was contacted by her husband three years after the war ended. He had since become attached to another woman and was deeply conflicted. "I do not know which I love best, you or Anna," he wrote to Spicer. "[T]ry and marry some good, smart man . . . and do it because you love me, and not because I think more of the wife I have got than I do of you."[9] Nor were parents always recognized by the children they had been forced to leave behind. "At firs' I was scared of her, 'cause I didn't know who she was," one child remembered of her mother. "She put me in her lap an' she most' nigh cried when she seen de back o' my head . . . where de lice had been an' I had scratched em."[10]

In 1865, the U.S. Army, charged with occupying and governing the defeated Confederacy, organized a special division to deal with the former slaves. The Freedmen's Bureau provided temporary relief, oversaw their labor, and adjudicated disputes with former masters. It was the first systematic welfare effort of the U.S. government for an oppressed racial minority. One of its tasks was to ensure that freedpeople had rights over and to their own children. On returning to the Union, southern states had passed laws, known as black codes, to limit the freedoms of newly emancipated slaves. Apprenticeship laws provided for the indenture of black children into servitude regardless of the wishes of their parents. Black mothers and grandmothers fought especially hard against the black codes. "We were delighted when we heard that the Constitution set us free," Lucy Lee of Baltimore explained, "but God help us, our condition is bettered but little; free ourselves, [but] deprived of our children. . . . Give us our children and don't let them be raised in the ignorance we have [been]."[11]

The deepest desire of the freedpeople was to have their own family farms. However, Congress was unwilling to reapportion the southern lands that might have established genuine black self-sufficiency. A few former slaves became homesteaders on public lands in Florida, Kansas, Texas, and Alabama, and a handful were able to acquire substantial property. But the overwhelming majority found that they had to continue to work for others, largely as agricultural labor. The fundamental dilemma of Reconstruction for most ex-slaves centered on their returning to work for white people: On what terms? With what degree of personal freedom? And for what compensation?

One of the most subtle and complex aspects of this dilemma concerned the disposition of black women's labor. During slavery, women worked alongside men in the fields (see p. 211). Black women began to leave field work immediately after emancipation, much to the dismay of white landowners who knew women's importance to the agricultural labor force. Some observers reported that black men, eager to assert the rights of manhood over their families, were especially determined that their wives not work for whites. Black women, who discovered that any assertion of autonomy toward white employers might be punished as unacceptable "cheekiness," had their own reasons for withdrawing their labor.

To achieve even a small degree of independence from direct white oversight, three out of four black families ended up accepting an arrangement known as sharecropping. Working on small farms carved out of the holdings of landowners, sharecropping families kept only a portion of the crops they grew. There were no foremen to drive and beat them, and they could work together as families. But in bad times, the value of their yield did not equal the credit that white landowners had extended them to cover their expenses, and most ended up in permanent indebtedness.

The ex-slaves were more successful in realizing their desire for education. Even before the war ended, black and white women from the North had gone south to areas occupied by the Union army to begin teaching the black population. Throughout Reconstruction, freedpeople built their own schools, funded by the Freedmen's Bureau and northern missionary societies, to gain the basics of

◆ **Winslow Homer,** *The Cotton Pickers* **(1876)**

In 1876, as federal Reconstruction was drawing to a close, renowned Boston-born painter Winslow Homer (1836–1910) went south to make sketches of African American women and children, which in turn became the basis for a series of powerful paintings. In *The Cotton Pickers*, Homer portrays African American women doing agricultural labor, which, along with domestic service, constituted their major postwar occupation. If the content of black women's labor stayed as it had under slavery, how might the meaning of that labor for them have changed with emancipation? *Winslow Homer,* The Cotton Pickers, *1876, Los Angeles County Museum of Art. Acquisition made possible through Museum Trustees: Robert O. Anderson, R. Stanton Avery, B. Gerald Cantor, Edward W. Carter, Justin Dart, Charles E. Ducommon, Camilla Chandler Frost, Julian Ganz Jr., Dr. Armand Hammer, Harry Lenart, Dr. Franklin D. Murphy, Joan Palevsky, Richard E. Sherwood, Maynard J. Toll, and Hal B. Wallis. Photograph © 2005 Museum Associates/LACMA.*

literacy. Edmonia Highgate, the daughter of fugitive slaves, was one of the many sympathetic women who taught in these schools. She was motivated by a sense of racial solidarity to return to the South, and she worked among former slaves for six years, until sheer exhaustion forced her to retire.[12]

Many of the colleges and universities that are now referred to as "historically black" began during the era of Reconstruction. Unlike long-standing prestigious white institutions, many of these institutions, for instance Howard University, established in Washington, D.C., in 1867, were opened to women as well as to men. In 1881, white multimillionaire John D. Rockefeller founded the Atlanta Baptist Female Seminary, an all-female school that later became Spelman College. While most of these institutions provided little more than a high school education throughout the nineteenth century, they nonetheless played a major role in educating black leaders. They educated women who went on to become teachers throughout the South. This fragile educational infrastructure helped to create a small southern black middle class in cities like Atlanta, Richmond, and New Orleans.

The right to vote awarded to ex-slave men by the Fourteenth and Fifteenth Amendments lay at the very core of ex-slaves' hopes for the future. During Reconstruction, freedmen's exercise of the ballot, protected by federal troops, helped to elect approximately two thousand black men to local, state, and national political office. Despite their own disfranchisement, black women understood the political franchise as a community rather than an individual right. They regularly attended political meetings and told men who had the vote how to use it. Southern white women, by contrast, regarded the enfranchisement of black men as yet another insult to their sex and their race.

White Women in the New South

At the end of the war, white women faced loss and defeat, not emancipation and hope for the future. Food shortages were compounded by the collapse of the economy. More than a quarter million southern white men died on Civil War battlefields, leaving one generation of widows and another that would never marry. Occupation by federal troops after the war deepened white southerners' feelings of humiliation. One historian argues that southern white women, who did not share men's sheer relief at getting off the battlefield, harbored greater resentment than southern white men toward the North.[13]

Elite white women felt the loss of their slaves acutely. If they wanted black men in their fields and black women in their kitchens, they had to concede to some of the freedpeople's new expectations for wages, personal autonomy, and respect. Elite white women began for the first time to cook and launder for themselves and their families. "We have most of the housework to do all the time," complained Amanda Worthington of Mississippi, "and . . . it does not make me like the Yankees any better."[14]

Non-elite white southerners were less affected by the withdrawal of slave labor, but because they lived much closer to the edge of subsistence, they suffered far more from the collapse of the economy and the physical devastation of the South. Economic pressures drove many into the same sharecropping arrangement and permanent indebtedness as ex-slaves. Poor southern white women and their children also provided the labor force for the textile mills that northerners and a new class of southern industrialists began building in the 1880s. Inasmuch as black people were not allowed to work in the mills, white women experienced textile work as a kind of racial privilege. Many poor white women believed as fervently as former plantation mistresses in the inviolability of racial hierarchies.

Even so, the collapse of the patriarchal slave system provided new opportunities for public life for those white women who chose to take them. Elite women became involved in the memorialization of the Confederacy. They raised funds, built monuments, and lionized the men who had fought for southern independence, all the while creating an expanded civic role for their sex. Poor farm women found their opportunities in the Grange, a social and educational movement that later fed into the rise of Populism (see pp. 412–14). With a very few exceptions, however, southern white women kept their distance from woman suffrage efforts, which reminded them all too much of the federal intervention to enfranchise their former slaves.

Racial Conflict in Slavery's Aftermath

Changes in gender and racial relations together generated considerable violence in the postwar South. Whites experienced African American autonomy as a profound threat. The Ku Klux Klan, founded in 1866 in Pulaski, Tennessee, terrorized freedpeople for asserting their new freedoms. Klan members sexually humiliated, raped, and murdered many freedwomen. In Henry County, Georgia, two Klansmen pinned down Rhoda Ann Childs; she told a congressional investigation in 1871, "[They] stretched my limbs as far apart as they could . . . [and] applied the Strap to my Private parts until fatigued into stopping, and I was more dead than alive." She was then raped with the barrel of a gun.[15]

Through such actions, white men were both punishing black men and attempting to reassert their slave-era control over black women's bodies. Black women were determined to defend themselves. An African American woman recalled that after the war her father vowed "never to allow his wife and daughters to be thrown in contact with Southern white men in their homes." Decades later, she felt the same: "There is no sacrifice I would not make . . . rather than allow my daughters to go in service where they would be thrown constantly in contact with Southern white men, for they consider the colored girl their special prey."[16] In an age when sexual propriety was still the essence of true womanhood, black women were determined to challenge the notion that they and the men of their race were sexually immoral.

Eventually, the region's hidden history of cross-racial sex took an even more deadly form. Whites charged that black men were sexual predators seeking access to white women. The irony, of course, was that under slavery, it was white men who had unrestricted sexual access to black women. Southern white women of all classes supported these charges against black men, and most northerners assumed that they were true. At the slightest suspicion of the merest disrespect to a white woman, black men could be accused of sexual aggression and lynched—killed (usually hanged) by mobs who ignored legal process to execute their own form of crude justice. Lynchings, often involving gruesome mutilation as well as murder, were popular events in the post-Reconstruction South, with white women and children attending amid a carnival-like atmosphere. In 1892, the high point of this practice, 160 African Americans were lynched.[17]

Ida B. Wells, an African American journalist from Memphis, Tennessee, inaugurated a campaign, eventually international in scope, to investigate and expose the false charges behind the epidemic of lynchings and to get leading white figures to condemn it. She recognized that allegations of black men's lewd behavior toward white women were closely related to assumptions of black women's sexual

◆ **Ida B. Wells with the Family of Thomas Moss**
In 1893, the date of this photograph, Ida B. Wells (standing left) was already an important figure for her courageous journalistic exposé of the lynchings of southern black men. She organized African American clubwomen to join her and challenged white reformers to speak out against this barbaric practice. With her are the widow and orphans of Thomas Moss, the Memphis shopkeeper whose murder inspired Wells's crusade. In 1895, Wells married Frederick Barnett, a Chicago newspaper publisher, and they raised four children. She remained a lifelong activist. *The University of Chicago Library, Special Collections Research Center, Ida B. Wells Papers.*

disreputability and contended that black women had a major role to play in challenging the system that led to lynchings. Her efforts helped to catalyze the organization of an African American women's reform movement. (See Documents: Ida B. Wells, "Race Woman," pp. 358–62.)

Southern blacks' efforts to claim their rights suffered many major setbacks in the late nineteenth century. One by one, all-white Democratic parties "redeemed" state governments from Republicanism and ended what they called "black rule," instituting devices to disfranchise black men, such as requiring voters to demonstrate literacy, to pay exorbitant poll taxes, or to prove that their grandfathers had been voters. By the beginning of the twentieth century, black voting had been virtually obliterated throughout the South.

Meanwhile, a new legal system of rigid racial separation in social relations was being put in place. Called Jim Crow, after a foolish minstrel character played by whites in black makeup, these laws and practices were a way to humiliate and intimidate black people. Legal segregation of the races had not been necessary under slavery, where black people had no rights, but now it became a way to reassert white domination. Recalling what enforced segregation felt like, a southern black woman wrote, "I never get used to it; it is new each time and stings and hurts more and more. It does not matter how good or wise my children may be; they are colored. . . . Everything is forgiven in the South but color."[18]

Segregation affected many things including education, public services, and public accommodations, but black women particularly resented Jim Crow regulations in public transportation. Wells began her career as a defender of her race in 1884 by suing the Tennessee railroad company that ejected her from a special "ladies" car and sent her instead to the "colored" car. Twelve years later, the Supreme Court considered a similar suit by Homer Plessy against a Louisiana railroad for its segregation policy. In *Plessy v. Ferguson* (1896), the Court characterized the entire Jim Crow regime as "separate but equal" and thus compatible with the Fourteenth Amendment's requirement of equality before the law. This constitutional defense of segregation survived for nearly sixty years. (See Appendix, p. A-26.)

FEMALE WAGE LABOR AND THE TRIUMPH OF INDUSTRIAL CAPITALISM

Industrial growth accelerated tremendously after the defeat of the slave system and the northern victory in the Civil War. Intense competition between industrialists and financial magnates gradually gave way to economic consolidation. By 1890, industries such as steel, railroads, coal mining, and meat production were dominated by a handful of large, powerful corporate entities. The mirror reflection of the growth of capital, the American working class also came into its own and organized to find ways to offset the power of its employers.

The growth of the female labor force was an important part of this development, although it flew in the face of the still-strong presumption that women belonged exclusively in their homes. Domestic service was the largest sector, but manufacturing labor by women, especially the industrial production of garments, with its distinctive and highly exploitative form of production, the sweatshop, was growing faster.

The dynamic growth of industrial society produced a level of class conflict in the last quarter of the nineteenth century as intense as any in American history. Starting in 1877, as the federal army retreated from the South and the first postwar depression receded, waves of protests by disgruntled workers shook the economy and drew a powerful and violent response from big business and government. Coming so soon after the Civil War, escalating class antagonism seemed to threaten national unity again, this time along economic rather than sectional lines. Women played a significant role in these upheavals and, in doing so, laid the groundwork for a female labor movement in the early twentieth century.

Women's Occupations after the Civil War

Between 1860 and 1890, the percentage of the nonagricultural wage labor force that was female increased from 10.2 to 17 percent (see Chart 6.1, Women and the Labor Force, 1800–1900). Since the population in these years increased enormously, the change in absolute numbers was even more dramatic: by 1890, 3.6 million women were working for pay in nonagricultural labor, more than twice the number in 1870. The average pay for women remained a third to a half of the pay for men. The great majority of white working women were young and unmarried. The outlines of black women's labor were somewhat different, remaining

◆ **Chart 6.1 Women and the Labor Force, 1800–1900**

Year	Percent of All Women in the Labor Force	Percent of the Labor Force That Is Female
1800	4.6	4.6
1810	7.9	9.4
1820	6.2	7.3
1830	6.4	7.4
1840	8.4	9.6
1850	10.1	10.8
1860	9.7	10.2
1870	13.7	14.8
1880	14.7	15.2
1890	18.2	17.0
1900	21.2	18.1

Sources: W. Elliot Brownlee and Mary M. Brownlee, Women in the American Economy: A Documentary History *(New Haven: Yale University Press, 1976).* Historical Statistics of the United States: Colonial Times to 1970, Part 1, Bicentennial Edition, *Bureau of the Census, U.S. Department of Commerce, 1975. "Marital and Family Characteristics of Workers," March 1983, U.S. Department of Labor.* Statistical Abstract of the United States, *Bureau of the Census, U.S. Department of Commerce, 1983 and 1992; Daphne Spain and Suzanne Bianchi,* Balancing Act *(New York: Russell Sage, 1996).*

largely agricultural until well into the twentieth century. Black women also were much more likely to work outside the home after marriage.

Much of what historians have written about working women of the nineteenth century, especially the numbers and statistics, is guesswork. Although women had been working for wages since the 1830s, it was not until 1890 that the U.S. census began to identify or count working women with any precision. After the Civil War, some states investigated female wage labor, framing their inquiries in moralistic terms. State labor bureaus paid a great deal of attention, for instance, to disproving the assertion that working women were inclined to prostitution. These statistical portraits were fleshed out by investigative reporting, usually by middle- or upper-class women, who went among the working classes to report on their conditions. (See Documents: The Woman Who Toils, pp. 363–68.)

Nonetheless, it is clear that, for white women, paid domestic work was on the decline. Domestic servants, who before the war were the majority of the white female labor force, constituted less than 30 percent by the end of the century. Working women had long been impatient with domestic service and left it whenever they could, usually for factory labor. After the Civil War, the end of slavery tainted personal service even more. Investigator Helen Campbell took testimony in the mid-1880s in New York City from women who had abandoned domestic service. "I hate the very words 'service' and 'servant,'" an Irish immigrant renegade from domestic labor explained. "We came to this country to better ourselves, and it's not bettering to have anybody ordering you around."[19]

As white women workers shifted out of domestic service, the percentage in manufacturing increased to 25 percent as of 1900. Women continued to work in the textile industry, and in the shoe industry women organized their own trade union, the Daughters of St. Crispin (named after the patron saint of their trade), but it survived only a few years. The biggest change in women's manufacturing labor was the rise of the garment industry, as the antebellum outwork system began to give way to more fully industrialized processes (see pp. 196–97).

The industrial manufacture of clothing depended on the invention of the sewing machine, one of the most consequential technological developments in U.S. women's history. The introduction of the sewing machine accelerated the subdivision of clothing production into discrete tasks. Thus a single worker no longer made an entire piece of clothing but instead spent her long days sewing sleeves or seams, incurring the physical and spiritual toll of endless, repetitive motion. Unlike the power looms and spindles of the textile mills, sewing machines did not need to be housed in massive factories but could be placed in numerous small shops. As sewing machines were also comparatively inexpensive, the cost of buying and maintaining them could be shifted to the workers themselves, who were charged rent or made to pay installments for them.

Profits in the garment industry came primarily from pushing the women workers to produce more for less pay. This system became designated as the "sweating" system, meaning that it required women workers to drive (or sweat) themselves to work ever harder. Women workers were usually paid for each piece completed, whereas men tended to be paid for time worked. Employers set a low piece rate, lowering it even further as women produced more. Often workers were charged for thread and fined for sewing errors. The work was highly seasonal, and periods of twelve-hour workdays alternated with bouts of unemployment. At the beginning of the Civil War, the average earnings of sewing women were $10 per week; by 1865, they were $5 per week.

Regardless of their ability or speed, women in the garment, textile, and shoe industries were generally considered unskilled workers, in part because they worked in a female-dominated industry, in part because they were easily replaced by other women, and in part because they learned their work on the job rather than through a formal apprenticeship. The higher pay associated with so-called skilled labor was reserved for trades that men dominated. A few women gained entrance to male-dominated trades, such as typesetting, where they earned up to $15 per week. Initially, women made their way into print shops by replacing male workers who were out on strike, but they were let go when the men came back to work. Eventually, the printers' union voted to admit women as equal members, only the second male trade union to do so.

In the 1870s, a new field began to open up for female wage earners: office work. Before 1860, the office environment had been totally male, filled by young men aspiring to careers in business or law. During the Civil War, young women began to replace men as government copyists and stenographers. The shift to female labor was accelerated by another crucial technological development, the typewriter. Women, with their smaller hands, were thought to be especially suited to typing. Office work required education and a command of the English language, adding to its prestige as an occupation for women. It also paid more than textile mills or garment sweatshops. Yet from the employers' perspective, hiring women rather than men to meet the growing demand for clerical labor constituted a considerable savings. By 1900, office work was still only 9 percent of the female labor force, but it was the fastest-growing sector, a harbinger of things to come in the twentieth-century female labor force (see the Appendix, p. A-39).

Who Were the Women Wage Earners?

Age and marital status were crucial elements in the structure of the female labor force. In 1890, three-quarters of white working women were unmarried. As a leading historian of working women puts it, "In the history of women's labor market experience in the United States the half century from about 1870 to 1920 was the era of single women."[20] Unlike working men, whose wages were supposed to provide for an entire family, these young women allegedly had no one but themselves to support. "Working girls" were expected to work for pay for only a few years, then marry and become dependent on the earnings of their husbands. This was the principle of the so-called family wage, which justified men's greater wages as much as it did women's lesser. Wage labor for women was meant to be an interlude between childhood and domestic dependence, while men expected to work throughout their adult lives.

The reality of working women's lives was considerably more complex. Approximately 10 to 15 percent of urban families were headed by single mothers

◆ **The Invention of the Typewriter**

A practical machine for mechanical writings—the typewriter—was devised just after the Civil War. Further changes were later made in the size of the machine and placement of the keyboard as well as the arrangement of the letters. This illustration from a manual on typewriting originally appeared with the caption "Operator sitting in correct position for rapid writing." From the beginning, women were envisioned as the major operators of this new technology. © *Corbis.*

and were acutely disadvantaged by the family wage system.[21] A working woman who was a wife and/or mother was considered at best an anomaly and at worst an indicator of family and social crisis. African American women wage earners were three times as likely as white women to be married, partly because their husbands' pay was so low and partly because many chose to work themselves rather than send their daughters into work situations where they would be vulnerable to sexual harassment from white men. In historical hindsight, African American women were pioneering the modern working women's pattern of combining wage labor and domestic responsibilities; but at the time, the high number of black working mothers was the object of much disparagement.

Most unmarried wage-earning women lived in their parents' homes, where, contrary to the ideal of the single male breadwinner, their earnings were crucial supplements to family support. However, perhaps as many as a third of single women wage earners lived outside of families. Carroll Wright, a pioneering labor statistician, reported in "The Working Girls of Boston" (1889), a Massachusetts Bureau of Statistics of Labor report, that in Massachusetts many young women workers were "obliged to leave their homes on account of bad treatment or conduct of [a] dissipated father or because they felt the need of work and not finding it at home, have come to [a large city]."[22] Philanthropists established charity boardinghouses to protect these so-called women adrift, who seemed vulnerable without parents or husbands to protect them. One of the major purposes of the Young Women's Christian Association (YWCA), formed soon after the Civil War, was to provide supervised housing for single, urban working women.

Responses to Working Women

Contemporaries' attempts to grapple with the growing female labor force contained a revealing contradiction. On the one hand, social observers contended that only women driven by sheer desperation should work outside the home. Other working women were taking work away from truly needy women and—even more disturbing—from male breadwinners. If young working women used any part of their pay to buy attractive clothing or go out with men, they were castigated for frivolity. "[Working girls] who want pin-money do work at a price impossible for the self-supporting worker, many married women coming under this head," observed journalist Helen Campbell.[23]

On the other hand, those women who were driven into wage labor by absolute necessity were so ill-paid, so unrelentingly exploited, as to constitute a major social tragedy. "All alike are starved, half clothed, overworked to a frightful degree," wrote the same Helen Campbell, "with neither time to learn some better method of earning a living, nor hope enough to spur them in any new path."[24] Sympathetic observers concluded that the only humane response was to remove young women from the labor force altogether. Wage-earning women were therefore criticized if they worked out of choice or pitied if they worked out of need. In either case, they seemed to be trespassing where they did not belong: in the wage labor force.

Set against middle-class social observers' steady chorus of criticism or lament, the lives and choices of working women hint at a different picture. Working girls objected to the constant supervision at philanthropic working girls' homes, stubbornly spent their wages as they pleased, engaged in recreational activities that were considered vulgar, occasionally continued to work even after they got married, and preferred their morally questionable factory jobs to the presumed safety of domestic service. Though they were criticized for taking jobs away from the truly deserving, many regarded themselves simply as women who liked to earn money, preferred the sociability of sharing work with others, chose the experience of manufacturing something new over endless domestic routine, and enjoyed their occasional moments of hard-earned personal freedom.

Class Conflict and Labor Organization

Women were part of all the dramatic strikes and labor conflicts of the late nineteenth century. During the nationwide rail strikes in 1877, in which workers protested layoffs and wage cuts, women were among the mobs that burned roundhouses and destroyed railroad cars. Women's involvement in such violent acts underlined the full fury of working-class resentment at the inequalities of wealth in postbellum America. "Women who are the wives and mothers of the [railroad] firemen," reported a Baltimore newspaper, "look famished and wild and declare for starvation rather than have their people work for the reduced wages."[25] President Rutherford B. Hayes sent federal forces, recently withdrawn from occupying the South, to suppress the riots. More than a hundred strikers were killed nationwide.

In the late 1870s, many angry workers joined the Knights of Labor, originally a secret society that became the largest labor organization of the nineteenth century. The Knights aimed to unite and elevate working people and to protect the country's democratic heritage from unrestrained capitalist growth. In 1881, the Knights, unlike most unions, admitted women (housewives as well as wage earners). At its peak, the Knights of Labor had 750,000 members, of whom some 10 percent were women. Its goal was to unite "the producing classes," regardless of industry or occupation or gender. Race was more complicated. In the South, the Knights admitted black workers in segregated local chapters, but in the West, the organization excluded Chinese men, whom it regarded as economic competitors rather than as fellow workers.

The Knights played a major role in the nationwide campaign to shorten the workday for wage earners to eight hours, a movement of obvious interest to women. On May 1, 1886, hundreds of thousands of workers from all over the country struck on behalf of the eight-hour day. At a related rally a few days later in Chicago's Haymarket Square, a bomb exploded, killing seven policemen. Although the bomb thrower was never identified, eight male labor leaders were charged with conspiracy to murder. Lucy Parsons, the wife of one of the accused, helped conduct their defense. An African American woman, Lucy had met her husband in Texas, where he had gone after the war to organize black voters for the

Republican Party. Defense efforts eventually won gubernatorial pardons for three of the accused men, although not in time to save Albert Parsons. The violence and repression unleashed by the Haymarket incident devastated the Knights of Labor. By 1890, it had ceased to play a significant role in American labor relations. The eight-hour workday would not be won for many decades.

After the collapse of the Knights, the future of organized labor was left to male-dominated trade unions and their umbrella organization, the American Federation of Labor (AFL), founded in 1886 by Samuel Gompers, a cigar maker from New York City. While the goal of the Knights was inclusive, to unify the producing classes, the purpose of AFL unions was exclusive, to protect the jobs of skilled and relatively well-paid labor from less-skilled, lower-paid workers. Most members of AFL unions regarded women workers as exactly this sort of threat: unskilled, underpaid workers who took men's jobs during strikes. Adapting the domestic ideal of true womanhood from the middle class, the AFL subscribed to the notion that women belonged in the home and that decent pay for a male worker was a wage sufficient to keep a wife out of the labor force.

Nonetheless, the late nineteenth-century labor movement did provide a few exceptional working women with the chance to begin speaking and acting on behalf of female wage earners. Leonora Barry and Mary Kenney were among the first women appointed by unions to organize other women workers. In 1886, the Knights of Labor designated Barry, a widowed Irish-born garment worker, to head its Woman's Department (see box, "Women in the Knights of Labor"). Although meeting with her might mean being fired, women workers around the country shared with Barry their complaints about wages and working conditions. Barry was their devoted advocate, but after two years, frustrated with the timidity of many working women and perhaps also with the limits of her support from the male leadership of the organization, she resigned her position.

Mary Kenney's trade was bookbinding. She joined an AFL union in Chicago and in 1891 was appointed the federation's first paid organizer for working women. She believed that working women should organize themselves but that they also needed the moral and financial support of middle- and upper-class women. The AFL was less committed to working women than the Knights, and Kenney was dismissed from her post after only six months. In the decades to come, many more female labor activists followed Barry and Kenney to play important roles in shaping women's history.

WOMEN OF THE LEISURED CLASSES

Paralleling the expansion of the American working class was the dramatic growth, both in numbers and wealth, of the middle and upper classes. For this reason, one of several terms used for the post-Reconstruction years is the Gilded Age. The term, first used by Mark Twain in a novel about economic and political corruption after the Civil War, captured both the riches and superficiality of the wealthier classes in the late nineteenth century. In the United States, with its proud

LEONORA BARRY
Women in the Knights of Labor

Leonora Barry (1849–1930) was one of the first female labor organizers. Her final report to the Knights of Labor expresses the ambivalence toward wage earning women that was so common in the late nineteenth century: they belonged at home but deserved equality in the labor force. In 1890, Barry, a widow when she began her assignment, resigned when she remarried.

I believe it was intended that man should be the breadwinner. But as that is impossible under present conditions, I believe women should have every opportunity to become proficient in whatever vocation they choose or find themselves best fitted for. When I took a position at [the Woman's Department's] head, I fondly hoped to weld together in organization a number of women as would be a power for good in the present, . . . I was too sanguine, . . . and I believe we now should . . . put more women in the field as Lecturers to tell women why they should organize as part of the industrial hive, rather than because they are women. There can be no separation or distinction of wage-workers on account of sex, and separate departments for their interests is a direct contradiction of this. . . . Therefore I recommend the abolition of the Woman's Department, believing as I now do that women should be Knights of Labor without distinction, and should have all the benefits that can be given to men—no more, no less.

SOURCE: Leonora Barry, Woman's Department, Knights of Labor, 1889, Report of the General Investigator, Proceedings of the General Assembly of the Knights of Labor, 1888.

middle-class ethic, the distinction between upper and middle class has always been hard to draw with precision, but in these years what was more important was the enormous and growing gap between those who lived comfortable, leisured lives and those who struggled with poverty. While the poor labored unceasingly, the upper class enjoyed unprecedented new wealth and influence, and the middle class imitated their values of material accumulation and display. For women of the leisured classes, the Gilded Age meant both new affluence and growing discontent with an exclusively domestic sphere.

New Sources of Wealth and Leisure

The tremendous economic growth of the post–Civil War era emanated from the railroads that wove together the nation and carried raw materials to factories and finished goods to customers. The great fortunes of the age were made especially

◆ **Mary Kenney O'Sullivan and Children**
Kenney left school at fourth grade, "as far," she said, "as any children of wage earners . . . was
expected to go,"[26] and became a skilled bookbinder. A natural labor organizer, she was
encouraged and supported by both clubwomen and male unionists. In 1894, she married
labor activist John F. O'Sullivan and had four children (one of whom died), but within a
decade she was widowed. She played a major role in the founding of the Women's Trade
Union League in 1903 and, like Ida B. Wells-Barnett, remained an activist throughout her
life. *The Schlesinger Library, Radcliffe Institute, Harvard University.*

in iron mining, steel manufacturing, and railroad building — and in financing
these endeavors. New technologies, government subsidies, cutthroat competition,
and the pressure on workers to work faster and more productively contributed to
this development. Dominated by a few corporate giants, this wealth was distributed very unevenly; in 1890 an estimated 1 percent of the population controlled
fully 25 percent of the country's wealth.[27] In New York City alone, the number of
millionaires went from a few dozen in 1860 to several hundred in 1865. Indeed,

many of the great American family fortunes were begun in the Gilded Age: John D. Rockefeller in oil, Cornelius Vanderbilt in railroads, J. P. Morgan in finance, and Andrew Carnegie in steel. One of the very few women to amass spectacular wealth on her own was Hetty Robinson Green. She began her financial career with a $10 million inheritance, which she multiplied tenfold through shrewd investment. Operating as she did in the man's world of high finance, her womanliness was suspect. The popular press played up her eccentricities, dubbing her "the witch of Wall Street" rather than one of the brilliant financiers of the epoch.

Wives of wealthy men faced no such criticism. On the contrary, they were regarded as the ultimate in womanly beauty and grace. In the world of the extremely wealthy, men's obligation was to amass money while women's was to display and spend it. Wealthy women were also responsible for the conduct of "society," a word that came to mean the comings and goings of the tiny upper class, as if the rest of the population faded into insignificance by contrast. In *The Theory of the Leisure Class* (1899), sociologist Thorstein Veblen astutely observed that upper-class women not only purchased expensive commodities but were themselves their husbands' most lavish and enviable possessions.

Shopping was a new and important role for leisure-class women in the postbellum years. Middle-class women, who previously had responsibility for a great deal of productive household labor, became active consumers. With the dramatic increase in the country's manufacturing capacity, their obligation was now to purchase rather than to produce, to spend rather than to economize. They flocked to the many department stores established in this period, grand palaces of commodities such as Marshall Field's in Chicago (founded in 1865), Macy's in New York (1866), Strawbridge and Clothiers in Philadelphia (1868), Hudson's in Detroit (1887), and May's in Denver (1888). They filled the elaborate interiors of their homes with furniture and decorative items. Even at a distance from the proliferating retail possibilities of the cities, mail order catalogs allowed rural women to look at, long for, and occasionally purchase the many commodities of the age.

Rising incomes lifted the burden of housekeeping off urban middle- and upper-class women in other ways. Cities laid water and sewer lines, but only in wealthy neighborhoods in which households could afford the fees; indoor plumbing and running water made housework easier for prosperous women. But the most important factor in easing the load of housekeeping for leisure-class women was undoubtedly the cheap labor of domestic servants. Despite constant complaints about the shortage of domestic help, middle-class families regarded having at least one or two paid domestic servants as a virtual necessity. The wealthy had small armies of them. Laundry, which required enormous energy and much time when done in an individual household, was sent out to commercial establishments, where poor and immigrant women pressed and folded sheets and linens in overheated steam rooms.

Another important factor in freeing middle- and upper-class women from domestic demands was the declining birthrate (see the Appendix, p. A-36). Between 1850 and 1890, the average number of live births for white, native-born

◆ **Rike-Kumler Co. Department Store, Dayton, Ohio**
Department store counters were one place where working- and leisure-class women met.
Neat dress, good English, and middle-class manners were job requirements, even though pay
was no better than for factory work. Customers like the woman being fitted for gloves in this
1893 photograph sat, but clerks stood all day, one of the conditions of their work to which
they most objected. © *Bettmann/Corbis.*

women fell from 5.42 to 3.87. African American birthrates were not recorded in
the federal census until several decades later, but by all impressionistic evidence,
they declined even more dramatically, as freedwomen took control of their lives
at the most intimate level. Ironically, birthrates declined in inverse proportion to
class status: the wealthiest, with money to spare, had proportionately fewer children than the very poor, whose earnings were stretched to the limit but who relied
on their children for income.

     In understanding the many individual decisions that went into the declining
birthrate among leisure-class women, the explanation is not obvious. There were
no dramatic improvements in contraceptive technology or knowledge in these

years. On the contrary, traditional means of controlling pregnancy—early versions of condoms and diaphragms—were banned by new laws that defined them as obscene devices; even discussions aimed at limiting reproduction were forbidden. Following the Comstock Act of 1873, which outlawed the use of the U.S. mails for distributing information on controlling reproduction, twenty-four states criminalized the dissemination of contraceptive devices.

Rather, declining birthrates seem to have been both a cause and an effect of the expanding sphere of leisure-class women. Women's decisions to limit their pregnancies reflected a growing desire for personal satisfaction and social contribution beyond motherhood. Even though maternity remained the assumed destiny of womanhood, many women were coming to believe that they could choose when and how often to become pregnant. In advocating "voluntary motherhood," Harriot Stanton Blatch encouraged women to choose for themselves when to have sexual intercourse (see box, "Voluntary Motherhood"). Reformers like Blatch did not yet envision the separation of women's sexual activity from the possibility of pregnancy, but they did believe that women should have control over both. The very term "birth control" and the movement to advance it came later in the twentieth century (see pp. 480–81), but basic changes in female reproductive behavior were already under way.

As women's reproductive lives changed, so did their understanding of their sexuality. To be sure, many restrictive sexual assumptions remained in place. Some physicians still regarded strong sexual desire in women as a disease, which they treated by methods ranging from a diet of bland foods to surgical removal of the clitoris. But the heterosexual double standard—that men's sexual desire was uncontrollable and that women's was nonexistent—was beginning to come under fire. By the end of the century, even the conservative physician Elizabeth Blackwell was writing in carefully chosen language that "in healthy, loving women, uninjured by the too frequent lesions which result from childbirth, increasing physical satisfaction attaches to the ultimate physical expression of love."[28]

Lesbianism, in the modern sense of women openly and consistently expressing sexual desire for other women, had not yet been named but in these years many leisure-class women formed intense attachments with each other. These "homosocial" relationships, as modern historians have designated them, ranged from intense, lifelong friendships to relationships that were as emotionally charged, as beset by jealousy and possessiveness, and quite possibly as physically intimate, as any heterosexual love affair. Mary (Molly) Hallock and Helena De Kay were two such friends. They met in 1868 as art students in New York and wrote frequently and passionately to each other. When Helena announced that she was marrying New York publisher Richard Gilder, Molly angrily wrote to him: "Until you came along, sir, I believe she loved me almost as girls love their lovers."[29]

Most of what we know about such homosocial relations comes from leisure-class women, perhaps because they wrote more letters that were preserved and handed down to families and archivists than working-class women did. But surely some working-class women experienced similar passions. A set of letters between

HARRIOT STANTON BLATCH
Voluntary Motherhood

In this 1891 speech, Harriot Stanton Blatch (1856–1940), daughter of Elizabeth Cady Stanton (see pp. 275–78), brilliantly exploited the nineteenth-century belief that motherhood was woman's highest vocation in order to argue for women's rights to control whether and when they had children. Although she used the term "race" here to mean humanity, she was relying on the racial "science" of the period, which emphasized the biological dimension of human progress.

Men talk of the sacredness of motherhood, but judging from their acts it is the last thing that is held sacred in the human species . . . men in laws and customs have degraded the woman in her maternity. Motherhood is sacred—that is, voluntary motherhood; but the woman who bears unwelcome children is outraging every duty she owes the race. . . . Let women but understand the part unenforced maternity has played in the evolution of animal life, and their reason will guide them to the true path of race development. . . . [Women] should refuse to prostitute their creative powers, and so jeopardize the progress of the human race. Upon the mothers must rest in the last instance the development of any species.

_____

SOURCE: Harriot Stanton Blatch, "Voluntary Motherhood," 1891, in Aileen S. Kraditor, comp., *Up from the Pedestal: Selected Writings in the History of American Feminism* (Chicago: Quadrangle Books, 1968), 167–75.

two African American women living in Connecticut during the 1860s offers the rare example of a cross-class homosocial relationship, moreover one that was strongly suggestive of physical intimacy. Rebecca Primus, a schoolteacher, and Addie Brown, a seamstress, domestic worker, and laundress, conducted what the historian of their bond calls "a self consciously sexual relationship" focused on breasts and their fondling.[30]

By the late nineteenth century, such intense bonds were coming under scrutiny from physicians. Recognizing the obvious erotic qualities of these intense same-sex relationships, neurologists sought to give them the dignity of scientific recognition, even as they characterized them as "unnatural" or "abnormal." Women-loving women who, in an earlier decade, would have believed unquestioningly in the asexual purity and innocence of their attachments, were beginning to read scientific writings about homosexuality and to wonder about the meaning and nature of their own feelings.

◆ **"Get Thee Behind Me, (Mrs.) Satan!"**
By 1872, when this cartoon appeared in *Harper's Weekly* magazine, suffragist Victoria Woodhull had gained considerable notoriety both for her dramatic pro-suffrage testimony before a congressional committee and for her bold critiques of sexual hypocrisy within the marriage relationship. Her proclamations and behavior won her the label of America's foremost "free lover." This image, created by the great nineteenth-century political cartoonist Thomas Nast, portrays her as the devil incarnate. He contrasts Woodhull to a heavily burdened drunkard's wife, who will be further weighted down by following her lead. *Library of Congress LC-USZ62-74994.*

The "Woman's Era"

Before the Civil War, women had formed charitable and religious societies and had worked together on behalf of temperance, abolition, and women's rights (see pp. 262–79). After the war, associational fervor among women was more diverse, secular, and independent of male oversight. Participation in Gilded Age women's societies provided numerous women with new opportunities for collective activity, intellectual growth, and public life. By the end of the nineteenth century, leisure-class women had almost totally commandeered nongovernmental civic life from men. Thus, another apt label for the post-Reconstruction years is the Woman's Era.

The women's club movement began in the Northeast just after the Civil War among white middle-class women. In 1868, New York City women writers formed a group they named Sorosis (a botanical term that suggested sisterhood) to protest their exclusion from an event held by male writers. Simultaneously, a group of Boston reformers led by Julia Ward Howe (author of "The Battle Hymn of the Republic") organized the New England Women's Club, dedicated to the cultivation of intellectual discussion and public authority for leisure-class women.

Despite their impeccable reputations, both groups were publicly lambasted for their unladylike behavior. "Woman is straying from her sphere," warned the *Boston Transcript*.[31]

Despite such criticisms, women's clubs thrived among those middle-aged married women whose childrearing years were behind them. The concerns of the women's club movement evolved from literary and cultural matters in the 1870s to local social service projects in the 1880s to regional and national federations for political influence in the 1890s. Many public institutions established in the Gilded Age — hospitals and orphanages as well as libraries and museums — were originally established by women's clubs. From the Northeast, the club movement spread to the West and then the South.

Clubs by their nature are exclusive institutions, and the sororal bonds of women's clubs reflected their tendency to draw together women of like background. In the larger cities, class differences distinguished elite women's clubs from those formed by wives of clerks and shopkeepers. Working women's clubs were rarely initiated by wage-earning women themselves but were likely to be uplift projects of middle- and upper-class clubwomen. Race and religion were especially important principles of association. German Jewish women and African American women organized separately from the mainstream women's club movement, which was largely white and Protestant. Generally, middle-class Jewish or African American women formed their own clubs both to assist poorer women and to cultivate their own skills and self-confidence.

The ethic of women's clubs was particularly compelling to African American women. They formed organizations not just to enlarge their horizons as women but to play their part in the enormous project of post-emancipation racial progress. "If we compare the present condition of the colored people of the South with their condition twenty-eight years ago," explained African American clubwoman Sarah J. Early in 1893, "we shall see how the organized efforts of their women have contributed to the elevation of the race and their marvelous achievement in so short a time."[32] By her estimate, there were five thousand "colored women's societies" with half a million members. Black women organized separately from white women because they were serving a different population with distinctive needs but also because they were usually refused admission into white women's clubs. Racism was alive and well in the women's club movement.

The relation of the Gilded Age women's club phenomenon to woman suffrage is complex. At first, white women who formed and joined clubs took care to distinguish themselves from the radicalism and notoriety associated with woman suffragists. Yet women's rights and woman suffrage were standard subjects for club discussion, and over time members came to accept the idea that women should have political tools to accomplish their public goals. Black clubwomen were less hesitant to embrace woman suffrage in light of their concerns over the disfranchisement of black men. Over time women's clubs incubated support for woman suffrage within a wide swath of the female middle class and prepared the way for the tremendous growth in the suffrage movement in the early twentieth century (see pp. 469–76).

The Woman's Christian Temperance Union

The largest women's organization of the Woman's Era was the Woman's Christian Temperance Union (WCTU). Following on women's temperance activities in the 1850s (see p. 264), the WCTU was formed in 1874 after a series of women's "crusades" in Ohio and New York that convinced local saloon owners to abandon the liquor trade. Initially focused on changing drinking behavior at the individual level, the organization soon challenged the liquor industry politically and undertook a wide range of public welfare projects such as prison reform, recreation and vocational training for young people, establishment of kindergartens, labor reform, and international peace. These projects and the ability of the WCTU to cultivate both organizational loyalty and individual growth among its members were characteristics it shared with women's clubs, but the WCTU was different in

◆ **Frances Willard Learns to Ride a Bicycle**

Frances Willard, president of the WCTU, combined sympathy with conventional Protestant middle-class women and an advanced understanding of women's untapped capacities. In 1895, "sighing for new worlds to conquer," she learned to ride a bicycle, one of the signature New Woman activities of the period. "Reducing the problem to actual figures," she methodically reported, "it took me about three months, with an average of fifteen minutes' practice daily, to learn, first, to pedal; second, to turn; third, to dismount; and fourth, to mount."[33] Willard, not yet sixty, died in 1898, after which the WCTU never regained its prominence or progressive vision. *Courtesy of the Frances E. Willard Memorial Library and Archives.*

crucial ways. On the one hand, it defined itself explicitly as Christian; on the other hand, it was racially more inclusive than the club movement. The writer Frances E. W. Harper (see p. 270) was one of several African American WCTU spokes-women, and black women were welcomed into the organization, though in sepa-rate divisions. The WCTU's centers of strength were less urban and more western and midwestern than those of women's clubs.

Finally, unlike the women's club movement, the WCTU was to a large degree the product of a single and highly effective leader, Frances Willard. Willard was born in 1839 and raised on a farm in Ohio. She never married. Determined to serve "the class that I have always loved and that has loved me always—the girls of my native land and my times,"[34] at age thirty-four she became the first Dean of Women at Northwestern University. In 1879, she was elected president of the WCTU, rapidly increasing its membership, diversifying its purposes, and making it the most powerful women's organization in the country. Disciplined and diplo-matic, she was able to take the WCTU to levels of political action and reform that the unwieldy mass of clubwomen could never reach. Notably, this included active advocacy of woman suffrage, which the WCTU formally and enthusiastically endorsed in 1884. "If we are ever to save the State," Willard declared, "we must enfranchise the sex . . . which is much more acclimatized to self-sacrifice for oth-ers. . . . Give us the vote, in order that we may help in purifying politics."[35]

Consolidating the Gilded Age Women's Movement

The endorsement of woman suffrage by the WCTU convinced Susan B. Anthony to encourage and draw together the pro-suffrage leanings developing within so many women's organizations. "Those active in great philanthropic enterprises," she insisted, "[will] sooner or later realize that so long as women are not acknowl-edged to be the political equals of men, their judgment on public questions will have but little weight."[36] Accordingly, in 1888, in honor of the fortieth anniver-sary of the Seneca Falls Convention, the National Woman Suffrage Association (NWSA) sponsored an International Congress of Women, attended by represen-tatives of several European countries and many U.S. women's organizations. Out of this congress came an International Council of Women and a U.S. National Council of Women, both formed in 1893. Both organizations were so broadly inclusive of women's public and civic activities as to admit anti-suffrage groups, and much to Anthony's disappointment, neither served as the vehicle for advanc-ing the prospects of woman suffrage.

Other overarching organizational structures were formed. In 1890, the NWSA and the American Woman Suffrage Association reconciled, forming the National American Woman Suffrage Association, which led the suffrage movement for the next thirty years. On the international level, U.S. suffragists joined with European colleagues to initiate the formation of an International Woman Suffrage Associa-tion in 1902. The associative impulse was constantly tending to greater and greater combination, amalgamating women in clubs, clubs in state federations, and state federations in national organizations. The vision shared by these federative efforts was of a unity of women so broad and ecumenical as to obliterate all differences between women. But the vision of all-inclusivity was a fantasy. For as women's social activism and public involvement grew, so did their ambitions and rivalries. Even as the National Council of Women was formed, the leaders of the venerable Sorosis club, who felt they should have been chosen to head this endeavor, set up a rival in the General Federation of Women's Clubs. Nor were federations any more racially inclusive than individual clubs. The General Federation of Women's Clubs refused to admit black women's clubs. In 1895, African American women's clubs federated separately as the National Association of Colored Women, and the next year the National Council of Jewish Women was formed.

The ambitious scope and unresolved divisions of "organized womanhood" were equally on display in Chicago in 1893 at the World's Columbian Exposition, America's first world's fair. The Board of Lady Managers, led by wealthy Chicagoan Bertha Palmer, received public funds to build and furnish a special Woman's Building. At the Congress of Representative Women, an elaborate weeklong event, more than eighty sessions addressed "all lines of thought connected with the progress of women." The promise of the Woman's Building was that "all organizations can come together with perfect freedom and entire harmony and discuss the problems presented, even from divergent points of view, with utmost friendliness."[37] But its conception, establishment, and management were rife with disagreement, power struggles, and frustrated ambitions. The Board of Lady Managers argued with Susan B. Anthony and Frances Willard about how prominent to make woman suffrage. Despite much rhetoric about the importance of women's work, wage-earning women were not invited to participate in the building's planning or to speak for themselves at the congresses. And the leadership of the Woman's Building was as white as its gleaming walls. African American women, proud of their achievements since emancipation, petitioned Palmer to include them in the planning and management—but to no end. Willing as always to speak uncomfortable truths to those in power, Ida B. Wells exposed racism at the fair in a pamphlet she coauthored with Frederick Douglass, *Reasons Why the Colored American Is Not in the World's Columbian Exposition* (1893). Women from indigenous cultures, including the American Eskimo, were "on display" on the fair's midway as exotics.

Looking to the Future

By 1890, a new, more modern culture was slowly gathering force under the complacent surface of late nineteenth-century America. The Gilded Age was organized around grand and opposing categories: home and work, black and white, capital and labor, virtue and vice, masculine and feminine. While nineteenth-century society subscribed to a rigid hierarchy of values and a firm belief in absolute truth, modernist convictions allowed for greater contingency and relativism in assessing people and ideas. The concept of morality, so crucial to nineteenth-century cultural judgment, was losing some of its coercive force, giving way to a greater emphasis on individuality, inner life, the free development of personality, and psychological variety.

◆ **The Woman's Building**
The Woman's Building was one of the most successful exhibits at the World's Columbian
Exposition in Chicago in 1893. Everything about it demonstrated the variety and extent of
women's achievements. The architect was twenty-two-year-old Sophia Hayden, and all the
interior adornments were designed by women. Books written by women filled the library,
and paintings by women lined the art gallery. This photograph shows the special organizational hall where the achievements of women in their various organizations and societies
were on display. © *Corbis.*

An important sign of this cultural shift was the growing displacement of the
ideal of the "true woman" by the image of the "New Woman," both in women's
rights circles and in popular representations of femininity. For modern women of
the late nineteenth century, true womanhood no longer seemed virtuous and
industrious but idle and purposeless. New Women pushed against the boundaries
of woman's sphere to participate in public life, whether by earning a wage, gaining an education, or performing community service. (See Visual Sources: The

Higher Education of Women in the Postbellum Years, pp. 369–78.) Their ethic emphasized "woman's work," a term that sometimes meant paid labor, sometimes public service, but always an alternative to exclusive domesticity.

Clubwoman and author Charlotte Perkins Gilman was the first great spokeswoman for the New Woman. Gilman went so far as to criticize the single family household and the exclusive dedication of women to motherhood. "With the larger socialization of the woman of today, the fitness for and accompanying desire for wider combination, more general interest, . . . more organized methods of work for larger ends," she wrote in her widely read *Women and Economics* (1898), "she feels more and more heavily the intensely personal limits of the more primitive home duties, interests, methods."[38] Gilman's writings emphasized a second element of the New Woman ethic, the importance of female individuation, of each woman realizing her distinctive talents, capacities, and personality. Individualism was a long-standing American value, but it had been traditionally reserved for men. Men were individuals with different abilities; women were members of a category with common characteristics. New Womanhood challenged this vision of contrasting masculinity and femininity and claimed the legacy of individualism for women.

At age seventy-seven, Elizabeth Cady Stanton stressed this dimension in her 1892 speech "The Solitude of Self," presented to a committee of the U.S. Congress and then to the National American Woman Suffrage Association. "The point I wish plainly to bring before you on this occasion," she began, "is the individuality of each human soul. . . . In discussing the rights of woman, we are to consider, first, what belongs to her as an individual, in a world of her own, the arbiter of her own destiny."[39] The speech was Stanton's swan song from suffrage leadership. Anthony's vision of a moderate, broad-based suffrage movement contrasted with Stanton's inclination to relentlessly challenge women's conventional values. A few years later, Stanton went so far as to lambaste the Bible for its misogyny. The greatest expression of her lifelong passion for individual women's freedom, "The Solitude of Self" looked forward to a future of women's efforts for emancipation that would be so different from the approach of the Woman's Era, so modern in its emphasis on the self and on psychological change, as to require a new name: feminism.

CONCLUSION: Toward a New Womanhood

The end of the Civil War ushered in a period of great conflict. Reconstruction sought to restore the Union and to replace sectionalism with a single sense of nationhood, but at its end in 1877 unity remained elusive for all Americans. Various terms for the post-Reconstruction era indicate its different aspects. In the South during Redemption, black and white women regarded each other over an embattled racial gulf, altered and intensified by emancipation. Meanwhile, in the America of the Gilded Age, a new divide had opened up between labor and capital. As the American economy became increasingly industrialized, the numbers and visibility of women wage earners grew, along with their determination to join in efforts to bring democracy to American class relations. For their part, middle- and upper-class women created what is called the Woman's Era as they pursued new opportunities in education, civic organization, and public authority.

Two other aspects of the changing face of America in the late nineteenth century are considered in Chapter 7: the massive immigration that underlay the growth, and much of the assertiveness, of the American working class; and the physical expansion and consolidation of the nation through the further incorporation of western lands. Women were important actors in the multifaceted political crisis in the 1890s, which brought together all of these phenomena — racial and class conflict, woman's expanding sphere, massive ethnic change, and the nation's physical expansion up to and beyond its borders. By 1900, women were poised on the brink of one of the most active and important eras in American history through women's eyes, the Progressive years.

DOCUMENTS

Ida B. Wells, "Race Woman"

I N THE YEARS AFTER 1877, when the federal protections of Reconstruction ended and the freed black population of the South was left on its own to resist resurgent white supremacy, a generation of exceptional female African American leaders emerged. Of these, none was more extraordinary than Ida B. Wells. Born in 1862 in Mississippi, she was orphaned at the age of sixteen by a yellow fever epidemic. Determined to assume responsibility for her siblings and to keep her family together, she found·work first as a teacher and then as a journalist. In 1889 in Memphis, she purchased part ownership of an African American newspaper, the *Free Speech.* Her goal was to expose and publicize the mistreatment of her people. In an age notable for its florid and euphemistic writing, Wells's style was straightforward and explicit. She was not afraid to use the word "rape" to describe the accusations against black men and the experiences of black women.

Wells was catapulted into the role that changed her life when an African American man she knew, Thomas Moss, was lynched by a Memphis mob in 1892 (see pp. 335–36). Although the practice of lynching had a long history elsewhere, in the South during this period, the accused were black and the mobs white. Wells concluded that Moss's "crime" had been the competition that his successful grocery business posed to whites. Over a hundred years later, we take for granted the connections that she was the first to make: between the postwar political and economic gains made by freed people and the brutal violence unleashed on them by resentful whites; and between the long history of sexual exploitation of black women during slavery and the inflammatory charges made after emancipation to justify lynching — that black men were sexual predators.

Perhaps the most remarkable element of Wells's analysis was her insistence that black and white people sometimes voluntarily chose to be each other's sexual partners. She was not particularly in favor of the practice. She was what was called in this period a "race woman," meaning that her concerns were less for integration than for the happiness and progress of African Americans. "A proper self-respect is expected of races as individuals," she later wrote, "We need more race love; the tie of racehood should bind us [through] . . . a more hearty appreciation of each other."[40] Nonetheless, she appreciated the difference between willing and coerced sexuality and defended the former while criticizing the latter. She understood that so long as interracial sex was concealed as a fact of southern life, black people would pay the deadly price.

Her investigations into the practice of lynching got her driven out of Memphis in 1892. This autobiographical account details the impact that her harrowing experience had on African American women in the North, who went on to form the National Association of Colored Women and to join in the work of exposing the true nature, extent, and causes of southern lynchings. Exiled from the South, she moved to Chicago, where in 1895 she married Frederick Barnett, also a journalist and activist, and continued to battle for justice for her race by working for greater political power for black people. She played an early role in organizing African American women to secure and use the right to vote. Her autobiography remained unfinished and unpublished until brought into print by her youngest child, Alfreda Duster, more than a century after her mother's birth.

As you read, consider what led Wells to undertake an expose of lynching and how doing so challenged the expectations of race and gender that she faced. What does Wells's analysis of the causes of and attitudes toward the lynching of African Americans reveal about the dynamics between whites and blacks several decades after the end of slavery?

IDA B. WELLS
Crusade for Justice: The Autobiography of Ida B. Wells (1970)

While I was thus carrying on the work of my newspaper, . . . there came the lynching in Memphis which changed the whole course of my life. . . .

Thomas Moss, Calvin McDowell, and Henry Stewart owned and operated a grocery store in a thickly populated suburb. . . . There was already a grocery owned and operated by a white man who hitherto had had a monopoly on the trade of this thickly populated colored suburb. Thomas's grocery changed all that, and he and his associates were made to feel that they were not welcome by the white grocer. . . .

One day some colored and white boys quarreled over a game of marbles and the colored boys got the better of the fight which followed. . . . Then the challenge was issued that the vanquished whites were coming on Saturday night to clean out [Thomas's] Colored People's Grocery Company. . . . Accordingly the grocery company armed

several men and stationed them in the rear of the store on that fatal Saturday night, not to attack but repel a threatened attack. . . . The men stationed there had seen several white men stealing through the rear door and fired on them without a moment's pause. Three of these men were wounded, and others fled and gave the alarm. . . . Over a hundred colored men were dragged from their homes and put in jail on suspicion.

All day long on that fateful Sunday white men were permitted in the jail to look over the imprisoned black men. . . . The mob took out of their cells Thomas Moss, Calvin McDowell, and Henry Stewart, the three officials of the People's Grocery Company. They were loaded on a switch engine of the railroad which ran back of the jail, carried a mile north of the city limits, and horribly shot to death. One of the morning papers held back its edition in order to supply its readers with the details of that lynching. . . . The mob took possession of the People's Grocery Company, helping themselves to food and drink, and destroyed what they could not eat or steal. The

SOURCE: Alfreda M. Duster, ed., *Crusade for Justice: The Autobiography of Ida B. Wells* (Chicago: University of Chicago Press, 1970), 47–82.

creditors had the place closed and a few days later what remained of the stock was sold at auction. Thus, with the aid of city and county authorities and the daily papers, that white grocer had indeed put an end to his rival Negro grocer as well as to his business. . . .

Like many another person who had read of lynchings in the South, I had accepted the idea meant to be conveyed—that although lynching was irregular and contrary to law and order, unreasoning anger over the terrible crime of rape led to the lynching; that perhaps the brute deserved death anyhow and the mob was justified in taking his life.

But Thomas Moss, Calvin McDowell and Henry Stewart had been lynched in Memphis, one of the leading cities of the South, in which no lynching had taken place before, with just as much brutality as other victims of the mob; and they had committed no crime against white women. This is what opened my eyes to what lynching really was. An excuse to get rid of Negroes who were acquiring wealth and property and thus keep the race terrorized and "keep the nigger down." I then began an investigation of every lynching I read about. I stumbled on the amazing record that every case of rape reported . . . became such only when it became public.

Many cases were like that of the lynching which happened in Tunica County, Mississippi. The Associated Press reporter said, "The big burly brute was lynched because he had raped the seven-year-old daughter of the sheriff." I visited the place afterward and saw the girl, who was a grown woman more than seventeen years old. She had been found in the lynched Negro's cabin by her father, who had led the mob against him in order to save his daughter's reputation. That Negro was a helper on the farm. . . .

It was with these and other stories in mind in that last week in May 1892 that I wrote the following editorial:

Eight Negroes lynched since last issue of the *Free Speech*. They were charged with killing white men and five with raping

white women. Nobody in this section believes the old thread-bare lie that Negro men assault white women. If Southern white men are not careful they will overreach themselves and a conclusion will be drawn which will be very damaging to the moral reputation of their women.

This editorial furnished at last the excuse for doing what the white leaders of Memphis had long been wanting to do: put an end to the *Free Speech*. . . .

Having lost my paper, had a price put on my life, and been made an exile from home for hinting at the truth, I felt that I owed it to myself and to my race to tell the whole truth now that I was where I could do so freely. Accordingly, the fourth week in June, the *New York Age* had a seven-column article on the front page giving names, dates and places of many lynchings for alleged rape. This article showed conclusively that my editorial in the *Free Speech* was based on facts of illicit association between black men and white women.

Such relationships between white men and colored women were notorious, and had been as long as the two races had lived together in the South. . . . Many stories of the antebellum South were based upon such relationships. It has been frequently charged in narratives of slave times that these white fathers often sold their mulatto children into slavery. It was also well known that many other such white fathers and masters brought their mulatto and quadroon children to the North and gave them freedom and established homes for them, thus making them independent.

All my life I had known that such conditions were accepted as a matter of course. I found that this rape of helpless Negro girls and women, which began in slavery days, still continued without . . . hindrance, check or reproof from church, state, or press until there had been created this race within a race—and all designated by the inclusive term of "colored."

I also found that what the white man of the South practiced as all right for himself, he assumed to be unthinkable in white women. They could and did fall in love with the pretty mulatto and quadroon girls as well as black ones, but they professed an inability to imagine white women doing the same thing with Negro and mulatto men. Whenever they did so and were found out, the cry of rape was raised, and the lowest element of the white South was turned loose to wreak its fiendish cruelty on those too weak to help themselves. . . .

The more I studied the situation, the more I was convinced that the Southerner had never gotten over his resentment that the Negro was no longer his plaything, his servant, and his source of income. The federal laws for Negro protection passed during Reconstruction had been made a mockery by the white South where it had not secured their repeal. This same white South had secured political control of its several states, and as soon as white southerners came into power they began to make playthings of Negro lives and property. This still seemed not enough "to keep the nigger down."

Here came lynch law to stifle Negro manhood which defended itself, and the burning alive of Negroes who were weak enough to accept favors from white women. The many unspeakable and unprintable tortures to which Negro rapists (?) [here Wells inserted a parenthetical question mark to indicate her skepticism of these charges] of white women were subjected were for the purpose of striking terror into the hearts of other Negroes who might be thinking of consorting with willing white women.

I found that in order to justify these horrible atrocities to the world, the Negro was branded as a race of rapists, who were especially after white women. I found that white men who had created a race of mulattoes by raping and consorting with Negro women were still doing so wherever they could; these same white men lynched, burned and tortured Negro men for doing the same thing with white women; even when the white women were willing victims.

That the entire race should be branded as moral monsters and despoilers of white woman-

hood and childhood was bound to rob us of all the friends we had and silence any protests that they might make for us. For all these reasons it seemed a stern duty to give the facts I had collected to the world. . . .

About two months after my appearance in the columns in the *New York Age,* two colored women remarked on my revelations during a visit with each other and said they thought that the women of New York and Brooklyn should do something to show appreciation of my work and to protest the treatment which I had received. . . . A committee of two hundred and fifty women was appointed, and they stirred up sentiment throughout the two cities which culminated in a testimonial at Lyric Hall on 5 October 1892.

This testimonial was conceded by the oldest inhabitants to be the greatest demonstration ever attempted by race women for one of their number. . . . The leading colored women of Boston and Philadelphia had been invited to join in this demonstration, and they came, a brilliant array . . . behind a lonely, homesick girl who was an exile because she had tried to defend the manhood of her race. . . .

So many things came out of that wonderful testimonial.

First it was the beginning of the club movement among the colored women in this country. The women of New York and Brooklyn decided to continue that organization, which they called the Women's Loyal Union. These were the first strictly women's clubs organized in those cities. Mrs. Ruffin of Boston, who came over to that testimonial . . . called a meeting of the women at her home to meet me, and they organized themselves into the Woman's Era Club of that city. Mrs. Ruffin had been a member of the foremost clubs among white women in Boston for years, but this was her first effort to form one among colored women. . . .

Second, that testimonial was the beginning of public speaking for me. I have already said that I had not before made speeches, but invitations came from Philadelphia, Wilmington, Delaware, Chester, Pennsylvania, and Washington, D.C. . . .

In Philadelphia . . . Miss Catherine Impey of Street Somerset, England, was visiting Quaker relatives of hers in the city and at the same time was trying to learn what she could about the color question in this country. She was the editor of *Anti-Caste,* a magazine published in England in behalf of the natives of India, and she was there-fore interested in the treatment of darker races everywhere. . . . [Thus happened] the third great result of that wonderful testimonial in New York the previous month. Although we did not know it at the time, the interview between Miss Impey and myself resulted in an invitation to England and the beginning of the worldwide campaign against lynching.

QUESTIONS FOR ANALYSIS

1. What were the underlying tensions and larger conflicts that led to the lynching of Thomas Moss?

2. What was the prevailing opinion about lynching that Wells was determined to challenge?

3. What did Wells see as the relationship between the long history of white men raping black women and the charges raised against black men of raping white women?

4. How did Wells's campaign contribute to the consolidation of the organized African American women's movement?

DOCUMENTS

The Woman Who Toils

THE LIVES AND LABORS of wage-earning women and leisure-class women intersected in numerous ways in the late nineteenth century. Maids, cooks, nannies, and laundresses provided the labor that made possible the elaborate homes and active social lives of leisure-class women. Working women and their children were the objects of the charitable and philanthropic projects that middle- and upper-class women, aiming for a larger role in community affairs, organized in these years. Above all, working women provided the labor to manufacture the food, clothing, and luxuries that distinguished the rich from the poor. As the authors of *The Woman Who Toils* wrote to wealthy women, working women provided "the labour that must be done to satisfy your material demands."[41]

By the end of the century, working-class women were also the subject of professional women's journalistic and sociological investigations, of which *The Woman Who Toils: Being the Experiences of Two Ladies as Factory Girls* (1903) is a notable example. The authors, Bessie and Marie Van Vorst, were upper-class women. Marie was born a Van Vorst, and Bessie married into the family. Neither went to college. Both were educated instead in the manner preferred by the upper classes for their daughters, by private tutors and at female academies. After Bessie's husband, Marie's brother, died, the two women, both still in their thirties, undertook together to establish greater economic independence for themselves. They moved to Paris and cowrote a novel about an upper-class American woman abroad. Their next collaborative effort was *The Woman Who Toils*, a journalistic account of the lives of wage-earning women. As upper-class New Women aspiring to independence, they were motivated by both their growing awareness of the lives of working-class women and their own authorial ambitions.

To research the book, they returned to the United States, assumed fictional identities, and took a series of working-class jobs. Marie worked in a New England shoe factory and a southern textile mill. Bessie became the Irishwoman "Esther Kelly" and took a job in a pickling factory in Pittsburgh, where she went from eagerness to exhaustion in a few short days. Moving from job to job in the factory, Bessie explored how different it felt to work for a preset daily wage and to work for payment by the piece—an arrangement that led workers to drive themselves to work faster. A day in the male workers' dining room allowed her to compare manufacturing to domestic service labor.

Throughout Bessie's account, the distance she maintained from the women she wrote about is evident. She and her sister-in-law chose a subtitle to clarify that they were still "ladies" despite their brief stint as factory girls. The young men with whom their coworkers associated, the recreation they sought, and the clothes they wore seemed to them "vulgar." Like most reformers, they did not endorse wage labor for women with children, a point emphasized by President Theodore Roosevelt in his introduction to their book. Nonetheless, Bessie came to appreciate the generosity of her coworkers, the pleasures of collective work, and the "practical, progressive" democracy of working-class life. Above all, it was the sheer physical demands of doing the job, descriptions of which are among the best parts of the Pittsburgh pickling section of *The Woman Who Toils*, that seem to have broken through her shield of gentility and brought her a measure of closeness to the women workers about whom she wrote.

As you read this account of working in the pickle factory, identify what Bessie Van Vorst finds attractive about the jobs she does and the women who do them, and what she finds repellent. Consider the points at which her class prejudices emerge, and the points at which she gets beyond them.

MRS. JOHN (BESSIE) VAN VORST AND MARIE VAN VORST
The Woman Who Toils: Being the Experiences of Two Ladies as Factory Girls (1903)

"What will you do about your name?" "What will you do with your hair and your hands?" "How can you deceive people?" These are some of the questions I had been asked by my friends.

Before any one had cared or needed to know my name it was morning of the second day, and my assumed name seemed by that time the only one I had ever had. As to hair and hands, a half-day's work suffices for their undoing. And my disguise is so successful I have deceived not only others but myself. I have become with desperate reality a factory girl, alone, inexperienced, friendless. I am making $4.20 a week and spending $3 of this for board alone, and I dread not being strong enough to keep my job. I climb endless stairs, am given a white cap and an apron, and my life as a factory girl begins. I become part of the ceaseless, unrelenting mechanism kept in motion by the poor....

My first task is an easy one; anybody could do it. On the stroke of seven my fingers fly. I place a lid of paper in a tin jar-top, over it a cork; this I press down with both hands, tossing the cover, when done, into a pan. In spite of myself I hurry; I cannot work fast enough — I outdo my companions. How can they be so slow? Every nerve, every muscle is offering some of its energy. Over in one corner the machinery for sealing the jars groans and roars; the mingled sounds of filling, washing, wiping, packing, comes to my eager ears as an accompaniment for the simple work assigned to me. One hour passes, two, three hours; I fit ten, twenty, fifty dozen caps, and still my energy keeps up....

When I have fitted 110 dozen tin caps the forewoman comes and changes my job. She tells me to haul and load up some heavy crates with pickle jars. I am wheeling these back and forth when the twelve o'clock whistle blows. Up to that time the room has been one big dynamo, each girl a part of it. With the first moan of the noon signal the dynamo comes to life. It is hungry; it has friends and favourites — news to tell. We herd down to a big dining room and take our places, five hundred of us in all. The newspaper bundles are unfolded. The menu varies little: bread and

SOURCE: Mrs. John Van Vorst and Marie Van Vorst, *The Woman Who Toils: Being the Experiences of Two Ladies as Factory Girls* (New York: Doubleday, Page & Co, 1903), 21–58.

jam, cake and pickles, occasionally a sausage, a bit of cheese or a piece of stringy cold meat. In ten minutes the repast is over. The dynamo has been fed; there are twenty minutes of leisure spent in dancing, singing, resting, and conversing chiefly about young men and "sociables."

At 12:30 sharp the whistle draws back the life it has given. I return to my job. My shoulders are beginning to ache. My hands are stiff, my thumbs almost blistered. The enthusiasm I had felt is giving way to numbing weariness. I look at my companions now in amazement. How can they keep on so steadily, so swiftly? . . . New girls like myself who had worked briskly in the morning are beginning to loiter. Out of the washing-tins hands come up red and swollen, only to be plunged again into hot dirty water. Would the whistle never blow? . . . At last the whistle blows! In a swarm we report: we put on our things and get away into the cool night air. I have stood ten hours; I have fitted 1,300 corks; I have hauled and loaded 4,000 jars of pickles. My pay is seventy cents. . . .

For the two days following my first experience I am unable to resume work. Fatigue has swept through my body like a fever. Every bone and joint has a clamouring ache. . . .

The next day is Saturday. I feel a fresh excitement at going back to my job; the factory draws me toward it magnetically. I long to be in the hum and whir of the busy workroom. Two days of leisure without resources or amusement make clear to me how the sociability of factory life, the freedom from personal demands, the escape from self can prove a distraction to those who have no mental occupation, no money to spend on diversion. It is easier to submit to factory government which commands five hundred girls with one law valid for all, than to undergo the arbitrary discipline of parental authority. I speed across the snow-covered courtyard. In a moment my cap and apron are on and I am sent to report to the head forewoman. . . .

She wears her cap close against her head. Her front hair is rolled up in crimping-pins. She has false teeth and is a widow. Her pale, parched face shows what a great share of life has been taken by daily over-effort repeated during years. As she talks she touches my arm in a kindly fashion and looks at me with blue eyes that float about under weary lids. "You are only at the beginning," they seem to say. "Your youth and vigour are at full tide, but drop by drop they will be sapped from you, to swell the great flood of human effort that supplies the world's material needs. You will gain in experience," the weary lids flutter at me, "but you will pay *with your life* the living you make."

There is no variety in my morning's work. Next to me is a bright, pretty girl jamming chopped pickles into bottles.

"How long have you been here?" I ask, attracted by her capable appearance. She does her work easily and well.

"About five months."

"How much do you make?"

"From 90 cents to $1.05. I'm doing piecework," she explains. "I get seven-eighths of a cent for every dozen bottles I fill. I have to fill eight dozen to make seven cents. . . ."

"Do you live at home?" I ask.

"Yes; I don't have to work. I don't pay no board. My father and my brothers supports me and my mother. But," and her eyes twinkle, "I couldn't have the clothes I do if I didn't work."

"Do you spend your money all on yourself?"

"Yes."

I am amazed at the cheerfulness of my companions. They complain of fatigue, of cold, but never at any time is there a suggestion of ill-humour. The suppressed animal spirits reassert themselves when the forewoman's back is turned. Companionship is the great stimulus. I am confident that without the . . . encouragement of example, it would be impossible to obtain as much from each individual girl as is obtained from them in groups of tens, fifties, hundreds working together.

When lunch is over we are set to scrubbing. Every table and stand, every inch of the factory floor must be scrubbed in the next four hours. . . .

The grumbling is general. There is but one opinion among the girls: it is not right that they should be made to do this work. They all echo the same resentment, but their complaints are made in whispers; not one has the courage to openly rebel. What, I wonder to myself, do the men do on scrubbing day. I try to picture one of them on his hands and knees in a sea of brown mud. It is impossible. The next time I go for a supply of soft soap in a department where the men are working I take a look at the masculine interpretation of house cleaning. One man is playing a hose on the floor and the rest are scrubbing the boards down with long-handled brooms and rubber mops.

"You take it easy," I say to the boss.

"I won't have no scrubbing in my place," he answers emphatically. "The first scrubbing day they says to me 'Get down on your hands and knees,' and I says — 'Just pay me my money, will you; I'm goin' home. What scrubbing can't be done with mops ain't going to be done by me.' The women wouldn't have to scrub, either, if they had enough spirit all of 'em to say so."

I determined to find out if possible, during my stay in the factory, what it is that clogs this mainspring of "spirit" in the women. . . .

After a Sunday of rest I arrive somewhat ahead of time on Monday morning, which leaves me a few moments for conversation with a piece-worker who is pasting labels on mustard jars. . . .

"I bet you can't guess how old I am."

I look at her. Her face and throat are wrinkled, her hands broad and scrawny; she is tall and has short skirts. What shall be my clue? If I judge by pleasure, "unborn" would be my answer; if by effort, then "a thousand years."

"Twenty," I hazard as a safe medium.

"Fourteen," she laughs. "I don't like it at home, the kids bother me so. Mamma's people are well-to-do. I'm working for my own pleasure."

"Indeed, I wish I was," says a new girl with a red waist. "We three girls supports mamma and runs the house. We have $13 rent to pay and a load of coal every month and groceries. It's no joke, I can tell you." . . .

Monday is a hard day. There is more complaining, more shirking, more gossip than in the middle of the week. Most of the girls have been to dances on Saturday night, to church on Sunday evening with some young man. Their conversation is vulgar and prosaic; there is nothing in the language they use that suggests an ideal or any conception of the abstract. . . . Here in the land of freedom, where no class line is rigid, the precious chance is not to serve but to live for oneself; not to watch a superior, but to find out by experience. The ideal plays no part, stern realities alone count, and thus we have a progressive, practical, independent people, the expression of whose personality is interesting not through their words but by their deeds.

When the Monday noon whistle blows I follow the hundreds down into the dining-room. . . . I am beginning to understand why the meager lunches of preserve-sandwiches and pickles more than satisfy the girls whom I was prepared to accuse of spending their money on gewgaws rather than on nourishment. It is fatigue that steals the appetite. I can hardly taste what I put in my mouth; the food sticks in my throat. . . . I did not want wholesome food, exhausted as I was. I craved sours and sweets, pickles, cakes, anything to excite my numbed taste. . . .

Accumulated weariness forces me to take a day off. When I return I am sent for in the corking-room. The forewoman lends me a blue gingham dress and tells me I am to do "piece"-work. There are three who work together at every corking-table. My two companions are a woman with goggles and a one-eyed boy. We are not a brilliant trio. The job consists in evening the vinegar in the bottles, driving the cork in, first with a machine, then with a hammer, letting out the air with a knife stuck under the cork, capping the corks, sealing the caps, counting and distributing the bottles. These operations are paid for at the rate of one-half a cent for the dozen bottles, which sum is divided among us. My two companions are earning a living, so I must work in dead earnest or take bread out of their mouths. . . .

There is a stimulus unsuspected in working to get a job done. Before this I had worked to make the time pass. Then no one took account of how much I did; the factory clock had a weighted pendulum; now ambition outdoes physical strength. The hours and my purpose are running a race together. But, hurry as I may, as we do, when twelve blows its signal we have corked only 210 dozen bottles! This is no more than day-work at seventy cents. With an ache in every muscle, I redouble my energy after lunch. The girl with the goggles looks at me blindly and says: "Ain't it just awful hard work? You can make good money, but you've got to hustle."

She is a forlorn specimen of humanity, ugly, old, dirty, condemned to the slow death of the over-worked. I am a green hand. I make mistakes; I have no experience in the fierce sustained effort of the bread-winners. Over and over I turn to her, over and over she is obliged to correct me. During the ten hours we work side by side not one murmur of impatience escapes her. When she sees that I am getting discouraged she calls out across the deafening din, "That's all right; you can't expect to learn in a day; just keep on steady." . . .

The oppressive monotony is one day varied by a summons to the men's dining-room. I go eagerly, glad of any change. . . . The dinner under preparation is for the men of the factory. There are two hundred of them. They are paid from $1.35 to $3 a day. Their wages begin upon the highest limit given to women. The dinner costs each man ten cents. The $20 paid in daily cover the expenses of the cook, two kitchen maids, and the dinner, which consists of meat, bread and butter, vegetables and coffee, sometimes soup, sometimes dessert. If this can pay for two hundred there is no reason why for five cents a hot meal of some kind could not be given to the women. They don't demand it, so they are left to make themselves ill on pickles and preserves. . . .

[In the dining room] I had ample opportunity to compare domestic service with factory work. We set the table for two hundred, and do a thousand miserable slavish tasks that must be begun again

the following day. At twelve the two hundred troop in, toil-worn and begrimed. They pass like locusts, leaving us sixteen hundred dirty dishes to wash up and wipe. This takes us four hours, and when we have finished the work stands ready to be done over the next morning with peculiar monotony. In the factory there is stimulus in feeling that the material which passes through one's hands will never be seen or heard of again. . . .

My first experience is drawing to a close. I have surmounted the discomforts of insufficient food, of dirt, a bed without sheets, the strain of hard manual labor. . . . In the factory where I worked men and women were employed for ten-hour days. The women's highest wages were lower than the men's lowest. Both were working as hard as they possibly could. The women were doing menial work, such as scrubbing, which the men refused to do. The men were properly fed at noon; the women satisfied themselves with cake and pickles. Why was this? It is of course impossible to generalize on a single factory. I can only relate the conclusions I drew from what I saw myself. The wages paid by employers, economists tell us, are fixed at the level of bare subsistence. This level and its accompanying conditions are determined by competition, by the nature and number of labourers taking part in the competition. In the masculine category I met but one class of competitor: the bread-winner. In the feminine category I found a variety of classes: the bread-winner, the semi-bread-winner, the woman who works for luxuries. This inevitably drags the wage level. The self-supporting girl is in competition with the child, with the girl who lives at home and makes a small contribution to the household expenses, and with the girl who is supported and who spends all her money on her clothes. It is this division of purpose which takes the "spirit" out of them as a class. There will be no strikes among them so long as the question of wages is not equally vital to them all. . . .

On the evening when I left the factory for the last time, I heard in the streets the usual cry of murders, accidents and suicides; the mental food of the overworked. It is Saturday night. I mingle with a crowd of labourers homeward bound, and with women and girls returning from a Saturday sale in the big shops. They hurry along delighted at the cheapness of a bargain, little dreaming of the human effort that has produced it, the cost of life and energy it represents. As they pass, they draw their skirts aside from us, the cooperators who enable them to have the luxuries they do; from us, the multitude who stand between them and the monster Toil that must be fed with human lives. Think of us, as we herd in the winter dawn; think of us as we bend over our task all the daylight without rest; think of us at the end of the day as we resume suffering and anxiety in homes of squalour and ugliness; think of us as we make our wretched try for merriment; think of us as we stand protectors between you and the labour that must be done to satisfy your material demands; think of us—be merciful.

QUESTIONS FOR ANALYSIS

1. What different sorts of women does Bessie Van Vorst meet in the factory, and how and why do their responses to their work vary?

2. Why does Van Vorst conclude that working women are passive in accepting their working conditions and unwilling to stand up for themselves in the way of working men? Do you think she is right?

3. How might the working women described in *The Woman Who Toils* have responded on reading the book? What accounts for your view?

4. In light of Van Vorst's final comments, how do you think her life and attitudes were changed by her experience as a factory girl?

The Higher Education of Women
in the Postbellum Years

WHENEVER WOMEN HAVE SOUGHT to improve their lives, almost invariably they have begun by aspiring to better education. "The neglected education of my fellow-creatures is the grand source of the misery I deplore," wrote British feminist Mary Wollstonecraft in 1792.[42] In the revolutionary era, grateful political leaders praised educated women for their role in mothering an enlightened (male) citizenry (see p. 146). Within fifty years, women were teachers in America's burgeoning system of public education. Even so, women continued to have far less access to education than men. Before the Civil War, women could rise no further than the high school level at all-female seminaries. Only Ohio's Oberlin College, an evangelical Protestant institution founded in 1833, admitted a few women to its regular baccalaureate course, most famously women's rights advocate Lucy Stone, who graduated in 1847. Even at Oberlin, however, most women students were educated in a special "ladies' program," with easier language and mathematics requirements than the baccalaureate course.

Two developments in the 1860s made higher education much more available to women. In 1862, the Morrill Land Grant Act provided federal lands to states and territories for the support of public institutions of higher education. While the act did not explicitly mention women, as one historian has explained, "taxpayers demanded that their daughters, as well as their sons, be admitted."[43] As coeducation spread, long-standing concerns that such easy association between the sexes would coarsen women students and distract men began to give way. The great land-grant universities established in the 1860s and early 1870s in Illinois, Nebraska, Kansas, Arkansas, Ohio, and California accepted women students. Public universities founded earlier—in Michigan, Indiana, Iowa, Missouri, and Wisconsin—changed their policies to admit women. Private universities such as Northwestern and the University of Chicago in Illinois, Stanford in California, and Tulane in Louisiana, and colleges such as Whitman in California, Colorado College, and Grinnell in Iowa, also followed the trend. By the end of the century, coeducational institutions granted college degrees to approximately four thousand women each year.

Because the land-grant universities were primarily in the Midwest and West, most coeducation occurred in these regions. The most important exception in the East was New York's Cornell University, which opened in 1868. Cornell, like virtually all other coeducational colleges and universities, nonetheless remained an institution shaped largely by the needs of men. Female students had to struggle

◆ **Figure 6.1 Chafing Dish Party, Cornell University (1904)**

to establish their own place, starting with where to live, since dormitories housed male students only. The establishment of sororities solved the problem in many state universities. At Cornell, benefactor Russell Sage donated a special women's building. Figure 6.1 is a 1904 photograph of Cornell women at a get-together called a "chafing dish party" in one of their rooms in Sage Hall. What do the activities, dress, and furnishings in the photograph indicate about these women's lives as college students? Consider also what the photograph suggests about the relations among women at a largely male institution.

After the Civil War, the establishment of all-women's colleges also increased women's opportunities for higher education. The first of these, Vassar College, opened in 1865, funded by a wealthy brewer from Poughkeepsie, New York, who wanted to create an educational institution "for young women which shall be to them, what Yale and Harvard are to young men."[44] Philanthropists endowed other all-female institutions, and by 1891 Smith and Wellesley colleges in Massachusetts, Bryn Mawr College outside Philadelphia, and Goucher College near Baltimore were graduating women with bachelor's degrees. (Mount Holyoke in Massachusetts, begun many years before as a female seminary, upgraded to college level in 1890.) These all-women institutions produced about sixteen hundred college graduates each year. Combining all-female and coeducational institutions, public and private, by 1890 women were approximately 40 percent of the total of college graduates—an extraordinary development in less than four decades.

There was much debate about whether women students received a better education and had a better collegiate experience at an all-women's college or at a coed-

◆ **Figure 6.2 Class in Zoology, Wellesley College (1883–1884)**
Courtesy of Wellesley College Archives, photo by Seaver.

ucational institution. To strengthen their claims to intellectual superiority, the top women's colleges were dedicated to providing a first-class education in the sciences, which were becoming increasingly important in modern higher education. The Wellesley College class pictured in Figure 6.2 is studying zoology. The students are examining a fish skeleton and a piece of coral to learn about animal physiology. This photograph, like so many photos of late nineteenth-century college women, is carefully posed. How does the deliberate positioning of the students convey the intellectual seriousness, intensity, and engagement of the scientific learning going on in this all-female classroom? Consider the simple and functional character of the students' clothes, especially compared to the elaborate and costly appearance of elite women engaged in less serious pursuits (see picture on p. 347).

Figure 6.2 also underscores the opportunities that all-female colleges in this period provided for the employment of educated women. Here, unlike in most coeducational schools, women could be professors and administrators. The zoology professor, the young woman seated at the center, is Mary Alice Wilcox, a graduate of Newnham College, the women's college of Britain's Cambridge University. Standing behind her and slightly to the right is Alice Freeman, the twenty-eight-year-old Wellesley College president. Freeman, an early graduate of the University of Michigan, was the first woman to head an institution of higher education in the United States. In 1886, she married Harvard professor George Herbert Palmer and resigned her position as college president. Why might women professors have been employed only at all-women's colleges? What difference do you think they made to women's experience of higher education? How might the youth of professors such as Wilcox and administrators such as Freeman have influenced the learning of these women students?

Concerns went beyond the intellectual. Did coeducation provide too many opportunities for undo familiarity between young unmarried men and women? Were women's colleges hotbeds for passionate female friendships? Anxiety that higher education would have a negative impact on women's health, in particular on their reproductive capacities, haunted the early years of women's higher education. In 1873 Dr. Edward Clarke published a controversial book, *Sex and Education*, in which he argued that higher education for women drained vital physical energy—literally blood—from the reproductive organs to the brain. Defenders of women's education rushed to challenge Clarke's argument that higher education endangered women's reproductive and maternal vocation. They undertook scientific studies of women college students to demonstrate that physical health and intellectual growth were not incompatible. Proponents of women's education were particularly anxious to prove that the menstruation of college girls was not disrupted by disciplined study.

To further counter the charge that higher education weakened women physically, but also to strengthen women's bodies as well as their minds, colleges added women's athletics and physical education to their curricula. Competition, however, was prohibited as unladylike, certainly between the sexes in coeducational institutions but even among the women themselves. Nonetheless, in the 1890s, soon after basketball was introduced among young men, a modified version of the game became the rage among college women. Figure 6.3 is a photograph of the team of the class of 1904 from Wells College, an all-women's college in Aurora, New York. In addition to their white-tie blouses the players are wearing loose, divided "bloomer" skirts. What in the photograph gives evidence of the physical freedom that sports brought to women's college experience? Why might the photographer have posed the team members with their hands folded, rather than in a more forceful representation of young women in action?

Black women faced extraordinary educational challenges. In the first years of emancipation, the overwhelming goal for ex-slaves was basic literacy. During Reconstruction, black educational institutions were founded, virtually all of them opened to women as well as men, but these schools provided secondary and vocational rather than baccalaureate education. Even the nation's premiere all-black college, Howard University, founded in Washington, D.C., in 1867, did not open its collegiate program until 1897 and did not graduate its first woman BA until 1901. In the same year, Atlanta's all-female Spelman College also granted its first BA degree (see pp. 332–34).

By 1900, an estimated 252 African American women held bachelor's degrees, but almost all had been granted by predominantly white institutions, one-quarter from Oberlin College alone. Committed to equal education by both race and gender, Oberlin had produced the very first black woman college graduate—Mary Jane Patterson—in 1862. Many of its black female graduates, including Mary Church Terrell and Anna Julia Cooper, went on to become leading spokeswomen for their race and their sex.

◆ **Figure 6.3** **Basketball Team, Wells College (1904)**
Wells College Archives, Louis Jefferson Long Library, Aurora, New York.

In southern black educational institutions, the dramatic downturn in race relations in the 1880s and 1890s had a discouraging impact on higher education for African Americans. Instead of striving for academic equality with white colleges, they concentrated on preparing their students for skilled trades and manual vocations. This approach to higher education was preached by Booker T. Washington, the era's premiere African American educator. Figure 6.4 is a photograph of a history class at Hampton Institute, a freedmen's school founded in 1868 in Virginia where Washington began his career, and a model for many similar institutions throughout the South. In a controversial experiment in interracial education, Hampton also began enrolling Native American students in 1878.

Freedpeople regarded the educational opportunities that Hampton and other such schools provided them as immense privileges. Speaking at the 1873 graduation, Alice P. Davis, born a slave in North Carolina in 1852, praised Hampton Institute as her alma mater: "[A] mother indeed she has been to us, for she has given us more instruction in these three years than our dear but illiterate mothers ever could."[45] Nonetheless, such institutions, which were often overseen by white benefactors, maintained strict controls over their black students, to train them in the virtues of industriousness and self-discipline. The young women were prepared for jobs as teachers, but also as domestic servants and industrial workers.

In 1899, Hampton's white trustees hired America's first important female documentary photographer, Frances Benjamin Johnston, who was white, to portray the students' educational progress. Her photographs were displayed at the Paris

◆ **Figure 6.4 Class in American History, Hampton Institute (1899–1900)**
Library of Congress LC-USZ62-38149.

Exposition of 1900, where they were much praised for both their artistic achievement and their depiction of racial harmony. Figure 6.4, entitled "Class in American History," is an exceptionally rich image for the diversity of its subjects and the complexity of its content. A white female teacher stands among her female and male, African American and Native American, students. All are contemplating a Native American man in ceremonial dress. He can be likened in some way to the scientific specimens in Figure 6.2. Consider what the man himself might have been thinking as he was exhibited to the gaze of both the photographer and the history class. Historian Laura Wexler has unearthed the name of one of the students, the young Indian woman standing at the far right: she is Adele Quinney, a member of the Stockbridge tribe.[46] What lessons were she and the other students being taught about American history by the living exhibit of traditional Indian ways placed before them? What do their precise posing and uniform dress suggest about the discipline expected of Hampton students? Above all, what does this single image capture about the forces at work in late nineteenth-century American society?

During the post–Civil War years, many "normal colleges" were established to concentrate exclusively on the training of teachers. Such schools provided a briefer, less demanding program of study than baccalaureate courses. With less competitive standards for admission and lower costs, they educated a much larger number of women students. The first teacher training institution supported with public funds was founded in 1839 in Framingham, Massachusetts. Normal colleges also benefited from the 1862 Morrill Act and were an important avenue of upward mobility for working-class immigrants, African Americans, and other people of color.

Many of these institutions survived into the twentieth century and became full-fledged colleges and universities. Figure 6.5 is a photograph of a class at Washington, D.C.'s Normal College, established in 1873. Because Washington was a

◆ Figure 6.5 **Science Class, Washington, D.C., Normal College (1899)**
Library of Congress LC-USZ62-14684.

southern town, public education there was racially segregated, and the Normal College enrolled only white students. Washington's Myrtilla Miner Normal School, founded in 1851 and named after a heroic white woman educator of African American girls, enrolled only African American students. The two schools remained separate and segregated until 1955, one year after the Supreme Court found segregated education unconstitutional in the case of *Brown v. Board of Education* (see p. 611). Then they were merged into the District of Columbia Teachers College, now named the University of the District of Columbia.

As in Figure 6.2, the students in Figure 6.5 are studying science, once again illustrating the importance of this subject in meeting the ambitions that the leaders of women's higher education had to offer young women a modern and intellectually challenging education. And yet the kinds of teaching and learning that went on in an elite college such as Wellesley and a teacher training institution such as the Normal School were very different. The former had a far more educated faculty and resources of equipment and specimens that the latter lacked. Consider what other differences can be detected by comparing this photograph with Figure 6.2. Figure 6.5 also invites comparison with Figure 6.4 because both photographs were taken by Frances Johnston. How has Johnston positioned her subjects in this picture, compared to those at Hampton Institute? What educational message is this different staging meant to communicate?

Like teachers, doctors were trained in specialized medical colleges. For most of the nineteenth century, a bachelor's degree was not a prerequisite to study medicine in the United States. Instead, students studied medicine at special medical schools and in undergraduate medical departments of large universities. The first major obstacle that women faced was gaining admission into these all-male programs of medical education. Anxieties about coeducation were particularly intense over the prospect of women sitting beside men at lectures about the human body. But women's desire for medical education was strong. Medicine, unlike other professions such as law or the ministry, fit comfortably with women's traditional role as healers. In 1849, after applying to a dozen major medical schools, Elizabeth Blackwell broke this educational barrier by graduating from Geneva Medical College in rural upstate New York.

One remedy was the establishment of all-female medical colleges. The Boston Female Medical College was established in 1849 by Dr. Samuel Gregory, who wanted to train women to attend their own sex in childbirth. Dr. Elizabeth Blackwell founded the Women's Medical College of New York in 1868 to help other women follow her into the profession. Such all-female schools played a major role in educating women physicians, but as they lacked adequate clinical resources and opportunities, women continued to demand admission to men's medical colleges, where they were eventually accepted.

By 1890, women represented between 15 and 20 percent of all medical students. After 1890, the number of medical colleges shrank, even as their standards rose. Educationally, the crucial change came in 1893 when the Johns Hopkins University in Baltimore established the first postgraduate medical course in the United States. A group of women, led by Mary Garrett, close friend of Bryn Mawr College dean

◆ **Figure 6.6 Graduating Class, Medical College of Syracuse University (1876)**
Prints & Photographs Department/Moorland-Spingarn Research Center, Howard University.

M. Carey Thomas, donated $500,000 to the new postgraduate medical college on the condition that women be admitted along with men. Overall, however, women began to lose access to medical education after 1890, and the percentage of women in most medical schools dropped by half or more by the turn of the century.

Figure 6.6 is a photograph of the 1876 class of the Medical College of Syracuse University, which in 1872 absorbed the resources of Geneva Medical College, Elizabeth Blackwell's alma mater. This medical class was impressively diverse, not only because four of the students were women but because one of them was

African American. Sarah Loguen (after marriage, Fraser) was the daughter of a fugitive slave who became an abolitionist. After graduation, she practiced medicine in Washington, D.C. Notice that the men look much more directly at the photographer than the women, several of whom look down or away. Does this photograph provide any hints about how the male students regarded their female colleagues or how the women felt about their presence in the medical classroom?

QUESTIONS FOR ANALYSIS

1. Nineteenth-century women's higher education proceeded along two parallel lines: the struggle for coeducation and the establishment of all-women's institutions. What were the advantages and disadvantages of each approach?

2. In what way did the motivations for and rewards of higher education differ for white and African American women?

3. How did the growth of higher education for women relate to other major postbellum developments in women's history discussed in this chapter?

Alice Austen:
Gilded Age Photographer

Tʜᴇ ᴘʜᴏᴛᴏɢʀᴀᴘʜs ᴏғ Alice Austen document in a remarkable way two dimensions of the lives of middle- and upper-class women in the Gilded Age: the elaborate patterns of recreation that their wealth allowed them, and the challenges they began to make to established gender conventions. In other words, Austen recorded the society she saw both as a leisure-class woman and as a New Woman.

Austen was born in 1866 to a comfortable middle-class family that had moved away from the crowds and bustle of New York City for Staten Island, then a rural suburb. The conventional appearance of the Austen family hid the disturbing conditions of Alice's birth: her father deserted her mother when she was born, and Alice was raised with no knowledge of this man, not even his name. Nonetheless, Alice was by all accounts a happy and curious child in a family of adults that doted on her. She did not go to college, but attended a private high school for girls. By her late teens, her life was focused not on education or occupation, but on recreation. Although there were many young men in her circle of friends, she never married, later commenting that she was "too good to get married . . . too good at sports, too good at photography, too good at mechanical skills."[47] She chose instead to spend her life with another unmarried woman, Gertrude Tate, whom she met in 1899.

Austen made herself into a skilled photographer. Her seafaring uncle presented her with her first camera when she was only ten, and taking pictures became the center of her life. She made more than five thousand photographs in her lifetime, beginning with the heavy chemically coated glass negatives used in the 1880s and ending with the much simpler roll film of the Kodak era. She took extraordinary care to set up her photographs and position her sitters, and did all the difficult work of developing and printing herself.

Yet, for all her commitment, dedication, and lifelong involvement with photography, Austen was an amateur, meaning she did not make her living with her camera. She published one tiny book of pictures of Manhattan street life, and she was paid for only a handful of other photographs. Even when her fortunes declined, it never occurred to her to turn to her photography to support herself. During the Depression of the 1930s, she mortgaged and then lost ownership of the house in which she had been raised. She and Gertrude sold their belongings and scraped together a living, but by 1950, she was officially declared a pauper and remanded to the New York City Farm Colony on Staten Island. Months before she died, she and her photographs were rediscovered by a young photographic historian named Oliver Jensen, who was researching a book later published as *The Revolt of American Women* (1952).

Figure 6.7, taken in 1886, is one of the earliest of Austen's images to have survived. Austen took pictures of her friends doing gymnastics and on bicycles as well as at tennis. Austen is the formally dressed young woman on the left. Instead of relaxing from playing tennis, as her friends were, Austen was busy setting up her picture, arranging the sitters' positions, making sure the light was perfect, and using a remote device to pull the shutter and take the picture—with herself in it. The others sat still for the exposure, but there is just a hint of movement in Austen. Under the racket to the lower left lay the cable by which Austen worked the shutter. In later pictures, she was able to better conceal the device. Why do you think that the faces of the young men and women in the photo are so open and their gaze at the camera so direct? Compare the expressions and poses of the

◆ **Figure 6.7 Alice Austen, Playing Tennis (1886)**
Alice Austen Collection, Staten Island Historical Society.

◆ **Figure 6.8 Alice Austen and Her Cousin (1894)**
Alice Austen Collection, Staten Island Historical Society.

women in this photograph to those in Figure 6.6. What do you suppose accounts for the differences in the two photos?

Figure 6.8, taken several years later, shows a more conventional scene of young people's leisure: Austen and her male cousin dressed up for the Annual Charity Ball at a local club. Austen was again the photographer, this time probably using a delayed-action shutter. The picture, taken in her family's parlor, features some of the elaborate furniture that filled Victorian homes. As an elderly woman looking at this photo, Austen described both figures as "looking as though we were shot out of a gun."[48] She remembered that she was concerned that the picture turn out well, but what other things might have been on her mind? How do this photograph and the relations between the figures compare to the scene in Figure 6.7?

The picture in Figure 6.9, of Austen and two of her friends dressed up as men, has become one of Austen's most famous photos. Like the Mexican artist Frida Kahlo, Austen became far better known and celebrated after her death than during her life. This photo, in the context of Austen's decision not to marry but to live her life with another woman, made her a historical icon for modern feminists

◆ **Figure 6.9** **Alice Austen and Friends Dress Up as Men (1891)**
Alice Austen Collection, Staten Island Historical Society.

and lesbians. "Maybe we were better looking men than women," Austen quipped many years later when she was shown the photograph.[49] How did the three girls make themselves look like men, and how successful were they? Austen is the standing figure holding the cigarette. Compare the look on her face in this picture with that in Figures 6.7 and 6.8. What do you think the joke here is?

In Figure 6.10, there is another masquerade going on, this time with actual masks. Twenty-five-year-old Austen, on the right, and her best friend at the time, Trude Eccleston, have literally let down their hair. The photograph is taken inside Eccleston's bedchamber, in the house of her father, an Episcopalian minister. The women, normally held to the rules of respectability in their public lives, recorded themselves in private playing with elements of female disreputability. What else besides the bedchamber setting suggests openly sexual women, perhaps even prostitutes? Compare this image with Figure 6.9. Which photograph represents a more daring leap of self-presentation and identity?

Eventually, Austen began to take her camera beyond the confines of her suburban friends and family. Her only published photographs were those she took in the late 1890s in Manhattan. She took photos of the leisure-class districts uptown, featuring the transom cabs and trolleys that carried shoppers and tourists around

◆ **Figure 6.10** **Alice Austen and Trude Eccleston Let Down Their Hair (1891)**
Alice Austen Collection, Staten Island Historical Society.

the city. However, the photos of people in Manhattan almost all concern those who lived downtown, in the working-class districts of the city. Most of them were probably immigrants.

Austen's pictures of New York City were taken at the same time that sociologists and social reformers were focusing on the plight of impoverished immigrants, but she did not intend her pictures to generate special sympathy or concern in the viewer. (See, for example, Visual Sources: Jacob Riis's Photographs of Immigrant Girls and Women, pp. 434–40.) Indeed, given her individualistic and leisure-class outlook, Austen may have been drawn by the vitality and individuality of her

◆ **Figure 6.11** **Alice Austen, *Hester Street, Egg Stand* (1895)**
Alice Austen Collection, Staten Island Historical Society.

immigrant subjects. Figure 6.11 was taken on Hester Street, the central shopping area of the Jewish Lower East Side. One woman is selling eggs, and the other may have been buying them. What do you think the smiling woman was thinking of the photographer, and what might Austen have been thinking about her? How does this picture compare with those that Jacob Riis took of New York immigrants at about the same time?

QUESTIONS FOR ANALYSIS

1. How do the photographs that Alice Austen took compare to those of the professional photographer Frances Benjamin Johnston, her contemporary, in Figures 6.4 and 6.5?

2. What was it about the camera that encouraged Austen and other women of her class to express their individual perspectives through photography?

3. What impact do these photographs have on your understanding of gender roles of American society in the late nineteenth century?

NOTES

1. Elizabeth Cady Stanton, "This Is the Negro's Hour," *National Anti-Slavery Standard*, November 26, 1865, reprinted in Elizabeth Cady Stanton, Susan B. Anthony, and Matilda J. Gage, eds., *History of Woman Suffrage* (Rochester, NY: Susan B. Anthony, 1881), 2:94.

2. Ellen Carol DuBois, *Feminism and Suffrage: The Emergence of an Independent Women's Movement in America, 1848–1869* (Ithaca: Cornell University Press, 1999), 63.

3. Ibid., 60.

4. Ibid., 175.

5. Elizabeth Cady Stanton to Lucretia Mott, April 1, 1872, in Theodore Stanton and Harriot Stanton Blatch, eds., *Elizabeth Cady Stanton as Revealed in Her Letters, Diary and Reminiscences* (New York: Harper and Brothers, 1922), 137.

6. Susan B. Anthony to Elizabeth Cady Stanton, November 5, 1872, Ida H. Harper Collection, Huntington Library, San Marino, CA.

7. Stanton, Anthony, and Gage, *History of Woman Suffrage*, 3:31.

8. Dorothy Sterling, ed., *We Are Your Sisters: Black Women in the Nineteenth Century* (New York: Norton, 1984), 313.

9. Lucy Chase to unknown correspondent, 1868, American Antiquarian Society, Worcester, Massachusetts, excerpted in Nancy Woloch, ed., *Early American Women: A Documentary History, 1600–1900* (Belmont, CA: Wadsworth, 1992), 401.

10. Sterling, *We Are Your Sisters*, 311.

11. Ibid., 314.

12. Ibid., 293–305.

13. Marilyn Mayer Culpepper, *All Things Altered: Women in the Wake of Civil War and Reconstruction* (Jefferson, NC: McFarland, 2002), 135.

14. Ibid., 123.

15. Tera W. Hunter, *To 'Joy My Freedom: Southern Black Women's Lives and Labors after the Civil War* (Cambridge: Harvard University Press, 1997), 33.

16. "The Race Problem: An Autobiography: A Southern Colored Woman," *The Independent* 56 (1904): 586–89.

17. Arthur F. Raper, *The Tragedy of Lynching* (Chapel Hill: University of North Carolina Press, 1933), 13–14.

18. "The Race Problem," 586–89.

19. Nancy Cott et al., eds., *Root of Bitterness: Documents of the Social History of American Women*, 2nd ed. (Boston: Northeastern University Press, 1996), 360.

20. Claudia Goldin, "The Work and Wages of Single Women: 1870 to 1920," National Bureau of Economic Research Working Paper, No. WO375, 1979, 1.

21. Linda Gordon, *The Great Arizona Orphan Abduction* (Cambridge, MA: Harvard University Press, 1999), 8.

22. Nancy Cott, ed., *Root of Bitterness: Documents of the Social History of American Women*, First Edition (Boston: Northeastern University Press, 1986), 319.

23. Helen Campbell, *Women Wage-Earners: Their Past, Their Present, and Their Future* (Boston: Roberts Brothers, 1893), 190.

24. Ibid., 191.

25. Quoted in Barbara Wertheimer, *We Were There: The Story of Working Women in America* (New York: Pantheon Books, 1977), 178.

26. Mary Kenney O'Sullivan, unpublished autobiography, Schlesinger Library, Harvard University, Cambridge, MA.

27. Gary B. Nash et al., *The American People: Creating a Nation and a Society*, brief 5th ed. (New York: Addison Wesley Longman, 2000), 481.

28. Elizabeth Blackwell, "On Sexual Passion in Men and Women," 1894, reprinted in Cott et al., *Root of Bitterness* (1986), 302.

29. Women's historians first encountered the De Kay/Hallock romance in Carroll Smith-Rosenberg's pathbreaking essay, "The Female World of Love and Ritual: Relations between Women in Nineteenth Century America," which can be found in her collection of essays, *Disorderly Conduct: Visions of Gender in Victorian America* (New York: Oxford University Press, 1985), 53–76. Their relationship also formed the basis of Wallace Stegner's Pulitzer Prize–winning 1971 novel, *Angle of Repose*. Winslow Homer is thought to have been infatuated with De Kay, and painted a lovely, haunting portrait of her "in repose." Hallock became an important writer and illustrator of the West (see p. 401). The quote is from Smith-Rosenberg, p. 57.

30. Karen Hansen, "'No Kisses Is Like Yours': An Erotic Friendship between Two African-American Women during the Mid-Nineteenth Century," *Gender History* 7 (1995): 153.

31. Karen Blair, *The Clubwoman as Feminist: True Womanhood Redefined, 1868–1914* (New York: Holmes and Meier, 1980), 34.

32. Sarah J. Early, "The Organized Efforts of the Colored Women of the South to Improve Their Condition," 1893, reprinted in Dawn Keetley and John Pettegrew, eds., *Public Women, Public Words*, vol. 1 (Madison, WI: Madison House, 1997), 316.

33. Frances E. Willard, *How I Learned to Ride the Bicycle: Reflections of an Influential 19th Century Woman*, ed. Carol O'Hare (1895; repr., Sunnyvale, CA: Fair Oaks, 1991), 17, 75.

34. Mary Earhart, *Frances Willard: From Prayers to Politics* (Chicago: University of Chicago Press, 1944), 93.

35. Suzanne Marilley, *Woman Suffrage and the Origins of Liberal Feminism in the United States, 1820–1920* (Cambridge, MA: Harvard University Press, 1996), 128–29.

36. Ellen Carol DuBois, ed., *The Elizabeth Cady Stanton–Susan B. Anthony Reader: Correspondence, Writings, Speeches*, rev. ed. (Boston: Northeastern University Press, 1992), 176.

37. Ellen Henrotin to May Wright Sewall, in Jeanne Madeline Weimann, *The Fair Women* (Chicago: Academy Chicago, 1981), 529.

38. Charlotte Perkins Gilman, *Women and Economics: A Study of the Economic Relation between Men and Women as a Factor in Social Evolution* (Boston: Small, Maynard & Company, 1898), 156.

39. Elizabeth Cady Stanton, "The Solitude of Self," 1892, http://historymatters .gmu.edu/d/5315 (accessed December 13, 2007).

40. Patricia Schechter, *Ida B. Wells-Barnett and American Reform, 1880–1930* (Chapel Hill: University of North Carolina Press, 2001), 62–63.

41. Mrs. John Van Vorst and Marie Van Vorst, *The Woman Who Toils: Being the Experiences of Two Ladies as Factory Girls* (New York: Doubleday, Page & Co., 1903), 58.

42. Alice Rossi, ed., *The Feminist Papers from Adams to de Beauvoir* (Boston: Northeastern University Press, 1988), 40.

43. Rosalind Rosenberg, "The Limits of Access," in John Mack Faragher and Florence Howe, eds., *Women and Higher Education: Essays from the Mount Holyoke College Sesquicentennial Symposia* (New York: Norton, 1988), 110.

44. Helen Lefkowitz Horowitz, *Alma Mater: Design and Experience in Women's Colleges from Their Nineteenth-Century Beginnings to the 1930s* (New York: Knopf, 1984), 29.

45. M. F. (Mary Frances) Armstrong, *Hampton and Its Students, by Two of Its Teachers, Mrs. M. F. Armstrong and Helen W. Ludlow* (New York: G. P. Putnam, 1874), 89–90.

46. Laura Wexler, *Tender Violence: Domestic Visions in an Age of U.S. Imperialism* (Chapel Hill: University of North Carolina Press, 2000), 168.

47. Ann Novotny, *Alice's World: The Life and Photography of an American Original, Alice Austen, 1866–1952* (Old Greenwich, CT: Chatham Press, 1976), 60.

48. Ibid., 51.

49. Ibid., 50.

SUGGESTED REFERENCES

General Works   A general introduction to women's history in the period from 1865 to 1900 is Eleanor Flexner, *Century of Struggle: The Woman's Rights Movement in the United States* (1975), which is still the best overall history of women's rights in the United States. The equivalent work on black women's history is Paula Giddings, *When and Where I Enter: The Impact of Black Women on Race and Sex in America* (1984), a pioneering synthesis of black women's history after slavery. Alice Kessler Harris's magisterial history of working women, *Out to Work: A History of Wage-Earning Women in the United States* (1982), gives excellent coverage to this period. A general history of sexuality that treats the nineteenth century is Estelle B. Freedman and John D'Emilio, *Intimate Matters: A History of Sexuality* (1997).

Woman Suffrage   For more on the woman suffrage movement in the postbellum era, Ellen Carol DuBois, *Feminism and Suffrage: The Emergence of an Independent Women's Movement in the United States, 1848–1869* (1978), focuses on the struggle over the Fourteenth and Fifteenth Amendments; DuBois, *Women's Rights, Woman Suffrage* (1998), considers the New Departure period. Ann D. Gordon, ed., *The*

Selected Papers of Elizabeth Cady Stanton and Susan B. Anthony, Vol. II, Against an Aristocracy of Sex, 1866–1873 (2000), is a compilation of the important writings of the two suffrage leaders over this period. See Barbara Goldsmith's biography of Victoria Woodhull, *Other Powers: The Age of Suffrage, Spiritualism, and the Scandalous Victoria Woodhull* (1998). Helen L. Horowitz, *Rereading Sex: Battles over Sexual Knowledge and Suppression in Nineteenth-Century America* (2002), is comprehensive.

Black Women in the South   For further research on African American women in the era of Reconstruction and Redemption, Tera W. Hunter's *To 'Joy My Freedom: Southern Black Women's Lives and Labors after the Civil War* (1997) focuses on black women in Atlanta. Evelyn Brooks Higginbotham, *Righteous Discontent: The Women's Movement in the Black Baptist Church, 1880–1920* (1993), examines the roots of the southern black middle class. Deborah G.White, *Too Heavy a Load: Black Women in Defense of Themselves, 1894–1994* (1994), analyzes the black women's club movement. Two recent biographies of antilynching crusader Ida B. Wells are Patricia Schechter, *Ida B. Wells-Barnett and American Reform, 1880–1930* (2001), and Linda McMurry, *To Keep the Waters Troubled: The Life of Ida B.Wells* (1998).

White Women in the South   The pioneering work on white women in the postbellum South is Anne Firor Scott, *The Southern Lady from Pedestal to Politics, 1830–1930* (1970). Marilyn Mayer Culpepper, *All Things Altered: Women in the Wake of Civil War and Reconstruction* (2002), provides many firsthand accounts of white women in the period. Dolores Janiewski, *Sisterhood Denied: Race, Gender, and Class in a New South Community* (1985), examines non-elite southern white women, especially as they moved into industrial labor. Laura Edwards, *Gendered Strife and Confusion: The Political Culture of Reconstruction* (1992), examines challenges raised to southern patriarchy by black and white women after the Civil War. Martha Hodes, *Black Men, White Women* (1994), examines the history of interracial sex in the South. Glenda E. Gilmore, *Gender and Jim Crow: Women and the Politics of White Supremacy in North Carolina, 1896–1920* (1996), focuses on late nineteenth-century insurgent racism.

Working Women in the North   For additional reading on women and work, Barbara Wertheimer, *We Were There: The Story of Working Women in America* (1977), provides a survey of women's work and labor activism, emphasizing but not limited to wage earners. Mary Blewett, *We Will Rise in Our Might: Workingwomen's Voices from Nineteenth-Century New England* (1991), weaves together primary sources into a historical overview of women workers, as does Rosalyn Baxandall and Linda Gordon, eds., *America's Working Women: A Documentary History, 1600 to the Present* (revised ed., 1995). Mary Blewett, *Men, Women, and Work: Class, Gender, and Protest in the New England Shoe Industry, 1780–1910* (1988), examines nineteenth-century working women in a single industry. So does Susan Levine, *Labor's True Woman: Carpet Weavers, Industrialization, and Labor Reform in the Gilded Age* (1984), which also examines women in the Knights of Labor. Marjorie

Davies, *Woman's Place Is at the Typewriter: Office Work and Office Workers, 1870–1930* (1981), examines the shift from male to female office workers. Joanne Meyerowitz, *Women Adrift: Independent Wage Earners in Chicago, 1880–1930* (1988), concerns the lives of working women who did not live in families. Alice Henry, *The Trade Union Woman* (1915), remains a basic resource for the history of women in the labor movement, as does Philip Foner, *Women and the American Labor Movement: From Colonial Times to the Eve of World War I* (1971). Kathleen Nutter, *The Necessity of Organization: Mary Kenney O'Sullivan and Trade Unionism for Women, 1892–1912* (2000), is a biography of the first woman organizer in the AFL.

Leisure-Class Women in the North   Upper-class women in the Gilded Age are discussed in Maureen Montgomery, *Displaying Women: Spectacles of Leisure in Edith Wharton's New York* (1998). The pathologies of shopping are analyzed in Elaine Abelson, *When Ladies Go A-Thieving: Middle-Class Shoplifters in the Victorian Department Store* (1989). Barbara Solomon, *In the Company of Educated Women: A History of Women and Higher Education in America* (1985), is a comprehensive history of women's higher education; Helen Horowitz, *Alma Mater: Design and Experience in Women's Colleges from Their Nineteenth-Century Beginnings to the 1930s* (1984), focuses on the all-female colleges. Sarah Deutsch, *Women and the City: Gender, Space, and Power in Boston, 1870–1940* (2000), examines women's activism and class relations in Boston, and Maureen Flanagan, *Seeing with Their Hearts: Chicago Women and the Vision of the Good City, 1871–1933* (2002), covers similar territory in Chicago. Anne Firor Scott, *Natural Allies: Women's Associations in American History* (1991), is a comprehensive study of women's associations. Karen Blair, *The Clubwoman as Feminist: True Womanhood Redefined, 1868–1914* (1980), is the first scholarly study of the women's club movement. The WCTU is the subject of Ruth Bordin, *Women and Temperance: The Quest for Power and Liberty, 1873–1900* (1990). The starting point for the history of women's romantic friendships is Lillian Faderman's *Surpassing the Love of Men: Romantic Friendship and Love between Women from the Renaissance to the Present* (1994). Also see Martha Vicinus, *Intimate Friends: Women who Loved Women, 1778–1928* (2004), and Lisa Duggan, *Sapphic Slashers: Sex, Violence and American Modernity* (2000). On the photography of Alice Austen, see Ann Novotny, *Alice Austen: The Life and Times of an American Original* (1976), and Laura Wexler, *Tender Violence: Domestic Visions in an Age of U.S. Imperialism* (1999).

For selected Web sites, please visit the *Through Women's Eyes* book companion site at bedfordstmartins.com/duboisdumenil.

7

Women in an Expanding Nation

CONSOLIDATION OF THE WEST, MASS IMMIGRATION, AND THE CRISIS OF THE 1890S

TWENTY-THREE-YEAR-OLD SHIGE KUSHIDA arrived in San Francisco in 1892. American influences had already reached her in Japan. She was Protestant, western-oriented, and one of the first women who dared to speak in Meiji, Japan, before a mixed audience of men and women. She intended to get an education in the United States and return to her home country, but her experience, like that of so many other immigrants, did not go according to plan. Instead of studying, she married another Japanese Christian and settled in Oakland. There she raised her children and became a leader of the Issei (first-generation Japanese American) community. She saw to it that her daughters got the education she did not.[1]

The life of Shige Kushida Togasaki illustrates two grand historical processes that were reshaping American society at the end of the nineteenth century. First, the United States was beginning an unprecedented wave of immigration, which brought with it tremendous social challenges and national transformations. Second, the western part of the continent was being consolidated into the American nation. The frontier—in the sense of a westward-moving line of American settlement—was entering its final stages and, according to the 1890 census, coming to a close. Western settlement, which seems like a quintessentially American phenomenon, and mass immigration, which brought the nation into greater interaction with the rest of the world, shared important links. Both involved enormous movements of people across oceans and continents, bringing different cultures into contact and sometimes into conflict. Both involved efforts to "Americanize," sometimes violently, different cultures into the national mainstream. Both developments were motivated at the individual level by hopes for better lives, greater prosperity, and more personal freedom. And yet both processes dashed hopes as much as they realized them, among the immigrant poor and especially among the Native Americans pushed aside by continuing westward expansion.

Mass immigration and the consolidation of the West together helped to set the stage for a major economic and political crisis in the 1890s, as discontented immigrants, farmers, and wage workers found ways to challenge what they saw as a failure of America's democratic promise, notably the unequal distribution of America's new wealth and the unwillingness of the two established political parties to offer any vision of a better social and political path. The resolution of the crisis in favor of corporate power and the established political parties prepared the way for America's first forays abroad as an imperial power.

In all these developments—western consolidation, mass immigration, the political and economic crises of the 1890s, and the beginnings of American imperialism— women were involved, active, influential, and, as a result, changed. In the great movements of people into and through American society in the late nineteenth century, men initially predominated, but women soon followed. When they did, families were formed and temporary population shifts became permanent new communities. By the early twentieth century, American women's participation in the radical challenges of the 1890s, along with their support for or criticism of their country's ventures abroad, had made them a significant new force in U.S. political life.

CONSOLIDATING THE WEST

American settlement reached the Pacific Coast before the Civil War, but the continent's broad heartland remained largely Indian territory. This changed in the last decades of the nineteenth century as white settlement and expansion

1890	Federal census declares that frontier line is "closed"
1891	**Queen Liliuokalani becomes monarch of nation of Hawaii**
1892	Immigrant receiving station established at Ellis Island in New York City harbor
1892	People's Party formed in St. Louis
1893	Illinois Factory and Workshop Inspection Act passed
1893	Frederick Jackson Turner delivers paper, "The Significance of the Frontier in American History"
1893	**Colorado women win equal voting rights with men**

1893–1894	National economic depression
1894	Pullman strike and national railroad disruption
1896	**Idaho women enfranchised**
1896	Populist Party collapses as William McKinley defeats William Jennings Bryan for president
1896	**Mary Harris ("Mother") Jones's fame as labor agitator begins**
1898	United States goes to war against Spain in Cuba
1898	United States annexes Hawaii
1899–1902	United States fights Filipino independence movement
1900	**Zitkala-Ša's autobiographical writings begin to appear in the *Atlantic Monthly***
1903	President Theodore Roosevelt speaks out against "race suicide"
1907	U.S. and Japanese governments issue "Gentlemen's Agreement" to limit Japanese immigration
1910	Mexican Revolution spurs immigration to the United States
1910	Angel Island immigrant receiving station established in San Francisco Bay

overtook the Great Plains. The tremendous postbellum growth in industrial capitalism traced in Chapter 6 had as one of its major consequences the steady integration of the entire continent into the national economy. The growth of the cross-continental railroad system constituted the infrastructure for a booming national market that could provide eager consumers throughout the country with the beef and wheat and lumber produced in abundance in the broad expanse of the trans-Mississippi West.

These western lands were consolidated as part of the American nation through two main processes, which were distinguished as much by their gender practices as by anything else. Large numbers of single men and a few women went west to realize quick profits or find jobs in the region's mines and on its cattle ranges. This form of American expansion has long been celebrated as the "Wild West" in national legend and popular culture. But there was also a "Family West" in which settlers domesticated the prairies of America's heartland. Women and women's labor were as fundamental to this West as men and men's labor were to the other.

Native Women in the West

Despite their differences, both kinds of westerners shared a basic premise: Indians would have to be removed to make way for the new settlers, for their economic ambitions, and for what they regarded as their superior civilization. Here, the U.S. Army, fresh from its victory over the Confederacy, was crucial. After 1865, federal forces moved with full strength against the western tribes to wrest control of the Great Plains and open these huge interior expanses to white settlement. Native American raids against encroaching white settlers provoked military retaliation in an escalating series of wars that wore away at Native unity and resources. There were occasional Indian victories, most famously the 1876 Battle of the Little Big Horn in Montana, in which assembled Lakota Sioux warriors annihilated the U.S. Seventh Cavalry commanded by George A. Custer. The army was able to keep Native peoples in a state of constant defense, wearing away at their ability to resist.

Bands of Native Americans who resisted pacification were regarded as "hostiles" who could be killed with impunity by Americans. Made up not only of male warriors but also of women and children, they moved constantly to elude pursuing troops. One of the last such groups was Geronimo's band of Warm Springs Apache. His female lieutenant, Lozen, exemplified the Native American practice of allowing exceptional individuals to cross the gender divide. Lozen never married, was skilled in tracking the enemy, and performed the spiritual and military duties of a true warrior. Her brother called her "strong as a man, braver than most, and cunning in strategy."[2] For almost a decade, she helped her people evade and attack the U.S. Army, until the Apaches finally surrendered in southern New Mexico in 1886.

The massacre at Wounded Knee Creek in South Dakota in the winter of 1890 is often cited as the tragic end to the so-called Indian Wars. Following their defeat at the Little Big Horn, army troops had relentlessly pursued the Lakota Sioux.

Deeply dispirited, the Lakotas began to practice a new religion, the Ghost Dance, which promised restoration of their traditional lands and lives. Male and female dancers alike wore special robes, said to be designed by a woman, that they believed would protect them against bullets fired by white people. Believing that the Ghost Dance signaled a new organized insurgency, skittish soldiers fired on a camp of mostly unarmed native people, killing many hundred. "Women with little children on their backs" were gunned down, one white witness to the Wounded Knee massacre recalled, and it was many days before their frozen bodies could be retrieved and buried in a mass grave.[3]

Assaults against the Plains Indians took forms other than outright military conflict. By the 1880s, hunters and soldiers with new high-powered rifles had decimated the buffalo herds that were the material basis of Plains Indians' traditional way of life. The Plains peoples were thus vulnerable to forced relocations on government reservations of the sort that had been pioneered in the 1850s among Pacific Coast tribes (see Map 7.1). Allegedly designed to protect Indians from aggressive white settlers, these reservations instead became "virtual prisons."[4] Unable to support themselves by either farming or hunting, reservation Indians were dependent on food and clothing doled out by federal agents, who often embezzled as much as they dispensed. Instead of their traditional role in gathering and preparing food, Indian women were relegated to standing in long lines, waiting for rations that frequently did not come.

After serving the U.S. Army as translator and scout, Sarah Winnemucca became a crusader against the reservation system (see pp. 258–59). Her people, the Paiute, had been grossly exploited by the government agent who administered their Nevada reservation and who refused to dispense stores allocated to them. They were then relocated to a reservation in Washington Territory, where they lived uneasily among other Native peoples. Winnemucca traveled from California to Massachusetts to describe the sufferings of her people to white audiences, and even met with President Rutherford B. Hayes, but to no avail.

In conjunction with establishing reservations, U.S. policy coerced Native children into government-run boarding schools to be forcibly reeducated in the values and ways of dominant American culture. By the 1890s, several thousand children per year were removed from their parents' control and sent to schools where they were made to stop dressing, speaking, thinking, and believing "like Indians." Half the students were girls, whose forcible reeducation was regarded as crucial to the cultural transformation of the Native population. All too frequently, Native girls' assimilation into American culture consisted of training in menial occupations and in American standards of domesticity, which they learned as servants in the homes of nearby white families.

The goal of such programs was to save the child by destroying the Indian, but the transformations sought were elusive. Evidence of repeated and harsh punishments testifies to the refusal of girls as well as boys to give up their Indian ways. One elderly Indian woman recalled later, "Two of our girls ran away . . . but they got caught. They tied their legs up, tied their hands behind their backs, put them in the middle of the hallway so that if they fell asleep or something, the matron

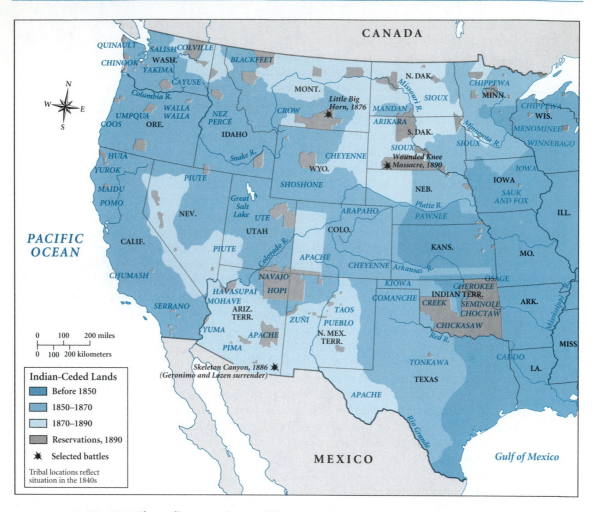

♦ **Map 7.1 The Indian Frontier, to 1890**
As settlers pushed westward after the Civil War, Native Americans put up bitter resistance but ultimately to no avail. Over a period of decades, they ceded most of their lands to the federal government. By 1890, they were confined to scattered reservations where the most they could expect was an impoverished and alien way of life. *Map reproduced courtesy of Colin Calloway.*

would hear them and she'd get out there and whip them and make them stand up again."[5] Parents and tribal leaders protested the brutality of this coercive Americanization, but they could not stop it.

Some Native American women, however, were able to acquire English literacy and other useful skills in the boarding school system. They worked in reservation agencies and became teachers. A few, such as the Yankton Sioux writer Gertrude Simmons Bonnin and the Omaha sisters Susan and Susette La Flesche, became public advocates for their people. Sponsored by the white women of the Woman's National Indian Association to attend the Women's Medical College of Pennsylvania, Susan La Flesche graduated in 1889 to become the first white-trained Native woman physician. She served her people for many years, both as a doctor and as a political leader. Susette La Flesche was a writer and speaker on behalf of Indian causes. She helped to convert several influential white women to the cause of Indian reform, including Helen Hunt Jackson, author of the influential exposé of government mistreatment of Native peoples, *A Century of Dishonor* (see box, "A Century of Dishonor"). Bonnin became a writer and activist for Native American causes (see Documents: Zitkala-Ša: Indian Girlhood and Education, pp. 422–26).

Protests against the corruptions of the reservation system led in 1887 to congressional passage of the Dawes Severalty Act, which divided reservation lands into allotments for individual Native families, the remaining acreage to be sold to non-Indians. Allotment was meant as a reform alternative to demeaning reservation existence, but the way the system played out by no means ended Native peoples' misery. Where land was not very fertile, Native American families could not support themselves; and where the land could be productively farmed, whites

◆ **Before and After Americanization**
These "before-and-after" pictures of Indian children at government-run boarding schools were common in the late nineteenth century and were sometimes sent to philanthropic donors to illustrate the schools' success in Americanizing Indians (see also Figure 6.4, p. 374). Within a little more than a year, these three girls sat on chairs, not the floor, and had lost their blankets and braids, but they retained their sad faces. The book on the lap of Sarah Walker, the girl on the right in the "after" photograph, was meant to indicate her literacy, but we cannot know whether she had really learned how to read. *© 2008 PFHC. Peabody Museum.* 2004.24.30439A; 2004.24.30440A.

HELEN HUNT JACKSON
A Century of Dishonor

Published five years after the nation's centennial, Helen Hunt Jackson's A Century of Dishonor *(1881) documents how U.S. Native American policy violated America's promise of liberty and freedom. The book helped catalyze public awareness of the corruptions and cruelties of the reservation system. Three years later, Jackson (1830–1885) drew on some of the same material for her popular California novel,* Ramona *(see p. 260).*

[W]e may hold nations to standards of justice and good faith as we hold men . . . [and that] a nation that steals and lies and breaks promises will be no more respected or unpunished than a man who steals and lies and breaks promises. . . . The history of the United States Government's repeated violations of faith with the Indians thus convicts us, as a nation, not only of having outraged the principles of justice, which are the basis of international law; and of having laid ourselves open to the accusation of both cruelty and perfidy; but of having made ourselves liable to all punishments which follow upon such sins — to arbitrary punishment at the hands of any civilized nation who might see fit to call us to account, and to that more certain natural punishment which, sooner or later, as surely comes from evil-doing as harvests come from sown seed.

To prove all this it is only necessary to study the history of any one of the Indian tribes. I propose to give in the following chapters merely outline sketches of the history of a few of them, not entering more into details than is necessary to show the repeated broken faith of the United States Government toward them. A full history of the wrongs they have suffered at the hands of the authorities, military and civil, and also of the citizens of this country, it would take years to write and volumes to hold. . . .

So long as there remains on our frontier one square mile of land occupied by a weak and helpless owner, there will be a strong and unscrupulous frontiersman ready to seize it, and a weak and unscrupulous politician, who can be hired for a vote or for money, to back him.

The only thing that can stay this is a mighty outspoken sentiment and purpose of the great body of the people. Right sentiment and right purpose in a Senator here and there, and a Representative here and there, are little more than straws which make momentary eddies, but do not obstruct the tide.

SOURCE: Helen Hunt Jackson, *A Century of Dishonor: A Sketch of the United States Government's Dealings with Some of the Indian Tribes* (New York: Harper and Brothers, 1881), 29–31.

managed to gain control. The allotment program also deepened the dependency of Indian women on their men, following the pattern of white society. In contrast to communal landholding and farming practices, the allotment program meant that women who chose to divorce their husbands risked the loss of economic resources under the control of male heads of household. A group of Hopi women vainly protested to the Bureau of Indian Affairs in 1894. "The family, the dwelling house and the field are inseparable" they wrote, "because the woman is the heart of these, and they rest with her."[6]

The Family West

As Native American control over the West weakened, American settlement across the vast continent continued apace. The passage of the Homestead Act in 1862 granted 160 acres to individuals willing to cultivate and "improve" the land. The railroads, themselves beneficiaries of federal largesse, also sold land to settlers to establish towns along their routes. Through this process, the broad central plains — from Minnesota to Montana to Oklahoma — were settled and Americanized. By the early twentieth century, one-quarter of the U.S. population lived west of the Mississippi.

This population was diverse. After Reconstruction, a small but steady stream of African American families was drawn west by the hope of independent farming. In all-black towns, such as Nicodemus, Kansas, and Langston, Oklahoma, African American women found ways to support their families that were less demeaning than working as domestic servants for white people. In Boley, Oklahoma, Lulu Smith started a dressmaking business; other women ran boardinghouses, catering services, and general stores.[7] European immigrants played a large role in western settlement, especially in the northern territories. In the late nineteenth century, in the period of mass immigration, one out of every two western settlers was foreign-born. The Homestead Act allowed land grants to immigrants who intended to become citizens. They, too, formed their own communities where they could live and speak and farm as they had in their home countries.

Meanwhile, in villages throughout New Mexico, Arizona, and southern California, Spanish-speaking women continued to live much as their mothers and grandmothers had. They maintained adobe homes and cultivated small plots, while the men in their families were increasingly drawn away to work in the mines, on the railroads, or on the commercial farms and ranches run by whites (known as Anglos). Ironically, while these Hispanic women were regarded by Anglo society as backward, they enjoyed considerable authority in their own communities. Local practices favored female property owning, and when widowed, women in these Hispanic enclaves preferred to head their own households rather than remarry. As the extension of the railroads brought national market pressures and a cash economy closer, however, the need for money became greater. Many of these women lost their distinctive advantages and followed their husbands into paid labor, as domestics in Anglo towns or agricultural wage laborers in Anglo fields.

◆ **San Juan Fiesta**

Many Spanish-speaking residents of the Southwest maintained their traditional village life into the late nineteenth century, even as their land and economic position were being lost to Anglo incursion. Religious holidays and life passages such as baptisms and marriages were extremely important, not just for the family but for the entire community. Women did the work of putting on these lavish events — the cooking and the making of fine clothes and also the fund-raising that made the occasions possible. This family fiesta in San Juan, a southern California town centered on its thriving mission-era church, took place about 1880. *Courtesy of the Autry National Center/Southwest Museum, Los Angeles, p.13250.*

Despite many differences, all these communities throughout the family-based West relied on women's unpaid labor, in striking contrast to the emphasis on middle-class female leisure and working-class female wage labor in the more urbanized parts of American society. Western women cooked, did laundry, and made clothes without benefit of many of the technological improvements available in more industrialized areas. While their husbands cultivated specialized commercial crops, the wives cared for animals and grew food for the family table. One Arizona woman described her morning chores: "[G]et up, turn out my chickens, draw a pail of water, . . . make a fire, put potatoes to cook, then brush and sweep half inch of dust off floor, feed three litters of chickens, then mix biscuits, get breakfast, milk, besides work in the house, and this morning had to go half mile after calves." She also contributed to her family's unending need for cash by churning twenty-four pounds of butter in four days. "Quit with a headache," she wrote in her diary. "Done too much work."[8]

Some women were inspired to try homesteading on their own. Perhaps as many as 15 percent of late nineteenth-century American homesteads were at some point controlled by women. Unmarried women who controlled their own

◆ Immigrants in the Great Plains

As with the growth of American industry, the settling of the Great Plains required immigrant labor and determination. The Homestead Act of 1862 made immigrants intending to become citizens eligible for federal land grants. Scandinavians were particularly drawn to homesteading. This Norwegian immigrant to Minnesota, Beret Olesdater Hagebak, sits alone in front of a small house made of sod, the most common building material available on the treeless plains. Her picture captures the difficult experience of immigrant farm women, who suffered both the cultural disorientation of immigration and the isolation of Plains farm life. *Photo by H. J. Chalmers, Minnesota Historical Society.*

homesteads combined two of the most irresistible resources for male settlers, land and female labor, and were besieged by marriage proposals. As one young Oklahoma woman wrote, as soon as she was awarded a claim, men started to court her: "The letters began pouring in—men wanting to marry me, men all the way from twenty-one to seventy-five."[9]

Western farm women did their homemaking in an environment where homes had to be built from scratch. On the plains, after spending the first few months living in temporary shelters, settler families would move into huts made of sod, the top layer of soil so dense with the roots of prairie grass that it could be cut into bricks. Women sprinkled their dirt walls and floors with water to keep down the dust, and decorated their unlikely homes as lavishly as they could, eager to banish the discomfort of being surrounded by dirt. Westering was an ongoing process; as families frequently moved and resettled on more promising land, it was left to the women to repeat the work of creating—both physically and emotionally—new home environments.

Of all the burdens for women settlers on the Great Plains, drudgery and loneliness seem to have been the worst, especially in the years when towns were still being established. Unlike their husbands, women rarely left the homestead—slaves, as some put it, to the cookstove and the washtub. Ignored when she complained that she "never got to go nowhere, or see anybody . . . or [do] anything but work," one Oklahoma woman packed up the children and fled. Overtaken by a wind and ice storm, she almost froze to death and ended up back at the homestead, disabled for life.[10]

The 1867 organization of the National Grange (the full title was the Order of the Patrons of Husbandry) helped to overcome women's isolation on the prairies. By the mid-1870s, three-quarters of the farmers of Kansas had joined.[11] Based on the premise that farm families had to cooperate to succeed against the corporate power of railroad and other monopolies, the Grange established farmer-run stores and grain elevators and promoted laws against unfair railroad rates. It also sponsored social and cultural events that enriched local community life and were of special importance to women, who played a prominent role in the Grange. Local chapters were required to have nine female members for every thirteen male members, and women served as officers and delegates to the national meetings. The sense of community that the Grange created prepared the way for more overtly political expressions of agricultural discontent, including the Farmers' Alliance in the late 1880s and the Populist movement of the 1890s (see pp. 411–13).

The "Wild West"

Alongside the families drawn by the promise of land and economic self-sufficiency were other westerners pursuing riskier schemes for getting rich. Both groups Americanized the West, but in different ways. While family settlement imported the American social and cultural values of industriousness and domesticity, these other westerners brought with them industrial capitalism, wage labor, and subor-

◆ On the Way to the Dance
Mary Hallock, the well-known late nineteenth-century artist and writer, got her start in New York literary circles, through her friendships with Helena De Kay and publisher George Gilder. In 1876, she married mining engineer Arthur Foote and spent all but the very last years of her long life in the West. She wrote and drew extensively out of these experiences, adapting the romantic conventions of Victorian literature to the excitement and exotic qualities of western life. This illustration accompanied a short story, written by Foote, provocatively entitled "The Rapture of Hetty." This image reinterprets the rituals of courtship where the wide open spaces of the West, rather than the flimsy buildings, dominate the landscape. How does Hallock's heroine subtly diverge from images of young women in the East? *From The Century, December 1891; courtesy of the Huntington Library, San Marino, CA.*

dination to growing corporate power. Despite their status as icons of individual freedom, the colorful cowboys of the cattle range and the grizzled miners of the gold and silver strikes were wage laborers and therefore suffered from wage dependence as much as industrial workers in New York and Chicago.

The contrasts between the Wild West and the Family West are particularly clear in terms of the radically different gender practices on which they rested. In the mines and cattle ranges, women wage earners were rare. Annie Oakley's riding and roping skills made her a featured player in Buffalo Bill Cody's Wild West Show in the 1890s, but cowgirls were a staple only in the Wild West of popular culture. The rapidly expanding female labor force found elsewhere in America existed in the West only in the largest cities, such as Denver, San Francisco, and Seattle.

There were other sorts of women in the Wild West, however. At first, most were prostitutes. Like the miners and cowboys who were their customers, they were black and white, English- and Spanish-speaking, native- and foreign-born. Initially, many of these women worked for themselves, as what one historian calls "proprietor prostitutes."[12] A few were able to earn or marry their way into respectable society. Others bought or rented brothels, hired other women, and became successful, if disreputable, businesswomen. In 1890, in Helena, Montana, one of the most prosperous real estate entrepreneurs was an Irish-born former prostitute, "Chicago Joe." But for most, prostitution was a thoroughly losing proposition. Two-thirds of prostitutes died young of sexually transmitted diseases, botched abortions, alcohol abuse, suicide, or homicide. As in other western businesses, the initial period of entrepreneurial exuberance was replaced by consolidated ownership. By the early twentieth century, men—pimps, landlords, and police—enjoyed most of the profits from western prostitution.

More respectable women—some rich, most poor—gradually began to move to western centers of industry. The wives of western mine owners lived in expensive, elegant homes, hired servants, and imported luxuries. The determination of a few to use their husbands' fortunes on behalf of their own social and philanthropic ambitions was legendary. Phoebe Appleton Hearst, whose husband got rich in the mines of California and Nevada, was a major benefactor of the University of California at Berkeley. Margaret (Molly) Tobin Brown, the daughter of Irish Catholic immigrants, married one of the rare individual prospectors to become wealthy off the mines. She bought and refurnished an elegant Denver mansion, hired tutors to teach her the ways of the upper class, and became a generous civic donor. In 1912, she survived the sinking of the ill-fated *Titanic*, earning herself the nickname of "Unsinkable Molly Brown."

At the other end of the class scale, wage-earning miners and cowboys also formed families. The immigrant copper miners of Anaconda, Montana, married the young Irish women who worked as domestic servants for their bosses or as waitresses in the local hotels. Mexican miners in Colorado brought their wives north to live with them and settled permanently in the United States. These working-class wives rarely took jobs outside the home, although they did earn money by feeding and housing single male miners, cowboys, and lumberjacks.

Western housewives lived with the constant fear of losing their husbands to violent death on the range or in the mines. Recognizing that unions would fight to raise wages and make working conditions safer, they were strong supporters of organized labor. They formed union auxiliaries that were very active during the militant strikes that rocked the region. In Cripple Creek, Colorado, miners' wives were involved in 1893 when the radical Western Federation of Miners won higher wages and in 1904 when the state militia drove union activists out of town. By far the most prominent female labor activist in the region was the legendary Irish-born Mary Harris ("Mother") Jones, who began her career as an organizer for miners' unions in the late 1890s. Mother Jones focused her attention on the miners—her "boys"—but she also understood the power of miners' wives and organized them into "mop and broom brigades" that were an effective tool against strikebreakers. Referring to one of the family dynasties most identified with corporate greed, Jones declared: "God Almighty made women and the Rockefeller gang of thieves made the ladies."[13]

Jones's contempt for female gentility notwithstanding, western working-class wives were as careful as women of the leisure classes to maintain a distinction between their own status as respectable women and the status of the disreputable women who had preceded them. Family life was gradually displacing the world of the dance halls and brothels. Respectable women took care not to live in the same areas as "fast" women. "If the world of work was divided into laborers and employers," writes one historian of the western female experience, "the world of women was divided into good women and bad."[14]

LATE NINETEENTH-CENTURY IMMIGRATION

While Americans were moving westward in the late nineteenth century, immigrants were pouring into the country, 27 million in the half century after 1880. These numbers dwarfed pre–Civil War immigration (see pp. 202–04). Five million came from Italy and an equal number from Germany, as well as 2 million Eastern European Jews, 1 million Polish Catholics, and 1 million Scandinavians. A small but growing number of Asians and Mexicans also came to the United States in these years. By 1910, Asians constituted 2 percent of all arriving immigrants. Numbers of Mexican immigrants are harder to determine. Until 1924, when the U.S. Border Patrol was established, the Mexican-U.S. border was virtually unregulated, and those crossing back and forth melded into already existing Spanish-speaking communities. This massive immigration turned the United States into an ethnically and religiously diverse people, no longer preponderantly English and Protestant but now broadly European, with a growing minority of resident Asians and Mexicans.

The gender patterns of these immigrations were complex. Among Slavic, Greek, and Italian immigrants, more men than women came to the United States. However, many men came as temporary workers and returned eventually to their homelands. As they did, and as more women came to marry those who remained, sex ratios tended to even out. Some groups, notably Eastern European Jews and new Irish immigrants, initially came in more gender-balanced numbers. Eventually, women constituted between 30 and 40 percent of all immigrants (see the Appendix, p. A-40) in these years.

The Decision to Immigrate

Women decided to leave their homelands and come to the United States for many reasons, some of which they shared with men. Faced with poverty, limited opportunity, and rigid class structures at home, families dispatched members to work in the United States and send money back. The booming U.S. economy had an insatiable need for workers in its factories, mines, and kitchens, and it lured men and women alike with its promises of high wages and easy prosperity. "This was the time . . . when America was known to foreigners as the land where you'd get rich," remembered Pauline Newman, who arrived from Lithuania in 1901. "There's gold on the sidewalk! All you have to do is pick it up."[15] Political persecution also pushed people out of their homelands. Jews began emigrating in large numbers in the 1880s to escape growing anti-Semitism in Eastern Europe, especially the violent, deadly riots called pogroms. Similarly, the upheavals that culminated in the Mexican Revolution of 1910 drove men and women north.

Young women also had their own distinctive reasons for emigrating. Many were drawn by the reputation that the United States was developing as a society that welcomed independence for women. A common story for young women of all groups involved fleeing from an overbearing, patriarchal father and from the threat of an arranged marriage. That was why Emma Goldman fled Russia in 1885. Upon arriving in the United States, she began a life of political activism that eventually made her the most notorious radical in the United States (see box, "Living My Life").

Other women came to the United States as wives or to become wives, to join husbands who had migrated before them or to complete marriages arranged in the old country. The Japanese government encouraged male immigrants to send back to Japan for women to marry. These women in turn sent letters and photographs to their potential husbands. This was a modern version of a traditional Japanese practice, but *shaskin kekkon* (literally, "photograph marriages") were regarded by Americans as akin to prostitution and still another indication of the allegedly low morals of Asians. Similar arrangements were common among European immigrants. Rachel Kahn came from Ukraine to North Dakota in 1894 to marry a Russian immigrant farmer with whom she had only exchanged pictures.[16]

Some women undoubtedly migrated for reasons so personal and painful that they were hidden from public view. Unmarried women who had become pregnant might flee or be sent away so that the scandal could be more easily hidden. The father of Lucja Krajulis's child would not marry her but sent her instead to the United States, where she was shuttled about among fellow Lithuanians.[17] During the 1910 Mexican Revolution, women in the countryside were raped by armed marauders, and crossing the border provided them escape from their shame.

The Immigrant's Journey

Having decided to move to the United States, immigrant women had many obstacles to negotiate. Passage in the steerage class of a transoceanic steamship in 1900 cost the modern equivalent of $400. It took ten to twenty days to cross from Italy to New York and twice as long from Japan to San Francisco, during which time passengers slept in cramped, unhealthy conditions below deck. One can only imagine the experience of pregnant women or mothers of infants. Photos of arriving immigrants show dazed women, with babies held tightly in their arms and older children clinging to their skirts.

EMMA GOLDMAN
Living My Life

Emma Goldman (1869–1940) was raised by an overbearing father and an uninterested stepmother. She was already interested in radical politics before she left Russia in 1885 to follow her sister Helena to become a garment worker in Rochester, New York. Within a few years she had become deeply involved with the anarchist movement. Her autobiography, Living My Life *(1931), is one of the most widely read life stories in American women's history.*

Helena also hated to leave me behind. She knew of the bitter friction that existed between Father and me. She offered to pay my fare, but Father would not consent to my going. I pleaded, begged, wept. Finally I threatened to jump into the Neva [River], whereupon he yielded. Equipped with twenty-five roubles — all that the old man would give me — I left without regrets. Since my earliest recollection, home had been stifling, my father's presence terrifying. . . . [Father] had tried desperately to marry me off at the age of fifteen. I had protested, begging to be permitted to continue my studies. In his frenzy he threw my French grammar into the fire, shouting: "Girls do not have to learn much! All a Jewish daughter needs to know is how to prepare gefüllte fish, cut noodles fine, and give the man plenty of children." I would not listen to his schemes; I wanted to study, to know life, to travel. Besides, I never would marry for anything but love, I stoutly maintained. It was really to escape my father's plans for me that I had insisted on going to America.

SOURCE: Emma Goldman, *Living My Life* (1931; New York: Courier Dover Publications, 1970), 1:11.

In 1892, the first federal receiving station for immigrants was established on Ellis Island in New York City harbor. The majority of immigrants were passed through quickly, although individuals judged "unfit" for admission could be isolated, confined, and eventually deported. Asian women were more likely to be kept for long periods at Angel Island, the equivalent site established in San Francisco Bay in 1910. Assumed to be sexually immoral, they were detained until they could establish their respectability by answering endless questions (for which they had carefully prepared) about themselves and the men they planned to marry. "Had I known it was like this," a thirty-year-old Chinese mother recalled, "I never would have wanted to come."[18]

Young European women in transit were regarded as sexually vulnerable rather than sexually immoral. Stories circulated of unaccompanied and disoriented immigrant girls tricked or forced into prostitution. This phenomenon was known at the time as "white slavery," a term that invoked memories of chattel (black) slavery. Feared as an international conspiracy to waylay and prostitute young women, white slavery was a major focus for anxieties about women and immigration. The actual extent of the practice is unknown.

Many immigrants kept on moving beyond their point of arrival in the United States, following friends or family or rumors of work. By the turn of the century, the populations of large midwestern cities such as Chicago and Milwaukee were preponderantly foreign-born. Numerous mining towns of the West were dense with immigrants as well. Many immigrants, wishing to retain something of their familiar homeland, preferred to live among people from their own village or region, but this could leave them ignorant of much about their new surroundings. Reformer Jane Addams told the poignant story of an Italian woman who had never seen roses in the few blocks of Chicago that she knew, thought they grew only in Italy, and feared that she would never enjoy their beauty again.[19]

Reception of the Immigrants

The United States' pride in its status as a nation of immigrants is embodied in New York harbor's Statue of Liberty, a giant female figure presented to the United States by the people of France in 1885 to represent the two countries' common embrace of liberty. The poem inscribed on the statue's base was written by Emma Lazarus, a descendant of Sephardic Jews who had arrived in the mid-seventeenth century. The words she wrote welcome the world's oppressed, those "huddled masses yearning to breathe free, / The wretched refuse of your teeming shore." But Lazarus's sentiment was not the norm. In the late nineteenth century, most native-born Americans regarded the incoming masses as disturbingly different aliens who could never assimilate.

Anti-immigrant legislation initially targeted Asians. The Page Law of 1875, the very first federal legislation meant to discourage immigration, was directed at Chinese women, on the assumption that most were prostitutes. In 1882, Congress passed a more comprehensive law, the Chinese Exclusion Act, which banned further immigration of Chinese laborers and their families. The few women who could prove that they were the wives or daughters of Chinese merchants already living in the United States were exempted. Once Chinese immigration had virtually ceased, Japanese workers began to come to the United States, but by the 1890s, anti-Asian sentiment on the West Coast had surfaced against them as well. In 1907, in the so-called Gentlemen's Agreement, the U.S. and Japanese governments agreed to restrict further immigration.

Laws against European immigrants, who were far more central to the U.S. economy, were not passed until 1921 and 1924, when highly restrictive national quotas were established, remaining in place until 1965 (see p. 761). Even before these laws, European immigrants were the targets of considerable prejudice and resentment. Degrading ethnic stereotypes were widely circulated as innocently amusing. (See Visual Sources: Women in the Cartoons of *Puck* Magazine, pp. 441–48.) Southern and Eastern European immigrants were seen as peoples whose strangeness and

State of California,
CITY AND COUNTY OF SAN FRANCISCO.

Chin Lung, a resident of San Francisco, being duly sworn according to law, deposes and says that he is a member of the firm of Sing Kee & Company No. 808 Sacramento Street in said City:

That his wife Leung Yee was a resident of this City for 5 or 6 years, and that she left this City per Steamship " *Belgic* " sailing for Hong Kong on the _____ day of October 1889.

That his daughter, Ah Kum, was born in San Francisco at No. 613 Dupont Street, in 1885, and left San Francisco with her mother in October 1889. *Chin Lung*

Subscribed and sworn to before me, this 14 day of *May* A.D. 1892
F. B. Hoyt
NOTARY PUBLIC.

◆ A Document of Chinese Immigration

Through diligent research, historian Judy Yung uncovered this sworn testimony given by her great-grandfather of her great-grandmother's immigration to the United States in 1892. She found that there were several strategic lies embedded within the document. First, his wife Leung Yee had not lived in the United States previously but was immigrating for the first time in 1892. Second, the daughter that she claimed on this document was in fact a young servant of the family. Such deceits were necessary—and common—to circumvent the prohibitions of the Chinese Exclusion Act of 1882. *File 12017/37232 for Leong Shee, Chinese Departure Application Case Files, 1912–1943, San Francisco District Office, Immigration and Naturalization Service, Record Group 85, National Archives and Records Administration—Pacific Region, San Bruno, CA.*

difference were fundamental, physical, and ineradicable. Religion was a major concern. The hundreds of thousands of Jews who arrived from Eastern Europe after 1880 were the first major group of non-Christians to settle in the United States. Even Catholics were regarded by American Protestants as so emotional and superstitious as barely to be fellow believers in Christ. Their devotion to a foreign pope was the source of much suspicion. Anti-Semitic and anti-Catholic attitudes abounded even among otherwise liberal-minded Americans. Susan B. Anthony could not understand by what logic "these Italians come over with the idea that they must be paid as much as intelligent white men."[20]

Americans were especially wary of immigrant gender relations, regarding their own attitudes as modern and those of the newcomers as Old World and patriarchal. They were particularly uneasy with the reproductive behavior of immigrant women. While the birthrates of native-born women had been falling for some time (see pp. 346–48), immigrant families were large. In 1903, President Theodore Roosevelt, concerned that immigrants' higher birthrates were overtaking those of native-born Americans, charged middle-class women who were working or going to college instead of having babies with responsibility for what he called "race suicide." "If the women do not recognize that the greatest thing for any woman is to be a good wife and mother," he declared in the introduction to *The Woman Who Toils* (see pp. 363–68), "why, that nation has cause to be alarmed about its future."[21] After some time in the United States, however, immigrant women started to want smaller families, too. Margaret Sanger, herself the daughter of Irish immigrants, founded the American birth control movement in the 1910s as a response to immigrant women's pleas for reliable ways to prevent unwanted pregnancy (see pp. 480–81).

Starting about 1910, settlement houses and other civic institutions initiated deliberate Americanization campaigns to assimilate immigrants into mainstream U.S. culture. While these programs did not regard immigrants as permanently alien to American society, they did look on their languages, religions, and cultural practices as foreign. Women's household routines were a particular object for reform, as were practices such as arranged marriages that seemed to violate American standards of family life. These Americanization programs became harsher during World War I, when nativism became much stronger and immigrants' patriotism was questioned.

Immigrant Daughters

Immigrant mothers and daughters confronted America very differently. Low wages made it difficult for immigrant men to meet the American standard of being the sole support of their families. Secondary wage earners were usually teenage children, not wives. Just as their families needed their earnings, the expanding labor force needed immigrant daughters' labor. Young girls were plunged immediately into the booming American economy, while their mothers remained largely homebound.

Young immigrant women predominated in the two largest categories of female wage labor, domestic labor and factory work. German, Polish, and Mexican girls met the late nineteenth-century middle-class demand for servants. By contrast, Italian parents did not want their daughters to work as servants in strange households and preferred that they take jobs where other family members could oversee their activities, such as in seasonal fruit picking.

Young immigrant women were also drawn into factory work, making their greatest contribution to the garment industry. The mass production of clothes in the United States could not have occurred without their labor. By 1890, one out of three garment workers was a woman, and most of those women were immigrants. Some — Russian Jews, Japanese, Italians — had worked in clothing factories in their home countries. New York and Chicago were the centers of the ready-made clothing industry in the United States, but garment factories filled with immigrant workers could be found throughout the country, from El Paso to San Francisco to Baltimore. Paid by the piece and pushed to work ever more quickly, young women earned low wages and risked occupational injuries. Sexual harassment was an additional problem for young immigrant women factory workers, as it was hard not to yield to the foremen who controlled their jobs.

Most of these young women workers lived with parents or other relatives, where intergenerational relations could be very tense. More than their brothers, girls were expected to turn over most of their wages to their parents. Mothers needed the money for household expenses, but daughters longed to spend some of their earnings on themselves. Disagreements did not end there. Daughters wanted to dress in the modern style, while mothers wanted them to look and behave like respectable girls in the old country. Battles could be even more intense with fathers. No one resisted Old World patriarchy more intensely than its daughters. The Russian Jewish novelist Anzia Yezierska wrote often of this theme. "Should I let him crush me as he crushed [my sisters]?" a character in her 1925 novel, *Bread Givers*, said of her father. "No. This is America. Where children are people. . . . It's a new life now. In America, women don't need men to boss them."[22]

Immigrant Wives and Mothers

While unmarried immigrant women were more likely to be wage earners than native-born women, the opposite was true of their mothers — very few of whom worked outside their homes. This behavior was not simply a carryover of Old World standards; Eastern European Jewish wives, for instance, had traditionally been shopkeepers or market vendors. Given the family wage system in the United States, however, adult immigrant women had difficulty finding paid work. Immigrant wives were nonetheless expected to contribute to the family economy. Because of the numbers of single male immigrants and the preference of many groups for living among people from their own country, boarding was very common among immigrants. Middle-class observers, who regarded familial privacy as sacred, condemned the immigrant practice of boarders living within families. Immigrants recognized the tensions but regarded them more tolerantly, and stories of liaisons between amorous boarders and discontented housewives were a source of much amusement in immigrant culture.

Women's housekeeping and childrearing tasks were daunting, both because of poverty and the surrounding alien culture. In densely populated cities, apartments were crowded and residents still relied on backyard wells and outdoor privies, augmented by public baths. Children playing on busy city streets required added supervision. Women hauled water up flights of stairs, purchased coal and wood for fuel, and fought a constant battle against ash and soot. Photographer Jacob Riis did pioneering work documenting these conditions. (See Visual Sources: Jacob Riis's Photographs of Immigrant Girls and Women, pp. 434–40.) Even so, American observers were frequently astonished at the levels of cleanliness immigrant women were able to maintain. While middle-class women dealt with their domestic obligations by hiring immigrant servants, immigrant women had no choice but to do their own scrubbing and ironing.

Immigrant mothers had responsibility for preserving customary ways against the tremendous forces working to Americanize them and their families. They continued to cook traditional foods and observe religious obligations, while their husbands and children entered into the American economic mainstream to make the family's living. As practices that were ancient and reflexive became deliberate and problematic, it fell to women to defend and perpetuate the old ways, thus laying the basis for what would eventually become American ethnic identity. Such practices constituted implicit resistance to the forces of Americanization and cultural homogenization. For the time being, however, such immigrant mothers were dismissed by their children as old-fashioned and quaint, their skills and knowledge irrelevant to the new world that their daughters mastered with such verve. Once again, Jane Addams subtly captured the emotional tenor of this role reversal in her description of the dilemma of immigrant women in search of runaway children in Chicago: "It is as if they did not know how to search for their children without the assistance of the children themselves."[23]

Despite these obstacles, adult immigrant women helped to construct lasting ethnic communities. In the mining town of Anaconda, Montana, Irish women, struggling to meet their family needs, nonetheless raised money to build St. Patrick's Catholic Church in 1888. This story was repeated in the immigrant neighborhoods within which the American Catholic church developed. Occasionally, immigrant wives' community activism took a political turn, as in 1902, when New York City Jewish women demonstrated against the rising cost of meat in the city's kosher markets. Like native-born middle-class women, late nineteenth-century immigrant women formed and joined associations, but for different reasons. They had been drawn to the United States by the promise of greater freedom, if not for themselves, then for their children. But they were learning that to realize that promise, they had to find ways to work together.

CENTURY'S END: CHALLENGES, CONFLICT, AND IMPERIAL VENTURES

For many of the women who immigrated to the United States or who migrated across the continent, the American dream remained elusive. Their frustrated hopes helped to fuel a dramatic crisis at century's end. The national economy, which had gone through a series of boom and bust cycles since the beginnings of industrialization in the 1830s, experienced its greatest economic crisis yet in 1893, as overextension of the railroad system, decline in gold reserves, and international collapse in agricultural prices set off a long, deep economic contraction that kept layoffs high, wages low, and economic growth stalled for four years. In the cities, the newest immigrants bore the brunt of massive unemployment and deep family disruption. In the agricultural heartland, crops could not be sold at a profit, and family farms failed. Factory workers and farmers were not natural allies; they were not even particularly sympathetic to each other. Nonetheless, the two groups moved together to confront the wealthy strata that ruled a complacent nation. The turmoil of the 1890s unleashed an unprecedented wave of industrial strikes and raised the prospects for a political movement, Populism, that mounted the first systematic challenge to entrenched political power since the rise of the Republican Party in the 1850s.

In the hotly contested presidential contest of 1896, the pro-business Republican candidate William McKinley defeated the Democratic-Populist nominee William Jennings Bryan, ending for the time being these challenges to entrenched power. In the wake of their victory, corporate leaders and Republican politicians brought the United States to join European nations in the race to acquire overseas colonies.

Women were active everywhere in the crises of the 1890s. They were the victims of desperate economic conditions, ardent supporters of strikes, spokeswomen for political challenges, and supporters and opponents of the new imperial ventures. In two especially important ways—winning the first victories for woman suffrage in the West and establishing settlement houses to assist urban immigrants—the decade brought American women to a new level of political prominence.

Rural Protest, Populism, and the Battle for Woman Suffrage

The years after Reconstruction were difficult for American farmers. With the dream of economic independence and self-sufficiency receding, farming families were driven into debt by the pressures of falling prices and rising costs. Culturally, rural Americans also felt that they were losing ground—and often their children—to the magnet of city life. The powerful railroad corporations that set rates for transporting their crops were a particular target of farmers' anger. "It is an undeniable fact that the condition of the farmer and their poor drudging wives is every year becoming more intolerable," Minnesotan Mary Travis complained in 1880. "We are robbed and crowded to the wall on every side, our crop [is] taken for whatever the middlemen are of a mind to give us, and we are obligated to give them whatever they have the force to ask for their goods or go without, and all this means so . . . much toil, and less help for the farmer's wife."[24]

The Grange led the way in the 1880s to the Farmers' Alliances. While continuing to encourage community life, the alliances emphasized the formation of farmers' buying and selling cooperatives to circumvent the powers of the banks and railroads. The Southern Alliance movement, which began in Texas in 1877, was particularly strong. In it, non-elite southern white women began to take a visible, public role. Southern black farmers organized separate Colored Farmers' Alliances, approximately half of whose 750,000 members were women. African American sharecroppers, who were trapped in debt because they had to acquire their supplies from their landlords at exorbitant credit rates, were particularly attracted to cooperatives. The People's Grocery in Memphis, the lynching of whose owner in 1892 catapulted Ida B. Wells into her reform career (see pp. 335–36), was probably one such cooperative enterprise.

By 1892, Farmers' Alliances in the Midwest came together with the Southern Alliance to form a new political party, ambitiously named the People's Party and commonly known as the Populists. Women were active in its meteoric life. Frances Willard, an important figure at the founding convention in St. Louis, brought the large and powerful Woman's Christian Temperance Union (WCTU) with her into the new effort. Several of the Populists' most successful organizers were also women. Kansan Mary Elizabeth Lease, daughter of Irish immigrants, was the fieriest of these radical female orators. "You wonder, perhaps, at the zeal and enthusiasm of the Western women in this reform movement," Lease proclaimed at the founding convention. "We endured hardships, dangers and privations, hours of loneliness, fear and sorrow; [w]e helped our loved ones to make the prairie blossom . . . yet after all our years of toil and privations, dangers and hardship upon the Western frontier, monopoly is taking our homes from us."[25]

The Populist insurgency lasted only four years, but it left an enduring mark on the history of women's rights. In the Reconstruction years, suffragists had fought for political rights via the U.S. Constitution (see pp. 326–27). During the 1890s, while national politics remained inhospitable to reform, the focus for woman suffrage, as for other democratic reforms, shifted to the state level. In several western states, the Populists endorsed woman suffrage, giving it new life.

The most important of these campaigns occurred in 1893, when the women of Colorado's suffrage societies, labor union auxiliaries, WCTU chapters, and Knights of Labor locals joined together to convince male voters to enfranchise them. In contrast to the violent, widespread class conflict in the western mining industry, the advocates of woman suffrage were proud of their ability to "work unitedly and well" for a common goal.[26] Middle- and upper-class women contributed money to hold giant women's rallies. Their respectability offset the charge that prostitutes' votes would further corrupt the world of politics. Suffragists linked their cause to struggling farmers and wage earners and asked for the vote as a tool against the entrenched power of railroads and mining corporations. "The money question has power to reach into the most sheltered home and bring want and desolation," Lease proclaimed. "Women have not invaded politics; politics have invaded the home."[27] Although suffragists had appealed to all parties, Populist support was crucial to victory. "There is less prejudice against and a stronger belief in equal rights in the newer communities," wrote suffrage journalist Ellis Meredith of this western victory. "The pressure of hard times, culminating in the panic of 1893, undoubtedly contributed to the success of the Populist Party and to its influence the suffrage cause owes much."[28] Three years later, Idaho women won a similar victory by an even greater margin.

Campaigns were also waged in Kansas and California, but they failed because of partisan conflict. In Kansas in 1894, two out of three male voters voted against woman suffrage and, according to Populist suffragist Annie Diggs, "the grief and the disappointment of the Kansas women were indescribable."[29] In 1896, the issue was put before the men of California. Seventy-six-year-old Susan B. Anthony went to the state to work for suffrage. At first, all three political parties endorsed the referendum, and labor, Socialist, Spanish-language, and immigrant newspapers also came out in its favor. But when national Populist leaders decided to campaign in the presidential election that year solely on the issue of currency reform ("free silver"), the political situation changed dramatically. The Democratic Party joined with the Populists to advocate basing the nation's currency on silver as well as gold, and the two parties "fused" behind the presidential candidacy of the charismatic Nebraskan orator William Jennings Bryan. Woman suffrage became a liability, and the Populists ceased to agitate on its behalf. Republicans turned against it, and the California referendum was defeated 45 percent to 55 percent. "We feel defeated, and it doesn't feel good," Anthony told a newspaper reporter. "But we must save ourselves for other States. 'Truth crushed to earth will rise again.'"[30]

In the South, woman suffrage, which had been held back by its association with black suffrage and with the Reconstruction-era effort to subordinate states' rights to federal authority, also got its first sustained support in the Populist era. In 1888, Texan Ann Other defended woman suffrage against its critics in the pages of the *Southern Mercury*, a Populist newspaper. "Those men who could think less of a woman because she took a judicious interest in the laws of her country would not be worth the while to mourn over," she wrote.[31]

Eventually, however, southern Populism was felled by the racial divisions inherited from slavery and deepening racial inequality at century's end. The threat of electoral cooperation between angry black and white farmers gave the final impetus to the new system of segregation and disfranchisement known as Jim Crow (see pp. 336–37). When southern suffrage campaigns resurfaced again in the twentieth century, they did so in the context of this aggressive racism, arguing for white women's votes as a means for countering black men's votes.

Nationally, the election of Republican William McKinley in 1896 signaled the defeat of the Populist movement. For women, however, the party's brief career had enormous consequences. The women of Colorado and Idaho now had full voting rights, in federal as well as state elections. Woman suffrage had become a live political issue, and its center had shifted from the Northeast, where the movement had begun, farther west, where male voters identified it with a more democratic political system. Having driven the People's Party from the electoral arena, the Republican Party absorbed some of its reform agenda. After 1896, the issue of woman suffrage passed into the hands of the reform-minded wing of the Republican Party, along with other Populist concerns, such as the impact of economic growth on the poor and the need for government regulation of corporations. As with the Populists, women activists and reformers would prove to be numerous and influential among these newly designated "Progressives" (see pp. 462–69).

◆ **Early Women Voters in Colorado, 1907**
In 1893, the Populist-controlled legislature of Colorado called for a referendum to amend the state constitution to enfranchise women voters, the first time that the issue had been put before large numbers of male voters. Colorado was a booming state, the center of the mining industry, home both to the owners of great fortunes and a large, militant working class. The woman suffrage referendum won with a strong majority, passing in over three-quarters of the counties. Women followed up their victory by voting in substantial numbers for state and federal offices. The pride that they took in their new status as active, voting citizens, is obvious in the faces and stances of these women, standing with male voters outside a Denver polling place. *Denver Public Library; Z-8811.*

Class Conflict and the Pullman Strike of 1894

Just as Populism was reaching its high point in 1893, the national economy collapsed, thousands of businesses failed, and nearly a quarter of wage workers lost their jobs. The nation's most severe depression to date exposed critical problems and deep social rifts. Women suffered, both as out-of-work wage earners and as wives of unemployed men. Federal and state governments, following the laissez faire principle of nonintervention in the marketplace, offered no help. Private charities provided a few paying jobs—street cleaning for men and sewing for women—but their efforts were inadequate to the need. Across much of the country, the winter of 1893–94 was one of the coldest ever recorded. Rosa Cavalleri, a recent immigrant from Italy to Chicago, recalled waiting in a line for free food: "Us poor women were frozen to death."[32] The spread of disease under such conditions — smallpox and typhoid in Chicago, diphtheria in New York — showed the middle and upper classes that, in a complex, modern society, misery and want could not be confined to one class: poverty put entire communities at risk.

For a handful, the moment promised a new American revolution. Amid rising working-class discontent, twenty-four-year-old Emma Goldman found her calling as a radical agitator and orator. She was already under suspicion for her role in the attempted assassination of the chairman of the Carnegie Steel Corporation during a violent strike at its Homestead, Pennsylvania, plant in 1892. The next year she led a phalanx of unemployed women in New York City. An advocate of anarchism, the political philosophy that condemned all government as illegitimate authority, she challenged the crowd, "Do you not realize that the State is the worst enemy you have? . . . The State is the pillar of capitalism and it is ridiculous to expect any redress from it."[33] She was arrested, tried, and sentenced to a year in prison for "inciting to riot." In jail, Goldman learned the trade of midwifery and became an advocate of sexual and reproductive freedom for working-class women.

The most dramatic of the strikes against falling wages and massive layoffs began in May 1894 at the Pullman Railroad Car Company just south of Chicago. Company founder George Pullman was proud of his paternalistic policy of providing for all his workers' needs; but now, determined to maintain profits, Pullman refused to lower rents in the company-owned housing, where employees were expected to live despite their diminished pay packets. Pullman's policy drew wives as well as women workers into the conflict. "Holding their babies close for shields," the antistrike *Chicago Tribune* reported of a workers' demonstration, "the women still break past the patrol lines and go where no man dares to step."[34] As railroad workers nationwide shut down the railroad system rather than transport Pullman cars, pressure grew on the federal government to intervene. President Grover Cleveland sent six thousand federal troops to quell riots and occupy the rail yards in Chicago. By early July, the strike was broken.

The Settlement House Movement

The Pullman strike also affected the future of middle- and upper-class women by putting a new development in female social reform, the settlement house movement, on the historical map. Settlement houses were pioneered in England in the 1880s by male college graduates who chose to live among and serve the urban poor. By 1890, settlement houses were beginning to appear in the United States, with the important difference that most of their participants were middle- and upper-class women. The most influential settlement house was Hull House, established in Chicago in 1889 by Jane Addams. (See Documents: Jane Addams and the Charitable Relation, pp. 427–33.)

Soon Hull House was serving several thousand people per week. Kindergarten and after-school classes helped immigrant mothers with child care and encouraged the spread of American values and culture. In contrast to later, more coercive forms of Americanization, however, Hull House valued immigrants for their home cultures as well. Creatively struggling with the gulf between immigrant mothers and their Americanized children, Jane Addams established the Hull House Labor Museum, where parents could demonstrate and explain to their children their traditional craft skills and thus "build a bridge between European and American experiences in such wise as to give them both more meaning."[35] Rooms were made available for union meetings and political discussion clubs. Immigrants in the neighborhood attended concerts and enjoyed the use of a gymnasium. A separate residence, named the Jane Club in homage to Addams, provided an alternative to commercial boardinghouses for young wage-earning women away from their families. "Hull-House is meant to be the centre for all the work needed around it," a sympathetic observer explained, "not committed to one line of work, but open to all that leads the way to a higher life for the people."[36]

The Pullman strike gave new prominence and impetus to the women of Hull House, who suddenly found themselves in the midst of Chicago's violent class conflict. Jane Addams, who had a reputation as an effective conciliator, was appointed to a special arbitration committee, but its members were unable to find a way to resolve the strike. Meanwhile, Florence Kelley, another Hull House member, was developing a more direct, long-term response to the frustration and demands of working-class immigrant families. The daughter of a Republican congressman and herself a Cornell University graduate, Kelley shared Addams's privileged background but had moved further beyond the expectations of women of her class. While living in Germany, she had become a socialist and corresponded with Karl Marx's collaborator, Friedrich Engels, about the condition of the Chicago poor. In 1892, she wrote him, "The most visible work is [being done] at the present moment by a lot of women who are organizing trade unions of men and women."[37] Kelley had come to Hull House to get away from an abusive husband and so knew something of wives' dependency. She deserves much of the credit for moving Hull House, and with it the entire settlement movement, decisively in the direction of modern social welfare reform.

Kelley crafted a body of protective labor laws designed to shield working-class families from the worst impact of the wage labor system. In 1893, she and others submitted a bill to the Illinois state legislature to prohibit the employment of children, constrain home-based manufacturing, and establish an eight-hour workday for adult women workers. Offered as a legislative response to the growing social and economic crisis of the poor, the Illinois Factory and Workshop Inspection Act was passed about a year before the Pullman strike. Kelley was appointed chief factory inspector for the state, and empowered to search out and prosecute violations of the new laws. She and her deputy inspectors, including the trade union activist Mary Kenney (see pp. 458–59), drew the attention of reformers, the state government, and labor unions to the extent and abuses of the sweating system in Illinois and helped to initiate a nationwide campaign to improve conditions in the garment industry. Many states began to pass similar factory and tenement inspection laws.

◆ **Jane Addams Reading to Her Nephew**
Jane Addams built her life as a reformer around the traditional womanly virtues of care, nurturance, and concern
for family life, expressed on a large, public stage. Although
she never married or became a mother, she was often
photographed with the immigrant children served by Hull
House. In her personal life, she was a devoted aunt. Buried
in this tender picture of Addams with her nephew Stanley
Linn, taken around 1894, is a tragedy. In the summer of
1894, with the railroads on strike, Addams's sister Mary
died before family members could reach her. Jane became
the legal guardian for Mary's children. Her biographer,
Victoria Brown, observes that the twin tragedies of the
Pullman strike and her sister's death took a considerable
toll on Addams, who looks older here than her thirty-four
years. *University of Illinois at Chicago, University Library Jane
Addams Memorial Collection (JAMC_000_0029_1703).*

Other provisions of the law were not so successful. Illinois garment manufacturers united in opposition to the eight-hour workday for women workers. In the
bitter aftermath of the Pullman strike, the Illinois Supreme Court ruled in 1895 that
limitations on the working hours of women were a violation of their individual freedom of contract, without "due process of law." Kelley's father had helped to write
the Fourteenth Amendment, which had enshrined the principle of due process in
the U.S. Constitution, and she railed against the 1895 decision as a perversion of
this principle, making it into "an insuperable obstacle for the protection of women
and children."[38] Ending child labor also proved extremely difficult, as immigrant
parents resisted efforts to deprive their families of young wage earners. But Kelley
had chosen her life's work—to find the political backing and constitutional basis
for social welfare provisions that would aid working-class women and families.

Women-based settlement houses soon appeared in other immigrant-dense
cities, among them the Henry Street Settlement in New York City, led by Lillian Wald;
Neighborhood House in Dallas; and the Telegraph Hill Neighborhood Association
in San Francisco. While many white settlement leaders personally believed in greater
racial justice, they yielded to the prejudices of the era and practiced racial segregation in the institutions they established. In the South, middle-class African American
women organized their own settlements, most notably Atlanta's Neighborhood

Union, organized in 1908 by clubwoman Lugenia Hope. In the North, all-black set-tlement houses were also organized. Ida B. Wells-Barnett set up the Negro Fellow-ship Association in a rented house on Chicago's south side. Hull House, which had experimented with a few black residents in the 1890s, switched in the twentieth cen-tury to encouraging and supporting a separate black settlement house, the Wendell Phillips House. Similar black-oriented settlement houses were Robert Gould Shaw House in Boston, Karamu House in Cleveland, and Lincoln House in New York City.

Epilogue to the Crisis: The Spanish-American War of 1898

In an atmosphere shaped by the crisis of the 1890s, the United States embarked on its first extracontinental imperialist efforts. Imperial advocates contended that the acquisition of overseas colonies could provide both new markets to revive the American economy and a military challenge to invigorate American manhood. In an influential paper entitled "The Significance of the Frontier in American His-tory," historian Frederick Jackson Turner considered the advantages of an impe-rial future for the United States. Mourning the end of an era in which the defin-ing national purpose was to conquer the American continent, and concerned that immigrants could not be fully Americanized in the absence of the frontier experi-ence, Turner suggested that overseas expansion might be a way for the United States to continue to pursue its Manifest Destiny and maintain its frontier spirit.

Turner made his remarks in 1893 at the World's Columbian Exposition in Chicago, the same exposition that featured the Woman's Building (see pp. 354–55). Throughout the fair, America's rising imperial aspirations were on display. The spa-tial organization of the grounds reflected the country's new ambitions for world leadership. At the center was the Court of Honor, where the United States wel-comed and joined the great nations of Europe. Meanwhile, on the riotous Midway Plaisance at the fair's periphery, belly-dancing Arabs, tribal Africans, and exotic Asians drew enormous crowds, fascinated and amused by the unprecedented spec-tacle of the world's strange variety of peoples. The implication was clear: the people on the Midway, albeit fascinating, were inferior, uncivilized, and backward and needed the stewardship of the United States and other advanced Christian nations.

Some of the earliest manifestations of this crusading sense of American national superiority had come from Protestant missionaries, among whom women were prominent. Since the 1830s, women with a strong religious vocation had been bringing American values and culture along with English language and Christian Bibles to the peoples of Asia and Africa. Women's overseas missionary efforts entered a new, more organized phase in 1883 when the Woman's Christian Temperance Union (WCTU) created a division to undertake international work. Mary Clement Leavitt, a former schoolteacher from New Hampshire, became the first of the WCTU's "round the world missionaries," traveling around the Pacific, from Hawaii to New Zealand and Australia to Burma, Madagascar, China, and India, to spread the ideas of temperance.

Some Asian women were able to use the resources and perspective of the WCTU missionaries to address their own problems as they understood them. In Japan, for instance, the WCTU's combined message of female purity and activism became the basis for an anticoncubinage movement, while the antiliquor arguments were initially ignored by women. Nonetheless, the assumption of American superiority and world leadership constituted a kind of "soft" imperialism. Frances Willard made the link explicit when she said, "Mrs. Leavitt has been to the women of Japan what U.S. naval and economic power has been to its commerce: an opening into the civilized world."[39]

Willard wrote those words in 1898, the year that the United States entered into its first explicitly imperial overseas war and acquired its first formal colonial possessions. The so-called Spanish-American War began in Cuba, which had long drawn American attention as a possible territorial acquisition. Cuban nationalists were showing signs of winning a prolonged insurgency against Spanish colonial control. In May, the United States joined the war on the side of the Cuban forces, ostensibly to avenge the destruction of the U.S.S. *Maine*, an American battleship blown up under suspicious circumstances in Havana harbor. (It was later determined that powder on the deck exploded, probably by accident.) Spain was quickly routed, but instead of supporting Cuban independence, the United States enforced a new type of foreign oversight on the island. While not making Cuba a formal colony, the Platt Amendment, passed by the U.S. Congress in 1902, gave the United States a supervisory role over Cuban affairs that it retained until 1934.

As Spanish imperial power collapsed further, the United States claimed as colonies other Spanish possessions, including Puerto Rico and Guam. U.S. forces found it most difficult to consolidate control over the rich prize of the Spanish Philippines, the gateway to trade across the Pacific and throughout Asia. An indigenous Filipino independence movement fought back against the Americans, who had come in 1898 to liberate and stayed to control. The Filipinos turned what at first appeared to be a quick U.S. victory into a long and deadly conflict, which U.S. forces brought to an end only in 1902 through considerable expenditure of life (see box, "Women of the Philippines"). Unlike Cuba, the Philippines became a formal U.S. colony and remained so until 1946.

Alongside the economic justification for imperial expansion in search of new markets, a restless, insecure, and aggressive masculinity played a significant role in America's decision to go to war. Rising New York politician Theodore Roosevelt thoroughly embodied this phenomenon. With the memory of Civil War death tolls receding, men like Roosevelt were eager to demonstrate a manliness they felt was being challenged by immigrant men and threatened by activist women. Newspapers encouraged popular support for intervention. In political cartoons, Americans were portrayed as the manly protectors of the Cuban people, who were regularly depicted as suffering women (see Figure 7.12, p. 447). These eager imperialists "regarded the war as an opportunity," says one historian, "to return the nation to a political order in which strong men governed and homebound women proved their patriotism by raising heroic sons."[40]

Most American women joined the clamor and supported intervention on what they believed was the side of the Cubans. Remembering female service in the Civil War, they raised funds for military hospitals. But when it came to the unprecedented taking of overseas colonies, opinion was much more divided. By

CLEMENCIA LOPEZ
Women of the Philippines

Clemencia Lopez and her husband, Sixto, were leading advocates of the cause of Philippine independence to the American people. She defended her people's dignity and sovereign rights in this 1902 address to the New England Woman Suffrage Association, many members of which were active in the Boston-based Anti-Imperialist League. Subsequently she became a student at Wellesley College, one of the first Filipinas to attend a U.S. college.

You will no doubt be surprised and pleased to learn that the condition of women in the Philippines is very different from that of the women of any country in the East, and that it differs very little from the general condition of the women of this country. Mentally, socially, and in almost all the relations of life, our women are regarded as the equals of our men. . . .

. . . [I]t would seem to me an excellent idea that American women should take part in any investigation that may be made in the Philippine Islands, and I believe they would attain better results than the men. Would it not also seem to you an excellent idea, since representation by our leading men has been refused us, that a number of representative women should come to this country, so that you might become better acquainted with us?

. . . You can do much to bring about the cessation of these horrors and cruelties which are today taking place in the Philippines, and to insist upon a more humane course. I do not believe that you can understand or imagine the miserable condition of the women of my country, or how real is their suffering. . . . [Y]ou ought to understand that we are only contending for the liberty of our country, just as you once fought for the same liberty for yours.

SOURCE: Clemencia Lopez, "Women of the Philippines," address to the New England Woman Suffrage Association, published in *Woman's Journal*, June 7, 1902.

nature a pacifist, Jane Addams recognized the threat that rising militarism posed to a more general spirit of reform. On the streets around Hull House, she observed, children were "playing war": "[I]n the violence characteristic of the age, they were 'slaying Spaniards.'"[41] Susan B. Anthony also opposed the war, while her longtime friend and political partner, Elizabeth Cady Stanton, took the opposite position and believed that colonization would civilize the Filipino people.

The annexation of Hawaii during the war illustrates other aspects of the many roles women played in the U.S. move toward empire. In 1891, Queen Liliuokalani became the reigning monarch of the sovereign nation of Hawaii. She had been educated by American Protestant missionaries, was a devout Congregationalist, spoke English, and was married to a white American. Wealthy American planters already had enormous economic power in Hawaii, but U.S. tariff policies put them at a disadvantage in selling their fruit and sugar, and they pressed for a formal U.S. takeover of the islands. Now that its monarch was a woman, they redoubled their claims that only annexation could assure Hawaii's stability and progress. The U.S. entry into the war against Spain created a political environment favorable to their aspirations, and in 1898 Congress voted to acquire Hawaii. Unlike Texas in 1845 and California in 1848, however, Hawaii did not become a state but was designated a colonial territory.

The response of U.S. suffragists was not to condemn this move, even though the deposed head of state was a woman, or to object that Congress was imposing a government on the islands instead of allowing its residents to organize their own. Rather, they protested Congress's intention to write a territorial constitution for the Hawaiians that confined political rights to men only. As one historian writes, suffragists "substituted a critique of imperialism with a critique of patriarchy, and in the process lent their tacit approval to America's colonial project."[42] Even when they seemed to defend the rights of women in the colonies, late nineteenth-century suffragists did so within a framework that assumed the superiority of American culture and their right, as white Americans, to play a role in the nation's expansive "civilizing" mission.

CONCLUSION: Nationhood and Womanhood on the Eve of a New Century

At the beginning of the twentieth century, most American women faced the new century with considerable optimism. Not so long before, their country had gone through a horrible Civil War, but now it had more than recovered. The settlement of the western half of the continental United States gave a sturdy new physicality to American claims of nationhood. The U.S. economy more than equaled that of England, Germany, and France combined. Many immigrants had taken great risks and come far to participate in this spectacular growth. Strong and confident, the United States, once a colony itself, ended the century by acquiring its own colonies. The country was on its way to becoming a world power.

As this new era of national development dawned, women's prospects looked especially promising. With the important exception of Native American women, most American women in 1900 were living more active, more public, more individualized, and more expansive lives than prior generations. As a group, they were prepared to make a major contribution to solving the problems that accompanied America's new prosperity and place in the world. In the coming era, they would achieve as much influence as in any period of U.S. history. Already the beneficiaries of American progress, they were about to become the mainstays of the Progressive era, in which America undertook the challenging task of both reforming and modernizing itself.

DOCUMENTS

Zitkala-Ša: Indian Girlhood and Education

THE NATIVE AMERICAN WRITER and activist known as Zitkala-Ša was born Gertrude Simmons in 1876. That same year, the Lakota Sioux achieved a stirring but brief victory over the U.S. cavalry at Little Big Horn. Her own band of Eastern Sioux, the Yanktons, had already been confined on a reservation in South Dakota, in the process of which her sister and uncle had died and her family had begun to disintegrate. At age eight, she overcame her grieving mother's reluctance and traveled to a Quaker-run school for Native children in Wabash, Indiana. Her three years there were deeply unhappy, after which she returned to the Yankton Reservation. But she found that she was not satisfied by the paths set out for her in either world, Native or white ("paleface" as she called it), and she began to search for her own way between them.

She resumed her education at Earlham College, another Quaker institution, and left her family again to teach at the most famous of the Indian colleges, Carlisle Institute in Pennsylvania. There she was beginning to find her voice — as orator and writer both — and sought ways to preserve and convey the experiences of her people to a broader American audience. Her career as a writer began in 1900 with the publication in the *Atlantic Monthly* of a series of autobiographical vignettes, excerpted below. To designate a kind of personal rebirth, she signed this work with a name that was both new and traditional, Zitkala-Ša, meaning Red Bird. She subsequently worked for the Bureau of Indian Affairs and married a Sioux man, Raymond Bonnin. Her essays were republished as 1921 as *American Indian Stories*. By this time, her interests and energies had shifted from the literary to the political. In 1911, she became one of the founders and leaders of the Society of American Indians (see p. 469).

Written early in her career — while she was still in her mid-twenties — these autobiographical writings powerfully convey the complex and contradictory nature of the pulls and pushes on Native young people of her transitional generation. Can you detect any literary devices that she uses to enrich her account? As you read this piece, consider how she portrays the attractions of the white world as an innocent child might understand them versus the reactions of their parents, who had already lost so much in the confrontation with white society. What turns her from an eager adventurer into a resentful and resisting young rebel?

ZITKALA-ŠA
American Indian Stories (1921)

INDIAN CHILDHOOD: THE BIG RED APPLES

The first turning away from the easy, natural flow of my life occurred in an early spring. It was in my eighth year; in the month of March, I afterward learned. At this age I knew but one language, and that was my mother's native tongue.

From some of my playmates I heard that two paleface missionaries were in our village. They were from that class of white men who wore big hats and carried large hearts, they said. Running direct to my mother, I began to question her why these two strangers were among us. She told me, after I had teased much, that they had come to take away Indian boys and girls to the East. My mother did not seem to want me to talk about them. But in a day or two, I gleaned many wonderful stories from my playfellows concerning the strangers.

"Mother, my friend Judéwin is going home with the missionaries. She is going to a more beautiful country than ours; the palefaces told her so!" I said wistfully, wishing in my heart that I too might go. . . . With a sad, slow smile, she answered: "There! I knew you were wishing to go, because Judéwin has filled your ears with the white man's lies. Don't believe a word they say! Their words are sweet, but, my child, their deeds are bitter. You will cry for me, but they will not even soothe you. Stay with me, my little one! Your brother Dawée says that going East, away from your mother, is too hard an experience for his baby sister."

Thus my mother discouraged my curiosity about the lands beyond our eastern horizon; for it was not yet an ambition for Letters that was stirring me. But on the following day the missionaries did come to our very house. . . .

Judéwin had told me of the great tree where grew red, red apples; and how we could reach out our hands and pick all the red apples we could eat. I had never seen apple trees. I had never tasted more than a dozen red apples in my life; and when I heard of the orchards of the East, I was eager to roam among them. The missionaries smiled into my eyes and patted my head. I wondered how mother could say such hard words against them.

"Mother, ask them if little girls may have all the red apples they want, when they go East," I whispered aloud, in my excitement. The interpreter heard me, and answered: "Yes, little girl, the nice red apples are for those who pick them; and you will have a ride on the iron horse if you go with these good people."

I had never seen a train, and he knew it.

"Mother, I am going East! I like big red apples, and I want to ride on the iron horse! Mother, say yes!" I pleaded. . . . With this they left us. Alone with my mother, I yielded to my tears, and cried aloud, shaking my head so as not to hear what she was saying to me. This was the first time I had ever been so unwilling to give up my own desire that I refused to hearken to my mother's voice.

There was a solemn silence in our home that night. Before I went to bed I begged the Great Spirit to make my mother willing I should go with the missionaries.

The next morning came, and my mother called me to her side. "My daughter, do you still persist in wishing to leave your mother?" she asked.

"Oh, mother, it is not that I wish to leave you, but I want to see the wonderful Eastern land," I answered. . . . My brother Dawée came for mother's decision. I dropped my play, and crept close to my aunt.

"Yes, Dawée, my daughter, though she does not understand what it all means, is anxious to

SOURCE: Zitkala-Ša, *American Indian Stories* (1921; repr., Lincoln: University of Nebraska Press, 1985), 39–56.

go. She will need an education when she is grown, for then there will be fewer real Dakotas, and many more palefaces. This tearing her away, so young, from her mother is necessary, if I would have her an educated woman. The palefaces, who owe us a large debt for stolen lands, have begun to pay a tardy justice in offering some education to our children. But I know my daughter must suffer keenly in this experiment. For her sake, I dread to tell you my reply to the missionaries. Go, tell them that they may take my little daughter, and that the Great Spirit shall not fail to reward them according to their hearts."

Wrapped in my heavy blanket, I walked with my mother to the carriage that was soon to take us to the iron horse. I was happy. I met my playmates, who were also wearing their best thick blankets. We showed one another our new beaded moccasins, and the width of the belts that girdled our new dresses. Soon we were being drawn rapidly away by the white man's horses.

SCHOOL DAYS OF AN INDIAN GIRL: THE LAND OF RED APPLES

There were eight in our party of bronzed children who were going East with the missionaries. Among us were three young braves, two tall girls, and we three little ones, Judéwin, Thowin, and I.

We had been very impatient to start on our journey to the Red Apple Country, which, we were told, lay a little beyond the great circular horizon of the Western prairie. Under a sky of rosy apples we dreamt of roaming as freely and happily as we had chased the cloud shadows on the Dakota plains. We had anticipated much pleasure from a ride on the iron horse, but the throngs of staring palefaces disturbed and troubled us.

On the train, fair women, with tottering babies on each arm, stopped their haste and scrutinized the children of absent mothers. Large men, with heavy bundles in their hands, halted near by, and riveted their glassy blue eyes upon us.

I sank deep into the corner of my seat, for I resented being watched. Directly in front of me, children who were no larger than I hung them-

selves upon the backs of their seats, with their bold white faces toward me. Sometimes they took their forefingers out of their mouths and pointed at my moccasined feet. Their mothers, instead of reproving such rude curiosity, looked closely at me, and attracted their children's further notice to my blanket. This embarrassed me, and kept me constantly on the verge of tears. . . .

It was night when we reached the school grounds. The lights from the windows of the large buildings fell upon some of the icicled trees that stood beneath them. We were led toward an open door, where the brightness of the lights within flooded out over the heads of the excited palefaces who blocked the way. My body trembled more from fear than from the snow I trod upon.

Entering the house, I stood close against the wall. The strong glaring light in the large whitewashed room dazzled my eyes. The noisy hurrying of hard shoes upon a bare wooden floor increased the whirring in my ears. My only safety seemed to be in keeping next to the wall. As I was wondering in which direction to escape from all this confusion, two warm hands grasped me firmly, and in the same moment I was tossed high in midair. A rosy-cheeked paleface woman caught me in her arms. I was both frightened and insulted by such trifling. I stared into her eyes, wishing her to let me stand on my own feet, but she jumped me up and down with increasing enthusiasm. My mother had never made a plaything of her wee daughter. Remembering this I began to cry aloud. . . .

I had arrived in the wonderful land of rosy skies, but I was not happy, as I had thought I should be. My long travel and the bewildering sights had exhausted me. I fell asleep, heaving deep, tired sobs. My tears were left to dry themselves in streaks, because neither my aunt nor my mother was near to wipe them away.

SCHOOL DAYS OF AN INDIAN GIRL: THE CUTTING OF MY LONG HAIR

The first day in the land of apples was a bitter-cold one; for the snow still covered the ground, and the trees were bare. A large bell rang for breakfast, its loud metallic voice crashing through the belfry overhead and into our sensitive ears. . . . And though my spirit tore itself in struggling for its lost freedom, all was useless.

A paleface woman, with white hair, came up after us. We were placed in a line of girls who were marching into the dining room. These were Indian girls, in stiff shoes and closely clinging dresses. The small girls wore sleeved aprons and shingled hair. As I walked noiselessly in my soft moccasins, I felt like sinking to the floor, for my blanket had been stripped from my shoulders. I looked hard at the Indian girls, who seemed not to care that they were even more immodestly dressed than I, in their tightly fitting clothes. While we marched in, the boys entered at an opposite door. I watched for the three young braves who came in our party. I spied them in the rear ranks, looking as uncomfortable as I felt.

A small bell was tapped, and each of the pupils drew a chair from under the table. Supposing this act meant they were to be seated, I pulled out mine and at once slipped into it from one side. But when I turned my head, I saw that I was the only one seated, and all the rest at our table remained standing. Just as I began to rise, looking shyly around to see how chairs were to be used, a second bell was sounded. All were seated at last, and I had to crawl back into my chair again. I heard a man's voice at one end of the hall, and I looked around to see him. But all the others hung their heads over their plates. As I glanced at the long chain of tables, I caught the eyes of a paleface woman upon me. Immediately I dropped my eyes, wondering why I was so keenly watched by the strange woman. The man ceased his mutterings, and then a third bell was tapped. Every one picked up his knife and fork and began eating. I began crying instead, for by this time I was afraid to venture anything more.

But this eating by formula was not the hardest trial in that first day. Late in the morning, my friend Judéwin gave me a terrible warning. Judéwin knew a few words of English; and she had overheard the paleface woman talk about cutting our long, heavy hair. Our mothers had taught us that only unskilled warriors who were captured had their hair shingled by the enemy. Among our people, short hair was worn by mourners, and shingled hair by cowards!

We discussed our fate some moments, and when Judéwin said, "We have to submit, because they are strong," I rebelled. "No, I will not submit! I will struggle first!" I answered.

I watched my chance, and when no one noticed, I disappeared. I crept up the stairs as quietly as I could in my squeaking shoes, — my moccasins had been exchanged for shoes. . . . On my hands and knees I crawled under the bed, and cuddled myself in the dark corner.

From my hiding place I peered out, shuddering with fear whenever I heard footsteps near by. Though in the hall loud voices were calling my name, and I knew that even Judéwin was searching for me, I did not open my mouth to answer. Then the steps were quickened and the voices became excited. The sounds came nearer and nearer. Women and girls entered the room. I held my breath and watched them open closet doors and peep behind large trunks. Some one threw up the curtains, and the room was filled with sudden light. What caused them to stoop and look under the bed I do not know. I remember being dragged out, though I resisted by kicking and scratching wildly. In spite of myself, I was carried downstairs and tied fast in a chair.

I cried aloud, shaking my head all the while until I felt the cold blades of the scissors against my neck, and heard them gnaw off one of my thick braids. Then I lost my spirit. Since the day I was taken from my mother I had suffered extreme indignities. People had stared at me. I had been tossed about in the air like a wooden puppet. And now my long hair was shingled like a coward's! In my anguish I moaned for my mother, but no one came to comfort me. Not a soul reasoned quietly with me, as my own mother used to do; for now I was only one of many little animals driven by a herder.

QUESTIONS FOR ANALYSIS

1. How do Zitkala-Ša's encounters with white society compare to those of Sarah Winnemucca in the 1840s (see pp. 287–90)?

2. Compare the response of the author to the noise and regimentation of her school to the experiences of European immigrants arriving into bustling, industrial American cities.

3. One scholar has characterized the assimilationist education offered by well-meaning white "friends of the Indian" as a kind of "tender violence."[43] Given Zitkala-Ša's account, what do you think of this term?

DOCUMENTS

Jane Addams and the Charitable Relation

JANE ADDAMS (1860–1935) was the leader of the American settlement house movement. After graduating in 1882 from Rockford Seminary in Illinois, she went to Europe in search of a larger purpose for her life. Like other daughters of wealthy families, she was looking for an alternative to the leisured, homebound life of the sort in which Alice Austen reveled (see Visual Sources: Alice Austen: Gilded Age Photographer, pp. 379–84). Restless leisure-class women like Addams did not require paid labor, but they did need work of large social purpose and a place and community in which to live. Visiting London, Addams learned of a "settlement" project of male college graduates who lived among and served the urban poor. She returned to Illinois, determined to establish a similar community of female college graduates dedicated to social service. In 1889 Addams persuaded a wealthy woman to donate a Chicago mansion, originally built by the Hull family and now in the center of a crowded immigrant district, for her planned settlement.

The reform-minded women who joined Addams to live and work in Hull House combined a palpable sympathy with the urban poor and a determination to find a nonrevolutionary solution to the era's class and ethnic conflicts. In Addams's words, they were determined "to aid in the solution of the social and industrial problems which are engendered by the modern conditions of urban life."[44] Their focus was especially on the welfare of women and children. They learned that in hard times poor women suffered the consequences of a double dependency—on men who could not be breadwinners and on governments that were slow to accept public responsibility for social welfare needs.

Addams wrote the essay excerpted here, "The Subtle Problems of Charity," in 1899, only a few years after the 1893 depression and 1894 Pullman Strike, before the success of her pioneering work at Hull House was widely acknowledged. The essay demonstrates Addams's dual vocation of empirical social observer and passionate social reformer. She actively struggled with the "perplexities" that plagued the efforts of leisure-class women like herself to respond to the needs of impoverished immigrants. In a society still imbued with a rigid morality, Addams displayed an impressive ability to avoid ethical absolutes in her understanding of immigrants' lives and choices.

Addams sought to interpret the long history of what she calls "the charitable relation." In the early nineteenth century, wealthy benefactors made sure that their money went only to the "worthy" poor, so as to encourage charity recipients to become self-supporting participants in a competitive, market-driven society. But Addams believed that these philanthropists treated their clients "exclusively as factors in the industrial system." By contrast, she advocated a more humanitarian ethic of "brotherhood and equality." She approached the problem of charity in broader terms, concerned that American political democracy should develop a social dimension. Her primary concern was not whether an individual was "worthy" of charity but the creation of constructive bonds and mutual understanding between those who need aid and those in a position to give it.

Simultaneous with this shift in the charitable ethic, the gender of those who dispensed philanthropic aid was changing. The traditional philanthropic leader had been a man who had succeeded in the struggle for individual wealth and gave in accordance with the values he credited for his own rise in society. But by the late nineteenth century, charity giving had become the responsibility of leisure-class women who had no direct experience with money making. In 1899, Addams was unsettled about the contradiction between leisure-class women's ignorance of material realities and the control they exerted over the lives of the needy poor who looked to them for necessary aid.

Contradictory intellectual frameworks can be detected in Addams's thinking about her relationship to the new immigrants. The beneficiary of expanding opportunities for higher education for women, Addams subscribed to the modern principles of progress and social science, which she used to make sense of the dilemmas she and other settlement house activists faced. She relied on Darwinian notions of evolution to characterize the inevitable and desirable development of society from the lower stages and backward cultures represented by European immigrants to the higher stages and superior cultures of the American bourgeoisie. Yet at the same time, she also regarded the "primitiveness" of these immigrant families as more natural, more basic, and in some ways more fundamentally human than the ways of her own class and culture. She felt that women of the middle and upper classes had lost touch with fundamental human needs and experiences that were instinctively understood by immigrant women.

Addams's analysis of the dilemmas of philanthropy was not limited to the problems of the charity givers but included the ethical dilemmas faced by the immigrant recipients. She resisted treating the immigrant poor as either passive or morally pure, seeing them instead as people struggling with their own contradictory values. In her view the new immigrants, like the larger American society into which they had come, quickly learned to respect economic success more than human compassion. Thus they admired but expected little from those who had achieved material wealth while they were polite to but contemptuous of the "good . . . and kind-hearted" women of wealth on whom they depended for crucial charitable aid.

Addams's concern with the relations between parents and children is also evident in this essay. She tended to see settlement house workers in the role of parents, sometimes beneficent, sometimes uncomprehending, of the childlike immigrants. This family-based model of class relations helped female settlement house activists legitimate their efforts at expanding their social authority: Addams and women like herself saw themselves as public "mothers." But as this essay makes clear, Addams also had considerable empathy for immigrant children. Within a few years, she would become a leader in the fight to ban child labor as well as to pass laws and regulations intended to move mothers out of the labor force so that they could devote themselves entirely to the rearing of their children.

By 1910 Jane Addams was the acknowledged head of the settlement movement and a leader in American philanthropy. In Hull House, she created a modern, progressive venue to which reformers from all over the world came, from British social democrat Sidney Webb to Japanese feminist Ichikawa Fusae. At times, she was misunderstood by both the poor and the rich for her determination to negotiate between the warring classes of turn-of-the-century American society, but her approach was widely influential on women and men alike. An instinctive revulsion at militarism, first evident during the Filipino-American conflict of 1899–1902, combined with the internationalism that she embraced at the neighborhood level in her Hull House work, led her to become, later in her career, a leader of the women's international peace movement (see Chapter 7).

Jane Addams
The Subtle Problems of Charity (1899)

Probably there is no relation in life which our democracy is changing more rapidly than the charitable relation, that relation which obtains between benefactor and beneficiary; at the same time, there is no point of contact in our modern experience which reveals more clearly the lack of that equality which democracy implies. We have reached the moment when democracy has made such inroads upon this relationship that the complacency of the old-fashioned charitable man is gone forever; while the very need and existence of charity deny us the consolation and freedom which democracy will at last give.

Formerly when it was believed that poverty was synonymous with vice and laziness, and that the prosperous man was the righteous man, charity was administered harshly with a good conscience; for the charitable agent really blamed the individual for his poverty, and the very fact of his own superior prosperity gave him a certain consciousness of superior morality. Since then we have learned to measure by other standards, and

the money-earning capacity, while still rewarded out of all proportion to any other, is not respected as exclusively as it was. . . .

Of the various struggles which a decade of residence in a settlement implies, none have made a more definite impression on my mind than the incredibly painful difficulties which involve both giver and recipient when one person asks charitable aid of another.

An attempt is made in this paper to show what are some of the perplexities which harass the mind of the charity worker; to trace them to ethical survivals which are held not only by the benefactor, but by the recipients of charity as well; and to suggest wherein these very perplexities may possibly be prophetic.

. . . The charity visitor, let us assume, is a young college woman, well-bred and open-minded. When she visits the family assigned to her, she is embarrassed to find herself obliged to lay all the stress of her teaching and advice upon the industrial virtues, and to treat the members of the family almost exclusively as factors in the industrial system. She insists that they must work

---

Source: Atlantic Monthly, February 1899, 163–78.

and be self-supporting; that the most dangerous of all situations is idleness; . . . [I]t often occurs to the mind of the sensitive visitor, whose conscience has been made tender by much talk of brotherhood and equality which she has heard at college, that she has no right to say these things; that she herself has never been self-supporting; that, whatever her virtues may be, they are not the industrial virtues; that her untrained hands are no more fitted to cope with actual conditions than are those of her broken-down family.

The grandmother of the charity visitor could have done the industrial preaching very well, because she did have the industrial virtues; if not skillful in weaving and spinning, she was yet mistress of other housewifely accomplishments. In a generation our experiences have changed — our views with them. . . .

A very little familiarity with the poor districts of any city is sufficient to show how primitive and frontier-like are the neighborly relations. There is the great willingness to lend or borrow anything, and each resident of a given tenement house knows the most intimate family affairs of all the others. The fact that the economic conditions of all alike is on the most precarious level makes the ready outflow of sympathy and material assistance the most natural thing in the world. There are numberless instances of heroic self-sacrifice quite unknown in the circles where greater economic advantages make that kind of intimate knowledge of one's neighbors impossible. . . .

The evolutionists tell us that the instinct to pity, the impulse to aid his fellows, served man at a very early period as a rude rule of right and wrong. There is no doubt that this rude rule still holds among many people with whom charitable agencies are brought into contact, and that their ideas of right and wrong are quite honestly outraged by the methods of these agencies. When they see the delay and caution with which relief is given, these do not appear to them conscientious scruples, but the cold and calculating action of the selfish man. This is not the aid that they are accustomed to receive from their neighbors. . . .

The only man they are accustomed to see whose intellectual perceptions are stronger than his tenderness of heart is the selfish and avaricious man, who is frankly "on the make." If the charity visitor is such a person, why does she pretend to like the poor? Why does she not go into business at once? . . . In the minds of the poor success does not ordinarily go with charity and kindheartedness, but rather with the opposite qualities. The rich landlord is he who collects with sternness; who accepts no excuse, and will have his own. There are moments of irritation and of real bitterness against him, but there is admiration, because he is rich and successful. . . . The charity visitor, just because she is a person who concerns herself with the poor, receives a touch of this good-natured and kindly contempt, sometimes real affection, but little genuine respect. . . .

When the agent or visitor appears among the poor, and they discover that under certain conditions food and rent and medical aid are dispensed from some unknown source, every man, woman and child is quick to learn what the conditions may be and to follow them. . . . The deception arises from a wondering inability to understand the ethical ideals which can require such impossible virtues, combined with a tradition that charity visitors do require them, and from an innocent desire to please. It is easy to trace the development of the mental suggestions thus received. The most serious effect upon the individual comes when dependence upon the charitable society is substituted for the natural outgoing of human love and sympathy, which, happily, we all possess in some degree. . . . The charity visitor has broken through the natural rule of giving, which in a primitive society is bounded only by the need of the recipient and the resources of the giver; and she gets herself into untold trouble when she is judged by the ethics of that primitive society.

The neighborhood understands the selfish rich people who stay in their own part of the town. . . . Such people do not bother themselves about the poor; they are like the rich landlords of the neighborhood experience. But this lady visitor, who pretends to be good to the poor, and certainly does talk as though she were kind-hearted, what does she come for, if she does not intend to give them things which so plainly are needed? The visitor says, sometimes, that in holding her poor family so hard to a standard of thrift she is really breaking down a rule for higher living which they formerly possessed; that saving, which seems quite commendable in a comfortable part of the town, appears almost criminal in a poorer quarter, where the next-door neighbor needs food, even if the children of the family do not. She feels the sordidness of constantly being obliged to urge the industrial view of life. . . . She says sometimes: "Why must I talk always on getting work and saving money, the things I know nothing about? . . ."

Because of this diversity in experience the visitor is continually surprised to find that the safest platitudes may be challenged. . . .

The subject of clothes, indeed, perplexes the visitor constantly, and the result of her reflections may be summed up something in this wise: The girl who has a definite social standing, who has been to a fashionable school or to a college, whose family live[s] in a house seen and known by all her friends and associates, can afford to be very simple or even shabby as to her clothes, if she likes. But the working girl, whose family lives in a tenement or moves from one small apartment to another, who has little social standing, and has to make her own place, knows full well how much habit and style of dress have to do with her position. Her income goes into her clothing out of all proportion to that which she spends upon other things. But if social advancement is her aim, it is the most sensible thing which she can do. She is judged largely by her clothes. . . .

Have we worked out our democracy in regard to clothes farther than in regard to anything else?

The charity visitor has been rightly brought up to consider it vulgar to spend much money upon clothes, to care so much for "appearances." . . . The poor naturally try to bridge the [class] difference by reproducing the street clothes which they have seen; they therefore imitate, sometimes in more showy and often in more trying colors, in cheap and flimsy material, in poor shoes and flippant hats, the extreme fashion of the well-to-do. They are striving to conform to a common standard which their democratic training presupposes belongs to us all. The charity visitor may regret that the Italian peasant woman has laid aside her picturesque kerchief, and substituted a cheap street hat. But it is easy to recognize the first attempt toward democratic expression.

The charity visitor is still more perplexed when she comes to consider such problems as those of early marriage and child labor. . . . She discovers how incorrigibly bourgeois her standards have been, and it takes but a little time to reach the conclusion that she cannot insist so strenuously upon the conventions of her own class, which fail to fit the bigger, more emotional, and freer lives of working people. . . .

The sense of prudence, the necessity for saving, can never come to a primitive, emotional man with the force of a conviction, but the necessity of providing for his children is a powerful incentive. He naturally regards his children as his savings-bank; he expects them to care for him when he gets old, and in some trades old age comes very early. . . . [A] tailor whom I know, a Socialist, always speaks of saving as a bourgeois virtue, one quite impossible to the genuine workingman. He supports a family, consisting of himself, a wife and three children, and his parents, on eight dollars a week. He insists that it would be criminal not to expend every penny of this amount upon food and shelter, and he expects his children later to take care of him. . . .

The struggle for existence, which is so much harsher among people near the edge of pauperism, sometimes leaves ugly marks on character, and the charity visitor finds the indirect results most mystifying. Parents who work hard and anticipate an old age when they can no longer earn, take care that their children shall expect to divide their wages with them from the very first. Such a parent, when successful, seizes the immature nervous system of the child and hypnotizes it, so to speak, into a habit of obedience, that the nerves and will may not depart from this control when the child is older. The charity visitor, whose family relation is lifted quite out of this, does not in the least understand the industrial foundation in this family despotism.

The head of a kindergarten training class once addressed a club of working-women, and spoke of the despotism which is often established over little children. . . . [O]ne [working woman] said, "Ah, of course, she [meaning the speaker] doesn't have to depend upon her children's wages. She can afford to be lax with them, because, even if they don't give money to her, she can get along without it." . . .

It is these subtle and elusive problems which, after all, the charity visitor finds most harassing. . . . The greatest difficulty is experienced when the two [ethical] standards come sharply together, and when an attempt is made at understanding and explanation. The difficulty of defining one's own ethical standpoint is at times insurmountable. . . .

A certain charity visitor is peculiarly appealed to by the weakness and pathos of forlorn old age. One of these poor old women was injured in a fire years ago. She has but the fragment of a hand left, and is grievously crippled in her feet. Through years of pain she had become addicted to opium. . . . Five years of tender care have done wonders for her. She lives in two neat little rooms, where with a thumb and two fingers she makes innumerable quilts, which she sells and gives away with the greatest delight. Her opium is regulated to a set amount taken each day. . . . [S]he was kept for two years in a suburb where the family of the charity visitor lived, and where she was nursed through several hazardous illnesses. . . . Her neighbors are constantly shocked by the fact that she is supported and comforted by "a charity lady," while at the same time she occasionally "rushes the growler,"° scolding at the boys lest they jar her in her tottering walk. The care of her has broken through even that second standard, which the neighborhood had learned to recognize as the

standard of charitable societies, that only the "worthy poor" are to be helped. . . . In order to disarm them, and at the same time to explain what would otherwise seem loving-kindness so colossal as to be abnormal, she tells them that during her sojourn in the suburb she discovered an awful family secret, a horrible scandal connected with the long-suffering charity visitor; that it is in order to prevent the divulgence of this that the ministrations are continued. Some of her perplexed neighbors accept this explanation as simple and offering a solution of a vexed problem. . . .

Of what use is all this striving and perplexity? Has the experience any value? It is obviously genuine, for it induces an occasional charity visitor to live in a tenement house as simply as the other tenants do. It drives others to give up visiting the poor altogether, because, they claim, the situation is untenable . . . the young charity visitor who goes from a family living upon a most precarious industrial level to her own home in a prosperous part of the city, if she is sensitive at all, is never free from perplexities which our growing democracy forces upon her.

We sometimes say that our charity is too scientific, but we should doubtless be much more correct in our estimate if we said that it is not scientific enough. . . . There is no doubt that our development of charity methods has reached this pseudo-scientific and stilted stage. We have learned to condemn unthinking, ill-regulated kind-heartedness, and we take great pride in mere repression, much as the stern parent tells the visitor below how admirably he is rearing the child who is hysterically crying upstairs, and laying the foundation for future nervous disorders. The pseudo-scientific spirit, or rather the undeveloped stage of our philanthropy, is, perhaps, most clearly revealed in this tendency to lay stress on negative action. "Don't give," "don't break down self-respect," we are constantly told. We distrust the human impulse, and in its stead substitute dogmatic rules for conduct . . . we forget that the accumulation of knowledge and the holding of convictions must finally result in the application

° Drinks alcohol.

of that knowledge and those convictions to life itself, and the course which begins by activity, and an appeal to sympathies so severe that all the knowledge in the possession of the visitor is continually applied, has reasonably a greater chance for ultimate comprehension.

For most of the years during a decade of residence in a settlement, my mind was sore and depressed over the difficulties of the charitable relationship. The incessant clashing of ethical standards, which had been honestly gained from widely varying industrial experience, — the misunderstandings inevitable between people whose conventions and mode of life had been so totally unlike, — made it seem reasonable to say that nothing could be done until industrial conditions were made absolutely democratic. The position of a settlement, which attempts at one and the same time to declare its belief in this eventual, industrial democracy, and to labor toward that end, to maintain a standard of living, and to deal humanely and simply with those in actual want, often seems utterly untenable and preposterous. Recently, however, there has come to my mind the suggestion of a principle, that while the painful condition of administering charity is the inevitable discomfort of a transition into a more democratic relation, the perplexing experiences of the actual administration have a genuine value of their own. . . .

The Hebrew prophet made three requirements from those who would join the great forward-moving procession led by Jehovah. "To love mercy," and at the same time "to do justly," is the difficult task. To fulfill the first requirement alone is to fall into the error of indiscriminate giving, with all its disastrous results; to fulfill the second exclusively is to obtain the stern policy of withholding, and it results in such a dreary lack of sympathy and understanding that the establishment of justice is impossible. It may be that the combination of the two can never be attained save as we fulfill still the third requirement, "to walk humbly with God," which may mean to walk for many dreary miles beside the lowliest of his creatures, not even in peace of mind, that the companionship of the humble is popularly supposed to give, but rather with the pangs and misgivings to which the poor human understanding is subjected whenever it attempts to comprehend the meaning of life.

QUESTIONS FOR ANALYSIS

1. Early in this essay, Addams speaks of the conditions in "the poor districts of any city" as "frontier-like." What does she mean by this? What were the similarities between the "settlement" of the West and "settlement" houses?

2. What is the "diversity of experience" that Addams witnessed in her work with immigrants in the neighborhood around Hull House, and how did it contribute to the ethical complexities about which she wrote?

3. The longest incident in this article is the story of the troubled old immigrant woman who was befriended and rescued by a leisure-class woman and then lied to her neighbors about her benefactor's motives. What does the incident reveal about the ethical dilemmas faced by charity recipients and charity givers alike, and about the obstacles that class inequalities posed to the creation of bonds between them?

4. How did Addams's experience as a member of the pathbreaking generation of women college graduates affect her perspective as a settlement house volunteer?

Jacob Riis's Photographs of Immigrant Girls and Women

I N THE DECADE 1880–1890, more than 5 million immigrants came through the port of New York, and many remained in the city, swelling its population by 25 percent. By 1890 nearly half of the city's dwellings were classified as "tenements," overcrowded urban slums where vulnerable and desperately poor people were overcharged for filthy, cramped, and unsanitary lodgings.

This rise in immigration coincided with new forms of social documentation. Pioneering social scientists provided statistics on the growing industrial labor force, including the women who were entering the workplace in unprecedented numbers. Local and state health bureaus collected information on the epidemic diseases such as diphtheria, cholera, and tuberculosis that threatened family life in the burgeoning cities. And photographers created searing images of the horrible living and working conditions of newly arrived immigrants. These new methods of documentation, informed by a rising sense of public responsibility for improving social conditions and alleviating poverty, allow us to look back through the perspectives of those who did the documenting, into the lives of late nineteenth-century immigrant girls and women.

One of the first series of photographs of immigrant women and children in the United States was produced in the 1880s and 1890s by a man who was himself an immigrant. Jacob A. Riis arrived in New York City from Denmark in 1870. After more than a decade struggling to earn a living, he found regular work as a newspaperman. He began as a police reporter, writing in a male-oriented, journalistic genre that sensationalized the seamy side of "downtown" life. Riis's own impulses, however, were more humanitarian and allied him with urban reformers, many of whom were women. He worked closely with Josephine Shaw Lowell, who founded the Charity Organization Society of New York State in 1882. His particular focus was "the slum," by which he meant not only the dilapidated tenement homes of the poor but the larger urban environment in which they lived and worked. He was especially concerned with children, and through them the mothers of immigrant families.

Convinced that only photographs could convey the shocking reality of urban poverty, Riis included them in *How the Other Half Lives: Studies among the Tenements of New York* (1890), a pioneering work of sociology that is still mined by historians and scholars for the insights it provides into urban immigrant life, nineteenth-century attitudes toward poverty and ethnicity, and the visual conventions of early documentary photography. Though the majority of the photographs deal with male subjects—homeless street boys, male vagrants, and gang members—Riis also took pictures of women and girls that give us glimpses of their lives. In its frequent resort to sensational and melodramatic conventions, *How the Other Half Lives* reflects its author's roots in mass commercial journalism, but it also skillfully adopts strategies from literary realism and the emerging field of social science to convey a probing portrait of poverty and its consequences.

Consistent with the late nineteenth-century's preoccupation with ethnic and racial characteristics, *How the Other Half Lives* is organized like a guided tour for the middle-class reader through the ethnic geography of lower New York. Not surprisingly, it invokes both positive and negative stereotypes in its descriptions and illustrations. Riis, as a northwestern European immigrant, had clear ethnic biases, but his prejudices were tempered by empathy and the recognition that "we are all creatures of the conditions that surround us."[45] His goal was to call attention to the plight of the poor, not to castigate them for their poverty.

Chapter V of Riis's book, "The Italian in New York," focuses on those who, as recent arrivals, were "at the bottom" of the economic and social hierarchy.[46] The frequently reproduced photograph shown in Figure 7.1 depicts the wife and infant child of a "ragpicker"—one who barely made a living by picking through public

◆ **Figure 7.1 In the Home of an Italian Ragpicker: Jersey Street**
Museum of the City of New York, the Jacob A. Riis Collection.

rubbish cans and dumps for rags to sell—in their subterranean home. Riis developed the innovative technology used to make this photograph, a new chemical process that produced a "flash" bright enough to light up dark and windowless areas.

The pose of the Italian mother and her tightly swaddled child, as well as her mournful, upturned gaze, is reminiscent of religious paintings of the Madonna and Child in which the Virgin Mary's sad expression foreshadows the suffering that awaits her infant son. In the chapter that includes this photograph, Riis offers an extended report, complete with comparative statistics, on the high mortality rates of infants and children in this Italian neighborhood. What other explanations can be offered for her upward look?

Italian families, no matter how poor, frowned on wives and mothers working outside the home. While the room in Figure 7.1 is sparsely furnished, what do the few items we see and their arrangement tell us about this woman and her daily life? In the text accompanying this photograph, Riis describes the Italian immigrant as "picturesque, if not very tidy."[47] Does his photograph support this characterization? What overall impression does it convey about Italian immigrant mothers? Also in the text relating to this image is Riis's description of Italian men as "hotheaded . . . and lighthearted" and of Italian women as "faithful wives and devoted mothers."[48] Note the man's straw hat hanging high on the wall. What are the possible explanations for the man's absence?

In Figure 7.2, Riis continues his progression through New York City's ethnic neighborhoods to "Jewtown," an area settled by large numbers of Eastern European Jews and marked by exceptional population density and industrial activity.

◆ **Figure 7.2 Knee Pants at Forty-Five Cents a Dozen—A Ludlow Street Sweater's Shop**
Museum of the City of New York, the Jacob A. Riis Collection.

As Riis notes, "Life here means the hardest kind of work almost from the cradle."[49] The "sweater" mentioned in the title of the photograph was a subcontractor who supplied garments to a larger manufacturer and hired other immigrants to do the work, often in his own tenement apartment. The ruthless competition to deliver finished goods at the lowest possible price pressured the sweater to offer impossibly low wages and push (or "sweat") workers to their physical limits during a working day that "lengthened at both ends far into the night."[50] While Riis criticizes the "sweater's . . . merciless severity"[51] in exploiting his fellow Jews, he concedes "he is no worse than the conditions that created him."[52]

Unlike the photograph shown in Figure 7.1, this photo was not posed and has no carefully arranged central figure. It catches its subjects off guard, and the blurring of some of their features suggests frantic activity and movement. The sweater is the moving figure with his back to the camera. The teenage girls in this picture are "greenhorns," newly arrived immigrant workers. One man looks up briefly from his work, but the other seems unwilling to lose a minute's time despite the photographer's presence. Piles of boys' short pants waiting to be finished are heaped on the floor and furniture. What visual clues tell us that this workshop is also a residence? What else goes on in this room? In what ways is it different from the living space of the Italian mother in Figure 7.1?

In contrast to the serious detachment of the adults, the young girl turns to smile directly into the lens and casually touches to her lips the long-bladed scissors she is using to cut the garments. Does this suggest she has not yet been disciplined to keep up with the brutal pace of piecework? Maybe Riis regarded her direct gaze as somewhat immodest, a consequence of work conditions that placed unsupervised young girls amid grown men. Or did she simply find pleasure in having her picture taken? In his second book, *The Children of the Poor* (1892), Riis noted that in contrast to adults, who resisted and feared being photographed, children loved posing for the camera and had a "determination to be 'took' . . . in the most striking pose they could hastily devise."[53] What other possible meanings can be suggested for this unusual and striking image of a young working woman?

Employers justified the low wages paid to female workers, which were inadequate for self-support, as supplements to a family income anchored by an adult male wage. Riis was sharply aware of the special hardships facing the unmarried, poor working women who had to live on their own. In his chapter "The Working Girls of New York," he describes the exploitation and harsh conditions they endured, sprinkling his narrative with tragic stories of underpaid and exhausted women workers driven to suicide, prostitution, and premature death. Like so many other late nineteenth-century reformers, Riis thought the best solution to working women's suffering was to get them out of the labor force. If they remained in it, their lives were bound to be intolerable.

Figure 7.3 is an unusual photograph of two adult women, past the age when even poor immigrant women were expected to leave the labor force. They are not driven by a supervisor as are the workers in Figure 7.2, but neither do they enjoy the camaraderie of other workers. How does their living space compare with that in the previous two photographs? What does their dress suggest about them?

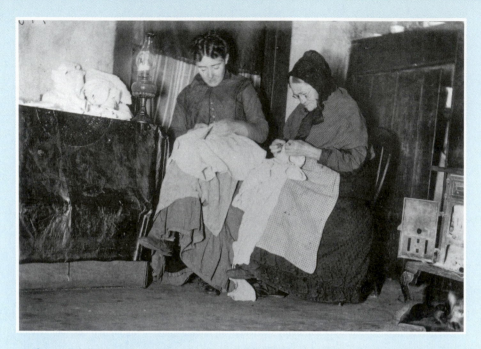

◆ **Figure 7.3 Sewing and Starving in an Elizabeth Street Attic**
Museum of the City of New York, the Jacob A. Riis Collection.

While we know little about these two women, the context of this photograph in *How the Other Half Lives* provides some help. Elsewhere in the narrative, Riis tells a heartrending story of two elderly sisters, the last of five siblings who had arrived from Ireland with their mother forty years before and who together made a scant living as lace embroiderers. When Riis encounters them, one of the sisters is crippled and the other, who had struggled to support them both, had recently been paralyzed in a fall. Now they were helpless and alone. How do the story, photograph, and title come together to reveal the conditions of aging women workers who had to support themselves through their own wage-earning capacities?

When wages were too low or unemployment too high, poor urban workers found themselves destitute and without shelter. Those who lacked even the pennies charged by commercial lodging houses ended up in overnight shelters in police stations. Of the half-million people seeking shelter in New York City in 1889, almost one-third sought refuge in makeshift facilities in police stations, and half of those were women. Riis knew firsthand about the filthy and dangerous conditions in the police station shelters. Recalling his own experience years before as a homeless vagrant in New York, he observed that "never was parody upon Christian charity more corrupting to human mind and soul than the frightful abomination of the police lodging-house."[54] He was particularly concerned when homeless women slept in the same room as men.

The photograph in Figure 7.4 was an illustration for an article Riis wrote for the *New York Tribune* in 1892, condemning the police station shelters. The West Forty-seventh Street police station was located in the aptly named Hell's Kitchen area of New York, and there is no doubt that Riis intended to shock readers with a graphic, unstaged photograph of women expelled from the domestic sphere, stripped of their dignity and privacy, eating and sleeping on filthy bare floors like animals. The extent of homelessness among women pointed to the collapse of working-class family life and indicated how deeply the combination of mass immigration, rapid urbanization, and economic collapse had rent the social fabric. Notice the details that reveal, perhaps unintentionally, how women manage to cooperate and care for their personal needs even under the harshest of circumstances. What do these details, and the facial expressions and postures of the women, reveal about social relations in this police station lodging room?

In *The Children of the Poor*, published originally as a series of articles in *Scribner's Magazine* in 1892, Riis turned his full attention to the group with whom he was most concerned, the children whose futures were being jeopardized by life in the tenements. Figure 7.5 is a rare individual portrait of an orphan, nine-year-old Katie, who attended the Fifty-second Street Industrial School, a charitable institution for indigent children. Although Katie did not earn wages, she was not spared hard work, for she cooked and cleaned for her three older working siblings. "In her person and work, she answered the question . . . why we hear so much about the

◆ **Figure 7.4 Police Station Lodgers: Women's Lodging Room in the West 47th Street Station**
Museum of the City of New York, the Jacob A. Riis Collection.

◆ **Figure 7.5 "I Scrubs": Katie Who Keeps House on West 49th Street**
Museum of the City of New York, the Jacob A. Riis Collection.

boys and so little about the girls," wrote Riis, "because the home claims their work earlier and to a much greater extent."[55] Consider Katie's clothing, posture, and expression. What do they suggest about her character and her prospects? In acknowledgment of Katie's contribution to her family's survival, Riis called Katie by the nickname often given to immigrant children who cared for younger siblings, "little mother." What does this tribute say about the economic role that mothers and other adult women played in the lives of poor families?

QUESTIONS FOR ANALYSIS

1. Riis clearly intended to shock comfortable Americans with his images of the slums. What might contemporaries have found most disturbing about his representations of immigrant women and girls?

2. Using Riis as an example, how would you evaluate the impact of documentary photography on middle-class America's reaction to poverty in the late nineteenth century? How do Riis's photographs of immigrants compare with the Alice Austen image on page 384?

3. Drawing on both Riis and Bessie Van Vorst (see Documents: The Woman Who Toils, pp. 363–68) as sources, in what ways did women's experience of poverty and underpaid labor in this period differ from that of men?

Women in the Cartoons of *Puck* Magazine

B Y 1900 AMERICAN LITERACY in English had risen to about 90 percent of white Americans and 50 percent of African Americans. Among both groups women were more literate than men. America's high literacy rate helped create a market for low-cost, mass-market print media.

The late nineteenth-century reading public was particularly fond of illustrated magazines that mixed words and images, political commentary and humor. Chief among these was *Puck* magazine, launched in the 1870s by German immigrant Joseph Keppler. *Puck* and magazines like it offer useful glimpses into popular opinions and cultural attitudes of the period, including assumptions about gender. *Puck* was famous for its cartoons, which included both serious commentaries on political issues and lighthearted jokes about social and cultural matters. Both political and humorous cartoons frequently portrayed women—but in quite different ways.

The changing face and place of women in American society provided rich material for *Puck*'s humor. Many jokes in *Puck*'s cartoons rested on stereotypes of women, from the mannish middle-class suffragist to the backward female immigrant. *Puck*'s humorous treatment of late nineteenth-century women contrasted sharply with the magazine's frequent use of female figures in its didactic political cartoons. Here political abstractions in female form were as reverent and conventional as the images of immigrant and native-born women were overstated and ridiculous.

The 1892 cartoon strip in Figure 7.6 ridicules ethnic stereotypes, especially about gender relations. Pedro, an Italian immigrant, praises America for its promise of liberty and freedom, despite his uncomplaining, overburdened wife. Then, an Irish policeman berates Pedro for the treatment of his wife, even though his own wife works over a washtub. How is the reader to recognize Italian and Irish immigrants? Is it the men or the immigrant groups that are being stereotyped and ridiculed? What is the implication about the superiority of gender relations among native-born Americans?

The contrast between native-born and immigrant women, especially as employer and servant in the middle-class household, is featured in Figure 7.7, also published in *Puck* in 1892. The Irish maid was such a stock cartoon figure that she was always drawn the same way. Notice the similarity to the 1852 drawing in Figure 4.5 (p. 237). In this cartoon, however, the native-born employer, while beautiful and well dressed, is also being ridiculed. How does the cartoonist make fun of this woman? In what ways does the contrast between mistress and maid set up the joke? What does the cartoon's title mean, about the woman as well as about the rolling pin?

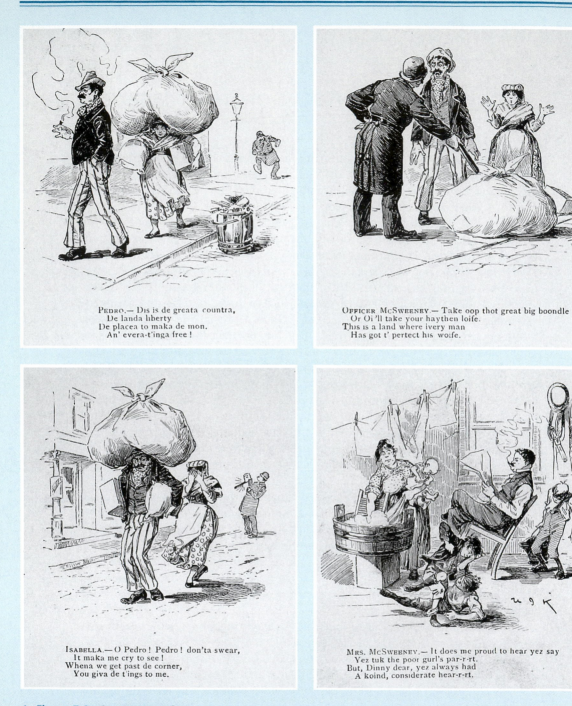

◆ **Figure 7.6 The Woman of It**
Collection of the New-York Historical Society, negative #76758d.

USEFUL AS WELL AS ORNAMENTAL.

NEW GIRL.— Please, Mum, I can't make pie-crust widout a rollin' pin.

MRS. DE KORATER.— You'll find it hanging in the parlor. Remove the ribbons and hooks, and scrape off the gold paint before you use it.

◆ **Figure 7.7 Useful as Well as Ornamental**
Collection of the New-York Historical Society, negative #76759d.

What does her name, "Mrs. de Korater," suggest about the role of middle-class women in America's consumer culture?

Puck also featured cartoons on women's demand for voting rights and entry into male-dominated professions. In Figure 7.8, a cartoon published in 1898, the woman away at her women's rights meeting sets up the joke. As far back as 1848, the great French cartoonist Honoré Daumier had used a similar image of a beleaguered husband, unmanned by the demands of childrearing in the absence of his wife, to warn of the chaos that public roles for women would bring to daily life. How does the cartoon subtly mock the absent woman's concerns with rights outside the household? How sympathetic is the cartoonist to the husband's hopes for a peaceful home and supportive wife? By changing the gender of the cradle-rocker from female to male, what does the cartoon suggest

◆ **Figure 7.8 Irony**
Collection of the New-York Historical Society, negative #76760d.

◆ **Figure 7.9 What We Are Coming To**
Collection of the New-York Historical Society, negative #76761d.

about the old sentimental claim about maternal power: "The hand that rocks the cradle is the hand that rules the world"?

By the late nineteenth century, women were making gains into heretofore all-male professions such as medicine. The legal profession, however, remained determinedly male, making the notion of a woman lawyer a good way to make fun of women's changing roles and a fine source of pictorial amusement. Many of *Puck*'s visual jokes about women's new roles used the same stereotype as the female attorney in Figure 7.9, a caricature that bore a striking resemblance to Susan B. Anthony, the venerable leader of the nineteenth-century women's rights movement (see p. 327 for a photograph of Anthony). How is the woman lawyer portrayed as crossing the line into mannishness? Office work continued to be a male-dominated vocation, yet the cartoonist makes the male secretary look less than manly; how?

In contrast to the negative way middle-class women's ambitions for political and economic equality were usually rendered, the New Woman's increasing athleticism and physical vitality were attractive to illustrators, most famously Charles Dana Gibson. The 1900 *Puck* cartoon in Figure 7.10 owes a great deal to the new standard of feminine beauty represented by the strapping and beautiful "Gibson girl." What elements of the illustration make for an image of womanhood that

◆ **Figure 7.10**
An Important Point

Collection of the New-York Historical Society, negative #76762d.

AN IMPORTANT POINT.

"I'm afraid we are a little slow yet."

"Possibly; but I'm sure we don't look slow!"

◆ **Figure 7.11 Unconscious of Their Doom**
Collection of the New-York Historical Society, negative #76763d.

was daringly sexy for the period? How does the dialogue between the two women undercut the visual portrayal of assertion and strength?

In the political cartoons so prominent in *Puck*, representations of actual women are rare, despite the growing involvement of women in politics. Instead, angels, goddesses, and madonnas are used as symbols for abstract concepts, such as national sovereignty or public virtue (see Visual Sources: Gendering Images of the Revolution, pp. 162–68). Ironically, cartoonists used women as symbols for the ideas and institutions of democratic political life from which actual women were excluded.

◆ **Figure 7.12 The Duty of the Hour: To Save Her Not Only from Spain but from a Worse Fate**
Culver Pictures.

Figure 7.11 features the powerful female figure "Columbia" to represent American democratic virtue and hope. Columbia was the female counterpart of Uncle Sam, who did not displace her as the personification of American nationhood until the 1920s. The dedication in 1885 of the Statue of Liberty gave Columbia new heft and importance. In this 1891 image she represents "human rights" as opposed to the "divine right" of monarchs, which she attacks by way of "education." What is the message about the future of American democracy as opposed to the outmoded European political order and its colonial minions? How does it benefit American democracy to be pictured as a woman?

Such uses of female imagery helped prepare the way for America to undertake its own imperial role by century's end. Mass media played a major role in stirring up popular enthusiasm for U.S. intervention in 1898 in the war between Cuba and Spain. The political cartoon in Figure 7.12 fuses visual and verbal clichés in support of Congress's declaration of war against Spain allegedly on Cuba's behalf. How does the cartoon play on the saying "Out of the frying-pan, into the fire"? How does the terrified dark-skinned young woman, who represents the national spirit of Cuba, contrast with the icon of Columbia in Figure 7.11? How does the female figure emphasize what many opinion makers saw as America's moral obligation to intervene on Cuba's behalf?

QUESTIONS FOR ANALYSIS

1. How do the *Puck* stereotypes of immigrant women compare to Jacob Riis's photographs of immigrant girls and women in Figures 7.1–7.5?

2. How does the symbolic use of female figures in late nineteenth-century political cartoons (Figures 7.11 and 7.12) contrast with the depictions of women in cartoons meant to amuse (Figures 7.6–7.10)?

3. How does the assumption that men should protect women function throughout these cartoons? Consider the stereotypes of immigrant women, the ridicule of native-born women entering public life, and the use of female representations to justify American imperial ambitions.

NOTES

1. Shige Kushida is mentioned in Mei Nakano, *Japanese American Women: Three Generations, 1890– 1990* (Berkeley: Mina Press, 1990). Our version of her life differs on the basis of information provided by Rumi Yasutake, Kobe University, author of *Transnational Women's Activism: The United States, Japan, and Japanese Immigrant Communities in California, 1859–1920* (New York: NYU Press, 2004).

2. Laura Jane Moore, "Lozen," in Theda Perdue, ed., *Sifters: Native American Women's Lives* (New York: Oxford University Press, 2001), 93.

3. Nelson Miles to George Baird, November 20, 1891, Baird Collection, Western Americana Collection, Beinecke Library, Yale University.

4. The term is from Alvin M. Josephy, *500 Nations: An Illustrated History of North American Indians* (New York: Knopf, 1994), 430.

5. Carolyn J. Marr, "Assimilation through Education: Indian Boarding Schools in the Pacific Northwest," http://content.lib.washington.edu/aipnw/marr.html (accessed June 28, 2004).

6. "A Man Plants the Fields of His Wife," in Ruth Barnes Moynihan, Cynthia Russett, and Laurie Crumpacker, eds., *Second to None: A Documentary History of American Women* (Lincoln: University of Nebraska Press, 1993), 2:82–83.

7. Linda Williams Reese, *Women of Oklahoma, 1890–1920* (Norman: University of Oklahoma Press, 1997), 152–53.

8. Diary of Lucy Hannah White Flake, excerpted in Joan M. Jensen, ed., *With These Hands: Women Working on the Land* (Old Westbury, NY: Feminist Press, 1981), 137–38.

9. Glenda Riley, *A Place to Grow: Women in the American West* (Arlington Heights: Harlan Davidson, 1992), 239.

10. Reese, *Women of Oklahoma*, 38.

11. Michael Lewis Goldberg, *An Army of Women: Gender and Politics in Gilded Age Kansas* (Baltimore: Johns Hopkins University Press, 1997), 40.

12. The term comes from Paula Petrik, *No Step Backward: Women and Family on the Rocky Mountain Mining Frontier, Helena, Montana, 1865–1900* (Helena: Montana Historical Society Press, 1987), 28.

13. Mother Mary Jones, *Autobiography of Mother Jones* (1925; repr., Chicago: C. H. Kerr, 1990), 204.

14. Elizabeth Jameson, "Imperfect Unions: Class and Gender in Cripple Creek, 1894–1904," in Milton Cantor and Bruce Laurie, eds., *Class, Sex, and the Woman Worker* (Westport: Greenwood Press, 1977), 171.

15. Joan Morrison and Charlotte Fox Zabusky, *American Mosaic: The Immigrant Experience in the Worlds of Those Who Lived It* (New York: E. P. Dutton, 1980), 9.

16. Linda Mack Schloff, *"And Prairie Dogs Weren't Kosher": Jewish Women in the Upper Midwest Since 1855* (St. Paul: Minnesota Historical Society Press, 1996), 28.

17. Edith Abbott, *Immigration: Select Documents and Case Records* (Chicago: University of Chicago Press, 1924), 719.

18. Him Mark Lai, Genny Lim, and Judy Yung, *Island: Poetry and History of Chinese Immigrants on Angel Island, 1910–1940* (San Francisco: San Francisco Study Center, 1980), 74.

19. Jane Addams, *Twenty Years at Hull-House,* edited with an introduction by Victoria Bissell Brown (1910; repr., Boston: Bedford/St. Martin's, 1999), 72.

20. Aileen Kraditor, *Ideas of the Woman Suffrage Movement, 1890–1920* (New York: Columbia University Press, 1965), 128.

21. Theodore Roosevelt, introduction to Mrs. John Van Vorst and Marie Van Vorst, *The Woman Who Toils: Being the Experiences of Two Ladies as Factory Girls* (New York: Doubleday, Page & Co., 1903), vii.

22. Anzia Yezierska, *Bread Givers* (1925; repr., New York: George Brazillier, 1975), 135.

23. Addams, *Twenty Years at Hull-House*, 166.

24. Ellen Carol DuBois, *The Elizabeth Cady Stanton–Susan B. Anthony Reader: Correspondence, Writings, Speeches*, rev. ed. (Boston: Northeastern University Press, 1992), 205.

25. Jensen, *With These Hands*, 157–58.

26. Susan B. Anthony and Ida H. Harper, eds., *History of Woman Suffrage* (Rochester, NY: Susan B. Anthony, 1902), 4:519.

27. Jensen, *With These Hands*, 147.

28. Ida H. Harper, ed., *History of Woman Suffrage* (New York: National American Woman Suffrage Association, 1922), 5:518.

29. Anthony and Harper, *History of Woman Suffrage*, 4:647.

30. "Women Keep Up Courage," *San Francisco Chronicle*, November 5, 1896. Thanks to Ann Gordon for the citation.

31. Marion K. Barthelme, ed., *Women in the Texas Populist Movement: Letters to the Southern Mercury* (College Station: Texas A&M Press, 1997), 111.

32. Moynihan, Russett, and Crumpacker, *Second to None*, 2:81.

33. Emma Goldman, *Living My Life*, ed. Richard and Anna Maria Drinnon (New York: New American Library, 1977), 122.

34. Kathryn Kish Sklar, *Florence Kelley and the Nation's Work* (New Haven: Yale University Press, 1995), 272.

35. Addams, *Twenty Years at Hull-House*, 156.

36. Alice Miller, "Hull House," *The Charities* (February 1892): 167–73.

37. Sklar, *Florence Kelley*, 215.

38. Ibid., 283.

39. Frances Willard, *The Autobiography of an American Woman, Glimpses of Fifty Years* (Chicago: Woman's Temperance Publishing Association, 1892), 431.

40. Kristin Hoganson, *Fighting for American Manhood: How Gender Politics Provoked the Spanish-American and Philippine-American Wars* (New Haven: Yale University Press, 1998), 11.

41. Allen Davis, *An American Heroine: The Life and Legend of Jane Addams* (New York: Oxford University Press, 1973), 140.

42. Allison Sneider, "Reconstruction, Expansion and Empire: The U.S. Woman Suffrage Movement and the Re-making of the National Political Community" (PhD dissertation, University of California–Los Angeles, 1999), 172.

43. Laura Wexler, *Tender Violence: Domestic Visions in an Age of U.S. Imperialism* (Chapel Hill: University of North Carolina Press, 2000).

44. Jane Addams, *Twenty Years at Hull-House*, 95.

45. Jacob A. Riis, *How the Other Half Lives: Studies among the Tenements of New York*, ed. David Leviatin (1890; repr. Boston: Bedford/St. Martin's, 1996), 61.

46. Ibid., 92.

47. Ibid., 91.

48. Ibid., 95.

49. Ibid., 129.

50. Ibid., 141.

51. Ibid., 140.

52. Ibid., 139.

53. Jacob A. Riis, *The Children of the Poor* (New York: Scribner's Sons, 1892), 82.

54. Jacob A. Riis, *The Making of an American* (New York: Macmillan, 1929), 150.

55. Riis, *Children of the Poor*, 80.

SUGGESTED REFERENCES

Women and Western Settlement   For an overall perspective on the consolidation of the West through the eyes of diverse groups of women, see the two excellent anthologies compiled by Susan Armitage and Elizabeth Jameson: *The Woman's West* (1987) and *Writing the Range: Race, Class, and Culture in the Women's West* (1997). Among many useful other books on this subject, see Glenda Riley, *A Place to Grow: Women in the American West* (1992); Ruth B. Moynihan, Susan Armitage, and Christiane Fischer Dichamp, eds., *So Much to Be Done: Women Settlers on the Mining and Ranching Frontier* (1990); and Julie Roy Jeffrey, *Frontier Women: The Trans-Mississippi West, 1840–1880* (1979). Linda Williams Reese, *Women of Oklahoma, 1890–1920* (1997), focuses on a single, interesting state. For two excellent local studies of women in the Wild West, see Marion Goldman, *Gold Diggers and Silver Miners: Prostitution and Social Life on the Comstock Lode* (1968), and Elizabeth Jameson, *All That Glitters: Class Conflict and Community in Cripple Creek* (1998). Two recent collections focus on Native American women in the West and cover a wide range of experiences: Theda Perdue, ed., *Sifters: Native American Women's Lives* (2001), and Nancy Shoemaker, ed., *Negotiators of Change: Historical Perspectives on Native*

American Women (1995). On the La Flesche sisters, see Norma Kidd, *Iron Eye's Family: The Children of Joseph La Flesche* (1969), and Benson Tong, *Susan La Flesche Picotte, MD: Omaha Indian Leader and Reformer* (1994). Helen Hunt Jackson's 1881 exposé, *A Century of Dishonor,* is still compelling. Valerie Mathes, *Helen Hunt Jackson and Her Indian Reform Legacy* (1997), also covers the formation of the Woman's National Indian Association.

On Mexican American women in the Southwest before the major waves of immigration in the twentieth century, see Sarah Deutsch, *No Separate Refuge: Culture, Class, and Gender on the Anglo-Hispanic Frontier in the American Southwest, 1880–1940* (1987), and Lisbeth Haas, *Conquests and Historical Identities in California, 1769–1836* (1995). Also, Linda Gordon's *The Great Arizona Orphan Abduction* (1999) examines ethnic and religious conflicts between Anglo and Hispanic women in southern Arizona.

Immigrant Women   The best general study on women and immigration is Donna Gabaccia, *The Other Side: Women, Gender, and Immigrant Life in the U.S., 1820–1990* (1994). Other general studies, concentrating mostly on European immigrants, include Katrina Irving, *Immigrant Mothers: Narratives of Race and Maternity, 1890–1925* (2000); Kristine Leach, *In Search of a Common Ground: Nineteenth and Twentieth Century Immigrant Women in America* (1995); and Doris Weatherford, *Foreign and Female: Immigrant Women in America, 1840–1930* (1986). For studies of women from particular groups, see the comparison of Italians and Eastern European Jews in Elizabeth Ewen, *Immigrant Women in the Land of Dollars: Life and Culture on the Lower East Side, 1890–1925* (1985), and Judith E. Smith, *Family Connections: A History of Italian and Jewish Immigrant Lives in Providence, Rhode Island, 1900–1940* (1985). Other studies of Jews include Susan Glenn, *Daughters of the Shtetl: Life and Labor in the Immigrant Generation* (1990), and Barbara Schreier, *Becoming American Women: Clothing and the American Jewish Experience* (1994). Linda Mack Schloff offers an unusual perspective in *"And Prairie Dogs Weren't Kosher": Jewish Women in the Upper Midwest since 1855* (1996). On Italian immigrant women, see Miriam Cohen, *Workshop to Office: Two Generations of Italian Women in New York City, 1900–1950* (1992), and Virginia Yans McLaughlin, *Family and Community: Italian Immigrants in Buffalo, 1880–1930* (1977). Hasia Diner considers Irish immigrant women in *Erin's Daughters in America: Irish Immigrant Women in the Nineteenth Century* (1983). Suzanne Sinke has researched an understudied group in *Dutch Immigrant Women in the United States* (2002).

For non-European immigrants, see *Chinese Women of America: A Pictorial History* (1986), *Unbound Feet: A Social History of Chinese Women in San Francisco* (1995), and *Unbound Voices: A Documentary History of Chinese Women in San Francisco* (1999), all by Judith Yung. See also Lucy Salyer, *Laws Harsh as Tigers: Chinese Immigrants and the Shaping of Modern Immigration Law* (1995). For Japanese women immigrants, see Mei Nakano, *Japanese American Women: Three Generations 1890–1990* (1990), and Evelyn Nakano Glenn, *Isssei, Nisei, War Bride: Three Generations of Japanese American Women in Domestic Service* (1986). On Mexican immigrant women, see Vicki Ruiz, *From Out of the Shadows: Mexican Women in Twentieth-Century America* (1998).

Women Reformers   On the history of women and the Populist revolt, see Rebecca Edwards, *Angels in the Machinery: Gender in American Party Politics from the Civil War to the Progressive Era* (1997), and Michael Lewis Goldberg, *An Army of Women: Gender and Politics in Gilded Age Kansas* (1997). For the western suffrage movement that Populism reinvigorated, see Rebecca Mead, *How the Vote Was Won: Woman Suffrage in the Western United States, 1868–1914* (2004). For southern Populism, see Marion K. Barthelme, ed., *Women in the Texas Populist Movement: Letters to the Southern Mercury* (1997), and Julie Roy Jeffrey, "Women in the Southern Farmers' Alliance: A Reconstruction of the Role and Status of Women in the Late Nineteenth-Century South," *Feminist Studies* 3:1/2 (1975): 72–91.

On the Pullman strike from a women's perspective, see Janice Reiff, "A Modern Lear and His Daughters: Gender in the Model Town of Pullman," *Journal of Social History* 23 (1997): 316–41. For the leadership of Hull House women in this period, see Victoria Bissell Brown, *The Education of Jane Addams* (2004), and Kathryn Kish Sklar, *Florence Kelley and the Nation's Work* (1995). The best general studies of settlement houses are Allen F. Davis, *Spearheads for Reform: The Social Settlements and the Progressive Movement, 1890–1914* (1967) and Mina Carson, *Settlement Folk: Social Thought and the American Settlement Movement, 1885–1930* (1990). Kathryn Sklar, "Hull House in the 1890s: A Community of Women Reformers," *Signs* 10 (1985): 658–77, considers the personal dimension of Hull House for its women residents. Joan Waugh, *Unsentimental Reformer: The Life of Josephine Shaw Lowell* (1994), examines a leading woman reformer in New York in the 1893 depression. Elizabeth Lasch-Quinn considers racism and racial segregation in the settlement house movement in *Black Neighbors: Race and the Limits of Reform in the American Settlement House Movement, 1890–1945* (1993).

On the female missionary contribution, see Patricia Hill, *The World Their Household: The American Woman's Foreign Mission Movement and Cultural Transformation, 1870–1920* (1985); Patricia Grimshaw, *Paths of Duty: American Missionary Wives in Nineteenth-Century Hawaii* (1987); and Ian Tyrrell, *Woman's World/Woman's Empire: The Woman's Christian Temperance Union in International Perspective, 1880–1930* (1991). On gender and late nineteenth-century imperialism, see Kristin Hoganson, *Fighting for American Manhood: How Gender Politics Provoked the Spanish American and Philippine-American Wars* (1998); Gail Bederman, *Manliness and Civilization: A Cultural History of Gender and Race in the United States, 1880–1917* (1995); Alison Sneider, *Suffragists in an Imperial Age: U.S. Expansion and the Woman Question, 1870–1929* (2008); and Laura Wexler, *Tender Violence: Domestic Visions in an Age of U.S. Imperialism* (2000).

For selected Web sites, please visit the *Through Women's Eyes* book companion site at bedfordstmartins.com/duboisdumenil.

8

Power and Politics

WOMEN IN THE PROGRESSIVE ERA, 1900–1920

THE DAY AFTER NEW YEAR'S DAY 1907, SEVERAL DOZEN women met in New York City determined to find a new way to get the drive for woman suffrage onto a winning path. Their leader, Harriot Stanton Blatch, was the daughter of the nineteenth-century leader of the demand for political equality, Elizabeth Cady Stanton. She was also a veteran of numerous reform campaigns organized by civic-minded and politically savvy women, with goals ranging from cleaning up municipal political corruption to improving the wages and working conditions of female workers. Woman suffrage had historically been a middle-class movement, but at this meeting wage-earning women, most of them trade union activists, were joining with leisure-class college graduates, professionals, and social reformers. Still, no woman of color was invited to attend.

A modernized cross-class movement for votes for women was one aspect of Progressivism, a period of intense reform activism from the late 1890s to the years just after the conclusion of the First World War in 1918. The Progressive era profoundly altered the role of government in American life. During these years, American liberalism, which had traditionally regarded government as a threat to citizens' rights, now came to embrace government as the ultimate guarantor of public welfare. Catalyzed by the devastating social consequences of industrial capitalism, the activists of this period battled for new labor laws and social welfare policies, arguing that the fate of society's most impoverished sector was linked to the general national welfare. Many socially conscious Americans, jolted by the crises of the 1890s, were ready to join in this new spirit of public stewardship.

Women played a leading role during the Progressive period. As one historian writes, "[W]omen filled the progressive landscape."[1] There is considerable irony in the public influence and power women wielded in these years, because most women would not become fully enfranchised until 1920, in the aftermath of World War I. But they were widely mobilized, organized, and ambitious. Indeed, the victory of votes for women was as much a result as a cause of women's political mobilization in the Progressive era. Earlier Gilded Age developments such as the steady increase of the female labor force, the growth of college education among women, and the spread of women's organizations laid the basis for women's dramatic rush into the public arena in the Progressive era.

Around the edges of the broad-based mass mobilization of Progressive-era suffragism was a smaller, more daring, and more modern approach to women's emancipation for which a new name was invented — feminism. While the achievement of the larger movement was to complete the campaign for equal political rights begun before the Civil War, early twentieth-century feminism foreshadowed the women's liberation movement of the 1960s.

THE FEMALE LABOR FORCE

A good way to start examining the dramatic changes in women's public lives in the Progressive era is to present a portrait of women workers. While the more obvious developments for women in this period were political, the underlying changes were economic, as the female labor force changed significantly.

The presence of large numbers of women in the workforce signaled the beginning of true modernity in female roles. Long a symbol of women's victimhood, the working woman came to stand for women's active presence in the larger world. The visibility and forcefulness of women

1913	**Alice Paul and Lucy Burns form the Congressional Union**
1913	**Ida B. Wells-Barnett organizes first all-black suffrage club, in Chicago**
1914	**"What Is Feminism?" mass meeting in New York City**
1914	World War I begins in Europe
1914–1919	Height of African American "Great Migration"
1915	**Woman's Peace Party formed**
1915	**Campaigns for woman suffrage fail in Massachusetts, New York, New Jersey, and Pennsylvania**
1915	**Jane Addams chairs International Council of Women peace meeting in The Hague**
1915	**Women's International League for Peace and Freedom founded**
1916	**Congressional Union becomes National Woman's Party (NWP)**
1916	**Margaret Sanger opens birth control clinic in Brooklyn**
1917	**Second New York referendum enfranchises women**
1917	**United States enters World War I; Montana Congresswoman Jeannette Rankin votes against declaration of war**
1917	Bolshevik Revolution ends Russian participation in war
1917	**Women's Council for National Defense established**
1917	**NWP members begin to picket the White House**
1917–1919	Urban race riots from St. Louis to Chicago
1918	Supreme Court overturns Keating-Owen Act limiting child labor
1918	Armistice ends World War I
1919	Eighteenth Amendment (Prohibition) ratified
1920	**Federal Woman's Bureau established**
1920	**Nineteenth Amendment (woman suffrage) ratified**

workers were particularly manifest through a series of spectacular strikes in the garment and textile industries, the first such sustained working women's movement since the antebellum years. Middle- and upper-class reformers made the concerns of working women central to their activities.

Continuity and Change for Women Wage Earners

In 1900, 18.3 percent of the labor force was female, but this figure was rising and would reach 21.4 percent in 1920.[2] More than half of the female working population was foreign-born and/or nonwhite. The wage rate for women workers was very low: in 1900, the average woman worker made about half of what the average male worker earned.[3] This disparity reflected the fact that men and women largely worked in different occupations and distinct industries, a highly structured sexual division of labor that limited working women's options even as it shaped the American labor force. Domestic service was still the largest category of female employment, but manufacturing was steadily gaining. The average working woman was young and unmarried. Mothers and wives who worked outside the home for wages were few; only among African Americans did they constitute a significant portion of women workers.

Against this general portrait, new areas of women's paid work were beginning to emerge in the early twentieth century. Clerical work, once entirely male and a form of apprenticeship in the business world, was a rapidly growing and desirable field for women. The work was clean and safe, and the wages regular. The demand for clerical workers to coordinate the movement of resources, finished goods, and finances through an increasingly complex national economy was expanding. Yet just as clerical work was being feminized, it was becoming mechanized and routinized, and thus losing its capacity to offer upward mobility. In the offices of mail order houses, banks, insurance companies, and large corporations, the labor of secretaries and typists was beginning to look like factory labor, at times even including the use of piece-rate payment.

Women were also gaining greater entry into some professional fields. The gradual opening up of professional opportunities for women constituted a partial solution to the vocational dilemma that Jane Addams's generation of college graduates had confronted. Overall, the professional sector comprised just 12 percent of the female labor force in 1920, but it played a major role in changing society's view of paid labor for women.[4] Women professional workers expected personal independence and upward mobility from their jobs, and they worked more out of choice than out of need. As such, they paved the way for a new, more positive attitude toward paid labor for women.

The one male-dominated professional field in which women had made any gains by the end of the nineteenth century was medicine; women were between five and six percent of the profession by 1900. The legal profession was far more hostile to women (compare Figures 6.6, p. 377, and 7.9, p. 444). In 1900, fewer than six hundred women were practicing law in the United States. But as women moved energetically into other aspects of public life, the number of women lawyers began to climb; by 1920, this number had tripled. Inez Milholland, one of the most glamorous figures in the American suffrage movement, applied to Harvard Law School after she graduated from Vassar in 1909 but was rejected. (Harvard Law did not admit its first woman until 1953.) Instead, she attended New York University Law School, where she specialized in labor, criminal, and divorce law.

In 1919, a group of New York City women lawyers were polled on their opinions about "the paradox of vocation and marriage" for women. The majority responded that women could continue professional life after marriage but should make family life a priority and put aside their profession while their children were small. A small minority believed that, with supportive husbands and enough paid household servants, it was possible to rear children and practice their professions simultaneously. Such a solution was available only to middle-class women who could hire maids and nannies. Even so, these professional women were beginning to grapple with the problem that would affect all working women later in the twentieth century.

More women found professional opportunities in the rise of new "female professions" where they did not have to break through a male monopoly. In these years, the profession of social work began to evolve out of the volunteer labor of women reformers in settlement houses. Practitioners were eager to upgrade traditional forms of benevolence by applying new social science methods. Sophonisba Breckinridge, a lawyer and the first American woman to receive a PhD in political science, convinced the University of Chicago to establish the Graduate School of Social Service Administration. By 1920, there were thirty thousand trained social workers, the majority of them women.

Nursing and teaching were the largest professions dominated by women. Since the Civil War, nursing had been shifting from a form of domestic service to a profession. Between 1900 and 1910, there was a tenfold increase in the number of professionally trained nurses. Many professional nurses worked as public health missionaries, going into immigrant homes to teach sanitation methods and to investigate epidemic disease. Teaching, a woman's occupation at the primary level since the 1830s, was also undergoing changes. In the Progressive era, teachers sought to upgrade their profession, ridding it both of intrusive moral constraints and political interference in hiring. Teacher training was moving from the two-year high-school-level institutions of the late nineteenth century to four-year truly collegiate institutions (see Figure 6.5, p. 375). In Chicago, Mary Haley, a second-generation Irish American, organized a powerful teachers' union, which removed control of appointments from local politicians.

African American women were also part of this move to professionalization, although the growing practice of segregation meant that African Americans were excluded from the white-run training programs and occupational associations that structured professions. In the field of nursing, black women responded by establishing their own schools and professional association, the National Association of Colored Graduate Nurses, formed in 1908. Ironically, Jim Crow provided opportunities for African American professional women in the separate institutions that served black communities, where they worked as librarians, physicians, and especially as teachers. Largely excluded from the National Educational Association, black women teachers formed their own teachers' organizations, through which they challenged racial discrimination in teachers' salaries.

Organizing Women Workers: The Women's Trade Union League

Despite the expansion of working opportunities for women in the clerical and professional strata, industrial workers, especially young immigrants, were considered the most representative working women of the Progressive era. Constituting 25 percent of the female labor force, they were a crucial factor in the tremendously productive power of the American economy and achieved an unprecedented level of public visibility. Many of the themes of the era—women's public prominence, their leadership of liberal causes, and their pursuit of independent lives—marked the women's labor movement of the Progressive period.

Working women received little assistance from the established trade union movement. The male-dominated American Federation of Labor (AFL), which provided the leadership of the trade union movement, regarded women wage earners not as potential union recruits but either as underpaid threats to their members' jobs or as pitiful victims of capitalist greed. If women were to improve their wages and working conditions through labor organization, they were going to have to find assistance from allies of gender, not of class.

The Women's Trade Union League (WTUL) formed in 1903 to meet this need. Modeled after a British organization of the same name, the WTUL hoped to reconcile women workers and the organized labor movement. It did so with the tacit permission of the AFL, the leaders of which were only too relieved to subcontract out the burden of organizing women workers. Membership was open to all committed to the labor organization of women, regardless of class or of union membership. The WTUL also aimed "to develop leadership among the women workers, inspiring them with a sense of personal responsibility for the conditions under which they work."[5]

The WTUL was a coalition of women trade union activists and leisure-class women (known as "allies"), primarily drawn from the settlement house movement. Mary Kenney O'Sullivan, who had begun her career in Chicago as a skilled bookbinder and had served as the AFL's first official female organizer, was one of its working-class founders (see p. 343). Another was Leonora O'Reilly, a garment worker from New York City with connections to the Henry Street Settlement. O'Reilly recruited two wealthy sisters also from New York City, Mary Dreier and Margaret Dreier Robins, who provided most of the financial resources for the WTUL throughout the 1910s. Major chapters emerged in Boston, New York City, and Chicago; smaller groups formed in Milwaukee, St. Louis, Kansas City, Philadelphia, and San Francisco.

The WTUL's interclass collaboration struck a different note from the antagonistic class relations between leisured and wage-earning women in the Gilded Age. Nonetheless, Leonora O'Reilly was concerned that the WTUL would become a "charity" organization in which middle-class women approached workers with

◆ **Margaret Dreier Robins and the Women's Trade Union League**
The Women's Trade Union League was established at a convention of the American Federation of Labor in 1903, bringing together leisure-class women and working-class women. The WTUL accepted the primacy of women's maternal obligations but recognized the reality of women's labor involvement. The organization worked for two main goals—a maximum eight-hour workday for women and a wage sufficient to allow a woman to support herself. Margaret Dreier Robins, pictured here talking to a group of Chicago's working women, was a wealthy progressive who served as the WTUL president from 1907 to 1922. *Chicago History Museum.*

"the attitudes of a lady with something to give her sister."[6] Despite the organization's commitment to developing working-class women's leadership abilities, formal control remained in the hands of leisure-class women until 1922, when Maud Swartz, a typesetter, took over as national president. Still, the WTUL was unique for its cross-class commitment to workers' empowerment.

While the WTUL worked hard on behalf of white and immigrant working-class women, its record was weak when it came to black women workers. Black workers, even more than white working women, faced hostility from the white men who led the American labor movement. They were not admitted into trade unions in this period, were hired at lower wages than white workers, and were employed as strike-breakers. The WTUL's association with the organized labor movement led it to go along with the AFL's racist antagonism to black workers throughout its early years.

After World War I the organization shifted its emphasis from trade union organization to the passage of state maximum workday hours and minimum wage laws for working women. The first director of the Women's Bureau of the Department of Labor, established in 1920, was Chicago WTUL member and shoe worker Mary Anderson. Later, Rose Schneiderman, a garment worker who labored for the league throughout her career, helped to shape New Deal policy toward working women and working families (see pp. 539–45).

The Rising of the Women

A wave of early twentieth-century strikes put the modern wage-earning woman on the labor history map. The most famous of these took place over the winter of 1909–10 in New York City in the shirtwaist (blouse) industry. The strike began when Local 25 of the International Ladies Garment Workers Union (ILGWU), a small male-dominated organization, struck several manufacturers over low wages and bad working conditions. Day after day, the picketers, most of them young Jewish and Italian women, were harassed by thugs their bosses had hired, arrested by police, and fined and jailed by local magistrates. Then they turned to the WTUL. When leisure-class women joined the picket line, they were subjected to the same disrespectful treatment as the striking workers, which made the newspapers take notice. (See Visual Sources: Parades, Picketing, and Power: Women in Public Space, pp. 490–97.)

The large clothing manufacturers were able to hold out against the workers by sending their unfinished garments to shops that the ILGWU was not targeting. Facing sure defeat, the union considered calling a general strike of the entire New York City shirtwaist industry. This was a daring strategy, especially in an industry in which the great majority of the workers were teenage immigrant girls who were not considered disciplined enough to sustain a long strike. Nonetheless, on November 22, 1909, more than fifteen thousand shirtwaist workers showed up at a mass meeting to discuss how to proceed against the manufacturers. As male labor leaders and leisure-class WTUL members on the stage hesitated to speak, seventeen-year-old shirtwaist maker Clara Lemlich spoke from the floor and galvanized the audience to walk off their jobs.

The next day, between twenty and thirty thousand workers, two-thirds of them Eastern European Jews, were on strike. The WTUL provided the strike pay, publicity, and legal support to keep the strike going. Some of the wealthiest women in New York City, including Ann Morgan, daughter of banking magnate J. P. Morgan, publicly endorsed the cause of the workers. The presence and commitment of young women on the picket line challenged the traditional image of women wage earners as passive victims. Even AFL president Samuel Gompers conceded that the strike demonstrated "the extent to which women were taking up with industrial life, their consequent tendency to stand together in the struggle to protect their common interests as wage earners, . . . and the capacity of women as strikers to suffer, to do, and to dare in support of their rights."[7]

After almost three months, the shirtwaist strike was settled. Many, but not all, of the manufacturers agreed to a fifty-two-hour workweek, no more fines for workers' mistakes, more worker involvement in setting wages, and even paid holidays. But they would not allow the ILGWU to represent the workers in future negotiations. Even so, the strike turned the ILGWU into a much more powerful labor organization. Individual working-class women, including Clara Lemlich and Rose Schneiderman, embarked on a lifetime of labor activism.

A tragic epilogue to the shirtwaist strike took place a little over a year later, highlighting why union recognition was so important to the workers. The Triangle Shirtwaist Company had begun locking the doors of its Manhattan factory after the workers arrived, to keep union organizers out and workers in. On March 25, 1911, a fire broke out on the tenth floor. Workers found that they were locked inside the building. Desperately they ran up to the roof. Some were able to escape, but 146 workers, more than a quarter of Triangle's employees, died. At a mass funeral held a few days later, Schneiderman delivered a bitter eulogy: "This is not the first time girls have been burned alive in this city. . . . Every year thousands of us are maimed. The life of men and women is so cheap and property is so sacred. There are so many of us for one job it matters little if [we] are burned to death."[8]

In 1912, labor militancy broke out again in the textile factories of Lawrence, Massachusetts. As in the garment industry, textile workers were overwhelmingly

◆ **Triangle Shirtwaist Fire**
The actual number of dead was 146. This gruesome newspaper photograph shows the broken bodies of young women who jumped to escape the fire because the doors were locked from the outside and the fire escapes pulled away from the building. A policeman leans over to identify and tag the victims. To the right is the building that housed the Triangle Shirtwaist Company, site of both the 1909–1910 strike and the 1911 fire. As Rose Schneiderman predicted, it survived long after the workers died. Currently, it is owned by New York University. No one was ever convicted of liability for the tragedy. New York Herald, *March 26, 1911.*

immigrant, but the textile industry employed entire families, including children. Textile workers labored long hours for very low wages. Much of the industry was located in company towns, where employers exerted total control and workers could find no local allies. When a Massachusetts law established a maximum of fifty-four working hours per week, Lawrence manufacturers cut the wages of their workers proportionately, and the workers struck.

Because the AFL was not interested in their plight, the workers turned to the Industrial Workers of the World (IWW), a radical socialist labor organization. One of the organization's most famous leaders was twenty-two-year-old Elizabeth Gurley Flynn, a single mother and an accomplished organizer and public speaker. In Lawrence, Flynn encouraged greater involvement among Italian women, whose enthusiasm for the struggle gave the lie to their reputation as cloistered and conservative peasants. Although members of the WTUL were eager to help in the Lawrence strike, the AFL's determination to stay clear of its rival, the IWW, made that impossible. Several founding members, including Mary Kenney O'Sullivan, quit in disgust.

The turning point in the strike involved the children of the town's workers. As police and militia attacks increased, Flynn decided it was time to relocate the younger children to the homes of out-of-town sympathizers. Children on their way to Philadelphia were beaten by Lawrence police, and their mothers were imprisoned for "neglect" by local courts. Nationwide outrage was so great that the employers were forced to agree to the strikers' demands for a fifty-four-hour week and wage increases as high as 25 percent (see Figure 8.1, p. 491). Ironically, the very magnitude of the Lawrence workers' victory contributed to the shift of much of the textile industry from New England to the South, in search of a more docile workforce.

The exceptional dedication and militancy of the women of the New York and Lawrence strikes—and other labor conflicts in Paterson, New Jersey; Chicago; and Atlanta—helped to transform the popular image of working women. No longer dependent on others to defend and protect them, they were now appreciated for the ability to fight their own battles. By the beginning of World War I, the number of women in trade unions had quadrupled. Even so, women remained a minority of the labor movement and had many obstacles—lack of male interest, middle-class condescension, and their own timidity—to overcome.

THE FEMALE DOMINION

The WTUL was connected to what one historian has named the "female dominion," the women's wing of reform movements in the Progressive era. Middle- and upper-class white women created a network of reform organizations, became active in partisan politics, and lobbied for legislation to benefit poor women and children. Largely excluded from those groups, African American women created their own institutions that promoted social welfare and self-help in their communities. Although black women faced obstacles unknown to white reformers, both groups demonstrated a strong commitment to women's involvement in the dramatic political changes of the early twentieth century.

Public Housekeeping

Female social reformers frequently drew on the image of "public housekeeping" to describe women's activism in the Progressive era. "The very multifariousness and complexity of a city government demand the help of minds accustomed to . . . a sense of responsibility for the cleanliness and comfort of other people," explained Jane Addams in 1906 of the reform work that women were doing in Chicago.[9] What once could be accomplished from within the home, it was argued, now required that women become leaders in the public realm.

Women's public housekeeping took many forms. Despite their disfranchisement, women worked to drive out corrupt machine politics and install reform mayors in various cities. They worked to improve slum housing and to establish public amenities in Boston and New York. The Civic Club of Charleston, South Carolina, established playgrounds and then convinced the city council to take them over. Many public libraries were founded by local women's clubs. Women were involved in the campaign to set health standards for food, especially for the notoriously impure milk supply, a particular threat to infants whose mothers did not breast-feed. Women played a major role in the establishment of special juvenile and family courts. Activist and budding historian Mary Beard chronicled the breadth and depth of this involvement in urban politics in her 1915 book, *Woman's Work in Municipalities* (see box, "Municipal Housekeeping").

These public housekeepers worked through existing national organizations such as the Woman's Christian Temperance Union and the General Federation of Women's Clubs and its state affiliates. But they also formed new, more focused groups. Of these, the most important was the National Consumers' League (NCL), formed in 1899 in New York City by Florence Kelley, and later expanded to chapters around the country. The NCL concentrated on working conditions for women and children.

Historians have developed the term "maternalism" to characterize the ideological core of women's reform concerns in the Progressive era.[10] Maternalist thinking had two parts. First, every sort of program advanced on women's behalf, even those having to do with women's wage labor, was justified on the grounds that society needed to protect maternal capacity. Second, the women who designed and advocated for these policies conceived of their own public involvement through the lens of motherhood. The dual meaning of "maternalism" obscured the different ways that standards of motherhood were applied to what were essentially two different classes of women, leisure-class policy makers and their working-class clients. The former legitimated themselves by expressing active maternal concern, wielded from within the public arena, while they viewed the beneficiaries of their policies as dependent and homebound mothers in need of protection. Thus, maternal power and maternal need were separated between two different classes rather than understood as linked and interdependent.

MARY BEARD
Municipal Housekeeping

Mary Ritter Beard (1876–1958) was deeply involved in many aspects of the women's movement in the Progressive era, from the Women's Trade Union League to the New York suffrage movement to the militant National Woman's Party. In 1915, she wrote her first book on the "municipal house-keeping" of civic-minded women, from which this passage is drawn. She went on to write and edit many books on the history of women—including America Through Women's Eyes *(1933), from which the title of this book is drawn—and to coauthor, with her husband, Charles Beard, pathbreaking works in American history. As she does here, she always emphasized women's active role in making history. How does Beard explain women's affinity for reforms she identifies as "municipal housekeeping"?*

In this expansion of municipal functions there can be little dispute as to the influence of women. Their hearts touched in the beginning by human misery and their sentiments aroused, they have been led into manifold activities in attempts at amelioration, which have taught them the breeding places of disease, as well as of vice, crime, poverty and misery. Having learned that effectively to "swat the fly" they must swat at its nest, women have also learned that to swat disease they must swat poor housing, evil labor conditions, ignorance, and vicious interests. . . .

Middle-class and upper-class women, having more leisure than middle- and upper-class men, have had greater opportunity for social observation and the cultivation of social sympathies, for the latter accompanies the former instead of preceding it, as all active emotions are the reflexes of experience. It is these women therefore who have seen, felt, experimented, learned, agitated, constructed, advised, and pressed upon the municipal authorities the need of public prevention of the ills from which the people suffer. In their municipal demands they have often had the support of women of the working class and of working men, among others, whose own preservation is bound up with legislation and administration to an ever-increasing degree. . . .

Whatever may be the outcome of the present tendencies in social service, it is certain that women are actively engaged in every branch of it: in organized charity, in all the specialized branches of kindred work, such as care for the several types of dependents and delinquents, in organizing women workers in the industries, in making social surveys and special investigation, and in creating the literature of social service.

SOURCE: Mary Beard, *Woman's Work in Municipalities* (New York: National Municipal League, 1915), 221–22.

Published by Votes-for-Women Publishing Co., Wilson Bldg., 127 Montgomery St., San Francisco 217

◆ **The Dirty Pool of Politics**
The image of civic-minded women sweeping out the dirt from the house of public life captures both the conventional and innovative nature of women's public activities in this period. The image was widely distributed by suffragists, suggesting that the link between politics and civic housewifery was an effective rhetorical tool with men and women alike. *Courtesy of the Bancroft Library, University of California, Berkeley, Selina Solomons Papers, BANC MSS C-B 773:7.*

Maternalist Triumphs: Protective Labor Legislation and Mothers' Pensions

Maternalist presumptions underlay policies designed on behalf of working women and mothers alike. One of reformers' first goals was to establish a legal maximum workday for working women. However, in 1905, in the case *Lochner v. New York*, the U.S. Supreme Court ruled that *any* attempt to regulate wage labor relations for men or women was an unconstitutional infringement on individual freedom of contract. At this point, the NCL reasoned that the courts might allow special labor laws only for women workers on the grounds that their future maternal capacity needed to be protected.

An opportunity to test this theory came in 1908 when an Oregon maximum-hours law only for women workers was challenged before the U.S. Supreme Court. Josephine Goldmark, NCL secretary, arranged for Louis Brandeis, her brother-in-law and later a member of the Supreme Court, to argue the case. The so-called Brandeis Brief proceeded on two grounds: (1) that "women are fundamentally weaker than men" in defending themselves against the assaults of wage labor and thus must rely on the state to safeguard them and (2) that protection of women's maternal capacity was necessary for the general welfare. In its 1908 decision, *Muller v. Oregon*, the Supreme Court accepted the argument that while men's working hours could not be regulated by law, women's could (see Appendix, pp. A-27–A-28). Within a decade, all but nine states had passed maximum hours laws for working women.

These so-called protective labor laws were widely applauded by women activists and working women alike. But there were some limits to this victory. Women in domestic and agricultural labor were for the most part excluded, which meant that the great majority of African American women were not covered. More generally, in exchange for a desired improvement in their working conditions, working women had been formally labeled weaker than men, without the same claim on individual rights. From this perspective, the underlying principle of one of the era's great achievements for women, protective labor laws, conflicted with those of another great success, equal political rights.

Other protective labor legislation for working women was passed on the basis of maternal capacity. After 1908, many states passed laws prohibiting women from working at night. Female printers and other skilled women workers whose jobs required night work protested. Laws that set minimum wages for women workers, so that any decrease in women's working hours would not result in lower earnings, were also passed, provoking controversy from employers who objected to the higher labor costs that minimum wage laws would incur. In a 1923 case entitled *Adkins v. Children's Hospital*, the U.S. Supreme Court reversed the logic of its earlier *Muller* decision and invalidated minimum wage laws for women, saying that women "are legally as capable of contracting for themselves as men."[11] The Court based this turnaround of perspective on the recently ratified Nineteenth Amendment to the Constitution giving women equal voting rights (see the Appendix, pp. A-28–A-29).

Most working women were still young, unmarried, and childless. The major forms of legislation directed at mothers themselves were maternal pension programs, to shield mothers who were unsupported by male breadwinners from having to go out into the workplace to earn money, allowing them to stay at home with their children. Thus, the two different reforms—legislation focused on working women's hours and pensions for nonworking mothers—were closely linked by the maternalist ethic that it was the government's responsibility to protect motherhood from the incursions of the wage labor system and to conserve women's best energies for bearing and raising children.

The first mothers' pension program was established in 1911 in Illinois. A limited number of single mothers, whose neediness was determined by the Juvenile Court, received monthly grants of $50. Almost from the beginning, the program generated tremendous concern over welfare fraud and battles over funding levels. Moreover, never-married mothers were considered morally unfit, as were those who did not meet "suitable home" standards. Not surprisingly, African American mothers barely appeared on the mothers' pension rolls, kept off by institutional prejudice and their own ignorance that these programs existed. By 1920, thirty-eight other states had established mothers' pension programs with similar structures.

Maternalist Defeat: The Struggle to Ban Child Labor

Ironically, the least successful of the maternalist programs was the one that seems the most basic and obvious: ending child labor. In 1900, an estimated 2 million underage children were reported to be working for wages. Given the youth of the female labor force, the line between women and child workers was not sharply drawn. Was a fourteen-year-old wage earner a child or a woman? (See Figure 7.5, p. 440.)

While state legislatures passed maximum-hours laws and mothers' pensions programs, the campaign to outlaw child labor was one of the first social welfare efforts to focus on the federal government. In 1912 Congress established a Children's Bureau in the Department of Labor, which became headquarters for the campaign to stop child labor. With little federal funding for its work, the Children's Bureau used women's clubs, especially those associated with the General Federation of Women's Clubs, to conduct surveys and to lobby for state and federal legislation for children. One measure of their success came in 1916 when Congress passed the Keating-Owen Act, which prohibited paid labor for children under sixteen.

What seemed like an amazingly quick victory in a key Progressive reform soon turned into defeat. Crucial industries such as textile manufacturing and mining relied on child workers and opposed the law. In addition, immigrant families depended heavily on the labor of their children and stubbornly resisted the perspective of middle-class social workers to eliminate it. (See Documents: Jane Addams and the Charitable Relation, pp. 427–33.) In 1918 the Supreme Court overturned the federal law as an unconstitutional violation of states' rights. Congress passed a constitutional amendment banning child labor in 1924, but its ratification failed, the victim of an energetic "anti"-campaign that labeled it as too "socialistic." It was not until 1938, with the anti-child-labor provision of the Fair Labor Standards Act, which the Supreme Court allowed to stand, that the practice of child labor in this country was outlawed.

Progressive Women and Political Parties

Despite the rhetoric of maternalism, many female reform activists were drawn to the traditionally male political arena. Even without the franchise, they involved themselves in the 1912 election in anticipation that their voting rights were just over the horizon.

Even though women tended to position themselves as nonpartisan, putting issues and candidates above party loyalty, they could be found in the ranks of all the major parties. Many politically active women reformers, such as the Dreier sisters of the WTUL, could be found in the reform wing of the Republican Party. In 1912 the reformers' candidate, former president Theodore Roosevelt, lost the Republican Party nomination to incumbent William Howard Taft. As a result, the reform forces bolted the party to create the independent Progressive Party. The Progressives supported woman suffrage and integrated women fully into all their activities. At the Progressive Party's national convention, the de facto leader of the women reformers, Jane Addams, was chosen to second Roosevelt's nomination as the party's presidential candidate. Most African American women, however, remained devoted to the regular Republicans, the party of Lincoln.

The 1912 presidential race also featured a strong Socialist candidate, Eugene V. Debs. While both the Progressive and Socialist Parties advocated woman suffrage and minimum wage laws for women, the Socialists' ultimate goal was working-class empowerment, whereas the Progressives sought interclass harmony. Socialist women came in different varieties. Kate Richards O'Hare, who had begun her reform career in Kansas as a temperance advocate, was a nationally prominent Socialist writer, journalist, and traveling lecturer. Rose Pastor Stokes, a Russian immigrant factory worker who made headlines when she married a wealthy New York reformer, was also prominent in the party.

In the 1912 election, Roosevelt received more popular votes than the regular Republican nominee, President William Howard Taft, but the winner of the election, profiting from the split in the Republican ranks, was the Democratic candidate, Woodrow Wilson. Wilson had a reputation as a reformer from his years as governor of New Jersey. Democrats did not have a record of cultivating female support, although this was beginning to change as full enfranchisement drew nearer. In New York State, for instance, a new generation of modern Democrats such as Robert Wagner, Al Smith, and Franklin Roosevelt (Theodore's distant cousin) were beginning to connect with women labor reformers. Debs won only 6 percent of the presidential vote, but Socialists were elected to local and state offices and even to Congress, marking the high point of electoral socialism in American history.

Outside the Dominion: Progressivism and Race

Race was a blind spot for white reformers in the Progressive era. Anti-Asian sentiment against Japanese immigration was strong and growing in the West. In the Southwest, the Mexican Revolution of 1910 swelled the numbers of Mexican immigrants—by 1920 they constituted 12 percent of the population of California—and nativist anxiety about these dark-skinned foreigners also grew stronger.

Inasmuch as the Progressive era coincided with the triumph of Jim Crow policies, however, the brunt of the era's racism fell on African Americans. In the South, white reformers advocated segregation and the disfranchisement of black men as a means to purge local political corruption. In the North, antiblack prejudice was reinforced by pseudoscientific theories of racial hierarchy. Even the most sympathetic whites saw the African American poor as less adaptable than European immigrants to urban industrial society. Given maternalist convictions about the importance of home-based childrearing, male breadwinning, and dedicated mothering, the tendency of black mothers to work outside the home seemed to white reformers to constitute an insurmountable barrier to their improvement.

Nonetheless, African American women shared the reform enthusiasms of the era. The small black middle class provided resources for the establishment of kindergartens for the children of working mothers and founded old-age homes for ex-slaves without families to care for them. By 1900, four hundred black women's clubs and societies were affiliated with the National Association of Colored Women (NACW). In addition to the antilynching work with which it had begun, the NACW had divisions for mothers' clubs, juvenile courts, domestic science, temperance, music, literature, and votes for women. Mary Church Terrell, an 1884 graduate of Oberlin College, was the association's first president. When the National Association for the Advancement of Colored People was founded in 1909, Terrell and Ida B. Wells-Barnett were the most prominent African American women admitted to the inner circle.

Two other important black women of the era were business entrepreneurs, a category that had no real equivalent among white women of the period. Louisiana-born Sarah Breedlove Walker went from being a laundress to the president of her own highly successful hair care business. As Madam C. J. Walker, she employed thousands of African American women who sold her products door-to-door. Virginia-born Maggie Lena Walker (no relation to Sarah) was the first woman president of a U.S. bank. Wealthy, philanthropic, community-minded, both women deeply identified with the progress of the women of their race. Maggie Walker described her "great all absorbing interest" as "the love I bear . . . our Negro women . . . blocked and held down by the fears and prejudices of the whites, ridiculed and sneered at by intelligent blacks."[12]

During the Progressive era, Native Americans also began to serve as public advocates for their people. A generation educated in white institutions had gained familiarity with the dominant culture and acquired the political skills needed to speak for themselves. Their goal was to undo the economic and political dependency that had resulted from late nineteenth-century Indian policy (see pp. 392–97). Gertrude Simmons Bonnin was the leading woman in this first generation of modern Indian activists (see Documents: Zitkala-Ša: Indian Girlhood and Education, pp. 422–26). Known by her Yankton Sioux name Zitkala-Ša, she advocated both preserving native culture from destruction and securing full rights of citizenship for native peoples. She became the secretary of the first secular national pan-Indian reform organization established by native peoples, the Society of American Indians.[13] Other native women also figured prominently in the Society of American Indians, but the society divided over numerous issues, including full citizenship rights for Native Americans, fearing that U.S. citizenship would weaken tribal communities. But in 1924, when Congress passed the 1924 Indian Citizenship Act, women were included, because by then the long battle for woman suffrage had come to a victorious end.

VOTES FOR WOMEN

The labor militancy of women workers and the public involvement of Progressive women reformers together fueled a great and final drive for women's enfranchisement. Ever since the constitutional amendments of the Reconstruction years (pp. 326–28), the woman suffrage movement had been accumulating advocates and reformulating its strategy. In 1890, the two rival suffrage societies, the

◆ **Madam C. J. Walker**
During the Progressive era, many wealthy women were also reformers and philanthropists, but only one earned her own fortune and was African American. Madam C. J. Walker, born Sarah Breedlove, was the daughter of ex-slaves and worked in the cotton fields before she built her immensely successful hair care and cosmetics business. Walker was active in the National Association of Colored Women and was the single largest contributor to the National Association for the Advancement of Colored People's antilynching campaign, which picked up from the earlier efforts of black club women. Walker died in 1919, and her daughter used the money her mother left her to become the most important black woman patron of the Harlem Renaissance. *Madam C. J. Walker Collection, Indiana Historical Society.*

National Woman Suffrage Association (founded by Elizabeth Cady Stanton and Susan B. Anthony) and the American Woman Suffrage Association (established by Lucy Stone and Henry Ward Blackwell), united as the National American Woman Suffrage Association (NAWSA). When Carrie Chapman Catt of Iowa took over the NAWSA presidency from Anthony in 1900, four states, all west of the Mississippi, had granted full voting rights to women.

A New Generation for Suffrage

A new generation of suffrage leaders was determined to expand the movement to the rest of the country and bring it into full conformity with the realities of urban, industrial, modern America. They rejected the outdated nineteenth-century term "woman suffrage" in favor of a more contemporary-sounding slogan, "votes for women." They drew in previously uninvolved classes of women, from the wealthy to the working class, and learned to play legislative politics to their own benefit. They established small, flexible suffrage societies and turned to the most advanced cultural methods and artistic styles, anything to get over the old-fashioned image from which their cause suffered.

The revived movement of the Progressive era came back to life in a series of campaigns for equal political rights at the state level. But appeals to male voters in one state after another were exhausting, repetitive, and, east of the Mississippi River, impossible to win. At this point, suffrage activists shifted their focus back to a federal constitutional amendment, the movement's original goal in the 1860s. Large but slow to change, NAWSA was challenged by a small, more aggressive group of activists, known as "militants" and "suffragettes" (the latter a derogatory term that British suffrage activists had turned into a label of pride). By the mid-1910s, these two wings of the movement had generated the right combination of female energy, male support, and political will to effect a constitutional amendment for women's political rights.

Why, then, did it take so long to win votes for women? Organized opposition is part of the answer. Ever since the 1890s, a few, mostly upper-class women actively opposed enfranchisement, either on the grounds that political rights would cost women their moral influence over men or that too many "unfit" women would vote. However, suffrage leaders were less concerned with the female anti-suffragists than with powerful male-led special interests — especially the liquor industry and manufacturers who exploited female and child labor — who worked against them from behind the legislative scenes.

But the really significant obstacles that had to be overcome were more elusive. Large numbers of women who otherwise had little in common had to unite in active pursuit of this single goal. Perhaps this was why, unlike the suffragists of Elizabeth Cady Stanton's day, the twentieth-century movement did not emphasize abstract justice, but instead stressed the many concrete purposes to which organized political power could be put. With a large, diverse movement of women demanding the vote, male politicians and legislators were gradually compelled to act. That votes for women was a reform long past due did not make its final achievement any less a triumph, the most successful mass movement for the expansion of political democracy in American history.

Diversity in the Woman Suffrage Movement

In terms of diversity, the greatest achievement of the twentieth-century woman suffrage movement was its extremely broad class base. Reform collaboration between middle-class reformers and working-class trade unionists greatly facilitated outreach to women wage earners in the suffrage movement. By 1910, several new suffrage organizations were focused on recruiting working women. In San Francisco, Maud Younger, a wealthy woman who organized food servers, established a Wage Earners Suffrage League; similar organizations were founded in Los Angeles, New York City, and elsewhere. More and more suffrage parades featured large divisions of working women, often marching under the banners of their trade or union. Pro-suffrage literature was printed in the languages of immigrants—Yiddish, German, Italian, Portuguese, and Spanish—and explained how votes for women would raise women's wages and improve their working conditions. Wage-earning women brought with them the support of male family members and coworkers, who began to see in votes for women a tool for their own class interests.

Simultaneously, women from the very highest class of society became involved in the movement. Their wealth came from their husbands, but, aspiring to power of their own, they used their money to gain entrée into the world of women's politics. One of the richest was Alva Belmont, who had divorced one millionaire, William Vanderbilt, in order to marry another, August Belmont. Their money paid the salaries of organizers, rented offices, and supported the publication of newspapers and leaflets. Relations between the wealthy and the wage earning were superficially sisterly. But wealthy suffragists expected to lead the movement, and working-class suffragists were suspicious of their motives. "We want the ballot for very different reasons," explained Los Angeles working-class suffragist Minna O'Donnell in 1908. "Our idea is self protection; you want to use it [to help] some one else."[14]

The growth of suffragism among young college-educated women, whose numbers had been increasing since the 1860s, was also a new development. The College Equal Suffrage League, formed by students and young alumnae at Radcliffe College in 1898 because the administration would not permit pro-suffrage speakers on campus, became a national organization in 1908 under the leadership of Bryn Mawr president M. Carey Thomas. College graduates provided the energy of youth in many other organizations.

In contrast to such bridges across the class gap, the suffrage movement was almost completely racially segregated. NAWSA repeatedly refused to condemn discrimination against African American women and allowed southern white affiliates to refuse them membership. In 1899, the last year of her presidency, Susan B. Anthony turned her back on her abolitionist past to declare that since "women are a helpless, disfranchised class," there was no point in challenging southern racism.[15] Southern suffrage leaders such as Kate Gordon of Louisiana and Laura Clay of Kentucky regarded the involvement of African American women as an outright threat to their plans to increase the political involvement of white women in their region. "The South will be compelled to look to its Anglo-Saxon women as the medium through which to retain the supremacy of the white race over the African," Belle Kearney of Mississippi hopefully predicted in 1903.[16]

Despite this discouragement, black suffragists continued to insist on their equal political rights (see box, "African Americans for Woman Suffrage"). For black women, achieving suffrage was a way to counter the disfranchisement of the men of their race. Starting in the 1890s, African American women began to assert their political rights aggressively from within their own clubs and suffrage societies. "If white American women, with all their natural and acquired advantages,

NANNIE BURROUGHS
African Americans for Woman Suffrage

Nannie Burroughs (1879–1961), whose mother was an emancipated slave, was one of the founders of the Woman's Convention of the National Baptist Convention, an important locale for the southern black women's movement. The Crisis, *the magazine of the recently formed National Association for the Advancement of Colored People, actively advocated woman suffrage. Writing in it, Burroughs made a very different sort of case than did white suffragists. What arguments did she offer for why African American women needed civic and political equality?*

When the ballot is put in the hands of the American woman, the world is going to get a correct estimate of the Negro woman. It will find her a tower of strength of which poets have never sung, orators have never spoken, and scholars have never written.

Because the black man does not know the value of the ballot, and has bartered and sold his most valuable possession, it is no evidence that the Negro woman will do the same. The Negro woman therefore needs the ballot to get back, by the wise use of it, what the Negro man has lost by the misuse of it. She needs to ransom her race. . . . She carries the burdens of the Church, and of the school and bears a great deal more than her economic share in the home.

Another striking fact is that the Negro woman carries the moral destiny of two races in her hand. Had she not been the woman of unusual moral stamina that she is, the black race would have been made a great deal whiter, and the white race a great deal blacker during the past fifty years. She has been left a prey for the men of every race, but in spite of this, she has held the enemies of Negro female chastity at bay. The Negro woman is the white woman's as well as the white race's most needed ally in preserving an unmixed race.

The ballot, wisely used, will bring to her the respect and protection she needs. It is her weapon of moral defense. Under present conditions, when she appears in court in defense of her virtue, she is looked upon with amused contempt. She needs the ballot to reckon with men who place no value upon her virtue, and to mould healthy public sentiment in favor of her own protection.

SOURCE: Nannie Helen Burroughs, "Black Women and Reform," *Crisis*, August 1915.

need the ballot," explained Adele Hunt Logan of Tuskegee, Alabama, "how much more do black Americans, male and female, need the strong defense of a vote to help secure their right to life, liberty and the pursuit of happiness?"[17]

Returning to the Constitution: The National Suffrage Movement

In the Reconstruction years, the suffrage movement had concentrated on getting woman suffrage recognized in the U.S. Constitution. Congress debated a woman suffrage amendment in 1878, but suffrage energies shifted to the state level soon after. The modern revival of the American suffrage movement began in a series of campaigns focused on enfranchisement in particular states (see Map 8.1). In Washington State, where women had briefly voted in the 1880s only to have their suffrage revoked by the territorial legislature, they regained the vote in 1910. The next year, California women won suffrage by less than five thousand votes. In 1915, campaigns were mounted in Pennsylvania, New Jersey, Massachusetts, and, most important, New York. Despite extraordinary efforts, the eastern campaigns of 1915 failed. New York suffragists blamed the size of the state, the prejudices of immigrant men, and the opposition of politicians. A second state referendum campaign, scheduled for 1917, was initiated right away. But some suffrage leaders were beginning to conclude that the state-by-state approach was futile. Even if every state could be won this way—and many, certainly the entire South, could not—the time and money required were prohibitive. At this point, the momentum of the movement shifted back to an approach that would enfranchise all American women: a constitutional amendment.

NAWSA was slow to make the shift to focus on a federal amendment. Anna Howard Shaw, who had replaced Carrie Chapman Catt as NAWSA president in 1906, was unwilling to redirect organizational resources from the influential state chapters to a centralized national campaign. In 1913, two young women college graduates, Alice Paul and Lucy Burns, convinced NAWSA leaders to allow them to take over work on a federal amendment. In their very first act, they signaled their intention to energize a national effort with the same kind of spectacular methods that had worked in state campaigns. They organized a suffrage parade in Washington, D.C. (see Figure 8.5, p. 495). They chose March 3, the day before Woodrow Wilson's inauguration, because then the nation's attention would be on the city. When the president-to-be disembarked from the train, he was told that the crowds he had expected to greet him were down on Pennsylvania Avenue, watching the suffragists. Within a few weeks, the suffrage amendment was being debated in the House of Representatives for the first time in seventeen years.

Fresh off this victory, Paul and Burns formed a new, smaller, more activist, and more disciplined national organization. They named it the Congressional Union because its goal was to pressure Congress to pass a woman suffrage amendment. Paul and Burns understood that the votes of women who were already enfranchised by successful state campaigns in the West provided an important tool for putting political pressure on Congress to move. Accordingly, in 1916 they adjusted the name of their organization to the National Woman's Party (NWP)

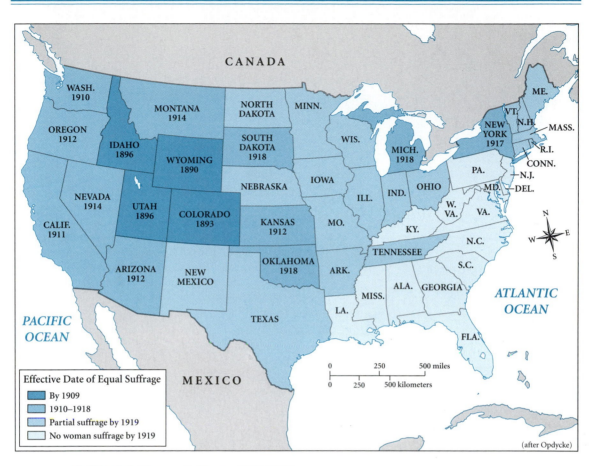

CANADA

WASH.
1910

OREGON
1912

IDAHO
1896

MONTANA
1914

NORTH
DAKOTA

MINN.

SOUTH
DAKOTA
1918

WIS.

MICH.
1918

ME.

VT.
NEW N.H.
YORK MASS.
1917
R.I.
CONN.
N.J.

WYOMING
1890

NEBRASKA

IOWA

PA.

MD. DEL.

NEVADA
1914

UTAH
1896

COLORADO
1893

ILL.

IND.

OHIO

W.
VA.

VA.

CALIF.
1911

KANSAS
1912

MO.

KY.

N.C.

ARIZONA
1912

NEW
MEXICO

OKLAHOMA
1918

ARK.

TENNESSEE

S.C.

ALA. GEORGIA

TEXAS

MISS.

LA.

ATLANTIC
OCEAN

PACIFIC
OCEAN

MEXICO

FLA.

0   250   500 miles

0   250   500 kilometers

Effective Date of Equal Suffrage

By 1909

1910–1918

Partial suffrage by 1919

No woman suffrage by 1919

(after Opdycke)

◆ **Map 8.1** **Woman Suffrage, 1890–1919**

The woman suffrage movement in the United States was fought on both the state and federal levels. States traditionally defined their electorates, but starting with the Fifteenth Amendment in 1870, the Constitution prohibited particular forms of disfranchisement. In 1893, Colorado amended its state constitution to include women as voting citizens. By 1914, ten other states, all in the West, had followed suit, granting their women full voting rights, including for president and Congress. The voting power of women in these "suffrage states" became a potent political lever for moving the national parties to support what became the Nineteenth Amendment, which prohibits states from disfranchising their citizens on the basis of sex.

to reflect the electoral focus of their strategy. That year, as President Wilson campaigned to be reelected, a corps of NWP activists fanned out through the West, urging women voters to withhold their votes from the Democrats until Wilson promised actively to back woman suffrage.

Although this tactic failed—Wilson won the election, including in states such as California where women voted—the NWP succeeded in redirecting suffrage

◆ **Votes for Women Graphics**
To advertise the October 1911 state referendum for votes
for women, California suffragists announced a contest for
the most beautiful image of the cause. B. M. Boye won with
her art nouveau graphic of a modern woman posed in
front of the Golden Gate, the mouth of the San Francisco
harbor. The sun setting in the West surrounds the woman's
head, like a halo. The suffrage message is carried not only
by the banner that she holds but also by the golden yellow
throughout the picture, the color chosen to designate the
pro-suffrage cause for the California campaign. *The
Schlesinger Library, Radcliffe Institute, Harvard University.*

energies to the national level. Even NAWSA loyalists who found the NWP's com-
bative methods distasteful were compelled to develop an alternative way for their
organization to push for federal-level enfranchisement. In 1915, NAWSA's most
politically savvy leader, Carrie Chapman Catt, reassumed the national presidency.
She mobilized NAWSA's enormous organizational structure in a concerted lobbying campaign for the federal amendment. Although the NWP and the NAWSA
were hostile to each other, belying the notion of a loving sisterhood on behalf of
suffrage, their two approaches were complementary, the former raising the political stakes by its radical efforts, the latter negotiating with congressmen to move
the amendment forward. Nonetheless, it took another five years, and the upheaval
of a world war, before the Constitution was amended to enfranchise women.

THE EMERGENCE OF FEMINISM

As the votes-for-women movement grew, an avant-garde approach to modernizing womanhood that emphasized women's autonomy was surfacing. To distinguish themselves from the more conventional suffragists, the women who took

◆ **Sacajawea Monument, Portland Oregon**
This statue of Sacajawea was commissioned in 1905 by the white women's clubs of Portland, Oregon, in recognition of the Shoshone guide and translator to the Lewis and Clark expedition, a hundred years before. The statue, by Denver sculptor Alice Cooper, was one of the first monuments to an actual historical woman in the United States. From this point on, Sacajawea's role as national symbol, both of the contribution of native people to American history, and their tragic fate at the hands of white settlers, began to grow. She is almost always represented as she is here: her baby on her back and her hand pointing the way west. *Hulton Archive/Getty Images.*

this approach began to use the term "feminist," borrowed from the French *feminisme*. "All feminists are suffragists," they explained, "but not all suffragists are feminists."[18] Their agenda was a broad one, moving beyond political rights and economic advancement to embrace female individuality, sexual freedom, and birth control.

The Feminist Program

Feminism was a cultural development more than an organized movement. Most of its adherents were middle-class college graduates, aspiring professionals, and artists, but female labor activists and immigrants were also in its ranks. From the moment of its inception, the definition of the word "feminism" was imprecise. On the one hand, feminists believed that women had all the capacities and talents of men; on the other, they believed that women's distinctive intelligence and powers had not yet been allowed to surface. Whether emphasizing similarities or differences with men, however, they agreed on feminism's power to disrupt the gender order. "Feminism was something with dynamite in it," Rheta Childe Dorr wrote. "It is the state of mind of women who realize that their whole position in the social order is antiquated . . . made of old materials, worn out laws, customs, conventions, fetishes, traditions and taboos."[19] Feminists were proud individualists, impatient with the female tradition of justifying all actions (including social reform) in terms of selfless, maternal service. (See Documents: Modernizing Womanhood, pp. 503–08.)

Unlike the votes-for-women movement, feminism placed the cutting edge of change in women's private lives, not in their public roles. Charlotte Perkins Gilman was a feminist favorite for her conviction that the family-oriented life of the middle class was narrow and inefficient, a point she explored in her path-breaking books *Women and Economics* (1890) and *The Home* (1903). Gilman championed collectivizing housework, and New York City feminist Henrietta Rodman organized a communal apartment house for women to realize this vision.

Other feminists challenged the Gilded Age premises of female sexual restraint by insisting that women had sexual desires as well as maternal capacities. They were influenced by British psychologist Havelock Ellis, one of the most eminent among a growing circle of "sexologists." Although similar to Sigmund Freud, the founder of modern psychoanalysis, in emphasizing the erotic nature of all humans, Ellis and others, including Swedish feminist Ellen Key, tended to romanticize sexuality by investing it with mystical qualities and insisting that sexual gratification was necessary for emotional health. In contrast to Freud, they also paid special attention to women's sexuality.

In the spirit of the new feminism, younger women claimed that previous generations of female activists fostered too much "sex antagonism" toward men, and that it was possible for advanced women and men to live and love together in mutual passion. Clustering in inexpensive, often immigrant urban neighborhoods, most famously New York City's Greenwich Village, they innovated new lifestyles, living with men in "free unions." A handful of women lived openly as lesbians in partnerships with other women that clearly were sexual, in contrast to the ambiguous homosocial relationships of the past (see p. 348).

Feminists' rejection of Gilded Age middle-class notions of sexual restraint was reinforced by broader trends in the society, especially urban popular culture. The fledgling film industry often portrayed women in ways that emphasized their sexual attractiveness to men, but also their own sexual natures. In vaudeville—live entertainment that featured a variety of comedic skits, song-and-dance acts, and novelty performances—female performers, including Eva Tanguay and Gertrude Hoffmann, became immensely famous and were noted for being independent, unconventional, strong women who were paid top dollar. And like the movies, vaudeville portrayed female sexuality. The enormous popularity of the "Salome" persona, a revealingly clad woman who performed an erotically charged dance number, highlighted women who embraced their sexuality as a source of power and pleasure.

Young working-class women were eager to take advantage of new urban commercial entertainments like dance halls, skating rinks, and amusement parks. Working-class women living apart from their families congregated in "furnished-room" districts of the nation's cities, which were often associated with prostitution and vice. These areas had a freer sexual climate that allowed experimentation and extramarital cohabitation, both with men and other women. Constrained by their poor wages, many young working-class women inhabited a culture in which

◆ **Kathleen McEnery,** *Going to the Bath* **(c. 1905–1913)** Kathleen McEnery (1885–1972) exhibited her paintings (including this one) in the famous 1913 New York Armory Show that introduced modern visual art to American audiences. McEnery, who also showed her paintings in an exhibit organized in 1915 for the benefit of the New York woman suffrage campaign, moved to Rochester to marry a local businessman and continued to be an active painter. The modernity and implicit feminism of her artistic vision is on display in the flat washes of color and the strong physiques of the bold female nudes. The two figures seem to be different perspectives on one woman, perhaps a suggestion of the multifaceted roles and selves of the New Woman. *Smithsonian American Art Museum, Washington, DC/Art Resource, NY.*

male suitors entertained them and bought them gifts in exchange for sexual favors. Elite urban women also began to frequent cabarets — the forerunners of today's nightclubs, where they learned syncopated dance steps in an atmosphere that suggested to some moral reformers "illicit sexuality."[20] The relative freedom of the urban environment and the attraction of popular amusements thus prompted early twentieth-century women to map out a new sexual terrain that coincided with feminists' articulation of sexuality as a crucial element of personal identity and fulfillment.

The Birth Control Movement

The most organized and politicized manifestation of cutting-edge feminism in the Progressive era was the campaign for birth control. Earlier women's rights champions had urged women to undertake pregnancy only voluntarily (see box, "Voluntary Motherhood," p. 349). Yet they regarded sexuality as fundamentally male, and they did not think it was important — or desirable — for women to have greater amounts of sexual intercourse freed of the threat of pregnancy. Emma Goldman was one of the first to speak widely on women's right to contraceptive information and methods, not only so that they could avoid unwanted pregnancy but also so that they could enjoy sexual intercourse.

In 1912, Margaret Sanger, a daughter of Irish immigrants, a trained nurse, and a Socialist, followed Goldman's lead to write and speak on behalf of women's right to control the frequency of their childbearing. She invented the term "birth control" to describe a practice that had long existed but had not been openly discussed or publicly advocated. Indeed, by the time Sanger began her work, birthrates among native-born white women had already fallen significantly. Sanger, like many feminists, viewed birth control as a means to women's autonomy. As she put it, "It is none of society's business what a woman shall do with her body."[21]

Yet Sanger's socialism also led her to focus on the problems of poor women. From her years of nursing, Sanger knew that immigrant women, without any access to private physicians, suffered the most from the public ban on discussions of contraception (see box, "The Story of Sadie Sachs"). At first, Sanger did not have a reliable contraceptive technology to promote. She concentrated instead on teaching young girls necessary reproductive and sexual information through a series of articles entitled "What Every Girl Should Know."

In sending her writings through the U.S. mail, Sanger fell foul of the Comstock anti-obscenity laws, which had been interfering with the spread of contraceptive information since the 1870s (see pp. 347–48). To avoid arrest, she fled to Europe, where a Dutch feminist doctor, Aletta Jacobs, taught her about the diaphragm (then known as a female pessary), an effective, female-controlled form of contraception. Sanger smuggled these devices into the United States and in 1916, in an immigrant neighborhood in Brooklyn, opened the first American birth control clinic. Days after the clinic opened, she was arrested for promoting birth control. After her 1917 trial and conviction, she served thirty days in jail.

She remained dedicated to the cause of birth control for the next forty years, but she engineered a compromise with physicians by agreeing that diaphragms should be available only through prescription. Contraception became more respectable and more widely disseminated in the 1920s (see p. 532), but in the prewar years, like feminism itself, birth control was a radical idea that challenged conventional notions of women's sexuality and reproduction.

THE GREAT WAR, 1914–1918

At the peak of the ferment of change prompted by Progressivism, suffragism, and feminism, international events dramatically altered the American political environment. In August 1914, war broke out in Europe, as a complex set of interlocking alliances pitted the Allied powers (Britain, France, and Russia) against the Central powers (Germany, and Austria-Hungary). Even before the United States entered the war nearly three years later, the conflict had already had a significant impact on American women. Labor shortages benefited working women. African American men and women began a large-scale exodus out of the rural South into the industrial cities of the North. Most of these economic opportunities faded at war's end, but women's political achievements were more lasting. The war bolstered women's claims to enfranchisement and propelled passage and ratification of the Nineteenth Amendment.

Pacifist and Antiwar Women

In the two years that the United States watched the war from the sidelines, peace advocacy among American women was widespread. NAWSA president Carrie Chapman Catt expressed the common sentiment that "when war murders the husbands and sons of women, . . . it becomes the undeniable business of women."[22] In August 1914, women marched silently and solemnly down the streets of New York City to protest the violence of war. Five months later, suffragist and feminist Crystal Eastman organized the Woman's Peace Party (WPP). With over twenty thousand women members, the WPP was dedicated to resolving the conflict in Europe through peaceful, negotiated means.

In the spring of 1915, WPP members joined a thousand women from twelve countries at an international peace conference of women in The Hague, Netherlands. Although transatlantic travel during wartime was dangerous, forty-seven American women sailed to Europe. Most were of the leisure class, but some working-class activists, such as Leonora O'Reilly, also attended. "For the first time in all the history of the world," wrote American journalist Mary Heaton Vorse, "women of warring nations and women of neutral nations had come together to lift up their voices in protest against war, through which the women and the workers gain nothing and lose all."[23] The organization they formed at The Hague, the Women's International League for Peace and Freedom, still exists today. The participants vowed to meet again when the war ended. For her role in this movement,

MARGARET SANGER
The Story of Sadie Sachs

Margaret Sanger (1879–1966), Socialist, feminist, and birth control pioneer, attributed her determination to dismantle the legal and cultural barriers keeping women from gaining access to contraceptive information to her experience as a visiting nurse among the immigrant working class in New York City. In her autobiography and elsewhere, she told the story of Sadie Sachs, who died of too many pregnancies and a self-induced abortion. Sanger did not blame individual men; she understood that the doctor and the husband in her story were trapped inside a system that regarded sexuality as a matter of morality rather than health and disregarded women's perspectives and needs. Who do you think was Sanger's intended audience for this story of Sadie Sachs?

Pregnancy was a chronic condition among women of [the immigrant working] class. Suggestions as to what to do for a girl who was "in trouble" or a married woman who was "caught" passed from mouth to mouth. . . . The doomed women implored me to reveal the "secret" rich people had, offering to pay me extra to tell them; many really believed I was holding back information for money. . . .

One stifling mid-July day of 1912 I was summoned to a Grand Street tenement. My patient was a small, slight Russian Jewess, about twenty-eight years old. . . . Jake Sachs, a truck driver scarcely older than his wife, had come home to find the three children crying and her unconscious from the effects of a self-induced abortion. He had called the nearest doctor, who in turn sent for me. . . .

After a fortnight Mrs. Sachs' recovery was in sight. . . . When the doctor came to make his last call, I drew him aside. "Mrs. Sachs is terribly worried about having another baby."

Jane Addams was awarded the Nobel Peace Prize in 1931, the first American woman so honored.

But peace was not in the offing and the United States inched closer to war. President Wilson's hopes for neutrality were literally sunk by German revival of unrestricted submarine warfare in the Atlantic, from which the United States was not spared. Wilson's position, as well as national sentiment, shifted toward entering the war. On April 6, 1917, Congress declared war on Germany and its allies.

Once the United States joined the war, women who opposed it were accused of political disloyalty, and the number and prominence of women speaking against militarism plummeted. Nonetheless, Jeanette Rankin, a suffragist from Montana and, in 1916, the first woman elected to the U.S. House of Representa-

"She may be," replied the doctor, and then he stood before her and said, "Any more such capers, young woman, and there'll be no need to send for me."

"I know, doctor," she replied timidly, "but," and she hesitated as it took all her courage to say it, "what can I do to prevent it?" . . . "Tell Jake to sleep on the roof." . . . [She turned to Sanger,] "He can't understand. He's only a man. But you do, don't you? Please tell me the secret, and I'll never breathe it to a soul. *Please!*" . . . I did not know what to say to her or how to convince her of my own ignorance; I was helpless to avert such monstrous atrocities. . . .

The telephone rang one evening three months later, and Jake Sachs' agitated voice begged me to come at once; his wife was sick again and from the same cause. . . . [When I arrived,] Mrs. Sachs was in a coma and died within ten minutes. . . . I left him pacing desperately back and forth, and for hours I myself walked and walked and walked through the hushed streets. . . . [The city's] pains and griefs crowded in upon me, . . . women writhing in travail to bring forth little babies; the babies themselves naked and hungry, . . . six-year-old children with pinched, pale, and wrinkled faces. . . . I knew I could not go back merely to keeping people alive. I went to bed, knowing that no matter what it might cost, I was finished with palliatives and superficial cures; I was resolved to seek out the root of evil, to do something to change the destiny of mothers whose miseries were vast as the sky.

SOURCE: Margaret Sanger, *Margaret Sanger: An Autobiography* (1938; repr., New York: Dover Publications, 1971), 88–92.

tives, voted against a formal declaration of war, for which she was turned out of office. Emily Balch was fired from her job as professor of economics at Wellesley College for challenging the government's right to draft young men to fight. Ida B. Wells-Barnett was threatened with jail for her efforts to defend black soldiers who had been convicted and executed for alleged insurrection in Texas. "I'd rather go down in history as one lone Negro who dared to tell the government that it had done a dastardly thing," she defiantly responded, "than to save my skin by taking back what I have said."[24]

After the 1917 Bolshevik Revolution, Russia negotiated a separate peace with Germany and left the war. This transformation of a former ally into a worker-run state intensified suspicion of American Socialists, who never recovered their pre-war vitality. Kate Richards O'Hare was sentenced to five years in federal prison for voicing the same kind of sentiments against mothers' being forced to sacrifice their sons to war that had been common a few years before. Emma Goldman was imprisoned for her antidraft speeches; after the war, along with hundreds of other

◆ American Women for Peace

Along with other members of the newly formed WPP, Jane Addams, second from the left behind the peace banner, arrives in The Hague, Netherlands, in April 1915. There she presided over an international women's peace meeting and formed a delegation to meet with the leaders of fourteen European nations to argue—in vain—for peace. Two years later, after the United States entered the war on the side of England and France, Addams remained a staunch advocate of peace, a position that then labeled her a dangerous radical. © *CORBIS.*

immigrant radicals, she was permanently deported from the United States and died in exile. When Eugene Debs ran again for president in 1920, he did so from federal prison, where he was serving time for his antiwar speeches.

Within the suffrage movement, it was the militant wing that resisted the atmosphere of wartime jingoism. Prior to U.S. entry into the war, NWP members had begun picketing the White House—the first American activists ever to do so—to add to the pressure on President Wilson to support a federal suffrage amendment (see Figure 8.6, p. 496). Although the NWP did not formally oppose the war, it refused to halt its activities once war was declared. On the contrary, it upped the ante, carrying signs provocatively addressed to "Kaiser Wilson," declaring that "Democracy Should Begin at Home." Peaceful protest was now perceived as the act of traitors.

From 1917 through 1919, 168 suffrage picketers were arrested, and 97 served up to six months in federal prison. Considering themselves political prisoners, many went on hunger strikes and were forcibly fed through tubes pushed down their noses into their stomachs. NWP leader Alice Paul was repeatedly interrogated by a prison psychiatrist, who wanted to prove that she was mentally ill rather than deeply dedicated to the cause of woman suffrage. She defied her interrogators and insisted that her opinions were political, not paranoid.

Preparedness and Patriotism

While antiwar women and militant suffragists persisted in their protests, the majority of American women, including middle-of-the-road suffragists, threw themselves into the war effort. Wilson had described the United States' role in idealistic terms, claiming World War I as a war for democracy to spread American ideals throughout the world. Following his lead, the majority of Americans believed that their country was fighting for the ideals of peace and freedom and against autocracy. They were sure that their government's purposes were good and that stronger government meant a better civic life. They hoped that war could be the fruition of many progressive hopes, and they were eager to help to make it so. (See Visual Sources: Uncle Sam Wants You: Women and World War I Posters, pp. 498–502.)

Activist women also viewed supporting the war as an opportunity to demonstrate not merely their patriotism but their claims to full citizenship. Carrie Chapman Catt set aside her long history of peace advocacy to lead NAWSA into active support for the war. "I am a pacifist, but not for peace without honor," she wrote in April 1917. "I'd be willing, if necessary, to die for my country."[25] Catt and others who supported the war pushed for the creation of the Women's Committee of the Council for National Defense (WCND) in 1917. Former NAWSA president Anna Howard Shaw became its head. Although ostensibly advisory, the women appointed to the WCND made it a channel for delivering women's energies to the war effort.

The WCND set up state and local branches of their organization, which in turn used women's organizations such as the Young Women's Christian Association, the Woman's Christian Temperance Union, and the General Federation of Women's Clubs to mobilize women's voluntary war work. The WCND also had a subdivision for "colored women," with African American poet Alice Dunbar-Nelson as its field representative. Women labor activists served on another subcommittee, Women in Industry; this was transformed after the war into the U.S. Woman's Bureau, led by Mary Van Kleeck.

Women's pro-war activities took many forms. Following the model of suffrage parades, women organized grand public marches to raise money for wartime "Liberty Bonds." They organized America's housewives to conserve meat, sugar, and wheat for the war effort. They raised relief funds for refugees in Europe. Several thousand women, organized by the American Red Cross, served as nurses and ambulance drivers on the battlefields of France.

Women were also active in what was called Americanization work. These were efforts to accelerate the assimilation of immigrants into American society, especially Germans, who were suspected of loyalty to America's opponents. In the Southwest, particular attention focused on Mexican immigrants, often regarded as potentially dangerous radicals because of the ongoing Mexican Revolution that began in 1910. Throughout the nation's cities, native-born women reformers taught English language, home, and health classes for immigrant women, while also instructing them in wartime food conservation measures.

The biggest contribution that women made to the war effort was through their labor. Although the United States did not enter the war until 1917, by 1915 the economy was already beginning to speed up to provision the Allies and prepare for possible American involvement. As European immigration was slowed to a halt by the naval war in the Atlantic, the accelerating needs of the labor force were met in part by white women workers. The female labor force increased to more than 10 million during the war years, and many women found new and better-paying opportunities in the railroad, steel, and other heavy industries.

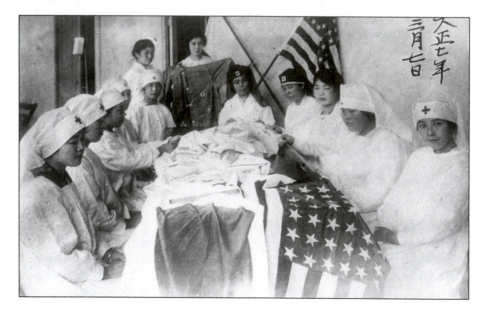

◆ Japanese Women's Auxiliary to the Los Angeles Red Cross
During World War I women actively supported mobilization by conserving food and raising funds for the Liberty Loan campaign, a major source of financing for the war. They also supported the American Red Cross, which not only sent nurses to the front but also provided warm garments and medical supplies for the troops. African Americans and immigrants, eager to express their patriotism, participated in these efforts. The women in this photograph were members of the Japanese Women's Auxiliary to the Los Angeles Red Cross, a group that took much pride in its work and its demonstration of loyalty to the United States.
Seaver Center for Western History Research Los Angeles County Museum of Natural History.

Harriot Stanton Blatch characterized the situation with brutal honesty: "When men go awarring, women go to work. War compels women to work. That is one of its merits."[26]

The Great Migration

World War I was an especially monumental turning point for African Americans, women and men alike. Many seized the opportunity provided by the demand for wartime labor to flee southern segregation and exploitation and head north. Two to three times as many southern blacks, perhaps five hundred thousand, migrated in the decade after 1910 as in the decade before. Chicago's black population increased by 150 percent, Detroit's by 600 percent, and New York City's by 66 percent. This profound shift in population between 1914 and 1920, from the South to the North and from rural to urban life, is known as the Great Migration.

Unlike European and Asian migrations, in which men represented the vast majority, women constituted almost half the number of African American migrants. Their reasons for migrating were in part economic. For the first time, African American women, who had been almost exclusively employed in domestic and agricultural labor, entered factory work, although usually in the dirtiest and most dangerous jobs and only for the brief period of wartime mobilization. "I'll never work in nobody's kitchen but my own anymore," one black woman optimistically declared.[27] Even in domestic labor, a woman could earn more in a day up North than in a week in the South. Going north also meant escaping the constant threat of sexual harassment to which they were exposed in the white homes in which they worked, and with it the lynching that loomed for any black man who tried to protect his wife or daughters. (See Documents: African American Women and the Great Migration, pp. 509–14.)

The new migrants needed aid in finding jobs and housing and adjusting to northern urban life. The NACW acted quickly to lift the burden, establishing a Women Wage Earners Association to assist migrating black women workers. The Young Women's Christian Association (YWCA) also responded by increasing the funding of its Division of Colored Work, designating $200,000 for work with young women in African American communities, and tripling the number of independent black branches. In 1919, the Women's Trade Union League, which had heretofore ignored the needs of African Americans, hired Irene Goins of Chicago as a special organizer for black women workers.

For the most part, however, black migrants met hostility in the North. In 1915, *Birth of a Nation*, one of the first great epics of the American film industry, presented a thoroughly racist account of the Civil War and Reconstruction, including a defense of lynching, to packed houses of white filmgoers across the United States. During and after the war, pent-up racial antagonism exploded in a series of race riots. In 1917 Ida B. Wells-Barnett risked her life to go to East St. Louis, Illinois, to investigate the 150 black people who were, in her words, "slaughtered" in a riot there. In 1919, another deadly riot erupted in her hometown of Chicago, after a white mob killed an African American child who had wandered onto a whites-only beach. But despite the violence and disappointment African Americans faced in the North, migration offered black women and their families improved economic opportunities and an escape from the dead-end life of the South.

Winning Woman Suffrage

The United States entered World War I just as momentum for woman suffrage was peaking. Militant suffragists of the NWP demonstrated daily outside the White House, while the NAWSA, under Carrie Chapman Catt's leadership, steadily lobbied Congress. The victory of woman suffrage in a second New York referendum in 1917 boosted prospects for national victory. Catt had predicted that once New York women were enfranchised, the state's congressional delegation, the largest in the country, would swing over to woman suffrage and "the backbone of the opposition will be largely bent if not broken."[28] She was right. Two months after woman suffrage won in New York, the House of Representatives passed a constitutional amendment establishing full voting rights for all American women. The NWP named it the Susan B. Anthony Amendment to signify the long battle that had to be fought to win it.

From the House, the Anthony Amendment went to the Senate, where it confronted the power and resistance of southern Democrats. With the Fourteenth and Fifteenth Amendments still rankling (see pp. 326–27), southern Democrats were opposed to any further federal involvement in voting rights. President Wilson, who finally yielded to pressure from suffragists, went to the Senate to appeal for passage. "We have made partners of women in this war," he pleaded. "Shall we admit them only to a partnership of suffering and sacrifice and toil and not to a partnership of privilege and right?" Nonetheless, when the Senate voted in October 1918, the amendment fell two votes short of passage.

That same month, the war ended in victory for the Allies. Wilson left for Paris to negotiate the peace and fight for the establishment of a "league of nations," a multinational organization to achieve, in his words, "mutual guarantees of political independence and territorial integrity to great and small states alike."[29] A small army of American women activists went with him in hopes of influencing the outcome of the peace conference. Many of these American women then traveled to Zurich to fulfill the promise they had made in The Hague in 1915 to reconvene the international women's peace movement after the war. When Wilson returned to the United States with the Versailles Treaty, which included establishment of the League of Nations among its provisions, he was unable to convince a skeptical Congress to ratify it, a defeat that literally destroyed him. In October 1919, he suffered a disabling stroke, and for the last year of his presidency, First Lady Edith Bolling Galt Wilson took on many of the tasks of her husband's office (and was widely maligned for overstepping her bounds).

Through all this, suffragists still had to find the support they needed in Congress and the nation for the Susan B. Anthony Amendment. Finally, in June 1919, they secured exactly the necessary two-thirds of Congress members to vote for the amendment and the measure went on to the states for ratification. NAWSA's structure of strong state divisions was crucial in winning endorsement from the necessary thirty-six states. Of these, the only southern states were Texas, Kentucky, Arkansas, Missouri, and Tennessee. (Georgia, Louisiana, Mississippi, and North Carolina did not formally ratify the woman suffrage amendment until the 1970s!) The final battle came down to Tennessee, one of the only southern states with a viable two-party system. The decisive vote came from a young Republican legislator named Harry Burn, in response to his mother's urging. "Don't forget to be a good boy," she wrote him, "and help Mrs. Catt put the 'Rat' in Ratification."[30]

On August 26, 1920, seventy-two years after the Seneca Falls Convention, the Nineteenth Amendment was added to the U.S. Constitution. Patterned after the Fifteenth Amendment, it reads, "The right of citizens of the United States to vote shall not be denied or abridged . . . on account of sex" (see the Appendix, p. A-15). But American women's struggles for political equality were not yet complete. The courts ruled that the amendment did not affect the political status of women in the American colonies of Puerto Rico and the Philippines, who had to undertake their own campaigns—lasting eight and sixteen years, respectively—for voting rights. Most African American women in the South found that when they tried to register to vote, they were stopped by the same devices used against black men. And for all American women, the battle for parity and power within political parties had just begun. It would take another seven decades for voting women to become a force to be reckoned with in American politics.

CONCLUSION: New Conditions, New Challenges

The gradual move of American women into public life that had begun in the middle of the nineteenth century reached its apex in the first decades of the twentieth. In few other periods of American history did women achieve greater public visibility and political influence. The inclusion of women's equal political rights in the U.S. Constitution, after almost three-quarters of a century of effort, crowned a host of women's other achievements in the Progressive era.

By the same token, crucial changes were taking place just under the surface. Not only were the numbers of female workers continuing to rise but the place of paid labor in women's lives was shifting dramatically. Women had entered the Progressive era under the banner of motherhood; they were leaving it, unbeknownst to many of them, under the banner of worker. The sexual revolution and the birth control movement of these years also signified grand changes to come in women's lives. All of these developments would play out in the next decades as women faced different sorts of challenges and began to envision new collective goals.

VISUAL SOURCES

Parades, Picketing, and Power:
Women in Public Space

ALTHOUGH AMERICAN WOMEN were never as tightly restricted to the private sphere of the home as nineteenth-century cultural prescriptions suggested, by the turn of the century, women's presence in the public arena had notably expanded. Working-class women had jobs in factories, shops, and offices and filled crowded city streets. They frequented dance halls and amusement parks. Leisure-class women shopped in department stores, attended college, and participated in reform activities. In this essay, we analyze women's increased public visibility by examining the ways in which two groups of women activists—working-class women strikers and leisure-class suffragists—took to the streets to march and picket, literally opening up new spaces for women in the society. Whether they were agitating for economic rights or for the vote, their public visibility had political and cultural significance. The bold occupation of public space was an important demonstration of women's legitimacy as political actors.

THE STRIKERS

Women laborers had participated in strikes and public demonstrations as early as the 1830s, when the mill girls of Lowell, Massachusetts, "turned out" in response to lowered wages (see pp. 199–203). Nonetheless, when New York City women shirtwaist workers began picketing in front of their factories in 1909, many observers found their behavior shocking. These mostly young Jewish and Italian women were not only challenging their employers but transgressing against conventional notions of appropriate feminine behavior. When the demonstrations expanded to a general strike of the entire industry and the leisure-class women of the Women's Trade Union League (WTUL) became involved, the newspaper coverage became more sympathetic. From this point on, the events of the strike were widely reported in the popular press. The women made good copy, and their leaders eagerly sought publicity for the cause.

By 1909, newspapers had the technology to illustrate their stories with photographs. Given the limitations of that technology, these pictures were usually posed and static; the dramatic moments captured on film that would become the hallmark of modern photojournalism were a thing of the future. The hybrid illustration in Figure 8.1 appeared in the *New York Evening Journal* on November 10, 1909. The photograph shows, as the newspaper caption puts it, "Girl Strikers: each of

40,000 Girls to Join Great Strike of New York Waistmakers

GIRL STRIKERS, EACH OF WHOM HAS BEEN ARRESTED FIVE TIMES FOR PICKETING.

◆ **Figure 8.1** "Girl Strikers," New York *Evening Journal* (November 10, 1909)

whom has been arrested five times for picketing." This somewhat formal picture is coupled with a drawing showing the action of police arresting the resisting women.

The photograph reveals something widely commented on in the newspaper reports. The women look fashionably dressed and, in particular, sport elaborate hats. People hostile to the strikers pointed to their clothing as evidence that the women were not suffering from dire poverty. Male union leaders and WTUL officials retorted that the clothes were cheap and bought through scrimping and going without food. Clara Lemlich was the only working woman to respond in the newspapers: "We're human, all of us girls, and we're young. We like new hats as well as any other young women. Why shouldn't we?"[31] Where critics of the strikers saw women dressed above their station, behaving in unladylike ways on the public streets, the strikers saw themselves as attractive, modern young women, willing to fight for their rights and a decent standard of living, dressed in their best to reflect the seriousness of their purpose and action.[32] Compare the photograph with the drawing. What response to the strikers did the newspaper editors seek to encourage by publishing this hybrid image?

The shirtwaist strike sparked dozens of garment industry strikes in other cities. Figure 8.2 portrays members of the Rochester, New York, branch of the Garment Workers Union as they picketed in the winter of 1912 for a cut in hours (but not pay), an end to subcontracting, and the union's right to represent the workers in negotiations with their employers. After four months — and the death of one seventeen-year-old striker shot by an excited employer — the workers won all their demands except union recognition. This image, in which the strikers are the only women in sight, suggests something of the transgressive meaning of women marching on picket lines. During the 1909 New York City shirtwaist strike, the

◆ **Figure 8.2 Members of the Rochester, New York, Branch of the Garment Workers Union (1913)**
From the Albert R. Stone Negative Collection, Rochester Museum & Science Center, Rochester, New York.

police conducted raids on brothels in the factory neighborhoods, pushing prostitutes into the street to mingle with the picketers. This effort to call into question the sexual respectability of union women proved a theme in many strikes. But note how the Rochester women posed themselves for this photograph. What attitude do they project about their right to take to the streets?

THE SUFFRAGISTS

For leisure-class suffragists to move into public space with their demonstrations was also difficult but for different reasons, as they were bound by standards of domestic propriety. The reputation for "respectability" that was key to their difference from the working class seemed endangered by such bold, forthright public activity. Precisely because public parades and demonstrations were such a radical move for leisure-class women, these events drew enormous crowds eager to see a mass violation of ladylike norms.

As the suffrage movement gathered steam in the early twentieth century, activists developed new promotional tactics and turned to the most advanced cultural methods and artistic styles, anything to get over the old-fashioned image from which their cause suffered. In their search to garner publicity and support,

◆ **Figure 8.3** **Votes for Women a Success (detail)**
The Historical Society of Pennsylvania.

they appropriated public spaces and used novel techniques. They turned up on tugboats and in touring cars, appeared in department store windows and movie theaters, had bonfires and dramatic pageants. In Seattle, Lucy Burns even distributed leaflets from a hot-air balloon. Figure 8.3, a photograph from the 1915 Pennsylvania state campaign, features a suffragist speaking before a group of working men at a factory gate. She holds in her hand a map indicating suffrage victories. What might be the significance of the decision to target working-class men? What do the body language and facial expressions of the men suggest about their receptivity to the speaker? What does the photograph reveal about the challenges facing suffragists who invaded spaces normally reserved to men?

Perhaps the most dramatic innovation designed to provide entertainment and spectacle was the suffrage parade. New York City, home to one of the largest and most well-funded suffrage movements, also featured the most impressive parades. The 1910 and 1911 parades, held right after the settlement of the shirtwaist strike and the deadly Triangle Shirtwaist Company fire, respectively, were specifically inspired by the public demonstrations of working women, which leisure-class allies had supported. In the 1911 suffrage march, labor organizer Leonora O'Reilly was a featured speaker. Banners highlighted both political and economic rights, and working girls were prominent in the ranks of the paraders. Harriot Stanton Blatch, chief organizer of the marches, understood the symbolic and dramatic possibilities of suffrage parades: "What could be more stirring than hundreds of women, carrying banners, marching—marching—marching! The public would be aroused, the press would spread the story far and wide, and the interest of our own workers would be fired."[33]

In 1912 and 1913, the New York City parades were many times more spectacular, no longer foregrounding working women but emphasizing instead the participation of women of all classes (though not always of all races) cooperating for the common cause of woman suffrage. Male supporters also marched. A bill authorizing a referendum to grant full voting rights to the women of New York was before the state legislature, and the parade was intended to impress voters and legislators alike with suffragists' determination and power. As Figure 8.4 indicates, the crowds watching the 1913 parade on Fifth Avenue were ten and twelve deep. How do the dress and organization of the marchers emphasize their unanimity and discipline?

◆ **Figure 8.4 Suffragists Marching down Fifth Avenue, New York City (1913)**
Milstein Division of United States History, Local History and Genealogy, The New York Public Library, Astor, Lenox, and Tilden Foundations.

◆ **Figure 8.5** **Suffrage Parade down Pennsylvania Avenue, Washington, D.C. (March 1913)**
Brown Brothers.

The most significant and highly publicized suffrage parade was held in Washington, D.C., in March 1913. This was not only the first suffrage parade to represent the movement on a national level but also one of the first such demonstrations held in the nation's capital on any issue. Extremely well organized by the young Alice Paul, just beginning her career as the leader of suffragism's militant wing (see pp. 474–75), the parade drew five thousand women from around the country. Banners identified some groups of marchers by their professions, from factory worker to lawyer. Other participants walked with women's clubs. Still others rode on floats that depicted women in roles of mother, worker, and citizen. The organizers required African American women to march at the back of the parade. The parade culminated at the steps of the U.S. Treasury building, where marchers enacted an allegorical pageant, with individual women performing the roles of America, Peace, Liberty, Hope, Justice, and Charity.[34] The *Washington Post* headline read: "Miles of Fluttering Femininity Present Entrancing Suffrage Appeal."[35] Although condescending, the newspaper's words vindicated the organizers' hopes that the attractiveness of the parade and its participants proved that suffrage and femininity were compatible.

The photograph in Figure 8.5 captures the start of the parade. The coordinated clothing of this group of marchers indicates the attention to matters of style. The woman to the far right is dressed in academic regalia, worn proudly by women college graduates in suffrage parades. To the left is Inez Milholland, the beautiful lawyer and suffragist, leading the parade from her white horse, as she had in New York City. The most striking aspect of the image, however, is the backdrop of the national Capitol. Although Washington, D.C., officials tried to locate the march in a less central site, Paul was adamant that it take place on Pennsylvania Avenue, in the customary place for official parades, and on the day before the presidential inauguration of Woodrow Wilson. What is the significance of the juxtaposition of the parade and the Capitol building in this image?

Ironically, the parade's greatest contribution to the suffrage cause may have been its disruption by enormous crowds of drunken men, the kind who always showed up for a presidential inauguration. The *Baltimore American* reported that the women "practically fought their way foot by foot up Pennsylvania Avenue through a surging throng."[36] Newspapers all over the country criticized not just the rowdy crowds but the police for failing to protect the marchers. The debacle led to a congressional hearing, which the suffragists skillfully exploited to generate favorable publicity for their cause. Even Anna Howard Shaw, former president of the National American Woman Suffrage Association who generally disapproved of radical tactics, knew how to make the most of the episode: "Do you suppose that if we were voters the police would have allowed the hoodlums to possess the streets while we marched?"[37]

A final example in 1917 of women's claim to public space for political ends comes full circle, back to picketing. Figure 8.6 shows the suffrage militants of the National Woman's Party picketing the White House during World War 1 (see pp. 484–85). College graduates, they identified themselves by their alma maters. Just as the working-class women illustrated in Figures 8.1 and 8.2 had hoped to attract publicity to their cause, these radical suffragists sought to embarrass President

◆ **Figure 8.6 National Woman's Party Picketers at the White House (1918)**
Library of Congress, LC-USZ62-31799.

Wilson by graphically pointing out the hypocrisy of a war fought for democracy while women at home were not enfranchised. More moderate suffragists criticized the radicals' tactics, but how might images such as this one have played a role in bringing Wilson around to support of the suffrage amendment?

QUESTIONS FOR ANALYSIS

1. Compare the photographs illustrating the strikers (Figures 8.1 and 8.2) and the suffragists (Figures 8.3 to 8.6). How did both groups take to the streets, and what commonalities and differences do their uses of public space reveal?

2. A major motivation behind picketing and parading was to capture publicity. What other purposes could these activities serve? What possibilities and dangers did the courting of publicity pose for strikers? For suffragists?

3. What does the popularity among women activists of these mass demonstrations suggest about the public involvement of women in the Progressive era?

Uncle Sam Wants You:
Women and World War I Posters

Prior to World War I, the federal government communicated with citizens primarily through press releases printed in newspapers. In April 1917, however, President Woodrow Wilson formed the Committee on Public Information (CPI) to promote public support for the war. The CPI established the Department of Pictorial Publicity, which drew on a well-established tradition of using posters for advertising as well as on the skills of well-known magazine illustrators. The federal government used other methods to build support for war needs such as conserving food, recruiting soldiers for the military and workers for war industries, and supporting Liberty Bond and Red Cross fund drives, but the posters were the most colorful and abundant device. Over 20 million copies of 2,500 different posters were produced during the war. State governments and civic associations such as the Red Cross also created these dramatic advertisements to "sell the war."

Wartime propaganda aimed at creating a strong sense of identification with the nation and an eagerness to support the military effort. Although building the army itself required the coercion of the draft, the government turned to persuasive measures when possible in keeping with the notion that the United States was going to "war for democracy." The posters reproduced here need to be understood as part of this massive drive to imbue Americans with intense loyalty and patriotism. There was a strong antiwar movement in the country, but dissent was repressed and many protestors were imprisoned and, if not citizens, deported (see pp. 483–84).

Women's efforts were central to the nation's call for patriotism. In the midst of the final stages of their drive for citizenship, many women saw themselves, if not quite as regular soldiers, as members of a volunteer army that blanketed the nation in support of various wartime mobilization drives. These activities required exceptional administrative skills, and for some leisure-class women this became full-time work.

Posters, of course, do not convey the complexity of these women's volunteer activity. The messages were simple. Women were urged to do their part as a demonstration of their citizenship, and their images were widely used to encourage all Americans to support the war. Given the eagerness with which women rushed into the public sphere to support the war, it is ironic that the majority of these images depicted traditional notions of womanhood.

Images of women have been used to represent the United States since the nation was founded. (See Visual Sources: Gendering Images of the Revolution, pp. 162–68). Posters used female representations to give a feminine face to war aims. A beautiful woman flanked by the U.S. flag or dressed in the Stars and Stripes represented the patriotism of a nation at war. Figure 8.7 depicts a beseeching woman wearing a cap that clearly echoes the American flag. In the backdrop is a European city with its church towers in flames, a potent reminder to Americans safe at home of the devastating war across the Atlantic. The poster in Figure 8.8 features a female form to indicate that America's honor needed fighting men to protect it. What conventional ideas of femininity do these posters mobilize to bolster their messages?

Posters also traded on images of female sexuality. The saucy young woman dressed in a military uniform in Figure 8.9, an image created by well-known artist Howard Chandler Christy, provocatively exclaims, "Gee!! I Wish I Were a Man." What does this image suggest about modern notions of female sexuality emerging in the prewar years? How does the cross-dressed figure communicate the proper roles of men and women in wartime?

Even when posters encouraged women to participate in war activities by buying Liberty Bonds, supporting the Red Cross, knitting socks for soldiers, or conserving food, the images rarely challenged traditional ideas of women's proper place. Figure 8.10, for example, is a recruitment poster for the Land Army, a voluntary organization formed to mobilize women as temporary farmworkers. How does it link labor on the home front to the war? How are the women agricultural laborers represented?

◆ **Figure 8.7** **"Let's End It—Quick with Liberty Bonds"** *(top)*
Library of Congress, LC-USZC4-9462.

◆ **Figure 8.8** **"It's Up To You. Protect the Nation's Honor. Enlist Now"** *(bottom)*
Library of Congress, LC-USZ62-87685.

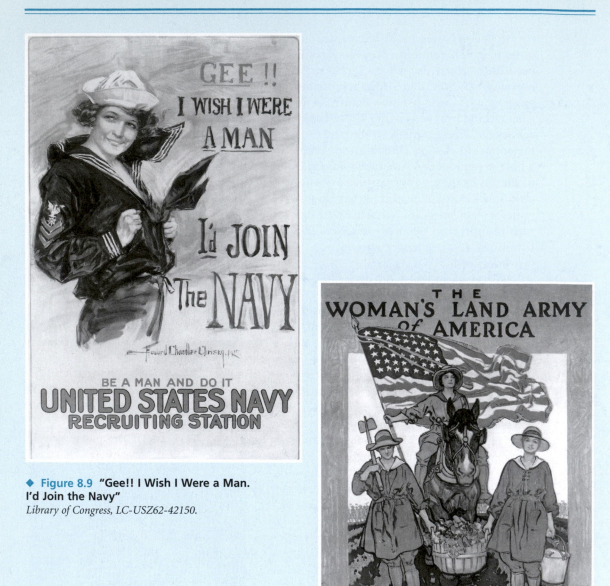

◆ **Figure 8.9** **"Gee!! I Wish I Were a Man.
I'd Join the Navy"**
Library of Congress, LC-USZ62-42150.

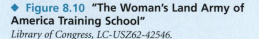

◆ **Figure 8.10** **"The Woman's Land Army of
America Training School"**
Library of Congress, LC-USZ62-42546.

Some posters depicted women supporting the war effort in the workforce. The government distributed one featuring a typist (typing now almost wholly a female occupation) with the caption "The Kaiser is afraid of you!" On occasion, posters acknowledged women who crossed conventional gender barriers when they took jobs in war work. These images were usually issued by the Young Women's Christian Association (YWCA), which produced its own posters. During the war, the YWCA continued its prewar activism on behalf of young working women and distributed the poster depicted in Figure 8.11 as part of its fund-raising campaign. In keeping with YWCA literature that praised women factory workers' vital contribution to defense, this image emphasizes female strength and solidarity. Note too the graphic style of this image. How does it compare to government posters intended to convey more conventional ideas about women's war contribution?

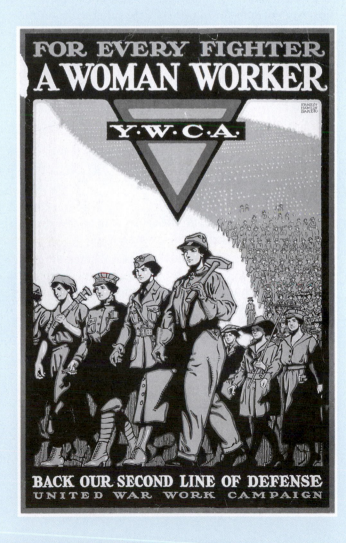

◆ **Figure 8.11**
"For Every Fighter a Woman Worker. Y.W.C.A."
Library of Congress, LC-USZC4-1419.

World War I poster art is also revealing for what it did not picture, in particular the way in which it supported existing racial hierarchies. Government and voluntary agencies worked in black communities to encourage support for war programs. Alice Dunbar-Nelson's report "Negro Women in War Work" (see p. 512), for example, detailed the fund-raising of the National Association of Colored Women, which raised close to $5 million in the third Liberty Loan drive. Yet despite the record of black women's participation, apparently no posters represented them or other women of color. Images of European immigrants appeared in a few World War I posters, but the diversity of American women was not reflected in this popular propaganda form.

War posters also failed to depict adequately the full range of ways in which women supported the war effort. The wartime growth in the wage labor force was rarely represented, and instead of images of women performing manual labor, most women depicted in posters were either icons for the nation or wartime volunteers. But if few posters challenged traditional expectations about women's domestic roles, women themselves did take advantage of wartime opportunities. Not only did working women temporarily break into traditionally male jobs, but suffragists used women's war service as a way of dramatically demonstrating their claim for full citizenship.

QUESTIONS FOR ANALYSIS

1. Figures 8.7 and 8.8 are both enlistment posters aimed at young men. What emotional responses do the artists seek to arouse in their intended audience? How are their methods alike, and how do they differ?

2. Until recently in the United States, only men officially served in combat, and it could be argued that by virtue of asking men to risk death, wartime gave them a heightened claim on citizenship. To what extent do these posters reinforce this notion? To what extent do they challenge it?

3. The Library of Congress's online catalog of prints and photographs offers an extensive number of World War I posters. Go to <loc.gov/rr/print/catalog.html>, find the World War I poster collection, and search for other poster images of women. What insights does your research give you about the representation of American women in World War I?

DOCUMENTS

Modernizing Womanhood

As the drive for the vote heated up in the years before World War I, another less sharply defined movement emerged among more radical women, who called themselves feminists (see p. 478). While women like Charlotte Perkins Gilman and Crystal Eastman supported the suffrage campaign, their ideas moved beyond women's political rights to include more modern themes of economic independence and more modern sexual relationships and marriages. Many feminists had socialist leanings and were associated with the struggles of working-class women; a few were union activists. Self-consciously rebellious, they viewed themselves as breaking from the suffocating conventions of respectable female behavior, demanding instead to be recognized, in the words of Edna Kenton, as "people of flesh and blood and brain, feeling, seeing, judging and directing equally with men, all the great social forces."[38]

In 1912, twenty-five feminists in New York founded a club they called Heterodoxy because it "demanded of a member that she should not be orthodox in her opinions."[39] Over the next two decades, Heterodoxy provided a lively environment for feminists to share their ideas. It was this group, under the leadership of Marie Jenney Howe, that called the first mass meeting on feminism, held in New York City's Cooper Union Hall on February 17, 1914. The range of ideas embodied in feminism, as well as the interest of many sympathetic males in the movement, is revealed in the following newspaper account.

Talk on Feminism Stirs Great Crowd (1914)

What is Feminism? Twelve speakers, six men and six women, attempted to answer the question in Cooper Union last night in what was called the first feminist mass meeting ever had. The People's Institute made the arrangements for the discussion. The auditorium was filled almost to capacity, and it was remarked that there were more men than women in the audience. The applause was frequent, and hearty. Many definitions of feminism were given, differing in details, but agreeing in the essential fact that the movement sought freedom for women.

There was Rose Young, who said that feminism to her was "some fight, some fate, and some fun," and there was Edwin Bjorkman, who said that feminism meant "that woman shall have the same right as man to be different." Henrietta Rodman said that when feminism was the vogue

Source: *New York Times*, February 18, 1914, 2.

women would lose such privileges as "the right to alimony and the right to be supported all of her life," and Will Irwin added that feminism would disprove "all of the bunk talked about the home and fireside."

George Middletown considered the subject of feminism from several points of view. He said in part:

"Feminism means trouble: trouble means agitation; agitation means movement; movement means life; life means adjustment and readjustment—so does feminism. Feminism is not a femaleness with fewer petticoats; it does not seek to crinoline men. It asks [for] a new fashion in the social garments of each. Feminism is a spiritual attitude. It recognizes that men and women are made of the same soul stuff. It places this above biological bosh.

"In another aspect feminism is an educational ideal. It asks that children be educated according to temperament and not according to maleness and femaleness. It asks that a girl be educated for work and not for sex. Feminism seeks to change social opinion toward the sex relation, not to advocate license, but to recognize liberty."

Rose Young, when her turn to speak came, said:

"To me feminism means that woman wants to develop her own womanhood. It means that she wants to push on to the finest, fullest, freest expression of herself. She wants to be an individual. When you mention individualism to some people they immediately see a picture of original sin, but the freeing of the individuality of woman does not mean original sin; it means the finding of her own soul.

"The first thing that we have to overcome is custom and convention, and the common attitude of mind, and then this fear of individuality will pass away. We have to compel conviction that woman is a human being."

This idea of the assertion of individuality by woman was dwelt upon by Edwin Bjorkman. He said that feminism meant that "woman should have the right to be a full-fledged personality and not merely a social unit."

"We want woman to have the same right as man to experiment with her own life," he said. . . .

"Feminism means revolution, and I am a revolutionist," said Frances Perkins.° "I believe in revolutions as a principle. It does good to everybody."

Max Eastman, as his contribution to the discussion, said:

"Feminism is the name for the newly discovered and highly surprising fact that it is just as important for a woman to be happy as a man. And one woman will be happy by going out and seeking adventures of her own and another will be happy staying at home and thinking about babies and baked beans. Both should be allowed to do what they want to do. There'll be a great deal more fun for everybody when women are universally active and free and independent."

Marie Jenney Howe, who was the Chairman of the meeting, said that feminism was "the entire woman movement," and she added that while men were held in prison by convention, custom, and tradition, "women were confined to one room in the prison and had to watch the men walk about in the corridors in comparative freedom."

"Feminism is simply part of the great world fight for freedom and justice and equality, and might better be called humanism," said George Creel.

"The basis of feminism, the basis of suffragism, the basis of all the modern movements making for progress lies in the labor movement," said Mrs. Frank Cochran, the only speaker who used her husband's name.

° At the time of the meeting a New York social reformer, Frances Perkins in 1933 became the first woman to head a federal cabinet office.

ALTHOUGH FEMINISTS most often published in radical journals, their writings also appeared in mass magazines. In 1913 *McClure's Magazine* noted that "no movement of this century is more significant or more deep-rooted than the movement to readjust the social position of women," and began a "department for women" to "represent the ideas of the more advanced thinkers of the feminist movement." High-profile suffrage activist and lawyer Inez Milholland wrote the articles. The following is an extract from her second essay.

INEZ MILHOLLAND
The Changing Home (1913)

PROPERTY RIGHTS IN WOMEN ARE DISAPPEARING

. . . The past fifty years, with their key discoveries in science, have unlocked the secrets of earth and air, have given us modern production and distribution, have brought the ends of the world together in an entirely new sort of neighborhood, with the beginnings of a new common understanding—have, in a word, expanded man's thought, feeling, and social power as the explorations of the sixteenth and seventeenth centuries expanded his geography.

These discoveries and the resultant harnessing of newly discovered natural laws, have made possible the "social surplus" of which the Socialists say so much. For the first time in human history, the race can produce enough of the necessaries of life to go round. While we have not yet arrived at such a fair distribution, the tendency of modern social and political effort is distinctly taking that direction all over the world.

And, coincidentally with the struggles of workers everywhere for a share in the fruits of life under the new conditions, we see woman, with individual economic independence at last in sight, stirring and striving to free herself from

SOURCE: "The Changing Home," *McClure's Magazine*, March 1913, 206–19.

property-subjection to man in industry, and in marriage itself.

THE HOME HAS BEEN REMOVED FROM THE WOMAN

It is still said, in some quarters, that "woman's place is the home"; but it is becoming increasingly difficult to understand the phrase. For the home, in the earlier sense of the term, has been pretty effectually removed from the woman. In the traditional idyllic home which apparently still exists in the fancy of many conservative thinkers (but which probably never existed as generally as these thinkers imagine), woman spun, wove, and made clothing, milked and churned, put up foods, and so on. Her duties were many, arduous, sometimes dignified and important. Her "sphere" was defined with some clearness. Within it she exercised a real authority. In addition, she bore and reared children. And she found time for all!

To-day, if woman is to "go back to the home" in the only sense that the phrase can possibly carry, she will have to follow it into the canning factory, the packing-house, the cotton and woolen mills, the clothing factory, the up-State dairy, the railroad that handles the dairy products, the candy factory, etc. As a matter of fact, she has already been forced in considerable numbers to follow these tasks into their new industrial environment. But, whereas in the home she had some authority and certain partnership rights, in industry she has no voice except as she can make herself heard through the medium of a trade union or (less directly) of the vote.

So the "home" has, in part, been removed, and the eight million women actually engaged in industry to-day indicate with some force that woman has had to go with it. To order her "back to the home" is, therefore, nonsense. It is like ordering the cab-driver, displaced by the taxicab chauffeur, back to the stage-coach to compete with the railroad.

MARRIAGE BY INTIMIDATION

No one, of course,—least of all the advanced feminist thinkers,—questions the imperative beauty and value of romantic love. Indeed, the hope is that marriage, far from being undermined or destroyed, can be made real and lasting. . . . What thoughtful women are distinctly beginning to object to is the time-honored belief that it is decent for a woman to bestow her sex, legally or illegally, in exchange for a guarantee of food, shelter, and clothing.

That millions of women have had to do precisely this in the past is too commonly known to be gainsaid. They have had to do it sometimes because there was no other way in which they could live according to reasonable standards of what living is, and sometimes, often, because the prevailing masculine ideal of the ornamental comparatively useless woman has withheld from them the training and equipment that would have enabled them to cope with life as it is.

But, now that the changing economic conditions have forced woman in some degree to meet life squarely and directly, and at the same time have begun to make some sort of economic independence seem possible for almost any individual, she is making the interesting discovery that she can in some measure subsist without throwing herself, legally or illicitly, on the mercy of the individual man. Accordingly, she is pressing and striving to increase her economic opportunity, even to gain some real economic authority; and at the same time she is getting a grip on the lever of political power. . . .

THE NEW POWER OF THE WAGE-EARNING WOMAN

. . . [T]hat this new condition carries with it a new social attitude toward divorce goes without saying. The promise of the new relationship between man and woman is that the deeply rooted, perennial mating instinct may begin to work more spontaneously and finely in conditions permitting freer choice. It is beginning to be recognized that real marriage can not be brought into existence through fear of want or through other social intimidation. . . .

A mere casual survey of current books and plays makes it evident that a calm, intelligent study of these elemental facts is rapidly taking the place of our traditional attitude of outward conformity tempered by inner panic. We are beginning to perceive that we can not successfully fit all of life into a preconceived mold; that our real task is to try, soberly and patiently, to learn what this strange substance we call life really is.

THE THEME OF SEXUAL LIBERATION, evident in Milholland's *McClure's* article, appeared repeatedly in feminist writing and was often accompanied by a call for the legalization of birth control. In this article from the radical journal *Birth Control Review*, Crystal Eastman discusses the far-reaching implications of women's control over reproduction. Eastman's concern for economic as well as sexual liberation reflects both her socialist and feminist sensibilities.

CRYSTAL EASTMAN
Birth Control in the Feminism Program (1918)

Feminism means different things to different people, I suppose. To women with a taste for politics and reform it means the right to vote and hold office. To women physically strong and adventuresome it means freedom to enter all kinds of athletic contests and games, to compete with men in aviation, to drive racing cars, . . . to enter dangerous trades, etc. To many it means social and sex freedom, doing away with exclusively feminine virtues. To most of all it means economic freedom,—not the ideal economic freedom dreamed of by revolutionary socialism, but such economic freedom as it is possible for a human being to achieve under the existing system of competitive production and distribution,—in short such freedom to choose one's way of making a living as men now enjoy, and definite economic rewards for one's work when it happens to be "home-making." This is to me the central fact of feminism. Until women learn to want economic independence, i.e., the ability to earn their own living independently of husbands, fathers, brothers or lovers,—and until they work out a way to get this independence without denying themselves the joys of love and motherhood, it seems to me feminism has no roots. Its manifestations are often delightful and stimulating but they are sporadic, they effect no lasting change in the attitude of men to women, or of women to themselves.

Whether other feminists would agree with me that the economic is the fundamental aspect of feminism, I don't know. But on this side we are surely agreed, that Birth Control is an elementary essential in all aspects of feminism. Whether we are the special followers of Alice Paul, or Ruth Law, or Ellen Key, or Olive Schreiner, we must all be followers of Margaret Sanger. Feminists are not nuns. That should be established. We want to love and to be loved, and most of us want children, one or two at least. But we want our love to be joyous and free—not clouded with ignorance and fear. And we want our children to be deliberately, eagerly called into being, when we are at our best, not crowded upon us in times of poverty and weakness. We want this precious sex knowledge not just for ourselves, the conscious feminists; we want it for all the millions of unconscious feminists that swarm the earth,—we want it for all women.

Life is a big battle for the complete feminist even when she can regulate the size of her family. Women who are creative, or who have administrative gifts, or business ability, and who are ambitious to achieve and fulfill themselves in these lines, if they also have the normal desire to be mothers, must make up their minds to be a sort of supermen, I think. They must develop greater powers of concentration, a stronger will to "keep at it," a more determined ambition than men of equal gifts, in order to make up for the time and energy and thought and devotion that child-bearing and rearing, even in the most "advanced" families, seems inexorably to demand of the mother. But if we add to this handicap complete uncertainty as to when children may come, how often they come or how many there shall be, the thing becomes impossible. I would almost say that the whole structure of the feminist's dream of society rests upon the rapid extension of scientific knowledge about birth control.

SOURCE: Blanche Wiesen Cook, ed., *Crystal Eastman on Women and Revolution* (New York: Oxford University Press, 1978), 46–49.

QUESTIONS FOR ANALYSIS

1. What role does women's economic independence play in feminist thought?
2. Why is birth control so crucial to the transformation in women's lives that feminists anticipated?
3. What changes in relationships and marriage did feminists promote?
4. Feminists were self-consciously "modern." What evidence do you see for this sensibility in these documents?

DOCUMENTS

African American Women
and the Great Migration

Between 1910 and 1930 African American men and women left the rural South in extraordinary numbers, some for cities in their own region but many more for urban centers in the North and Midwest. This move profoundly shaped the black experience. The number of women migrants nearly equaled that of men. For both men and women the impulse to leave stemmed from a combination of factors, with the lure of jobs in the North during the war and postwar years particularly important.

THE EXPERIENCE OF MIGRATION

Poor African Americans left behind few private papers for the historical record, so historians are fortunate to be able to turn to letters that southern migrants wrote to black newspapers like the *Chicago Defender* and the *Atlanta Journal*, as well as to letters written to potential employers and friends and family back home. The letters reproduced here were collected in 1919 and published in the *Journal of Negro History*.° Letter A, written by an Anniston, Alabama, man in 1917, makes it clear that the Great Migration was a family affair and that women expected to join men in getting paid work, a point made in many men's letters.

Women's letters reveal a variety of concerns. A wife hopes to find out about work for her family in letter B, which also suggests the desperate conditions of poor southern blacks and their fear of reprisal from southern whites for leaving. Her unwillingness to "say more" makes it frustrating for the historian. Would a franker letter refer to the sexual assault so many black women experienced? Or to her fear for the men of her family and the omnipresent threat of violence or lynching? More commonly, women who wrote concentrated on economic issues and detailed their own work experience and skills, which were usually in some form of domestic service (letter C).

° The names of the writers are not provided in these letters because the editor wished to protect their privacy and perhaps to prevent identification by whites from their hometowns.

Women who wrote letters seeking jobs expected to find familiar work as domestics, but as wartime labor shortages increased, factories began to hire African American women in manufacturing jobs. Letter D details work in a meatpacking house. Written by a woman who had already migrated to Chicago to a friend back home, encouraging letters like this helped fuel further migration.

A. Letter from Anniston, Alabama (April 26, 1917)

Dear Sir:
Seeing in the Chicago Defender that you wanted men to work and that you are not to rob them of their half loaf; interested me very much. So much that I am inquiring for a job; one for my wife, auntie and myself. My wife is a seamster, my auntie a cook I do janitor work or common labor. We all will do the work you give us. Please reply early.

B. Letter from McCoy, Louisiana (April 16, 1917)

Dear Editor [of the *Chicago Defender*]:
I have been takeing your wonderful paper and I have saved [each edition] from the first I have received and my heart is upset night and day. I am praying every day to see some one that I may get a pass [a free railway ticket] for me, my child and husband I have a daughter 17 who can work well and myself. please sir direct me to the place where I may be able to see the parties that I and my family whom have read the defender so much until they are anxious to come dear editor we are working people but we cant hardly live here I would say more but we are back in the jungles and we have to lie low but please sir answer and I pray you give me a homeward consolation as we haven't money enough to pay our fares.

C. Letter from Biloxi, Mississippi (April 27, 1917)

Dear Sir:
I would like to get in touch with you a pece of advise I am unable to under go hard work as I have a fracture ancle but in the mene time I am able to help my selft a great dele. I am a good cook and can give good recmendation can serve in small family that has light work, if I could get something in that line I could work my daughters a long with me. She is 21 years and I have a husband all so and he is a fireman and want a positions and too small boy need to be in school now if you all see where there is some open for me that I may be able too better my condission anser at once and we will com as we are in a land of starvation. From a willen workin woman. I hope that you will healp me as I want to get out of this land of surfing [suffering] I no there is som thing that I can do here there is nothing for me to do I may be able to get in some furm where I don't have to stand on my feet all day I don't know just whah but I hope the Lord will find a place now let me here from you all at once.

SOURCE: *Journal of Negro History*, October 1919, 329, 426, 457–58, and July 1919, 318, 333.

D. *Letter from Chicago, Illinois* (undated)

My dear Sister:

I was agreeably surprised to hear from you and to hear from home. I am well and thankful to say I am doing well. The weather and everything else was a surprise to me when I came. I got here in time to attend one of the greatest revivals in the history of my life—over 500 people joined the church. We had a Holy Ghost shower. You know I like to have run wild. It was snowing some nights and if you didnt hurry you could not get standing room. Please remember me kindly to any who ask of me. The people are rushing here by the thousands and I know if you come and rent a big house you can get all the roomers you want. You write me exactly when you are coming. I am not keeping house yet I am living with my brother and his wife. My son is in California but will be home soon. He spends his winter in California. I can get a nice place for you to stop until you can look around and see what you want. I am quite busy. I work in Swifts packing Co. in the sausage department. My daughter and I work for the same company—We get $1.50 a day and we pack so many sausages we dont have much time to play but it is a matter of a dollar with me and I feel that God made the path and I am walking therein.

Tell your husband work is plentiful here and he wont have to loaf if he want to work. . . .Well goodbye from your sister in Christ.

P.S. My brother moved the week after I came. When you fully decide to come write me and let me know what day you expect to leave and over what road and if I dont meet you I will have some one ther to meet you and look after you. I will send you a paper as soon as one come along they send out extras two and three times a day.

AFRICAN AMERICAN WOMEN AND WORLD WAR I

THE WAR YEARS OPENED UP MORE WORK OPPORTUNITIES as the following essay by Alice Dunbar-Nelson, the Women's National Council of Defense field representative for black women, indicates. Primarily designed to praise the contributions of black women to the war effort, the essay mostly concerns middle-class black women volunteering in the Red Cross or Young Women's Christian Association or raising money for war bonds. In this passage, however, Dunbar-Nelson summarizes the impact of migration and war on women's job opportunities. The widow of poet Paul Dunbar, Dunbar-Nelson was already an important author when this essay was published. She went on to become one of the founding figures of the Harlem Renaissance (see pp. 534–35).

ALICE DUNBAR-NELSON
Come Out of the Kitchen, Mary (1919)

For generations colored women have been working the fields of the South. They have been the domestic servants of both the South and the North, accepting the positions of personal service open to them. Hard work and unpleasant work has been their lot, but they have been almost entirely excluded from our shops and factories. Tradition and race prejudice have played the largest part in their exclusion. The tardy development of the South and the failure of the colored woman to demand industrial opportunities have added further values [factors]. Clearly, also, two hundred years of slavery and fifty years of industrial boycott in both the North and the South, following the Civil War, have done little to encourage or to develop industrial aptitudes. For these reasons, the colored women have not entered the ranks of the industrial army in the past.

But war expediency, for a time at least, partially opened the door of industry to them. . . .

"Come out of the kitchen, Mary," was the slogan of the colored woman in war time. She doffed her cap and apron and donned her overalls. Some States, such as Maryland and Florida, specialized in courses in motor mechanics and automobile driving. The munitions factories took the girls in gladly. Grim statistics prove that their scale of wages were definitely lower than a man's doing the same work, and sad to say a considerable fraction below that of white girls in the same service, although Delaware reports some very high-priced, skilled ammunition testers, averaging seven to twelve dollars a day. The colored girls blossomed out as switchboard operators, stock takers, wrappers, elevator operators, subway porters, ticket choppers, track-walkers, trained signalers, yard-walkers. They went into every possible kind of factory devoted to the production of war materials, from the most dangerous posts in munitions plants to the delicate sewing in aeroplane factories. Colored girls and colored women drove motor trucks, unloaded freight cars, dug ditches, handled hardware around shipways and hardware houses, packed boxes. They struggled with the discomforts of ice and fertilizing plants. They learned the delicate intricacies of all kinds of machines, and the colored woman running the elevator or speeding a railroad on its way by signals was a common sight. . . .

A strange thing about . . . [women's industrial work] was that there was no perceptible racial disintegration and the colored women bore their changed status and higher economic independence with much more equanimity than white women on a corresponding scale of living. The reason for this may perhaps be found in the fact that the colored woman had a heritage of 300 years of work back of her. Her children were used to being left to shift for themselves; her home was used to being cared for after sundown. The careful supervision of the War Work Council and the Council of Defense over the health and hours of the woman in industry averted the cataclysm of lowered vitality and eventual unfitness for maternity.

The possible economic effect of this entrance into the unknown fields of industry on the part of the colored woman will be that when pre-war conditions return and she is displaced by men and is forced to make her way back into domestic service, the latter will be placed on a strictly business basis and the vocation of housekeeping and home-making will be raised to the dignity of a profession.

SOURCE: Alice Dunbar-Nelson, "Negro Women in War Work," in *The American Negro in the World War* (1919; repr., New York: Arno Press, 1969), 394–97.

Although Alice Dunbar-Nelson seemed resigned to black women's return to domestic work after the war—if perhaps on better terms—black sociologist Forrester B. Washington was far more openly critical of this likely outcome.

FORRESTER B. WASHINGTON
The Last to Be Employed . . . the First to Be Released (1919)

Everyone is aware that almost as soon as the armistice was signed, the cancellation of war orders began, and factories engaged in production dependent upon the continuation of hostilities commenced to release their women employe[e]s. But it is not generally known that in the majority of plants in Chicago the first persons to be released were colored women. If only those were discharged who had taken soldiers' positions, it is doubtful if any serious distress would be caused the colored people; but the fact is that many colored people who had obtained their positions as a result of the labor vacuum caused by the cessation of immigration a year or two before we entered the war are now being discharged as well as those hired more recently. The history of the experiences of colored women in the present war should make fair-minded Americans blush with shame. They have been universally the last to be employed. They were the marginal workers of industry all through the war. They have been given, with few exceptions, the most undesirable and lowest paid work, and now that the war is over they are the first to be released.

It is especially significant that Chicago, which now has the third largest negro population in the country, should be the most inconsiderate in its treatment of the colored woman worker. As a matter of fact, the country as a whole has not treated the colored working woman according to the spirit of democracy. The essential difference between Chicago and elsewhere is that in the other cities the colored woman made some little progress into the skilled and so-called semiskilled industries. In Chicago, while she did get into many occupations into which she had never gained entrance before, they were only the marginal occupations. She became the bus girl in the dairy lunches, the elevator girl, the ironer in the laundry, etc. Now she is being discharged rapidly from even these menial and low-paid positions. . . .

The American employer in his treatment of colored women wage-earners should square himself with that democratic ideal of which he made so much during the war. During those perilous times white and black women looked alike in the factory when they were striving to keep the industry of the country up to 100 per cent production, just as white and black soldiers looked alike going over the top to preserve the honor of the country. Moreover, organized labor cannot afford to sink below the high standard to which it rose during the war.

If either the American employer or the American laborer continues to deny the colored woman an opportunity to make a decent living, the Bolshevik cannot be blamed for proclaiming their affirmation of democratic principles a sham.

SOURCE: Forrester B. Washington, "Reconstruction and the Colored Woman," *Life and Labor 9*, no. 1 (Jan. 1919): 3–7, reproduced in Eric Arnesen, *Black Protest and the Great Migration: A Brief History with Documents* (Boston: Bedford, 2003), 151–53.

QUESTIONS FOR ANALYSIS

1. What insights do these documents give you about African American women's motivation for migration? About their subsequent experiences in the workforce?

2. What advantages did these women find in the North? What challenges and hardships?

3. Judging from these documents, how would you characterize the impact of World War I on African American women?

4. What comparisons can you draw between women's experiences during the Great Migration and the turn-of-the-century wave of European immigration discussed in Chapter 7?

NOTES

1. Nancy S. Dye, "Introduction," in Nancy S. Dye and Noralee Frankel, eds., *Gender, Class, Race, and Reform in the Progressive Era* (Lexington: University Press of Kentucky, 1991), 1.

2. Lynn Wiener, *From Working Girl to Working Mother: The Female Labor Force in the United States, 1820–1980* (Chapel Hill: University of North Carolina Press, 1985), 4.

3. Estelle B. Freedman, *No Turning Back: The History of Feminism and the Future of Women* (New York: Ballantine Books, 2002), 162.

4. Nancy Cott, *The Grounding of Modern Feminism* (New Haven: Yale University Press, 1987), 350.

5. Barbara Mayer Wertheimer, *We Were There: The Story of Working Women in America* (New York: Pantheon, 1977), 271.

6. Elizabeth Anne Payne, *Reform Labor and Feminism: Margaret Dreier Robins and the Women's Trade Union League* (Urbana: University of Illinois Press, 1988), 48.

7. Meredith Tax, *The Rising of the Women: Feminist Solidarity and Class Conflict, 1880–1917* (New York: Monthly Review Press, 1980), 222.

8. Ibid., 235.

9. Susan B. Anthony and Ida H. Harper, eds., *History of Woman Suffrage* (Rochester, NY: Susan B. Anthony, 1902), 4:178.

10. An early use of this term can be found in Seth Koven and Sonya Michel, eds., *Mothers of a New World: Maternalist Politics and the Origins of Welfare States* (New York: Routledge, 1993).

11. Alice Kessler-Harris, *Out to Work: A History of Wage-Earning Women in the United States* (New York: Oxford University Press, 1982), 198.

12. Darlene Clark Hine and Kathleen Thompson, *A Shining Thread of Hope: The History of Black Women in America* (New York: Broadway Books, 1998), 202.

13. Ruth Spack, "Dis/engagement: Zitkala-Ša's Letters to Carlos Montezuma, 1901–1902," *Melus* 26 (April 2001): 173.

14. Rebecca Mead, *How the Vote Was Won: Woman Suffrage in the Western United States, 1868–1914* (New York: New York University Press, 2004), 123–24.

15. Paula Giddings, *When and Where I Enter* (New York: William Morrow, 1984), 126.

16. Dawn Keetley and John Pettegrew, eds., *Public Women, Public Words: A Documentary History of American Feminism* (Madison, WI: Madison House, 1997–2002), 2:157.

17. Ibid., 2:164.

18. Christine Stansell, *American Moderns: Bohemian New York and the Creation of a New Century* (New York: Metropolitan Books, 2000), 228.

19. Rheta Childe Dorr, *A Woman of Fifty* (New York: Funk and Wagnalls, 1924), 286–69.

20. John D'Emilio and Estelle B. Freedman, *Intimate Matters: a History of Sexuality in America* (New York: Harper and Row, 1988), 213.

21. Ibid., p. 322.

22. Harriet Human Alonso, *Peace as a Women's Issue: History of the U.S. Movement for World Peace and Women's Rights* (Syracuse: Syracuse University Press, 1993), 61.

23. Mary Heaton Vorse, *A Footnote to Folly: Reminiscences of Mary Heaton Vorse* (New York: Farrar & Rinehart, 1935), 82.

24. Alfreda M. Duster, ed., *Crusade for Justice: The Autobiography of Ida B. Wells* (Chicago: University of Chicago Press, 1970), 370.

25. Carrie Chapman Catt, "Organized Womanhood," *Woman Voter*, April 1917, 9.

26. Harriot Stanton Blatch, *Mobilizing Woman Power* (New York: Woman's Press, 1918), 88–90.

27. Maurine Greenwald, *Women, War, and Work: The Impact of World War I on Women Workers in the United States* (Westport, CT: Greenwood Press, 1980), 24.

28. Quoted in Eleanor Flexner, *Century of Struggle: The Woman's Rights Movement in the United States* (Cambridge: Belknap Press, 1959), 291.

29. Woodrow Wilson, Fourteen Points speech, in Arthur S. Link et al., eds., *The Papers of Woodrow Wilson* (Princeton, NJ: Princeton University Press, 1984), 45:536.

30. Flexner, *Century of Struggle*, 336.

31. Susan Glenn, *Daughters of the Shtetl: Life and Labor in the Immigrant Generation* (Ithaca: Cornell University Press, 1991), 165.

32. Nan Enstad, *Ladies of Labor, Girls of Adventure: Working Women, Popular Culture, and Labor Politics at the Turn of the Twentieth Century* (New York: Columbia University Press, 1999), 84–160.

33. Harriot Stanton Blatch and Alma Lutz, *Challenging Years: The Memoirs of Harriot Stanton Blatch* (New York: G. P. Putnam's Sons, 1940), 129.

34. Sarah J. Moore, "Making a Spectacle of Suffrage: The National Woman Suffrage Pageant, 1913," *Journal of American Culture* 20 (1997): 89–103.

35. Linda J. Lumsden, "Beauty and the Beasts: Significance of Press Coverage of the 1913 National Suffrage Parade," *Journalism and Mass Culture Quarterly* 77 (2000): 595.

36. Flexner, *Century of Struggle*, 269.

37. Linda J. Lumsden, "Beauty and the Beasts: Significance of Press Coverage of the 1913 National Suffrage Parade," *Journalism and Mass Communication Quarterly* 77 (2000): 595, 597.

38. Cott, *Grounding of Modern Feminism*, 36.

39. Ibid., 51.

SUGGESTED REFERENCES

General Works   No period in U.S. women's history has generated greater and more varied scholarship than 1900–1920. For a general overview on women and Progressivism, see the collection edited by Noralee Frankel and Nancy S. Dye, *Gender, Class, Race, and Reform in the Progressive Era* (1991); and Dorothy and Carl J. Schneider, *American Women in the Progressive Era, 1990–1920* (1993).

Women Workers   Overviews of the history of working women include Claudia Goldin, *Understanding the Gender Gap: An Economic History of American Women* (1992); Alice Kessler Harris, *Out to Work: A History of Wage-Earning Women in the United States,* 20th anniv. ed. (2003); and Leslie Woodcock Tentler, *Wage-Earning Women: Industrial Work and Family Life in the United States, 1900–1930* (1979). In *Daughters of the Shtetl: Life and Labor in the Immigrant Generation* (1991), Susan A. Glenn explores Jewish and Italian immigrant women in the garment industry and addresses the sources of their militancy. Nan Enstad brings the tools of cultural history to bear on women's labor history in *Ladies of Labor, Girls of Adventure: Working Women, Popular Culture, and Labor Politics at the Turn of the Twentieth Century* (1999). Eileen Boris examines wage earning in domestic settings in *Home to Work: Motherhood and the Politics of Industrial Homework in the United States* (1994).

On women in the clerical field, see Sharon Harman Strom, *Beyond the Typewriter: Gender, Class, and the Origins of Modern American Office Work, 1900–1920* (1992). On women in the legal profession, see Virginia Drachman, *Sisters in Law: Women Lawyers in Modern American History* (1998). Susan M. Reverby surveys the nursing profession in *Ordered to Care: The Dilemma of American Nursing, 1850–1945* (1987). Rosalind Rosenberg looks at the first generation of professional women social scientists in *Beyond Separate Spheres: Intellectual Roots of Modern Feminism* (1982). Stephanie Shaw has written a general history of black professional women workers in the Jim Crow era in *What a Woman Ought to Be and Do* (1995). Darlene Clark Hine considers the history of black women in nursing in *Black Women in White: Racial Conflict and Cooperation in the Nursing Profession, 1890–1950* (1989).

Women's labor activism in the Progressive era is well studied. Meredith Tax's *The Rising of the Women: Feminist Solidarity and Class Conflict, 1880–1917* (2001) provided the title for a section of Chapter 8. David Von Drehle offers fresh insights into the New York City Triangle Shirtwaist Company fire in *Triangle: The Fire That Changed America* (2003). Also see Annelise Orleck, *Common Sense and a Little Fire: Women and Working-Class Politics in the United States, 1900–1965* (1995). The Women's Trade Union League is the subject of Nancy Schrom Dye's *As Equals and as Sisters: Feminism, the Labor Movement, and the Women's Trade Union League of New York* (1980).

Social Housekeeping   The term "female dominion" used for women's social reform activism in this period comes from Robyn Muncy, *Creating a Female Dominion in American Reform, 1890–1935* (1991). On "maternalism," see the collection compiled by Seth Koven and Sonya Michel, *Mothers of a New World: Maternalist Politics and the Origins of Welfare States* (1993). Two studies of child welfare programs in this period are Linda Gordon, *Pitied but Not Entitled: Single Mothers and the History of Welfare, 1890–1935* (1994); and Molly Ladd-Taylor, *Mother-Work: Women, Child Welfare, and the State, 1890–1930* (1994). Mothers' pensions are the subject of Joanne Goodwin's study, *Gender and the Politics of Welfare Reform: Mothers' Pensions in Chicago, 1911–1929* (1997). Protective labor legislation is one of the few aspects of U.S. women's history that has been examined in a comparative historical context; see Ulla Wikander, Alice Kessler-Harris, and Jane Lewis, eds., *Protecting Women: Labor Legislation in Europe, the United States, and Australia, 1880–1920* (1995). Vivien Hart, *Bound By Our Constitution: Women, Workers and the Minimum Wage* (1994), also uses comparative tools.

For women and political parties, Melanie Gustafson has written a comprehensive history of *Women and the Republican Party, 1854–1924* (2001). (There is no comparable history of women and the Democratic Party.) See Mari Jo Buhle's *Women and American Socialism, 1870–1920* (1981) for coverage of the American Socialist Party.

On African American women in the Progressive era, see Cynthia Neverdon-Morton, *Afro-American Women of the South and the Advancement of the Race, 1895–1925* (1989); also Jacqueline Anne Rouse, *Lugenia Burns Hope: Black Southern Reformer* (1989). Much of the material on this subject is in article form. Important anthologies include Vicki Ruiz and Ellen Carol DuBois, eds., *Unequal Sisters: A Multicultural Reader in U.S. Women's History,* 3rd ed. (2000); Sharon Harley and Rosalyn Terborg Penn, eds., *The Afro-American Woman's Struggles and Images* (1978); and Darlene Clark Hine et al., *"We Specialize in the Wholly Impossible": A Reader in Black Women's History* (1995). On Native American activism during the Progressive era, see Frederick Hoxie, *Talking Back to Civilization: Indian Voices from the Progressive Era* (2001). The Society for American Indians is examined in Hazel Hertzberg, *The Search for an American Indian Identity: Modern Pan-Indian Movements* (1971), and Lucy Maddox, *Citizen Indians: Native American Intellectuals, Race & Reform* (2005).

Woman Suffrage   The history of woman suffrage is another well-studied topic. For an unequaled overview of this complex subject, see Eleanor Flexner and Ellen Fitzpatrick, *Century of Struggle: The Woman's Rights Movement in the United States,* enl. ed. (1996). Additional scholarship is found in Jean Baker, ed., *Votes for Women: The Struggle for Suffrage Revisited* (2002), and Marjorie Spruill Wheeler, ed., *One Woman, One Vote: Rediscovering the Woman Suffrage Movement* (1995). Sara Hunter Graham examines the National American Woman Suffrage Association in *Woman Suffrage and the New Democracy* (1996). For the radical wing of militant suffragists, see Linda G. Ford's *Iron-Jawed Angels: The Suffrage Militancy of the National Woman's Party, 1912–1920* (1991); also see Christine Lunardini, *From Equal Suffrage to Equal Rights: Alice Paul and the National Woman's Party, 1910–1928* (1986). Rosalyn Terborg-Penn considers black women's suffrage involvement in *African American Women in the Struggle for the Vote, 1850–1920* (1998). On the New York suffrage movement, see Ellen Carol DuBois, *Harriot Stanton Blatch and the Winning of Woman Suffrage* (1997). Gayle Gullett focuses on the California movement in *Becoming Citizens: The Emergence and Development of the California Women's Movement, 1880–1911* (2000). On the theatricality of the woman suffrage parades, see Susan A. Glenn, *Female Spectacle: The Theatrical Roots of Modern Feminism* (2000). The anti-suffrage movement is the subject of Susan E. Marshall, *Splintered Sisterhood: Gender and Class in the Campaign against Woman Suffrage* (1997).

The Rise of Feminism   On the feminist movement that emerged in the 1910s, the place to start is Nancy F. Cott, *The Grounding of Modern Feminism* (1987). Christine Stansell considers the Greenwich Village milieu in *American Moderns: Bohemian New York and the Creation of a New Century* (2000). Ellen Kay Trimberger examines one New York feminist marriage of the period in *Intimate Warriors: Portrait of a Modern Marriage, 1899–1944* (1991). Susan Glenn, *Female Spectacle,* and Sharon R. Ullman, *Sex Seen: The Emergence of Modern Sexuality in America* (1997), discuss popular culture and new sexual patterns. On urban working-class women, see Kathy Peiss, *Cheap Amusements: Working Women and Leisure in Turn-of-the-Century New York* (1986), and Joanne J. Meyerowitz, *Women Adrift: Independent Wage Earners in Chicago, 1880–1930* (1988). A general study on the history of sexuality is John D'Emilio and Estelle B. Freedman, *Intimate Matters: a History of Sexuality in America* (1989).

Linda Gordon studies the birth control movement in *The Moral Property of Women: A History of Birth Control Politics in America* (2002). The most recent major biography of Margaret Sanger is Ellen Chesler's *Woman of Valor: Margaret Sanger and the Birth Control Movement in America* (1992). On Charlotte Perkins Gilman, see Ann Lane's biography, *To Herland and Beyond: The Life and Work of Charlotte Perkins Gilman* (1990).

Women and World War I   On the topic of women during World War I, see Maurine W. Greenwald, *Women, War, and Work: The Impact of World War I on Women Workers in the United States* (1980). Carrie Brown's *Rosie's Mom: Forgotten Women Workers of the First World War* (2002) includes extraordinary photographs. Kathleen Kennedy examines female dissenters in this period in *Disloyal Mothers and Scurrilous Citizens: Women and Subversion during World War I* (1999). Harriet Hyman Alonso is the major historian of the women's peace movement; see her *Peace as a Women's Issue: A History of the U.S. Movement for World Peace and Women's Rights* (1993).

On the Great Migration of African Americans in this period, see Elizabeth Clark-Lewis, *Living In, Living Out: African American Domestics and the Great Migration* (1994), and Joe William Trotter Jr., ed., *The Great Migration in Historical Perspective: New Dimensions of Race, Class, and Gender* (1991).

For selected Web sites, please visit the *Through Women's Eyes* book companion site at bedfordstmartins.com/duboisdumenil.

9

Change and Continuity

WOMEN IN PROSPERITY, DEPRESSION, AND WAR, 1920–1945

FROM ONE PERSPECTIVE, WOMEN'S EXPERIENCES IN the period from 1920 to 1945 seem marked more by change than by continuity. Popular culture icons graphically capture the differences between the decades. The young, devil-may-care flapper with her short dress, rouged face, and rolled stockings symbolized the New Woman of the 1920s. Rebelling against the restraint of Victorian womanhood, the flapper eagerly embraced the growing consumer culture, with its emphasis on leisure and materialism, of this largely prosperous era. For the following decade, the most powerful icon is Dorothea Lange's widely reproduced photograph of a migrant mother, who symbolized Americans' dignified suffering as they weathered the devastating economic crisis of the 1930s. The migrant mother embodied, too, the popular assumption that woman's most important role during the Great Depression was an extension of her traditional responsibilities of maintaining the home and family. Images of women during World War II seemingly point in yet a third direction. "Rosie the Riveter"—the cheerful, robust woman in overalls working in the defense industry, taking on new and challenging work to serve her country in time of need—emphasized female independence and strength outside the home.

But although each decade had its distinctive qualities, overarching developments, especially in work and politics, link these seeming disparities into the larger trends in American women's history. In the immediate aftermath of the Nineteenth Amendment, women plunged into the responsibilities of active citizenship and struggled to carve out a base for political power and influence. Female participation in the paid labor market continued to grow, especially with respect to the growing numbers of working women who were also wives and mothers. Finally, cultural expectations for women shifted in two crucially related areas, consumerism and sexuality. Both of these shifts had implications for women's family lives as well. Yet despite these changes in women's lives, another theme also emerges, that of continuity with the past. Racial and ethnic prejudice continued to limit women's opportunities in the workforce and women's access to political influence. And for all women, traditional expectations about women's primary role in the home persisted, serving as the filter through which change would affect their lives.

PROSPERITY DECADE: THE 1920s

Looking on the surface, the 1920s appear to have been a decade of progress and prosperity. Industrial growth and international economic expansion created a society more affluent than ever before. An explosion of consumer goods, from mass-produced cars to gleaming bathroom fixtures and electrical kitchen appliances, helped to transform daily lives and gave women more power and pleasure as consumers. Underlying the bright prosperity of the decade, however, were darker currents. Many Americans continued to live below or near the poverty line. Farm families suffered from low prices and high indebtedness for most of the decade, and many rural women endured harsh, isolated lives. Cities provided more opportunities, but here, too, poor wages and living conditions, especially for Mexican Americans and African Americans, separated the haves from the have nots.

Relatively few commentators in the 1920s delved beneath the surface image of prosperity to analyze the lives of those who did not participate in the boom times. The same superficiality characterized the widely held image of the New Woman. In the popular mind, women had

1933	Prohibition repealed
1935	National Youth Administration (NYA) created
1935	National Labor Relations (Wagner) Act passed
1935	Social Security Act passed
1935	Works Progress Administration created
1935	Congress of Industrial Organizations founded
1936	*United States v. One Package of Japanese Pessaries* legalizes the dissemination of contraceptive information
1936	**Mary McLeod Bethune appointed to head the National Youth Administration's Division of Negro Affairs**
1937	Japan invades China
1937	**Women create the Emergency Brigade in Flint, Michigan, strike**
1938	Fair Labor Standards Act passed
1939	World War II breaks out in Europe
1941	Fair Employment Practices Commission established
1941	United States enters World War II after Japan attacks Pearl Harbor
1942	**Women recruited into war industries**
1942	**Women's Army Corps given formal military status**
1942	Japanese immigrants and their citizen children interned
1942– 1945	**Rationing increases women's domestic responsibilities**
1943	Congress extends the right of naturalization to Chinese immigrants
1945	Harry S. Truman becomes president after Roosevelt's death
1945	United States drops atomic bombs on Hiroshima and Nagasaki
1945	Japan surrenders, ending World War II

become liberated—by the freedom of wartime, by the exercise of the vote, by participation in the workforce, and by experiments with a new sexual morality. The image was an exaggerated generalization of the experience of young, urban, prosperous white women who were glamorized in the popular media. But contemporaries were correct that most women's lives had changed significantly since the nineteenth century, even though the goals of autonomy and equality remained elusive.

The New Woman in Politics

In 1920 women political activists were poised for a great adventure. With the energy they had brought to the suffrage campaign, women from all groups were now prepared to make women's votes count. African American women focused on using the new national amendment to extend suffrage in the South and on lobbying for a federal antilynching law. In 1920 white women formed the League of Women Voters (LWV), which emphasized lobbying, voter education, and get-out-the-vote drives in the overall mission to train women to be good citizens. An astute recognition of the growing importance of national organizations' lobbying efforts in Washington, D.C., led fourteen women's organizations to form the Women's Joint Congressional Committee, with the goal of promoting legislation backed by the member organizations. On the local and state levels, women also pursued their agendas, supporting child and women's labor laws, health and safety legislation, municipal reform, and a broad extension of women's legal rights. The lobbying efforts of these women's groups underline the importance of women activists in pioneering twentieth-century interest-group politics.

In addition to working through their organizations, activist women debated among themselves as to how, and whether, they should act within the Democratic and Republican parties. The argument that women were unsullied by the corruption of political parties had been a common one in the suffrage battle, and many women had grave reservations about working within the established party system. Indeed, like its precursor, the National American Woman Suffrage Association, the LWV was established as a nonpartisan group that refrained from supporting political parties or their candidates. While some former suffragists attempted to exert influence within the Republican and Democratic parties, others followed Alice Paul's lead into the National Woman's Party (NWP). Always a single-issue organization, the NWP focused exclusively on passage of an Equal Rights Amendment (ERA). First introduced in Congress in 1923, the ERA stated: "Men and women shall have equal rights throughout the United States and every place subject to its jurisdiction."

At first glance, the optimism of white women activists seems justified. In 1920 both Democrats and Republicans recognized women's issues in their platforms, presumably taking women at their word that they planned to use their combined votes as a powerful political tool. And they opened up places within the organizational structure of their parties for female members, although the positions granted were rarely equal in terms of power or influence. As the *New York Times* magazine *Current History* summed it up, "Where there is dignity of office but little else, or where there is routine work, little glory, and low pay, men prove willing to admit women to an equal share in the spoils of office."[1] Women became office-holders, although only a handful were elected to the House of Representatives (a high of seven in 1928). Suffrage veteran and newspaper magnate Ruth Hanna McCormick's 1928 effort to become the first woman elected to the Senate was blocked by influential Republicans, including former California Progressive leader Hiram Johnson. But hundreds served at the state level in legislatures and executive positions earmarked as women's jobs, such as secretary of education and secretary of state. Women were more numerous in local governments, in part because many of these positions were nonpartisan and thus seemingly more in keeping with ideas that women should operate "above politics." Despite these inroads, female officeholders generally worked within the context of prevailing assumptions that women should relegate themselves to women's issues, or "municipal housekeeping," the same assumption that limited their ability to wield much power within their political parties.

Women reformers also had mixed success in their lobbying activities. Many states passed laws urged by women activists, including those that expanded women's legal rights and those directed at maternalist social reform, such as child labor laws and wage and hour protective laws for women. At the federal level, the women's lobby saw an early success in the Sheppard-Towner Act of 1921, which gave matching funds for states to provide health care and other services for mothers and children. Yet by the end of the decade, progress had slowed, especially on the national level. The Child Labor Amendment—passionately advocated after the Supreme Court invalidated a second national child labor law in 1921—failed to be ratified, and most national legislation supported by women lobbyists was unsuccessful. Congress cut the Sheppard-Towner Act's appropriations and ended its once-promising program in 1929.

Moreover, the women's rights movement itself was deeply divided as to tactics and goals. By decade's end, many women activists were disillusioned and embittered. Ironically, some of the problems hindering a sustained feminist movement grew out of the success of the suffrage battle. Before national suffrage was achieved, a great many women—equally excluded from this basic right of citizenship—came under the same umbrella of "votes for women." Once the Nineteenth Amendment was ratified, the lines that divided women—class, race, age, ideology—became more significant. By gaining the individual right they had so vigorously sought, they laid the groundwork for the fracturing of female communities. As one activist ruefully put it in 1923, "The American woman's movement, and her interest in great moral and social questions, is splintered into a hundred fragments under as many warring leaders."[2]

This was particularly evident in the ferocious debate over the Equal Rights Amendment (see boxes, "Arguing for the ERA" and "Arguing against the ERA"). Under the leadership of Alice Paul, the NWP focused so exclusively on the ERA as a means of achieving political and economic equality with men that it appropriated the newly coined term "feminism" to refer to its specific agenda. Women

ALICE PAUL
Arguing for the ERA

At the height of the Equal Rights Amendment battle, foes and supporters debated each other in print. In March 1924 the Congressional Digest *featured an exchange between Alice Paul and Mary Van Kleeck, "Is Blanket Amendment Best Method in Equal Rights Campaign?" Here, Paul (1895–1977), founder of the National Woman's Party and foremost supporter of the ERA, argues for the amendment. Why does she think the ERA is so necessary?*

The Woman's Party is striving to remove every artificial handicap placed upon women by law and by custom. In order to remove those handicaps which the law can touch, it is endeavoring to secure the adoption of the Equal Rights Amendment to the United States Constitution. . . .

1. **A National Amendment Is More Inclusive Than State Legislation.**
   The amendment would at one stroke compel both federal and state governments to observe the principle of Equal Rights, for the Federal Constitution is the "supreme law of the land." The amendment would override all existing legislation which denies women Equal Rights with men and would render invalid every future attempt on the part of any legislators or administrators to interfere with these rights.

2. **A National Amendment Is More Permanent Than State Legislation.**
   The national amendment would establish the principle of Equal Rights permanently in our country, in so far as anything can be established permanently by law. Equal Rights measures passed by state legislatures, on the other hand, are subject to reversal by later legislatures.

3. **The Campaign for a National Amendment Unites the Resources of Women, Which Are Divided in Campaigns for State Legislation.**
   In the campaign for a national amendment the strength of the Equal Rights forces is concentrated upon Congress and is therefore more effective than when divided among forty-eight state campaigns.

SOURCE: "Who Won the Debate over the Equal Rights Amendment in the 1920s?" Women and Social Movements in the United States, 1775–2000, Center for the Study of Women and Gender at the State University of New York at Binghamton, http://womhist.binghamton.edu/era/doc16.htm (accessed March 17, 2004).

interested in broader social reform were alarmed at this "blanket amendment," which they feared would undermine the protective labor laws that they had worked so hard to achieve in the states. Although not unsympathetic to the plight of working-class women, ERA supporters countered that such legislation treated women as invalids and could limit their economic opportunity. The controversy revealed differing attitudes about women's nature and the meaning of equality. Social reformers such as Julia Lathrop and Frances Perkins also cared about extending women's legal rights, but they nonetheless stressed the distinctiveness of their sex. They believed that biological attributes justified protective legislation. Moreover, their sense of women's moral superiority and special maternal qualities, rooted in the nineteenth-century ideology of separate spheres, shaped their commitment to social reform.

Other factors besides differences over the ERA would hamstring the development of a strong feminist movement. Young, middle-class white women often seemed more interested in the pleasures of consumption and leisure than in the social commitment involved in pursuing women's rights and social reform. If these women felt both ERA and anti-ERA supporters were quaintly old-fashioned, black women reformers found their white counterparts largely unresponsive to their concerns. This split emerged most concretely at a 1921 NWP meeting, where sixty black women representing the National Association of Colored Women were refused convention time to raise the subject of the failure of southern states to acknowledge the voting rights of black women. Alice Paul insisted that this was a "race issue," not a "woman's issue." The African Americans, led by Addie Hunton, field secretary for the National Association for the Advancement of Colored People (NAACP), countered by reminding the convention that "five million women in the United States cannot be denied their rights without all the women of the United States feeling the effect of that denial. No women are free until all women are free."[3] Although this and other setbacks in the effort to secure the vote in the South led African American women to de-emphasize the voting issue, they persisted in their broad agenda of improving the lives of all African Americans; in particular, they continued their antilynching activities by working for federal legislation and even, in some cases, forging alliances with southern white women. Though some women could come together in interracial cooperation, the limited vision of white leaders such as Paul as to what constituted "women's issues" shut off possibilities for a broader, more inclusive conception of a feminist movement.

While the difficulties women reformers faced arose in part from women's disunity, a far more serious problem was the decade's conservative political climate. Observers in the 1920s, citing declining overall voting participation during the decade (roughly half of those eligible voted), assumed that women's nonvoting accounted for the decline. With only sparse data of voting by sex available, many historians have echoed this assumption. More recent studies, however, maintain that women's participation in elections varied significantly by location and by election. Women in states that only recently had enfranchised them seem to have participated in fewer numbers than those living in states such as California, where women had longer experience with the electoral process. Notably, men's voting

MARY VAN KLEECK
Arguing against the ERA

Mary Van Kleeck (1883–1972), a noted labor reformer who had served as the first head of the Women's Bureau in the U.S. Department of Labor, was the director of industrial studies at the Russell Sage Foundation. Like other activists concerned about women workers, she adamantly opposed the ERA because of its perceived threat to protective labor laws for women. Why does she think the ERA would be so damaging?

We hold that many important steps toward the goal of removing all sex-prejudice are beyond the reach of law and would be unaffected by this amendment. . . .

   We believe that if this amendment were passed many separate statutes in state and in nation would be required to put its intent into effect. These statutes, we are convinced by experience, can be enacted without any constitutional amendment. . . . The time taken to enact and ratify the amendment would only postpone the passage of these laws which we must have anyway.

   . . . If this vague provision for equal rights for men and women were to be included in the Constitution, the time-consuming efforts of judges to define its meaning for each new statute may be expected to nullify for the next century the effect of present and future laws designed to open up larger opportunities to women. Some of our laws which do not apply alike to men and therefore appear to perpetuate legal discriminations

decreased in this period as well, following a long-standing trend of declining engagement in partisan politics. Jane Addams ruefully commented in 1924 that the question should not be "Is Woman Suffrage Failing?", but rather, "is suffrage failing?"[4] That both men and women were failing to vote in large numbers points to a political climate of disaffected or uninterested citizenry, and it is this broader context of American politics, not women's failures as voters, that offers the most compelling explanation for the difficulties women reformers faced.[5]

   A related problem was a political climate hostile to reform that made it impossible to sustain the prewar enthusiasm for progressive measures. On the national scene, the Republicans dominated the White House and Congress, and, reflecting in part the party's ties to corporate business interests, resisted efforts to expand federal regulatory powers. Federal prohibition of alcohol, following ratification of the Eighteenth Amendment in 1919, further increased many Americans' wariness of intrusive social reforms. Prohibition met with vigorous opposition. Many Americans resented and circumvented the law, and others worried that the

against women — such as mothers' pensions and certain provisions for the support of children — do so only superficially. Actually these laws are intended to protect the home or to safeguard children. They do not contemplate an artificial segregation of women as a group apart from their social relationships. In sweeping away laws like these on the superficial ground that they perpetuate sex disabilities, we should be deliberately depriving the legislature of the power to protect children and to preserve the right of mothers to be safeguarded in the family group.

The amendment would jeopardize laws like these for women in industry because they do not also apply to men. The proposal to include men in them will indefinitely postpone their extension[.] Yet in the opinion of women in industry these laws which insure tolerable conditions of work should come first in any genuine bill of equal rights for women. Women in industry ask for the substance of freedom. . . .

We hold that the amendment is unnecessary because the right of suffrage has already given women the power to secure legislation and accomplish all that the amendment is supposed to make possible. . . . We hold that besides being unnecessary it is dangerous because its vagueness jeopardizes what we have and indefinitely retards what we have still to gain.

SOURCE: "Who Won the Debate over the Equal Rights Amendment in the 1920s?" Women and Social Movements in the United States, 1775–2000, Center for the Study of Women and Gender at the State University of New York at Binghamton, http:// womhist.binghamton.edu/era/doc16.htm (accessed March 17, 2004).

ineffectual effort to control alcohol consumption had fostered contempt for the legal system. That women reformers were so closely associated with the controversial amendment surely fueled hostility to the social reforms women activists promoted in the 1920s. Finally, the widening prosperity of the period may well have influenced many Americans to turn toward new consumer and leisure pleasures and away from political engagement and concern for the nation's poor.

Perhaps most damaging to reform and especially women's part in it was the "Red Scare" of 1919 to 1921. Prompted initially by the Russian Revolution of 1917 and the fear that the fledgling U.S. Communist Party was plotting a revolution to topple this nation's government, Americans succumbed to a hysteria in which wild-eyed Bolsheviks seemed to be lurking around every corner. The Red Scare led to the deportation of "suspicious" immigrants, the suppression of the labor movement, and massive violations of civil liberties. It also helped to fuel the growth of the second Ku Klux Klan, an organization opposed to immigrants, Catholics, Jews, and blacks that achieved significant popularity and influence in the early 1920s. Finally, the Red Scare contributed to the passage of restrictive immigration laws of the 1920s and became a weapon for opponents of reform legislation, who could now argue that efforts to increase government's role in regulating the economy or protecting workers and the poor would lead America down the same path as Russia.

Red Scare hysteria particularly focused on a number of women's groups, including those in the Women's Joint Congressional Committee and the Women's International League for Peace and Freedom, which they claimed were spreading bolshevism in the United States. Jane Addams in particular came in for forceful criticism. Opponents' attempts to discredit women reformers with claims that they were Bolsheviks point to a further dilemma facing women activists. Preeminent among the opponents of reform were right-wing women's organizations. The Women Sentinels of the Republic was a small but vocal group that opposed social reform as the forerunner of bolshevism. The Daughters of the American Revolution, initially interested in women's social reform efforts, had by mid-decade also taken up the antiradical hysteria. Women in an auxiliary of the all-male Ku Klux Klan supported some reforms such as Prohibition but, like other right-wing women's groups, promoted what was called "one-hundred-percent Americanism" and were suspicious of the liberal goals of the women's lobby.

With these counterpressures, then, it is not surprising that the reform agenda of women's groups stalled at the nation's Capitol, and it is impressive that women activists accomplished as much as they did on the local and state levels. In the process they helped to keep the reform spirit alive, if not well, and created a crucial bridge to the social welfare reforms of the 1930s introduced by President Franklin D. Roosevelt's New Deal.

Women at Work

Although women's expanding political opportunities contributed to the sense of a New Woman in the 1920s, changes in work were equally important—and were similarly mixed in offering women genuine independence (see Visual Sources: Women at Work, pp. 570–83). World War I had brought short-term opportunities in a variety of jobs for women, but these opportunities were not sustained. After the war, as before, women's work was characterized by sex segregation, clustered in job categories dominated by women. In the 1920s, 86 percent of women workers concentrated into ten job classifications, jobs in which they made less money and had lower status and fewer skills than men. (See Chart 9.1 for women's occupational distribution from 1900 to 1940; for more data on women's participation in the labor force, see Tables 2–4 in the Appendix.) As one historian neatly summed it up, "Women were invited into the workforce and again invited not to expect too much of it."[6]

The growing acceptance of women in the workforce is evident in the hard statistics. Their participation in paid labor grew from 21 percent in 1900 to 25 percent in 1930. Not only did more women work, but the percentage of married women in the labor force doubled, rising from 5.6 to 11.7 percent. This increase

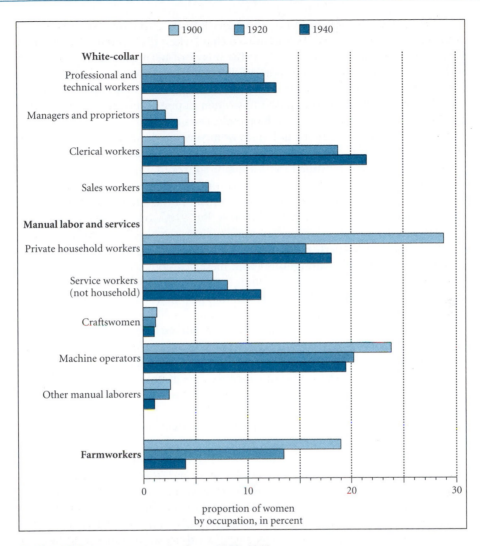

◆ **Chart 9.1 Women's Occupations, 1900–1940**
Source: U.S. Bureau of the Census, Historical Statistics of the United States, *Part 1, table D 182–232*; Statistical Abstract of the United States, 1985 (*Washington, DC: GPO, 1984*), *table 673; 1991 (*Washington, DC: GPO, 1991*), *table 652.*

resulted in part from compulsory education laws that kept children from taking jobs to help out the family, a trend that particularly affected immigrant wives. Also contributing to the rise of working wives were new consumer standards, which required more family income.

Despite the dramatic increase in the number of married women in the labor force, only 10 percent of all wives worked during the 1920s. Yet their presence signaled a trend that would grow steadily in the future, and in the 1920s the development was significant enough to spark heated controversies. Marriage experts such as Ernest Groves announced that "when the woman herself earns and her maintenance is not entirely at the mercy of her husband's will, diminishing masculine authority necessarily follows."[7] Even observers sympathetic to working wives tended to criticize those who elected to pursue careers allegedly for personal satisfaction, as opposed to women in poorer households who were compelled to join the workforce to help make ends meet.

Married or single, as more and more women entered the labor force, the idea of women's proper place profoundly shaped their work experiences and opportunities. Factory work continued to be a major source of employment, especially among immigrant daughters, but the most rapidly expanding field was clerical work. The emergence of the modern corporation in the late nineteenth century transformed office work and office personnel. By 1910, women already held most stenographic and typing positions, and in the 1920s they increased their presence as clerks and bookkeepers. As clerical work became increasingly dominated by women, or "feminized," assumptions about these positions changed as well. While men might enter the lower rungs of white-collar work as the first stepping-stone to climbing their way up the corporate ladder, jobs that women filled rarely had the same potential for upward mobility.

Status and salaries were low within the feminized white-collar hierarchy; nonetheless, many women viewed these jobs as welcome opportunities and flocked to the commercial courses offered in the public high schools. European immigrant daughters, whose level of education was improving in part because of mandatory education laws, now had more options than factory work. Middle-class workers—who would have found factory work and domestic service demeaning—also staffed the modern office, and their high visibility helped to improve the respectability of women working. Women of color, however, faced office doors that were largely closed to them. Black women found positions only in a small number of black-owned firms. Japanese and Chinese American women also experienced discrimination in finding office work.

Similar patterns of sexual and racial discrimination appeared in the professions. The professional woman attracted much publicity in the 1920s as an exemplar of the New Woman, yet the percentage of working women in the professions was still small (see Chart 9.1). Women professionals tended to cluster in teaching, nursing, and the expanding field of social work. Even in these increasingly feminized fields, women met with discrimination. Although eight of ten teachers were women, for example, only one in sixty-three superintendents was female. For women of color, the barriers were particularly high, and they made few inroads in this period. The percentage of black women working in the professions, for example, barely rose from 2.5 percent in 1920 to 3.4 percent in 1930.

While educated women struggled to find meaningful work in the professions, the vast majority of American women worked at far less satisfying labor. Black women had been optimistic that migration to the North would provide well-paid factory work. But even in the boom time of World War I, their jobs were the least desirable ones and usually did not last after the war had ended and soldiers had returned to the workforce. In the 1920s, some black women managed to find jobs in industries such as Chicago's packing plants and slaughterhouses, where researcher Alma Herbst found them seasonally employed in the hog-killing and beef-casing departments and working "under repulsive conditions."[8]

Most African American women, however, engaged in agricultural labor, laundry work, or domestic service. Seeking to improve control over their work lives, they increasingly refused jobs as live-in servants. The change to day work allowed these women to carve out some control over their work lives and their private time. As Mayme Gibson put it, "When I got work by the days I'd work in jobs where I'd be doing all the cleaning, my way. Nobody's be looking over your shoulder, saying what you was to do. People took daywork to finally get to work by theyself; to get away from people telling you how to do every little thing."[9] While day work offered an improvement over live-in situations, domestic work continued to be highly exploitative, with poor wages and conditions.

Like black women, Mexican American women were heavily concentrated in domestic labor. In 1930, the first date in which census figures reported people of Mexican descent separately, 44 percent of Mexican women who worked were servants. Some urban women found semiskilled factory work. A 1928 study of Los Angeles reported "that in some cases the wife or mother sought the work; in others, the young daughters. In either case, poverty was the immediate incentive." Most worked in "packing houses and canneries of various kinds, followed by the clothing, need trades, and laundries."[10] Outside the cities, many Mexicanas and their American-born daughters worked with their families in agricultural labor. Next to black women, Japanese women were the most likely women of color to work outside the home; about 30 percent worked for wages. Most were married and, like Mexican Americans, worked either as family farm laborers or as domestic servants.

For all women of color, even the educated, the double burden of race and gender translated into few job options. In contrast, most white women, especially native-born ones who had office and professional employment, had cleaner, better paying, less demanding work. Despite these significant differences, all women faced a hierarchical labor market that devalued women's work. As Emily Blair put it at the end of the decade, summarizing her and other feminists' disappointment over women's failure to make significant economic advances in the 1920s, "The best man continued to win, and women, even the best, worked for and under him. Women were welcome to come in as workers, but not as co-makers of the world. For all their numbers they seldom rose to positions of responsibility or power."[11]

The New Woman in the Home

As significant as changes in the public realm of politics and work were for women, the most dramatic transformation in women's lives emerged in the private worlds of home, family, and personal relationships. Contemporaries in the 1920s either celebrated or condemned what was widely viewed as a female sexual revolution. At the center of the revolution was the young, emancipated flapper with her bobbed hair, skimpy clothes, and penchant for outrageous dancing and drinking.

Although the image of the flapper was glamorized in movies and in the pages of popular novelist F. Scott Fitzgerald, many young women across class and racial lines eagerly adopted the flapper clothing style and danced to jazz music their elders found alarmingly erotic. Even more unnerving was their sexual activity. Rejecting the Victorian moral code, young unmarried women increasingly engaged in "petting"—a term that encompassed a wide range of sexual play short of intercourse. And the generation who came of age in the 1920s was significantly more likely than their mothers to have engaged in premarital intercourse.

But if daughters were experimenting sexually, many of their mothers, too, were carving out new roles in what historians have called the "affectionate family." Smaller families were becoming the norm for the urban middle class, but fewer children did not mean less maternal responsibility. Modern mothers, aided by a bounty of household appliances made possible by the widespread electrification of homes in this period, were expected to maintain their homes and raise their children with new efficiency and skill. Increasingly important was their role as consumers. *Photoplay* magazine ran an ad that summed up popular opinion of the New Woman in the home: "Home Manager—Purchasing Agent—Art Director—Wife. She is the active partner in the business of running a home. She buys most of the things which go to make home life happy, healthful, and beautiful."[12] The rosy images of advertising aside, most homemakers continued to have time-consuming responsibilities. Indeed, expectations about careful shopping, cleaner homes, and healthier children may have increased, rather than lightened, women's domestic burdens. Also in the 1920s, a new emphasis on the marriage partnership being a mutually satisfying sexual relationship emerged. A 1930 sociological study, *New Girls for Old*, encapsulated the new way of thinking: "After hundreds of years of mild complaisance to wifely duties, modern women have awakened to the knowledge that they are sexual beings. And with this new insight the sex side of marriage has assumed sudden importance."[13]

Changing ideas about female sexuality were furthered in part by the increasing availability and respectability of reliable birth control, especially the diaphragm. When reformer Margaret Sanger began her drive to legalize the dissemination of contraceptives in 1912, she initially concentrated on helping poor women to control their fertility (see pp. 480–81). By the 1920s, however, discouraged by conservative opposition to her plans for birth control clinics for the poor, she began to target elite and middle-class audiences and to emphasize the erotic potential for women by separating sex from reproduction. Sanger was instrumental in liberalizing state laws to make contraceptives more available, although the requirement that a physician dispense contraceptives meant that they were more likely to be readily available to prosperous white women.

Changing conceptions about female sexuality had been evident in the prewar years, especially among radical feminists and some urban working-class young women (see pp. 478–79). By the 1920s, these new ideas had filtered to a broad middle-class audience. Crucial to the popularization of these ideas was the rapid expansion of the mass media, especially motion pictures. Popular movies featured stars like Clara Bow, who had "It" (the catchphrase for sexual appeal), and

◆ Movies, Sex, and Consumerism

Movie moderns like Joan Crawford, pictured here in a scene from *Our Dancing Daughters* (1929), conveyed a sense of physical freedom, energy, and independence. They helped to promote new notions of female sexuality that were often tied to the burgeoning consumer culture. Here the screen itself simulates a department store window as Crawford's character, Diana, stands in front of her mother's perfume collection extravagantly displayed in a luxurious dressing room. *Courtesy of the Academy of Motion Picture Arts and Sciences.*

attracted audiences with displays of female flesh—bare arms and legs—and sensual love scenes. Despite heightened attention to sexuality, movies rarely condoned adultery or promiscuity. While some plots titillated with the escapades of "bad" girls, these women usually paid for their sins; the heroines who resisted temptation were rewarded at the end by marriage or a renewal of their marriage commitment.

Another way in which movies and other forms of mass media, most notably advertising, simultaneously promoted a new sexuality while limiting it was the close association drawn between sexuality and consumer goods. Advertising featured a variety of images of women, but one of the most ubiquitous was the glamorous female, made sexy by the products she purchased. The 1920s also witnessed an explosion of beauty shops, expanding from five thousand in 1920 to forty thousand in 1930, along with a corresponding 400 percent leap in the sale of cosmetics. Thus, just as women were being encouraged to explore their sexuality, they were also being encouraged to identify it with particular standards of beauty and with the purchase of consumer goods and to see its goal as the happily adjusted marriage. In the process, the radical egalitarian potential of women's sexual liberation that earlier feminists had hoped for was muted.

There were other indications that the sexual revolution was less revolutionary than it seemed. Young women might engage in petting, for example, but prevailing norms discouraged intercourse except as a prelude to marriage between engaged couples. A double standard for men and women persisted, and women could get a reputation for being "fast," which could damage their marriage prospects. Moreover, not everyone embraced the new sexuality. Divorce case records in the 1920s reveal that some wives, traditionally reared, could not comfortably accept the new sexual code, much to the dismay of their husbands, who had anticipated a highly sexualized marriage. Among Italian immigrant daughters, a very low rate of illegitimacy persisted into the 1930s, an indication that many of these young women remained outside the peer culture that sanctioned sexual activity for unmarried women.[14]

The concentration on women's sexuality in the twenties also disconcerted many women's right activists, for whom sexuality had never been a site for the achievement of equality. They worried that the pursuit of sexual pleasure and recreation led women away from more serious concerns such as civic reform and women's rights. Many older activists, who came of age in a time when homosocial bonding was especially common among educated, professional women, were also disconcerted that the new psychology of sexuality focused on the erotic dimension of close relationships between women, in part because it became increasingly common for hostile critics to dismiss militant feminists as repressed lesbians. For women more comfortable with same sex sexuality, sophisticated urban environments gave them opportunities to live the lives they wanted, but the relentless celebration of heterosexuality may well have been disconcerting.

For many African American women reformers, who had labored for decades to protect black women from sexual exploitation and to counter the stereotype of black women as promiscuous, celebrating female sexuality was also problematic. During the Harlem Renaissance, a major cultural movement of black authors and artists who sought to articulate a distinct black contribution to American culture, women writers such as Jessie Fauset, Nella Larsen, and Zora Neale Hurston similarly were sensitive to the sexualized portrayal of black women. But in another major expression of black culture, female jazz and blues singers such as Bessie Smith, Ida Cox, and Ma Rainey often presented an exuberant sense of women's enjoyment of their sexuality that spoke of resistance to sexual objectification and domination by men. Some songs featured a woman demanding that her lover pay attention to her needs, such as "One Hour Mamma," in which Ida Cox reminded her partner that she wanted "a slow and easy man" who "needn't ever take the lead."[15] Others suggested lesbian desire, such "Prove It on Me Blues," in which Ma Rainey sang, "Went out last night with a crowd of my friends / They must've been women, 'cause I don't like no men."[16]

The sexual dimension of the New Woman, like her participation in politics and the workforce, was thus complex. New developments in both public and private spheres ushered in significant changes, although these were filtered through the lens of class, race, and ethnicity and were accompanied by continued emphasis on women's roles as wives and mothers. A coalescence of factors in the 1920s—an expanding role in the workplace, new political opportunities, a more sexualized marriage, and the growing importance of the consumer culture—did not give women full economic and political equality or personal autonomy, but it did give their lives a modern contour, putting in motion the trends that would characterize women's lives for the rest of the twentieth century.

DEPRESSION DECADE: THE 1930s

Although the fabled prosperity of the 1920s was never as widespread as popular memory has it, the contrast between that decade and the economic hardships faced by Americans in the 1930s is striking. In 1933 unemployment figures had reached 25 percent and the U.S. gross national product (GNP) had been cut almost in half. A stunning stock market crash in late October 1929 had helped precipitate the Great Depression, particularly by damaging the nation's banking system, but long-standing weaknesses in the economy accounted for the Depression's length and severity. A prolonged agricultural depression and a decline in certain "sick" industries such as textiles and mining were just two points of underlying vulnerability. An unequal distribution of the nation's wealth—in 1929, 40 percent of the population received only 12.5 percent of aggregate family income, while the top 5 percent of the population received 30 percent—meant that once the Depression began, the majority of people were unable to spend the amount of money that was needed to revive the economy. The Great Depression became self-perpetuating, and for ten years it left what one observer has called "an invisible scar" running through the lives of millions of Americans.

If our most familiar female icon of the 1920s is the flamboyant flapper, then the counterpart for the Depression decade of the 1930s is Dorothea Lange's haunting photograph of Florence Owens, titled "Migrant Mother." Owens was part of a

◆ **Migrant Mother**

This evocative 1936 photograph of Florence Owens by Farm Security Administration photographer Dorothea Lange captured one of the tragic outcomes of the Great Depression: the
massive migration of farm families from the drought-ravaged Great Plains. At least 350,000
victims of the dust bowl headed west in the 1930s, half of them settling in rural areas where
they worked for low wages as migratory farm laborers. In 1960, Lange reminisced about the
photograph: "She told me her age, that she was thirty-two. She said that they had been living
on frozen vegetables [picked from] surrounding fields, and birds that the children killed. She
had just sold the tires from her car to buy food. There she sat in that lean-to tent with her
children huddled around her, and seemed to know that my pictures might help her, and so
she helped me. There was a sort of equality about it." Years later, a more complicated story
emerged. Lange had promised the woman, whose name she did not know, that the photographs would not be published but would be used to help the migrants. Decades later,
Owens resented the photograph's widespread distribution and the fact that she never
received any money from its publication. She also felt it misrepresented her as a dustbowl
"Okie." Of Cherokee descent, she and her family originally migrated to California in the
1920s. Hard times led them to migrant farm work in 1931. She survived the crisis, as did her
children, and she remarried and led a comfortable middle-class life in California. *Library of
Congress LC-USF34-009058-C.*

massive exodus of farm families from the southwestern plains states, where farmers, already suffering from low crop prices in the 1920s, were devastated by a prolonged drought in the 1930s that had created the "dust bowl" and countless family tragedies. The image potently evokes the hardships embodied in the sterile statistics of the era, a period in which overall unemployment rose as high as 30 percent, banks closed by the thousands, and hundreds of thousands of Americans lost their homes and farms. Even if a woman was not among the down and out, she could identify with the fear and uncertainty of the migrant woman. But just as the flapper only scratches the surface of the experience of women in the 1920s, the migrant mother was just one facet of a complex mosaic of American womanhood.

At Home in Hard Times

Even more so than in good times, class and race proved powerful determinants of women's experience in the Great Depression. While elite and middle-class families experienced downward mobility and emotional and material hardships, it was the nation's working-class and farm families who suffered most from the economic crisis. Not only did they face a greater likelihood of losing their jobs or farms, but they also had fewer resources to draw on. African Americans were among the greatest losers. They were the first fired in industrial jobs and the hardest hit among the rural southern Americans so devastated by the farm crisis. Mexican and Asian American farmers and workers in the West and Southwest also experienced high rates of unemployment and low wages. Like African Americans, they met with discrimination from city, state, and federal agencies that provided relief payments to the impoverished. Indeed, resistance to subsidizing unemployed immigrant workers led to a drive to deport Mexican immigrants, especially in Texas and California. In the 1930s, Los Angeles lost one-third of its Mexican population, many of whom were citizen children of immigrant parents. This deportation movement led to significant disruption in communities, placing heavy burdens on women and families already coping with economic dislocations.

The Depression was also a heavily gendered experience. Although women's participation in the workforce had been steadily increasing in the early twentieth century, most observers continued to regard women's proper place as the home. Thus, policymakers, sociologists, and popular writers alike interpreted the unemployment crisis of the 1930s as primarily a male dilemma, emphasizing "the forgotten man" and worrying about the psychological impact of unemployment for American traditions of masculine individualism. Sociological studies such as *The Unemployed Man and His Family* (1940) emphasized the familial disruption that resulted when men lost jobs and often sacrificed their dominant position in the household. Observers may have been correct that the crisis was harder on men than on women. As sociologists Helen and Robert Lynd put it in their widely read 1937 study of "Middletown" (Muncie, Indiana), "The men, cut adrift from their usual routine, lost much of their sense of time and dawdled helplessly and dully about the streets; while in the homes the women's world remained largely intact and the round of cooking, housecleaning, and mending became if anything more absorbing."[17]

These tasks became more absorbing because so many women had to juggle fewer resources and become adept at making do. Magazines ran articles on cooking with cheaper ingredients, and ads aimed at female consumers touted moneysaving products and offered advice for preparing nutritious "7 cents' breakfasts." For poor women, the burdens of homemaking were exacerbated by problems of poor sanitation and substandard housing—problems especially for minority women and poor white rural women. In many social groups, homemaking was made more complicated and stressful by the presence of extended kin, as families coped with reduced income by combining households.

Other issues shaped the households women inhabited. Unemployment for men often strained marriages, especially ones that had been patriarchal. Desertion rates rose, but rates for divorce, an expensive proposition, did not. Another measure of the Depression's impact was the decline in fertility rates, dropping, for example, from eighty-nine to seventy-six live births per thousand women of childbearing age between the years 1930 and 1933 (see Chart 1, p. A-36). The trend toward smaller families and the use of contraception, evident among more prosperous families in the 1920s, spread to many working-class families in the 1930s, as fewer children became an economic necessity and after access to legal birth control was facilitated by a 1936 decision (*United States v. One Package of Japanese Pessaries*) invalidating federal laws that had prohibited the dissemination of contraceptive information.

Women and Work

Although contemporaries viewed women's primary responsibility to be maintaining the home in hard times, women as workers constitute an important part of the Depression story. Hostility toward the idea of married women going to work intensified in the 1930s, evident in public opinion polls such as the one conducted by George Gallup in 1936, which asked if married women should work if their husbands were employed; 82 percent of the respondents said no, although there was less opposition to wives in very low-income families who worked.[18] Legislation reflected this attitude. The 1932 National Economy Act required that when workforce reductions occurred, the first let go should be those who already had a family member in the government's employ. While this legislation did not specifically target women, it led to the firing of thousands of them. State and local governments echoed this trend, as did many private companies. Most school districts did not hire wives as teachers, and half of them fired women when they married. For those women who did work, wages shrank in the 1930s; women also continued to earn less than men—in 1935 they earned approximately 65 cents for every dollar of men's wages.[19]

Despite this discrimination, women's desire and need to work increased and their participation in the workforce grew modestly, inching up from 25 percent in 1930 to 27 percent in 1940. More striking was the increase of married women workers. In 1930, 12 percent of wives worked; in 1940, 17 percent.[20] While women also experienced devastating unemployment, especially in the early hard years of the Depression, white women at least found jobs far more quickly than their male counterparts. Sex segregation in the workforce ironically assisted them. Heavy industrial jobs, the domain of men (where women counted for less than 2 percent of all workers), were the most affected by the Depression, while light industry, usually associated with female operatives, recovered more quickly as the decade progressed. More significantly, opportunities in clerical work expanded in part because the federal agencies of the New Deal designed to cope with the Depression almost doubled the number of federal employees.

In contrast to white women, black women lost jobs during the 1930s. One traditional field for black women—farm labor—constricted as hundreds of thousands of sharecroppers and wage workers were thrown out of work in the South. Mechanization further eliminated farm jobs. At the same time, opportunities in the other major area of employment for black women—domestic work—shrank and competition grew. In New York City and elsewhere, "slave markets" provided a particularly potent example of the harsh conditions. Black women would stand on street corners waiting for white women to drive by and hire them for a day's heavy labor for less than $2.00. Whatever their jobs, black women were almost certain to earn less than other groups. The average wage per week of white women in Texas factories, for example, was $7.45, while Mexican women took home $5.40 and black women only $3.75.[21]

The patterns of work in the 1930s underlined the broad trends becoming clear in the previous decade. Participation of women, especially married women, in the workforce increased, but it did so in sex-segregated labor markets that limited women's occupational mobility and income. Moreover, that market was further segregated by race and ethnicity, with white women dominating the rapidly expanding clerical workforce. Jobs in agriculture decreased, but they were still a significant source of work for women of color, as were domestic labor and semi-skilled industrial work, especially that related to garment and food processing. The restricted nature of women's job opportunities would not be challenged—and then only temporarily—until the United States entered World War II in 1941.

Women's New Deal

As American women and men coped with hard times, they sought strong political leadership. They found it in President Franklin D. Roosevelt. In 1932, as the Depression deepened, Roosevelt defeated Republican incumbent Herbert Hoover handily and came to Washington, D.C., with a clear mandate to act forcefully to bring about recovery and relieve suffering. He brought to the presidency a charisma and a willingness to experiment with programs that directly assisted the needy. Labeling these programs a "New Deal" for Americans, Roosevelt pushed an enormous amount of legislation through Congress. Roosevelt's New Deal agencies contributed to his immense popularity, a popularity that the efforts of his wife, Eleanor Roosevelt, enhanced. A gifted woman with a long-standing commitment to social reform, Eleanor called herself "the eyes and ears of the New Deal," perhaps an implicit reference to her husband's limited physical mobility. (He was

◆ **Eleanor Roosevelt and the Women's Press Corp**
Eleanor Roosevelt, seated at center, is surrounded by women reporters, who particularly
appreciated the First Lady because of the access she gave them to the White House. She instituted women-only press conferences that helped them counter the prevailing sexism they
faced in their profession and allowed her to publicize her interest in New Deal programs and
social reform. One appreciative newspaper woman said, "Never was there such a gift from
heaven for the working press." *Stock Montage.*

severely crippled from polio.) She crisscrossed the nation promoting the New
Deal, pushed Roosevelt to pay more attention to the plight of African Americans,
and gathered around her a group of activist women particularly concerned about
the hardships women and children faced during the Depression. (See Documents:
Women's Networks in the New Deal, pp. 563–69.) Despite her efforts, however,
most New Deal programs slighted or discriminated against women.

The National Industrial Recovery Act (NIRA) reflected the way in which the
New Deal reinforced existing assumptions about women's subordinate role in the
workforce. Passed in 1933 and designed to stimulate recovery, this pivotal piece of
legislation established codes that set wages, hours, and prices in the nation's major

economic sectors. Jobs described as "light and repetitive" were those usually assigned to women, and 25 percent of the codes explicitly permitted differential wages between men and women, anywhere from 5 to 25 cents per hour. Clerical workers in many fields were excluded, and farm and domestic workers were not covered at all.

Despite such shortcomings, the New Deal did help some women workers, especially in its efforts to provide protection for organized labor. The 1920s had been a low point for unions, which suffered from the postwar Red Scare and corporate antiunion drives. Union membership stood at a mere 12 percent of the workforce at the end of the decade. The NIRA, however, contained provisions that legitimized unions and helped to spark hundreds of organizing drives that tapped into the widespread discontent of workers. Women were particularly active in the International Ladies Garment Workers' Union, which conducted organizing drives in sixty cities, increasing its size by 500 percent between 1933 and 1934. When in 1935 the Supreme Court, arguing that the NIRA represented an unconstitutional delegation of power to the executive, invalidated the act, the New Deal replaced its labor provisions with the National Labor Relations Act, known as the Wagner Act. This legislation again galvanized unionization campaigns and contributed to the success of a new national union federation, the Congress of Industrial Organizations (CIO), which in 1935 had broken off from the more conservative American Federation of Labor (AFL). The CIO, influenced in part by the significant presence of Communist Party members among its organizers, many of whom were women, concentrated on mass production industries. Women especially benefited from union inroads in light industries such tobacco and paper products manufacturing. In 1924, 200,000 women belonged to a union; by 1938, the figure was 800,000.

Women actively participated in strikes, both as workers and as wives of male strikers. In 1933, poor wages and working conditions led to a long and bitter strike by eighteen thousand cotton workers in California, most of whom were Mexicans associated with the Cannery and Agricultural Workers Industrial Union. Women participated by preparing and distributing food among the strikers, but they were also active on the picket line. They taunted strikebreakers, urging them to join the strike, yelling out in Spanish, "Come on out, quit work, we'll feed you. If you don't, we'll poison all of you." This confrontation ended in violence as many women armed themselves with knives and lead pipes.[22]

Women also played a crucial role in the 1937 Flint, Michigan, sit-down strike against General Motors. When the men sat down at their machines, their wives as well as women workers (who were not included in the occupation of the factory because of concerns about sexual propriety) organized the Women's Emergency Brigade. They fulfilled the traditional female role of providing food for the men, but then they moved beyond that role to stage a women's march of seven thousand and to create other diversions that allowed men to expand the strike to another GM plant. Brigade leader, autoworker, and socialist Genora Johnson Dollinger explained, "This was an independent move. It was not under the direction of the union or its administrators—I just talked it over with a few women—

the active ones—and told them this is what we had to do."[23] The successful strike ended with GM's recognition of the United Auto Workers union. Thus, as supporters and as workers, women played an important role in the labor radicalism that shaped the 1930s.

The federal government's new involvement in protecting working-class Americans through labor legislation was matched by its unprecedented intervention in providing relief for those made destitute by the Depression. Although most policy makers perceived of the unemployment crisis as primarily a male one, an inner circle of female New Dealers, aided by Eleanor Roosevelt, insisted that the government pay attention to the "forgotten woman." (See Documents: Women's Networks in the New Deal, pp. 563–69.) A central figure was Ellen S. Woodward, who headed the Women's and Professional Projects Division of several agencies that provided federal relief for the unemployed—the Federal Emergency Relief Administration (FERA), Civil Works Administration (CWA), and Works Projects Administration (WPA). Woodward worked hard to get women included in programs that created jobs for the unemployed. A small number of professional women, such as librarians, social workers, teachers, and nurses, were accommodated in federal projects, and some artists and writers found employment in programs such as the Federal Theater Project, headed by Hallie Flanagan. But the vast majority of women needing help (almost 80 percent in 1935) were unskilled, and for them the work-relief jobs clustered in traditional women's work of sewing, canning, and domestic labor.

In addition to offering individual employment, these programs benefited the community. Between 1933 and 1937, women made over 122 million articles that were distributed to the poor free of charge. They provided the food for highly successful free school lunch programs. Librarians created card catalogs and oversaw Braille transcription projects. Handicraft programs drew on regional variations. In Texas, women were given leather to make coats and jackets; in Arizona, Native American women fashioned copperware: in Florida, women produced hats, handbags, and rugs for the tourist industry.

Yet, despite these benefits and Woodward's promise that "women are going to get a square deal," New Deal programs were riddled with discrimination against women. Most programs focused on male unemployment and treated women as subordinate earners who ideally should be in the home. To be eligible for work relief, they needed to prove that they were heads of family, and if a husband was physically able to work, whether he had found work or not, women were unlikely to be given federal jobs. Some young women found jobs with the National Youth Administration (NYA), but they were excluded from the Civilian Conservation Corps, which put 2.5 million young men to work conserving the nation's parks and natural resources. Only after Eleanor Roosevelt intervened were similar camps set up for women, but these accommodated only eight thousand young women.

This type of discrimination provoked protest from women's groups as well as the unemployed. One woman wrote to the Roosevelts to complain: "I should like to know why it is that men can be placed so easily and not women."[24] The answer to that question lay in part with local administrators, who often resisted finding

◆ WPA Training for Household Workers
Most telling of the ways in which New Deal programs reinforced existing stereotypes concerning minority women were the programs for domestic training. When Ellen S. Woodward set about to deal with the problem of unemployed domestics, she wanted to have a training program that would elevate these women's position and give them both dignity and skills. But by shunting minority women to these programs, the New Deal reinforced both race- and sex-segregated labor patterns. *Franklin D. Roosevelt Presidential Library and Museum.*

work for women, particularly work that challenged traditional notions of women's proper domestic roles. When women found positions, the jobs invariably fell into low-paying categories. New Deal agencies, then, not only followed sex segregation policies based on traditional notions of women's proper place in the home but also helped to institutionalize them.

Similarly, New Deal agencies replicated the discrimination based on race and ethnicity found in the private labor market. Relief policies were designed to help the poor, and indeed, most minority groups benefited from them to some degree.

◆ **More Social Security for the American Family**
Labor Secretary Frances Perkins, the first woman cabinet member in the United States, played a critical role in the drafting and implementation of the landmark Social Security Act of 1935. Despite this fact, the legislation acted under the assumption that women were dependents, not workers themselves, as this poster suggests. *Franklin D. Roosevelt Presidential Library and Museum.*

But despite official guidelines that tried to limit racial discrimination, federal agencies rarely challenged the policies of local administrators. On many Native American reservations, officials often were even more indifferent to the problem of work relief for women than to native peoples in general. In the racially segregated South, local New Deal agencies resisted giving black women jobs during harvest periods when cheap farm labor was in demand. When African American women could get federal jobs, they were usually in segregated programs and were routinely given the most menial work. In San Antonio, a three-part caste system was in operation. African American women were formally segregated from projects that could employ white or Mexican women, but an informal process kept white and Mexican women from working together in sewing or canning rooms.

That the New Deal both assisted women especially in their family responsibilities and reinforced their inequality as wage workers was most dramatically evident in the Social Security Act of 1935. This pathbreaking legislation owed much to women reformers, especially Secretary of Labor Frances Perkins. It provided a federal pension plan and federal-state matching fund programs for unemployment assistance and for aid to dependent mothers and children. Neither domestic workers nor farmworkers—two major employment options for poor women—were covered by the program, however, and women who worked in the home as mothers and housewives were similarly excluded. A 1939 amendment to Social Security further institutionalized inequality. Married working women were taxed at the same rate as their husbands, but because there was a family limit to benefits, a wife's benefits were reduced if her wages and her husband's exceeded the family limits. In addition, widows and their children received benefits when a husband and father died, but a married woman's dependents did not. In common with other New Deal programs, then, Social Security operated under the assumption of women's subordinate place in the labor market and their primary role in the home.

Despite its mixed record in terms of racial and gender discrimination, the New Deal did assist a wide variety of Americans in coping with the devastating effects of the Great Depression. It facilitated the growth of unions, put millions of people to work, and institutionalized the modest welfare provisions of the Social Security Act. One thing it failed to accomplish was to end the Depression. The return of prosperity would not come until the advent of World War II, when the demand for war production set American factories back to work and created full employment.

WORKING FOR VICTORY: WOMEN AND WAR, 1941–1945

In the late 1930s, as the militarism of Germany, Italy, and Japan rose to a crescendo, most Americans adamantly opposed being drawn into war. This remained true even after Germany, under Adolf Hitler, invaded Poland in 1939 and France and Britain, the United States' allies in World War I, declared war on the Axis powers, Germany and Italy. Despite the official neutrality mandated by Congress, the United States offered financial and other material assistance to its former allies and began its own defense buildup. Public sentiment remained high against becoming involved in the war, but December 7, 1941, shattered that resistance. When Japan, which had signed an alliance with the Axis, executed a devastating surprise air attack on the American naval base and fleet at Pearl Harbor, Hawaii, killing 2,400 Americans, Congress declared war on Japan. Within days, Germany and Italy declared war on the United States, and the United States in turn declared war on those nations. The United States entered a global conflagration being fought in Europe, Asia, and Africa that would last until 1945.

The global war and the massive mobilization it entailed had a tremendous impact on American women. By undercutting patterns of sex-segregated labor—perfectly symbolized by the poster image of "Rosie the Riveter" and offering women new independence and responsibilities—it produced significant changes, both in the workplace and in the domestic arena. Yet to a striking degree Americans continued to reiterate traditional notions about woman's proper sphere in the home even as they challenged these ideas in daily life. And, as was the case during the Depression, race, ethnicity, and gender discrimination continued to shape American women's experience.

Women in the Military

Despite a long tradition of exceptional American women edging their way onto the battlefield, donning the nation's uniform was a particularly male act that served to shape definitions of ideal masculinity. As the American military establishment geared up for World War II, it initially resisted incorporating women into the service. Eventually, military necessity, as well as pressure from women's groups under the leadership of Congresswoman Edith Nourse Rogers of Massachusetts, led to the acceptance of female military recruits. Thousands of men were thus made available for combat. The Women's Army Corps (WAC) attracted 140,000 recruits; 100,000 served in the navy's Women Accepted for Volunteer Emergency Service (WAVES); 23,000 were in Marine Corps Women's Reserve (MCWR); and 13,000 enlisted with the Coast Guard Women's Reserve (SPAR: from the motto Semper Paratus, Always Ready). Another 76,000 served as army or navy nurses.

In the service, women's jobs typically followed the conventional patterns of peacetime. While some women worked as mechanics and welders and in other skilled jobs that broke the gender barrier, most filled jobs as clerks, telephone operators, dieticians, and in other routine assignments. A particularly vital role filled by women was nursing, often in exceptionally dangerous circumstances, just behind the front in all the major theaters of the war—North Africa, Europe, and Asia. While the military welcomed nurses, it resisted commissioning women as doctors—despite the severe shortage of physicians—until April 1943, fifteen months after America's entry into the war.

Black women experienced racial discrimination at the hands of the federal government's segregated military establishment. Because the navy prohibited African American men from serving in any but menial positions, it also refused to incorporate black women into its ranks until 1944, almost at the end of the war. Black nurses were commissioned in the army, and 10 percent of WACs were African American, but they lived and worked in segregated units and had less access to training and skilled jobs than white women. Black nurses were allowed to attend only to African Americans or prisoners of war, and they were often assigned to menial, not skilled, patient services.

All women in the service encountered a public that was ambivalent about the gender challenges presented by women in uniform. Oveta Culp Hobby, a prominent Houston woman who became director of the WACs, had to counter pervasive rumors of sexual immorality and drunkenness among servicewomen. Although some of the rumors focused on lesbianism among recruits, referring to the "queer damozels of the Isle of Lesbos," most critics alleged promiscuity among heterosexual women.[25] The WACs distributed publicity praising the women's high moral character, but the agency also refused to distribute contraceptives to women in the service, in contrast to the policy adopted for men that was designed to prevent the spread of venereal disease. For women and men alike, the military also adopted a harsh policy toward homosexuality, making "homosexual tendencies," as diagnosed by a psychiatrist, sufficient grounds for dismissal from the service. However, although World War II military service offered many women and men opportunities to participate in a discreet lesbian and gay subculture, relatively few servicepeople were discharged on these grounds.

Equally as pressing as concerns about sexual immorality was the worry that servicewomen were sacrificing their femininity by usurping men's roles. In an effort to put these fears to rest, the *New York Times* reported in 1945 that the WAC "will always be a civilian at heart," and predicted that "the most important postwar plans of the majority of women in the WAC include just what all women

◆ **Breaking Down the Sex and Color Lines: African American WAC Officers in World War II**

This 1943 photograph features a group of African American nurses drilling at the first Women's Army Corps Training Center in Fort Des Moines, Iowa. Leading the group is Charity Adams, a former teacher from South Carolina who rose to the rank of major in the WACs. Her autobiography details pride in her accomplishments and the women who served with her, but also unstinting criticism of the segregation she and other black women experienced. After reporting a particularly brutal exchange with a white male colonel who criticized her severely for attending an officer's club—for, as he put it, she might be an officer, but "you are still colored and I want you to remember that"—Adams commented, "I suspect that I knew it all before, but having lived under circumstances in which I had learned how to avoid confrontation and humiliation, I had not fully recognized what obstacles we had to overcome." *National Archives NWDNS-111-SC-238651.*

want—their own homes and families."[26] Similarly, Colonel Hobby, while insisting that women in the service be treated with respect, reiterated traditional notions of women's proper place by asserting that military women were developing "new poise and charm," and that they "were only performing the duties that women would ordinarily do in civilian life."[27]

One duty that women rarely took on in civilian life was eagerly embraced by the members of the Women Airforce Service Pilots (WASP). The U.S. government refused to militarize this agency, a measure of just how threatening the idea of women performing high-status "male" jobs was. Instead, these pilots were civil servants without military rank, privileges, or uniforms. Drawing on an eager applicant pool of over 25,000 women, the air force accepted 1,074 as WASPs, all of whom had pilot's licenses and experience, unlike most men accepted for training as military pilots. Of these, two were Mexican American, two Chinese American, and one Native American. The lone African American who applied was urged to withdraw her application by WASP director Jacqueline Cochran, who explained that she wanted to avoid controversy at a time when the program had not yet been officially put in place.

WASP pilots ferried and tested planes and participated in maneuvers and training. Although they did not participate in combat, thirty-eight women lost their lives on duty. The WASPs performed invaluable services, but they were disbanded in December 1944, before the end of the war, because of pressure from civilian male pilots and veterans groups, which resented potential female competition in an elite male field. WASPs were not eligible for veterans benefits until a congressional act passed in 1977 finally gave them partial recognition for what they had accomplished.

Working Women in Wartime

Just as the military establishment was reluctant to incorporate women into the armed services, so too employers did not initially welcome female workers into defense industries. But by mid-1942, as more male workers were drafted into the army, the reality of labor scarcity started to erode resistance to female war workers. Women became the objects of a massive propaganda campaign to urge them to do their bit for Uncle Sam. Writers for popular magazines such as the *Saturday Evening Post* adopted story lines and recommendations from the government's Office of War Information to reinforce the importance of women taking advantage of training programs and employment opportunities. Posters and newsreels echoed the message: "The More Women at Work the Sooner We'll Win."

Women responded eagerly to expanded job opportunities, not just in defense industries but in other sectors of the economy as well. (See Visual Sources: Women at Work, pp. 570–83.) After the hardships of the Depression, with some 3 million women unemployed as late as 1940, a burgeoning demand for labor put the unemployed to work and created jobs that provided new opportunities for women coming into the labor market for the first time. Between 1940 and 1945, almost 5 million new female workers entered the labor force, representing a 43 percent increase in women workers.[28] In 1944, an estimated 37 percent of adult women worked in the paid labor force. In a particularly important trend that foreshadowed postwar developments, older, married women provided the largest numbers of new workers, while there was little change in women between twenty and thirty years of age. Traditional jobs in light industry and clerical work expanded, and for white women, professional positions also became more readily available. As male farmers went off to war, women increased their presence in agriculture by 8 percent, as women, many of them organized in the U.S. Department of Agriculture's Women's Land Army, helped to harvest the nation's crops.

Women's participation in the defense industry was particularly significant because it broke down sex-segregated labor patterns. Women were trained in skilled jobs such as welders, riveters, and electricians. Their successes were widely touted, but publicity about these many Rosie the Riveters emphasized that women had maintained their femininity. One plant personnel manager, for example, commented that "we like the girls to be neat and trim and well put together. It helps their morale. It helps our prestige too."[29] Further, defense jobs were for the war's duration only, something women were doing allegedly for service, not for their own economic or personal goals. Thus, what could have been a dramatic development that challenged sex segregation in the labor market was robbed of its more radical potential.

Nonetheless, defense work did improve women's economic situation. The federal government's National War Labor Board (NWLB) issued General Order Number 16 in November 1942, calling for equal wages for women when the work they were doing was comparable to men's. Women's groups had pressured the NWLB, but the main motivation for the order was a desire not to undercut men's wages while women were temporarily taking on male jobs. Unions adopted a similar approach. Women's participation in unions rose from 9.4 percent of union members before the war to 22 percent in 1944. Although some left-wing unions' nondiscriminatory policies stemmed from genuinely egalitarian goals, most unions supported equal pay primarily with the goal of preserving male privileges. Moreover, older patterns of male and female classifications for jobs persisted, as well as seniority-based pay scales that served to assure higher wages for men.

For African American women, war job opportunities presented a mixed lot. Defense industries resisted hiring black women until it became absolutely necessary. In Detroit's war industries in 1943, of ninety-six thousand jobs filled by women, women of color held only one thousand.[30] Not until later that year did wartime manufacturers begin to hire black women. These possibilities for breaking into better-paying industrial work—the first since World War I—were undeniably exciting and helped to create another large migration out of the South. This time, in addition to the cities of the Midwest and North, African Americans branched out into the West, especially southern California. In this burgeoning center of defense manufacturing, as many as twelve thousand African Americans arrived monthly in the peak year of 1943 (see Map 9.1).

War jobs allowed many black women to escape the drudgery and poor wages of domestic work. However, they were often denied training and, even with training, assigned to less desirable positions, such as work in foundries and outside labor gangs. Although some of the treatment they received reflected employer racism, white women frequently resisted working with black women, in particular refusing to share toilet, shower, and meal facilities. In some cases, white women even went on strike over these issues, reflecting more a desire to maintain social distance between the races and a deep-seated belief that black women were "unclean" than fears about economic competition.[31]

Many black women protested the discrimination they encountered. Black organizations such as the NAACP fostered this new militancy, as did black newspapers. In Los Angeles, publisher Carlotta Bass used the pages of the *Eagle* to call for more jobs for African Americans. In concert with the NAACP, Bass organized a march in July 1942 against the local U.S. Employment Services office to insist that black women be given jobs in war industries, a tactic that eventually helped to integrate southern California defense plants. Black women also turned to the Fair Employment Practices Commission (FEPC), filing 25 percent of the complaints it received. This federal agency, charged with assuring that defense industries and

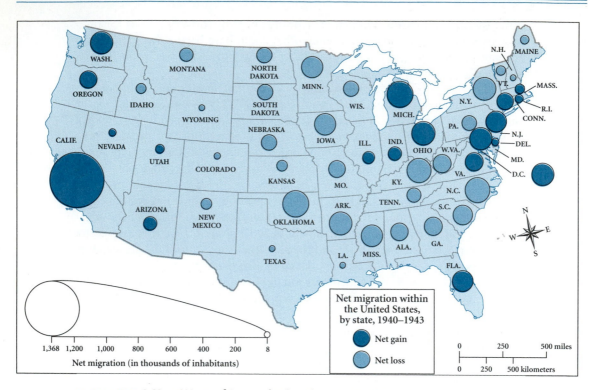

◆ **Map 9.1 A New Wave of Internal Migration, 1940–1943**
Almost 15 million people changed residence during the war years, with half of them moving
to another state. While the movement of African Americans out of the rural South was the
most dramatic example of this internal migration, whites, Mexican Americans, and Native
Americans also headed for the nation's cities. Migrants found exciting job opportunities in
defense industries, but they had to cope with the stresses of relocating and overcrowded,
often inadequate housing, problems that fell especially on women's shoulders.

training programs did not discriminate, had been created in 1941 in response to
determined black protest and a threat to lead a march on Washington, D.C. A significant development in the history of civil rights, the FEPC nonetheless had limited success. The imperative of keeping war production up to speed meant that the
FEPC had few tools for disciplining discriminating companies, and it rarely succeeded in forcing defense contractors to hire black women.

Nonetheless black women benefited significantly from war opportunities. The
percentage of black women employed in domestic service decreased from 60 percent in 1940 to 45 percent in 1944, and their participation in the industrial workforce increased from 7 to 18 percent for the same period. They also obtained more
white-collar work in the federal government, especially in Washington, D.C. However, black women's low seniority usually meant that as the war wound down, they
were the first fired. Margaret Wright, a skilled worker for Lockheed Aircraft, a major
defense contractor, was laid off at the war's end; later she sadly recalled, "I had to

fall back on the only other thing that I knew, and that was doing domestic work."[32] By 1950, some of the gains made in breaking away from domestic work had eroded: 50 percent of African American working women were still in domestic service. After the war, however, some women were able to hold on to higher paying industrial and clerical work. Even for those who went back to domestic work, the migration from the impoverished rural South offered at least the hope for a better life.

Other women of color found expanded opportunities in the war years and faced less discrimination than African Americans. In the Midwest, Mexicans, who before the war had difficulty finding industrial work and were routinely asked for their citizenship papers, found that employers "stopped asking for proof of legalization because they needed all the workers they could find for the war effort."[33] Not only did these women secure jobs in defense industries, but they also found that the labor scarcity improved their circumstances in other industrial jobs. Food processing, which was traditionally characterized by low status and pay, was vital to the war effort, and the United Cannery, Agricultural, Packing, and Allied Workers of America union in California was able to use the war emergency to push usually resistant employers for pay concessions and other benefits, including in one instance a plant nursery for children of employees.

Native American women's employment also expanded during the war. About one-fifth of adult women on reservations left to take jobs, and those who stayed behind increased their duties, helping to maintain farming and tribal businesses such as the timber industry. The Bureau of Indian Affairs, under John Collier, a New Dealer who had constructed a more humanitarian and liberal Native American policy (though still perpetuating a patronizing attitude toward Indians), publicized Native American contributions to the war effort, as did the journals of off-reservation boarding schools, which supplied most of the young women who went into defense work.[34]

For Chinese American women, the war offered unusual opportunities. Jobs in defense industries represented a significant economic improvement over working in family businesses or in food processing or garment industries. Unlike many other groups of women, Chinese American defense industry workers were young and unmarried. Before the war, these second-generation women had found most jobs outside Chinatown closed to them, despite their American education and English language proficiency. Their improved job prospects stemmed in part from the labor scarcity but also from a reduction in the racial prejudice against the Chinese now that China was a U.S. ally in the war against Japan. Even on the West Coast, where Asian Americans were most densely populated and where prejudice ran extremely high, the Chinese became the "good" Asians. Symbolic of this change in attitude was the 1943 congressional decision to abolish the legal strictures prohibiting Chinese aliens from becoming naturalized citizens. For Chinese women and their families, then, World War II facilitated more integration into mainstream American society as well as improved economic opportunities.[35]

For most Japanese American women, especially those in the West, the situation was bleak. Following decades of anti-Japanese sentiment on the West Coast,

◆ **Keeping the Home Fires Burning**
Much wartime publicity was given to women who took jobs in the defense industry or
served in the military, but another valued role for women was the faithful wife or mother
who patriotically sent off her menfolk to fight. Magazine articles offered advice on the types
of letters women should write to help maintain their fighting men's morale. Here, Rose Ong,
a San Francisco seamstress, is shown with pictures of her six sons, all of whom were in the
military. For Mrs. Ong and her family, World War II marked a watershed of new acceptance
into mainstream American life. *National Archives 208 MO-74R-19075.*

the Japanese bombing of Pearl Harbor touched off a firestorm of suspicion
directed at the Japanese in the United States. Despite the absence of any evidence
of sabotage or disloyalty, President Roosevelt, encouraged by military leaders and
western politicians, issued Executive Order 9066, mandating the internment of
over 110,000 people of Japanese descent, more than two-thirds of whom were
native-born American citizens. In ten remote camps in California, Arizona, Utah,
Colorado, Wyoming, Idaho, and Arkansas the Nisei (the Japanese term for second-
generation Japanese Americans) and the Issei (their parents) lived in stark barracks behind barbed wire. Prisoners without trial, incarcerated because of race,
the internees found the experience bewildering and humiliating.

Women continued as best they could with their familial duties, trying to supplement the unappetizing and inadequate food provided in the mess tent, keeping

clothes clean without the benefit of running water in their barracks, and above all struggling to keep the family unit together in the face of the disruption of relocation and camp life. Ironically, internment may have offered slight benefits to young Nisei women. They worked in the camps as clerks or teachers for the same low wages as their fathers and brothers, giving them some small taste of economic equality and independence. Within the camps, peer groups exerted strong pressure as teenage girls tried to keep up with the latest fashions on the outside and socialized with young men. The strong patriarchal authority of the Japanese household further eroded when the Nisei began to leave the camps in 1942 after the government determined that an individual Nisei's loyalty could be sufficiently investigated and determined. Some obtained permission to go to college in regions outside the West; an estimated 40 percent of those who became students were women. Others secured jobs in the Midwest and on the East Coast, with the most likely type of work being domestic service, although some found employment in manufacturing. After Nisei men were urged to volunteer for military service to "prove" their loyalty, some Nisei women followed suit and became WACs or military nurses.

War and Everyday Life

Far removed from the experience of Japanese internment, most American women faced very different sorts of pressures connected to everyday life on the home front. When men went off to join the military, wives often followed them while they were in training stateside, living in makeshift accommodations and coping with a sense of impermanency and an uncertain future.[36] Other women migrated either alone or with their families in search of better-paying jobs in cities, confronting the challenges of adjustment to new surroundings. These included scarce housing in boom areas, a particularly pressing problem for black women and Mexicans, who were also subject to housing discrimination.

The new environment also could be liberating, especially for single women. New jobs offered higher income and a sense of independence that led to more sexual experimentation. As one young war worker expressed it, "Chicago was just humming, no matter where I went. The bars were jammed, and unless you were an absolute dog you could pick up anyone you wanted to." Observers worried about this trend, pointing out that it was not prostitutes but "amateurs" who were undermining morality and spreading sexually transmitted disease.[37] Although promiscuity was probably not as great as critics feared, women did experience more personal freedom. Particularly notable were opportunities for lesbian women. Leaving provincial hometowns for large cities, they found other women who identified as lesbians. A woman who called herself "Lisa Ben," an anagram of "lesbian," reported that she moved from a ranch in northern California to a job in Los Angeles, ending up in a boardinghouse occupied by young single women and asking herself, "Gee, I wonder if these are some of the girls I would very dearly love to meet." They apparently were; Ben stayed in Los Angeles after the war and became part of the discreet lesbian bar scene that emerged there and in other major cities during the war years.[38]

Despite the sexual experimentation, conventional expectations about marriage and family remained unaltered. The number of marriages escalated, with the Census Bureau estimating that between 1940 and 1943 a million more families were formed than would have been expected in peacetime. Fertility spiked as well, after the low levels of the Depression, with the birthrate rising from 19.4 per 1,000 in 1940 to 24.5 per 1,000 in 1945 (see Chart 1, p. A-36). Popular culture reiterated respect for the domestic ideal. While movie heroines were often portrayed as self-reliant and independent war workers or army nurses, the message remained that women at war were only temporarily outside their proper place of home and family.

Whether they worked or not, married women faced ongoing responsibilities in the household. Although released from the extreme restraints of making do in the hard times of the 1930s, homemakers still worked hard. Consumer goods such as sugar, meat, and shoes were rationed, and housewives had to organize their shopping carefully. Home appliances that might have lightened their load were not being produced because factories and workers were needed for war production—though manufacturers continued their advertising campaigns to keep up consumer desire. A vacuum cleaner company promised, "A day is coming when this war will be done. And on that day, like you, Mrs. America, Eureka will put aside its uniform and return to the ways of peace . . . building household appliances."[39]

For women who worked, household burdens proved particularly difficult. Limited hours for shopping after their workday ended was one source of frustration. Nor could women expect any help from absent husbands and sons during their "second shift" at home. Child care posed another problem. Some corporations, faced with high turnover and absenteeism, offered nurseries. The federal government mounted a limited program of day care centers, but these were underutilized, in part because women associated federal programs with New Deal assistance to the down and out and in part because of cultural resistance to the idea of strangers taking care of one's children. Most women relied on friends and family members for help with child care.

As the war drew to a close in 1945, people expressed growing fear about the long-term roles of Rosie the Riveter and her colleagues and the implications for the postwar family. Anthropologist Margaret Mead reported that soldiers contemplating their return to the United States worried, "Well, mostly we've been wondering whether it's true that women are smoking pipes at home."[40] Americans foresaw that women were in the workforce to stay, and agencies like the U.S. Department of Labor's Women's Bureau still worked to improve their wages and opportunities. But most opinion makers advocated reinstating women to their rightful place, the home, so that returning GIs could expect full employment and a stable family life. Industrial leader Frederick Crawford pronounced, "[F]rom a humanitarian point of view, too many women should not stay in the labor force. The home is the basic American institution."[41]

Surveys of women working during the war indicated that a significant number—a Women's Bureau survey reported three of four women—had hoped to continue to work outside the home after the war.[42] But with demobilization women were laid off in large numbers. Gladys Poese Ehlmann recalled the shock of her dismissal from Emerson Electric Company in St. Louis: "[T]he war was over on August 14 and we went in on the 15th. They lined us up and had our paychecks ready for us."[43] Accounting for 60 percent of the dismissals in heavy industry, women were fired at a rate 75 percent higher than men. But although women's participation in the workforce dropped, this decline was short-lived. Women lost better-paid positions and most of the high-status jobs that had challenged sex-segregated labor patterns. But within a few years of the armistice, 32 percent of women were back in the labor force, and more than half of them were married. The war had not eroded cultural ideas about women's primary role in the home and their secondary status as wage earners, but it had been a vehicle for sustaining and even accelerating a process of increased female participation in the workplace.

CONCLUSION: The New Woman in Ideal and Reality

The images called up at the start of this chapter—the 1920s flapper, the 1930s migrant mother, and the 1940s Rosie the Riveter—capture the distinctive qualities of these three decades. But while the eras of prosperity, depression, and war affected women in different ways, we can still discern broad trends for the period as a whole that reveal the trajectory of twentieth-century women's lives.

Between 1920 and 1945, women worked in greater numbers, and more wives and mothers contributed to this trend, but they did so in the context of discriminatory sex-segregated labor patterns and unequal opportunities for women of color. In politics, women also witnessed important changes. Women now had the vote in all states, with the significant exception of African American women in the South, who like southern black men were largely disfranchised. In most states, women also enjoyed other legal rights—the right of married women to own property and obtain divorces and the right of all non-disenfranchised women to serve on juries.

Although women did not sustain the ambitious hopes that followed the successful suffrage campaign, they could claim smaller victories. Reformers in the 1920s struggled against a repressive political climate to sustain their social justice agenda and, in the Depression years, became active and valued participants in the New Deal. Not as influential in the war years, they nonetheless left a permanent mark on public policy, especially in their Women's Bureau and Social Security activities.

Patterns in the home are less clearly defined. The Depression and war had contradictory effects on marriage, divorce, and fertility rates. Trends of the 1920s toward increased emphasis on female sexuality persisted, but they did so in the context of an abiding cultural ideal that assumed that this sexuality would be confined in the context of marriage and the home.

As Americans faced the realities of a complex postwar world, these themes of women's lives at home and in the workplace and political arena would do more than continue. They would eventually erupt in dramatic challenges to prevailing notions of women's proper place.

D O C U M E N T S

Young Women Speak Out

Hᴵꜱᴛᴏʀɪᴀɴꜱ ʜᴀᴠᴇ ᴍᴀɴʏ ᴡᴀʏꜱ of exploring the new patterns in women's lives concerning sexuality, marriage, and work in the 1920s. Magazine and newspaper articles repeatedly analyzed the "New Woman." Movies featured "dancing daughters" and working girls. Advertisements encouraged women to enjoy new freedoms and new consumer goods. Sociologists conducted surveys and studies, such as Phyllis Blanchard and Carlyn Manasses's appropriately titled *New Girls for Old* (1930), which spoke frankly about sexuality.

To hear what young women themselves had to say about the New Woman, we can turn to evidence historians rarely examine—advice columns. The first modern sustained advice column appeared in the *New York Evening Journal* in 1898 and was largely a sales gimmick intended to attract women readers who might purchase products on the advertising pages. Marie Manning, writing under the name of Beatrice Fairfax, became an instant success because, according to Fairfax, the column was "the only medium through which [women] could discuss their perplexities and get an impartial answer from an unknown and unprejudiced person."[44]

In the 1920s and 1930s, young women continued to seek such help. The themes vary in the following letters—one set from *Photoplay* and probably written by white women, and another from a San Francisco Japanese newspaper, the *New World Sun*. As you read the letters, consider how they reveal the struggles women encountered as they adjusted to new social expectations and sought outside, rather than parental, assistance.

LETTERS TO CAROLYN VAN WYCK

Iɴ ᴛʜᴇ 1920ꜱ, Cᴀʀᴏʟʏɴ Vᴀɴ Wʏᴄᴋ's column ran in *Photoplay*, a glossy magazine that featured articles on movies and the stars' lives, advice on clothes and cosmetics, and even articles on household furnishings to help readers emulate the lives of their favorite movie personalities. Van Wyck's answers incorporated both modern and more conventional ideas about women's roles. She was sympathetic to the desire to flirt and have a good time but consistently warned young women against being "cheap." She spoke approvingly of a "wise divorce," which she described as much fairer and squarer than a "miserable marriage." Yet she generally reinforced the notion of marriage as the ultimate goal for young women, arguing in 1927 that it is the "happy ending (no matter what you young moderns say!) of the love story."

Van Wyck solicited letters on specific topics. She described the March 1927 theme as follows: "Should a Wife Work? Working Girls when they get married often want to be working wives. They don't want kitchen duty and no wages but a real outside job and real wages. Then the fun begins, for many a husband objects to such arrangement. Now I'm stepping into the fray."

Dear Carolyn Van Wyck:

I'm married and just eighteen. My husband is only a boy of nineteen, so you can imagine how strange we feel, away from family and friends. He is making a small salary, and I'd like to work to help out. He says that it's because I feel I'm not getting what I want of our marriage. It isn't true. I love him more than life and I want to work to help him. He thinks I'd rather work than be with him. I would work only during his working hours. I have a chance at a job that needs only my afternoons. I worked before I was married. I honestly believe we'd be happier if we had more money. Still my husband protests. Please advise me.

M. T.

IN RESPONSE, VAN WYCK AGREED that wives should work if they wanted to, but she insisted that the woman who loves her husband "must see that their common interests always supersede her personal interest in her work." Compare this young wife's predicament to the young wife in the 1925 advertisement in *Good Housekeeping* (see Figure 9.1, p. 571).

If young married couples were struggling with issues of money and relationships, so too were young single working women. One letter addressed what Van Wyck claimed was a common concern: "Whether or not to be a gold-digger!" She thought the interest was probably generated by the popular 1925 book *Gentlemen Prefer Blondes*, with the oft-quoted line from the heroine Lorelei Lee, "[A] kiss on the hand is thrilling, but a diamond bracelet lasts forever."

Dear Carolyn Van Wyck:

What do you think of golddiggers? Do you think a girl should be one? I was brought up in the country and taught no nice girl would take gifts from a man, unless she was engaged to him, much less deliberately work him for presents. Now I am alone, a working girl in a large city. The girls in my office are constantly augmenting their incomes through men's pocketbooks, and getting away with it. They call me an idiot for not doing the same. What do you think?

M. A. B.

VAN WYCK RESPONDED WITH A LENGTHY criticism of the trend, concluding, "For what does it profit a girl if she lose all the real beauty of life and win a fur coat?"

Yet another working woman felt her friends were too modern in paying their own way on dates.

Dear Carolyn Van Wyck:

I live in a small city and most of the girls in my crowd work. I myself am a wage earner. We are all eager to get a good time out of life, but here's the trouble. Many of my friends pay their own way when they go out with boys. The boys, you see, don't make much money. And they argue that, if the girl pays her share, they can have snappier parties. Somehow I can't seem to do that — perhaps that is why my friends have more dates than I. I'm not entirely manless, but I wonder if I'd have more fun if I were less old-fashioned on this money matter. Please tell me. Do you think a girl should pay her own way?

Myrtle

VAN WYCK WAS SYMPATHETIC TO the desire to be thoughtful of young men's pocketbooks, but she insisted in August 1927 that "men . . . like to own a sense of importance, of power. And paying the dinner check, tipping not wisely but too well, bringing an occasional nosegay of valley lilies or a box of French bon-bons, is their way of flaunting this sense. And so, Myrtle, continue to be old-fashioned!"

Perhaps even more pressing an issue than who paid for dates was women's sexual behavior, a common theme in Van Wyck's column. The following letter in March 1926 encapsulates the dilemma of the desire to explore sexuality in the context of a persistent sexual double standard.

Dear Carolyn Van Wyck:

Petting is my biggest problem. The boys all seem to do it and don't seem to come back if you don't do it also. We girls are at our wits' end to know what to do. All the boys want to pet. I've been out with nearly fifty different ones and every one does it. I thought sometimes it was my fault but when I tried hardest to keep from it they were all the worse. As yet I've never been out with anyone that got beyond my control. It may sound simple, but the minute I say that it is mean to take advantage because they are stronger they all seem to respect my wishes. I've tried getting mad; but it doesn't do any good. I don't seem to know what I want out of life. I want the thrills. I get a kick out of petting and I think all girls do no matter how much they deny it. What's to be done? The boys all like it and I can't seem to make myself dislike it and am not afraid of any of the men I know. . . . It makes me wonder how on earth you are to get a husband who respects you because you don't pet if you get turned down every time because you won't, before they have time to appreciate your sterling qualities. I'm sure that I don't want to marry anyone who is too slow to want to pet. But I want to discover what is right. Please help me.

[unsigned]

IN THIS CASE, VAN WYCK once again sympathized with the problem the writer faced and claimed she must make her own decision. She added, however, "It seems to me much better to be known as a flat tire and keep romance in one's mind than to be called a hot date and have fear in one's heart."

LETTERS TO DEIDRE

SOME ETHNIC NEWSPAPERS also had advice columns directed toward young people, which emphasized letters from young women. Historian Valerie Matsumoto has uncovered a rich source of such letters.[45] In San Francisco's *New World Sun*, Mary Oyama Mittwer was "Dear Deidre" in the 1930s, a decade later than the *Photoplay* columns reproduced on the preceding pages. Her correspondents were Nisei, young second-generation Japanese American men and women. These writers' questions repeated many of the same issues that mainstream young women raised with Carolyn Van Wyck, but they did so in the context of assimilation and intergenerational conflicts that reflected their immigrant background. Both urban and rural Nisei from numerous states wrote to "Dear Deidre," and they often offered advice of their own to fellow letter writers. Deidre was generally sympathetic to young women's desire to be up-to-date and "modern," but she consistently urged them to find a medium between Japanese and American values.

Letters concerning intergenerational tensions surfaced frequently in letters to Deidre. In a 1937 column entitled "Parents Tell Nisei Too Much What to Do," a twenty-year-old college sophomore wrote:

Dear Deidre:

I feel myself quite dependent upon my parents. Therefore, my next question is: Am I dominated over by my parents? For instance, when she (my mother) tells me how I should dress, how I should make up, dress my hair, how I should or should not act in public, where I should go, what I should do, and every bit of anything that concerns me. Most of the time she is right. If ever I should oppose any of her advice, she would say that she has experienced more and that she does not want me to get into trouble.

According to Japanese teachings, children should listen to what parents say and do as they say, which is to be "Oya koh-ko." She tells me that parents teach good things most of the time and SOMETIMES they make mistakes. If you can give me answers by personal letter or through your daily column, I would be very happy and then may seek out a way to prevent my parent's domineering over me—if I can. . . .

Yours truly,
S. N.

DEIDRE'S RESPONSE UNDOUBTEDLY DISAPPOINTED S.N. She noted that when children are truly adults and out on their own, parents should recognize their maturity. But Deidre did not consider a twenty-year-old college student fully adult; she remarked, "[A]s for your parents, I hardly think that they are trying to dominate or to oppress you; and no doubt your mother's advice is sound and most of what she says is right. Yes, and she is more experienced than you in the knowledge of the world (having seen more), and you are wise to be 'oya koh-ko' and to follow her counsel."

Like S. N.'s letter, "An Educated Girl Faces a Problem," published in 1937, reveals distinctive issues the Nisei generation faced. The marriages of most mothers of Nisei women had been arranged ones, and few Issei (first-generation Japanese Americans) had received much education. Progressive Miss, as the writer called herself, had an invalid father and was the eldest of three sisters, and thus had a responsibility for their welfare. She cast her problem, however, in the context of a decision about whether to marry a man she was attracted to but with whom she had little in common.

Miss Deidre:

. . . Now to get back to my problem, it's this: To marry or not to marry my current love and boy friend. To go back a little to ancient history, my ex-boy friend and first love, many years back, was a brilliant and well educated man. Our friendship and love, while it lasted, was quite perfect and beautiful, but for some perverse reason on my part, we broke up.

After that, I went around with several others, but not very seriously. Most of my pals of the opposite sex were all college graduates and the above-average type of men. I respected and admired them, but did not fall in love. Finally, I met my second and current boyfriend, who is totally unlike any that I have ever known before. I like him *very much* although we have little in common. He is fond of me and perfectly devoted.

The thing that worries me is: can marriage be based upon mere liking or "love" so-called— when there is so very, very little in common?

Progressive Miss

INSTEAD OF OFFERING ADVICE TO Progressive Miss, Deidre published two long letters from readers, one who called herself Farmer's Daughter and the other Voice of the Rockies. The first writer urged Progressive Miss to marry the man, emphasizing that he could offer her a comfortable life. And, reflecting traditional Japanese ideas about familial responsibility, she also commented that Progressive Miss's financially secure marriage could allow her to pave the way for her younger sisters' marriages. Voice of the Rockies also encouraged Progressive Miss to marry, but she emphasized instead an idealized notion of romantic love and the way in which time would allow it to blossom.

While Progressive Miss worried about the basis for a good marriage, letter writer Modern Miss raised questions about marriage itself. In "In Defense of Nisei 'Bachelorettes,'" written in 1936, she was reacting to a column in the newspaper about Nisei "spinsters."

Dear friend Deidre:

So many of our Nisei young men are surprisingly backward in this respect and are too afraid or lack the open mind to think out such ideas for themselves without being influenced to a great extent by the old Japanese ideas. It makes me chuckle when I hear these old dodoes smugly calling themselves "Americanized" when they are anything but Americanized or modern in their thinking.

Now, to get back to the point about "bachelorettes": I have no use for any rash person, man or woman, who makes such sweeping statements as: "ALL women are born to fulfill biological duties to this world," etc. Ridiculous! Any one with common sense realizes that there are exceptions to every statement and rule. ALL women are NOT necessarily "born for marriage." Most women, yes, I grant; but NOT "all women." Are all men born to be fathers? No, well, then, for the same reason, all women are not born to be mothers. . . .

In the sensible American society of today there is no stigma attached to the unmarried women. In conservative Japanese society and in our backward Nisei society there seems to be a sort of "unwritten question mark" hovering over the unmarried misses' heads, like a sort of an invisible halo. Why this silly fact should be, I don't know, unless it's a hangover from the unprogressive old Japanese thinking, or rather I should say the OLD Oriental mode of thinking.

What makes me laugh is that some of our elders think that all our bachelorettes are either: (1) dying to get married, (2) unhappy, restless and dissatisfied, or else (3) thinking of catching a man and getting married from the time they are born.

The fact is: (1) they are NOT dying to get married—far from it; they love their own work, are independent and don't intend to get married until they find the RIGHT man (which is more than some of our Issei women did), (2) Our bachelorettes are happy and having a good time out of life. Oftentimes, they are happier than those disillusioned, frustrated-in-life, young matrons who married too soon (or to the wrong man) because they feared public opinion and being labeled an "oldo missu," (3) ALL girls do NOT necessarily think of getting married. Although many do, still there are exceptions who have no intention whatsoever of getting married or even wanting to get married.

I know several charming, talented, gifted girls who have NO intention of marrying, because they want to devote their life to their work, and because they have not so far met a man of equal talent and ability whom they might be able to fall in love with. In other words, they won't marry until they can meet a man they can love BETTER than their careers. Don't think they lack boyfriends because they have admirers, swains and proposals galore. They turn down proposals because they are afraid that marriage will hinder their work, or that too much interest in a man will turn their mind away from their art. So much for that. . . .

Modern Miss

DEIDRE'S RESPONSE WAS TO ACKNOWLEDGE that there were many "charming and talented misses who had no particular desire for marriage." Then she continued, "We have known extreme cases where one or two have looked upon matrimony, as a yoke of bondage to be avoided as long as possible! At any rate, it is our personal opinion that no one need worry about the 'old maid problem.' Sooner or later they all get married anyway. It's just a case of some girls taking a longer time to make up their minds than others. No need for busybodies on the sidelines to worry . . . yokei na osewa!"

QUESTIONS FOR ANALYSIS

1. To what extent do the letters to Carolyn Van Wyck and Deidre support the notion of the New Woman in the 1920s and 1930s? To what extent do they contradict this notion?

2. Compare the themes emphasized in the two sets of letters. In what ways do Nisei women's concerns reflect their family's immigrant past?

3. Why might young women write to total strangers about such pressing personal questions rather than turn to parents and friends?

D O C U M E N T S

Women's Networks in the New Deal

D URING THE PROGRESSIVE ERA of the early twentieth century, white women reformers operated within a political network of shared goals. Their common "maternalist" outlook advocated a special female interest in expanding state power in support of humanitarian reform (see pp. 462–66). Through a multitude of organizations, ranging from the National Consumers League to the National Women's Trade Union League, they worked together to support the abolition of child labor, mothers' pensions, women's wage and hour laws, and the suffrage campaign. In addition to well-known activists in this "female dominion" of reform, like Jane Addams and Florence Kelley, thousands of women supported the reform agenda through local clubs and membership in the General Federation of Women's Clubs.

During the 1920s, when the climate for reform was less hospitable, the women's dominion nonetheless persisted, working through the Women's Joint Congressional Committee to achieve temporary successes like the Sheppard-Towner Act (see p. 523). But it was not until the election of Franklin D. Roosevelt in 1932 and his implementation of the New Deal that women activists had a significant opportunity to influence national public policy. The Roosevelt administration appointed numerous women with experience in Progressive-era organizations to high federal positions, helping to create a network of almost thirty women in Washington, D.C., who collaborated on a female-focused social reform agenda. Although many of them were concerned with advancing women's rights, broad-ranging social reform, rather than feminism, was their primary agenda. As Secretary of Labor Frances Perkins explained, "I was much more deeply touched by the problems of poverty, the sorrows of the world, the neglected individuals, the neglected groups, and the people who didn't get on well in this great and good civilization."[46] Despite these women's high profiles in public life, an organized movement for women's equal rights would not appear until well after World War II.

Former Hull House volunteer and executive secretary of the New York Consumers League, Perkins occupied the most powerful position of the group, becoming the first woman to serve in a presidential cabinet. Her department was a force behind New Deal legislation that secured the rights of organized labor, and it was crucial in developing Social Security (1935) and the Fair Labor Standards Act (1938). Even more ambitious than the women-backed labor legislation of the Progressive era, which had mostly focused on the states, the Fair Labor Standards Act established federal minimum wages and maximum hours for women and men, and it finally restricted child labor.

Another major appointment, Ellen Sullivan Woodward, headed up women's programs under various New Deal agencies (1933–1936) targeted toward the unemployed. Woodward later served as a member of the Social Security Board (1938–1946). One of Woodward's first undertakings, a White House conference in November 1933 on the emergency needs of women, brought in representatives from women's organizations to discuss the problems of hundreds of thousands of women in need of urgent assistance. Woodward hoped to "mobilize women's inherent capacities for community housekeeping."[47]

Women's prominent place in the New Deal in part stemmed from practical politics. Male Democrats recognized that female voters could help the party and the New Deal, as the following excerpt by Molly Dewson indicates. Another crucial factor was the presence of Eleanor Roosevelt. Before her husband became president, Eleanor had been involved in social welfare reform in New York. Her work with the Women's Trade Union League had brought her into contact with working-class women such as Rose Schneiderman, who became a personal friend and staunch supporter of the New Deal. Eleanor Roosevelt brought unprecedented activism and ability to the role of First Lady. Highly visible in public, she wrote daily news columns, contributed frequently to women's magazines, spoke often on the radio, gave weekly press conferences, and nurtured the group of women activists who supported social reform. Roosevelt was also, for her time, unusually forward-thinking in her concern for racial justice, far more so than her husband. African American women were not part of the same network as Perkins and Woodward, but Eleanor was close to and supportive of Mary McLeod Bethune, a black educator who used her position as head of the National Youth Administration's Division of Minority Affairs to push the New Deal to pay more attention to African Americans' needs.

The documents that follow reflect a profound sense of excitement about opportunities in the New Deal for advancing the cause of social reform and optimism about women's participation in government and politics. By the late 1930s, even before U.S. entry into World War II, the New Deal began to lose momentum, and with it women's roles in Roosevelt's administration and in the Democratic Party diminished.

ELEANOR ROOSEVELT

IN A 1940 *GOOD HOUSEKEEPING* ARTICLE, Eleanor Roosevelt attempted to answer the question "What have women accomplished for human betterment with the vote?" She acknowledged that women had made only partial progress in having political influence, but consider the ways in which Roosevelt argues that women in government had helped to bring about significant change.

No revolution has come about because women have been given the vote, and it is perfectly true that many women are not thrilled by their opportunity to take part in political-party work. . . .

The women, however, are gradually increasing their activities. There are more women in civil-service positions and there are more women in rather inconspicuous but important positions

SOURCE: Mrs. Franklin D. Roosevelt, "Women in Politics," *Good Housekeeping*, March 1940, 45, 68.

in city, state, and federal governments where technical knowledge is required.

When I went to Washington, I was so much impressed by the work they were doing that I started to have parties for women executives in various departments, and I discovered an astonishing number of women doing very important work, but getting comparatively little recognition because government is still a man's world.

As a result of this, however, I find the influence of women emerging into a more important sphere. There was a time when no one asked: "What will the women think about this." Now that question comes up often. . . .

Looking for concrete achievements, I feel we can really credit to the women only one over this period of years, and that is the one already mentioned — the government's attitude of concern for the welfare of human beings. On the whole, more interest is now taken in social questions. The government is concerned about housing, about the care of citizens who temporarily are unable to take care of themselves, about the care of handicapped children, whether handicapped by poor homes or by straitened circumstances. This is the general change, which I attribute to the fact that men had to appeal for the vote of the women and have therefore taken a greater interest in subjects they feel may draw women to their support.

ROSE SCHNEIDERMAN

Rose Schneiderman had worked her way from cap maker in a sweat shop to president of the Women's Trade Union League. But she considered her appointment in 1933 to the National Recovery Administration (NRA), the administrative board of the National Industrial Recovery Act, the high point of her career, in part because of the act's assistance to organized labor. In this passage from her autobiography *All for One* (1967), she describes the code-making process of the NRA. What accounts for her obvious excitement about being a New Dealer?

The object of the three advisory boards was to formulate codes for all the different industries for the President's approval. These codes would set up conditions of employment, wages and hours, and would also contain a provision known as 7-A, giving workers the right of collective bargaining by representatives of their own choosing. To do this, hearings, presided over by deputy administrators, were held for every industry. A member of each of the three advisory boards was present at each hearing to safeguard the interest of his constituents. Employers and trade union leaders appeared as witnesses. I was appointed to represent the Labor Board when codes affecting working women were discussed.

Of course, I was very excited and pleased about my appointment. . . . The next two years were the most exhilarating and inspiring of my life. Working hours were of no account. Most of the time there were hearings all day long and in the evening, too. I left the office late every night, tired but happy over the job the Labor Board was doing.

Eleanor Roosevelt took part in everything that was happening. She was intensely interested

SOURCE: Rose Schneiderman with Lucy Goldthwaite, *All for One* (New York: Paul S. Eriksson, 1967), 195–99.

in the housing situation and in the distribution of food to the needy and the work of the W.P.A. [Works Progress Administration]. But with it all, there was always time for friendship and to help those who needed her.

It was fun to be included in some of the White House parties. Shortly after F.D.R. was elected, the Gridiron Club, composed of newspapermen, gave one of its famous dinners to which no woman has ever been invited. Mrs. Roosevelt decided that she would give one for the newspaper women in Washington and for a few other friends, so while the President was the guest of honor at the men's dinner, we had a very gay evening with satirical skits on current events as amusing, I am sure, as those given by men at their dinner.

MOLLY DEWSON

MOLLY DEWSON, WHO HAD BEEN ACTIVE in the New York Consumers League, became the head of the Women's Division of the Democratic National Committee in 1932, and she played an important role in bringing out the female vote for Franklin D. Roosevelt in his first election. Her reward was political patronage for women. She succeeded in getting women appointed to positions in the Democratic Party and also to government positions. Two of her most significant lobbying efforts were on behalf of Frances Perkins and Ellen S. Woodward. Another important activity was her "Reporter Plan" to maintain support for the New Deal among women. The plan called for each county to appoint women to serve as "Reporters of each Federal agency." Their role was to educate themselves about that agency's activities and to share that understanding in local communities through speeches, discussion groups, and the like. Dewson eventually accepted federal appointments herself, most notably serving on the Social Security Board from 1937 to 1938. How does this segment of her unpublished 1949 autobiography explain its title, "An Aid to an End"?

I was going to put my energies into organizing the women to learn specifically what F.D.R. was trying to accomplish and tell others about it so that he would have understanding support in the states, but until January [1933?] I would work to get worthwhile government positions for Democratic women who had demonstrated the capacity to fill them adequately. There were some sixty-five on my list of "key women" whose political work deserved recognition either by the federal or the state governments and whose assistance in future party work was essential. . . .

[Dewson provides pages of typed lists of women appointed to a wide range of government positions including Ruth Byran Owen of Florida, minister to Denmark; Judge Florence F. Allen of Ohio, who was appointed to the U.S. Sixth Circuit Court; Antoinette Funk, New Mexico's Assistant Commissioner, General Land Office; and Edna Bushman, Deputy Collector, Internal Revenue, San Jose, Texas. Another lengthy list details women appointees to special New Deal agencies, an

SOURCE: Molly Dewson, "An Aid to an End," in Women in National Politics microfilm collection, Schlesinger Library, reel A3, vols. 39 and 40, pp. 124, 130, 135, 140–41.

accomplishment she particularly valued because of her deep commitment to social reform.]

Many additional and important, although temporary, appointments were made in the New Deal agencies created to meet the national emergency, to move the country off its dead center, to end certain deplorable practices, to care for those wiped out by the Great Depression and to give people a basic modicum of security. Skilled executives, trained specialists and lawyers were necessary to develop and administer these agencies. . . .

In three years Roosevelt had set a new trend. At last women had their foot inside the door. We had the opportunity to demonstrate our ability to see what was needed and to get the job done while working harmoniously with men.

I believe the work of the women I have listed compared well with that of the best men and was much better than the average man's performance.

But it is true that the number of trained and experienced women to choose from is still very much smaller than the pool of well-equipped men. Also women are bucking a deeply founded prejudice. It takes at least a generation for an idea to penetrate, yet it is fast becoming a commonplace for women to strike out in all fields whether it is an economic necessity or not.

One day in 1935 Mary Anderson [head of the Women's Bureau] and I were sitting side by side at a small luncheon in the women's University Club. I said, "This is a pleasant dining room for private parties." Mary answered nostalgically, "I have very pleasant memories of this place. The women in the top government positions used to lunch here regularly on certain days. Now there are so many of them they would need a hall, so we don't get together any more."

MARY McLEOD BETHUNE

AFRICAN AMERICAN WOMEN LEADERS in the 1930s continued to work for women's rights in the context of the broader struggle for justice for all members of their race. Mary McLeod Bethune was in this tradition. A prominent educator, Bethune had founded Bethune-Cookman College, served as president of the National Association of Colored Women, and established the National Council of Negro Women in 1935. Bethune began her New Deal experience as an adviser to the National Youth Administration but soon became the director of the Division of Minority Affairs, later called the Division of Negro Affairs. Years later, Bethune recounted, "[I] visualized dozens of Negro women coming after me, filling positions of high trust and strategic importance. God, I knew, would give me the requisite strength, wisdom and administrative ability to do the job."[48] In that role, Bethune energetically tried to expand black leadership in the NYA and to pressure the Roosevelt administration to provide equal opportunities for blacks in all New Deal programs, not just in the NYA. What does the following document indicate about Bethune's commitment to the New Deal?

Proceedings of the Second National Youth Administration Advisory Committee Meeting (1936)

I want first of all to express on the part of the Negro people, our appreciation for the vision of our illustrious President, and his committee, in extending to the nation this NYA program. In my opinion, and I think I am thinking in terms of thinking Negro people, I believe it to be one of the most stabilizing projects for the benefit of the American of tomorrow, than possibly any one thing that we have done. . . .

The Negro views with deep interest the national program for all youth and approves most highly its objectives. More particularly is the Negro interested in those phases of the program, which for the first time in the history of the nation, affords to Negro youth through Federal benefits, larger opportunities for education, productive work and cultural and wholesome recreation.

SOURCE: Audrey Thomas McCluskey and Elaine M. Smith, eds., *Mary McLeod Bethune: Building a Better World, Essays and Documents* (Bloomington: Indiana University Press, 1999), 216.

DESPITE THE NEW DEAL'S ultimate shortcomings in addressing the inequities blacks experienced, Bethune remained a loyal supporter of both Roosevelts. In describing Eleanor Roosevelt, she claimed that she "has done more to better race relations and to give the 'human touch' to the affairs of state and the democratic struggle than any other woman I have known."[49]

The following is a formal letter to President Roosevelt. Written in 1940, as the United States began mobilizing its industrial productivity anticipating the advent of war, Bethune wrote in her position of president of the National Council of Negro Women. Although not a participant in the white women's New Deal, Bethune had a strong base of power among black women's organizations. What is she asking of Roosevelt in this letter? What claims does she make about African American women and why?

My dear Mr. President:

At a time like this, when the basic principles of democracy are being challenged at home and abroad, when racial and religious hatreds are being engendered, it is vitally important that the Negro, as a minority group in this nation, express anew his faith in your leadership and his unswerving adherence to a program of national defense adequate to insure the perpetuation of the principles of democracy. I approach you as one of a vast army of Negro women who recognize that we must face the dangers that confront us with a united patriotism.

We, as a race, have been fighting for a more equitable share of those opportunities which are fundamental to every American citizen who would enjoy the economic and family security which a true democracy guarantees. Now we come as a group of loyal, self-sacrificing women who feel they have a right and a solemn duty to serve their nation.

In the ranks of Negro womanhood in America are to be found ability and capacity for leadership, for administrative as well as routine tasks,

SOURCE: McCluskey, 173–74.

for the types of service so necessary in a program of national defense. These are citizens whose past records at home and in war service abroad, whose unquestioned loyalty to their country and its ideals, and whose sincere and enthusiastic desire to serve you and the nation indicate how deeply they are concerned that a more realistic American democracy, as visioned by those not blinded by racial prejudices, shall be maintained and perpetuated.

I offer my own services without reservation, and urge you, in the planning and work which lies ahead, to make such use of the services of qualified Negro women as will assure the thirteen and a half million Negroes in America that they, too, have earned the right to be numbered among the active forces who are working towards the protection of our democratic stronghold.

Faithfully yours,
Mary McLeod Bethune

QUESTIONS FOR ANALYSIS

1. Frances Perkins once commented, "Those of us who worked to put together the New Deal are bound together by spiritual ties no one else can understand." What was the basis for the bond of the New Deal's women's network?

2. What distinctive contribution did Eleanor Roosevelt think women had brought to public life since getting the vote?

3. To what extent are the concerns expressed by Mary McLeod Bethune different from those of the white women associated with the Roosevelt administration?

4. Although the women's network did not forge an organized feminist movement, it did further some feminist aims. How do these documents reflect the concern to advance women's rights?

Women at Work

Since 1830, every period in American history has seen a rise in the numbers of working women, but during the years from 1920 through 1945 growth in numbers also meant fundamental changes in women's labor force participation. By 1920, 24 percent of women worked, and by 1947, two years after the war, when employment patterns had stabilized, that figure was 29 percent. For the period 1920–1945, we can see specific developments, even marks of "progress"—the expansion of the clerical field and contraction of agricultural work; the increased presence of wives and mothers in paid labor; women's growing presence in unions; and an expansion of women's opportunities in skilled factory work. Categories of class, race, and ethnicity continued to segment the female labor market, however, and popular values concerning women's work continued to view women as subordinate wage earners—an attitude that reinforced a sex-segregated labor market that devalued all working women as "temporary" and unskilled, regardless of their status. Even at the height of World War II, when demands for women's labor dramatically broke through traditional employment barriers, this static idea of women's proper place continued to shape profoundly their work experiences and opportunities.

The visual sources reproduced here feature two types of images. The first are advertisements from popular magazines; the second are documentary photographs. Comparing the two reveals the growing disparity between the reality of women's work and cultural values that continued to stress that women's proper place was in the home.

ADVERTISEMENTS

In the 1920s, the advertising industry experienced an extraordinary boom, as advertising agencies adopted some of the techniques developed during World War I to promote the war effort and applied them to the business of selling to consumers the vastly expanded products that rolled off the assembly lines of American factories. Growing more sophisticated, advertisers recognized that women had become the family's purchasing agent, and so they targeted the female buyer with ads featuring women placed in general family journals such as the *Saturday Evening Post* or in women's magazines such as *Good Housekeeping*.

These advertisements depicted women almost exclusively as housewives in the context of their home and children or as purchasers of personal products and fashions. The relatively infrequent depictions or acknowledgment of women's paid labor fell into predictable patterns. Consider Figure 9.1, a 1925 ad encouraging

"**John was worried about bills—Till I Helped Him**"

Earned $600 in 4 Months

Mrs. Ray Altschuler, of New York, earned $600.00 in four months. Mrs. Alice Loomis, in far off Hawaii, virtually paid for her home —by telephone calls and pleasant chats with people interested in entertaining and inspiring reading.

Mrs. Florence M. Caffee, of Wyoming, reports that her work for us has earned her several hundred dollars.

Thousands are earning money, and exercising a cultural influence in their communities, by pleasant spare time work through telephone calls, letters and personal chats. Our instructions by mail make it easy for you. If an addition to the monthly income will be welcome, let us explain without obligation, our money-making plan.

SHE was a young wife who thought her husband could miraculously stretch his income to meet all of her desires. When the sober awakening came, she learned that a wage-earner can bring in only so much. She found out too why so many women are joining hands with the men of the household to make dreams come true. Instead of frittering away her spare hours, she is now a money-earner through the IMC way.

This case is typical of hundreds of couples who have found in our plan a means to become savers instead of owers. The time seems to have passed when one person's income is sufficient for the needs of a family. Let us tell you of this plan that enables thousands of men and women, boys and girls, to turn their spare time into cash —without experience, without capital, without interfering with their regular duties.

Mail Coupon Today!

Dept. GH-H825
International Magazine Co., Inc.
119 West 40th Street, N. Y. C.

YES, I would like to earn some extra money in my spare time. Without obligation to me, please send the details of your money-making plan.

Name..

Street and Number.........................

City............................State.........

◆ **Figure 9.1 A Young Wife Earns Extra Money**
Good Housekeeping, *August 1925, p. 174.*

women to sell magazine subscriptions. Although the text suggests that wives can contribute to the family income "in their spare time" and by "joining hands with the men of the household to make dreams come true," both the image and the text suggest women's distinctly subordinate status. Consider the message in the ways in which husband and wife are positioned and in their facial expressions. What do the image and the text together suggest about attitudes toward wives and husbands as "money earners"? What is the significance of the way in which the ad correlates women's paid labor to family goals?

When ads depicted women in the workplace, by far the most common image was that of the secretary, a reflection of the burgeoning ranks and high visibility of office workers in the years after World War I. Figure 9.2 shows an ad in which Palmolive soap directed its attention to the "Business Girl." In this 1928 image,

the demure and tidy appearance of the young woman reflected the respectability of clerical work for young, white, unmarried women and the importance of a feminine appearance. How does the text distinguish Palmolive from other soaps? What message is the advertiser trying to convey by emphasizing "Dollars-and-Cents Value" and "'That Schoolgirl Complexion'"?

The rare ad images of professional women in the 1920s and 1930s were almost always of a nurse promoting products related to health and cleanliness. Figure 9.3, a 1937 ad for the scouring powder Bon Ami, depicts a beautiful, even glamorous, young woman in a crisp nursing uniform. Juxtaposed with her elegance is the labor she's performing—cleaning a bathtub. Why did Bon Ami choose the figure of a nurse to help sell its product? What does the image suggest about popular perceptions of the nursing profession?

In magazines directed at white audiences, the only images of black working women were as domestic servants. The 1935 ad shown in Figure 9.4 illustrates a short story of a white woman, Helen, and her frustration with her black maid, Ella May, who "plumb forgot" to wash out her dish rag and towels. The problem is resolved when Helen's friend Marian, who does her own housework and is therefore more knowledgeable about helpful products, urges Helen to buy Red Cross (paper) towels for Ella May

◆ **Figure 9.3** "A nurse meets all sorts of bathtubs"
Saturday Evening Post, *1937.*

◆ **Figure 9.4 Ella May Learns about Red Cross Towels**

to use on messy jobs. Note that the photographic image of Ella May at the top indicates a chastened look as she listens to her employer criticize her, while in the final cartoon image she is smiling happily. Why did the advertiser choose to introduce a black maid into the story rather than simply having one housewife educate another about the virtues of paper towels? What does the ad suggest about popular perceptions of black domestic workers?

If ads in the 1920s and 1930s portrayed working women in customarily subordinate and sex-segregated jobs, advertisements in the World War II era branched out significantly. White women appeared engaged in defense factory work and in a variety of jobs traditionally viewed as the preserve of men. Texts accompanying the ads often explained that women had stepped in to fill the void left by male workers who joined the military, and the women depicted were young and attractive, indicating that doing "men's work" did not endanger femininity. That married women were taking defense jobs was a common theme in wartime ads. In the 1943 ad for the Pennsylvania Railroad reproduced in Figure 9.5, for example, "Mrs. Casey Jones" is shown wearing overalls and holding an oversized hammer and wrench. The name is a reference to railroad engineer John Luther "Casey" Jones (1864–1900), immortalized as a hero in a popular ballad. The ad tells readers, "You will find these women, not merely in expected places, such as offices, telephone exchanges

Meet <u>MRS.</u> Casey Jones

CASEY'S gone to war...so Mrs. Jones is "working on the railroad!"

She is putting in a big day's work oiling and swabbing down giant engines, cleaning and vacuuming cars, handling baggage, selling tickets, moving through the aisles as a trainman.

In fact, she is doing scores of different jobs on the Pennsylvania Railroad — and doing them well. So the men in the armed forces whom she has replaced can take comfort in the fact Mrs. Casey Jones is "carrying on" in fine style.

Since the war began, Pennsylvania Railroad has welcomed thousands of women into its ranks of loyal, busy and able workers. They are taking a real part in the railroad's big two-fold job of moving troops and supplies and serving essential civilian needs during the war emergency.

You will find these women, not merely in expected places, such as offices, telephone exchanges and ticket windows . . . you will find them out where "man-size" jobs have to be done: in the round house, in the shops, in the yards, in the terminals, in the cars.

We feel sure the American public will take pride in the way American womanhood has pitched in to keep the Victory trains rolling!

BUY UNITED STATES
WAR BONDS AND STAMPS

★ ★ PENNSYLVANIA RAILROAD
Serving the Nation

★ 34,547 in the Armed Forces   ★ 43 have given their lives for their country

◆ **Figure 9.5** **Mrs. Casey Jones**
Saturday Evening Post, September 18, 1943, 93. By permission of American Premier Underwriters (formerly Penn Central Corporation).

and ticket windows . . . you will find them out where 'man-size' jobs have to be done." But consider the other images and the text. How do they suggest that her job is only temporary? What popular interpretation of married women's wartime work does this ad reveal?

DOCUMENTARY PHOTOGRAPHS

Documentary photographs of ordinary working women multiplied dramatically in the post–World War I years. Producing images was made easier by technological advancements such as the availability of rolls of film and faster lenses that allowed photographers to capture people and events more spontaneously. The interest of federal agencies in investigating and documenting work and social life also fostered more attention to photographing ordinary Americans. After its inception in 1920, the Women's Bureau of the U.S. Department of Labor not only conducted surveys but also commissioned photographs of a wide range of employment situations. During the Great Depression, the New Deal's Farm Security Administration (FSA) became a potent force in documenting the lives of Americans throughout the nation. Created in part to promote the New Deal itself, the FSA's photography project dramatically conveyed both the nation's pervasive poverty and the efforts of the federal government to help Americans weather the crisis. Many FSA photographers were exceptionally talented and brought artistic skill as well as compassion for their subjects to their work. Of these, a number were women. Marion Post Wolcott recorded the details of people's daily lives, particularly women's work. Dorothea Lange, who called herself a "photographer-investigator," was especially noted for her documentation of migrant workers in the West, with "Migrant Mother" perhaps the most famous photograph (see p. 536). Even after the Depression ended, the government stayed in the business of photographing Americans at work as part of its Office of War Information propaganda effort.

Figures 9.6 and 9.7 capture an aspect of women's work ignored in advertisements: farm labor and food processing. The numbers of Americans involved in agricultural labor declined steadily in the twentieth century, a reflection of both the mechanization of farm work and the growing importance of the industrial and commercial sectors of the economy. Whereas in 1880 the U.S. Census had listed 19 percent of adult working women as employed in agriculture, by 1920 that figure was 13 percent, and by 1940, 3 percent. However, these statistics do not take into account the many rural women who labored without pay in family-owned farms, performing both household tasks and field work

Among agricultural wage laborers, race was a determining factor. In 1930, more than 20 percent of African American, Japanese, and Mexican working women were farm laborers, as opposed to 5 percent of working white women. Filipinas and Native American women also commonly worked in the fields. Rural Japanese and Mexican women, who worked on their small family-held farms in the West, supplemented the family income by working for wages in local food-processing plants. In the South, black women and their families continued as

◆ **Figure 9.6** Ben Shahn, "Picking Cotton" (1935)
Library of Congress LC-USF-3301-006218.

sharecroppers, struggling through the crushing conditions of drought and depression to eke a living out of the land.

Both Figures 9.6 and 9.7 were produced under the auspices of the FSA. The well-known painter Ben Shahn took the haunting photograph in Figure 9.6 in 1935. While many pictures of field workers emphasized the backbreaking nature of their labor, Shahn chose to photograph a young black girl as she paused at her work as a cotton picker. What impact is Shahn striving for with this image in an Arkansas cotton field? In what ways does his photograph increase the viewer's empathy for the young woman?

Mexican immigrant women had the double burden of working while trying to maintain their families in harsh, substandard living conditions. In addition to working in the fields, they also clustered in jobs packing fruits and vegetables, as Figure 9.7 indicates. This 1938 picture, taken in Brentwood, California, by Dorothea Lange, seems less obviously posed than Figure 9.6, but here, too, the women are aware of the photographer. In another photograph taken at the same time, Lange captured a wider view of the packing shed that emphasized unpleasant working conditions and showed the women and a handful of men hard at work. For this photograph Lange focused on the women themselves. What was Lange attempting to capture? What does the image suggest about the way in which these women created a communal spirit despite the arduous nature of fruitpacking work?

◆ **Figure 9.7** **Dorothea Lange, "Women Packing Apricots" (1938)**
Library of Congress LC-USF34-018316-E.

Figure 9.8, a 1939 photograph of an Atlanta, Georgia, domestic servant taken by Marion Post Wolcott, captures one of the most common yet least frequently photographed forms of paid female labor, domestic service. Although in the twentieth century, the percentage of women employed as domestics declined overall, for the years 1920 through 1945, roughly 20 percent of all women workers still fell into this category. By 1920, the percentage of native-born and foreign-born white women domestics had dropped dramatically, leaving the field to be dominated by women of color. In 1920, 40 percent of black women were domestic workers, a percentage that rose to almost 60 percent in 1940. Native Americans and Mexican Americans also clustered in domestic work, although better job opportunities for these groups expanded during World War II to a greater extent than for African Americans.

This racial pattern points to the importance of hierarchical relationships in constructing a multicultural history of American women. The definition of middle-class status for white women included freedom from household drudgery, a freedom gained by the purchase of household appliances and by the employment of other women to do the domestic labor. Many middle-class and elite white

◆ **Figure 9.8** Marion Post Wolcott, "Negro Domestic Servant" (1939)
Library of Congress LC-USF34TO1-051738-D.

women's ability to entertain, to enjoy leisure, or to take paid employment often depended on their ability to secure the cheap, easily exploitable labor of women of color. The image in Figure 9.8 hints at this dynamic, as the work of the black maid—in doing the dishes, keeping the kitchen spotless, and caring for the white infant—offers her employer freedom from household tasks. Might the photographer be calling our attention to the fact that the black woman, who was surely old enough to be a mother, was caring for a white baby instead of her own child? How does this photograph's representation of a black servant contrast with the advertisement in Figure 9.4? Are there are any parallels between this photograph and the daguerreotype in Figure 4.11 (p. 245) of the nineteenth-century family with their "slave nurse"?

For most of the 1920s, an era of weak unions, few women (one in thirty-four) participated in organized labor. A new militancy emerged late in the decade, however, when textile workers in North Carolina rebelled in spontaneous strike, setting off a wave of union organizing that persisted into the 1930s and 1940s.

Figure 9.9, an FSA photograph taken by Jack Delano in 1941, shows the determined stance of United Textile Workers' Union women picketing in Greensboro, Georgia, as a lone policeman or perhaps company guard looks on. Other unions, mostly notably the International Ladies Garment Workers' Union, made even more headway in the Depression, prompting organizer Anna Weinstein to say, "Now the girls have a power stronger than the bosses to back them. We are no longer robots. We are independent. We are strong. No longer can a boss cheat us out of pay. We now have the courage to tell him he is doing wrong and he must stop."[50]

Although the Greensboro women are not elegantly dressed, their clothing does not necessarily reveal that they are factory workers. What do their clothing choices suggest about their image of themselves as strikers? Compare this photograph with the depiction of striking shirtwaist workers in 1909 (see Figure 8.1, p. 491). How does the ability to capture women actively on the picket line enhance the photographer's power to depict striking women's militancy? What does the photograph reveal of Delano's own attitude toward the strikers?

While some women were able to organize to improve their work lives, the harsh times of the Depression created more opportunities for exploitative labor.

◆ **Figure 9.9** **Jack Delano, "Striking Georgia Textile Workers" (1941)**
Library of Congress LC-USF33-020936-M2.

◆ **Figure 9.10** **Mexican American Garment Workers in Texas (1934)**
National Archives 86G-6E-8.

A glutted labor market and the presence of poor Mexican women in the West and Southwest led garment manufacturers to return to the late nineteenth-century practice of putting out piecework to women in their homes. Figure 9.10 shows Mexican American women in Texas working on fabric cut in New York City and sent to them in bundles. The photographer makes it clear that the three women are gathered in a home. But the positions of the women and the bundles of cloth indicate that the women are engaged in commercial sewing. The man's hat hanging on the wall suggests that there might be a male breadwinner in the family but that women's paid labor is nonetheless necessary. Compare this to a photograph with a similar theme from the turn of the century, Jacob Riis's "In the Home of an Italian Ragpicker" (see Figure 7.1, p. 435). What similarities do you find in these depictions of piecework? How have conditions changed?

Women's job opportunities significantly improved during World War II. The 1945 image of two female riveters engaged in defense work in Figure 9.11 suggests the dramatic changes in women's work during the war. The imperatives of defense industry not only challenged traditional sex segregation and gave white women an opportunity to work in highly skilled industrial jobs, but they also created inroads in racial hierarchies that had limited most African American women to domestic labor. While magazine advertisements like that in Figure 9.5 continued to depict white women exclusively, documentary photographers, most of whom worked for the FSA, created an extensive record of white and black women's defense work during World War II. These images were usually posed and intended to highlight women's patriotic participation in the war effort.

The image in Figure 9.11 originally appeared in the black journal *Opportunity* and, like many wartime defense work photographs, was to some extent idealized.

◆ **Figure 9.11 Rosie the Riveters (1945)**
General Research Division, Schomburg Center for Research in
Black Culture, The New York Public Library, Astor, Lenox, and
Tilden Foundations.

Defense firms resisted hiring any women in the first half year after Pearl Harbor, and even after a severe labor shortage forced them to turn to white women, the firms still balked at hiring black women, who were the last hired and first fired, tended to have the least skilled and least desirable industrial jobs, and encountered significant discrimination from white employees as well as employers (see pp. 549–51). Yet none of these tensions surface in this photograph of two women riveting. In what ways does this posed image indicate a collegial working relationship between the women? Why might a magazine with a black readership choose this particular image to represent black women defense workers?

Wartime photographs of working women documented their contribution to the war effort, but neither the government nor employers expected women's expanded job opportunities to be permanent, an assumption that was also reflected in wartime advertisements (see Figure 9.5). But World War II labor shortages did result in some permanent changes. Although few women maintained the same level of skilled industrial work after the war, many were able to continue in some industrial jobs, especially in the textile and auto industries. Wartime need also helped to open up the clerical field to many women of color. African American, Chinese American, and Nisei women, for example, obtained jobs working for the federal government during the war, and for black women in particular civil service was an important avenue of employment in the postwar period. These small gains, however, should not obscure the fact that sex- and race-segregated labor patterns that relegated women to lower-paid and lower-skilled jobs continued to be the norm in the post–World War II years.

QUESTIONS FOR ANALYSIS

1. What do the advertising images suggest about popular attitudes concerning women and work?

2. In what ways are the advertising images similar to those of the documentary photographs? How are they different?

3. What sorts of jobs were most likely to be considered women's work? Why is sex-segregated labor such an important concept for understanding the broader meaning of women's increased participation in the workforce in this period?

4. How did the Great Depression and World War II affect women's work lives?

5. How did the job experiences of white women and women of color vary? In what ways were they similar?

NOTES

1. Dorothy M. Brown, *Setting a Course: American Women in the 1920s* (Boston: Twayne, 1987), 69.

2. Ibid., 50.

3. Paula Giddings, *When and Where I Enter: The Impact of Black Women on Race and Sex in America* (New York: Quill Press, 1988), 169.

4. Nancy F. Cott, *The Grounding of Modern Feminism* (New Haven: Yale University Press, 1987), 102.

5. Kristi Andersen, *After Suffrage: Women in Partisan and Electoral Politics before the New Deal* (Chicago: University of Chicago Press, 1996); Cott, *The Grounding of Modern Feminism*, 104–8, 318–19.

6. Alice Kessler-Harris, *Out to Work: A History of Wage-Earning Women in the United States* (New York: Oxford University Press, 1982), 248.

7. Lynn Y. Weiner, *From Working Girl to Working Mother: The Female Labor Force in the United States, 1820–1980* (Chapel Hill: University of North Carolina Press, 1985), 104.

8. Jacqueline Jones, *Labor of Love, Labor of Sorrow: Black Women, Work, and the Family, from Slavery to the Present* (New York: Basic Books, 1985), 177.

9. Elizabeth Clark-Lewis, *Living In, Living Out: African American Domestics in Washington, D.C., 1910–1940* (Washington, DC: Smithsonian Institution Press, 1994), 157.

10. Paul S. Taylor, "Mexican Women in Los Angeles Industry in 1928," *Aztlan* 11 (1980): 116 (originally written in 1929).

11. Emily Newell Blair, "Discouraged Feminists," *Outlook and Independent* 158 (July 8, 1931): 303.

12. *Photoplay* 29 (February 1926): 105.

13. Phyllis Blanchard and Carlyn Manasses, *New Girls for Old* (New York: Macaulay, 1930), 196.

14. Elaine Tyler May, *Great Expectations: Marriage and Divorce in Post-Victorian America* (University of Chicago Press, 1980); John D'Emilio and Estelle B. Freedman, *Intimate Matters: A History of Sexuality in America* (New York: Harper & Row, 1988).

15. Hazel V. Carby, "'It Jus Be's Dat Way Sometime': The Sexual Politics of Women's Blues," *Radical America* 20 (1986), 9–22.

16. Christina Simmons, "Women's Power in Sex Radical Challenges to Marriage in the Early-Twentieth Century United States," *Feminist Studies* (Spring 2003) 29: 188.

17. Robert S. and Helen Merrell Lynd, *Middletown in Transition: A Study in Cultural Conflicts* (New York: Harcourt, 1937), 178–79.

18. Kessler-Harris, *Out to Work*, 257.

19. Susan Ware, *Holding Their Own: American Women in the 1930s* (Boston: Twayne, 1982), 27.

20. Weiner, *From Working Girl to Working Mother*, 4–6.

21. Jones, *Labor of Love*, 209.

22. Devra Weber, *Dark Sweat, White Gold: California Farm Workers, Cotton, and the New Deal* (Berkeley: University of California Press, 1994), 95–96.

23. Ware, *Holding Their Own*, 47.

24. Ibid., 48.

25. Melissa A. Herbert, "Amazons or Butterflies: The Recruitment of Women into the Military during World War II," *Minerva* 9 (1991): 50–68.

26. Ibid., 7.

27. Susan Hartmann, *The Home Front and Beyond: American Women in the 1940s* (Boston: Twayne Publishers, 1982), 42.

28. Kessler-Harris, *Out to Work*, 276.

29. Ibid., 288.

30. Karen Tucker Anderson, "Last Hired, First Fired: Black Women Workers during World War II," *Journal of American History* 69 (1982): 85.

31. Eileen Boris, "'You Wouldn't Want One of 'Em Dancing with Your Wife': Racialized Bodies on the Job in World War II," *American Quarterly* 50 (1998): 77–108.

32. Paul Spickard, "Work and Hope: African American Women in Southern California during World War II," *Journal of the West* 32 (1993): 75.

33. Richard Santillán, "Rosita the Riveter: Midwest Mexican American Women during World War II, 1941–1945," *Perspectives in Mexican American Studies* 2 (1989): 132.

34. Grace Mary Gouveia, "'We Also Serve': American Indian Women's Role in World War II," *Michigan Historical Review* 20 (1994): 153–82.

35. Xiaojian Zhao, "Chinese American Women Defense Workers in World War II," *California History* 25 (1996): 138–53.

36. Elaine Tyler May, "Rosie the Riveter Gets Married," in Lewis A. Erenberg and Susan E. Hirsch, eds., *The War in American Culture: Society and Consciousness during World War II* (Chicago: University of Chicago Press, 1996), 128.

37. D'Emilio and Freedman, *Intimate Matters*, 261.

38. Ibid., 290.

39. Hartmann, *The Home Front and Beyond*, 200.

40. Margaret Mead, "The Women in the War," in Jack Goodman, ed., *While You Were Gone: A Report on Wartime Life in the United States* (New York: Simon and Schuster, 1946), 278.

41. May, "Rosie the Riveter Gets Married," 140.

42. Julia Kirk Blackwelder, *Now Hiring: The Feminization of Work in the United States, 1900–1995* (College Station: Texas A&M University Press, 1997), 137.

43. Nancy Baker Wise and Christy Wise, *A Mouthful of Rivets: Women at Work in World War II* (San Francisco: Jossey-Bass, 1994), 182.

44. Lynne Olson, "Dear Beatrice Fairfax," *American Heritage* (May/June 1992): 93.

45. Valerie Matsumoto, "Desperately Seeking 'Deidre': Gender Roles, Multicultural Relations, and Nisei Women Writers of the 1930s," *Frontiers* 12 (1991): 19–32, and "Redefining Expectations: Nisei Women in the 1930s," *California History* 73 (1974): 44–53.

46. Susan Ware, *Beyond Suffrage: Women in the New Deal* (Cambridge: Harvard University Press, 1981), 15.

47. Martha H. Swain, Ellen S. Woodward: *New Deal Advocate for Women* (Jackson: University Press of Mississippi, 1995), 45.

48. Mary McLeod Bethune, "My Secret Talks with FDR," *Ebony* IV, April 1949, 42–51.

49. Ibid.

50. James R. Green, *The World of the Worker: Labor in Twentieth-Century America* (New York: Hill and Wang, 1980), 167.

SUGGESTED REFERENCES

General Works   A number of broad studies offer insights to women's experiences for the period 1920–1945. For politics, see Robyn Muncy, *Creating a Female Dominion in American Reform, 1890–1935* (1991), and Lois Scharf and Joan M. Jensen, eds., *Decades of Discontent: The Women's Movement, 1920–1940* (1987). On issues of sexuality and marriage, see, for example, Beth Bailey, *From Front Porch to Back Seat: Courtship in Twentieth-Century America* (1988); Ellen Chesler, *Woman of Valor: Margaret Sanger and the Birth Control Movement in America* (1992); Lillian Faderman, *Odd Girls and Twilight Lovers: A History of Lesbian Life in Twentieth-Century America* (1991); and John D'Emilio and Estelle B. Freedman, *Intimate Matters: A History of Sexuality in America*, 2nd ed. (1997). For women's work lives, see Julia Kirk Blackwelder, *Now Hiring: The Feminization of Work in the United States, 1900–1995* (1997); Miriam Cohen, *Workshop to Office: Two Generations of Italian American Women in New York City, 1900–1950* (1993); Evelyn Nakano Glenn, *Issei, Nisei, War Bride: Three Generations of Japanese American Women in Domestic Service* (1986); Barbara J. Harris, *Beyond Her Sphere: Women and the Professions in American History* (1978); Darlene Clark Hines, *Black Women in White: Racial Conflict and Cooperation in the Nursing Profession, 1890–1950* (1989); Susan Estabrook Kennedy, *If All We Did Was to Weep at Home: A History of White Working-Class Women in America* (1979); Alice Kessler-Harris, *Out to Work: A History of Wage-Earning Women in the United States* (2003); and Phyllis Palmer, *Domesticity and Dirt: Housewives and Domestic Servants in the United States, 1920–1945* (1989). For African American women, see Paula Giddings, *When and Where I Enter: The Impact of Black Women on Race and Sex in America* (1984); Jacqueline Jones, *Labor* *of Love, Labor of Sorrow: Black Women, Work, and the Family, from Slavery to the Present* (1986); and Kimberley L. Phillips, *Alabama North: African-American Migrants, Community, and Working-Class Activism in Cleveland, 1915–45* (1999). Valerie J. Matsumoto, *Farming the Home Place: A Japanese American Community in California, 1919–1982* (1993); Judy Yung, *Chinese Women of America: A Pictorial History* (1986); and Judy Yung, *Unbound Feet: A Social History of Chinese Women in San Francisco* (1995), treat the experiences of Asian American women. For information on Mexican American women, see Vicki L. Ruiz, *From Out of the Shadows: Mexican Women in Twentieth-Century America* (1998), and George Sánchez, *Becoming Mexican American: Ethnicity, Culture, and Identity in Chicano Los Angeles, 1900–1945* (1993).

The 1920s   For sources that specifically address the 1920s, see Dorothy M. Brown's general study, *Setting a Course: American Women in the 1920s* (1987). For postsuffrage political issues, Kristi Andersen, *After Suffrage: Women in Partisan and Electoral Politics before the New Deal* (1996); Nancy F. Cott, *The Grounding of Modern Feminism* (1987); and J. Stanley Lemons, *The Woman Citizen: Social Feminism in the 1920s* (1990), are especially valuable. Excellent insights on work are available in Susan Porter Benson, *Counter Cultures: Saleswomen, Managers, and Customers in American Department Stores, 1890–1940* (1986); Elizabeth Clark-Lewis, *Living In, Living Out: African American Domestics in Washington, D.C., 1910–1940* (1994); Margery W. Davies, *Woman's Place Is at the Typewriter: Office Work and Office Workers, 1870–1930* (1982); Lisa M. Fine, *The Souls of the Skyscraper: Female Clerical Workers in Chicago, 1870–1930* (1990); Angel Kwolek-Folland, *Engendering Business: Men and Women in the Corporate Office, 1870–1930* (1994); and Sharon Hartman Strom, *Beyond the Typewriter: Gender, Class, and the Origins of Modern American Office Work, 1900–1930* (1992). Themes of consumption and sexuality are analyzed in Hazel V. Carby, "'It Jus Be's Dat Way Sometime': The Sexual Politics of Women's Blues," *Radical America* 20 (1986): 9–22; Kathy Peiss, *Hope in a Jar: The Making of America's Beauty Culture* (1998); and Ellen Kay Trimberger, "Feminism, Men, and Modern Love: Greenwich Village, 1900–1925," in Ann Barr Snitow, Christine Stansell, and Sharon Thompson, eds., *Powers of Desire: The Politics of Sexuality* (1983).

The 1930s   An excellent general study of women in the Depression is Susan Ware, *Holding Their Own: American Women in the 1930s* (1982). See also Jeane Eddy Westin, *Making Do: How Women Survived the '30s* (1976). On women and work, see Lois Scharf, *To Work and to Wed: Female Employment, Feminism, and the Great Depression* (1980); and Devra Weber, *Dark Sweat, White Gold: California Farm Workers, Cotton, and the New Deal* (1994). Studies that explore women and the New Deal include Julia Kirk Blackwelder, *Women of the Depression: Caste and Culture in San Antonio, 1929–1939* (1984); Julie Boddy, "Photographing Women: The Farm Security Administration Work of Marion Post Wolcott," in Lois Scharf and Joan M. Jensen, eds., *Decades of Discontent: The Women's Movement, 1920–1940* (1987); Blanche Wiesen Cook, *Eleanor Roosevelt,* 2 vols. (1992, 1999); Joyce Ross, "Mary McLeod Bethune and the National Youth Administration: A Case Study of Power Relationships in the Black Cabinet of Franklin D. Roosevelt," *Journal of Negro His-*

tory 60 (1975): 1–28; Sandra Schackel, *Social Housekeepers: Women Shaping Public Policy in New Mexico, 1920–1940* (1992); Martha H. Swain, *Ellen S. Woodward: New Deal Advocate for Women* (1995); Susan Ware, *Beyond Suffrage: Women in the New Deal* (1981); and Susan Ware, *Partner and I: Molly Dewson, Feminism, and New Deal Politics* (1987). A valuable essay on the experience of Japanese American women is Valerie Matsumoto, "Redefining Expectations: Nisei Women in the 1930s," *California History* 73 (1994): 44–53.

World War II   For World War II, see the following general works: Karen Anderson, *Wartime Women: Sex Roles, Family Relations, and the Status of Women during World War II* (1981); D'Ann Campbell, *Women at War with America: Private Lives in a Patriotic Era* (1984); Susan M. Hartmann, *The Home Front and Beyond: American Women in the 1940s* (1982); Emily Yellin, *Our Mothers' War: American Women at Home and at the Front During World War II* (2004); and Margaret Higonnet et al., eds., *Behind the Lines: Gender and the Two World Wars* (1987). Women's military service is treated in Grace Mary Gouveia, "'We Also Serve': American Indian Women's Role in World War II," *Michigan Historical Review* 20 (1994): 153–82; Gail M. Gutierrez, "The Sting of Discrimination: Women Airforce Service Pilots (WASP)," *Journal of the West* 35 (1996): 153–82; Melissa A. Herbert, "Amazons or Butterflies: The Recruitment of Women into the Military during World War II," *Minerva* 9 (1991): 50–68; and Martha S. Putney, *When the Nation Was in Need: Blacks in the Women's Army Corps during World War II* (1992). Valuable accounts of women in the workforce are Karen Tucker Anderson, "Last Hired, First Fired: Black Women Workers during World War II," *Journal of American History* 69 (1982): 82–97; Eileen Boris, "'You Wouldn't Want one of 'Em Dancing with Your Wife': Racialized Bodies on the Job in World War II," *American Quarterly* 50 (1998): 77–108; Sherna Gluck, *Rosie the Riveter Revisited: Women, the War, and Social Change* (1988); Vicki L. Ruiz, *Cannery Women, Cannery Lives: Mexican Women, Unionization, and the California Food Processing Industry, 1930–1950* (1987); Richard Santillán, "Rosita the Riveter: Midwest Mexican American Women during World War II, 1941–1945," *Perspectives in Mexican American Studies* 2 (1989): 115–47; Paul Spickard, "Work and Hope: African American Women in Southern California during World War II," *Journal of the West* 28 (1993): 70–79; and Nancy Baker Wise and Christy Wise, *A Mouthful of Rivets: Women at Work in World War II* (1994). Studies dealing with minority women's experiences in wartime include Maureen Honey, ed., *Bitter Fruit: African American Women in World War II* (1999); Valerie Matsumoto, "Japanese American Women during World War II," *Frontiers* 8 (1984): 6–14; and Xiaojian Zhao, "Chinese American Women Defense Workers in World War II," *California History* 25 (1996): 138–53. On reconversion, see Elaine Tyler May, "Rosie the Riveter Gets Married," in Lewis A. Erenberg and Susan E. Hirsch, eds., *The War in American Culture: Society and Consciousness during World War II* (1996).

For selected Web sites, please visit the *Through Women's Eyes* book companion site at bedfordstmartins.com/duboisdumenil.

10

Beyond the Feminine Mystique

WOMEN'S LIVES, 1945–1965

IN DECEMBER 1955, A MIDDLE-AGED AFRICAN AMERICAN woman in Montgomery, Alabama, was arrested for refusing to give up her seat to a white passenger. Rosa Parks's protest against segregation sparked the Montgomery bus boycott, one of the pivotal events of a resurgent postwar civil rights movement. Parks's story signals the importance of women in the civil rights movement, certainly, but Parks, a department store seamstress, is also significant because she was a working woman. In the postwar era, female participation in the paid labor force expanded dramatically and became a defining characteristic of many more women's lives.

Parks's life is one indication of how the period of 1945 to 1965 was rife with tensions and contradictions. Mainstream cultural values of the "feminine mystique" emphasized women's domestic and maternal roles. Yet women worked outside the home and participated in civic activism that encompassed labor unions, politics, and civil and women's rights. Other contradictions are evident in the contrast between Americans' celebration of unprecedented prosperity and their deep anxieties about the Cold War and nuclear arms race. Cold War fears contributed to a repressive social and political climate that inhibited dissenting voices and reinforced traditional expectations about women's familial roles. Yet despite the conservative temper of this era, women activists helped to launch the civil rights movement and began to challenge the discrimination women faced in the workplace and public life.

FAMILY CULTURE AND GENDER ROLES

Two overarching themes shaped Americans' lives in the postwar era. The first, the Cold War between the Soviet Union and the United States, led to a sense of insecurity and anxiety that encouraged conformity to political and social norms. The second, the United States' extraordinary prosperity, prompted tremendous optimism about the nation's material progress. Both anxiety and affluence contributed to a popular conception of the family as a source of social stability and prosperity and reinforced traditional notions of women's place in the home.

The New Affluence and the Family

One startling measure of the nation's post–World War II prosperity was the growth in the gross domestic product (GDP), from $213 billion in 1945 to more than $500 billion in 1960. Not everyone enjoyed this new affluence. Many Americans, but especially nonwhite minorities, continued to live economically marginalized lives, and in 1959, 22 percent of all Americans still lived below the poverty line. Yet most Americans experienced a rising standard of living, with average family income almost doubling in the years between 1945 and 1960. Veterans pursued upward mobility through the Servicemen Readjustment Act of 1944, or GI Bill, which provided federal assistance through home and student loans to returning military personnel. The GI Bill was particularly significant for assisting children of European immigrants in leaving behind the poverty of urban ethnic enclaves to become middle-class suburbanites. Although educational and economic differences still created clear class distinctions between blue-collar and white-collar workers, many of the former benefited from their unions' success in negotiating improved benefits, such as health insurance and automatic cost-of-living wage adjustments.

Affluence contributed to an emphasis on domesticity and the nuclear family. With more discretionary funds,

Americans spent money on homes, raising the percentage of homeownership in the country from 43 percent of families in 1940 to 62 percent in 1960. Many of these homes were located in new suburban developments that created a haven for the new domesticity. However, much postwar housing remained racially segregated both by law and custom. To furnish their homes and garages, families bought electrical appliances, cars, and the exciting new form of at-home entertainment, televisions. New housing construction, road building, and consumer goods fueled the burgeoning postwar economy. Advertisers, manufacturers, and public policy makers all considered consumer purchasing power crucial to prosperity. They extolled the family as the bedrock of the nation's economic well-being and targeted women as its purchasing agent. *Life* magazine captured the essence of this understanding with a 1958 cover that featured thirty-six babies and the caption "Kids—Built-in Recession Cure."

Figures on marriage and fertility for the postwar era suggest Americans' enthusiasm for family and domestic life. Temporarily reversing the long trend since early in the nineteenth century toward fewer children, family size between the war and the early 1960s went up, creating a "baby boom" (see Chart 10.1). More Americans married and married younger, further spiking the birthrate. In the 1930s, women gave birth to 2.4 children on average; in the 1950s, that number increased to 3.2. More babies were born between 1948 and 1953 than had been born in the previous thirty years. In these years, the divorce rate briefly turned downward, a pattern unique in the twentieth century. Pent-up desires for traditional family life denied to many in the Great Depression and war years undoubtedly played a part, while the pervasive celebration of family life in popular culture may also have shaped young couples' decisions.

◆ **Chart 10.1** The American Birthrate, 1860–1980

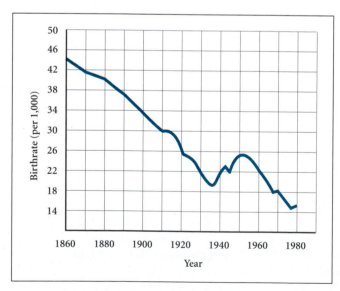

The Cold War and the Family

While prosperous families lay at the heart of America's material success, a stable family order was also credited with a crucial role in giving the United States the upper hand in the Cold War. World War II had barely ended before the two former allies, the Soviet Union and the United States, began facing off for what became a global struggle lasting almost fifty years. Representing the conflicting systems of capitalism and communism, each side attempted to achieve dominance in world geopolitics. In the United States, President Harry S. Truman articulated the doctrine of "containment," which called for resisting the spread of Communist governments in countries around the world. The Cold War became hot in Korea between 1950 and 1952, in the first major overseas armed conflict in American history not authorized by congressional declaration. The newly formed United Nations sent troops, primarily supplied by the United States, to defend the U.S.-backed government in the south of Korea against encroachment by the Communist regime in the north. The war ended with a cease-fire that left Korea divided by a demilitarized zone between North and South Korea that is still in existence. The Cold War also spawned an escalating nuclear arms race. The terrible power of atomic destruction unleashed when the United States dropped bombs on Hiroshima and Nagasaki, Japan, became a mushrooming threat to the peoples of the world as the U.S. and Soviet governments matched their militant rhetoric with competition to stockpile nuclear weapons.

The Cold War had a chilling effect on U.S. domestic politics. In the late 1940s and early 1950s, the nation was immersed in a hunt for Communists within its borders, led by the House Un-American Activities Committees (HUAC) and U.S. Senator Joseph McCarthy. McCarthy's search for Communists in high places was more symptom than cause of the new witch hunts. Other politicians and leaders also called for purging American institutions of "internal subversives." The most notorious manifestations of the period's "Red Scare" were a federal loyalty program that scrutinized thousands of public employees and widely publicized congressional hearings held by the HUAC to investigate Communist influence in American life. Women and men lost jobs and had their civil liberties violated on the basis of flimsy evidence.

In 1950, U.S. representative Helen Gahagan Douglas was red-baited (accused of being a Communist) and pushed from politics because of her support for causes such as rent control laws and federal regulation of oil drilling. Douglas lost a hotly contested U.S. Senate race in California to future president Richard M. Nixon, who hinted at what he thought were her pro-Communist sympathies by saying that "she was pink down to her underwear."[1] Unions and mainstream liberal organizations, including the American Association of University Women and the National Council of Negro Women, purged their membership of Communists and "fellow travelers"—people deemed sympathetic to communism. The intensity of the Red Scare began to ebb after 1954, when Senator McCarthy, overreaching by investigating the U.S. army, was formally censured by the Senate for unbecoming

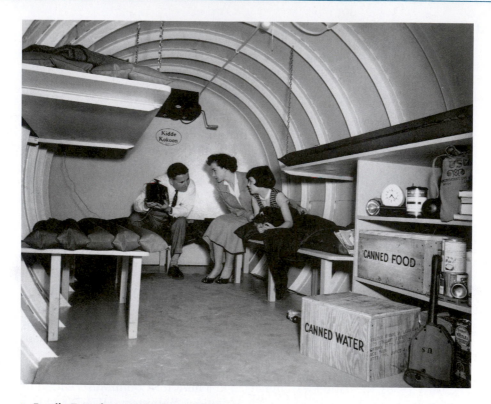

◆ **Family Togetherness in the Cold War Era**

As the Cold War spread fears of nuclear warfare, many Americans, encouraged by the federal government, built fallout shelters in their front and back yards. Magazines and newspapers frequently ran articles that featured pictures of 1950s families posed in their shelters, reflecting the strong emphasis on family culture in the era. This 1955 image depicts mother, father, and daughter in a "Kidde Kokoon," a shelter manufactured by Walter Kidde Nuclear Laboratories of Garden City, New York. The shelter cost $3,000 and was outfitted with such items as canned food and water, a chemical toilet, a radiation detector, and a face respirator. © *CORBIS.*

conduct. But anxieties about subversion and dissent continued to shape the political climate for many years to come.

The Red Scare targeted a great many others as well. The hysterical hunt for Communists was accompanied by an attack on lesbians and gay men as alleged security risks and subversive presences in government employment. Executive Order 10450, issued in 1953, tightened the federal government's loyalty program (established in 1947) and explicitly included "sexual perversion" as grounds for dismissal. Applicants for federal jobs were asked, "Have you ever had, or have you now, homosexual tendencies?" and a rule in the *Federal Personnel Manual* read, "Persons about whom there is evidence that they have engaged in or solicited others to engage in homosexual or sexually perverted acts with them, without evidence of rehabilitation . . . are not suitable for Federal employment."[2] While the majority of people fired or not hired under these loyalty investigations were men, women felt the pervasive risk of exposure, too. Private employers also were unwilling to hire or retain homosexuals. Middle-class lesbians kept their sexual identity private if they wanted to maintain their jobs.

In addition to anxieties over homosexuality, the postwar era witnessed a continuation of fears about women's sexual promiscuity. The 1953 publication of Alfred Kinsey's *Sexual Behavior in the Human Female,* the follow-up to Kinsey's *Sexual Behavior in the Human Male* (1948), shocked many Americans with its statistics: 50 percent of the women surveyed admitted to premarital intercourse, 90 percent to "petting," and 28 percent to what Kinsey termed "homosexual tendencies." Kinsey's findings—as well as other evidence, such as the growth of an urban lesbian subculture centered in working-class bars and a rise in premarital pregnancies—signaled changes in sexual behavior. Yet taboos against female sexuality outside of heterosexual marriage remained strong, as did a double standard that excused male sexual adventures before marriage while prizing premarital female virginity. In the face of challenges to these norms, leading experts championed early marriages to reduce premarital experimentation and firm gender roles in the home to ensure the heterosexuality of children.

Indeed, one key aspect of the postwar culture of conformity was an emphasis on the nuclear family as a bastion of social order, one that would help Americans resist the menace of communism and provide shelter in the midst of an uncertain world. Employers and returning soldiers had been eager to send women back to the home to restore traditional gender patterns. Meshing with anxieties flowing from the disruptions of World War II, Cold War fears of atomic annihilation and Soviet expansion reinforced what was a revised and revived cult of domesticity. And just as social stability presumably led to family order, family dysfunction was deemed responsible for social problems. An apparent postwar rise in crime among children, referred to as "juvenile delinquency," was blamed on working mothers and weak fathers. (See Documents: "Is a Working Mother a Threat to the Home?" pp. 644–48.)

With this concentration on the family came a strong emphasis on rigid gender roles—on men's role as breadwinners and women's as wives and mothers. Many psychologists insisted that "maturity" entailed a willing acceptance of one's biologically determined social roles. Parents who turned to the best-selling child-rearing book *Baby and Child Care* (1946), by Dr. Benjamin Spock, learned that working mothers damaged their children: "If a mother realizes clearly how vital [a mother's] care is to a small child, it may make it easier for her to decide that the extra money she might earn, or the satisfaction she might receive from an outside job, is not so important, after all."[3] In educational films such as *A Date with Your Family,* high school students viewed a mother and daughter dutifully catering to men as they prepared and served a meal. And in movies such as *The Best of Everything* (1959), filmgoers followed a plot that not only depicted career women's sterile lives but also warned young women that "love, even when it's bad, is the best of everything." While some television shows pictured men struggling to control their scheming and adventuresome wives, others portrayed women as

COSMOPOLITAN

SEPTEMBER 1953 · 35¢

SEX BEHAVIOR OF WOMEN

A First Look at Kinsey's New Report

SHEREE NORTH

See "Nothing Sacred" by James H. Street

Another Terrific Murder Novel by Sebastian Blayne

◆ **The Kinsey Report**

Despite the report in Alfred Kinsey's *Sexual Behavior in the Human Female* (1953) that 50 percent of American women admitted to engaging in premarital intercourse, taboos against women's sexuality outside of marriage remained strong. At the same time, the report signaled a real change in Americans' sexual behavior. Kinsey's findings were widely publicized, as evident in this cover of *Cosmopolitan* magazine. *Courtesy of the Hearst Corporation.*

content wives and mothers. (See Visual Sources: Television's Prescriptions for Women, pp. 628–43.)

Rethinking the Feminine Mystique

In 1963 Betty Friedan captured the essence of this postwar ideology of female domestic containment in her best-selling book *The Feminine Mystique*. Arguing that millions of American women were suffering from "the problem that has no name," a malaise brought about by the limited aspirations to which society restricted women, Friedan indicted the "feminine mystique" of popular culture. Excoriating mass media for encouraging women to develop a sense of personal creativity through the use of cake mixes and floor waxes, she similarly lambasted psychologists for prescribing tranquilizers for "neurotic" women rather than examining the social bases of their unhappiness. She criticized popular magazines for disseminating the feminine mystique at every turn, while denying that women were interested in reading about political, international, and social issues. Friedan argued that such attitudes denied women a sense of an autonomous self. *The Feminine Mystique* sold over 3 million copies, a clear indication that Friedan had tapped into many women's frustrations over their prescribed roles (see box, "The Problem That Has No Name").

Despite the impact of Friedan's book, recent critics have pointed out that she vastly overstated the pervasiveness of this restrictive domestic ideal. Rarely acknowledging that the women she described were affluent and white, she glossed over the significant differences that class, race, and ethnicity produced and neglected the increasing number of women entering the paid workforce. Among black women, working wives and mothers had long been valued and understood as virtually essential to families hoping to achieve middle-class status. Images and articles promoting the feminine mystique were largely absent from *Ebony*, the major African American popular magazine of the period. Instead, *Ebony* featured women who fought racial discrimination and achieved success in business, politics, and the arts, although it was careful to note the importance of these women's family roles and their attention "to the needs of their husbands and children."[4]

Even among middle-class white women, Friedan overstated her case. Articles in popular magazines directed at white women often depicted successful career women, including those who combined work and marriage. Writers encouraged women to be active in community affairs and held up as models women who achieved "great pride and accomplishment and the satisfaction of 'doing a job.'"[5] Moreover, in contrast to Friedan's claim that magazines ignored women's discontent, they gave extensive attention to wives' dissatisfaction with their married lives and their housework obligations. In advice columns like the *Ladies' Home Journal*'s "Can This Marriage Be Saved?" letter writers testified to the drudgery of household chores and the stresses entailed in unrelenting domesticity. Nevertheless, the advice dispensed uniformly encouraged women to find psychological tools to help them adjust to the gendered expectations of middle-class marriage, rather than challenge the expectations themselves.[6]

BETTY FRIEDAN
The Problem That Has No Name

In The Feminine Mystique *(1963), Betty Friedan (b. 1921) condemned the media, educators, professionals, and the culture as a whole for defining domesticity and motherhood as the only appropriate goals for women. Based on these two excerpts, what arguments did Friedan present for challenging conventional expectations about women's proper roles?*

If I am right, the problem that has no name stirring in the minds of so many American women today is not a matter of loss of femininity or too much education, or the demands of domesticity. It is far more important than anyone recognizes. It is the key to these other new and old problems which have been torturing women and their husbands and children, and puzzling their doctors and educators for years. It may well be the key to our future as a nation and a culture. We can no longer ignore that voice within women that says: "I want something more than my husband and my children and my home." . . .

. . . With a vision of the happy modern housewife as she is described by the magazines and television, by the functional sociologists, the sex-directed educators, and the manipulators dancing before my eyes, I went in search of one of those mystical creatures. Like Diogenes with the lamp, I went as a reporter from suburb to suburb, searching for a woman of ability and education who was fulfilled as a housewife. . . .

In one upper-income development where I interviewed, there were twenty-eight wives. Some were college graduates in their thirties or early forties; the younger wives had usually quit college to marry. Their husbands were, to a rather high degree, engrossed in challenging professional work. Only one of these wives worked professionally; most had made a career of motherhood with a dash of community activity. Nineteen out of the twenty-eight had had natural childbirth. . . . Twenty of the twenty-eight breastfed their babies. At or near forty, many of these women were

The most ironic corrective to Friedan's assessment is that the author was not the simple housewife and unwitting victim of domestic confinement that she claimed to be. Friedan had a background in radical politics; had been a journalist for the United Electrical, Radio and Machine Workers Union; and in the 1940s and 1950s had frequently written about racial and gender discrimination in the workforce. Thus she knew about women workers but chose not to discuss them in her book. She obscured her past probably because of the anti-Communist preoccupations of the era and because portraying herself as an angry casualty of the feminine mystique made for a more marketable book.

pregnant. The mystique of feminine fulfillment was so literally followed in this community that if a little girl said: "When I grow up, I'm going to be a doctor," her mother would correct her: "No, dear, you're a girl. You're going to be a wife and mother, like mummy."

But what was mummy really like? Sixteen out of the twenty-eight were in analysis or analytical psychotherapy. Eighteen were taking tranquilizers; several had tried suicide; and some had been hospitalized for varying periods, for depression or vaguely diagnosed psychotic states. ("You'd be surprised at the number of these happy suburban wives who simply go berserk one night, and run shrieking through the street without any clothes on," said the local doctor, not a psychiatrist, who had been called in, in such emergencies.) Of the women who breastfed their babies, one had continued, desperately, until the child was so undernourished that her doctor intervened by force. Twelve were engaged in extramarital affairs in fact or in fantasy.

These were fine, intelligent American women, to be envied for their homes, husbands, children, and for their personal gifts of mind and spirit. Why were so many of them driven women? Later, when I saw this same pattern repeated over and over again in similar suburbs, I knew it could hardly be coincidence. These women were alike mainly in one regard: they had uncommon gifts of intelligence nourished by at least the beginnings of higher education — and the life they were leading as suburban housewives denied them the full use of their gifts.

It was in these women that I first began to notice the tell-tale signs of the problem that has no name; their voices were full and flat, or nervous and jittery; they were listless and bored, or frantically "busy" around the house or community. They talked about "fulfillment" in the wife-and-mother terms of the mystique, but they were desperately eager to talk about this other "problem" with which they seemed very familiar indeed.

SOURCE: Betty Friedan, *The Feminine Mystique* (1963; repr., New York: Dell, 1974), 27, 224–26.

These limitations do not decrease *The Feminine Mystique*'s value as a historical source. Not only was the book important in the revival of feminism in the 1960s, but it also captured a crucial aspect of mainstream Cold War cultural values about women. The ideology of the feminine mystique is best understood as a prescription for female behavior promulgated by those Americans most eager to reinforce rigid gender roles as a means of creating social order. This eagerness may well have stemmed from the challenges posed by working women to conventional expectations.

Women and Work

These challenges were most evident in women's changing employment patterns. As the baby boom suggests, women embraced motherhood in the 1950s, but they also poured into the paid labor market in what many observers at the time called a revolutionary development. In 1940, 25 percent of women worked; by 1960 the figure had climbed to 35 percent.

More dramatic was the growth in the percentage of married women in the labor force. In 1940, only 17 percent of wives worked; by 1960, 32 percent of wives earned wages, constituting fully 61 percent of the female labor force (see the Appendix, Table 2, on p. A-37). While all groups of women held jobs outside the home, particularly significant was the growth in wage earning of middle-class white married women, the very group assumed to be most in the grip of the feminine mystique. White wives' participation in the workforce more than doubled between 1940 and 1960, rising from 14 to 30 percent, while for black wives the increase was smaller but began at a higher level, going from 32 percent in 1940 to 47 percent in 1960. In a reversal of older patterns, educated women were more likely to work than those without high school and college degrees.

Mothers also increased their participation in the workforce. One of the most significant developments was the trend toward older women entering the workforce when their children reached school age. By having children at younger ages, mothers found themselves positioned to join the labor force. Because advances in health care meant Americans were living longer, women could expect to work for twenty or more years after their children began going to school.

The expanded availability of jobs, created by a burgeoning economy and fueled by the growth of the consumer culture, also affected women's work patterns. White-collar fields dominated by women for decades—clerical work, sales, nursing, social work, and teaching—grew dramatically. Service sector jobs—so-called pink-collar work, such as food service, personal care, and beauty salon work—also multiplied and became increasingly feminized. In blue-collar employment, women had lost many skilled positions in heavy manufacturing at the end of World War II, but they found other fields opening up: the lower ranks of the printing industry, positions in industrial assembly, and jobs as delivery personnel and bus and taxi drivers.

Improvements in the opportunities for women of color were particularly notable. Although the absolute numbers were small, black women in the 1950s attended college at a rate higher than either white women or black men. After decades of discrimination, they found more white-collar clerical work opening up to them, as did Latinas and Chinese American and Japanese American women. Because of their high degree of education, Nisei (second-generation Japanese American) women also made strides in teaching, social work, and civil service.

For all these improvements, poor women of color still had limited options. Although the percentage of black women workers employed as domestics dropped significantly, from 60 percent in 1940 to 42 percent in 1950, a substantial minority continued to work in low-paid, devalued labor, as did many Latina and Asian

◆ **Dishing It Out—a 1950s Waitress**
So-called pink-collar jobs—food and personal service jobs such as waitressing and hair-dressing—and low-skilled white collar jobs were a significant source of women's employment in the postwar years, as the service sector of the economy expanded and women's participation in the workforce grew. Food service was one of the most sex-segregated areas of employment. While in 1900 approximately 33 percent of the 100,000 people who waited tables were women, by 1970, 92 percent of the 1 million food servers were women. Unlike other pink-collar workers, waitresses were well represented in unions, with about 25 percent of them organized in the 1950s. Unions, as well as a strong sense of occupational identity, helped offset the arduous nature of their work and gave many waitresses and waiters more autonomy in the workplace. *Peter Sickles/SuperStock.*

women. Immigrant women, because of lack of language and other skills as well as discrimination, found few jobs available to them. In 1943 Congress repealed the Chinese Exclusion Act of 1882, in deference to America's World War II alliance with China. As a result of this and the War Brides Act of 1945 and the 1953 Refugee Relief Act, between 1948 and 1965, approximately forty thousand Chinese women immigrated to the United States. Most clustered in Chinatowns in the nation's cities, especially New York and San Francisco. There they worked in family enterprises as well as the garment industry, which was a crucial source of income. Puerto Rican women, part of a vastly expanded post–World War II migration from Puerto Rico mostly to New York City, also concentrated in the garment trade, an industry that was in decline. The results were low wages, poor working conditions, and erratic employment. These poorer women's restricted options underline an important characteristic of the "revolutionary" aspect of women's

◆ **Puerto Rican Garment Worker in New York City**
After World War II, Puerto Rican immigration to the
United States swelled dramatically, facilitated by cheap
airfares to New York City and the fact that Puerto
Ricans were citizens because their nation was an
American-controlled territory. Women migrated in
large numbers, lured by plentiful low-skilled manufac-
turing and garment industry jobs. *Archives of the Puerto
Rican Diaspora. Centro de Estudios Puertorriqueños, Hunter
College, CUNY.*

work after World War II. While certainly many women of color had new opportunities, the most dramatic change was the entrance into the labor market of white
married women who could take advantage of new service and clerical jobs that
offered "respectable" employment.

Women's increased employment also stemmed from changes in employment
practices. Well aware of the expanding labor market and concerned about finding
qualified workers, employers not only willingly hired women but also dropped
the "marriage bar" that had operated in many fields. Moreover, they restructured
the nature of the work market by making part-time jobs widely available for the
first time to tap a rich vein of labor power.

Employers who enticed married women with more flexible schedules and
other incentives had encouragement from administrators in the U.S. Department
of Labor, including its Women's Bureau, and other public policy makers. Maintaining economic prosperity and keeping the upper hand over the Soviet Union
in the Cold War motivated employment experts to evaluate the labor market carefully. Many insisted that "womanpower" needed to be exploited efficiently as a
means of promoting U.S. productivity and competitiveness. Alice Leopold, head
of the Women's Bureau in the mid-1950s, emphasized the need to compete with
communism by training American women in new skills. "Women," she noted, "are
becoming increasingly important in the development of our country's industry,
in scientific research, in the education field, and in the social sciences."[7]

This recognition framed the work of two important agencies in the 1950s. The National Manpower Council (NMC), a private group with close ties to government agencies and corporations, used conferences and publications to draw attention to women's employment. At a 1951 conference on "Women in the Defense Decade," held in the midst of the Korean War, the American Council on Education tackled the "urgent question . . . about just how and in what respects women could serve the defense of the nation,"[8] leading to the 1953 creation of the Commission on the Education of Women (CEW).

In both groups, organizers walked a tightrope between what they viewed as national needs and the dominant ideology about women's place. Sensitive to the prevailing gender norms, they took care not to be viewed as undermining traditional roles. A 1955 CEW report explicitly stated that its recommendations concerning women "must not detract from the importance of their roles as wives and mothers."[9] Yet both groups also encouraged training and education for women and criticized discriminatory labor patterns that limited full use of the nation's womanpower.

Despite the attention paid to promoting women's opportunities in the workforce, changes in attitudes were slow in coming. Public schools continued to track young women into traditional female occupations such as clerical work. And little headway occurred in breaking down racial discrimination in employment. Neither the NMC nor the CEW addressed the limited economic opportunities for women of color, focusing their attention almost exclusively on white women. For all women, sex-segregated labor patterns, and the inequality embedded in them, persisted. Indeed, one historian argues that by emphasizing part-time work, the NMC reinforced women's marginal status in the workplace.[10] These groups legitimated married women's participation in the workforce but barely scratched the surface of the discrimination women faced.

Changes in the labor market and encouragement on the part of employers and the government are crucial factors in understanding the growth in women's work outside the home, but this development was also fundamentally a question of personal choice. Scattered evidence suggests the complicated processes that undergirded these choices. Nurses, the largest category of female professional labor, described themselves as taking advantage of new work opportunities to serve their community.[11] At the same time, they emphasized that their home responsibilities came first, and it was only the flexibility of nursing that allowed them to work for wages. In contrast, many working-class women apparently felt less need to justify working, admitting that they took paid labor to get out of the house in addition to providing assistance to their families.

The degree of family need may have been the crucial factor in most married women's decisions to seek employment. Poor women of color—as they had done for decades—worked to make ends meet. For others, paid labor made life easier for their families and, in particular, enabled them to participate in the burgeoning consumer economy and enter the middle class. A survey of unionized women indicated that a significant number of them took jobs to finance their children's education or to make house payments. Contemporary observers echoed these explanations. A 1957 Ford Foundation study, *Womanpower*, reported that "the desire to achieve a richer life for the family has such widespread approval that it provides a generally acceptable reason for married women whose responsibilities at home do not absorb all their time and energy to go to work."[12] Similarly, in 1956 *Look* magazine concluded: "No longer a psychological immigrant to man's world, she works rather casually as a third of the U.S. labor force, and less toward a big career than as a way of filling a hope chest or buying a new home freezer. She gracefully concedes the top job rungs to men."[13] *Look*'s assessment fittingly summed up prevailing assumptions about women's work. Acknowledging a significant shift in labor patterns, it minimized its impact on women's role in the home, a belief that sustained the persistent discrimination that the rising tide of working women encountered.

WOMEN'S ACTIVISM IN CONSERVATIVE TIMES

No matter how observers minimized the implications of women's work outside the home, it represented a potentially significant challenge to cultural norms. Still other evidence of women's engagement in the public world was the wide range of activism that flourished in the postwar era. Organized feminism remained weak, but women participated in a variety of efforts to improve their work lives and to contribute to their communities. Their activism, like women's participation in the workforce, laid the seeds for challenging the prevailing ideas of women's role in the family, the workplace, and public life.

Working-Class Women and Unions

While the increased participation of middle-class women in the labor market was one of the most striking characteristics of the postwar era, working-class women's struggle to maintain the gains they had made during World War II was an important aspect of women's activism. Unionized women in industry led the way in challenging layoffs, poor pay, restricted job opportunities, and other discriminatory policies. And in some industries, black and white women came together to challenge the racial discrimination that African American women faced in the workplace.

Women of the United Packinghouse Workers of America (UPWA) exemplified a female activism that not only sought to improve working women's opportunities in the 1950s but also laid the groundwork for working-class women's participation in the feminist movement of the 1960s. Like many other Congress of Industrial Organization (CIO) unions, the UPWA had theoretically embraced an egalitarian stance in the 1930s and 1940s and actively recruited black men and white and black women. Women, however, did not always find their union sympathetic to their concerns. As in most industries during World War II, sex-segregated labor patterns broke down in the big meatpacking houses, with women taking on heavy work formerly reserved for men. But after the war, the companies

◆ **Women and Union Activism**

Like women in the UPWA and the UE, women in the United Auto Workers (UAW) fought hard in the postwar era to counter discriminatory employment practices. One of the most militant groups emerged in 1947 in the Detroit area, where women created Region 1-A's Women's Committee, which spawned similar committees elsewhere. This photograph captures Region 1-A's Women's Committee conference in November 1955, a period in which tensions over the impact of automation on women was one of several issues that concerned female union leaders. Although it appears that only a few African Americans are present in this picture, black women were active in the UAW and pursued twin goals of workers' rights for African Americans and for women. *Walter P. Reuther Library, Wayne State University.*

largely reverted to prewar job classifications that limited women's opportunities and wages, and union men did not challenge employers' decisions to lay off women in large numbers, regardless of their seniority rights.

Despite the UPWA's failure to support women during postwar reconversion, the national leadership had become more sympathetic by the 1950s, in part because women made up a significant percentage (approximately 20 percent) of the union. Women drew on the union's Anti-discrimination Department—which also addressed racial discrimination—to bolster their efforts at improving their work lives. This department organized women's conferences, sponsored a woman's column in the union's newspaper, and served as a clearinghouse for grievances.

African American women became some of the most militant female activists in many unions. Women like UPWA member Addie Wyatt of Chicago often built on their positions as community leaders. Wyatt recalled, "[In my church] women were always leaders. They were preachers, they were officers . . . and whatever was necessary in the church to do, women and men always did it in partnership. And I always thought that was right."[14] As Wyatt rose to prominence in the union—eventually becoming president of her local chapter—she turned her attention to the struggle for racial justice and served as a labor adviser to civil rights leader Martin Luther King Jr. Other black UPWA women were active on the local level, drawing their colleagues into drives against segregation and other discriminatory policies in their communities.

Wyatt and other black women focused in part on challenging the discrimination black women faced in the packing houses. Joined by many white women union members, they successfully protested racial discrimination in hiring as well as the packers' policy of racially segregating departments, where white women had cleaner, better paid positions such as bacon slicers, while black women were relegated to dirty work such as cleaning feces from sausage casings.

These women concentrated on breaking down racial barriers, but they also recognized some of their shared concerns as working women. They addressed the problems that kept women from being active in the union and made clear connections between women's domestic lives and their work lives. At a 1954 conference, UPWA leader Marian Simmons pointed out, "[M]erely satisfying the needs of women on the job would not be enough. Just now with women working in the plants and having to go home to all the household drudgery and assuming the full responsibility of taking care of children during non-working hours and providing for their keep during working hours, it is impossible for [them] to exercise [their] full freedom and equality. We have to map out a plan by which women can be free to exercise [their] full talents and inclinations."[15]

UPWA women tackled a number of issues specifically focused on women's employment concerns. They negotiated contracts calling for equal pay for equal work—a provision that affected relatively few women, however, as it applied to men and women doing the same jobs, when most women were clustered in low-paying "women's work." The next logical step in achieving better wages for women—challenging the gendered structure of the workplace—was more problematic, in part because men resisted but also because women were divided on the issue. UPWA women had long supported the concept of protective labor legislation for women and opposed the Equal Rights Amendment, which they viewed as something for elite working women that did not speak to their concerns. Slow to challenge sex-typed work, they sought instead to improve women's wages and conditions within their separate work sphere.

In the immediate postwar years, Mexican women were particularly active in organizing workers in the cannery industry in California and became leaders in a struggle between the more conservative union affiliated with the AFL's Teamster Union and the groups associated with the CIO, the Food, Tobacco, Agricultural and Allied Workers of America (FTA, formerly UCAPAWA). The FTA was among the most egalitarian of labor unions and had organized southern tobacco workers, as well as southwestern food processors, a large proportion of whom were women. The union was sensitive to women's needs and in California during the war had been successful in negotiating nurseries for workers' children. In the postwar era, the issue was union survival. Weakened from the internal struggle and recalcitrant employers, the union was further undercut by Red-baiting. The FTA was branded as "Red," and the Immigration and Naturalization Service deported six of its organizers, including longtime activist Luisa Moreno, because of claims that they were Communists. As with many other unions that appeared too radical, the CIO expelled the FTA from its membership, leading to its eventual demise. However, many of its women leaders became community activists; Julia Luna Mount, for example, became a grassroots organizer around community issues in East Los Angeles.

Most women unionists in the late 1940s and 1950s concentrated on improving their work opportunities and wages, primarily in the context of jobs carved out as women's work. They called for fair treatment as workers but rarely framed their analysis in terms of women's equality. Class more than gender was their lens for understanding their circumstances, although certainly black women had a more complicated analysis due to the racial inequality they routinely faced. But the struggles of this era and the recalcitrance of both corporate employers and male unionists would culminate in a far more activist movement for women's rights in the 1960s and beyond.

Middle-Class Women and Voluntary Associations

More affluent women were also activists in the postwar years. The cultural values that discouraged middle-class women from working outside the home sanctioned the long tradition of their participation in voluntary associations outside the domestic sphere. In the postwar era, middle-class women participated in a wide range of civic and political activities, sometimes in mixed-sex groups such as the American Civil Liberties Union (ACLU), the National Association for the Advancement of Colored People (NAACP), or Parent-Teacher Associations (PTAs), and sometimes in all-female groups such as the Young Women's Christian Association (YWCA) and the League of Women Voters (LWV). As was the case with working-class union leaders, middle-class women's organizations rarely tackled questions of women's rights, but their activism nonetheless belies the stereotype of the bored or self-satisfied housewife cut off from the larger world outside the home.

In the 1950s, many women's organizations shifted their focus away from gender issues. Cold War anxieties over Communism and the domestic ideology of the

1950s put pressure on organizations to moderate their interests in women's rights and in social reform more generally. Changing demographics also fostered the retreat from previous agendas. Both the LWV and the American Association of University Women (AAUW) expanded dramatically in the postwar era, bringing an influx of suburban housewives who had less interest in women's issues than did older members. The LWV moved away from endorsing legislation and narrowed its focus to voter education and local civic issues. The AAUW membership showed less interest in an action-oriented agenda to promote women's educational advancement and focused instead on local study groups.

In other organizations, interest in promoting women's rights was redirected to a growing concern with the civil rights movement. The YWCA's long-standing concern with working-class women helped prepare it to focus on racial inequality. Spurred by black women in its ranks, it eliminated its own organizational segregation and forged alliances in support of black women's civil rights efforts. In the context of the 1950s, this modern reform activity led critics to label YWCA women as "subversive." Other organizations with religious affiliations, such as the National Council of Catholic Women and the National Council of Jewish Women (NCJW), also became involved in racial justice issues. The NCJW's interest in civil rights was particularly deepened by the shock of the Holocaust. The extermination of 6 million Jews by Adolf Hitler's Nazi regime fostered a belief that racism in all its forms needed to be combated vigorously.

The National Council of Negro Women (NCNW) also witnessed significant changes in this era. Founded during the Great Depression by Mary McLeod Bethune (see p. 567) with the idea of creating a political pressure group that could agitate for black women's political and economic advancement, the NCNW fell on hard times in the 1950s. It had difficulty attracting young women, in part because it had gained the reputation of being interested only in black professional women. By the mid-1960s, the NCNW revived, but it did so by downplaying women's rights in favor of community service and civil rights.

Women also found outlets for civic activism in conventional political organizations, working for both the Democratic and Republican parties. One important example was the National Federation of Republican Women, a group founded in 1937 that consisted of local clubs composed mostly of white middle- and upper-class women, although other women, including some African Americans, joined as well. In the postwar era, leaders emphasized women's domesticity, arguing that their concerns for home and family and religious and moral values were exactly what were needed in promoting a patriotic anticommunism that focused on what one leader called the "moral issue of a free America."[16] The federation served a vital role for the Republicans by taking over what was often called the "housework" of the party: grassroots organizing. Working in their local neighborhoods, women, mostly homemakers, became precinct workers. Their tasks included ringing doorbells, registering voters, sending out mailings, and babysitting on election day. In 1956, they orchestrated Operation Coffee Cup featuring small social gatherings in women's homes that allowed them to meet local candidates or watch television together as the national ticket of Dwight D. Eisenhower and Richard

◆ **I Like Ike**

Even as popular culture celebrated the 1950s "stay-at-home" wife and mother, many women, liberal and conservative alike, were active in public life. Groups of women, most of them homemakers, organized Operation Coffee Cup to rally support for Dwight D. Eisenhower's presidential candidacy for a second term. In 1956, enthusiastic women supporters pictured here gathered around the campaign's popular slogan "I Like Ike." *Bettmann/CORBIS.*

M. Nixon spoke to a group of women. Although the federation consisted of both moderate and conservative women, in some areas, notably suburban southern California in the early 1960s, it became the seedbed for a militant sector of the party that sought more right-wing policies, particularly in calling for a more aggressive foreign policy and in demanding reduced federal domestic programs and expenditures. In 1964 these women and their grassroots activities were crucial to the Republican nomination of Senator Barry Goldwater, whose unsuccessful campaign historians now cite as the origin of the modern right wing of the Republican Party (see p. 736).

Other conservative women participated in new organizations such as the Minute Women of the USA, Pro-America, and Women for Constitutional Government, founded to tackle what they viewed as pervasive Communist subversion of American ideals. In their local communities, these women investigated politicians, teachers, and school boards and focused attention on international issues, including U.S. participation in the United Nations, which they viewed as undermining America's sovereignty. In the domestic political realm, they were on the lookout for liberals whom they considered too sympathetic to communism and opposed the Democrats' efforts to extend the welfare state established by the New Deal, which they called "creeping socialism." They promoted their ideas within the mainstream organizations to which they belonged, such as the PTA, and they red-baited liberal groups such as the AAUW and the YWCA. Women in these small radical groups networked with more moderate right-wing organizations such as the Daughters of the American Revolution and helped to fuel and perpetuate the Red Scare. Even after the intensity of the Red Scare abated, these women continued to be active in conservative anti-Communist groups and, like the National Federation of Republican Women, became important contributors to the growth of the right wing within the Republican Party.

On the other side of the political spectrum was a new entry in the long-standing female pacifist tradition. Women Strike for Peace (WSP) came into the public spotlight on November 1, 1961, when over fifty thousand American women in at least forty communities staged a one-day peace demonstration protesting the nuclear arms race and the Soviet Union's and the United States' proposed resump-

◆ **Women Strike for Peace**
The antinuclear group Women Strike for Peace (WSP) began by literally striking—walking out of their kitchens and off their jobs. As the group's numbers swelled, women engaged in lobbying, petitioning, and picketing. This 1962 photo captures WSP members' attempt to stop atmospheric testing in Nevada. *Swarthmore College Peace Collection; photo by Harvey Richards.*

tion of atmospheric testing of bombs after a three-year moratorium. Over the next year, the WSP sponsored peace vigils, petition drives, forums, and letter-writing campaigns. Although the media often characterized WSP members as "simple housewives and mothers," many had a long history of activism. Some had connections to the Communist Party, and many had been active in the Committee for a Sane Nuclear Policy (SANE), an organization that had been founded to challenge the proliferation of nuclear weaponry and that had been damaged by red-baiting. Other members had abandoned the Women's International League for Peace and Freedom (see p. 481), which they found too hierarchical to achieve its aims.

Despite WSP members' concerted efforts to present themselves as merely concerned middle-class mothers, their activism drew the attention of HUAC, which summoned fourteen women to a congressional hearing in December 1962. As WSP women prepared to be grilled on their political affiliations and opinions, they determined that they would not give in to any HUAC demands that they identify Communists in the organization. When the committee called its first witness, Blanche Posner, a volunteer in WSP's New York office, all the WSP women stood with her as a gesture of solidarity. Much to the consternation of the interrogators, they applauded witnesses' comments and seemed not so much defiant as slightly mocking. The women frequently suggested to their questioners that the "male mind" simply could not understand their refusal to have a structured organization with clearly defined leaders and membership lists. They repeatedly invoked their maternal role. As Posner put it, "I don't know, sir, why I am here, but I do know why you are here, because you don't quite understand the nature of this movement. This movement was inspired and motivated by mothers' love for their children. . . . When they were putting their breakfast on the table, they saw not only the Wheaties and milk, but they also saw [radioactive traces of] strontium 90 and iodine 131. . . . They feared for the health and life of their children. This is the only motivation."[17]

The women's conduct made the hearings a media embarrassment for HUAC. Major newspapers featured articles with such titles as "Peace Gals Make Red Hunters Look Silly" and "It's Ladies Day at Capitol: Hoots, Howls and Charm."[18] The hearings strengthened rather than crippled the WSP, which in the following year claimed some credit for President John F. Kennedy's decision to agree to a limited test ban treaty with the Soviet Union. The organization went on to play an important role in the early years of the anti–Vietnam War movement, but its rhetoric of maternalism gradually subsided as WSP women felt the powerful influence of the younger activists of the women's liberation movement.

That a group with such radical political ideas could make use of rhetoric that aligned so well with the feminine mystique sheds light on the complexity and contradictions of postwar female activism. Like other working- and middle-class women activists, WSP members wielded public influence and power but did not overtly challenge the primacy of women's domestic roles. The influence of the feminine mystique, coupled with the anti-Communist climate that stifled dissent, explains why women's activism was not accompanied by feminist questioning of women's unequal position in American society.

A MASS MOVEMENT FOR CIVIL RIGHTS

Women who supported the civil rights movement through their unions or through middle-class organizations like the YWCA were responding to one of the most potent movements for social change of the twentieth century, the civil rights campaign of the postwar years. Going against the tide of the era's political conservatism, black women and men fought against the system of white supremacy in the South. Joined by white liberals sympathetic to their cause, they achieved substantial gains but met with much frustration as well. Both black and white women were major activists in the civil rights movement, and, although women's rights took a back seat to the issue of race, the civil rights movement nonetheless proved a seedbed for the resurgence of feminism in the late 1960s.

As late as a week before the most famous public moment of the civil rights movement — the August 28, 1963, March on Washington, which attracted an unprecedented two hundred thousand black and white demonstrators — no woman had been invited to speak from the platform. At the last minute, Rosa Parks and a few other women were added to the program, but their participation was clearly an afterthought. The charismatic Martin Luther King Jr. overshadowed all other speakers, male and female, with his "I Have a Dream" speech. Historians have only recently begun to reconstruct women's substantial contributions to the postwar civil rights movement. Some were blue-collar unionists, others college and high school students; some were well-educated professionals, others illiterate sharecroppers. In their search for racial justice, they rarely focused on specific concerns of women, but their gender shaped the nature of the activism they engaged in — both creating opportunities and imposing limits — as they helped to forge the modern civil rights movement. (See Documents: Women in the Civil Rights Movement, pp. 649–57.)

Challenging Segregation

At first the movement focused specifically on the South, where widespread racial violence and economic exploitation left millions of African Americans economically, socially, and politically deprived. Racism, moreover, was institutionalized. Since the late nineteenth century, southern states enforced Jim Crow laws establishing a rigid system of segregation where everything from water fountains to public schools was designated for either "whites" or "colored." In all southern states, the majority of African Americans were also disfranchised through poll taxes and stringent literacy requirements. This legalized apartheid system, which denied blacks virtually any protection under the law, came under relentless attack in the postwar era.

World War II helped to set the stage for radical racial change. Continuing migration out of the South, new job opportunities, and military service gave black men and women heightened expectations. By successfully lobbying the federal government to establish the Fair Employment Practices Commission in 1941, African American leaders established a beachhead, albeit one with limited impact, in the struggle to force the national government to take responsibility for enforc- ing the Fourteenth and Fifteenth Amendments. Further, as more African Ameri- cans moved outside the South to regions where they could finally vote, they expanded their political base and gained influence with national politicians in both parties. This influence helped to bring about the desegregation of the army during the Korean War. The Cold War, too, created a new climate, as the shocking inequities faced by African Americans became a common refrain in the Soviets' argument that American democracy was a sham.

In the immediate postwar period, national organizations, especially the NAACP and the Congress of Racial Equality (CORE, founded during World War II), battled disfranchisement and segregation, joined by unions that worked to counter economic discrimination against black people, such as the UPWA. The movement against segregation is usually dated from the 1954 Supreme Court decision in *Brown v. Board of Education of Topeka*, a case brought by the NAACP on behalf of elementary school student Linda Brown and others. The *Brown* deci- sion effectively overturned the 1896 decision *Plessy v. Ferguson*, which had legit- imized the southern pretense of a "separate but equal" system (see p. 337). The *Brown* decision found that segregated schools were inherently unequal and thus violated the Fourteenth Amendment, infusing African Americans with new hope. In the aftermath, their efforts to organize resistance to the southern racial system multiplied (see the Appendix, pp. A-28–A-29).

Thurgood Marshall, who later became the first black Supreme Court justice, led the NAACP team that won the *Brown* case. Constance Baker Motley, the first African American woman to be appointed to the federal judiciary (1966), was the only woman on the legal team. Black women were more in the forefront of the many local struggles to compel school boards to comply with the Court's deci- sion. Of all these confrontations, the one that drew the most national attention occurred in Little Rock, Arkansas. In 1957, with the support of the Little Rock Board of Education, nine black students, six of them young women, registered to attend the all-white Central High School. For their determination, the young people and their families were subjected to considerable violence. One of the young women, Melba Patillo, later recalled that she was threatened with sexual assault as she walked back from school but did not dare tell her parents for fear they would withdraw her from the desegregation effort. Arkansas governor Orval Faubus sent the state National Guard to block the black students' entry. It was not until President Dwight D. Eisenhower, concerned about the defiance of federal law, sent U.S. troops to protect the students that they were able to enter the school. Their victory, however, was only temporary. The following year, Faubus closed the school system rather than integrate it, a tactic that was not checked by the federal courts for several years. Although parts of the Upper South desegregated their school systems voluntarily, by 1964 only 2 percent of southern blacks attended integrated schools, a measure of the deep resistance *Brown* evoked among many southern whites.

Throughout the Little Rock students' ordeal, one local woman organized their efforts and provided much-needed support. Daisy Bates was in many ways typical of black female activists throughout the twentieth century. A successful business-woman and civic leader — she and her husband owned the local black newspaper, the *State Press* — Bates had long been active in the NAACP, serving as president of the Arkansas branch in 1953. While federal troops remained to guard the students throughout the school year, each day Bates ushered the students to their high school and provided crucial leadership within the black community.

Efforts to integrate higher education also were hard-fought battles in which women had high visibility. In 1956, Autherine Lucy became the first black student to be admitted to the University of Alabama, only to be expelled three days later "for her own protection" against relentless white brutality and official intransigence. Seven years later Vivian Malone, along with a black male student, succeeded in integrating that university. At the University of Georgia, Charlayne Hunter, later a nationally prominent television newswoman, broke the racial barrier of that state's higher education system in 1961.

A year after the *Brown* decision, the Montgomery, Alabama, bus boycott became the second great watershed in invigorating the postwar civil rights movement. African Americans stayed off the buses of Montgomery for 381 days until the U.S. Supreme Court struck down the city's system of segregated public buses. The boycott had its origins on December 1, 1955, when Rosa Parks — whose historic action was described at the start of this chapter — refused to give up her seat to a white passenger, a daily humiliation required of black bus riders. Parks was not simply a tired woman whose arrest unwittingly sparked a massive protest. She had been active in the local NAACP for fifteen years, and her decision to make this stand against segregation was part of a lifelong commitment to racial justice. For some time local NAACP leaders had wanted to find a test case to challenge Montgomery's bus segregation in the courts. Parks, a respectable, hardworking, middle-aged woman, fit the bill perfectly.

On the night of Parks's arrest, a group working independently of the NAACP sprang into action. The Women's Political Caucus (WPC), consisting primarily of black professional women, had been founded in 1946 to focus on challenging disfranchisement and segregation in Montgomery. According to one member, well before Parks's arrest, "We had all the plans and we were just waiting for the right time."[19] WPC president Jo Ann Robinson used the organization's extensive network to duplicate and distribute flyers announcing a boycott. At a community meeting the evening after Parks's arrest, the boycott was formally organized and endorsed. Shortly afterward a twenty-six-year-old minister newly arrived in town, Martin Luther King Jr., was selected to head up the Montgomery Improvement Association (MIA), an agency created in response to the boycott.

Men, particularly ministers, who traditionally were at the center of black southern leadership, predominated in the MIA, and women largely were excluded from formal leadership positions, an exclusion they rarely questioned. But women were nonetheless pivotal to the success of the boycott. They not only initiated the boycott but also formed its backbone. Ever since 1884, when Ida B. Wells (see p. 337) had challenged her ejection from a Tennessee railroad car, black women had been in the forefront of battles to desegregate public transportation. Much more than men, women depended on public transportation to travel to their jobs as domestic servants in white households. During the Montgomery bus boycott, some were able to take advantage of a carpool system created by women activists, but most walked. In addition to their personal sacrifices, other women helped the boycott by raising funds and providing food for mass meetings. As one WPC leader put it, the "grassroots support" was "a hundred percent among the women."[20]

Women as "Bridge Leaders"

Montgomery women demonstrated a pattern repeated in other civil rights activities. Men monopolized the formal leadership roles and mediated among the community, the media, and government officials. Women were far more likely to have unofficial positions, yet they served vital functions in organizing and inspiring their local communities. One scholar terms this pattern "bridge leadership."[21] The role of bridge leader became increasingly significant as the struggle took on a new trajectory. While not neglecting the older methods of pursuing legal battles in the courts and lobbying legislators, the movement increasingly became a *mass* movement. In boycotts, sit-ins, demonstrations, and marches, women repeatedly served as bridge leaders.

Ella Baker exemplified the bridge leader. A well-educated southerner who migrated to New York in the 1920s, Baker became active in the NAACP, eventually becoming director of the branch offices. An extraordinary woman and gifted speaker, Baker was committed to bringing about social change by mobilizing grassroots resistance. In 1957 she began to work for the Southern Christian Leadership Conference (SCLC), an organization of black ministers under the direction of Martin Luther King Jr. The SCLC reluctantly appointed Baker an "acting" executive director until a suitable male executive could be found. She accepted the position but clearly chafed at the male-dominated leadership structure and hierarchical style. She later said, "I had known . . . that there would never be any role for me in a leadership capacity with SCLC. Why? First, I'm a woman. Also, I'm not a minister."[22]

Perhaps Baker's most lasting contribution was her central role in the establishment of the Student Nonviolent Coordinating Committee (SNCC, pronounced "snick"). SNCC had emerged from yet another kind of mass protest, the sit-in movement that started in 1960 in Greensboro, North Carolina, when four male students took seats at the "whites only" lunch counter at the local Woolworth's store, determined to "sit in" until they were served. Their protest eventually drew in hundreds of students, women and men, blacks and whites. Their goal was both economic disruption and publicity for the movement. They showcased the tactics of nonviolent resistance, a doctrine popularized by King but originating with the Indian nationalist leader Mahatma Gandhi. Students stoically withstood taunts and physical abuse in a steadfast determination to overcome oppression. The successful Greensboro sit-in sparked a wave of sit-ins in fifty-four cities that helped to desegregate many public facilities in the Upper South. The Deep South, however, especially Alabama and Mississippi, remained resistant.

ELLA BAKER
Bigger Than a Hamburger

Ella Baker (1903–1986), one of the most influential activists in the civil rights movement, served a particularly important role in advising Student Nonviolent Coordinating Committee members. In this 1960 article, she describes their goals. What are her most important points?

The Student Leadership Conference made it crystal clear that current sit-ins and other demonstrations are concerned with something much bigger than a hamburger or even a giant-sized Coke.

Whatever may be the difference in approach to their goal, the Negro and white students, North and South, are seeking to rid America of the scourge of racial segregation and discrimination—not only at lunch counters, but in every aspect of life.

In reports, casual conversations, discussion groups, and speeches, the sense and the spirit of the following statement that appeared in the initial newsletter of the students at Barber-Scotia College, Concord, N.C., were re-echoed time and again: "We want the world to know that we no longer accept the inferior position of second-class citizenship. We are willing to go to jail, be ridiculed, spat upon and even suffer physical violence to obtain First Class Citizenship."

By and large, this feeling that they have a destined date with freedom, was not limited to a drive for personal freedom, or even freedom for the Negro in the South. Repeatedly it was emphasized that the movement was concerned with the moral implications of racial discrimination for the "whole world" and the "Human Race."

In her role as SCLC acting director, Baker convened a meeting of over three hundred college students to help form an organization to orchestrate their future efforts. Following Baker's precept that strong leaders were not necessary for a strong movement, SNCC emerged as a nonhierarchical organization, with rotating officers. Although women were active in all the civil rights organizations, SNCC gave women the greatest opportunity to participate and influence the civil rights movement (see box, "Bigger Than a Hamburger").

SNCC men and women participated in the Freedom Rides of 1961, which CORE organized to challenge segregated interstate bus travel and bus terminals in the South. On May 14, 1961, a group consisting of black and white men and women boarded a bus in Washington, D.C., headed to New Orleans. In Anniston and Birmingham, Alabama, the activists encountered vicious mob violence. A pivotal bridge leader in the Freedom Rides was Diane Nash, a young black SNCC

This universality of approach was linked with a perceptive recognition that "it is important to keep the movement democratic and to avoid struggles for personal leadership."

It was further evident that desire for supportive cooperation from adult leaders and the adult community was also tempered by apprehension that adults might try to "capture" the student movement. The students showed willingness to be met on the basis of equality, but were intolerant of anything that smacked of manipulation or domination.

This inclination toward group-centered leadership, rather than toward a leader-centered group pattern of organization, was refreshing indeed to those of the older group who bear the scars of the battle, the frustrations and the disillusionment that come when the prophetic leader turns out to have heavy feet of clay.

However hopeful might be the signs in the direction of group-centeredness, the fact that many schools and communities, especially in the South, have not provided adequate experience for young Negroes to assume initiative and think and act independently accentuated the need for guarding the student movement against well-meaning, but nevertheless unhealthy, over-protectiveness.

Here is an opportunity for adult and youth to work together and provide genuine leadership—the development of the individual to his highest potential for the benefit of the group.

SOURCE: "Bigger Than a Hamburger," *Southern Patriot*, June 1960, p. 4.

activist who had earlier led the Nashville sit-ins. (See Documents: Women in the Civil Rights Movement, pp. 649–57.) After the violence in Birmingham, some SCLC leaders called for an end to the rides, but Nash interceded, insisting, "[I]f they stop us with violence, the movement is dead."[23] The rides continued. The unwillingness of Alabama's officials to protect the freedom riders eventually led President John F. Kennedy to send federal marshals to Alabama to protect them. He later ordered the Interstate Commerce Commission to enforce desegregation on interstate bus routes. Even though they never made it to New Orleans, the riders had succeeded in integrating interstate bus travel.

Voter Registration and Freedom Summer

Women activists like Nash faced violence, harassment, and degrading jail conditions. By far the most challenging—and dangerous—activities were the voter organizing drives that took place deep in the rural South. In 1960 SNCC had begun a voter registration drive in Mississippi, where, although African Americans represented 45 percent of the population, only 5 percent of black adults were registered to vote. In 1962, registration efforts heated up after the SCLC, SNCC, the NAACP, and CORE established the Council of Federated Organizations (COFO) to oversee voting registration drives in Mississippi.

As they struggled to overcome the reluctance of local blacks to risk their livelihood or personal safety to register to vote, the activists also encountered stiff resistance from local whites. Viewed as outside agitators, they experienced harassment, intimidation, and deadly violence. But they were usually able to rely on a small number of local community leaders — often women — who provided shelter, moral support, and valuable personal contacts, at great personal risk to themselves. (See Documents: Women in the Civil Rights Movement, pp. 649–57.)

The most famous of these local leaders was Fannie Lou Hamer of Sunflower County, Mississippi. Hamer worked on a large cotton plantation. There, despite having only a sixth-grade education, she exhibited natural leadership capacities that eventually elevated her to a position as a kind of forewoman for her boss and an influential person in the local black community. Motivated by the desire to make blacks full citizens, Hamer joined SNCC and, after a year of effort, finally registered to vote in 1963. "We just got to stand up now as Negroes for ourselves and for our freedom," she insisted, "and if it don't do me any good, I do know the young people it will do good."[24] Despite the loss of her job and threats to her life, she became an organizer and spokeswoman for the Mississippi voter registration effort. She was renowned for her outspoken and charismatic style and for her passion and skill as a politically inspirational singer. Hamer was an exemplar of the rural black southern women who were pillars of the southern civil rights movement. But appreciation for their strength must not obscure the considerable personal sacrifices these women endured. Until she died in 1977, Hamer suffered both physically and emotionally from the ramifications of a brutal 1963 beating she received as punishment for her commitment to the civil rights movement.

Despite such heroism, southern black voter registration was stalled by fear, violence, and the determined resistance of white political leaders. In the spring of 1964, COFO devised a plan to import one thousand volunteers from outside the South, primarily white students, to register black voters in the Deep South. Freedom Summer, as the plan was called, was meant not only to infuse new energy into the voter registration drive but to use these white students to focus media and federal attention on southern recalcitrance. Trained in nonviolent resistance and warned about the dangers involved, the first volunteers arrived in June 1964. Violence overshadowed Freedom Summer. Four volunteers were killed, eighty beaten, and more than a thousand arrested. Thirty-seven churches were bombed and burned.

The recruitment of white northern students created tension within the movement. Some of these highly educated whites tried to assume leadership positions and had to be reminded that they had come to help, not to take charge. The presence of white women raised particular issues. A handful of southern white women had been active in the civil rights movement from the very beginning, including older women like Virginia Foster Durr and Anne Braden, who had a lifelong commitment to challenging segregation, and younger activists like Joan Browning, who was a freedom rider, and Casey Hayden, who was an early member of SNCC. (See Documents: Women in the Civil Rights Movement, pp. 649–57.) During Freedom Summer, however, the number of white women, estimated at somewhere between one-third and one-half of the volunteers, increased dramatically. Any sort of closeness or intimacy between black men and white women constituted a highly charged trigger for white racists' anger. White women and black men had their own reasons for engaging in these flirtations and sexual liaisons, but black women often resented them, and they contributed to racial divisions in the early years of the women's liberation movement.

The climax of southern voter registration efforts and Freedom Summer was a bold challenge to the all-white Mississippi Democratic Party. Mississippi blacks organized a delegation of the newly formed Mississippi Freedom Democratic Party (MFDP) to attend the Democratic National Convention in Atlantic City in August 1964. They demanded that they replace the all-white state group as the

◆ **Fannie Lou Hamer**
Fannie Lou Hamer, one of the most charismatic civil rights figures, was active in SNCC in Mississippi and came to national attention as a delegate of the Mississippi Freedom Democratic Party to the 1964 Democratic National Convention in Atlantic City. Under pressure from President Johnson, the networks cut off live coverage of Hamer's passionate speech, in which she asked "Is this America?" but the speech later made network news. Standing next to Hamer are Eleanor Holmes (later Norton) and Ella Baker (far right). *Matt Herron/Take Stock.*

official Mississippi delegation. Hamer testified before the convention's rules committee about the violence and beatings she suffered in order to register to vote. Despite the extraordinary power of her story, the party leadership, including President Lyndon Johnson and Vice President Hubert Humphrey, with the tacit approval of more moderate black leaders, chose to seat the all-white delegation and to offer the MFDP two "at-large" seats. The MFDP rejected this proposal as a compromise that did not address the illegality of Mississippi's systematic denial of blacks' access to the political process. Deeply disillusioned, the MFDP delegates returned to Mississippi. Although Hamer and others continued their activism on behalf of southern black economic and political empowerment, the civil rights movement as a whole never recovered its optimism after the disappointment in Atlantic City.

Sexism in the Movement

When Hamer returned home in the fall of 1964, SNCC was faltering, beset by a wide range of tensions, including the influx of new white members who had stayed on after Freedom Summer and questions about the viability of nonviolent resistance in the face of relentless persecution. A discussion paper written by Casey Hayden and Mary King, two longtime, highly respected white members of SNCC, drew parallels between the subordination of blacks and the subordination of women in society. Hayden and King criticized SNCC for not "recognizing that women are the crucial factor that keeps the movement running on a day-to-day basis [or giving women] equal say-so when it comes to day-to-day decision making."[25] The paper received virtually no attention at the time, but historians now regard it as an important document linking women's participation in the civil rights movement to the women's liberation movement of the late 1960s (see box, "Women in the Movement").

Was SNCC sexist? Were women relegated to minor positions and not taken seriously by male leaders? Many black women had established themselves as a powerful presence in SNCC, but white women, especially the new student volunteers, were viewed, and usually viewed themselves, as playing supportive roles. In retrospect it seems that males monopolized formal leadership positions, but few women now claim that they experienced any resentment at the time. For black women, race was of utmost importance, and few acted in the context of bettering the position of black women specifically. Even those white women who criticized male domination of the movement remember above all that participating in the civil rights movement proved personally and politically liberating. Harriet Tanzman, a University of Wisconsin student who first went south during Freedom Summer, explained, "I was able to do things I never knew I could do. I mean it took the best of us, the movement, whether we were eighteen or twenty-five. It empowered our lives."[26]

In numerous ways, the civil rights movement was fundamental in helping to revive the feminist movement, discussed in Chapter 11. It gave middle-class white women exposure to role models of female public activism and leadership, like Ella

Baker and Fannie Lou Hamer, and opportunities to envision themselves operating outside the rigid gender norms of middle-class culture. What might be called implicit feminist impulses underlay their willingness to undertake the risks of civil rights activism. Rita Schwerner Bender (the wife of Mickey Schwerner, one of four activists killed during Freedom Summer) was a member of CORE in Brooklyn before heading to Mississippi in 1964. In 1994, she recalled her decision to join the movement: "I did not see myself as saving anyone, but I did have a view of saving myself from a split-level house."[27] The empowerment that Tanzman and other women described later led many to challenge the patriarchal nature of their society.

Tensions within SNCC exacerbated by Freedom Summer and its aftermath were part of a larger change in the direction of the civil rights movement. The Atlantic City disappointment exposed the degree to which the Johnson administration temporized about protecting African Americans' constitutional rights. Repeatedly, as activists faced violence and intimidation, the Justice Department intervened only when forced by massive media exposure of violence against peaceful demonstrators. Despite years of agitation, Congress resisted passing a Civil Rights Act until 1964, when President Lyndon Johnson pushed it through as homage to the assassinated John F. Kennedy. Brutality to demonstrators in Selma, Alabama, was followed by passage of the Voting Rights Act of 1965, which threw out the literacy tests used to keep blacks out of southern Democratic parties and authorized the U.S. attorney general to intervene in counties where less than 50 percent of the black voting-age population was registered. But for many young blacks, this was too little too late. Breaking from more moderate leaders like Martin Luther King Jr., in the late 1960s militant blacks turned from the goal of integration to "black power," an explicitly male-dominated phase of the civil rights movement. Rejecting the "beloved community" of black/white unity in the heady first days of civil rights radicalism, SNCC demanded that whites leave the organization to be run entirely by blacks for goals of their own choosing.

A Widening Circle of Civil Rights Activists

As African Americans mounted their civil rights struggle, Mexican Americans intensified their own drive to fight prejudice and attain legitimacy in American society. Here, too, women made significant contributions that have been obscured by the attention given to male leaders.

After World War II, Mexican Americans in Texas, California, and some states in the Midwest sought to improve their communities, increase their political influence, and challenge de facto segregation and economic and educational discrimination. One of the most dynamic organizations of the period was the Community Service Organization (CSO), founded in 1947 and based primarily in California. The CSO had wide-ranging goals of fostering civil rights, improving health care and living conditions, and developing leadership skills in urban Mexican communities. Historians estimate that close to half of the CSO's members were women, most of whom participated with their husbands. Men dominated

CASEY HAYDEN AND MARY KING
Women in the Movement

Casey Hayden (b. 1939) and Mary King (b. 1940) anonymously distributed a document titled "Position Paper: Nov. 1964" during an SNCC retreat in Waveland, Mississippi. The statement symbolizes the close connection between young white women's civil rights activism and the emergence of the women's liberation movement later in the decade. What were their concerns?

Staff was involved in crucial [SNCC] constitutional revisions at the Atlanta staff meeting in October. A large committee was appointed to present revisions to the staff. The committee was all men.

Two organizers were working together to form a farmers league. Without asking any questions, the male organizer immediately assigned the clerical work to the female organizer although both had had equal experience in organizing campaigns.

Although there are some women in Mississippi projects who have been working as long as some of the men, the leadership group in COFO is all men. A woman in a field office wondered why she was held responsible for day-to-day decisions, only to find out later that she had been appointed project director but not told.

A fall 1964 personnel and resources report on Mississippi projects lists the number of people on each project. The section on Laurel, however, lists not the number of persons, but "three girls."

One of SNCC's main administrative officers apologizes for appointment of a woman as interim project director in a key Mississippi project area. . . .

Any woman in SNCC, no matter what her position or experience, has been asked to take minutes in a meeting when she and other women are outnumbered by men.

The names of several new attorneys entering a state project this past summer were posted in a central movement office. The first initial and last name of each lawyer was listed. Next to one name was written: (girl).

Capable, responsible, and experienced women who are in leadership positions can expect to have to defer to a man on their project for final decision-making.

formal leadership positions, while women played subordinate but nonetheless vital roles, including most of the clerical work. Helen Chávez, wife of César Chávez, who became the most significant Chicano activist of his time, recalled that daily she recorded in longhand her husband's dictated reports and that for meetings, "I would address all the envelopes and address the postcards."[28] Women

A session at the recent October staff meeting in Atlanta was the first large meeting in the past couple of years where a woman was asked to chair.

Undoubtedly this list will seem strange to some, petty to others, laughable to most. The list could continue as far as there are women in the movement. Except that most women don't talk about these kinds of incidents, because the whole subject is [not] discussible—strange to some, petty to others, laughable to most. The average white person finds it difficult to understand why the Negro resents being called "boy," or being thought of as "musical" and "athletic," because the average white person doesn't realize that *he assumes he is superior*. And naturally he doesn't understand the problem of paternalism. So too the average SNCC worker finds it difficult to discuss the woman problem because of the assumptions of male superiority. Assumptions of male superiority are as widespread and deep rooted and every much as crippling to the woman as the assumptions of white supremacy are to the Negro. Consider why it is in SNCC that women who are competent, qualified, and experienced, are automatically assigned to the "female" kinds of jobs such as typing, desk work, telephone work, filing, library work, cooking, and the assistant kind of administrative work but rarely the "executive" kind. . . .

This paper is presented anyway because it needs to be made know[n] that many women in the movement are not "happy and contented" with their status. . . . What can be done? Probably nothing right away. . . . [But] maybe sometime in the future the whole of the women in this movement will become so alert as to force the rest of the movement to stop the discrimination and start the slow process of changing values and ideas so that all of us gradually come to understand that this is no more a man's world than it is a white world.

November, 1964

SOURCE: Alexander Bloom and Wini Breines, eds., *"Takin' It to the Streets": A Sixties Reader* (New York: Oxford University Press, 1995), 45–47.

also turned their energies to citizenship education programs, voter registration drives, and fund-raising. In the latter, their efforts reflected the gendered nature of their activism. They often raised money through sales of items such as Mexican tamales or *pan dulce* (sweet rolls). The CSO Reporter described another quintessential 1950s social gathering that these Mexican American women adapted to their cause: "A series of Tupper Ware parties with a percentage of sales given to CSO are being conducted under the able leadership of Ursula Gutierrez."[29]

Some Mexican women worked outside these patterns of gendered activism. Dolores Huerta began her career doing volunteer work for the Mexican American

◆ **Dolores Huerta**

Dolores Huerta is most famous for her role as cofounder with César Chávez of the United Farm Workers in 1962. Huerta played a leading role in organizing workers and negotiating contracts. In the late 1960s, she spearheaded a national boycott of grapes that forced growers to sign a contract with the union. Here she is shown in 1962 registering farmworkers. *Walter P. Reuther Library, Wayne State University.*

community but later served as a paid lobbyist for CSO and, in 1962, cofounded the United Farm Workers with César Chávez. Another prominent woman, Hope Mendoza, had been active in the International Ladies' Garment Workers Union and, like women in the UE and UPWA, was militant in her defense of women workers. Chairing the CSO's labor relations committee, she brought her labor expertise and extensive contacts to the CSO's efforts to support Mexican American workers. Among other things, she educated workers to the value of unions, raised funds, and interviewed politicians seeking the CSO's endorsement. Mendoza's high-profile activities were exceptional, but many other women in the CSO shared her union experience. Although most women in the organization stayed within traditional female boundaries, many more women followed the more assertive paths of Huerta and Mendoza in the late 1960s and 1970s as the Chicano movement for Mexican American empowerment gathered force (see pp. 680–81).

WOMEN AND PUBLIC POLICY

While the civil rights movement forged ahead, encouraging many young women to begin to question the cultural assumptions that reinforced women's subordination, other women focused on public policy issues, especially discrimination in the workforce. The creation of the President's Commission on the Status of Women in 1961 proved a turning point. It not only focused renewed attention on the problems employed women faced but also helped to create a network of activists committed to addressing working women's rights.

The Continuing Battle over the ERA

The community of women interested in promoting women's legal rights and economic opportunities faced many obstacles in the years following World War II. With the feminine mystique holding sway over much of American culture and the Red Scare promoting conformity, the social and political climate hampered serious questioning of women's roles. Nonetheless, professional lobbyists for organizations like the YWCA, the AAUW, and the National Federation of Business and Professional Women (BPW) formed a female network attentive to policy developments in Washington that kept alive concerns over women's rights. Throughout the late 1940s and 1950s, however, these women were divided by the longstanding debate over the Equal Rights Amendment (ERA). Their division on this issue discouraged fresh approaches to questions concerning women's growing, yet fundamentally unequal, participation in the workforce.

The battle lines were similar to those of the 1920s, when the ERA was first introduced (see pp. 523–27). The National Woman's Party, with strong support from career women in the BPW, argued for the amendment as a device that would strike down all manner of laws and policies that fettered women's rights as free and equal individuals. Opposing the ERA were most of the staff of the federal Women's Bureau and the women's organizations traditionally allied with it, such as the League of Women Voters and the YWCA. Women labor union leaders formed a particularly adamant group in opposition to the ERA.

All of these opponents believed that the ERA endangered protective labor legislation, which ever since its inception in the Progressive era had emphasized women's distinctiveness, especially in their maternal function. By the 1950s, Women's Bureau leaders had retreated somewhat from their emphasis on promoting more protective legislation in the various states and had moved toward fostering equal pay laws and challenging some discriminatory policies. They no longer had to defend special minimum wage and maximum hour laws for women since the Fair Labor Standards Act of 1938 had extended these protections to men.

Under the Republican administration of Dwight D. Eisenhower, Republican politicians, including many women, joined with anti-union conservative business interests to support the ERA because they viewed protective labor legislation as an intrusion of the government into the labor market. Alice Leopold, appointed by Eisenhower as the new head of the Women's Bureau, was a supporter of the amendment. Nonetheless, Women's Bureau staffers and their traditional allies continued to condemn the ERA, their commitment heightened by the anti-union climate of the 1950s and by the affiliation of some with the Democratic Party, which remained resolutely anti-ERA.

A Turning Point: The President's Commission on the Status of Women

It was in part to deflect attention away from the ERA that Esther Peterson, who became head of the Women's Bureau in 1961, proposed a commission on the status of women. Appointed by Democrat John F. Kennedy, Peterson had strong union ties and enthusiastically supported the new president's program for revived activism on the part of the federal government, especially on behalf of disadvantaged Americans. Kennedy pledged to "get this country moving again" with a "New Frontier" to continue the liberal reforms started by Franklin Roosevelt's New Deal. Peterson prevailed on Kennedy to establish the President's Commission on the Status of Women (PCSW) in late 1961, with the hope that it would particularly advance the cause of working women.

Eleven men and fifteen women drawn from leaders in women's organizations, unions, business, education, and politics comprised the PCSW, which was chaired by former first lady Eleanor Roosevelt. Supplementing the commission were dozens of subcommittees that brought many women activists into the process of research and deliberation on issues ranging from inequities in wage rates and limited job opportunities to the particular problems of poor black women and of working mothers. As activists like Peterson pushed an agenda to assist working women, many members of the commission worried lest their efforts be interpreted as undermining women's maternal roles by encouraging them to work. Indeed, the executive order creating the commission revealed the contradictions implicit in its task. The commission was responsible for "developing recommendations for overcoming discriminations in government and private employment on the basis of sex and for developing recommendations for services which will enable women to continue their roles as wives and mothers while making a maximum contribution to the world around them."[30]

Not surprisingly, the PCSW's final report, published in 1963, outlined moderate proposals for the most part. It recommended child care tax benefits for low-income working mothers and improved maternity benefits. It called for state and federal governments to promote women's education and job training and endorsed equal pay for equal work. The PCSW recommended an executive order to require private employers to give women "equal opportunities," a strikingly vague mandate already established for federal employment. It proposed expanding provisions of existing legislation to improve women's social security benefits

◆ **Eleanor Roosevelt Meets with President John F. Kennedy**
In 1961, Women's Bureau head Esther Peterson convinced new president John F. Kennedy
to establish the President's Commission on the Status of Women (PCSW), which brought
together many activists for women and civil rights, including attorney Pauli Murray. The
PCSW chair was former First Lady Eleanor Roosevelt; in this photograph, a clearly energetic
Roosevelt engages Kennedy in conversation. *Franklin D. Roosevelt Presidential Library and Museum.*

and bring more women under the coverage of the Fair Labor Standards Act of
1938, a change that would particularly benefit poor black and Chicana women. In
keeping with the Women's Bureau's long-standing commitment to protective legislation, it endorsed a forty-hour workweek for women, with overtime pay beyond
forty hours. The PCSW also addressed the need for states to repeal outdated laws
that limited the rights of women to serve on juries or control their own property.

The commission did not endorse the ERA but offered as an alternative a recommendation that the Fourteenth Amendment (see Appendix, p. A-14) be understood as protecting women's equal rights. Pauli Murray, an African American civil
rights attorney who served on the Subcommittee on Political and Civil Rights and
had long been active in promoting black and women's rights, formulated this
argument for the PCSW, explicitly drawing a connection between the discrimination women faced and the civil rights movement, claiming that "arbitrary discrimination against women violated the Fourteenth Amendment in the same way
racial bias did."[31] Despite Murray's insightful analysis, the commission omitted

any discussion of a race-gender analogy—presumably because it was too controversial—and simply urged the Supreme Court to legitimate the Fourteenth Amendment's applicability to women, which it did within the decade.

One legacy of the PCSW was passage of federal "equal work for equal pay" legislation. The Equal Pay Act of 1963 offered significantly less than the Women's Bureau or its female union supporters had hoped for. It rejected the concept of equal pay for comparable work, substituting instead the proviso that women working in identical jobs with men—a relatively small class of workers—must be paid equally. The act also limited its applicability to those occupations already covered by the 1938 Fair Labor Standards Act, a measure that failed to include women's jobs in the agricultural and domestic service sectors. Despite its limits, the Equal Pay Act resulted in concrete gains for some women and at least theoretically committed the federal government to the recognition that women's labor had equal value to men's.

Still, few concrete results followed the commission's recommendations. Its importance was in the way in which it focused attention, however ambivalently, on the varied discriminations that women faced. It was instrumental in encouraging many activists to retreat from an interpretation that emphasized sexual difference and the need for laws to protect women toward an approach that favored equal rights and promoted the government's role in challenging discrimination against women. The PCSW's deliberations also encouraged a network of women activists interested in promoting women's rights and spawned dozens of state commissions on the status of women, which in turn created a community of women throughout the country addressing similar concerns. Pauli Murray explained, "Like-minded women found one another, bonds developed through working together, and an informal feminist network emerged to act as leaven in the broader movement that followed."[32]

CONCLUSION: The Limits of the Feminine Mystique

American women in the postwar era lived in conservative times. Cold War fears stifled dissent, labeled labor unions and civil rights activity "subversive," and contained women and men in rigid gender roles to maintain family and social order. Certainly many women's lives were limited by this dominant ideology, yet women's lives were more diverse and complex than mainstream cultural prescriptions indicate. Women's place might have been in the home, but it was also in the workforce, as both public officials and employers eagerly sought to fuel American productivity and achieve the upper hand in the Cold War. Women may have been shunted into sex-segregated jobs, but participation in the workforce and the discrimination experienced there would have long-term implications for their consciousness.

Other signs that women's roles were not as constrained as popular images of the era suggest are evident in women's central role as bridge leaders in the burgeoning civil rights movement, as well as the persistent efforts of working-class union women to fight for fair treatment on the job. Middle-class women, too, in a wide range of voluntary associations and political activity represented women's desire to engage as citizens in the world outside their homes. These different forms of activism, combined with initiatives from the federal government's Women's Bureau, especially the President's Commission on the Status of Women, helped lay the groundwork for the resurgence of feminism in the late 1960s that would have a powerful impact on many women's domestic and public lives.

VISUAL SOURCES

Television's Prescriptions for Women

THANKS TO CABLE NETWORKS LIKE Nickelodeon and TV Land, viewers today have access to some well-known 1950s television programs and commercials. Some critics explain the popularity of these shows and advertisements by suggesting that for some present-day viewers they are camp entertainment, amusing in their outdated, unintended humor, but for others they evoke a nostalgic sense of simpler, more innocent times. Historians who study 1950s television delve more deeply into the medium and its message and, as with any other historical source, examine both the televised images and the assumptions of the people who created programming and advertising. This essay explores women and television in the 1950s by looking first at the way in which television programming and advertising targeted and understood the female viewer and second at the images of women conveyed in the decade's situation comedies. While advertising tended to reinforce key aspects of the feminine mystique, especially a relentless depiction of white middle-class women's role in the home, situation comedies of the 1950s displayed a more diverse and complex rendering of women and their families.

Television was a novelty until after World War II. Some national programming began to appear in 1947, and then during the years 1948–1950 the new medium took off: by 1951 there were 107 stations in 52 cities. Rising prosperity and a burgeoning consumer culture facilitated Americans' eager embrace of TV. By 1955, 65 percent of the nation's households had televisions, and by 1960 that figure had grown to 90 percent. National networks dominated television from the medium's inception, and network executives, along with their programs' sponsors, viewed television's purpose as the selling of products. This commercial motivation encouraged the networks to promote television as family entertainment and in the process to reinforce conventional notions of women's roles as housewives and mothers.

Many observers in the postwar years argued that television viewing would bring families together, thus stabilizing the home. Women's magazines ran articles discussing how women might integrate the "box" into their homes. While some authors addressed decorating problems that arose in making room for a large appliance, others explored the placement of the television in the context of family leisure-time patterns. They noted that the TV set was quickly displacing the piano as a source of family entertainment and that it was usurping the role of the fireplace as the focal point for social interaction. The TV had become, many argued, an electric hearth, the heart of family "togetherness."

ADVERTISEMENTS

The idea of the television as a means of bringing families together appeared in many advertisements for television sets. Figure 10.1 depicts a comfortable middle-class home with an elegant TV as part of its attractive furniture. The family

◆ **Figure 10.1**
Advertisement for Motorola Television (1951)
Gaslight Advertising Archives, Inc.

clusters around the Motorola TV in a semicircle, watching a program designed for family viewing, the variety show starring singer Dinah Shore (who was the television spokeswoman for Chevrolet cars, suggesting another element of the flourishing consumer market of the period). That the mother alone is standing is typical of many depictions of television viewers. Why do you think advertisers chose to show the mother standing? What does the posture and position of the woman suggest about her role in the family? How does the text above the image reinforce the television's familial function?

Although the television industry generally assumed that its family audience was white and largely middle class, manufacturers did aggressively market television sets to African Americans and routinely ran ads in *Ebony*, a popular black magazine founded in 1942. Blacks were negatively stereotyped in television programming (see Figure 10.7, p. 636), but they were interested in buying sets, perhaps because they could enjoy entertainment in their homes rather than suffer the indignity of segregation in public venues. Some ads were identical to those that appeared in white mainstream periodicals, such as a May 1953 advertisement in *Ebony* that featured glamorous white brides framed by an Admiral TV set, with text noting that a television made a "memorable wedding gift."

Other advertisers attempted to adapt to their black audience. Figure 10.2 is an example of one of a number of 1953 RCA Victor advertisements that featured

◆ **Figure 10.2 Advertisement for RCA Victor Television (1953)**
Gaslight Advertising Archives, Inc.

African Americans watching television. Another ad in this series depicts the Dinah Shore television show (as in Figure 10.1), but this ad displays black singer Eartha Kitt, a frequent performer on network variety shows. Notice that the woman is once again standing, this time in the effort to help her husband select a station, now made easier by an automatic dial. Compare Figures 10.1 and 10.2. How do these advertisements for televisions reinforce conventional roles for male and female viewers?

Televisions were often depicted as bringing families together, but some critics worried that the new medium would create new sources of familial conflict, as parents and children and husbands and wives collided over control of the set. Television advertisers themselves often tackled this theme. Their solution, as Figure 10.3 indicates, was multiple television sets! Consider the two-part construction of this 1955 General Electric ad. Why might the advertiser have chosen to use a cartoon to portray family conflict? How does the photograph depict stereotypical gender roles?

Women's primary roles as housewives became a predominant theme for network executives and sponsors in the early years of television. They were eager to attract women viewers because of their responsibilities as family purchasing agents. One executive noted, "We're after a specific audience, the young housewife — one cut above the teenager — with two to four kids, who has to buy the clothing, the food, the soaps, the home remedies."[33] As the television industry saw it, the dilemma was whether daytime programming geared to this specific audience would be compatible with women's patterns of household labor. Unlike radio, they feared, television needed to be watched with some degree of concentration. These hesitations were finally overcome by 1952, when the networks began to offer a full range of daytime programs that included soap operas, quiz shows, and magazine-style variety shows. As the 1955 *Ladies' Home Journal* ad in Figure 10.4 indicates, they explicitly marketed their daytime lineup to women by emphasizing that the programs did not interfere with their household duties. Read the descriptions of the seven shows watched by the young housewife in a single morning. How do they attempt to persuade women that television watching hastens rather than hinders their household work? What assumptions does this advertisement make about women's domestic labor?

One program the ad in Figure 10.4 featured was *Home*, a magazine-style variety show modeled after NBC's *Today* program, which debuted in 1952, aired between 7 and 9 A.M., and offered short segments of news and entertainment designed for the whole family, plus features on fashion and homemaking directed toward women. Inspired by *Today*'s success, in 1954 NBC introduced *Home*, expressly for women. *Newsweek* noted that NBC's president, Sylvester Laflin (Pat) Weaver, sought to tap the advertising market that women's magazines enjoyed. "It is inconceivable to me," Weaver noted, "that all that advertising money spent on women's products . . . has been allowed to escape [from television]."[34] In keeping with that idea, *Home* segments were generally tied to specific sponsors and commercials, and indeed NBC described the program's set as "a machine for selling."[35]

NEW! 32-lb. G-E Personal TV—goes where you go! So light, carry it easily from room to room ...kitchen, bedroom, patio, den. Take it along on trips...to the country. Amazingly bright picture—low price. Models from $99.95.

NEW! G-E 24-inch TV. Show your friends the biggest, brightest picture ever! Smart space-saving cabinet. Enjoy G-E "Daylight Power"—famous G-E Aluminized Tube—Super-power transformer—Hi-contrast, dark safety glass.

NEW! G-E Clock-TV! Watch late shows till the sandman comes—Clock-TV turns itself off automatically. Wakes you in A.M. Reminds you of favorite programs. Yet costs less than other TV without this useful feature!

Prices include Federal Excise Tax, one-year warranty on picture tube. 90-days on parts. Subject to change without notice.

WHEN Dad wants to watch the game...Mom and Sis, the cooking show...there's too much traffic for one TV to handle. It's easy to have a TV for everyone at G.E.'s new low prices. Starting at $99.95, two now cost less than millions paid for one. You'll thrill to G-E "Daylight Power" that makes the picture so clear you can view with shades up, lights on...even in the open. See G.E.'s new 32-lb. portable that "goes where you go," the Automatic Clock-TV, the mammoth 24-inch model. All low-priced at your G-E Television dealer. General Electric Company, Radio & Television Department, Electronics Park, Syracuse, New York.

See G.E. on TV: "Warner Bros. Presents" (ABC-TV) and "The 20th Century Fox" Hour (CBS-TV)

Progress Is Our Most Important Product

GENERAL ELECTRIC

◆ **Figure 10.3** Advertisement for General Electric Television (1955)
Gaslight Advertising Archives, Inc.

WHERE
DID THE
MORNING
GO?

Time for lunch already?
Where did the morning go?
The chores are done, the
house is tidy ... but it hasn't
seemed like a terribly
tiring morning.

First there was breakfast, and that was pleasant. We all got the news from "TODAY," and Dave Garroway had some fascinating guests. The children were still laughing about J. Fred Muggs when they left for school.

Then I sat Kathy down in front of "DING DONG SCHOOL" and I didn't have to worry about her while I tidied up. Miss Frances got her interested in finger-painting, and after the program Kathy just went on playing quietly.

"WAY OF THE WORLD" had the second installment of the new story, and I couldn't miss that. It's like a magazine serial — you keep looking forward to the next episode. And beautifully acted, with new stars for every new story.

I think I started the ironing while I watched "THE SHEILAH GRAHAM SHOW". First she discussed the latest Hollywood news and gossip. Then she interviewed William Holden, and showed parts of his exciting new movie.

And I finished the ironing while I watched "HOME". I couldn't *count* the good ideas I've had from Arlene Francis and her expert assistants on health, home decorating, gardening and food. I added a few things to my shopping list.

Any morning of any day, "THE TENNESSEE ERNIE FORD SHOW" can brighten things up for me. Tennessee Ernie and his talented friends joke, sing and share the fun with everyone ... at the studio and at home.

And then "FEATHER YOUR NEST", where that lovely couple won a living room suite, and Bud Collyer and Janis Carter were so nice to them. And I think that it's a wonderful idea that viewers at home can win prizes, too.

The morning was a pleasure instead of drudgery. And yet I have everything done ... I haven't really wasted a second. It's the way I like to have the morning go.
EXCITING THINGS ARE HAPPENING ON

NBC
TELEVISION
a service of RCA

◆ **Figure 10.4** *Ladies' Home Journal* **Advertisement for NBC (1955)**
Gaslight Advertising Archives, Inc.

◆ **Figure 10.5** Advertisement for Betty Crocker (1952)

Courtesy of General Mills Archives.

The line between programming and commercials was often blurred in shows geared to "Mrs. Consumer." This was evident in programs featuring Betty Crocker, General Mills' mythical spokeswoman, who was portrayed by a series of actresses on both radio and television. Figure 10.5 features actress Adelaide Hawley, who appeared in the 1952 ABC daytime programs *Bride and Groom* and *Betty Crocker Star Matinee*. In the former, a couple was married on-screen and Betty gave tips to brides on fixing their grooms' favorite foods, foods that featured General Mills products. Her television appearances featured this verse:

> American homemakers
> Keepers of the hearth
> Whose hands and hearts are filled
> With the day-to-day cares and joys
> That, taken with one another
> Make homemaking a woman's
> Most rewarding life.[36]

How does Figure 10.5 illustrate this verse? What does it suggest about the relationship between popular media and the "feminine mystique"?

SITUATION COMEDIES

This section examines the depiction of women in situation comedies (sitcoms), which, in contrast to the genres discussed above, were shown in the evening and geared to the whole family. The images reproduced here, of course, do not adequately convey the dynamic medium of TV. They do not capture motion, dialogue, or laugh tracks. Missing, too, is the importance of audience familiarity with the shows' characters, another crucial aspect shaping how Americans experienced sitcoms. These photographs, mostly publicity stills, nonetheless stand as emblems of popular sitcoms' depiction of women and the family in this era. With a very few exceptions, such as *Our Miss Brooks*, a comedy starring Eve Arden as a schoolteacher, adult white women characters in sitcoms did not work outside the home and were portrayed as housewives, despite the number of married women entering the paid workforce. Beyond this common thread, these programs offered strikingly diverse images of the American family.

The networks adopted many sitcoms from successful radio programs. Two of these starred African Americans. *Beulah* aired on ABC from 1950 to 1953 and portrayed a maid and the white family she worked for, the Hendersons. Over the life of the series on radio and television, three well-known black actresses played Beulah: Louise Beavers, Hattie McDaniel, and Ethel Waters. Figure 10.6 shows Louise Beavers as Beulah. Two other black characters appeared regularly in the series: Beulah's boyfriend, Bill, an oafish man who ran a fix-it shop but seemed to spend most of his time in his girlfriend's kitchen, and Oriole, her scatterbrained friend who worked for the white family next door. Although some of the comedy derived from Beulah's persistent, yet fruitless, efforts to convince Bill to marry her, the major focus of the series was Beulah's nurturing her white family and solving their small dilemmas. A classic "mammy" figure, her catchphrase was "Somebody bawl fo' Beulah?" In one episode her southern cuisine (she was described as the "queen of the kitchen") helped Mr. Henderson impress a business client. In another, she taught Donnie, the family's son, to jive dance.

◆ **Figure 10.6 Scene from *Beulah***
Photofest.

Although some African Americans took pleasure in seeing an African American star on television, other individuals and groups, including the NAACP, criticized the series for perpetuating degrading stereotypes. Does Beulah appear to be part of the family? In what ways does Figure 10.6 reinforce racial hierarchies of the day? Contrast this image with the slave nurse in Figure 4.11 (p. 245).

A more famous sitcom with black cast members was *Amos 'n' Andy* (1949–1953), which starred men but featured a number of women. On the original radio show, two white men who had created the series played the title characters, but on television the cast was all African American. Even before the show aired, the NAACP launched a protest over bringing the radio program, which many blacks found degrading because of its racist stereotypes, to television. In response to this pressure, CBS modified Amos, one of the title characters, by making him and his wife, Ruby, models of middle-class propriety. To fill the comedic void, however, the series gave enhanced attention to George ("the Kingfish") Stephens, with his fractured English and his scams to avoid work and get rich quick. The unambitious and none-too-smart Andy served as the victim of many of the Kingfish's schemes.

The major female character was the Kingfish's wife, Sapphire, played by Ernestine Wade, who had also performed the role in radio. For the most part Sapphire was a shrew, a caricature of the domineering wife who routinely threw her husband out of the house. In Figure 10.7, she is shown waiting to pounce on the Kingfish as he attempts to sneak into their home. An even more negative portrayal of black women emerged with Sapphire's large and loud-mouthed mother, "Mama." As the Kingfish described her, "Andy, you take de venom of a cobra, de disposition of a alligator and de nastiness of a rhinoceros. . . . Put 'em all together dey spell Mother!"[37] Partially as a result of NAACP pressure and partly because of

◆ **Figure 10.7**
Scene from *Amos 'n' Andy*
Everett Collection.

declining ratings, CBS canceled the show in 1953. Compare Sapphire and her husband to the loving black couple shown in Figure 10.2. What might account for the striking differences in these two popular culture depictions? After at first perpetuating negative stereotypes of black women as either mammies or shrews, sitcoms subsequently treated them as invisible. African Americans would not reappear in sitcoms for another decade, and it was not until 1968, when Diahann Carroll appeared as a nurse in *Julia*, that a black woman starred in a series.

A number of early sitcoms featured white immigrant families, most notably *The Goldbergs* (1949–1954). CBS adopted the show from the popular radio program of the same name, which starred Gertrude Berg as Molly Goldberg. Berg also wrote the scripts for the program, which she said was modeled after the experiences of her mother and grandmother. The show explored the domestic crises of a Jewish family living in the Bronx and their circle of neighbors. Molly dominated the show, and part of the humor was her accented English and eccentric phrasing: "Enter, whoever. If it's nobody, I'll call back."[38]

◆ **Figure 10.8 Scene from *The Goldbergs***
Photofest.

A stereotypical Jewish mother, Molly eagerly turned her nurturing skills to solve friends' and family members' problems. Each show began with Molly leaning out her apartment window to shout across the airshaft, "Yoo-hoo, Mrs. Bloom." Inside the family circle, a key theme was the aspiration for assimilation and the American middle-class dream. Significantly, assimilation was often cast in terms of consumption. In one show Molly disapproves of her daughter-in-law's plan to buy a washing machine on the installment plan. "I know Papa and me never bought anything unless we had the money to pay for it," Molly says. Her son convinces her she is wrong, and by the end she is suggesting that the family buy two cars in order to "live above our means—the American way."[39]

Figure 10.8 shows Molly in her dining room, where she is serving the guest of honor, well-known television personality Arthur Godfrey. Molly is depicted as nurturing and the family as close-knit. The room's decor is old-fashioned, as is Molly for the most part. At a time when many upwardly mobile Jews were leaving the crowded cities and the ethnic neighborhoods their parents and grandparents had created, the cozy world of the Goldbergs was increasingly anachronistic. Why might this disparity contribute to the appeal of the program?

A less sentimental rendering of the urban family was *The Honeymooners* (1955–1956), in which Jackie Gleason played bus driver Ralph Kramden, a dreamer who always missed realizing his hopes for a more comfortable life. Audrey Meadows played Alice, his long-suffering and practical wife. Marital bickering between the two was a constant in the series. The stance of Alice in Figure 10.9 as she looks disapprovingly at Ralph, with their friends Norton and his wife, Trixie, in the background, conveys some of this tension. One of Ralph's catchphrases, "One of these days, Alice, one of these days, pow! Right in the kisser!" suggests even more. Plots frequently involved Alice's disappointment over their limited income and the drabness of the apartment, completely devoid of the consumer goods that most Americans were eagerly acquiring in this period. The show generally closed with a harmonious resolution, but the overarching tone was nonetheless one of male-female conflict, with Alice fighting back.

Marital disputes also served as the focal point for the humor in one of the most beloved sitcoms of early television, *I Love Lucy* (1951–1961). Lucille Ball's character, Lucy, is married to Ricky Ricardo, played by Ball's real-life husband, Cuban bandleader Desi Arnaz. In the process of the show, they have a baby, Little Ricky, whose TV birth coincided with the birth of the couple's real son. Lucy seemingly represents a stereotypical dizzy female. Childish and impractical, she is juxtaposed to Ricky's usually mature demeanor. She constantly is forced to defer to his decisions as head of the family and resorts to wheedling, deception, and "feminine wiles" to get her way. But like the Kramdens, the Ricardos' marital disagreements prove fodder for most plots. Lucy eternally desires a job in show business and constantly hankers for consumer items, from kitchen appliances to Parisian frocks. Ricky proves the obstacle on both counts.

Many plots focus on Lucy's schemes to get a job, yet repeatedly she humiliates herself as she fails in each attempt. A particularly revealing episode for its

◆ **Figure 10.9** **Scene from *The Honeymooners***
Photofest.

comments on male-female roles is the show in which Lucy and her best friend, Ethel, wager with Ricky and Ethel's husband, Fred, that men's work is easier than women's labor in the home. They trade places, and while Ricky and Fred make a mess of homemaking (Figure 10.10, top), Lucy and Ethel look for work. In the middle image of Figure 10.10, a clerk in an employment agency reads a list of jobs, and the women realize they have no training for any of them except perhaps candy making. They get jobs making chocolates, but their incompetence leads to their demotion to packing on an assembly line. They do well at first, but they fall behind as the conveyer belt speeds up and start eating the chocolate instead of packing it (Figure 10.10, bottom). At the end of the episode, both men and women agree to call the bet off and to return to their accustomed roles.

◆ **Figure 10.10 Scenes from *I Love Lucy***
Photofest.

Some critics argue that, far from reinforcing the feminine mystique, with its emphasis on women's roles as housewives and mothers, *Lucy* subverts it. For if Lucy is a housewife, she is not a contented one, as her quest for employment suggests. Conversely, others maintain that despite her aspirations, she fails at her forays into the workplace, and the storylines generally end with her return to her housewifery role and her acceptance of Ricky's authority. Do you think the images shown in Figure 10.10 suggest subversion or reinforcement of the feminine mystique? How do you suppose contemporary audiences interpreted the squabbles between Lucy and Ricky?

Sitcoms that featured working-class or minority families had almost disappeared by the mid-1950s. And, with the exception of *I Love Lucy*, so, too, had programs that traded on marital bickering and themes concerning domestic power. As more and more real American women went into the workforce, the networks offered up sitcoms that idealized the family and reinforced women's prescribed role in the home. Unlike Lucy, the mothers in *The Adventures of Ozzie and Harriet, The Donna Reed Show, Leave It to Beaver,* and *Father Knows Best* lead contented lives with serene marriages. Their husbands are successful breadwinners, and their homes are spacious and well furnished. They are rarely depicted as performing arduous household labor, but their immaculate houses are a reflection of their womanly skills.

Although ostensibly comedies, the humor in these sitcoms was sometimes barely discernible. Plots usually revolved around the dilemmas of childrearing as parents strove to teach children social and moral lessons. *Father Knows Best* (1954–1963), the first of this genre, led the way among sitcoms that promoted middle-class family values. Figure 10.11 shows the mother, Margaret Anderson (played by Jane Wyatt), joining in a prayer around the family dinner table. In what ways are the Andersons similar to and different from the families shown in the earlier sitcoms?

Father Knows Best was aptly named. In the episode titled "Kathy Becomes a Girl," the youngest daughter, Kathy, learns that boys do not like tomboys. As her father explains, "Being dependent — a little helpless now and then" was a sure ploy designed to win men.[40] An even more telling statement about the ideal female role came in a show that uncharacteristically featured Margaret expressing a degree of dissatisfaction with her lot. As her children and her husband are winning trophies for various activities, Margaret is forced to acknowledge that she has never received a medal for anything. To compensate, she takes up fishing and plans to compete in a tournament. Her chances are good, her coach tells her, because so few women compete. Ready for the competition, she falls, injures herself, and misses the contest. Her children seek to cheer her up with a series of tributes to her motherly skills and homemade awards, such as a frying pan emblazoned with the title "Most Valuable Mother." The episode received a 1958–1959 directing Emmy.

Neither advertising nor sitcom images should be taken as an accurate reflection of American women. What they offer are insights into how television portrayed women. The inherently commercial nature of television facilitated advertising and

◆ **Figure 10.11 Scene from *Father Knows Best***
Everett Collection.

programming that featured women's role as housewives and the purchaser of consumer goods for her family. Sitcoms, too, had close commercial links. When Molly Goldberg left her window at the start of the show, she returned to her kitchen and launched into a commercial for Sanka coffee, the program's sponsor. Although early sitcoms acknowledged some diversity among Americans, with a few exceptions most women were portrayed in their domestic roles. As the example of *Lucy* indicates, tensions over these roles often served as the comedic plot. But despite the reality of women's increased participation in the workforce, by the second half of the 1950s, TV sitcoms idealized the middle-class family and the stay-at-home mother and thus served as a powerful reinforcement of the cultural prescriptions of the feminine mystique.

QUESTIONS FOR ANALYSIS

1. What messages do the spatial arrangements, figure positions, and clothing styles in the advertisements (Figures 10.1–10.5) suggest about popular perceptions of the middle-class family and women's role in it?

2. Why did advertisers think these ads would sell consumer goods and network programming?

3. To what extent do the images from the sitcoms (Figures 10.6–10.11) reflect American diversity in terms of ethnicity, race, or class?

4. In what ways have television messages about gender roles changed since the 1950s?

DOCUMENTS

"Is a Working Mother a Threat to the Home?"

D URING THE 1950S, PUBLIC POLICY EXPERTS extensively studied the question of the working wife and mother (see p. 593). While there was widespread assumption that the growing number of mothers in the workforce was an irreversible phenomenon, officials and experts differed as to whether this new trend would have adverse effects on children, the family, and the social order in general. Popular magazines intently followed the debate and offered extensive coverage on working wives and mothers. The gamut of responses ran from the ex–working mother who reported, "I am now a better mother. I know I am a happier one,"[41] to the office worker and mother of two who explained her decision to go back to work in part by noting, "Some vital part of me wasn't being used."[42] Men chimed in as well. One man exulted over being married to a working mother who combined a successful career with a happy home, while another insisted that the career woman "may find many satisfactions in her job, but the chances are that she, her husband and her children will suffer psychological damage, and that she will be basically an unhappy woman."[43] In 1958 the *Ladies' Home Journal* assembled a forum of experts and mothers to address the question of whether mothers of young children should work. The following is an excerpt from that forum.

Should Mothers of Young Children Work?

[MODERATOR] MISS [MARGARET] HICKEY: Traditionally, in our country, marriage and motherhood have been considered difficult, full-time jobs — as well as satisfying ones. Married women and mothers who worked outside the home did so only for really pressing reasons: because they had to support their families; because there was a war on; because they were driven by great ambition or talent.

But recently a change seems to be taking place. Women no longer are working entirely from necessity or to satisfy a driving ambition, but rather from choice. Today one out of three wives is a wage earner. And, even more startling — one out of five of the mothers of small children is now working outside the home.

This situation raises many questions, but the one most asked by mothers is the basic personal one: Should I or shouldn't I work? Mrs. Easton, will you tell us what you wrote us some time back — in one of the letters that started us thinking of this forum today?

SOURCE: "Should Mothers of Young Children Work?" *Ladies' Home Journal* 75 (November 1958): 58–59, 154–56, 158–61.

MRS. EASTON: Well, as you said, I always thought it was out of necessity that mothers went to work. Then, looking around me, I couldn't help noticing that a lot of my neighbors didn't *have* to work, but they did. So then I began wondering, who is right—are they or am I? Where are mothers needed? Are they needed at home or is it better to be out making some money? I want to feel I am someone who does the right thing. So I wrote to the JOURNAL. . . .

MISS HICKEY: Secretary Mitchell, what do you think the national need is—does the country need women jobholders today?

SECRETARY [OF LABOR JAMES P.] MITCHELL: Yes, it does. Our economy would suffer severely if women left the labor force. By 1965, we expect to have a population of 193,000,000—an increase of 20,000,000 people. This means that if we are to have the standard of living we have now, and increase it, which we must, and if we are to maintain our defense, which we must, we will need a work-force increase of 10,000,000 people—half of which we expect will be women.

MISS HICKEY: So we have grown dependent on women workers. But from your statistics, Mr. Mitchell, do you think that this group will have to include the mothers of small children?

SECRETARY MITCHELL: Let me say first that I think it is very right that we in this country have freedom of choice, unlike the communist world, where there is no such thing. I would not want to say to anyone whether he or she should work or not. But it is my hope that the women workers we need will *not* be sought or encouraged to come from the group who are mothers. It seems to me that in our world a mother's place—and I hope this is not heresy in this group—is in the home.

Of course, there *are* times in a nation's history, such as war, when everyone has to be asked to work outside the home. But I believe strongly that no nation should ever forget that the very primary, fundamental basis of a free society is the family structure—the home—and the most vital job is there. . . .

[CHILD PSYCHOLOGIST] DR. [JOHN] BOWLBY: [on the impact on children whose mothers work] I don't mean to say that all small children of working mothers are necessarily deprived of mothering, but clinical evidence shows clearly that you can't bring up a child adequately if you leave him first with this person and then with that one in the first years of his life. The trouble is that we know there are serious risks, and as yet we have too little knowledge of the safety margin.

MRS. ERNEST LEE [A STENOGRAPHER AND MOTHER OF THREE]: My children are older now, six to nine, but in the past few years I have had four different sitters with them. They have shown no bad effects. Every once in a while they say, "Mommy, I wish you were not working," but then they say, "When we get our house you won't be."

If I didn't work to help pay the rent now and to save for a home of our own later—well, we'd have to live in one of those overcrowded cramped places where there are gangs and profane language and no safe place for the kids to play. Or my husband would have to work two jobs and the children would never see him. This way at least we all have the evenings together and a decent place to live. Isn't this important? . . .

DR. BARTUSKA: Well, I started out as just a career girl. In premedical school I thought I would never marry, and then, in medical school, my plans changed very drastically because I met my husband-to-be and almost before I knew it I *was* married. I was still in medical school when I had my first baby. . . . But things went well and I thought that as long as I had gotten that far, I might as well go ahead and get the state boards, so I did, and I had another child and still no trouble, so I decided I might as well get a specialty, so I did that and now I do cancer research and am a fellow in endocrinology, and have another child, and things still go along smoothly.

If the children had seemed to need me in some way really I would have just given all this up but for some reason I still cannot understand they appear well adjusted and the happiest children I know. I am amazed that it has worked out as well as it has. . . .

MRS. [ROY] DAVIS [A NURSE WHO WORKS AT NIGHT "AND RUNS HER HOUSE BY DAY"]: Until I had my first child I worked full time. Then I worked part time until I had my second child, then I retired for a while, but my husband had to let his profession slide—he is a lawyer—and take another job to supplement our income—so I went back to work.

I feel that the father is almost as important as the mother to the child, and by my working at night I saw the children in the daytime and he saw them in the later afternoon. Together we have done everything. We have not even had household help. We agreed on a ten-year plan ending in June, 1958, to get him through law school, to begin a family, and pay the ten-year mortgage on our home. Our family is here, our practice started. . . .

[SOCIOLOGIST] DR. [MIRRA] KOMAROVSKY: Unfashionable as it is today to defend women's education, I think it is on the right track. All women's colleges have courses in child psychology and in sociology of the family, and men's colleges should follow suit. I don't think it is the job of the college to teach housekeeping skills. The best preparation for family life, is, after all, a liberal-arts education. A woman has to have her own mind awakened before she can awaken the mind of her child, and I don't think that colleges devalue homemaking. In any event, they don't succeed! About 20 per cent of Barnard's seniors are married by Commencement Day. . . .

SENATOR [FRANK J.] LAUSCHE: If our way of life is to survive, we must keep the family intact. We must give it importance.

A woman needs cultivation of the mind for a unified personality. She needs a vocation to turn to in times of need. But over and above everything else, she needs to give attention and devotion to the family.

Outside jobs are the symptoms of deeper problems. We must remove the forces which break down the home. The housewife, the mother, needs more than housework to keep her occupied. She needs education, books, intellectual companion-ship. In short, she needs a rounded life so that she will be a good influence on her children and a helpful companion to her husband. . . .

[EVANGELIST] DR. [WILLIAM F.] GRAHAM: I think all of us would agree that we do accept some of the principles at least of the Bible, and the most fundamental one is that the first marriage was performed by God Himself and God instituted the marriage relationship and the family relationship before the school and before the government and before any other institution.

And in instituting marriage, He also gave rules and regulations concerning marriage and the home and the family. Many of these regulations we have violated, and I think we are paying for these violations.

The Bible was not against women working outside the home; it recognized the necessity and the value of this in special cases. But the whole trend of the Bible is found in the second chapter of Titus, in which it says that a woman, a family woman, should be a keeper at home. . . .

In short, I agree with the Bible. A mother should be at home during the formative years of her children unless she is a widow or in some financial straits which make it absolutely imperative for her to earn something outside the home. . . .

DR. KOMAROVSKY: But good relationships are not incompatible with being a working mother. I asked a group of students who were children of working mothers whether they thought their relationships with their mothers were affected by her working. And one girl spoke very movingly about how proud she was that her mother was a teacher—that it made her proud to help her mother in the home care of her brother, and that it was awfully exciting when her mother came home and had fascinating things to say about what had happened to her that day. "I feel very close to my mother and we are a very close family. My ideal in life is to be like my mother," this girl said.

[PSYCHOLOGIST] MRS. [FLORIDA] SCOTT-MAXWELL: This is the type of woman who is very valiant, but I would say is perhaps distorted by having her children and her career. She creates an atmosphere of activity, of achievement, but I think it very doubtful if she could teach her daughter any deep feminine wisdom this way.

The thing that is lacking is something that is very intangible but very real, very creative, that I can only call a feminine oneness with the depths of life. It isn't something that can be organized into a lesson, but if you have had deep experiences of life, feeling experiences of its sorrow and meaning, then you are a woman and you can pass this on to your daughters, and give strength to your husband and sons.

MISS HICKEY: Mrs. Phillips, would you like to comment on this? You were trained to be a schoolteacher, but you chose instead to be a mother in the home.

MRS. [CHARLES R.] PHILLIPS [A STAY-AT-HOME MOTHER OF FOUR]: Well, I do feel that as a mother there are things I can give my children that no one else can, and there are moments when if you are not with them, the moment will never come again. I am glad that I have a career they could be proud of if I had to go to work, but since I don't work, I feel that by staying home I am setting an example to my three daughters of what is right for a woman to do. . . .

[LADIES HOME JOURNAL EDITOR] MISS [JOAN] YOUNGER: There seems to be general agreement that ideally, mothers of small children should work at home. May I ask, then, who will pay the bills for those mothers whose only choice is to go out to work or starve?

SENATOR LAUSCHE: We have an aid-to-dependent-children program paid for jointly by the states and the Federal Government for those families who are deserted for left bereft by fathers. It works quite well in my home state of Ohio.

MISS HICKEY: In many states, however, it is most inadequate. Why, in Mississippi the average monthly payment to a recipient is only $7.53. In Washington State, with the highest average payment, it is $42.49 — a little less than $10 a week. It is no wonder that some mothers waive the public assistance payment in favor of a job outside the home. I have been watching with great interest the children's allowance program in Canada. There, all parents, regardless of need, are given small allowances to aid in the care of their children, to buy shoes for school, to get medicine, that sort of thing.

SENATOR LAUSCHE: I think that basically this is regimentation. I think the more you take away from the individual the necessity of independent effort, the more you take away his character. . . .

MISS HICKEY: It is difficult to decide how many of America's working mothers would see real deprivation by staying home. There are perhaps three million mothers of young children working. The majority of these are in low-income brackets — that is, under average. But what seems like an economic necessity to one family may not to another.

[COLLEGE PROFESSOR] DR. [LYNN] WHITE: The mothers I know who work do so either for self-expression or for a certain [rise?] in their standard of living rather than out of sheer necessity. . . .

MRS. DAVIS: Like all working mothers, I am constantly asking myself if I am doing the right thing. But, with us, it seemed either to wait for children until we were too old to have them, or for my husband to work at two jobs—

DR. WHITE: Mrs. Davis, I was filled with appalled admiration as I listened to your schedule of nursing at night and housework by day. But it is not in the proper sense an economic necessity. You are seeking what for you is the ideal physical setting of life. And I suspect that no matter what we say here, a lot of people will go on seeking this thing. . . .

MRS. SCOTT-MAXWELL: Meanwhile, we have come back to the responsibility of the individual mothers. There is an enormous responsibility upon them to become conscious of the situation—

MRS. GOULD: To feel the importance of their role and the value of it—

MRS. SCOTT-MAXWELL: Women need to live their public side, and their private side, and they must have every help in find the right balance of the two.

QUESTIONS FOR ANALYSIS

1. What do critics of working mothers suggest are the most serious drawbacks of their participation in the labor market?

2. What justifications are offered for the presence of mothers in the workforce?

3. How do you reconcile the extensive attention to working mothers in this era with Betty Freidan's complaints about the "feminine mystique" (pp. 595–97)?

4. What is the significance of the discussion of aid to dependent children, and how does that discussion relate to the history of mothers' pensions discussed on p. 466?

DOCUMENTS

Women in the Civil Rights Movement

As HISTORIANS EXAMINE THE LIVES of American women of the last half of the twentieth century, they are able to draw on a wider variety and number of sources than historians researching earlier periods. The documents presented in this essay are either autobiographical accounts or oral histories. Both types offer us the woman's own words and understanding of her participation in the civil rights movement. But, as with all types of historical sources, the reader needs to evaluate the document's strengths and shortcomings. How does the narrator's commitment shape her recollection? Does she have an ax to grind? Is she anxious to justify or exaggerate her actions? Need we be concerned that her memory is accurate? And in the case of oral histories, has the interviewer unduly influenced the narrative?

AUTOBIOGRAPHICAL ACCOUNTS

Septima Clark (1898–1987), a Charleston, South Carolina, schoolteacher, had been active in the civil rights movement before she went to the Highlander Folk School in 1954 in Tennessee, a left-wing, biracial institution interested in labor and community organizing. She became Highlander's director of education and established, with Esau Jenkins and Miles Horton, an innovative Citizenship School for prospective voters. Like Ella Baker (see pp. 614–15), Clark emphasized grassroots mobilization and the importance of listening to the needs and interests of the people the civil rights movement was trying to engage. Clark's program, which was later transferred to the Southern Christian Leadership Council (SCLC), trained hundreds of local activists—more than half of them women—who in turn ran their own workshops.

The key to the program was teaching blacks how to read and write so they could attempt the difficult process of registering to vote. The southern states used a poll tax system to keep both poor blacks and whites from registering to vote, but the most widespread technique was a literacy test that included trick questions and such devices as asking the prospective voter to interpret a selected passage from the state constitutions.

In the following passage from her second autobiography, *Ready from Within*, originally published in 1986, Clark describes a school set up in the early 1960s at the Dorchester Cooperative Community Center in McIntosh, Georgia, where recruits from all over the South were brought for workshops. What were the most serious problems Clark and her group encountered?

SEPTIMA CLARK

Once a month, for five days, we'd work with the people we had recruited, some of whom were just off the farms. . . . We went into various communities and found people who could read well aloud and write legibly. They didn't have to have a certificate of any kind. I sat down and wrote out a flyer saying that the teachers we need in a Citizenship School should be people who are respected by the members of the community, who can read well aloud, and who can write their names in cursive writing. These are the ones that we looked for.

We brought those people to the [Dorchester Cooperative Community] center in Liberty County, Georgia. While they were there, we gave them the plan for teaching in a citizenship school. We had a day-by-day plan, which started the first night with them talking, telling us what they would like to learn. The next morning we started off with asking them: "Do you have an employment office in your town? Where is it located? What hours is it open? Have you been there to get work?"

The answers to those things we wrote down on dry cleaner's bags, so they could read them. We didn't have any blackboards. That afternoon we would ask them about the government in their home town. They knew very little about it. They didn't know anything about the policemen or the mayor or anything like that. We had to give them a plan of how these people were elected, of how people who had registered to vote could put these people in office, and of how they were the ones who were over you.

We were trying to make teachers out of these people who could barely read and write. But they could teach. If they could read at all, we could teach them that c-o-n-s-t-i-t-u-t-i-o-n spells constitution. We'd have a long discussion all morning about what the constitution was. We were never telling anybody. We used a very non-directive approach.

The people who left Dorchester went home to teach and to work in voter registration drives. They went home, and they didn't take it anymore. They started their own citizenship classes, discussing the problems in their own towns. "How come the pavement stops where the black section begins?" Asking questions like that, and then knowing who to go to talk to about that, or where to protest it.

The first night at the Liberty County Center we would always ask people to tell the needs of the people in their community. The first night they gave us their input, and the next morning we started teaching from what they wanted to do.

But what they wanted varied. We had to change. Down in the southern part of Georgia some women wanted to know how to make out bank checks. One woman told the workshop that somebody had been able to withdraw a lot of money from her account because she did not know how to make out her own check and check up on her own account. . . .

So we started teaching banking. We brought in a banker, and he put the whole form up on the board and showed them how to put in the date and how to write it out. He told them, "Don't leave a space at the end of the check. Somebody else could write another number in there. When you finish putting down the amount, take a line and carry it all the way to the dollar mark."

[Clark summed up the impact of the voter registration drive and the 1965 Voting Rights Act, which had eliminated the literacy test.]

After that, people in Alabama did not have to answer twenty-four questions. They could register to vote if they could sign their name in cursive. It didn't take us but twenty minutes in Selma, Alabama, to teach a woman to write her

SOURCE: Cynthia Stokes Brown, ed., *Ready from Within: Septima Clark and the Civil Rights Movement* (1986; repr., Trenton, NJ: Africa World Press, Inc., 1990), 63–70, 77–79.

name. The white students took her to the courthouse. She wrote her name in cursive writing and came back with a number that meant she could register to vote. This is the way we did it.

We had 150 of those schools in Selma, paying those teachers $1.25 an hour, two hours, each morning, five days a week. The Marshall Field Foundation furnished the money for that, and we did it for three solid months. At the end of three months, we had 7002 persons with a number that gave them the right to vote when the federal man came down in August. We worked from May 18 to August 15. That was in 1965, because in 1966 we went to the vote. . . .

In Selma, anybody who came to our meeting lost their job. Fifty or more did. Some of them got their jobs back later, but some never did. . . . But even with that kind of harassment, the Citizenship Schools really got into full force. There were 897 going from 1957 to 1970. In 1964 there were 195 going at one time. They were in people's kitchens, in beauty parlors, and under trees in the summertime. I went all over the South, sometimes visiting three Citizenship Schools in one day, checking to be sure they weren't using textbooks, but were teaching people to read those election laws and to write their names in cursive writing.

One time I heard Andy Young say that the Citizenship Schools were the base on which the whole civil rights movement was built. And that's probably true. . . .

[Clark, like Ella Baker, later expressed frustration over the male domination of the civil rights movement.]

I was on the Executive Staff of SCLC, but the men on it didn't listen to me too well. They liked to send me into many places, because I could always make a path in to get people to listen to what I have to say. But those men didn't have any faith in women, none whatsoever. They just thought that women were sex symbols and had no contributions to make. That's why Rev. Abernathy would say continuously, "Why is Mrs. Clark on this staff?"

Dr. King would say, "Well, she has expanded our program. She has taken it into eleven deep south states." Rev. Abernathy'd come right back the next time and ask again. I had a great feeling that Dr. King didn't think much of women either. . . .

But in those days I didn't criticize Dr. King, other than asking him not to lead all the marches [so other leaders could be developed]. I adored him. I supported him in every way I could because I greatly respected his courage, his service to others, and his non-violence. The way I think about him now comes from my experience in the women's movement. But in those days, of course, in the black church men were always in charge. It was just the way things were. . . .

I see this as one of the weaknesses of the civil rights movement, the way the men looked at the women. . . .

Out of these experiences I felt I wanted to be active in the women's liberation movement. [At the encouragement of a white civil rights activist, Virginia Durr, Clark went on to participate in the National Organization for Women.]

Although the vast majority of civil rights activists were black, some whites, many of them women, also participated. Sandra "Casey" Hayden (b. 1939) came from a small town in Texas where she lived with her divorced mother and grandmother, both strong women and highly influential in her life. Her activism began at the University of Texas through the Young Women's Christian Association (YWCA), an organization that fostered social activism on many college campuses in the 1950s and that Hayden described as a place where she was "grounded in a democratic manner of work, exposed to and educated about race." She was an early and valued member of the Student Nonviolent Coordinating Committee (SNCC). In this passage from an autobiographical essay, "Fields of Blue" (2000), she discusses some of her activities in Atlanta as the organization's northern coordinator during 1963. What is the significance of her emphasis on the ideal of community?

CASEY HAYDEN

I threw myself into my work, developing Friends of SNCC groups on campuses and in cities. Initially, SNCC was kept alive largely through spontaneous donations. Now we were looking for sustaining support. This position was a good fit for me. I was trained to organize and administer programs, had been on a northern campus and knew what was needed to sustain support there, and had an enormous number of contacts by now through the Y, the NSA [National Student Association], SDS [Students for a Democratic Society — see p. 673], the Northern Student Movement, and all the traveling I'd done. I sent out field reports and instructions on how to organize, created mailing lists and key supporter lists, answered piles of correspondence and endless phone calls, responded to emergencies in the field, and laid the groundwork for Dinky Romilly and Betty Garman, white women I knew from other organizations, who followed me in this position. . . . I did all my own work in SNCC. At this point, bringing into being a program and a network, I did the head work and the hands-on work. I thought we turned hierarchy upside down by throwing out that division of labor. This was true for me throughout my years with the organization. I was never a secretary in SNCC and never had one. I worked long hours with no days off, feeling responsible for the staff in the field whose lives were daily at risk. I visited the field,

including Greenwood, where I attended the First Greenwood Mississippi Freedom Folk Festival. Traveling in an integrated car, we took turns hiding under blankets on the floor in the back. Once there, we sat with local people on planks in an open field to listen to local talent, and Pete Seeger and Bob Dylan. Whites in pick-ups circled the field, rifles on display in racks on the rear windows. . . .

In meetings and out, I saw our first task as creating relationships among ourselves, holding our community together. A style, an ethic, was implied. I stuck around endlessly, we all did, until some level of understanding was reached, at which point we could act. This was called coming to consensus. Once this broad consensus was reached, I didn't argue with people about what they should do. There was more than enough to do, and plenty of room for experimentation. If folks were willing to risk their lives, that was enough. They should be able to choose how they would die. I did try to do what I said I'd do. That was accountability, synonymous with self-discipline. To my recollection everyone operated like this, for some time.

Integration worked both ways. I was breaking the barrier between people with my own body, integrating the black community. I thought I was getting the better side of the deal. . . . Our struggle was to break down the system, the walls, of segregation. This implied no barriers in our relations with each other. Once we broke down the barriers between ourselves, we were in a new space together, in community. This was our radi-

SOURCE: Constance Curry et al., *Deep in Our Hearts: Nine White Women in the Freedom Movement* (Athens: University of Georgia Press, 2000), 349–50, 365–66.

cal truth. Our radical truth was an experience, not an idea. That was SNCC's great genius.

[Hayden comments on the SNCC position paper she coauthored in 1964 with another white woman, Mary King (see box, pp. 620–21).]

The paper aimed to bring forward the fact that sexism was comparable to racism, a novel idea at the time—so novel, in fact, that the word sexism didn't exist in our lexicon. . . . [A]s the paper has entered the literature of feminism over the years, some historians have wondered if it exposed a struggle for power or leadership. Nonsense. We [the authors] were all white. None of us

were after leadership. That was for blacks. I believe we were speaking not for our private self-interest, but for all women, to share what we saw: that gender is a social construct, as is race. There was no written feminist critique on the left in our generation. We were the first. It is a good critique, in many ways, and brave, a fine example of how the tools developed in analyzing racism were translated, inside SNCC itself, into an analysis of gender. We had pierced the racist bubble and were seeing clearly. All things were open to question. As Bernice Reagon has said, "SNCC was where it could happen."

ORAL HISTORIES

ALTHOUGH WE HAVE ONLY a handful of memoirs written by women civil rights activists, a growing collection of oral histories has expanded historians' access to a wide range of women who participated in the movement. Oral accounts, like memoirs, if recorded long after the events described, are sometimes marred by faulty memories or influenced by the person conducting the interview. Nonetheless, they give invaluable insights into the experiences and feelings of historical actors whose voices are often unheard in more traditional documentary sources.

This first selection is drawn from an interview conducted by historian and filmmaker Henry Hampton with Diane Nash (later Bevel), one of the best known of the women SNCC activists. Nash (b. 1938), an African American who left Chicago to attend Fisk University in Nashville, describes her early involvement in the movement, at the Nashville sit-ins in 1960. Why is this account so powerful?

DIANE NASH

The sit-ins were really highly charged, emotionally. In our non-violent workshops, we had decided to be respectful of the opposition, and try to keep issues geared toward desegregation, not get sidetracked. The first sit-in we had was really

SOURCE: Henry Hampton and Steve Fayer, comps., *Voices of Freedom: An Oral History of the Civil Rights Movement from the 1950s through the 1980s* (New York: Bantam, 1990), 57–59, 82–83.

funny, because the waitresses were nervous. They must have dropped two thousand dollars' worth of dishes that day. It was almost a cartoon. One in particular, she was so nervous, she picked up dishes and she dropped one, and she'd pick up another one, and she'd drop it. It was really funny, and we were sitting there trying not to laugh, because we thought that laughing would be insulting and we didn't want to create that kind of atmosphere. At the same time we were scared to death. . . .

After we had started sitting in, we were surprised and delighted to hear reports of other cities joining in the sit-ins. And I think we started feeling that power of the idea whose time had come. Before we did the things that we did, we had no inkling that the movement would become as widespread as it did. I can remember being in the dorm any number of times and hearing the newscast, that Orangeburg had demonstrations, or Knoxville, or other towns. And we were really excited. We'd applaud, and say yea. When you are that age, you don't feel powerful. I remember realizing that with what we were doing, trying to abolish segregation, we were coming up against governors, judges, politicians, businessmen, and I remember thinking, "I'm only twenty-two years old, what do I know, what am I doing?" And I felt very vulnerable. So when we heard these newscasts, that other cities had demonstrations, it really helped. Because there were more of us. And it was very important.

The movement had a way of reaching inside you and bringing out things that even you didn't know were there. Such as courage. When it was time to go to jail, I was much too busy to be afraid.

[As an SNCC activist, in 1961 Nash became involved in the Freedom Rides. Here, she describes her leadership role when violence threatened to stop the rides and Nash insisted that they go forward (see pp. 614–15).]

A contingent of students left Nashville to pick up the Freedom Ride where it had been stopped. Some of the students gave me sealed letters to be mailed in case they were killed. That's how prepared they were for death.

The students who were going to pick up the Freedom Ride elected me coordinator. As coordinator, part of my responsibility was to stay in touch with the Justice Department. Our whole way of operating was that we took ultimate responsibility for what we were going to do. But it was felt that they should be advised, in Washington, of what our plans were. Some people hoped for protection from the federal government. I think Jim Lawson cautioned against relying on federal protection.

I was also to keep the press informed, and communities that were participating, such as Birmingham, Montgomery, Jackson, and Nashville. And I coordinated the training and recruitment of more people to take up the Freedom Ride.

[Nash later became a rider herself and was jailed in Jackson, Mississippi, in 1961.]

ORAL HISTORIES ARE PARTICULARLY VALUABLE for capturing the stories of older rural women who offered indispensable aid to the activists who came to their communities. In this selection, published in 1983, Mary Dora Jones reminisces about taking in Freedom Summer workers in Marks, Mississippi. The interviewer is the Pulitzer Prize–winning journalist Howell Raines, who later became executive editor of the *New York Times*. What does Jones's account convey about disagreements within the African American community and the dangers facing those African Americans who supported the civil rights activists?

MARY DORA JONES

MARY DORA JONES: I had about several blacks and four whites in my house, wouldn't nobody else take 'em.

RAINES: In Marks?

JONES: Right . . . they really move. They comes in, they mean business. They didn't mind dyin', and as I see they really mean business, I just love that for 'em, because they was there to help us. And since they was there to help us, I was there to help them. . . .

RAINES: Did that cause you any problems in the community. . . . opening your home up?

JONES: Oh, really, because they talkin' about burnin' my house down. . . . Some of the black folks got the news that they were gonna burn it down. . . . My neighbors was afraid of gettin' killed. People standin' behind buildin's, peepin' out behind the buildin's, to see what's goin' on. So I just told 'em. "Dyin' is all right. Ain't but one thing 'bout dyin'. That's make sho' you right, 'cause you gon' die anyway." . . . If they had burnt it down, it was just a house burned down.

RAINES: That's the attitude that changed the South.

JONES: So that's the way I thought about it. So those kids, some of 'em from California, some of 'em from Iowa, some of 'em from Cincinnati, they worked, and they sho' had them white people up there shook up.

RAINES: . . . [Y]oungsters that came in, particularly the white ones from outside the South, did they have a hard time adjusting . . . ?

JONES: They had a hard time adjustin' because most all of the blacks up there didn't want to see 'em comin' . . . said they ain't lettin' no damn civil rights come. "If they come up here to my house, I'm gon' shoot 'em."

See this is what the black folks were sayin', and those kids had went to the preachers' houses,

they had done went to the deacons' houses, they had done went to the teachers' houses, all tryin' to get in. Some of 'em come in around five o'clock that evenin', landed in my house. I give 'em my house, "My house is yo' house." I was workin' for a man, he was workin' at the Post Office, and he and his wife was beggin' me everyday, "Don't fool with them Communists."

RAINES: The white people?

JONES: That's what they was tellin' me, those kids was Communists. I said, "Well, I tell you what. I don't think they no more Communist than right here where I am, because if they Communists, then you Communists. They cain't hurt me no mo' than I already been hurt." Anything that helped the peoples, then I'm right there. So I didn't stop, although I got him scared to fire me. He would have fired me, but I got him scared to fire me. . . .

RAINES: This was your white boss?

JONES: This was my white boss I was working for. His wife was sick, and every day the wife would talk to me about those people, askin' me where they lived. I said, "Well, they ain't livin' at yo' house. Why you want to know where they live?" So she said, "They ain't livin' with you?" And I said, "Well, I'm payin' the last note on the house," just like that. And I never did tell her.

Finally one day she brought me home, and it was a car sittin' there in my driveway, and two white men was in there, and there were some sittin' on the porch. She put me out and she went on back. When I went to work the next morning, she say, "Mary, was them, ah, civil rights people at yo' house?" I said, "Now when you turned around and stopped and they were sittin' there, you oughta been askin' 'em what they was. They'da told you."

And I never did tell 'em anything. So it went on some, she said, "Ain't but one thing I hate about it, this intermarriage." And I said, "Well, ain't no need in worryin' about that, because if you wanna worry about that, you oughta been talkin' to your granddaddy."

SOURCE: Howell Raines, *My Soul Is Rested: Movement Days in the Deep South* (New York: Putnam, 1977), 279–81.

EARLINE BOYD of Hattiesburg, Mississippi, had been involved in the NAACP in her community even before civil rights activists came to her town for the voter registration drive. In this interview, conducted in 1991 by Dr. Charles Bolton of the University of Southern Mississippi's Civil Rights in Mississippi Oral History Project, she describes some of the harassment African Americans active in civil rights faced. What insights does she offer about women's participation in the movement?

EARLINE BOYD

EARLINE BOYD: There was the pressure on people about jobs or they would try and intimidate them in different ways.

I remember one man lost his job. He had been working for one of the white funeral homes here and his wife was very active in it. When they found out that she was marching that day going to the courthouse—that's where we were marching to that particular day—when he went back to work the people—I don't remember exactly what they said to him, but I do know that she his wife told him just to give that job up and not to go back anymore. So evidently they had said things to him, had made him know that they did not want him. He didn't go; it was his wife who was doing the marching and was active in the movement.

So it was hard on people and a lot of people was afraid, you know, to take a step towards trying to work with the movement. I don't remember where I was working then, but it didn't have any effect on me, on my job at the time. And I would just go whenever they had it and it was kind of hard. Now some people probably, well, the ones that was working for people who didn't want them to go, I'm sure they gave them a lot of hard times. So that was my way of getting started in the movement.

DR. CHARLES BOLTON: Were a lot of women involved? It sounds like the women maybe were more involved than the men.

BOYD: There were more women involved than men in the movement.

BOLTON: Why do you think that is?

BOYD: Well, I guess the man was the person who was really head of the household and needed a job. Women worked but I guess they felt like it would be easier for them to go and not lose their job than for men. Even so, like I said about this man who lost his job when the person that he was working for found out that his wife was going, then he started talking to him. And of course, his wife was working for herself and had her own day care center. So it wouldn't bother her. And he stopped working there, and I don't know where he went to work after that. But later on I do remember that he started working for himself too.

SOURCE: "Civil Rights in Mississippi Digital Archive," Mississippi Oral History Program of The University of Southern Mississippi, interview conducted August 29, 1991, http://anna.lib.usm.edu/%7Espcol/crda/oh/ohboydrp.html (accessed January 29, 2003).

QUESTIONS FOR ANALYSIS

1. What insights do these accounts offer about the distinct experiences of women in the civil rights movement?

2. What kinds of leadership skills did these movement women display?

3. Can you find specific examples in these documents that suggest any of the pitfalls historians face in drawing upon remembrances as sources?

4. To what extent do these documents reveal the obstacles facing civil rights activists?

5. What clues do these documents provide as to the relationship between the civil rights movement and the emergence of the feminist movement in the late 1960s?

NOTES

1. James T. Patterson, *Grand Expectations: The United States, 1945–1974* (New York: Oxford University Press, 1996), 223.

2. David K. Johnson, *The Lavender Scare: The Cold War Persecution of Gays and Lesbians in the Federal Government* (Chicago: University of Chicago Press, 2004), 196.

3. Jessica Weiss, *To Have and to Hold: Marriage, the Baby Boom, and Social Change* (Chicago: University of Chicago Press, 2000), 57.

4. "Wright Girls Combine Careers and Marriage," *Ebony*, January 1951, 74.

5. Joanne Meyerowitz, "Beyond the Feminine Mystique: A Reassessment of Postwar Mass Culture, 1946–1958," in Joanne Meyerowitz, ed., *Not June Cleaver: Women and Gender in Postwar America, 1945–1960* (Philadelphia: Temple University Press, 1994), 240.

6. Eva Moskowitz, "'It's Good to Blow Your Top': Women's Magazines and a Discourse of Discontent, 1945–1960," *Journal of Women's History* 8 (Fall 1996): 66–98.

7. Alice Kessler-Harris, *Out to Work: A History of Wage-Earning Women* (New York: Oxford University Press, 1982), 304.

8. Susan M. Hartmann, "Women's Employment and the Domestic Ideal in the Early Cold War Years," in Joanne Meyerowitz, ed., *Not June Cleaver: Women and Gender in Postwar America, 1945–1960* (Philadelphia: Temple University Press, 1994), 88.

9. Ibid., 90.

10. Julia Kirk Blackwelder, *Now Hiring: The Feminization of Work in the United States, 1900–1995* (College Station: Texas A&M University Press, 1997), 162–63.

11. Susan Rimby Leighow, "An 'Obligation to Participate': Married Nurses Labor Force Participation in the 1950s," in Meyerowitz, ed., *Not June Cleaver*, 37–56.

12. Weiss, *To Have and to Hold*, 55.

13. Sara M. Evans, *Born for Liberty: A History of Women in America* (New York: Free Press, 1989), 254.

14. Bruce Fehn, "African-American Women and the Struggle for Equality in the Meatpacking Industry, 1940–1960," *Journal of Women's History* 10 (Spring 1998): 50.

15. Ibid., 58–59.

16. Catherine E. Rymph, *Republican Women: Feminism and Conservatism from Suffrage through the Rise of the New Right* (University of North Carolina Press: Chapel Hill, 2006), 117.

17. Amy Swerdlow, *Women Strike for Peace: Traditional Motherhood and Radical Politics in the 1960s* (Chicago: University of Chicago Press, 1993), 110.

18. Ibid., 117.

19. Belinda Robnett, *How Long? How Long? African-American Women in the Struggle for Civil Rights* (New York: Oxford University Press, 1997), 59.

20. Ibid., 67.

21. Ibid., 17–32.

22. Ibid., 94.

23. Ibid., 104.

24. Clayborne Carson, *In Struggle: SNCC and the Black Awakening of the 1960s* (Cambridge: Harvard University Press, 1995), 74.

25. Sara Evans, *Personal Politics: The Roots of Women's Liberation in the Civil Rights Movement and the New Left* (New York: Knopf, 1979), 86–87.

26. Debra L. Schultz, *Going South: Jewish Women in the Civil Rights Movement* (New York: New York University Press, 2001), 83.

27. Ibid., 9.

28. Margaret Rose, "Gender and Civic Activism in Mexican American Barrios in California: The Community Service Organization, 1947–1962," in Joanne Meyerowitz, ed., *Not June Cleaver*, 181.

29. Ibid., 190.

30. Patricia G. Zelman, *Women, Work, and National Policy: The Kennedy-Johnson Years* (Ann Arbor: UMI Research Press, 1982), 28.

31. Linda Kerber, *No Constitutional Right to Be Ladies* (New York: Hill and Wang, 1998), 192.

32. Alice Kessler-Harris, *In Pursuit of Equity: Women, Men, and the Quest for Economic Citizenship in Twentieth-Century America* (New York: Oxford University Press, 2001), 234.

33. William Boddy, *Fifties Television: The Industry and Its Critics* (Urbana: University of Illinois Press, 1990), 20.

34. *Newsweek*, March 15, 1954, 93.

35. Lynn Spigel, *Make Room for TV: Television and the Family Ideal in Postwar America* (Chicago: University of Chicago Press, 1992), 83.

36. Jim Hall, *Mighty Minutes: An Illustrated History of Television's Best Commercials* (New York: Harmony, 1984), 47.

37. Melvin Patrick Ely, *The Adventures of Amos 'n' Andy* (New York: Free Press, 1991), 211.

38. Rick Mitz, *The Great TV Sitcom Book* (New York: Richard Marek, Publishers, 1992), 14.

39. George Lipsitz, "The Meaning of Memory, Family, Class and Ethnicity in Early Network Television Programs," in Lynn Spigel and Denise Mann, eds., *Private Screenings: Television and the Female Consumer* (Minneapolis: University of Minnesota Press, 1992), 78.

40. Susan J. Douglas, *Where the Girls Are: Growing Up Female with the Mass Media* (New York: Times Books, 1994), 36.

41. Violet Brown Weingarten, "Case History of an Ex-Working Mother," *New York Times*, September 20, 1953, 54.

42. Gerry Murray Engle, "I Chose Work," *Good Housekeeping*, November 1953, 299.

43. David Yellin, "I'm Married to a Working Mother," *Harper's*, July 1956, 34–37; Robert Coughlan, "Modern Marriage," *Life*, 41 (December 24, 1956): 116.

SUGGESTED REFERENCES

General Works   Two books offer overviews of women's history for this era: Rochelle Gatlin, *American Women Since 1945* (1987), and Eugenia Kaledin, *American Women in the 1950s* (1984). A lively oral history is Brett Harvey, *The Fifties: A Women's Oral History* (1993). Joanne Meyerowitz, ed., *Not June Cleaver: Women and Gender in Postwar America, 1945–1960* (1994), offers a valuable anthology of recent historical essays that challenge the primacy of the feminine mystique for understanding the period.

Marriage, Family, and Cold War Culture   A starting point for understanding the impact of the Cold War on American families is Elaine Tyler May, *Homeward Bound: American Families in the Cold War Era* (1988). Other insights on marriage, sexuality, and the family may be found in Wini Breines, *Young, White, and Miserable: Growing Up Female in the Fifties* (1992); Stephanie Coontz, *The Way We Never Were: American Families and the Nostalgia Trap* (1992); Lillian Faderman, *Odd Girls and Twilight Lovers: A History of Lesbian Life in Twentieth-Century America* (1991); Steven Mintz and Susan Kellogg, *Domestic Revolutions: A Social History of American Family Life* (1988); Eva Moskowitz, "'It's Good to Blow Your Top': Women's Magazines and a Discourse of Discontent, 1945–1960," *Journal of Women's History* 8 (1996): 66–98; and Jessica Weiss, *To Have and To Hold: Marriage, the Baby Boom, and Social Change* (2000). For a valuable primary source on working-class women, see sociologist Mirra Komarovsky's *Blue-Collar Marriage* (1967).

Popular culture is engagingly discussed by Susan J. Douglas in *Where the Girls Are: Growing Up Female with the Mass Media* (1994). See also William Boddy, *Fifties Television: The Industry and Its Critics* (1990); Robin P. Means Coleman, *African American Viewers and the Black Situation Comedy: Situating Racial Humor* (2000); Gerald Jones, *"Honey, I'm Home!" Sitcoms: Selling the American Dream* (1992); George Lipsitz, "The Meaning of Memory: Family, Class, and Ethnicity in Early Network Television Programs," in Lynn Spigel and Denise Mann, eds., *Private Screenings: Television and the Female Consumer* (1992); and Lynn Spigel, *Make Room for TV: Television and the Family Ideal in Postwar America* (1992).

For the feminine mystique, begin with Betty Friedan, *The Feminine Mystique* (1963), followed by Daniel Horowitz's insightful assessment, *Betty Friedan and the Making of* The Feminine Mystique (1998); Susan M. Hartmann, "Women's Employment and the Domestic Ideal in the Early Cold War Years," in Joanne Meyerowitz, ed., *Not June Cleaver*, 84–102; and Joanne Meyerowitz, "Beyond the Feminine Mystique: A Reassessment of Postwar Mass Culture, 1946–1958," in Joanne Meyerowitz, ed., *Not June Cleaver*, 229–62.

Women and Work   Three important overviews of women and work that include valuable material on the postwar era are Julia Kirk Blackwelder, *Now Hiring: The Feminization of Work in the United States, 1900–1995* (1997); Alice Kessler-Harris, *Out to Work: A History of Wage-Earning Women* (1982); Lynn Y. Weiner, *From*

Working Girl to Working Mother: The Female Labor Force in the United States (1985). On the popular debate concerning women and work, see Kathryn Keller, *Mothers and Work in Popular American Magazines* (1994). A number of books analyze women's participation in the labor movement: see Dorothy Sue Cobble's *Dishing It Out: Waitresses and Their Unions in the Twentieth Century* (1991) and *The Other Women's Movement: Workplace Justice and Social Rights in Modern America* (2004); Dennis A. Deslippe, *"Rights, Not Roses": Unions and the Rise of Working-Class Feminism, 1945–1980* (2000); and Nancy F. Gabin, *Feminism in the Labor Movement: Women and the United Auto Workers, 1935–1975* (1990). Specialized articles on the topic include Bruce Fehn, "'Chickens Come Home to Roost': Industrial Reorganization, Seniority, and Gender Conflict in the United Packinghouse Workers of America, 1956–1966," *Labor History* 34 (1993): 324–41; Lisa Kannenberg, "The Impact of the Cold War on Women's Trade Union Activism: The EU Experience," *Labor History* 34 (1993): 309–23; and Leah F. Vosko and David Witwer, "'Not a Man's Union': Women Teamsters in the United States during the 1940s and 1950s," *Journal of Women's History* 13 (2001): 169–92. On African American women and work, see Bruce Fehn, "African-American Women and the Struggle for Equality in the Meatpacking Industry, 1940–1960," *Journal of Women's History* 10 (1998): 45–69; Paula Giddings, *When and Where I Enter: The Impact of Black Women on Race and Sex in America* (1984); and Jacqueline Jones, *Labor of Love, Labor of Sorrow: Black Women, Work, and the Family, from Slavery to the Present* (1985). On Mexican cannery workers, see Vicki L. Ruiz, *Cannery Women, Cannery Lives: Mexican Women, Unionization, and the California Food Processing Industry, 1930–1950* (1987).

Middle-Class Women's Activism   For an overview of this subject, consult Leila J. Rupp and Verta Taylor, *Survival in the Doldrums: The American Women's Rights Movement, 1945 to the 1960s* (1987). Specialized studies include Susan Levine, *Degrees of Equality: The American Association of University Women and the Challenge of Twentieth-Century Feminism* (1995); Faith Rogow, *Gone to Another Meeting: The National Council of Jewish Women, 1893–1993* (1993); Susan Lynn, *Progressive Women in the Conservative Times: Racial Justice, Peace, and Feminism, 1945 to the 1960s* (1992); Amy Swerdlow, *Women Strike for Peace: Traditional Motherhood and Radical Politics in the 1960s* (1993); Susan Ware, "American Women in the 1950s: Nonpartisan Politics and Women's Politicization," in Louise A. Tilly and Patricia Gurin, eds., *Women, Politics, and Change* (1990), 281–99; and Deborah Gray White, *Too Heavy a Load: Black Women in Defense of Themselves, 1894–1994* (1999). For the importance of women to conservative politics, see Lisa McGirr, *Suburban Warriors: The Origins of the New American Right* (2001), Catherine E. Rymph, *Republican Women: Feminism and Conservatism from Suffrage through the Rise of the New Right* (2006), Michelle Nickerson, "'The Power of a Morally Indignant Woman': Republican Women and the Making of California Conservatism," *Journal of the West* 42 (Summer 2001): 35–43; and a conference paper by Laura Pierce, "'Civic Watchdogs in High Heels': Women's Patriotic Organizations and Anti-Communism in the United States, 1945–1965" (paper presented at meeting of the Organization of American Historians, Memphis, 2003).

Women and Civil Rights   After being largely invisible in the history of the civil rights movement, women activists are the subject of a growing literature. A number of general works offer insights about women's experiences. See especially Charles M. Payne, *I've Got the Light of Freedom: The Organizing Tradition and the Mississippi Freedom Struggle* (1995), and the oral history collections of Henry Hampton and Steve Fayer, comps., *Voices of Freedom: An Oral History of the Civil Rights Movement from the 1950s through the 1980s* (1990), and Howell Raines, *My Soul Is Rested: Movement Days in the Deep South Remembered* (1983). For the concept of bridge leaders, see Belinda Robnett, *How Long? How Long? African-American Women in the Struggle for Civil Rights* (1997). A useful anthology of articles is Vicki L. Crawford, Jacqueline Anne Rouse, and Barbara Woods, eds., *Women in the Civil Rights Movement: Trailblazers and Torchbearers, 1941–1964* (1990), but see also articles such as Bernice McNair Barnett, "Invisible Southern Black Women Leaders in the Civil Rights Movement: The Triple Constraints of Gender, Race, and Class," *Gender and Society* 7 (1993): 162–82; Carolyn Calloway-Thomas and Thurmon Garner, "Daisy Bates and the Little Rock School Crisis: Forging the Way," *Journal of Black History* 26 (1996): 616–28; Aprele Elliott, "Ella Baker: Free Agent in the Civil Rights Movement," *Journal of Black Studies* 26 (1996): 593–603; and Cynthia Griggs Fleming, "Black Women Activists and the Student Nonviolent Coordinating Committee: The Case of Ruby Doris Smith Robinson," *Journal of Women's History* 4 (1993): 64–82. Biographies of major leaders include Douglas Brinkley, *Rosa Parks* (2000); Chan Kai Lee, *For Freedom's Sake: The Life of Fannie Lou Hamer* (2000); and Barbara Ransby, *Ella Baker and the Black Freedom Movement: A Radical Democratic Vision* (1993). Valuable autobiographies are Cynthia Stokes Brown, ed., *Ready from Within: Septima Clark and the Civil Rights Movement* (1990), and Jo Ann Robinson, *The Montgomery Bus Boycott and the Women Who Started It: The Memoir of Jo Ann Gibson Robinson* (1987). For white women in the movement, see Joan C. Browning, "Trends in Feminism and Historiography: Invisible Revolutionaries: White Women in Civil Rights Historiography," *Journal of Women's History* 8 (1996): 186–204; Constance Curry et al., *Deep in Our Hearts: Nine White Women in the Freedom Movement* (2000); Virginia Foster Durr, *"Outside the Magic Circle": The Autobiography of Virginia Foster Durr* (1985); Catherine Fosl, *Subversive Southerner: Anne Braden and the Struggle for Racial Justice in the Cold War South* (2002); and Debra L. Schultz, *Going South: Jewish Women in the Civil Rights Movement* (2001). For a crucial assessment of the relationship between the civil rights movement and second wave feminism, see Sara Evans, *Personal Politics: The Roots of Women's Liberation in the Civil Rights Movement and the New Left* (1979).

Scholarship on Mexican American women for this period is still sparse, but see Vicki Ruiz, *From Out of the Shadows: Mexican Women in Twentieth-Century America* (1999); Margaret Rose, "Women in the United Farm Workers: A Study of Chicana and Mexicana Participation in a Labor Union, 1950–1990," PhD dissertation,

University of California, Los Angeles (1988); Margaret Rose, "Gender and Civic Activism in Mexican American Barrios in California: The Community Service Organization, 1947–1962," in Joanne Meyerowitz, ed., *Not June Cleaver*, 177–200; and Richard Santillán, "Midwestern Mexican American Women and the Struggle for Gender Equality: A Historical Overview, 1920s–1960s," *Perspectives in Mexican American Studies* 5 (1995): 79–119.

Women and Public Policy   A number of books address the issues that framed the President's Commission on the Status of Women. See Cynthia Harrison, *On Account of Sex: The Politics of Women's Issues, 1945–1968* (1988); Linda Kerber, *No Constitutional Right to Be Ladies* (1998); Alice Kessler-Harris, *In Pursuit of Equity: Women, Men, and the Quest for Economic Citizenship in Twentieth-Century America* (2001); Kathleen A. Laughlin, *Women's Work and Public Policy: A History of the Women's Bureau, U.S. Department of Labor, 1945–1970* (2000); Judith Sealander, *As Minority Becomes Majority: Federal Reaction to the Phenomenon of Women in the Work Force, 1920–1963* (1983); and Patricia G. Zelman, *Women, Work, and National Policy: The Kennedy-Johnson Years* (1982).

For selected Web sites, please visit the *Through Women's Eyes* book companion site at bedfordstmartins.com/duboisdumenil.

11

Modern Feminism and American Society

1965–1980

IN 1966, A GROUP OF SIXTEEN WOMEN MET IN WASH-ington, D.C., to create the National Organization for Women (NOW) to "bring women into full participation in the mainstream of American society." Two years later, Alice Peurala, who worked for U.S. Steel in Chicago, was denied a higher-paying job in the mill; after her boss told her, "We don't want any women on these jobs," she filed an antidiscrimination suit with a government agency, a case she won in 1974.[1] In 1968, members of a guerrilla street group staged a dramatic protest at the Miss America pageant, in which they crowned a live sheep and tossed symbols of women's oppression — curlers, bras, and makeup — into a "freedom trash can." That same year, African American women formed the Black Women's Liberation Committee. In 1970, Chicana activists created the Comisión Femenil Mexicana with the purpose of "organizing women to assume leadership positions within the Chicano movement and in community life."[2]

These disparate events highlight the emergence of a multifaceted feminism that flourished in the late 1960s and 1970s. The feminism of women associated with NOW took inspiration from the civil rights movement and was rooted in the early 1960s activism that had focused on women's employment rights. Different visions of feminism stemmed from the protest movements of the 1960s in which young men and women took to the streets to demand an end to the war in Vietnam while others demanded racial justice through a variety of nationalist power movements. Exhilarated to be part of the ambitious activism of the period but frustrated by their exclusion from its leadership, women had begun by 1968 to insist that equality and liberation should characterize the relations between the sexes, as well as among races and nations. As African American writer and activist Toni Cade (later Bambara) put it, "mutinous cadres of women" in all sorts of protest organizations were "getting salty about having to . . . fix the coffee while the men wrote the position papers and decided on policy."[3]

Out of this combination of excitement and frustration came "women's liberation," a new kind of feminism rooted in 1960s experiences and perspectives. Initially concentrated on gaining equality for women within the protest movements of black power, Chicanismo, and the New Left, women's liberation soon challenged the condition of women in the larger society. In conjunction with NOW, women's liberation made feminism into a mass movement. Sometimes called the "second wave" (the "first wave" having been the feminism associated with the woman suffrage movement of the Progressive era — see pp. 476–81), this modern feminism outlived its 1960s origins to become one of the most important social and political forces of the late twentieth century.

ROOTS OF SIXTIES FEMINISM

In 1960, "feminism" was often a term of derision or contempt, if it was used at all. By decade's end, Americans were hearing a great deal about it. A diverse group of women — young and old, working class and privileged, heterosexual and lesbian, white and women of color — all contributed to a resurgent feminism. Rooted in the social upheavals surrounding the civil rights movement, the Vietnam War, and the counterculture, the new feminism that emerged in the second half of the 1960s signaled the beginning of a transformative era in women's history.

The Legacy of the Civil Rights Movement

The revival of feminism in the 1960s first emerged clearly among a group of women associated with the National Organization for Women (NOW), founded in 1966. This version of feminism owed much to the civil rights movement and a dramatic legislative milestone: the passage of the Civil Rights Act of 1964. Pressure from the civil rights movement had led to a call for an omnibus federal act forbidding discrimination on the grounds of race. While Congress was debating the legislation, members of the National Woman's Party encouraged U.S. Representative Howard Smith of Virginia, a supporter of the Equal Rights Amendment (ERA), to propose an amendment to the bill that would extend federal civil rights protection to women. Smith did so, in large measure because as a white southerner he opposed the Civil Rights Act and thought the inclusion of sex would undermine support for the legislation. Once the bill was introduced in the House, however, the few women congressional representatives, notably Martha Griffiths of Michigan, backed it, with support from many women activists such as African American lawyer Pauli Murray, who saw the amendment as a way of fighting both "Jim Crow" and "Jane Crow."

The Women's Bureau staff, led by Esther Peterson (see p. 624), initially withheld support for the amendment because they worried that if the Civil Rights Act applied to women it would undermine state protective legislation, but also because they feared damage to the African American cause, which the bureau viewed as the more serious form of discrimination. Once the measure went to the Senate, however, President Lyndon B. Johnson backed the amendment to assure the entire bill's swift passage, and Peterson and Women's Bureau allies came on board. Title VII of the Civil Rights Act of 1964, prohibiting employment discrimination based on race, sex, national origin, or religion, became law.

The Equal Employment Opportunity Commission (EEOC), the agency established to implement Title VII, estimated that in the first year of its operation, grievances about sex discrimination constituted an unexpected 37 percent of its complaints. Women, many of them rank-and-file union members, complained about unequal benefits and pay, discrimination in hiring and firing, restrictive state protective legislation, and separate union seniority lists. The commission, however, concentrated on racial discrimination and gave little priority to women's complaints, making the EEOC an ineffective tool to counter sexual discrimination in the workplace.

NOW and Liberal Feminism

Discontent with the failures of the EEOC erupted in the 1966 Third Annual Conference on the Status of Women. By then, a groundswell of women, whose growth began among the President's Commission on the Status of Women and the state commissions and was reinforced by labor union and civil rights activists, had emerged to insist on women's equal rights. Their consciousness had also been raised by the 1963 publication of Betty Friedan's *The Feminine Mystique* (see pp. 595–97).

As a result, sixteen women held an impromptu meeting to create an outside pressure group; thus the National Organization for Women was founded with Friedan as its first president. Although NOW is often described as a white middle-class organization, African Americans, such as Pauli Murray and Aileen Hernandez (who was NOW's second president), participated from the very beginning. In addition, labor union members such as Dorothy Haener of the United Auto Workers were also crucial to the organization's success (see box, "National Organization for Women's Statement of Purpose").

The creation of NOW put women's civil rights on the political map. Self-consciously modeling their organization after the National Association for the Advancement of Colored People, the founders expected NOW to act primarily as a lobbying and litigating group to promote women's political and economic rights, but its goals gradually expanded. In 1967, for example, the organization endorsed women's right to reproductive freedom. The breadth of NOW's agenda was symbolized by its national Women's Strike for Equality on August 26, 1970. Commemorating the fiftieth anniversary of the Nineteenth Amendment granting woman suffrage, the strike focused on drawing attention to abortion rights, child care, and equal educational and economic opportunity. By 1974, NOW boasted seven hundred chapters, forty thousand members, and an annual budget of $300,000. Especially outside of large cities and college towns, women — inspired by the growing media visibility of women's liberation in the early 1970s — turned to the only organization they could find, NOW, and in the process broadened it from a lobbying group to a mass membership organization.

Other liberal organizations were also important in spreading the feminist message. In 1968, women who described themselves as "less radical" than the feminists in NOW — primarily because of their unwillingness to support abortion rights — created the Women's Equity Action League (WEAL). WEAL focused on discrimination in education and the workforce and lobbied extensively in Washington, D.C. Dozens of older women's organizations, such as the National Council of Jewish Women, the National Council of Negro Women, and the American Association of University Women, also supported specific legislative campaigns. Women in labor unions continued their commitment forged in the postwar years to improving working-class women's job opportunities. Many were active in NOW and, in 1974, they founded the Coalition of Labor Union Women (CLUW) to bring women's issues to the forefront of the labor movement. A host of mixed-sex organizations, with a strong interest in social justice causes, including the American Civil Liberties Union, the Young Women's Christian Association and the National Council of Churches, also helped bring feminism to the mainstream.

Historians often describe NOW and groups that supported much of its agenda as representing "liberal" feminism because it focused on bringing about women's formal equality through legal and political means, a process that paralleled other twentieth-century liberal reform movements. These groups continued many of the issues and approaches that previous phases of feminism had begun, and many of their members had been working on women's issues for decades. By contrast, the feminism known as "women's liberation" drew on a younger generation and

NATIONAL ORGANIZATION FOR WOMEN
Statement of Purpose (1966)

When NOW was founded in 1966, Betty Friedan wrote the organization's mission statement, extracts of which are reproduced here. How does the statement characterize the impediments facing women's equality, and how does it propose to address them?

We, men and women who hereby constitute ourselves as the National Organization for Women, believe that the time has come for a new movement toward true equality for all women in America, and toward a fully equal partnership of the sexes, as part of the world-wide revolution of human rights now taking place within and beyond our national borders.

The purpose of NOW is to take action to bring women into full participation in the mainstream of American society now, exercising all the privileges and responsibilities thereof in truly equal partnership with men. . . .

NOW is dedicated to the proposition that women, first and foremost, are human beings, who, like all other people in our society, must have the chance to develop their fullest human potential. We believe that women can achieve such equality only by accepting to the full the challenges and responsibilities they share with all other people in our society, as part of the decision-making mainstream of American political, economic and social life.

We organize to initiate or support action, nationally, or in any part of this nation, by individuals or organizations, to break through the silken curtain of prejudice and discrimination against women in government, industry, the professions, the churches, the political parties, the judiciary, the labor unions, in education, science, medicine, law, religion and every other field of importance in American society. . . .

WE BELIEVE that the power of American law, and the protection guaranteed by the U.S. Constitution to the civil rights of all individuals, must be effectively applied and enforced to isolate and remove patterns of sex discrimination, to ensure equality of opportunity in employment and education, and equality of civil and political rights and responsibilities on behalf of women, as well as for Negroes and other deprived groups.

We realize that women's problems are linked to many broader questions of social justice; their solution will require concerted action by many groups. Therefore, convinced that human rights for all are indivisible, we expect to give active support to the common cause of equal rights for all those who suffer discrimination and deprivation, and we call upon other organizations committed to such goals to support our efforts toward equality for women. . . .

WE BELIEVE that it is as essential for every girl to be educated to her full potential of human ability as it is for every boy—with the knowledge that such education is the key to effective participation in today's economy and that, for a girl as for a boy, education can only be serious where there is expectation that it will be used in society. We believe that American educators are capable of devising means of imparting such expectations to girl students. Moreover, we consider the decline in the proportion of women receiving higher and professional education to be evidence of discrimination. . . .

WE REJECT the current assumptions that a man must carry the sole burden of supporting himself, his wife, and family, and that a woman is automatically entitled to lifelong support by a man upon her marriage, or that marriage, home and family are primarily woman's world and responsibility—hers, to dominate—his to support. We believe that a true partnership between the sexes demands a different concept of marriage, an equitable sharing of the responsibilities of home and children and of the economic burdens of their support. We believe that proper recognition should be given to the economic and social value of homemaking and child-care. To these ends, we will seek to open a reexamination of laws and mores governing marriage and divorce, for we believe that the current state of "half-equity" between the sexes discriminates against both men and women, and is the cause of much unnecessary hostility between the sexes.

WE BELIEVE that women must now exercise their political rights and responsibilities as American citizens. They must refuse to be segregated on the basis of sex into separate-and-not-equal ladies' auxiliaries in the political parties, and they must demand representation according to their numbers in the regularly constituted party committees—at local, state, and national levels—and in the informal power structure, participating fully in the selection of candidates and political decision-making, and running for office themselves.

IN THE INTERESTS OF THE HUMAN DIGNITY OF WOMEN, we will protest, and endeavor to change, the false image of women now prevalent in the mass media, and in the texts, ceremonies, laws, and practices of our major social institutions. Such images perpetuate contempt for women by society and by women for themselves. We are similarly opposed to all policies and practices—in church, state, college, factory, or office—which, in the guise of protectiveness, not only deny opportunities but also foster in women self-denigration, dependence, and evasion of responsibility, undermine their confidence in their own abilities and foster contempt for women. . . .

> WE BELIEVE THAT women will do most to create a new image of women by acting now, and by speaking out in behalf of their own equality, freedom, and human dignity—not in pleas for special privilege, nor in enmity toward men, who are also victims of the current, half-equality between the sexes—but in an active, self-respecting partnership with men. By so doing, women will develop confidence in their own ability to determine actively, in partnership with men, the conditions of their life, their choices, their future and their society.
>
> _SOURCE:_ "The National Organization for Women's 1966 Statement of Purpose," National Organization for Women, http://www.now.org/history/purpos66.html (accessed August 4, 2007).

considered itself revolutionary, seeking changes that went beyond civil rights and formal equality to cultural transformation.

WOMEN'S LIBERATION AND THE SIXTIES REVOLUTIONS

All of the upheavals collectively known as the "sixties revolutions" played a role in the emergence of women's liberation. The counterculture of youthful radicals who defied conventional norms of sexual behavior and criticized both the nuclear family and the middle-class ethos of success helped to fuel feminist critiques of the subordinate status of women within the family and their call for a feminist sexual revolution. At the same time, the political ferment ignited by Black Power advocates and other groups that promoted nationalist movements in opposition to the white-dominated power structure of American life, offered women's liberationists a model for challenging male power. Finally, the antiwar movement directed against U.S. involvement in Vietnam mobilized tens of thousands of Americans to challenge the federal government and gave impetus to radical feminists' calls for taking on another kind of authority by dismantling patriarchy.

Sexual Revolution and Counterculture

The introduction in 1960 of the birth control pill, along with the confidence that modern medicine could cure any sexually transmitted disease (proved tragically wrong by the AIDS epidemic that began two decades later), forged a conviction that sexual relations no longer had unwanted consequences and could be indulged in casually and freely. The sixties atmosphere of sexual liberation pushed women past the expectations of earlier generations that marriage and motherhood were both their goal and their fate. But the ethic of sexual liberation set different sorts of restraints on women. What sexual liberation meant before women's liberation is captured in images of women in miniskirts and go-go boots, with exaggerated eye makeup and long straight hair, signaling their availability to men. Women were not supposed to be sexual adventurers themselves so much as rewards for the men who crashed through the barricades of respectability.

By the late 1960s, young people had expanded sexual liberation into a broader challenge to the very foundations of their parents' way of life. The "counterculture," as this diffuse phenomenon was known, went beyond the "hippie" lifestyle of sex, drugs, and rock 'n' roll to experiment with new forms of living. Instead of following in the path of the idealized, hard-working, male-headed, nuclear family of the 1950s, the counterculture encouraged the creation of "communes," groups determined to find different forms of intimacy and interdependence. These deliberately created communities (latter-day versions of the utopian communities of the 1830s and 1840s — see pp. 264–66) retained more of the gender divisions of the larger society than they cared to admit. Nonetheless, the countercultural ambition to replace the traditional middle-class family with a radically different alternative set the stage for an explicitly feminist revolt against expected norms of domesticity and motherhood.

Black Power and SNCC

Changes in the civil rights movement also had an impact on the emergence of women's liberation. African Americans, deeply frustrated by the slow federal response to their demands, were further dispirited by a wave of black ghetto riots in the summer of 1965. Then, when Martin Luther King Jr. was assassinated in Memphis, Tennessee, in April 1968, the nonviolent phase of the modern civil rights movement died with him. The assassination in June that year of Robert Kennedy, whose campaign for the Democratic presidential nomination championed African American and Chicano civil rights, also traumatized black leaders, many of whom now turned away from the goal of racial integration and concentrated instead on cultivating black leadership, sensibility, and mass empowerment. Their spirit of militant collective antiracism spread to other communities of color. Young Mexican American civil rights advocates created the era of Chicano nationalism. Mostly urban Native Americans formed the American Indian Movement in 1969, and Asian Americans established a Pan Asian movement. Coming together under the term "third world" — borrowed from the term for developing countries outside the Cold War orbits of the first world (highly developed industrialized Western nations) and the second world (the Soviet Union and other Communist nations) — these radical activists saw themselves as part of a larger uprising against America's traditions of white supremacy.

Of all these forms of militant antiracism, the most influential was black power. In contrast to earlier, southern-based civil rights activism, the black power movement thrived in northern cities. Black power advocates adopted a black nationalist philosophy, which, although it did not call for an independent state, did seek to consolidate a sense of peoplehood among African Americans. A major inspiration for black power was the philosophy of Malcolm X, a renegade leader of the Nation of Islam (whose members were commonly known as Black Muslims) who challenged the goal of integration and the message of black inferiority it subtly conveyed. He was assassinated in 1965. In 1966 the Student Nonviolent Coordinating Committee (SNCC) became a black power organization, voting to expel its white members and embracing the goal of black self-determination. That same year, the Black Panther Party was formed in Oakland, California, and quickly became known for insisting on the right to community self-defense, with weapons if necessary, against police abuse.

The impact of the black power movement on the emergence of women's liberation was complex. Black power had a decidedly masculine caste, in contrast to the earlier phases of civil rights activism, in which African American women had been prominent as local leaders (see pp. 611–15). Black nationalism tended to cast women as mothers of a new peoplehood rather than as political actors themselves. Black men were to lead and defend their people; black women were to give birth to and nurture them. Nonetheless, there were significant female figures in the black power era, notably Angela Davis, a philosophy professor who went underground to escape FBI charges that she had aided a black prisoner revolt in Marin County, California. Yet black power's emphasis on self-determination rather than integration, on the group rather than the individual, provided the model for the emerging women's liberation movement. Black power ideas inspired women's liberation by insisting that true freedom could be won only when the oppressed and the activist were one and the same, when subordinate people sought to liberate themselves rather than look to powerful saviors.

◆ **Angela Davis and Black Power**
The face of Angela Davis, framed by the halo of her natural Afro hairstyle, is one of the signature female images of the era. Sought by the FBI for her alleged role in a 1970 revolt of black militant prisoners in Marin County, California, she gave herself up after a few months in hiding and spent over a year in federal prison. There, using only the resources available, she wrote one of the earliest historical analyses of the position of women within slavery. In 1972 she was acquitted of all charges. ©*Bettmann/CORBIS.*

The War in Vietnam and SDS

Even more than sexual liberation and black power, however, the U.S. war in Vietnam provided the immediate context for the appearance of the women's liberation movement. The presence of U.S. armed forces in Vietnam began to escalate in 1961, as part of President John F. Kennedy's decision to intervene in the civil war there between a Communist government in the north and an anti-Communist regime in the south. In 1965, President Lyndon B. Johnson began sending ever-larger numbers of combat troops and ordered the bombing of Hanoi, the capital of North Vietnam. By the time U.S. forces withdrew in 1973, approximately 2.8 million Americans had served in Vietnam. Of these, an estimated seven thousand were women. Among the approximately sixty thousand Americans who died in Vietnam were eight military nurses and fifty-six women working with organizations ranging from the Red Cross to the CIA.

In general, however, the Vietnam War—fighting in it or fighting against it—was an intensely male experience. By the mid-1960s, the possibility of being called up through the draft hung like a cloud over the lives of nearly all young men in the United States. As opposition against the war grew, men could pursue alternative forms of heroism: by refusing to be drafted, by publicly burning their draft cards, or by leaving the United States. Women who opposed the war were their supporters. "Hell no, we won't go" was the slogan of men in the draft resistance movement. "Girls say yes to guys who say no" was the female equivalent. In the many giant demonstrations against the Vietnam War, women were fully half of the rank and file.

The major organization behind the antiwar protests was Students for a Democratic Society (SDS). Formed in 1962 by forty college students meeting at Port Huron, Michigan, SDS protested against America's hypocritical claim to be the bastion of democracy. Impatient with what they regarded as the outdated, class-based politics of the previous generation of left-wing activists (the "Old Left"), SDS activists declared themselves the "New Left." After white students left SNCC, many joined SDS.

Even more than SNCC, SDS tended strongly to reserve leadership roles for men. By 1967, largely in response to SDS men's hostility to women's issues, SDS women began to meet separately from men, following the model of the black power movement. "Women must not make the same mistake that blacks did at first of allowing others . . . to define our issues, methods and goals," an anonymous group of women SDSers announced. "The time has come for us to take the initiative in organizing ourselves for our own liberation."[4]

By 1969, an estimated 2 million Americans, women and men, had taken to the streets in cities all over the country to protest the war. In the spring of 1970, antiwar demonstrations closed down many college campuses. Tragically, in May 1970 National Guard troops killed four students, two of whom were women, and wounded nine others at Kent State University in Ohio; later that month, two young men at Jackson State University in Mississippi were killed by local police. Rebellion at home combined with mounting American casualties in Vietnam to

◆ **Women against War**

Although the most common images of antiwar protesters in the Vietnam era focus on college students, Americans of all sorts protested the war in Indochina. Among the first were members of Women Strike for Peace (WSP), a group that had taken up the antinuclear cause in the 1950s (see pp. 608–09). This photograph of an April 1972 "die-in" in New York City captures the dramatic techniques prevalent in antiwar demonstrations of the 1960s and 1970s. Here, WSP women are protesting President Nixon's bombing of Cambodia while specifically targeting International Telephone & Telegraph because of its defense contracts with the military. *Swarthmore Peace Collection; photo by Dorothy Marder.*

increase the pressure on President Richard Nixon to find some way out of what now appeared to be an unwinnable war, although the United States would not withdraw from Vietnam until 1973.

Significantly, the first national political event at which the radical women's liberation movement made its appearance was a women's antiwar demonstration, organized in January 1968 by Women Strike for Peace (WSP). Named the "Jeanette Rankin Brigade" in honor of the first woman elected to the U.S. Congress, who had cast her vote against both world wars, the Washington, D.C., demonstration drew five thousand women, including eighty-seven-year-old Rankin. A group of younger women, determined to leave behind older traditions of female activism, organized a protest within the protest. They criticized the WSP for the link between pacifism and motherhood on which it relied. "You have resisted our roles of supportive girlfriends and tearful widows," read the leaflet they distributed. "Now you must resist approaching Congress playing these same roles that are synonymous with powerlessness."[5]

IDEAS AND PRACTICES OF WOMEN'S LIBERATION

Women's liberationists approached the challenge of greater freedom for women in a manner radically different from that which NOW had laid out two years before. Well educated, confident of an affluent future, politically alienated, and disdainful of sexual restraints, many young people in the 1960s had no faith in the older generation's ability to create a better world. "We want something more, much more, than the same gray, meaningless, alienating jobs that men are forced to sacrifice their lives to," wrote Robin Morgan in criticism of NOW's goal of integrating women into the American mainstream.[6] The young women who had come through the movements of the sixties envisioned a different kind of emancipatory politics for their sex and they offered new theories and new approaches to that emancipation. Their goal — and in many ways their achievement — was to revolutionize consciousness and culture, not to reform law and public policy. Determined to bring about a dramatic shift in the fabric of history, they did not form a single overarching organization but rather declared themselves a "movement."

Consciousness-Raising

These new activists wanted to transform consciousness, and they did so even with the term "feminism." Viewing it as too old-fashioned and circumscribed to describe their movement, they adopted a term of their own making: "women's liberation." This term pointed to freedom for women without limits and without pragmatic considerations of what was politically feasible. Small women's liberation groups surfaced in 1968 and 1969 in many places throughout the country. Much has been written about New York City, but early and influential groups emerged as well in smaller (often college) towns such as Chapel Hill, North

Carolina; Iowa City; and Gainesville, Florida. Women's liberation periodicals published in Seattle and Baltimore were read in Los Angeles and Boston. Spontaneity and the lack of centralized direction or national organization were hallmarks of women's liberation.

A key component of women's liberation was a practice called consciousness-raising, which consisted of small groups of women — perhaps a dozen women meeting weekly — sharing personal and private aspects of their lives in order to understand female subordination. Accumulating their personal experiences into collective truths could free women from the belief that their lives were abnormal or that they were to blame personally for their alienation from norms of femininity. Ultimately, consciousness-raising rested on the conviction that "the personal is political," that the massive power inequities from which women suffered could be found in the tiniest details of daily existence. No longer was it trivial that husbands refused to change the baby's diapers, that construction workers harassed women on the streets, or that women felt inhibited from telling their boyfriends what they wanted sexually.

Groups of women's liberationists also worked to raise consciousness among a larger female public through dramatic public actions. They picketed and sat in at magazines from *Playboy* to *Ladies' Home Journal* in protest of their perpetuation of degrading stereotypes of women. The most famous such protest took place in Atlantic City, New Jersey, at the 1968 Miss America pageant, the site of a notorious "bra-burning" episode that has come down through history as a symbol for women's liberation. In reality, no bras were actually burned at the demonstration.

Sexual Politics

Of all the changes in women's lives that came out of these consciousness-raising efforts, perhaps the most pervasive was the revisioning of sexuality from a thoroughly female point of view. No longer were feminist women willing to regard their own sexuality solely in terms of how sexy they appeared to men. Instead they concentrated on exploring their own desires. They suggested that intercourse might not be as good a way for women to experience sexual pleasure as it was for men. Rejecting widespread diagnoses of female frigidity, women's liberation celebrated the possibilities of the clitoris. "What we must do is redefine our sexuality," wrote Anne Koedt in her widely read article "The Myth of the Vaginal Orgasm"[7] (see pp. 723–24). Masturbation, long a favorite topic among young men, now became a subject of experimentation and discussion among women.

The most radical change in sexual thinking and behavior centered around lesbianism. The powerful new assertion of women's sexual desires, coupled with the exploration of the richness of women's relationships, encouraged many women's liberationists to pursue sexual relations with each other. "We were putting our energy into each other and slowly falling in love with each other," explained Marilyn Webb of Washington, D.C.[8] At the 1970 Congress to United Women in New York City, a group of lesbians took over the meeting, proudly declaring themselves the "Lavender Menace" and challenging the women in the audience to acknowledge, accept, and even explore same-sex love. The legitimization of lesbianism within women's liberation was facilitated by the argument that loving women was as much a political identity as a sexual one. "Feminism is the theory, lesbianism is the practice," declared New Yorker Ti-Grace Atkinson.[9]

The lesbian community was transformed not only by the women's liberation movement but also by the gay power movement. The campaign for gay rights had exploded on the scene after a police raid on a New York City working-class gay bar, the Stonewall, on June 27, 1969. Instead of the customary acquiescence, men and a small number of women fought back with beer cans and bottles. During the subsequent two-day riot, the protesters chanted "gay power," a slogan modeled after "black power." The results were electrifying. The gay liberation movement spread quickly throughout the nation's cities; public demonstrations often were held in conjunction with protests against the Vietnam War.

In the early 1970s, many young lesbians worked from within the feminist movement, arguing that the root of discrimination against lesbians could be found in the oppression of women, and that an ideological commitment to women loving women was the only way to quash patriarchal power and achieve female liberation. Novelist Rita Mae Brown expressed this view powerfully: "I became a lesbian because the culture that I live in is violently anti-woman. How could I, a woman, participate in a culture that denies my humanity? . . . To give a man support and love before giving it to a sister is to support that culture, that power system."[10] With their passionate commitment to creating a "lesbian nation," these radicals advocated lesbianism on the basis of political ideology. This ideology, which reflected the growth of a style of politics based on group identity, sometimes led to conflict between gay men and women and also between heterosexual and lesbian feminists, even as it strengthened lesbian communities.

Although the link between women's liberation and lesbianism is strong in popular memory, most women liberationists remained heterosexual. Indeed, women's liberation encouraged utopian ambitions for revolutionizing intimate relations so that men and women could be genuine and full partners. One goal was that women would no longer need to choose between their own needs and ambitions and their love of men. Some marriages were shattered by the rise of women's liberation, but others were initiated or remade on an explicit basis of equality and mutuality. The women's liberation practice of women not taking their husband's names upon marriage began to spread among women in general.

Radical Feminist Theory

As women attempted to put into practice the ideas that emerged from consciousness-raising, feminists devised radical liberation theories. The central project was to understand the structures of universal male dominance. "Our society, like all other historical civilizations, is a patriarchy," declared feminist writer

◆ **Kate Millett of Women's Lib**
Artist Alice Neel was almost seventy
when she painted this portrait of
feminist Kate Millett for *Time* in
1970. The painting, as well as the
feminists' eagerness to promote
women artists, helped to bring the
talented Neel recognition that had
long eluded her. The cover and the
accompanying story on Millett and
her book *Sexual Politics* suggests
how significant the feminist movement had become in popular media
by the beginning of the 1970s. *Time
& Life Pictures/Getty Images.*

Kate Millett in *Sexual Politics* (1970).[11] One of the boldest statements came from
Shulamith Firestone, a twenty-four-year-old whose book *The Dialectic of Sex: The
Case for Feminist Revolution* (1970) became an international best-seller. Like many
radical feminists, Firestone worked from a left-wing framework garnered from
her background as a student radical. Marxist theorists spoke of the dialectic, or
contradiction, of class; Firestone wrote of the "dialectic of sex." The most basic
human conflict was not economic but sexual, she contended, and its roots were
nothing less than the biological distinction between the sexes.

Other theorists took the opposite tack, challenging the idea that differences
between men and women were rooted in nature and thus fundamentally
unchangeable. They documented the different ways that various societies formulated this distinction and how vigorously our own society worked to teach young
children to be appropriately masculine or feminine. Part of the problem, they
observed, lay with the word "sex" itself. Because it referred both to the biological
capacity for human reproduction and the behavioral and psychological differences of men and women, it confused what was anatomical and what was social.
To distinguish the two, women's liberation writers revived the obscure grammatical term "gender" for what anthropologist Gayle Rubin described in 1975 as "a set
of arrangements by which the biological raw material of human sex and procreation is shaped by human, social intervention."[12]

DIVERSITY, RACE, AND FEMINISM

Concerns with racial and ethnic diversity also reflected the influence of the civil rights movement on the first generation of women's liberation activists. Early anthologies such as *Sisterhood Is Powerful* (1970) included selections from African American, Latina/Chicana, and Asian American women to substantiate the claim that sisterhood was all-inclusive. Nonetheless, there was little cross-racial organizing within women's liberation. While white women withdrew from New Left groups to form their own all-female collectives, women of color tended to remain within mixed-sex (but racially separatist) organizations, unwilling to give up personal and political alliances with besieged male allies. As historians have begun to explore the feminism of other women of color more deeply, it is clear that Latinas, Asian American women, and Native American women, as well as black women, challenged sexism within their own organizations and promoted issues of particular concern to women, especially reproductive rights and access to community welfare services. Although many women of color associated with predominantly white organizations, those associated with racial nationalist groups felt ambivalent about allying with mainstream feminist women.

African American Women

For African American women, the concentration on male-female unity was especially strong in response to the 1965 publication of a federal report, "The Negro Family: A Case for National Action," authored by Daniel Patrick Moynihan, then assistant secretary in the U.S. Department of Labor. The Moynihan Report characterized the competence and power of African American women, in their families and in their communities, as "pathological," a holdover from slavery still affecting black Americans. The report was intended to aid in the advancement of African Americans, but written as it was before the emergence of women's liberation, it did so by blaming black women for single-parent households and rising male unemployment. Here was a federally authorized report calling for greater male authority in the black community as a way to bring it into line with the larger society.

But the Moynihan Report alone would not have had such a powerful impact if it had not been for long-standing strains of racial antagonism within the history of American feminism, reaching back through the white-dominated women's movement of the early twentieth century to the Reconstruction era split over black suffrage (see pp. 472–74 and 326–28). Further exacerbating relations with white women was black women's resentment at sexual relations between black men and white women in the civil rights movement. Put simply, many African American women did not trust white advocates of women's liberation to be truly inclusive in their struggle for freedom for women. One of the major challenges confronting the revived feminist movement was to face this history, overcome this distrust, and create a more inclusive, diverse women's freedom movement.

Despite their mistrust of white women's liberationists, women of color shared an interest in many feminist issues. Within the women's caucuses that they formed in their mixed-sex groups, they discussed and wrote about male chauvinism, reproductive freedom, and sexual exploitation. Simmering resentments about the treatment of women within SNCC led to the formation of the Black Women's Liberation Committee in 1968. "We can't talk about freedom and liberation," explained one of the committee's founders, Frances Beal, "and talk about putting women down."[13] The group later expanded to include Puerto Rican and Asian American women and renamed itself the Third World Women's Alliance.

One of African American women's most distinctive contributions to the activism of the period focused on the struggle for welfare rights. State welfare recipients had risen significantly in the postwar era, and most states, fueled by racially charged (and false) stereotypes that most women receiving Aid to Dependent Children (ADC) were black single mothers of illegitimate children, had cut benefits and tried to force women into the labor force (forty-eight percent of ADC recipients in 1961 were African American).[14] In many places local agencies instituted humiliating home visits and "morals" tests. In protest against poverty and the indignities of public assistance, women, the majority of whom were African American, created local welfare rights organizations such as Los Angeles's Aid to Needy Children (ANC), Mothers Anonymous, and Milwaukee's Welfare Rights Organization. In 1966, the same year NOW was founded, these groups staged protests in twenty-five cities (including Chicago, Newark, Los Angeles, Louisville, New York, and Columbus, Ohio), and later that year were brought together as the National Welfare Rights Organization (NWRO), which had both male and female leadership. Eventually women in the NWRO, spurred on by sexism within the organization and a desire to give poor working women more voice, became explicitly more defined as feminist (see box, "Welfare Is a Women's Issue").

Latina Activism

When Chicanas began to explore feminist ideas, they felt unwelcome in white-dominated women's groups but were charged by male comrades with being *vendidas* (traitorous sellouts) for allegedly following Anglo ideas. Chicanas particularly resented the argument that the truly authentic and politically devoted Mexican American woman was one who remained focused on her family. Many criticized what they saw as the Chicano movement's emphasis on *machismo*, arguing that it undermined women's ability to participate in the struggle for racial pride and justice.

To draw attention to women's issues, Anna Nieto-Gomez and other Chicanas at California State University at Long Beach founded the Hijas de Cuauhtémoc (Daughters of Cuauhtémoc, an Aztec emperor) in 1971, named after a 1911 Mexican women's rights group that the Cal State students rediscovered. Later that year the Hijas de Cuauhtémoc and six hundred other Chicanas from all over the country gathered in Houston for the First National Chicana Conference, crowding into workshops with titles such as "Sex and the Chicana" and "Marriage Chicana Style."

Although productive, the conference also highlighted the tensions surrounding Chicana feminism: a significant number of delegates walked out, claiming that the organizers were too closely allied with white feminists. This tension was never really resolved for Chicana activists. Writing in 1973, Nieto-Gomez commented on the intimidation faced by "people who define themselves as Chicana feminists." They were frustrated by the belief that "if you're a Chicana you're on one side, if you're a feminist, you must be on the other side. They say you can't stand on both sides."[15] Not surprisingly, most Chicanas worked from within the larger Chicano movement in organizations such as the paramilitary Brown Berets and the student group Movimiento Estudiantil Chicano de Aztlán (MEChA) on behalf of welfare rights, reproductive freedom, and community control of social services.

Women in the Puerto Rican Young Lords Party had an agenda similar to that of other Latina activists and were unusually successful in pressuring their organization to take their concerns seriously. Anger over sexism in the movement in 1970 prompted them to make the personal political by calling for a "no-sex strike" against male leaders with whom they had personal relations until their demands were met. The result was that the Young Lords' central committee passed a resolution that explicitly endorsed women's rights.[16] In 1971, the following statement appeared in a Young Lords' publication: "Third World women have an integral role to play in the liberation of all oppressed people. In the struggle for national liberation they must press for the equality of women. The woman's struggle is the revolution within the revolution."[17]

Asian American Women

Asian American women's activism was forged in Asian American groups that emerged in the 1960s around the issues of racial pride, identity, and particularly the Vietnam War. Women formed a number of local organizations, especially in Los Angeles and the San Francisco area, but mostly worked from within the broader Asian American movement. They were especially adamant about challenging insidious stereotypes of Asian women. The first issue of *Gidra*, a Los Angeles Asian American movement newspaper, featured an article by Dinora Gil in which she insisted, "It is not enough that we must 'kow tow' to the Yellow male ego, but we must do this by aping the Madison Avenue and Hollywood version of *White* femininity. All the peroxide, foam rubber, and scotch tape will not transform you into what you are not. . . . Whether this is a conditioned desire to be white, or a desperate attempt to attain male approval, it is nothing more than Yellow Prostitution."[18]

Native American Women

Native American women participated extensively in the militant activism of their people in the late 1960s and 1970s. In 1969, a group of Native Americans began a two-year occupation of an abandoned federal penitentiary on Alcatraz Island in San Francisco Bay to protest the policies of the Bureau of Indian Affairs and to

JOHNNIE TILLMON
Welfare Is a Women's Issue

Johnnie Tillmon helped to establish a Los Angeles welfare rights group in 1963 and then in 1972 was one of the founders of the National Welfare Rights Organization and served as its chair beginning in 1972. Her state-ment on welfare as a woman's issue appeared in Ms. *magazine and was widely reproduced in the feminist press. Why does Tillmon consider welfare a woman's issue?*

I'm a woman. I'm a black woman. I'm a poor woman. I'm a fat woman. I'm a middle-aged woman. And I'm on welfare.

In this country, if you're any one of those things — poor, black, fat, female, middle-aged, on welfare — you count as less than as a human being. If you're all those things, you don't count at all except as a statistic.

I am a statistic.

I am 45 years old. I have raised six children.

I grew up in Arkansas, and I worked there for fifteen years in a laun-dry, making about $20 or $30 a week, picking cotton on the side for car-fare. I moved to California in 1959 and worked in a laundry there for nearly four years. In 1963 I got too sick to work anymore. Friends helped me to go on welfare. . . .

There are millions of statistics like me. Some on welfare. Some not. And some, really poor, who don't even know they're entitled to welfare. Not all of them are black. Not at all. In fact, the majority — about two-thirds — of all the poor families in this country are white.

Welfare's like a traffic accident. It can happen to anybody, but espe-cially it happens to women.

And that is why welfare is a women's issue. For a lot of middle-class women in this country, Women's Liberation is a matter of concern. For women on welfare it's a matter of survival.

Forty-four per cent of all poor families are headed by women. That's bad enough. But the *families* on A.F.D.C. aren't really families. Because

draw attention to the historic oppression of Native Americans. One of the main leaders to emerge was LaNada Means, a Shoshone-Bannock, who had also been active in antiwar demonstrations in Berkeley. Wilma Mankiller, who later became the first female principal chief of the Cherokee Nation, initially became involved in the Native American movement during the occupation of the island. Then, in 1973, reservation-based activists at the Pine Ridge Reservation, supported by the urban-based American Indian Movement (AIM), organized against local corrup-tion. Women were particularly prominent. Ellen Moves Camp, a local activist,

99 percent of them are headed by women. That means there is no man around. In half the states there really can't be men around because A.F.D.C. says if there is an "able-bodied" man around, then, you can't be on welfare. If the kids are going to eat, and the man can't get a job, then he's got to go. So his kids can eat.

The truth is that AFDC is like a super-sexist marriage. You trade in *a* man for *the* man. But you can't divorce him if he treats you bad. He can divorce you, of course, cut you off anytime he wants. . . .

The man runs everything. In ordinary marriage sex is supposed to be for your husband. On AFDC you're not supposed to have any sex at all. You give up control of your own body. It's a condition of aid. You may even have to agree to get your tubes tied so you can never have more children just to avoid being cut off welfare.

The man, the welfare system, controls your money. He tells you what to buy, what not to buy, and how much things cost. If things—rent, for instance,—really cost more than he says they do, it's just too bad for you. . . .

If I were president, I would solve this so-called welfare crisis in a minute and go a long way toward liberating every woman. I'd just issue a proclamation that "women's" work is *real* work.

In other words, I'd start paying women a living wage for doing the work we are already doing—child-raising and housekeeping. And the welfare crisis would be over, just like that. Housewives would be getting wages, too—a legally determined percentage of their husband's salary—instead of having to ask for and account for money they've already earned.

For me, Women's Liberation is simple. No woman in this country can feel dignified, no woman can be liberated, until all women get off their knees. That's what N.W.R.O. is all about—women standing together, on their feet.

SOURCE: Johnnie Tillmon, "Welfare Is a Women's Issue," *Liberation News Service* (No. 415), February 26, 1972, reprinted in Rosalyn Baxandall et al., eds., *America's Working Women: A Documentary History, 1600 to the Present* (New York: Vintage, 1976), 355–58.

asked, "Where are our Men? Where are our defenders?"[19] Within days, they had occupied the Wounded Knee Trading Post, at the site of a devastating massacre in 1890, remaining for seventy-one days; however, the activities of women tended to be obscured by high-profile male AIM leaders.

Some women activists did speak out against the sexism they encountered within groups such as AIM, but others emphasized men and women working together within the movement against white oppression. Although most held aloof from the women's movement, in 1977, at the National Women's Conference

◆ **Chicana Activism**

Mexican American women were highly visible in the Chicano/a movement of the 1970s. Here women demonstrate at the state capitol in Sacramento, California, at a 1971 rally that was the culmination of a 600-mile trek that had begun in Calexico, California. Called "La Marcha de la Reconquista," the march sought to call attention to discrimination against Mexican Americans. *Bettmann/CORBIS.*

(see pp. 698–99), a group of Native American women issued a communication that called for federal policies to ensure tribal rights and sovereignty and to improve Native American health and education. They brought an emphasis on spirituality to the feminist movement by invoking the traditional power of "American-Indian and Alaskan Native women," pointing out that they "have a relationship to the Earth Mother and the Great Spirit as well as a heritage based on the sovereignty of Indian peoples."[20]

Women of Color

Walking a careful line between embracing and challenging the premises of women's liberation, between promoting and criticizing their own communities and cultures, women of color raised fundamental issues. They asked in what way white women wanted to be equal, and to whom. The Third World Women's Alliance posed the following question: "Equal to white men in their power and ability to oppress Third World people?"[21] While women's liberation theory emphasized the overwhelming role of patriarchal power in the subordination of women, women of color insisted that the reality of inequality was more complex and that their lives were shaped by the intersections of race, class, and sex.

The feminism of women of color took a major step toward articulating this notion with the publication in 1977 of "A Black Feminist Statement," authored by the Combahee River Collective, a Boston-based group of African Americans, many of them lesbians. They insisted that their "sexual identity combined with their racial identity to make their whole life situation and the focus of their political struggles unique."[22] They named their approach, which focused on their own oppression rather than the suffering of others, "identity politics." Their formulation encouraged a multiplicity of feminist voices, reflecting a diversity of women's experiences, rather than the unitary statement of a single, common "women's oppression" that had characterized the early white-dominated women's liberation years. Over time, these new, diverse approaches to women's lives and demands helped to shift the center of feminist energy and authority away from the white middle-class women with whom it had begun.

THE IMPACT OF FEMINISM

As the ideas and experiences of women of color suggest, there were multiple forms of feminism and tensions among women activists over race, class, sexual orientation, and ideology. None of these tensions were ever completely resolved, but by the early 1970s at least women's liberation and NOW had moved closer to form a common feminist movement, with the former contributing the issues and the militant stance and the latter the organizational structure and focus on institutional and legislative change. By the end of the decade, feminists could point to significant improvements in women's lives, especially in their economic and educational opportunities and their ability to exercise more control over their bodies and reproductivity.

Challenging Discrimination in the Workplace

Feminist lobbying resulted in a raft of important federal actions on women's rights issues in the early 1970s, including legislation clarifying the inclusion of women in earlier civil rights legislation such as the 1963 Equal Pay Act and Title VII of the 1964 Civil Rights Act, which had created the Equal Employment Opportunity Commission (EEOC). An important piece of economic legislation was the 1974 law that "prohibited discrimination on the basis of sex or marital status during credit transactions."[23] And, in 1978 Congress passed the Pregnancy Discrimination Act, which recognized the increased participation of mothers in the workforce and gave pregnant women explicit protection against workplace discrimination under the Civil Rights Act. Another valuable tool in the fight for equality emerged in 1971 when the Republican administration of President Nixon issued guidelines for federally contracted employment that went beyond banning discrimination by race and gender to authorize "affirmative action" in hiring. This process of expanding women's rights received crucial reinforcement when the Supreme Court began to rule that legal discrimination by gender was unconstitutional, including in cases where the law favored women over men. The first of these cases, *Reed v. Reed* (1971), involved an Idaho state law that gave fathers preference over mothers in control over the estate of a deceased child. The court found this discrimination by gender irrelevant to the purposes of the law and ruled it unconstitutional. (See the Appendix, p. A-31.)

With the Civil Rights Act's inclusion of discrimination against women clarified by further legislation, NOW, WEAL, and feminist lawyers both inside and outside of government increased their pressure on the EEOC. NOW's Legal Defense and Education Fund assisted women in bringing lawsuits against their employers. Women were also helped by the Women's Rights Project of the American Civil Liberties Union, cofounded by future Supreme Court Justice Ruth Bader Ginsberg. The most notable successes included challenges to the steel and airline industries, to AT&T, and to Sears, Roebuck and Company where the focus was primarily on overturning patterns of sex-segregated labor that kept women clustered in low-paying jobs. (See Visual Sources: Feminism and the Drive for Equality in the Workplace, pp. 701–10.)

Symbolic of the change in attitude of the EEOC was the appointment in 1977 of Eleanor Holmes Norton to head the commission. Norton, an African American attorney who was a protégée of Pauli Murray (see pp. 625–26) and a seasoned activist in the civil rights and feminist movements, pushed the EEOC to even greater efforts on behalf of minorities and white women. She was responsible for establishing guidelines against sexual harassment in the workplace so that finally in 1985 the Supreme Court agreed that harassment violated women's civil rights. One historian summed up her accomplishments as follows: "By the time Norton left the EEOC, American workplaces looked and felt very different than they had in 1964 when Title VII passed."[24]

As significant as national efforts were, local activists were central to the campaign against discrimination: they organized demonstrations against companies, picketed newspapers that ran sex-segregated help-wanted ads, and staffed telephone hotlines to offer advice about workplace discrimination. Some of these activities were sponsored by women's liberation groups. For example, the Chicago Women's Liberation Union sponsored both the Action Committee for Day Care to promote public support for child care for working women and Women Employed to help clerical workers organize for better pay, wider job opportunities, and general respect as workers.

Activism also emerged in the workplace when women coworkers came together to share grievances. This consciousness-raising led them to demand change, ranging from the right to wear pants to work to an end to what became known as the "glass ceiling" against advancement. As one historian has put it,

◆ **Two Women Activists—Then and Now**

Attorneys Ruth Bader Ginsburg and Eleanor Holmes Norton were two women central to the fight for equal legal rights for women and racial minorities. Ginsburg cofounded the Women's Rights Project of the American Civil Liberties Union in 1972, and Norton, also active in the ACLU, became director of the EEOC in 1977. Thirty years later, the two women have become major figures in American political life. In 1993 Ruth Bader Ginsburg became the second woman to serve on the U.S. Supreme Court, and in 1990 Norton became a representative to the U.S. Congress, a position she still holds. *Sources: Top row: l, Bettmann/CORBIS; r, Reuters/CORBIS. Bottom row: l, Bettmann/CORBIS; r, Congressional Quarterly/Getty Images.*

"Women were organizing in steel plants and auto factories, in banks and large corporations, in federal and university employment, in trade unions and professional associations, and in newspaper offices and television networks."[25] Among the most highly publicized activist groups was the *New York Times* Women's Caucus, started in 1972. Not only did the women employees draw up a list of grievances concerning discrimination in pay, promotion, and opportunities, but they also challenged the sexist language in the newspaper. Eventually the *Times* agreed to establish an affirmative action program and to compensate women workers for past pay inequities. Similar grassroots organizing allowed women to break ground in other white-collar professions, as well as in skilled blue-collar jobs (see Visual Sources: Feminism and the Drive for Equality in the Workplace, pp. 701–12).

Another approach to challenging workplace discrimination sought to address the concerns of poor women that had been raised by the national welfare rights organizations. In cities throughout the United States, women established organizations such as Wider Opportunities for Women (Washington, D.C.) and Advocates for Women (San Francisco) to help poor women break into the male domain of construction work by taking advantage of federal funds for job training programs. Women of color provided leadership as well as the clientele for many of these organizations. In 1979, over ninety of these employment centers came together to create the Women's Force Network, which in turn established the Construction Compliance Task Force.

The gains for working women were nonetheless not as dramatic as the lawsuits, agitation, and organizations fighting against discrimination might suggest. Although sex segregation in the labor force declined and newspapers stopped running ads for sex-segregated jobs, patterns of sex segregation, especially in low-paying service and clerical work, did not disappear and women at the lowest rungs of clerical work saw fewer of the gains. Women made inroads into skilled blue-collar work in the 1970s and even more in the 1980s. Despite some incursions into fields such as mining, firefighting, and construction work, however, many jobs traditionally associated with masculinity nonetheless remained resistant to women's employment (see Documents: Women's Liberation, pp. 713–27). Elite professionals experienced the most improvement in the 1970s: the number of female lawyers more than quadrupled between 1970 and 1980, while the number of physicians and surgeons more than doubled. Women also significantly improved their representation in middle-class professional and managerial positions.

Ironically, as some women achieved success in employment, women as a whole were worse off financially in the 1970s, primarily because of a worsening economic climate. After decades of prosperity and international dominance, the U.S. economy faltered in the 1970s, because of the high cost of the Vietnam War as well as rising competition from Japan and Europe. An energy crisis, prompted by the 1973 Middle East embargo on oil imports to nations that supported Israel, further eroded the economy, bringing in its wake high inflation and repercussions for automakers and related industries. As jobs disappeared, heavy industry regions, especially in the Midwest, began a process that scholars term "deindustrialization." The inflationary crisis, accompanied by increased unemployment (which reached 9 percent in 1975), led to hard times for many American families and was a crucial factor in bringing more working wives and mothers into the workforce (see Appendix, Table 2, on p. A-38).

Another factor that profoundly affected women economically was the rise in the percentage of female-headed households, which was in turn a reflection of higher divorce rates and an increase in the numbers of single mothers. Because of long-standing patterns of workplace discrimination, women heads of households generally had far fewer economic resources and options than men: "In 1976, one out of every three families headed by women was living below the officially defined poverty level, compared with only one of eighteen husband-wife families."[26] The position of African American women who headed households was far worse than white women's. In 1981, 52.9 percent of black women lived in poverty, while 27.4 percent of white women's households did. Dubbed the "feminization of poverty," this reality indicated the difficulties feminists faced in addressing the deep structural and institutional problems that kept women unequal in the economy.[27]

◆ **College Women Athletes Go the Distance**
In this photograph from the 2000 National Collegiate Athletic Association (NCAA) Outdoor Track and Field Championships in Durham, North Carolina, college women athletes are shown running the women's 5,000-meter race. Kara Wheeler (number 515) of the University of Colorado won the event. In the center is Amy Yoder of the University of Arkansas and on the right Marty Hernandez of Brigham Young University. The passage in 1972 of Title IX, which prohibits sex discrimination in federally funded programs, transformed the world of female athletics. Since 1972, women's participation has increased by 400 percent in college sports and by 800 percent in high school sports. Despite these developments, women's programs still lag behind men's: currently male athletic programs at NCAA institutions receive 36 percent more funding than women's.
AP/Photo/Erik Perel.

Equality in Education

One way to promote long-term economic benefits for women was to improve their educational opportunities. In 1972, feminists succeeded in introducing Title IX of the Education Amendments Act, which prohibits sex discrimination in federally funded educational programs. Title IX passed with very little fanfare and took several years to become effective, but eventually led to a revolution in education, especially in high school and college athletics, by requiring that women's sports be funded at equivalent levels to men's sports. Title IX, as well as pressure placed on institutions of higher learning to adopt affirmative action policies, also brought tangible results in graduate programs. Between 1972 and 1980, the proportion of women among students who earned PhDs expanded from 16 to 30 percent, while the percentages of women in medical school and law schools grew, respectively, from 10 to 34 percent and from 11 to 26 percent (see Chart 11.1).[28]

But equally important as challenges to discrimination in the schools, the content of education reflected the impact of the feminism, especially the women's liberation movement. Charging that the standard college curriculum ignored women's presence, women faculty and students laid the basis for a different sort of education. Time-honored generalizations were reexamined for their applicability to women. "Did women have a Renaissance?" asked historian Joan Kelley Gadol. (The answer was no.) Examination of entire disciplines revealed hidden assumptions about the gendered nature of reason and intellectual authority. The natural and physical sciences were found to be particularly unfriendly to women. To challenge the existing canon of appropriate topics for study, in the early 1970s graduate students began writing doctoral dissertations on the history of women, comparative anthropology of sex roles, and forgotten women writers and artists. Simultaneously, Title IX of the federal Education Amendments Act increased pressure on university administrations to hire women to remedy the colossal gender inequity in faculty staffing. Women's studies programs were established, initially

◆ **Chart 11.1 Degrees Granted to Women, 1950–1980**

	Bachelor's Degrees		Doctoral Degrees	
	Number	*% of Total*	*Number*	*% of Total*
1950	103,217	23.9	643	9.7
1960	136,187	35.0	1,028	10.5
1970	343,060	41.5	3,976	13.3
1980	456,000	49.0	10,000	30.3

Prior to World War II, in 1940, women comprised 41.3 percent of college graduates (although only 13 percent of those receiving doctoral degrees). The Servicemen's Readjustment Act of 1944 (popularly known as the GI Bill of Rights) led to a sharp increase in college enrollments but a decrease in the overall percentage of women. This chart dramatically illustrates the shift in women's higher education from 1950 to 1980, in large part because of the efforts of women's rights activists in the 1960s and 1970s. *Sandra Opdycke, The Routledge Historical Atlas of Women in America (New York: Routledge, 2000), 132.*

on the very margins of legitimate academic study. The first such programs were founded in 1969 at Cornell University and San Diego State University. By 1973, there were over eighty programs and one thousand courses around the country.

Women's Autonomy over Their Bodies

The feminist movement also significantly transformed women's ability to exercise control over their own bodies. Determined to implement fundamental changes in gender relations, women's liberation groups sought to address the long-standing but unacknowledged oppression of women in their relationships with men and in the family. They particularly addressed women's health and reproductivity as well as the issues of abuse and violence.

One major concern was to bring rape and other sorts of violence against women dramatically into public light. Before women's liberation, rape victims were often suspected of dressing or behaving in provocative ways, and their testimony was distrusted by police and courts. Husbands were legally sheltered from rape prosecution on the grounds that sexual service was a wife's conjugal obligation. As women broke the silence around rape, it soon became clear how many sexual assaults went unreported. Women's liberationists held "speak-outs," in which they went public with their own experience as rape victims, and established crisis centers to help other women find support. They undertook state-by-state campaigns to make sexual assault within marriage a crime. They established shelters for wives who were battered and exposed the common police practice of keeping the lid on domestic violence.

Another indication of women's determination to uproot patriarchy emerged in their protest against the medical system's treatment of women. The authority of physicians, roughly 90 percent of whom were male, routinely went unchallenged, and women's complaints were often treated as psychological rather than physical. Focusing less on women becoming doctors and more on wresting the control of women's health from the hands of professionals altogether, some women's liberationists learned the skills of midwifery and encouraged women to give birth at home, not in obstetrical wards. Carol Downer of Los Angeles specialized in teaching women how to do safe self-abortions at early stages of pregnancy. The Boston Women's Health Collective, none of whose members were doctors, became expert on the topics of women's bodies and needs and produced a short book, *Women and Their Bodies* (1970), which eventually became the large, multiedition *Our Bodies, Ourselves*. Its approach to women's health proved so empowering that it outgrew the resources of the original collective and was turned over to a commercial publisher for broader distribution.

The campaign to give women more control over their bodies also focused on the newest dimension of feminism, women's quest for sexual self-determination and in particular its relationship to abortion. Since no form of contraception was 100 percent reliable (the birth control pill came close, but the side effects posed significant complications), legal and safe access to abortion was important to heterosexually active women who wanted to have full control over whether, when, and how often they became pregnant. Although many states allowed doctors to perform what were called "therapeutic" abortions, in the postwar years access to these procedures had become increasingly cumbersome and expensive. By 1970, when it was estimated that 1 million American women a year had illegal abortions, an abortion reform movement surfaced that sought to widen the legal loophole that allowed doctors to perform medically necessary abortions.[29] The feminist movement aimed to go further, insisting that abortion was not a matter of medical practice or criminal law but a highly personal decision that belonged only to the woman who was pregnant. The movement to reform abortion laws was thus transformed by the rising tide of feminism into the movement to repeal them.

Starting in 1967 in Colorado, some states began to liberalize their abortion laws, and in 1971, New York State completely decriminalized abortion in the first six months of pregnancy. But as the majority of state legislatures resisted these changes, abortion activists turned to the federal courts to challenge abortion laws. Norma McCorvey, a young, single pregnant mother, was willing to be the plaintiff in such a case, even though it meant she would have to carry her pregnancy to term. She took the pseudonym "Jane Roe" and with her lawyers challenged the highly restrictive abortion laws of Texas. They won at the lower level, but the State of Texas appealed the decision to the U.S. Supreme Court.

On January 22, 1973, the Supreme Court ruled seven to two in favor of Jane Roe (see Appendix, pp. A-31–A-33). *Roe v. Wade* was the most important Supreme Court case concerning women's rights since *Minor v. Happersett*, a century before (see the Appendix, p. A-25). The decision effectively threw out as unconstitutional all state laws making abortion a crime. But the decision was not without its troubling aspects and effectively invited the states to rewrite their laws to restrict abortion more narrowly after the first trimester of pregnancy. With this inviting loophole, the battle for abortion rights began in earnest (see pp. 737–41).

Meanwhile, women of color were beginning to draw attention to another aspect of the problem of reproductive freedom. Throughout the 1960s, many poor women, especially those dependent on government aid, were subject to tremendous pressure from physicians and social workers to allow themselves to be sterilized by tubal ligation, often while lying on the delivery table in the midst of labor. Among women on welfare, on Native American reservations, and in the U.S. colony of Puerto Rico, sterilization statistics reached as high as one-third of women of childbearing age, a figure that activists equated to racial genocide. Pointing out the irony that many states were willing to fund sterilization of poor women but were not willing to provide crucial health care for their families, they linked the issue to their broader demands for community control of social services, including health, welfare, and education.

In response to the groundswell of complaints about coerced sterilization, in 1974 the Department of Health, Education and Welfare issued guidelines requiring a three-day waiting period between granting consent and getting the operation. Even so, a great deal of patient advocacy at the local level was necessary to ensure that women understood the situation and had granted truly informed consent. The fight against sterilization abuse was important in clarifying that women

◆ **Fighting for Reproductive Rights**

By the mid-1970s, feminists' understanding of reproductive rights had moved beyond access to contraception and abortion to encompass the campaign against coercive sterilization, an abuse with its origins in public health officials' desire to control the childbearing of women in the welfare system. As this poster suggests, unwanted sterilization especially affected women of color: Native Americans, blacks, Puerto Ricans, and Chicanas. Because of the efforts of groups like the Committee for Abortion Rights and Against Sterilization, the U.S. Department of Health, Education and Welfare created guidelines that eventually halted these practices.

must be able to make their own choices about their reproductive lives rather than have decisions forced on them by public regulations, institutional policy, or economic exigency. The campaign enlarged the abortion repeal movement into something larger and more basic, a movement for comprehensive reproductive rights for all women. Despite the early successes of this campaign, a drive to reverse the movement toward reproductive freedom began almost immediately and would fuel the rise of conservative politics in the late 1970s and 1980s (see pp. 744–46).

CHANGING PUBLIC POLICY AND PUBLIC CONSCIOUSNESS

Just as feminism helped to improve women's opportunities and secure their rights to reproductive control and self-determination, it also made its mark on American politics and on public consciousness. In their drive to change public policy, feminists engaged as political actors in lobbying, demonstrations, and lawsuits, but they also sought more explicit influence in national party politics and mounted a massive campaign to pass the Equal Rights Amendment. At the same time, both in the patterns of daily life and in the content of popular culture, we can track the ways in which feminism entered into the mainstream of American society in the 1970s.

Women in Party Politics

Women's political activism in the 1970s needs to be understood in the context of tumultuous national politics of the era. Richard Nixon had been elected president in 1968 (and reelected in 1972) by promising to achieve "peace with honor" in Vietnam. Nixon simultaneously negotiated with and bombed the North Vietnamese, but his actions only deepened protests at home. In 1973 the troops began to come home through a negotiated cease-fire with the North Vietnamese. Nixon had also won support by playing upon the resentment that many white middle Americans—a group he called the "silent majority"—harbored toward the disruptions of the 1960s. A potent backlash was forming against youth radicalism, antiwar protest, the counterculture, and racial nationalism. Many voters north and south resented programs like affirmative action and busing to end segregated schooling. Still others balked at the monetary cost of the "Great Society" social welfare programs established by President Johnson. At the same time, Americans were coping with the failure in Vietnam, the energy crisis, and economic decline.

Despite being a candidate who promoted "law and order," Nixon contributed to a sense of disorder by plunging the country into a constitutional crisis. In 1972 Nixon's Committee to Reelect the President (known by the acronym CREEP) arranged for a covert break-in at the Democratic National Committee's headquarters in the Watergate apartment complex in Washington, D.C. The Watergate burglars were arrested, and, when they went on trial, evidence of high-level involvement in the episode, as well as a host of political "dirty tricks," began to accumulate. Despite the administration's cover-up efforts, in the summer of 1974, Congress began to draw up articles of impeachment. To avoid this fate, Richard Nixon resigned, becoming the only American president to do so during his term in office.

The lasting legacies of the Watergate scandal were profound, including both widespread public distrust of government and recognition of the political power wielded by the news media. Thus the women's movement of the 1970s bucked a trend of conservatism and pessimism. It was remarkable for its successes and for its optimism about the possibilities for social change, even as its successes helped fuel backlash politics.

To facilitate women's more equal participation in the political process, in 1971 a diverse group of women, including NOW stalwarts such as Betty Friedan, congressional representatives Bella Abzug and Shirley Chisolm, and civil rights activist Fannie Lou Hamer (see p. 616), came together to create the National Women's Political Caucus. Its purpose was the election of women to political office and the use of political influence to affect public policy. Its ambitious goals were to eliminate "racism, sexism, institutional violence and poverty through the election and appointment of women to public office, party reform, and the support of women's issues and feminist candidates across party lines."[30] The caucus attracted a diverse group of women, including African Americans, Chicanas, Native Americans, and Puerto Ricans, and although they were not always in accord on specific agenda items, the group was responsible for significant gains in women's representation.

Pressured by the NWPC, the 1972 Democratic National Convention had three times as many women delegates as in 1968 and included numerous women's demands in its platforms, including support for the ERA and national funding for child care. Women Republicans to a lesser extent also saw their influence increase within their party. The NWPC chose to support liberal Democrat George McGovern in the hope that his successful candidacy would result in significant gains for women. They also vigorously backed an impressive but unsuccessful effort to give Texan Frances "Sissy" Farenthold the vice presidential nomination. The NWPC, however, lost an opportunity to make a dramatic statement in support of women officeholders when it failed to back New Yorker Shirley Chisholm, who had been elected in 1968 as the first African American woman representative to the U.S. Congress and now mounted a serious campaign for the Democratic nomination for president, the first woman and the first African American to do so. On the national level, the NWPC helped to increase women's influence in both political parties, especially the Democratic National Committee, but met with little immediate success in terms of electing women to public office.

The Reemergence of the ERA

Among the most potent political issues for feminists in the 1970s were the Equal Rights Amendment (ERA) and reproductive rights. The ERA, which sought to amend the Constitution to prohibit the denial of legal equality on the basis of gender discrimination, had first been proposed in 1923 (see pp. 522–26). Organized d long opposed the ERA for endangering protective labor legislation, but ake of the feminist upheaval of the sixties, the composition of the forces against the ERA changed dramatically. In 1973, urged on by female labor ts, the American Federation of Labor–Congress of Industrial Organizations CIO) formally switched its position to support the ERA. In the wake of this ge, working women became a mainstay of the pro-ERA movement.

This switch in labor's attitude toward the ERA flowed directly from profound changes in the place and prospects of women in the labor force. (See Visual Sources: Feminism and the Drive for Equality in the Workplace, pp. 701–12.) Equal access to all occupations and equal pay for equal work were the most widely supported elements of the feminist agenda, and the ERA appeared to be just the tool to ensure economic justice for women. In 1972, the ERA easily passed both houses of Congress, and within a year thirty of the necessary thirty-eight states had ratified the amendment. As victory seemed imminent, few could foresee the long and protracted battle over the ERA and how it would lead to the emergence of an antifeminist movement (see pp. 735–41).

Feminism Enters the Mainstream

Although we may chart concrete developments spurred on by the feminist movement—especially those related to public policy—evaluating changes in women's consciousness, women's private lives, and public opinion is far more difficult. Nonetheless, demographic changes for the 1970s are striking. In contrast to the trend of the 1950s, women in the 1970s married later and had children later. Divorce rates rose dramatically in this era (from 2.2 per thousand marriages in 1960 to 4.8 per thousand in 1975).[31] The number of children born to single women increased significantly (for the period 1960–1964 premarital first-child births constituted 10.3 percent of all first births, while for the period 1975–1979 the figure was more than double, at 25.7 percent), and the number of couples cohabitating outside of marriage more than quadruped between 1970 and 1984.[32] Survey data also suggest a rise in premarital sex, as well as an expanded repertoire of sexual behavior. At the same time as these changes in family structure emerged, women's participation in the workforce continued its twentieth-century upward trajectory, growing in the decade of the 1970s from 43.5 to 51.1 percent. Even more striking was the increase in the percentage of mothers in the workforce (40.8 to 50.1 percent).[33]

But to what extent may these changes be credited to feminism? Most scholars argue that the rise in women's participation in the workforce was prompted in part by the nation's economic decline of the era. Divorce increases may have been promoted by the feminist ideological critique of the family but were also influenced by many women's increased wage-earning capacity and to liberalization in state divorce laws. Similarly, changes in sexuality must be understood in part as a result of the technology of the birth control pill as well as the related sexual revolution.

Nonetheless, feminism undoubtedly sparked many changes in personal life. In 1972 *Life* magazine featured a cover story on feminist Alix Kate Shulman's marriage contract, in which she and her husband agreed, among other things, that both "had an equal right to his/her own time, work, values, and choices." The article was later reprinted in *Redbook*, and by 1978, according to one historian, "even *Glamour* magazine was explaining how to write your own marriage contract."[34] Opinion polls conducted during the 1970s and early 1980s also suggested that many Americans had changed their views on working mothers and embraced more egalitarian notions of household responsibilities. Moreover, by 1970, 40 percent of American women were willing to say to pollsters that they favored "efforts to change and strengthen women's status in society."[35] Working women particularly favored changes, and African American women were twice as likely as white women to be supportive.

What two scholars have termed the epoch's "cultural validation of erotic pleasure"[36] may well have spread to women in general through feminist arguments about sexual double standards and women's sexual empowerment. As one young woman said, "I may have had an unusual upbringing, but . . . I have the same needs and moods as a man, and I am not going to let some chauvinist pig stifle them."[37] One measure of this legitimation of women's sexuality was the popularity of fiction that presented women's erotic lives in explicit language from a decidedly feminist point of view. Erica Jong's novel *Fear of Flying* (1973) featured a woman's "uninhibited odyssey," which one critic characterized as a "decidedly new way of thinking about women."[38] Feminist and gay power movements also were instrumental in the decisions of homosexual couples to live openly together and to begin the campaign for legal access to civil union and gay marriage.

Another way of gauging feminism's impact is to examine its permeation of mainstream popular culture. One major breakthrough was the emergence of *Ms.*, a glossy, mainstream national feminist magazine that began publication in 1972. The term "Ms." was revived by feminists in the 1970s so that women would no longer need to advertise their marital status by having to choose between the appellations "Miss" and "Mrs.," and was itself a reflection of the way in which feminism would help to challenge unnecessarily gendered language. Under the editorship of journalist Gloria Steinem, *Ms.* magazine matured to feature high production values and commercial advertisements carefully chosen for their non-exploitive portrayal of women.

Elsewhere in the media, early feminist agitation often met with condescending coverage with women's liberation activists' more radical critiques of patriarchy sensationalized or trivialized. Yet there were sympathetic treatments of the movement, especially concerning liberal feminists' attention to economic discrimination. In 1970, an eleven-hour sit-in of the offices of the *Ladies' Home Journal* forced that magazine to run an eight-page spread on the movement, with articles written by feminists themselves. Later in the 1970s, *McCall's* featured a column titled "Betty Friedan's Notebook" as well a regular series titled "The Working Woman." However, critics have noted that even sympathetic treatments of feminist issues in the mainstream magazines tended to dilute the feminist message by stressing women's need to change from within rather than to focus on challenging patriarchy or changing society.

A similar process may be seen in television. Sitcoms of the 1950s primarily featured white middle-class families and the happy (usually) homemaker. In the 1970s, those shows' characters were still largely white and middle class but offered broader possibilities in their representations of women that reflected the influence of contemporary feminist issues. In *Maude* (1972–1978), Bea Arthur played a middle-aged feminist who in many ways was a caricature that antifeminists loved to hate: loud, domineering, and opinionated. However, the most controversial episode, aired in the 1972–73 season, featured a sympathetic portrayal of Maude's decision to get an abortion. By far the most popular "new woman" on television in the 1970s was Mary Richards of the *Mary Tyler Moore Show* (1970–1977). Richards was a single thirty-ish career woman who settled in Minneapolis, determined, as the show's theme song put it, to "make it on her own." One of the series' writers described the writers' assumption that Mary "represented a new attitude, that you could be single and still be a whole person, that you didn't need to be married to have a complete life."[39] The show explicitly touched on feminist themes, including the centrality of Mary's friendship with her neighbor, Rhoda, and Mary's chagrin that, although she got the job as associate producer of a TV news program, her pay was less than the man who preceded her. Despite this sympathetic treatment, it is easy to overstate the feminist sensibilities of the *Mary Tyler Moore Show*. Although Mary didn't have a husband or children, she was consistently nurturing and other-directed in her relationships with her coworkers. The show's modern approach to the single career woman allowed the producers (and advertisers) to tap into a young, sophisticated viewing audience without seriously challenging traditional notions of womanly virtues. Shows like *Mary Tyler Moore* thus reflected aspects of feminism but also co-opted its more radical potential. Despite these limits, the media reflects the way in which modern feminism became increasingly mainstream in the 1970s.

The growing influence of feminism in the mainstream was also evident in the National Women's Conference held in Houston in 1977. The meeting, a follow-up to the first International Year of Women held in 1975 (see Documents: Women's Liberation, pp. 713–27), received funding from the federal government, and two former First Ladies, Lady Bird Johnson and Betty Ford, as well as then–First Lady Rosalynn Carter, presided over the opening services. Gloria Scott, national president of the Girl Scouts of America, also made opening remarks. African American congressional representative Barbara Jordan's keynote address similarly reflected feminism's incorporation into the mainstream. Jordan noted, "None of the goals stated in this conference are incompatible with the goals of America. The goals of this conference, as a matter of fact, sound like stanzas to 'America the Beautiful.'"[40]

Jordan overstated the case. Many of the ideas presented at the conference were still radical to many, if not most, Americans. An important event in the development of American feminism, the conference brought together a diverse range of attendees: one-third were women of color. The high point of the meeting was the approval of the comprehensive National Women's Agenda, which called for action against domestic violence and rape, ratification of the ERA, reproductive freedom

◆ **National Women's Conference in Houston (1977)**
In 1977, the U.S. government authorized funds for a National Women's Conference, held in Houston that same year. The conference brought together a diverse range of participants: one-third were women of color, and one-fifth were conservative women. The conference passed the comprehensive National Women's Agenda calling for ratification of the ERA, reproductive freedom, lesbian rights, support for the rights of women of color, and action against domestic violence and rape. Second from left is tennis champion Billie Jean King; in the center is then–New York Congresswoman Bella Abzug; next to her are three young Houston-area athletes; at the far right is Betty Friedan. *Copyright © 1978 Diana Mara Henry: dianamarahenry.com.*

and lesbian rights, and a unified statement of the importance of rights for women of color. Coretta Scott King offered a hopeful vision of the future, declaring, "Let the message go forth from Houston . . . and spread all over this land. There is a new force, a new understanding, a new sisterhood against all injustice that has been born here. We will not be divided and defeated again."[41]

But even as feminists celebrated, they recognized that the Houston meeting also exposed a growing threat to feminist goals. As the various states elected representatives to the conference, conservative forces, including anti-abortion and anti-ERA activists, had mobilized and managed to secure about 20 percent of the delegates.

At the same time right-wing activist Phyllis Schlafly organized a counterconvention in Houston and founded a new conservative coalition she dubbed the "Pro-Family movement." The counterconvention at Houston did not disrupt the National Women's Conference, but its attendees' activities were a harbinger of a resurgent conservatism that would transform the American political climate in the next two decades.

CONCLUSION: Feminism's Legacy

The 1960s and 1970s proved an era of extraordinary ferment for women. Politically and culturally, the radical movements of the sixties and early seventies — from black power, the counterculture, and the antiwar movement to Chicano, Native American, and Asian American nationalism — were fundamental to women's history, reigniting a long-dormant feminist tradition and encouraging a new generation to rethink the meaning of freedom for women. Despite divisions and disappointments, the various strands of feminist activism led to improvements in many women's economic and political equality and changed the consciousness of millions who in turn challenged conventional notions about women's role in the home, family, and workplace. It might seem that feminism caused the deep economic and social changes in American women's lives, but it is more accurate to say that it resulted from them. Feminism gave millions of women a framework for interpreting their lives and served as a catalyst for mobilizing women for social and political change. Above all, from the special perspective of this book — revisioning American history through women's eyes — the modern feminist revival marked a tremendous increase in women's determination to take an active, conscious role in the shaping of American society.

VISUAL SOURCES

Feminism and the Drive for Equality in the Workplace

Dᴜʀɪɴɢ Wᴏʀʟᴅ Wᴀʀ ɪɪ, ᴀʟᴛʜᴏᴜɢʜ ᴡᴏᴍᴇɴ entered the workforce in large numbers and took on high-skilled blue-collar jobs that had formerly been closed to them, no feminist movement existed to rally women in sustaining their gains or in defense of their economic rights. When increasing numbers of women, including mothers of young children, continued their march into the workforce in the postwar years, sex-segregated labor patterns returned and women's work continued to be devalued. In the 1960s, however, the liberal women's movement associated with NOW and WEAL became a crucial engine for challenging deeply rooted discriminatory patterns, especially sex segregation, in the workplace. Women did not benefit equally or at the same rate of change, but legal challenges as well as consciousness-raising about women's rights and capabilities produced a dramatic expansion of their employment opportunities. As witness to these changes, photographs abounded in the 1970s that graphically documented the transformation in women's work. This essay explores a selection of these images. They record areas in which women achieved significant success as well as those in which change came far more slowly.

Photos by Lester Sloan—Newsweek

Stews on the job and on the march

◆ **Figure 11.1 Flight Attendants Protest Discriminatory Practices (1974)**
Lester Sloan.

◆ **Figure 11.2 AT&T Advertises for Telephone Operators**
Courtesy of AT&T Archive and History Center.

One of the most powerful tools for women seeking equal rights as paid labor-ers was Title VII of the 1964 Civil Rights Act (see pp. 685–86), but it was of little use until feminists put pressure on the Equal Employment Opportunity Commis-sion (EEOC) to take seriously the constant stream of complaints women began filing as soon as the commission was established. Among the early challengers were flight attendants who faced demeaning circumstances in which they were treated as servants. But bread-and-butter issues tied to sex segregation in what one critic called a "pink-collar ghetto" were the most potent concerns. Airlines hired women exclusively and placed strict limits on weight, appearance, and age. They also refused to hire women of color and married women. Discontented flight

◆ **Figure 11.3 AT&T Promotes Women Installers**
Courtesy of AT&T Archive and History Center.

attendants recognized that employment practices that defined a job as appropriate only to young, unmarried women devalued their work and provided justification for poor wages and disrespectful treatment. In 1968 the EEOC finally ruled in favor of an attendant who had filed suit against American Airlines for mandatory retirement. Other discriminatory practices were also disallowed over a period of years and finally, in 1971, the U.S. Court of Appeals ruled that "female-only" hiring practices of the airlines were discriminatory.

Although these legal successes changed the face of the flight attendant workforce dramatically in the 1970s, opening up the career to women of color and to men, the profession still suffered from low wages, long hours, and recalcitrant airlines, problems that increased flight attendants' union activism and helped spur the growth of pink-collar unions in this era. Flight attendants also continued their complaints about airlines' advertising campaigns that sexualized them. A National Airlines series enticed passengers with the slogan "I'm Debbie [or Susan or Betty], Fly Me." (National also required attendants to wear buttons that said "Fly Me.") Even worse, Continental Airlines ads featured stewardesses who promised that "we really move our tail for you."[42] Frustration with this sexual objectification led to the creation of Stewardesses for Women's Rights (SFWR) in 1972. Reflecting the influence of women's liberation, the group announced that it hoped to "raise the consciousness of stewardesses" to their "'slut-in-service-to-America' status." They vowed "to fight the demeaning treatment to which 35,000 stewardesses are subjected by airlines, crews, and male passengers[;] . . . to enforce airline compliance with Federal affirmative action guidelines[;] . . . to improve the economic status of stewardesses[;] . . . [and] to increase the promotional opportunities for stewardesses."[43]

The two images in Figure 11.1 are from *Newsweek*'s 1974 article on SFWR as the organization sought to draw attention to health problems faced by flight attendants, including excessive fatigue and exposure to hazardous cargo. The image on the left shows members of SFWR, and the one on the right shows "Stews on the Job." What might have been *Newsweek*'s goal in juxtaposing these images? What does the photograph on the left suggest about the breadth of the influence of feminism in the early 1970s?

Other major targets of discrimination suits were the nation's phone companies. The major focus of complaint was sex-segregated labor policies that excluded women from highly skilled and better-paid jobs and funneled them into poorly rewarded positions, such as operators and clerks. Lorena Weeks, a working mother and a nineteen-year veteran telephone operator employed at Southern Bell in Georgia, was refused her 1966 request to be transferred to a better job as a "switchman": she filed a complaint with the EEOC. In court, when the company claimed that state law barred women and minors from lifting more than thirty pounds, "Weeks pointed out that her typewriter, which supervisors made her move, weighed more than that."[44] She won the case in 1971, when the U.S. Court of Appeals observed that Title VII of the Civil Rights Act prohibits such "stereotyped characterization" and "rejects just this type of romantic paternalism as unduly Victorian and instead vests individual women with the power to decide whether or not to take on unromantic tasks."[45]

Especially far-reaching was the success of women who challenged the behemoth AT&T, which employed more women than any other company in the country. A twenty-five-thousand-page government study concluded that the Bell system was "without a doubt, the largest oppressor of women workers in the United States."[46] By 1973, the company had agreed to significant restitution ($38 million to thirteen thousand women of all races and to two thousand minority men) and had transformed its hiring policies. Even before the settlement was finalized, AT&T embarked on an advertising campaign that emphasized affirmative action. Consider the 1972 advertisements in Figures 11.2 and 11.3. The first one explains that AT&T wants to hire male operators and the second shows a woman in a job formerly reserved for men. What clues do the images provide to indicate the kind of employment climate the company wishes to project? At the time, both of these ads would have been startling to many viewers. Do they have any shock value today? Does one seem more jarring than the other? If so, why do you think that is?

Other women challenged the sex segregation of one of the most dangerous fields of employment—mining. In the seventeenth century, Virginia slave women apparently engaged in some mine work, and labor shortages during the Great Depression and World War II gave some women opportunities in Appalachian coalfields. But in general, mining was historically one of the most jealously protected male occupations. Many states had laws prohibiting women's work as miners, and unions, employers, and male miners all resisted women's entrance into this male-dominated job category. In addition, notions of women's proper place in the home were particularly rigid in Appalachian community culture, where mining was a significant part of the economy. Beginning in the early 1970s, some individual women successfully challenged companies that refused to hire them. Then, in 1978, a group of Tennessee women created the Coal Employment Project and, working with NOW, won a massive class action suit against the coal operators for sex discrimination. As a result, individual women received financial compensation and over 830 women were hired in the mines. By 1980 there were 3,871 women miners, but this number represented only 3 percent of the total miners in the nation.

Although the numbers were small, these women provide insights into the experiences of women who sought to break down employment barriers in this era. Because working-class women were excluded from the only significant skilled-labor job in the Appalachian coal-mining areas, they had few job options beyond domestic work or low-paid service employment. Many poor women were on welfare. Most of the women who bucked community disapproval to become miners did so because the job paid the best wages available in their region, and they recognized that the sex-segregation patterns of the mining industry limited their ability to earn a living wage. Even though mining jobs brought in more income, women who did become employed in the mines faced hostility and sexual harassment underground. They also found themselves relegated to low-level work that offered few options for advancement. Although many women worked well together and created bonds of friendship, sometimes across racial lines, their limited numbers and the nature of their jobs made it difficult to create women's work communities that could mitigate some of the hardships of their labor.

The photograph in Figure 11.4 was taken by labor photographer Earl Dotter in 1976 in Vansant,

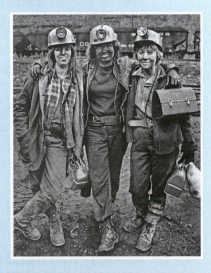

◆ **Figure 11.4 Women in the Coal Mines**
Earl Dotter Photojournalist.

Virginia. Many of Dotter's images emphasize the hardship and danger of coal work, but this one strikes a different tone. What do the women's expressions and bearing suggest concerning their feelings about their work? Does the photograph give any clues as to why it was so difficult for women to challenge the sex segregation of coal mining? How might their reactions have been different if there had only been one of them?

Firefighting, a job as arduous and dangerous as mining, also saw small but symbolically significant challenges to male monopoly in the 1970s. Some women served as firefighters in the face of severe labor shortages during World War II, but for several decades after the war fire departments did not employ women as career personnel. According to one account, Arlington County Virginia hired the first woman career firefighter, Judith Livers, in 1974. The following year, a handful of cities followed suit and small numbers of women found jobs as firefighters throughout the country. The barriers, however, remain high to this day, and women still constitute a tiny percentage of professional firefighters (3.3 percent in 2005).

Figure 11.5 is a photograph of the Kansas City, Missouri, Fire Department's first three women firefighters, Carolyn Y. Mitchell, Anne K. Wedow, and Kathleen Kline, who were hired in 1977. Efforts to desegregate firefighting were occurring at the same time, and Mitchell was one of the very few African American women firefighters in the nation. In 1988 she told an *Ebony* reporter, "They tried to make it as

◆ **Figure 11.5 Kansas City Firefighters**
The Kansas City Star.

hard as possible. . . . They'd isolate you, wouldn't talk to you. They even make up special rule for me, like 'you can't watch television or read the newspaper' while on duty."[47] Mitchell's experiences in fighting multiple levels of discrimination were apparently shared by other African American firefighters.[48] Mitchell persisted, however; she was a leader in her union and served in the fire department until her retirement in 2003. Kline and Wedow eventually became battalion chiefs who actively fought gender discrimination in the fire department. In a 1988 lawsuit against the city for sex discrimination, they complained "about strippers performing at fire stations, female employees being fondled, and male firefighters watching X-rated videos while on duty."[49] That case led to the implementation of sensitivity training in the department. Then, in 2002, they filed another lawsuit claiming discrimination over inadequate fire gear for women and other issues. Not only did they win the original case, but—aided by Legal Momentum, the successor to NOW's Legal Defense and Education Fund—they won again when the city appealed.

Before joining the fire department, Mitchell was a seasonal clerk for the city, while Wedow had worked as a city parking attendant for three years. Kline's earlier employment is not known. Does their previous work history give you any evidence as to why Mitchell and Wedow might have sought out firefighting as a career? Does the photograph offer any indication of how the three women felt about becoming firefighters?

For many women in white-collar work, the struggle to break down sex-segregated labor patterns was just as difficult as that undertaken by blue-collar workers. Women were traditionally shunted into low-level office work, while men monopolized management positions. In many instances in the 1970s, office workers met with significant success in unionizing to gain some power in negotiations with employers and in their struggle to open up managerial positions to women. One of the most intransigent sectors, however, proved to be the banking industry, which became the site of one of most publicized strikes mounted by women during the 1970s.

Like other banks throughout the nation, Citizens National Bank of Willmar, Minnesota, routinely kept women out of high-status and well-paid work in the bank: only one woman was a bank officer (and she made $4,000 less annually than the men she supervised), while no men were tellers or clerks. In 1977, when the bank passed over its experienced women workers to hire a man with no training at a salary higher than all but one of the women employees, the women protested to their employers, to no avail. Like countless other women workers, they filed a complaint with the EEOC and sought the assistance of the local NOW chapter. At the same time, they created their own union, the first bank employees' union in the state. The bank, however, was adamant in its refusal to engage in collective bargaining or address the women's concerns. In response, eight women employees went out on strike and organized a picket line in the freezing Minnesota winter (see Figure 11.6). Their strike garnered publicity from all over the world, and they received letters from other women who pleaded, "You can't stop, you can't stop. Please understand you're doing this for all of us." As one striker, Ter Wisscha, proudly recalled, "It wasn't very long before it wasn't our strike anymore."[50]

◆ **Figure 11.6 The Willmar Eight**
Minnesota Historical Society.

In the end, after two long years, the strike failed. As a result of the EEOC's recommendation, the women received a small economic settlement in return for an agreement not to sue, but the National Labor Relations Board did not endorse the strikers' demand for reinstatement of their jobs. The bank rehired only one of the strikers at a job that paid less than the one she had left. Nor did the strike or subsequent unionizing efforts elsewhere make significant progress for women in banking or undercut the industry's sex-segregation patterns. Today, women represent 75 percent of the banking industry, but only 10 percent of all banking officers. Yet the strike, which became the subject of a moving documentary, *The Willmar Eight*, is viewed as important in part for its demonstration of the broad impact of feminism in the 1970s, even among women who did not call themselves feminists. Does Figure 11.6 offer any clues as to why the strike became so well-known? How does this picket line of white-collar workers compare to the striking textile workers depicted on pages 491 and 580? Do their picket signs offer us any sense of how they view themselves as workers?

During the first decade of the feminist movement, women workers made perhaps the most significant gains when they broke down barriers that had largely excluded them from professional occupations such as law and medicine (see p. 686). Less numerous but nonetheless noteworthy pioneer professionals were women who became ordained as rabbis or ministers in this era. As the seventeenth-century story of Anne Hutchinson indicates (see pp. 74–76), women have been spiritual leaders throughout American history, but rarely have they become leaders in organized religion. During the 1970s feminist theologian Mary Daly urged women to leave their patriarchal churches and create new communities of religious women. But most women sought change from within. Black and white women were active within the National Council of Churches of Christ and its allied group Church Women United, which agitated for more women leaders and attention to women's issues within the churches. The struggle to gain acceptance for female clerics met with mixed success. Catholic women failed in their 1975 (and subsequent) call for women's acceptance into the priesthood. However, as early as 1970, some Lutheran denominations ordained women, and in 1976 the Episcopalian church bowed to pressure and agreed to women's ordination.

Jewish women as a group were highly attracted to the feminist movement, and it is not surprising that they would exert pressure for change within Judaism. Especially among reform and conservative congregations, the two largest wings of American Judaism, and in the smaller group of Reconstructionists, feminists succeeded in bringing women's issues into their congregations and religious practices. Conservative women established Ezrat Nashim in 1972 to press for equality in Jewish religious observance, but it was not until 1985 that Conservatives began to ordain women. The movement for female ordination had to counter a three-thousand-year-old tradition of male leadership in which the rabbi was revered above all for his great learning. In 1972, Sally Preisand, a Reform Jew who studied at Hebrew Union College in Ohio, became the first American woman to be ordained as a rabbi. Preisand did not start her quest for ordination from an explicitly feminist perspective, but she became a central figure among Jewish feminists who sought equality within the Jewish faith.

◆ **Figure 11.7 Rabbi Sally Preisand**
The Jacob Rader Marcus Center of the American Jewish Archive.

Figure 11.7 is a photograph of Preisand in 1972. The power of this photograph might not be immediately evident to anyone not familiar with Judaism. It shows Preisand with the central ritual object of Jewish practice, the first five books of the Old Testament, handwritten on a parchment scroll. The rabbi's job is to teach the contents of the Torah and the long interpretive tradition that accompanies it. Why might some religions have been easier to integrate at the clerical level than

◆ **Figure 11.8** "Hire him. He's got great legs."
Legal Momentum, formerly known as NOW LDEF.

others? Is the image of a woman presiding over public religious practice still somewhat shocking?

Everywhere Americans turned in the 1970s, they saw images that challenged conventional notions of women's proper place, especially women's proper place in the workforce. A final example of this challenge comes from NOW's Legal Defense and Education Fund (LDEF), which in the early 1970s mounted an advertising campaign to raise public consciousness about the employment discrimination women faced. With the help of free creative services from J. Walter Thompson and other advertising agencies, in 1973 the LDEF ran a series of print ads that appeared in mainstream magazines such as *Time, Saturday Review,* and *Business Week,* as well as thirty-second television commercials. In both cases the advertisements appeared as free-of-charge public service ads. Midge Kovacs, head of the Image Committee of NOW, was responsible for the campaign; she commented, "We hope it will make all Americans aware of the limited aspirations of girls and the limited opportunities for women, and that they will act to do something about both."[51]

◆ **Figure 11.9** "This healthy, normal baby has a handicap. She was born female."
Legal Momentum, formerly known as NOW LDEF.

The two print ads reproduced in Figures 11. 8 and 11.9 take two different approaches. What point is being stressed in "Hire him. He's got great legs"? How is that point different from the one stressed in the ad featuring the baby? In what ways and for whom would the two ads have been effective? Kovacs later commented that she regretted that the initial ad series contained no images of women of color. Several years later, the LDEF ran the advertisement in Figure 11.10. Besides the race of the two children, what are the differences in the ways in which Figures 11.9 and 11.10 attempt to convey their messages? One of the rationales behind the LDEF campaign was to counter the pervasive sexism in advertising, including those that devalued women's work. How successful do you think these advertisements were in meeting this challenge?

◆ **Figure 11.10** "When I grow up, I'm going to be a judge, or a senator or maybe president."
Legal Momentum, formerly known as NOW LDEF.

QUESTIONS FOR ANALYSIS

1. How do these images convey the changing nature of women's work in the 1970s?

2. To what extent do they reflect the impact of feminism?

3. How do the images presented here compare with those in Visual Sources: Women at Work (pp. 570–83)?

4. This essay has emphasized change. Taking into account the chapter's analysis of the women's work in this period, what other sorts of images would be necessary to convey the broad contours of women's paid labor, especially in those areas where change was less dramatic?

DOCUMENTS

Women's Liberation

Women's liberation activism produced an immense amount of feminist literature, most of which was published in organizational journals and newsletters. The late 1960s and 1970s saw an explosion of these periodicals, with eighty-five debuting in 1970 alone. Many of these were modeled after the underground newspapers that had been the staple of the New Left, and were the result of New Left women's frustration over the control and content of these newspapers. One of the most famous of the early feminist salvos, Robin Morgan's "Goodbye to All That," grew out of this anger. Morgan detailed how women engineered the takeover of the New York newspaper *Rat*, whose sometimes pornographic articles, graphics, and advertising were demeaning to women. She explained, "No more, brothers. No more well-meaning ignorance, no more co-optation, no more assuming that this thing we're all fighting for is the same: one revolution under man, with liberty and justice for all."[52]

These alternative periodicals spread feminist ideology, with its commitment to collective rather than individual identity and to the elimination of hierarchical structures. As one scholar has noted, the writers "were not communicating about something outside themselves, as mass media journalists might. They were communicating about their own ideas, activities, and the growing movement among women."[53] Fortunately, much of the early, ephemeral women's liberation literature survives in major archives with online access. These archives include Duke University's Documents from the Women's Liberation Movement and the Chicago Women's Liberation Herstory Project. Their survival is in part a result of feminists' recognition that they were making history, a point evident in the comments of the editors of *Notes from the First Year*, a publication of New York Radical Women: "We needed a movement periodical which would expand with the movement," and "reflect its growth accurately, and in time become a historical record, functioning politically as much as did Stanton's and Anthony's Revolution exactly a century ago."[54]

The documents excerpted here demonstrate some key themes of the early women's liberation movement: its roots in New Left politics and racial and ethnic nationalist movements, the critique of patriarchy, the ambivalence of women of color toward white feminists, the ideology of political lesbianism, the call for women to exert control over their sexuality, the technique of consciousness-raising, and the recognition that the "personal is political." Women's liberationists are often termed "radical feminists," in part to distinguish them from the liberals associated with NOW. As you read these documents, all written between 1969 and 1971, consider why they might have been considered radical when they were published. Do they still seem radical today? Why or why not?

WOMEN BEGAN TO ABANDON the New Left in early 1969, frustrated with male leaders' unwillingness to take gender issues and sexism seriously. Scores of organizations sprang up, from the Redstockings in New York City to the Chicago's Women's Liberation Union to Gainesville Women's Liberation in Gainesville, Florida. In theorizing about feminism, women liberationists articulated a feminist ideology that reflected both their socialist roots and their innovative critique of patriarchy. In 1969 Ellen Willis, cofounder with Shulamith Firestone of the Redstockings, wrote "Letter to the Left" for the left-wing journal *The Guardian*, which refused to publish it. What are her criticisms of the male leaders of the left? What is the importance of her analogy to the black power movement?

ELLEN WILLIS
Letter to the Left (1969)

You say, "the basic misperception is that our enemy is man, not capitalism." I say, the basic misperception is the facile identification of "the system" with "capitalism." In reality, the American system consists of two interdependent but distinct parts—the capitalist state and the patriarchal family.

The social organization for the production of commodities is the property system, in this case the capitalist state. The social organization for the production of new human beings is the family system. And within the family system, men function as a ruling class, women as an exploited class. Historically, women and their children have been the property of men (until recently, quite literally, even in "advanced" countries). The mistake many radicals make is to assume that the family is simply part of the cultural superstructure of capitalism, while both capitalism and the family system make up the material substructure of society. It is difficult to see this because capitalism is so pervasive and powerful compared to the family, which is small, weak, and has far less influence on the larger economic system than vice versa. But it is important for women to recognize and deal with the exploited position in the family system for it is primarily in terms of the family system that we are oppressed *as women*. If you really *think* about our exploitation under capitalism—as cheap labor and as consumers—you will see that our position in the family system is at the root.

Our position here is exactly analogous to the black power position, with male radicals playing the part of white liberals. Blacks answered "We can't work together because you don't understand what it is to be black; because you've grown up in a racist society, your behavior toward us is bound to be racist whether you know it or not and whether you mean it or not. . . . If you as whites want to work on eliminating your own racism, if you want to support our battle for liberation, fine. If we decide that we have certain common interests with white activists and can form alliances with white organizations, fine. But we want to make the decisions in our own movement." Substitute man-woman for black-white and that's where I stand. With one important exception: while white liberals and radicals always understood the importance of the black liberation struggle, even if their efforts in the blacks' behalf

SOURCE: Ellen Willis, "Letter to the Left," in Rosalyn Baxandall and Linda Gordon, *Dear Sisters: Dispatches from the Women's Liberation Movement* (New York: Basic Books, 2000), 51.

were often misguided, radical men simply do not understand the importance of our struggle. Except for a hip vanguard movement, men have tended to dismiss the woman's movement as "just chicks with personal hang-ups," to insist that men and women are equally oppressed, though maybe in different ways, or to minimize the extent and significance of male chauvinism ("just a failure of communication"). All around me I see men who consider themselves dedicated revolutionaries, yet exploit their wives and girl friends shamefully without ever noticing a contradiction.

T HE THIRD WORLD WOMEN'S ALLIANCE emerged from an earlier organization, the Black Women's Alliance, founded by Frances Beal and other women in SNCC (see pp. 613–15). The term "third world" was drawn from the language of geopolitics to characterize underdeveloped nations and peoples and outside of the "first world/second world" antagonisms of the Cold War. As the following statement indicates, the group changed its title and broadened its focus when Puerto Rican and Asian women joined. The organization, probably numbering about two hundred, had members in Cambridge, Massachusetts, and New York City and lasted through the 1970s. Like later organizations founded by women of color, it emphasized the intersection of race, class, and gender in understanding the oppression they experienced. Why does the statement stress the myth of the black matriarchy (see p. 679)? What criticisms does it make of white feminists? What premises do they share with white feminists?

THIRD WORLD WOMEN'S ALLIANCE
Statement (1971)

The Third World Women's Alliance started about December, 1968. Within SNCC (Student Nonviolent Coordinating Committee) a Black women's liberation committee was established and a number of women who had been meeting over a period of a few months decided that we would be drawing in women from other organizations, and that we would be attracting welfare mothers, community workers, and campus radicals—so we decided to change the name to the Black Women's Alliance. As of now, the organization is independent of SNCC and at the same time SNCC has decided to retain its women's caucus.

We decided to form a Black women's organization for many reasons. One was and still is, the widespread myth and concept in the Black community of the matriarchy. We stated that the concept of the matriarchy was a myth and that it has never existed. Our position would be to expose this myth. There was also the widespread concept that by some miracle the oppression of slavery for the Black woman was not as degrading, not as horrifying, not as barbaric [as for men]. However, we state that in any society where men are not yet free, women are less free because we are further enslaved by our sex.

SOURCE: Baxandall and Gordon, *Dear Sisters*, 65.

Now we noticed another interesting thing. And that is, that with the rise of Black nationalism and the rejection of white middle class norms and values, that this rejection of whiteness — white cultures, white norms and values — took a different turn when it came to the Black woman. That is, Black men defined the role of black women in the movement. They stated that our role was a supportive one; others stated that we must become breeders and provide an army; still others stated that we had kotex power or pussy power. We opposed these concepts also stating that a true revolutionary movement enhances the status of women.

Now one of the changes that have taken place in the organization, is that we recognize the need for Third World solidarity. That is, we could not express support for Asia, Africa and Latin America and at the same time, ignore non-Black Third World sisters in this country. We found that we would be much more effective and unified by becoming a Third World Women's organization. So our group is opened to all Third World sisters because our oppression is basically caused by the same factors and our enemy is the same. The name of the organization has been changed to reflect this new awareness and composition of the group — THIRD WORLD WOMEN'S ALLIANCE.

Some women in the movement cannot understand why we exclude whites from our meetings and programs. The argument that we are all equally oppressed as women and should unite as one big family to confront the system is as artificial as the argument that Third World women should be fighting on only one front.

And to the white women's liberation groups we say . . . until you can deal with your own racism and until you can deal with your OWN poor white sisters, you will never be a liberation movement and you cannot expect to unite with Third World peoples in common struggle.

Most white women involved in liberation groups come from a middle-class and a student thing. They don't address themselves to the problem of poor and working class women, so there is no way in the world they would be speaking for Third World women. There are serious questions that white women must address themselves to. They call for equality. We answer, equal to what? Equal to white men in their power and ability to oppress Third World people?

It is difficult for Third World women to address themselves to the petty problems of who is going to take out the garbage, when there isn't enough food in the house for anything to be thrown away. Fighting for the day-to-day existence of a family and as humans is the struggle of the Third World woman. We are speaking of oppression, we don't need reforms that will put white women into a position to oppress women of color or OUR MEN in much the same way as white men have been doing for centuries. We need changes in the system and attitudes of people that will guarantee the right to live free from hunger, poverty, and racism. Revolution and not reform is the answer.

To some extent, Chicanas' feminism was similar to that of African Americans in that it was rooted in the nationalist movement of Chicanos and Chicanas that flourished in the late 1960s and 1970s. Here, too, women were leery of associating with white feminists yet felt frustrated by the sexism they experienced from Chicano men. In 1969, at a women's workshop at the Chicano Youth Liberation Conference in Colorado, Chicanas issued a statement, saying, "It was the consensus of the group that the Chicano woman does not want to be liberated."

Although subsequent scholarship has suggested that these women were primarily concerned with indicating that they did not want to identify with white feminism, the statement proved highly controversial among Chicanas and helped to generate an upsurge in Chicana feminism. Two years later in Houston, at the first national conference of Chicanas, the tone had changed dramatically. In the following selection, Mirta Vidal, an Argentinean-born socialist, describes the issues raised at the Houston conference. "La Raza," which literally means "the race," is the term militant Chicanos and Chicanas invoked to describe the unity of people of Mexican descent. How did Chicanas describe the nature of the oppression they experienced? How did they get beyond the charge that women's liberation was a "white woman's thing"?

MIRTA VIDAL
New Voice of La Raza: Chicanas Speak Out (1971)

At the end of May 1971, more than 600 Chicanas met in Houston, Texas, to hold the first national conference of Raza women. For those of us who were there it was clear that this conference was not just another national gathering of the Chicano movement.

Chicanas came from all parts of the country inspired by the prospect of discussing issues that have long been on their minds and which they now see not as individual problems but as an important and integral part of a movement for liberation.

The resolutions coming out of the two largest workshops, "Sex and the Chicana" and "Marriage—Chicana Style," called for "free, legal abortions and birth control for the Chicano community, controlled by *Chicanas*." As Chicanas, the resolution stated, "we have a right to control our own bodies." The resolutions also called for "24-hour child-care centers in Chicano communities" and explained that there is a critical need for these since "Chicana motherhood should not preclude educational, political, social and economic advancement."

SOURCE: Alma M. Garcia, ed., *Chicana Feminist Thought: The Basic Historical Writings* (New York: Routledge, 1997), 21–24.

While these resolutions articulated the most pressing needs of Chicanas today, the conference as a whole reflected a rising consciousness of the Chicana about her special oppression in this society. . . .

In part, this awakening of Chicana consciousness has been prompted by the "machismo" she encounters in the movement. . . .

This behavior, typical of Chicano men, is a serious obstacle to women anxious to play a role in the struggle for Chicano liberation. The oppression suffered by Chicanas is different from that suffered by most women in this country. Because Chicanas are part of an oppressed nation if they are subjected to the racism practiced against La Raza. Since the overwhelming majority of Chicanos are workers, Chicanas are also victims of the exploitation of the working class. But in addition, Chicanas, along with the rest of women, are relegated to an inferior position because of their sex. Thus, Raza women suffer a triple form of oppression: as members of an oppressed nationality, as workers, *and* as women. Chicanas have no trouble understanding this. At the Houston Conference 84 percent of the women surveyed felt that "there is a distinction between the problems of the Chicana and those of other women."

On the other hand, they also understand that the struggle now unfolding against the oppression of women is not only relevant to them, but *is* their struggle. Because sexism and male chauvinism are so deeply rooted in this society, there is a strong tendency, even within the Chicano movement, to deny the basic right of Chicanas to organize around their own concrete issues. Instead they are told to stay away from the women's liberation movement because it is an "Anglo thing."

We need only analyze the origin of male supremacy to expose this false position. The inferior role of women in society does not date back to the beginning of time. In fact, before the Europeans came to this part of the world women

enjoyed a position of equality with men. The submission of women, along with institutions such as the church and the patriarchy, was imported by the European colonizers, and remains to this day part of Anglo society. Machismo—in English, "male chauvinism"—is the one thing, if any, that should be labeled an "Anglo thing."

When Chicano men oppose the efforts of women to move against their oppression, they are actually opposing the struggle of every woman in this country aimed at changing a society in which Chicanos themselves are oppressed. They are saying to 51 percent of this country's population that they have no right to fight for their liberation.

ALTHOUGH WOMEN IN RADICAL MOVEMENTS often challenged men for the sexism evident in the movements they led, much feminist literature was meant for women and was specifically designed to their raise consciousness concerning sexism. Bread and Roses, a socialist feminist group founded primarily by white women in Boston in 1969, was one of the earliest women's liberation organizations. The name refers to the history of working women's struggles in the United States and highlights the historical consciousness that accompanied the growth of women's liberation (see pp. 675–78). The following document is a leaflet distributed at a pro–child care demonstration in Boston in 1970. Bread and Roses women supported community child care, so how do you explain their critique of the demonstration? What do the words they offer as starting points for discussions with friends suggest about their perspectives?

BREAD AND ROSES
Outreach Leaflet (1970)

Sisters
We are living in a world that is not ours—"it's a man's world." We feel our lives being shaped by someone or something outside ourselves; because we are females we are expected to act in certain

ways and do certain things whether or not it feels right to *us*. We have had to teach ourselves to run off our real feelings and real desires—to be "realistic"—in other words, to accept the place we have been given in the world of men.

But it's no good—deep in our guts we know this. Cooking and cleaning and children have not given us the fulfillment the ladies' magazines

SOURCE: Baxandall and Gordon, *Dear Sisters*, 35.

promise even after we've followed all their recipes. Our most honest selves know there is more to it than being hung-up when our emotions fight against a [male partner's] casual sexual affair. Why have we always assumed it was *our* fault if the "new morality" wasn't satisfying us? What does it mean when men whistle at us on the street?

We are waking up angry and shocked, amazed that we didn't realize before. Women begin to name enemies: men, capitalism, families, neurosis, technology, etc. And in various ways we start trying to make changes. Some women — such as those who have expressed themselves in the platform of this march — look to the state and federal legislation to give us the unrestricted humanity which has been denied us for so long. They have decided to "work within the system." In other words, they say, "Let us into the world you men live in. Give us your education and your jobs and your public positions. Free us with child-care programs designed in your offices." Is this really what we want? How about female generals in Vietnam? DO WE WANT EQUALITY IN THE MAN'S WORLD, OR DO WE WANT TO MAKE IT IN A NEW WORLD?

Women being ourselves and believing in ourselves, women finding the strength to live how we feel, *powerful* women, can lead the way to create a new kind of politics, a new life.

To join the Women's Liberation Movement, begin by talking with friends. Here are some words which might help to get started:

date-bait community-controlled childcare centers fathers my boss castrating woman *Playboy* rape fashions marriage high school abortions doctors pretending orgasms masculinity self-reliance

---

F OR MANY FEMINIST THEORISTS, one persistent problem was how to analyze the oppression of women in way that clarified that the problem was not individual men, but rather the larger structure of patriarchy. In the following article, published in 1970, Boston activist Dana Densmore takes on the simplistic critique that feminists are men-haters who think that men are the enemy. If men are not the enemy, who or what is? What is your analysis of her advice to women for overcoming their oppression?

DANA DENSMORE
Who Is Saying Men Are the Enemy? (1970)

The question "Are men the enemy?" has always struck me as a curious one.

If enemies are perceived as that force against which one does battle and against whom (having killed off sufficient numbers) one wins, the concept is obviously inappropriate.

It is clear to me that in its form "I object to your attitude that men are the enemy" the issue is a dishonest one: it is an attempted smear or a defensive counterattack against the force of our analysis. . . .

It makes it appear that if we do anything but embrace all men, whatever their individual

SOURCE: Dawn Elizabeth Keetley and John Charles Pettigrew, eds., *Public Women, Public Words: A Documentary History of American Feminism* (Madison, WI: Madison House Publishers, 1997), 3:182–84.

attitude, as our friends and allies, treating them as allies however they treat us, if we so much as speak of men generally as "our oppressors," then it must be that we regard them as "enemies" in the sense of an opponent so all-powerful and implacable that he must be killed in order to be neutralized.

Of course we couldn't kill off all men if we wanted to, but the point is that it isn't necessary and we know it. It is the situation men and women find themselves in, the structures of society and the attitudes of women, that make it *possible* for men to oppress.

Given power and privileges, told by society that these are not only legitimate but the essence of his manhood, it is not surprising that a man should accept an oppressor's role. But if women refused to cooperate, and if they demanded changes in the structures, institutions and attitudes of society, then men, whatever their desires, could not and therefore would not oppress women. . . .

The distinction is often made in the female liberation movement between an "enemy" and an "oppressor." The real enemy, I think we all agree, is sexism and male supremacy; a set of attitudes held by men and women and institutionalized in our society (and in all societies throughout history). . . .

If the minds of the women are freed from these chains, no man will be able to oppress any woman. No man can, even now, in an individual relationship; all the woman has to do is walk out on him. And ironically enough, that is exactly what would force the men to shape up fastest. Not very many men could tolerate being deserted, especially over a political issue. And all that's needed is for the woman to learn enough respect for herself to be unwilling to live with a man who treats her with contempt.

Men are not our "enemies" and we should refuse to play "enemy" games with them. If they ridicule us or try to smear us or isolate us, we must laugh and walk out. "Winning rounds" with individual men will not bring our final victory closer and cannot change contempt and terror into a generous respect. Challenges by individual women to individual men have always been met the same way: threats, ridicule, smears, repression. These are the prescribed ways for men to defend their "manhood" against "castrating females."

ALTHOUGH MANY LESBIANS PARTICIPATED in the gay liberation front spearheaded by the Stonewall Rebellion in 1969, many lesbian activists worked within the women's liberation movement. In articulating an ideology of lesbian feminism, they not only shaped lesbians' feminism but contributed to heterosexual feminists' critique of patriarchal power and to the notion that the bonds of sisterhood link women together. Radicalesbians evolved from a group calling itself Lavender Menace, in reference to the disparaging term used by NOW leader Betty Friedan in 1970. Later that year the group electrified the Second Congress to United Women by taking over open microphones, removing their shirts to reveal T-shirts emblazoned with "Lavender Menace," and distributing their manifesto, "The Woman Identified Woman." The document makes few references to sexual intimacy between women and instead emphasizes "political lesbianism" (see pp. 676–77). How does the document explain lesbianism as a political choice? Why do Radicalesbians consider the woman-identified woman essential to feminism?

RADICALESBIANS
The Woman Identified Woman (1970)

What is a lesbian? A lesbian is the rage of all women condensed to the point of explosion. She is the woman who, often beginning at an extremely early age, acts in accordance with her inner compulsion to be a more complete and freer human being than her society—perhaps then, but certainly later—cares to allow her. These needs and actions, over a period of years, bring her into painful conflict with people, situations, the accepted ways of thinking, feeling and behaving, until she is in a state of continual war with everything around her, and usually with her self. She may not be fully conscious of the political implications of what for her began as personal necessity, but on some level she has not been able to accept the limitations and oppression laid on her by the most basic role of her society—the female role. The turmoil she experiences tends to induce guilt proportional to the degree to which she feels she is not meeting social expectations, and/or eventually drives her to question and analyze what the rest of her society more or less accepts. She is forced to evolve her own life pattern, often living much of her life alone, learning usually much earlier than her "straight" (heterosexual) sisters about the essential aloneness of life (which the myth of marriage obscures) and about the reality of illusions. To the extent that she cannot expel the heavy socialization that goes with being female, she can never truly find peace with herself. For she is caught somewhere between accepting society's view of her—in which case she cannot accept herself—and coming to understand what this sexist society has done to her and why it is functional and necessary for it to do so. Those of us who work that through find ourselves on the other side of a tortuous journey through a night that may have been decades long. The perspective gained from that journey, the liberation of self, the inner peace, the real love of self and of all women, is something to be shared with all women—because we are all women.

It should first be understood that lesbianism, like male homosexuality, is a category of behavior possible only in a sexist society characterized by rigid sex roles and dominated by male supremacy. Those sex roles dehumanize women by defining us as a supportive/serving caste *in relation to* the master caste of men, and emotionally cripple men by demanding that they be alienated from their own bodies and emotions in order to perform their economic/political/military functions effectively. Homosexuality is a by-product of a particular way of setting up roles (or approved patterns of behavior) on the basis of sex; as such it is an inauthentic (not consonant with "reality") category. In a society in which men do not oppress women, and sexual expression is allowed to follow feelings, the categories of homosexuality and heterosexuality would disappear.

But lesbianism is also different from male homosexuality, and serves a different function in the society. "Dyke" is a different kind of put-down from "faggot," although both imply you are not playing your socially assigned sex role . . . are not therefore a "real woman" or a "real man." The grudging admiration felt for the tomboy, and the queasiness felt around a sissy boy point to the same thing: the contempt in which women—or those who play a female role—are held. And the investment in keeping women in that contemptuous role is very great. Lesbian is a word, the label, the condition that holds women in line. When a woman hears this word tossed her way, she knows she is stepping out of line. She knows that she has crossed the terrible boundary of her sex role. She recoils, she protests, she reshapes her actions to gain approval. Lesbian is a label invented by the Man to throw at any woman who dares to be his equal, who dares to challenge his prerogatives (including that of all women as part of the exchange medium among men), who dares to assert the primacy of her own needs. To have the label applied to people active in women's liberation is just the most recent instance of a long history; older women will recall that not so long ago, any woman who was successful, independent, not orienting her whole life about a man, would hear this word. For in this sexist society, for a woman to be independent means she *can't be* a woman — she must be a dyke. That in itself should tell us where women are at. It says as clearly as can be said: women and person are contradictory terms. For a lesbian is not considered a "real woman." And yet, in popular thinking, there is really only one essential difference between a lesbian and other women: that of sexual orientation — which is to say, when you strip off all the packaging, you must finally realize that the essence of being a "woman" is to get fucked by men. . . .

Women in the movement have in most cases gone to great lengths to avoid discussion and confrontation with the issue of lesbianism. It puts people up-tight. They are hostile, evasive, or try to incorporate it into some "broader issue." They would rather not talk about it. If they have to, they try to dismiss it as a "lavender herring." But it is no side issue. It is absolutely essential to the success and fulfillment of the women's liberation movement that this issue be dealt with. As long as the label "dyke" can be used to frighten women into a less militant stand, keep her separate from her sisters, keep her from giving primacy to anything other than men and family — then to that extent she is controlled by the male culture. Until women see in each other the possibility of a primal commitment which includes sexual love, they will be denying themselves the love and value they readily accord to men, thus affirming their second-class status. As long as male acceptability is primary — both to individual women and to the movement as a whole — the term lesbian will be used effectively

against women. Insofar as women want only more privileges within the system, they do not want to antagonize male power. They instead seek acceptability for women's liberation, and the most crucial aspect of the acceptability is to deny lesbianism — i.e., to deny any fundamental challenge to the basis of the female. It should also be said that some younger, more radical women have honestly begun to discuss lesbianism, but so far it has been primarily as a sexual "alternative" to men. This, however, is still giving primacy to men, both because the idea of relating more completely to women occurs as a negative reaction to men, and because the lesbian relationship is being characterized simply by sex, which is divisive and sexist. On one level, which is both personal and political, women may withdraw emotional and sexual energies from men, and work out various alternatives for those energies in their own lives. On a different political/psychological level, it must be understood that what is crucial is that women begin disengaging from male-defined response patterns. In the privacy of our own psyches, we must cut those cords to the core. For irrespective of where our love and sexual energies flow, if we are male-identified in our heads, we cannot realize our autonomy as human beings. . . .

It is the primacy of women relating to women, of women creating a new consciousness of and with each other, which is at the heart of women's liberation, and the basis for the cultural revolution. Together we must find, reinforce, and validate our authentic selves. As we do this, we confirm in each other that struggling, incipient sense of pride and strength, the divisive barriers begin to melt, we feel this growing solidarity with our sisters. We see ourselves as prime, find our centers inside of ourselves. We find receding the sense of alienation, of being cut off, of being behind a locked window, of being unable to get out what we know is inside. We feel a real-ness, feel at last we are coinciding with ourselves. With that real self, with that consciousness, we begin a revolution to end the imposition of all coercive identifications, and to achieve maximum autonomy in human expression.

O NE OF THE MOST COMPELLING IDEAS to emerge from women's liberation was the notion that the "personal is political." Nowhere was this more explicit than with respect to women's sexuality. In consciousness-raising groups, women exchanged intimate details and recounted daily experiences, in the hopes of realizing that many of the experiences that women thought were unique to them (and about which they may have been embarrassed or ashamed) were actually part of larger pattern of intimate sexism. By assessing the ways in which societal pressures shaped sexual behavior and reinforced male domination over women, women's liberationists situated the private world of sexuality in the political context of male/female inequalities. At the same time, they encouraged women to move beyond a mentality of victimization and to empower themselves sexually and otherwise.

Anne Koedt, a member of New York Radical Women, published "The Myth of the Vaginal Orgasm" in 1970. Freudian psychology had long insisted that women's orgasms were either good—to the degree that they were the direct result of intercourse—or bad—because they came from clitoral stimulation. Scientific studies of the way that women actually achieve orgasms challenged the idea of two different female orgasms, one located in the vagina and the other in the clitoris. Koedt drew on this research in the essay excerpted here. How did the physiological experience of women's sexual climax fit with the women's liberation agenda? How did it coincide with growing interest in lesbianism? Why do you think this article made such a powerful impression when it was published?

ANNE KOEDT
The Myth of the Vaginal Orgasm (1970)

Whenever female orgasm and frigidity are discussed, a false distinction is made between the vaginal and the clitoral orgasm. Frigidity has generally been defined by men as the failure of women to have vaginal orgasms. Actually the vagina is not a highly sensitive area and is not constructed to achieve orgasm. It is the clitoris which is the center of sexual sensitivity and which is the female equivalent of the penis.

I think this explains a great many things: First of all, the fact that the so-called frigidity rate among women is phenomenally high. Rather than tracing female frigidity to the false assumptions about female anatomy, our "experts" have declared frigidity a psychological problem of women. Those women who complained about it were recommended psychiatrists, so that they might discover their "problem"—diagnosed generally as a failure to adjust to their role as women.

The facts of female anatomy and sexual response tell a different story. Although there are many areas for sexual arousal, there is only one area for sexual climax; that area is the clitoris. All orgasms are extensions of sensation from this area. Since the clitoris is not necessarily stimulated sufficiently in the conventional sexual positions, we are left "frigid."

SOURCE: Anne Koedt, "The Myth of the Vaginal Orgasm," in Rosalyn Baxandall and Linda Gordon, eds., *Dear Sisters: Dispatches from the Women's Liberation Movement* (New York: Basic Books, 2000), 158.

Aside from physical stimulation, which is the common cause of orgasm for most people, there is also stimulation through primarily mental processes. Some women, for example, may achieve orgasm through sexual fantasies, or through fetishes. However, while the stimulation may be psychological, the orgasm manifests itself physically. Thus, while the cause is psychological, the effect is still physical, and the orgasm necessarily takes place in the sexual organ equipped for sexual climax, the clitoris. The orgasm experience may also differ in degree of intensity—some more localized, and some more diffuse and sensitive. But they are all clitoral orgasms.

All this leads to some interesting questions about conventional sex and our role in it. Men have orgasms essentially by friction with the vagina, not the clitoral area, which is external and not able to cause friction the way penetration does. Women have thus been defined sexually in terms of what pleases men; our own biology has not been properly analyzed. Instead, we are fed the myth of the liberated woman and her vaginal orgasm—an orgasm which in fact does not exist.

What we must do is redefine our sexuality. We must discard the "normal" concepts of sex and create new guidelines which take into account mutual sexual enjoyment. While the idea of mutual enjoyment is liberally applauded in marriage manuals, it is not followed to its logical conclusion. We must begin to demand that if certain sexual positions now defined as "standard" are not mutually conducive to orgasm, they no longer be defined as standard. New techniques must be used or devised which transform this particular aspect of our current sexual exploitation.

CALLING ATTENTION TO WOMEN'S ROLE in the family, and especially their responsibility for child care and housework, was another compelling way in which feminists demonstrated that the personal is political and brought their critique of patriarchy close to home. Pat Mainardi penned a witty critique of male privilege in the home for the journal *Redstockings* in 1970. How did she combine down-to-earth advice to women in their daily struggles over who would wash the dishes or change the diapers with an analysis of the power struggles between women and men? Do you think her critique is still valid today? Why or why not?

PAT MAINARDI
The Politics of Housework (1970)

Though women do not complain of the power of husbands, each complains of her own husband, or of the husbands of her friends. It is the same in all other cases of servitude; at least in the commencement of the emancipatory movement. The serfs did not at first complain of the power of the lords, but only of their tyranny.

—JOHN STUART MILL, *On the Subjection of Women*

Liberated women—very different from Women's Liberation! The first signals all kinds of goodies, to warm the hearts (not to mention other parts) of the most radical men. The other signals—HOUSEWORK. The first brings sex without marriage, sex before marriage, cozy housekeeping arrangements ("I'm living with this chick") and the self-content of knowing that you're not the kind of man who wants a doormat instead of a woman. That will come later. After all, who wants that old commodity anymore, the Standard American Housewife, all husband, home and kids? The New Commodity; the Liberated Woman, has sex a lot and has a Career, preferably something that can be fitted in with the household chores—like dancing, pottery, or painting.

On the other hand is Women's Liberation—and housework. What? You say this is all trivial? Wonderful! That's what I thought. It seemed perfectly reasonable. We both had careers, both had to work a couple of days a week to earn enough to live on, so why shouldn't we share the housework? So I suggested it to my mate and he agreed—most men are too hip to turn you down flat. You're right, he said. It's only fair. Then an interesting thing happened. I can only explain it by stating that we women have been brainwashed

more than even we can imagine, [p]robably too many years of seeing television women in ecstasy over their shiny waxed floors or breaking down over their dirty shirt collars. Men have no such conditioning. They recognize the essential fact of housework right from the very beginning. Which is that it stinks.

Here's my list of dirty chores: buying groceries, carting them home and putting them away; cooking meals and washing dishes and pots; doing the laundry; digging out the place when things get out of control; washing floors. The list could go on but the sheer necessities are bad enough. All of us have to do these things, or get someone else to do them for us. The longer my husband contemplated these chores, the more repulsed he became, and so proceeded the change from the normally sweet, considerate Dr. Jekyll into the crafty Mr. Hyde who would stop at nothing to avoid the horrors of housework. As he felt himself backed into a corner laden with dirty dishes, brooms, mops and reeking garbage, his front teeth grew longer and pointier, his fingernails haggled and his eyes grew wild. Housework trivial? Not on your life! Just try to share the burden.

So ensued a dialogue that's been going on for several years. Here are some of the high points: "I don't mind sharing the housework, but I don't do it very well. We should each do the things we're best at." MEANING: Unfortunately I'm no good at things like washing dishes or cooking. What I do best is a little light carpentry, changing light bulbs, moving furniture (how often do you move furniture?). ALSO MEANING: Historically the lower classes (black men and us) have had hundreds of years experience doing menial jobs. It would be a waste of manpower to train someone else to do them now. ALSO MEANING: I don't like the dull, stupid, boring jobs, so you should do them.

SOURCE: Pat Mainardi, "The Politics of Housework," CWLU Herstory Project, http://www.cwluherstory.org/classic-feminist-writings/the-politics-of-housework.html (accessed November 16, 2007).

"I don't mind sharing the work, but you'll have to show me how to do it." MEANING: I ask a lot of questions and you'll have to show me everything every time I do it because I don't remember so good. Also don't try to sit down and read while I'M doing my jobs because I'm going to annoy hell out of you until it's easier to do them yourself."

"We used to be so happy!" (Said whenever it was his turn to do something.) MEANING: I used to be so happy. MEANING: Life without housework is bliss. No quarrel here. Perfect Agreement. . . .

"Housework is too trivial to even talk about." MEANING: It's even more trivial to do. Housework is beneath my status. My purpose in life is to deal with matters of significance. Yours is to deal with matters of insignificance. You should do the housework.

"This problem of housework is not a man-woman problem. In any relationship between two people one is going to have a stronger personality and dominate." MEANING: That stronger personality had better be me.

"In animal societies, wolves, for example, the top animal is usually a male even where he is not chosen for brute strength but on the basis of cunning and intelligence. Isn't that interesting?" MEANING: I have historical, psychological, anthropological and biological justification for keeping you down. How can you ask the top wolf to be equal?

"Women's liberation isn't really a political movement." MEANING: The revolution is coming too close to home. ALSO MEANING: I am only interested in how I am oppressed, not how I oppress others. Therefore the war, the draft and the university are political. Women's liberation is not.

"Man's accomplishments have always depended on getting help from other people, mostly women. What great man would have accomplished what he did if he had to do his own housework?" MEANING: Oppression is built into the system and I, as the white American male,

receive the benefits of this system. I don't want to give them up.

Participatory democracy begins at home. If you are planning to implement your politics, there are certain things to remember.

1. He is feeling it more than you. He's losing some leisure and you're gaining it. The measure of your oppression is his resistance.

2. A great many American men are not accustomed to doing monotonous, repetitive work which never issues in any lasting, let alone important, achievement. This is why they would rather repair a cabinet than wash dishes. If human endeavors are like a pyramid with man's highest achievements at the top, then keeping oneself alive is at the bottom. Men have always had servants (us) to take care of this bottom stratum of life while they have confined their efforts to the rarefied upper regions. It is thus ironic when they ask of women—Where are your great painters, statesmen, etc.? Mme. Matisse ran a military shop so he could paint. Mrs. Martin Luther King kept his house and raised his babies.

3. It is a traumatizing experience for someone who has always thought of himself as being against any oppression or exploitation of one human being by another to realize that in his daily life he has been accepting and implementing (and benefiting from) this exploitation; that his rationalization is little different from that of the racist who says, "Black people don't feel pain" (women don't mind doing the shitwork); and that the oldest form of oppression in history has been the oppression of 50 percent of the population by the other 50 percent.

4. Arm yourself with some knowledge of the psychology of oppressed peoples everywhere, and a few facts about the animal kingdom. I admit playing top wolf or who runs the gorillas is silly but as a last resort men bring it up all the time. Talk about bees. If you feel really hostile bring up the sex life of spiders. They have sex. She bites off his head. The psychology of oppressed peoples is not silly. Jews, immigrants, black men and all women have employed the

same psychological mechanisms to survive; admiring the oppressor, glorifying the oppressor, wanting to be like the oppressor, wanting the oppressor to like them, mostly because the oppressor held all the power. . . .

9. Beware of the double whammy. He won't do the little things he always did because you're now a "Liberated Woman," right? Of course he won't do anything else either. . . .

I was just finishing this when my husband came in and asked what I was doing. Writing a paper on housework. Housework? he said. Housework? Oh my god how trivial can you get? A paper on housework.

QUESTIONS FOR ANALYSIS

1. In what ways do these documents suggest the diverging concerns of white feminist women and feminist women of color? What similarities do they indicate?

2. Women's liberation pioneered the concept of consciousness-raising for feminists. What do these documents suggest about the themes addressed in consciousness-raising?

3. Compare the writings of these feminists to those of the early twentieth century on pages 482–83 and 503–08. To what extent are the similar and in what ways do they differ?

NOTES

1. Nancy MacLean, *Freedom Is Not Enough: The Opening of the American Workplace* (Cambridge: Harvard University Press, 2006), 130.

2. Francisca Flores, "Conference of Mexican Women in Houston—Un Remolino," in Alma M. Garcia, ed., *Chicana Feminist Thought: The Basic Historical Writings* (New York: Routledge, 1997), 160.

3. Toni Cade, ed., *The Black Woman: An Anthology* (New York: New American Library, 1970), 107.

4. "To the Women of the Left," in Rosalyn Baxandall and Linda Gordon, eds., *Dear Sisters: Dispatches from the Women's Liberation Movement* (New York: Basic Books, 2000), 29.

5. "Burial of Weeping Womanhood," in Rosalyn Baxandall and Linda Gordon, eds., *Dear Sisters: Dispatches from the Women's Liberation Movement* (New York: Basic Books, 2000), 25.

6. Robin Morgan, ed., *Sisterhood Is Powerful: An Anthology of Readings from the Women's Liberation Movement* (New York: Random House, 1970), xxxv.

7. Anne Koedt, "The Myth of the Vaginal Orgasm," in Rosalyn Baxandall and Linda Gordon, eds., *Dear Sisters: Dispatches from the Women's Liberation Movement* (New York: Basic Books, 2000), 158.

8. Quoted in Alice Echols, *Daring to Be Bad: Radical Feminism in America, 1967–1975* (Minneapolis: University of Minnesota Press, 1989), 212.

9. Ibid., 238.

10. Quoted in Lillian Faderman, *Odd Girls and Twilight Lovers: A History of Lesbian Life in Twentieth-Century America* (New York: Columbia University Press, 1991), 207.

11. Kate Millett, *Sexual Politics* (New York: Avon, 1970), 25.

12. Gayle Rubin, "The Traffic in Women: Notes on the 'Political Economy' of Sex," in Joan W. Scott, ed., *Feminism and Theory* (New York: Oxford University Press, 1996), 111.

13. Quoted in Benita Roth, *Separate Roads to Feminism: Black, Chicana, and White Feminist Movements in America's Second Wave* (New York: Cambridge University Press, 2004), 90.

14. Premilla Nadasen, *Welfare Warriors: The Welfare Rights Movement in the United States* (New York: Routledge, 2005), 7.

15. Benita Roth, *Separate Roads to Feminism: Black, Chicana, and White Feminist Movements in America's Second Wave* (Cambridge: Cambridge University Press, 2004), 157.

16. Jennifer Nelson, *Women of Color and the Reproductive Rights Movement* (New York: New York University Press, 2003), 120.

17. Michael Abrahamson, *Palante: Young Lords Party* (New York: McGraw-Hill, 1971), 117.

18. Susie Ling, "The Mountain Movers: Asian American Women's Movement in Los Angeles, *Amerasia* 15 (1989), 56.

19. Paul Chaat Smith and Robert Allen Warrior, *Like a Hurricane: The American Indian Movement from Alcatraz to Wounded Knee* (New York: New Press, 1996), 199.

20. Beatrice Medicine, "The Native American Woman: A Perspective," *ERIC/CRESS* (March 1978): 95.

21. Third World Women's Alliance, "Statement" (1968), in Rosalyn Baxandall and Linda Gordon, eds., *Dear Sisters: Dispatches from the Women's Liberation Movement* (New York: Basic Books, 2000), 65–66.

22. Combahee River Collective, "A Black Feminist Statement," in Dawn Keetley and John Pettegrew, eds., *Public Women, Public Words: A Documentary History of American Feminism* (Madison: Madison House, 2002), 3:77.

23. Rita J. Simon and Gloria Danziger, *Women's Movements in America: Their Successes, Disappointments, and Aspirations* (New York: Praeger, 1991), 149.

24. MacLean, *Freedom Is Not Enough,* 145.

25. Nancy MacLean, "The Hidden History of Affirmative Action: Working Women's Struggles in the 1970s and the Gender of Class," *Feminist Studies* 25, no. 1 (Spring 1999), online at ProQuest (accessed July 16, 2007).

26. Winifred D. Wandersee, *On the Move: American Women in the 1970s* (Boston: Twayne, 1988), 133.

27. Ibid., 136.

28. Mary Ann Millsap, "Sex Equity in Education," in Irene Tinker, ed., *Women in Washington: Advocates for Public Policy* (Beverly Hills: Sage, 1983), 116.

29. Flora Davis, *Moving the Mountain: The Women's Movement in America since 1960* (Urbana: University of Illinois Press, 1999), 158.

30. Sara M. Evans, *Tidal Wave: How Women Changed America at Century's End* (New York: Free Press, 2003), 62.

31. Gerald C. Wright and Dorothy M. Stetson, "The Impact of No-Fault Divorce Law Reform on Divorce in American States," *Journal of Marriage and the Family* 40 (1978): 575.

32. *Statistical Abstract of the United States, 2000,* Allcountries.org, http://www.allcountries.org/uscensus/146_marital_status_of_women_15_to.html (accessed October 24, 2007); Sara R. Rix, *The American Woman 1987–1988: A Report in Depth* (New York: W. W. Norton, 1987), 74.

33. Rix, *The American Woman 1987–1988,* 107–08.

34. Stephanie Coontz, *Marriage: A History* (New York: Viking Press, 2005), 255.

35. Cited in Myra Marx Ferree and Beth B. Hess, *Controversy and Coalition: The New Feminist Movement across Three Decades of Change,* 3rd ed. (New York: Routledge, 2000), 8.

36. John D'Emilio and Estelle B. Freedman, *Intimate Matters: A History of Sexuality in America* (New York: Harper and Row, 1988), 337.

37. Ibid., 336.

38. Susan M. Hartmann, *From Margins to Mainstream: American Women and Politics since 1960* (New York: Knopf, 1989), 70.

39. Bonnie J. Dow, *Prime Time Television: Television, Media Culture, and the Women's Movement Since 1970* (Philadelphia, University of Pennsylvania, 1996), 25.

40. Donald R. Martin and Vicky Gordon Martin, "Barbara Jordan's Use of Language in the Keynote Address to the National Women's Conference," *Southern Speech Communication Journal* 49 (1984): 322.

41. Evans, *Tidal Wave*, 141.

42. Dorothy Sue Cobble, *The Other Women's Movement: Workplace and Justice and Social Rights in Modern America* (Princeton, NJ: Princeton University Press, 2004), 209, 210.

43. Kathleen M. Barry, *Femininity in Flight: A History of Flight Attendants* (Durham, NC: Duke University Press, 2007), 192.

44. Nancy MacLean, *Freedom Is Not Enough: The Opening of the American Workplace* (Cambridge: Harvard University Press, 2006), 124.

45. Ibid., 124.

46. Ibid., 132.

47. *Ebony* 43 (March 1988): 136.

48. Janice D. Yoder and Patricia Aniakudo, "Outsider within the Firehouse: Subordination and Difference in the Social Interactions of African American Women Firefighters," *Gender and Society* 11 (June 1997): 324–41.

49. "$285,000 Awarded to KC Female FF," *FireTimes*, January 12, 2002, http://www.firetimes.com/story.asp?FragID=1195 (accessed August 9, 2007).

50. Minnestoa AFL-CIO, "Workday Minnesota," http://www.workdayminnesota.org/index.php?article_1_70 (accessed August 10, 2007).

51. *New York Daily News*, February 10, 1973, p. 14.

52. Baxandall and Gordon, *Dear Sisters*, 53.

53. Martha Allen, "The Development of Communication Networks Among Women, 1963–1983," Women's Institute for Freedom of the Press: History of Women's Media, http://www.wifp.org/womensmediach3.html (accessed November 24, 2007).

54. Ibid.

SUGGESTED REFERENCES

General Works   Three scholars of U.S. women's history have recently published studies of women's history in the last third of the twentieth century that emphasize the powerful influence of the feminist revival: Sara M. Evans, *Tidal Wave: How Women Changed America at Century's End* (2003); Estelle B. Freedman, *No Turning Back: The History of Feminism and the Future of Women* (2002), which situates U.S. women's history in a global context; and Ruth Rosen, *The World Split Open: How the Modern Women's Movement Changed America*, 2nd ed. (2007).

Feminist Movements   Judith Sealander, *As Minority Becomes Majority: Federal Reaction to the Phenomenon of Women in the Work Force, 1920–1963* (1983); and Patricia G. Zelman, *Women, Work, and National Policy: The Kennedy-Johnson Years* (1982), offer a sense of the issues that framed the origins of NOW. The history of NOW is yet to be written, but see Rosen, *The World Split Open,* and Friedan's own account in *It Changed My Life: Writings on the Women's Movement* (1976). An account of the diversity of support for feminism among a variety of more mainstream organizations may be found in Susan M. Hartmann, *The Other Feminists: Activists in the Liberal Establishment* (1998).

One of the earliest studies of women's liberation, published while the movement was still thriving, is *The Politics of Women's Liberation* (1975), by feminist activist and political scientist Jo Freeman. Sarah Evans's influential *Personal Politics: The Roots of Women's Liberation in the Civil Rights Movement and the New Left* (1979) examines the influence of the civil rights and New Left movements on the rediscovery of feminism in the late 1960s. Alice Echols's collection of essays, *Shaky Ground: The Sixties and Its Aftershocks* (2002), considers relations of gender and race within the counterculture. Echols has also written a critical historical analysis of the tensions between different early women's liberation approaches in *Daring to Be Bad: Radical Feminism in America, 1967–1975* (1989). Flora Davis's *Moving the Mountain: The Women's Movement in America since 1960* (1999) is a more narrative history that interweaves the history of women's liberation with that of the National Organization for Women. In *Controversy and Coalition: The New Feminist Movement across Three Decades of Change*, 3rd ed. (2000), Myra Marx Ferree and Beth B. Hess go beyond the emergence of women's liberation to trace the development and influence of contemporary feminism through the rest of the century. Judith Ezekiel's *Feminism in the Heartland* (2002) examines women's liberation in Dayton, Ohio. Amy Erdman Farrell provides a history of *Ms.* magazine in *Yours in Sisterhood: Ms. Magazine and the Promise of Popular Feminism* (1998).

A classic collection of feminist documents is *Sisterhood Is Powerful* (1970), edited by Robin Morgan. Three newer collections of historical documents from the women's liberation movement are Nancy MacLean, *The American Women's Movement 1945–2000: A Brief History with Documents* (Boston: Bedford/St. Martin's, 2009), Dawn Keetley and John Pettegrew, eds., *Public Women, Public Words: A Documentary History of American Feminism*, vol. 3, *1960 to the Present* (2002), and Rosalyn Baxandall and Linda Gordon, eds., *Dear Sisters: Dispatches from the Women's Liberation Movement* (2000). Individual memoirs have begun to appear, for instance, Susan Brownmiller, In *Our Time: A Memoir of Revolution* (1999); Sheila Tobias, *Faces of Feminism: An Activist's Reflections on the Women's Movement* (1997); and Karla Jay, *Tales of the Lavender Menace: A Memoir of Liberation* (1999). Rachel Blau DuPlessis and Ann Snitow, eds., *The Feminist Memoir Project: Voices from Women's Liberation* (1998), offers a collection of briefer reminiscences. Florence Howe, ed., *The Politics of Women's Studies: Testimony from Thirty Founding Mothers* (2000), focuses on one of the more lasting aspects of the second wave.

The starting point for a history of lesbians is Lillian Faderman, *Odd Girls and Twilight Lovers: A History of Lesbian Life in Twentieth-Century America* (1991). For a path-breaking study of a working-class lesbian community, see Elizabeth Lapovsky Kennedy and Madeline D. Davis, *Boots of Leather, Slippers of Gold: The History of a Lesbian Community* (1993). John D'Emilio, *Sexual Politics, Sexual Communities: The Making of a Homosexual Minority in the United States, 1940–1970*, 2nd ed. (1998), and David K. Johnson, *The Lavender Scare: The Cold War Persecution of Gays and Lesbians in the Federal Government* (2004), offer insights on early gay efforts to counter discrimination, and Martin Duberman explores the origins of the gay liberation movement in *Stonewall* (1993).

The first source for the role of women of color and their response to the rise of women's liberation is Toni Cade's *The Black Woman: An Anthology* (1970). Michele Wallace's *Black Macho and the Myth of the Superwoman* (1990) is a new edition of a controversial 1979 critique of sexism in the black liberation movement. Gloria T. Hull et al., *All the Women Are White, All the Blacks Are Men, but Some of Us Are Brave* (1982), offers excerpts from many pioneering black feminist writings, and Patricia Hill Collins's *Black Feminist Thought: Knowledge, Consciousness, and the Politics of Empowerment* (2000) analyzes this literature. *Ain't I a Woman: Black Women and Feminism,* by bell hooks (1981), is one of the earliest modern African American feminist analyses. A very interesting dialogue between black and white feminists is found in Gloria I. Joseph and Jill Lewis, *Common Differences: Conflicts in Black and White Feminist Perspectives* (1981). See also Winifred Breines, *The Trouble Between Us: An Uneasy History of White and Black Women in the Feminist Movement* (2006). For the welfare rights movement, see Premilla Nadasen, *Welfare Warriors: The Welfare Rights Movement in the United States* (2005), and Annelise Orleck, *Storming Caesar's Palace: How Black Mothers Fought Their Own War on Poverty* (2005). Jennifer Nelson analyzes the broadening of the reproductive rights issue in *Women of Color and the Reproductive Rights Movement* (2004).

Alma García, ed., *Chicana Feminist Thought: The Basic Historical Writings* (1997), is the best primary source for feminism within the Chicano/Chicana movement. Material on women in the Puerto Rican Young Lord's Party is available in Michael Abrahamson, *Palante: Young Lords Party* (1971), and in Jennifer Nelson, *Women of Color and the Reproductive Rights Movement.* For personal accounts of the Asian American movement, see Steve Louie and Glenn K. Omatsu, eds., *Asian Americans: The Movement and the Moment* (2000). Two essays on Asian American women are Susie Ling, "The Mountain Movers: Asian American Women's Movement in Los Angeles," *Amerasia* 15 (1989), and Miya Iwataki, "The Asian Women's Movement: a Retrospective," *East Wind* (1983). For Native American women, a brief summary is available in Bea Medicine, *The Native American Woman: a Perspective* (1978). For a personal reminiscence, see Mary Crow Dog, *Lakota Woman* (1991).

For a range of writings from all groups of women of color, see Cherríe Moraga and Gloria Anzaldúa, eds., *This Bridge Called My Back: Writings by Radical Women of Color* (1979), and the subsequent volume, edited by Gloria Anzaldúa and Ana Louise Keating, *This Bridge We Call Home: Radical Visions for Transformation* (2002). In *Separate Roads to Feminism: Black, Chicana, and White Feminist Movements in America's Second Wave* (2004), Benita Roth offers a very useful comparative analysis of the three movements. Larua Pulido, *Black, Brown Yellow and Left: Radical Activism in Los Angeles* (2007), includes material on women's activism in her local study of Los Angeles radicalism of the era.

Impact of Feminism   On women in the labor force, an excellent overview that extends to the late twentieth century is Julia Kirk Blackwelder, *Now Hiring: The Feminization of Work in the United States, 1900–1995* (1997). For an analysis of the campaigns to address discrimination in the workplace, the starting point should be Nancy MacLean, *Freedom Is Not Enough: The Opening of the American Workplace* (2003), which covers the recent history of affirmative action. See also MacLean's article, "The Hidden History of Affirmative Action: Working Women's Struggles in the 1970s and the Gender of Class," *Feminist Studies* 25 (Spring 1999). Another valuable study is Dorothy Sue Cobble, *The Other Women's Movement: Workplace and Justice and Social Rights in Modern America* (2004), which emphasizes how active working-class women were in the drive for economic equality. Studies of specific occupations and women's battles include Virginia G. Drachman, *Sisters in Law: Women Lawyers in Modern American History* (1998); Mary Roth Walsh, *Doctors Needed: No Women Need Apply* (1977); Marjorie A. Stockford, *The Bellwomen: The Story of the Landmark AT&T Sex Discrimination Case* (2004); Kathleen M. Barry, *Femininity in Flight: A History of Flight Attendants* (2007); Dorothy Sue Cobble, *Dishing It Out: Waitresses and Their Unions in the Twentieth Century* (1991); and Suzanne E. Tallichet, *Daughters of the Mountain: Women Coal Miners in Central Appalachia* (2006). Two valuable oral history accounts of women who broke down barriers are Mary Lindenstein Walshok, ed., *Blue-Collar Women: Pioneers on the Male Frontier* (1981), and Marat Moore, *Women in the Mines: Stories of Life and Work* (1996). On women religious leaders, see Mark Chaves, *Ordaining Women: Culture and Conflict in Religious Organization* (1999) and Pamela Nadell, *Women Who Would Be Rabbis: A History of Women's Ordination 1889–1985* (1998).

The most useful study of women's political activism is Susan M. Hartmann, *From Margin to Mainstream: American Women and Politics Since 1960* (1996). Also helpful is a survey of women of the period, Winifred D. Wandersee, *On the Move: American Women in the 1970s* (1983). Irene Tinker, ed., *Women in Washington: Advocates for Public Policy* (1983), offers a collection of essays by women lobbyists and activists of the era. Susan M. Hartmann, *The Other Feminists: Activists in the Liberal Establishment* (1998), analyzes the permeation of feminism within many "mainstream" organizations. For women and television, see Bonnie J. Dow, *Prime Time Television: Television, Media Culture, and the Women's Movement Since 1970* (1996), and Ella Taylor, *Prime-Time Families: Television Culture in Post-War America* (1991). On changes in family and personal life, see two books by Stephanie Coontz, *The Way We Really Are: Coming to Terms with America's Changing Families* (1997) and *Marriage: A History* (2006), as well as John D'Emilio and Estelle B. Freedman, *Intimate Matters: A History of Sexuality in America* (1988).

For selected Web sites, please visit the *Through Women's Eyes* book companion site at bedfordstmartins.com/duboisdumenil.

12

U.S. Women in a Global Age

1980–PRESENT

IN 1993, PRESIDENT BILL CLINTON NOMINATED corporate lawyer Zoe Baird to be the first woman attorney general of the United States. But Baird's nomination foundered when it was discovered that she and her husband had employed an undocumented immigrant couple from Peru, Lillian and Victor Cordero, to serve as nanny and driver, and that they had failed to pay Social Security taxes for the couple. After a media firestorm, Baird withdrew her name from consideration and Janet Reno, a single woman with no children or household help, became attorney general instead. The Corderos divorced and, under pressure from the Immigration and Naturalization Service, returned to Peru. The incident, while largely forgotten now, highlights important aspects of women's experiences in recent history.

Baird's nomination itself suggests the dramatic change in women's professional and political opportunities since the beginning of the feminist movement in the 1960s. That Baird, unlike male cabinet appointees, was grilled about her child care providers, also reveals that the double standard about which parent was responsible for children and their care persisted, despite women's widespread entrance into the workplace. Finally, the fact that Baird paid Lillian Cordero $250 a week while her own household income was $600,000 a year indicates the wide disparity among working women's experiences and highlights the centrality of immigrant women to the functioning of millions of prosperous American households.

Baird's and Cordero's stories highlight several themes addressed in this chapter. One is women's changing roles in the home and their experiences in the workplace over the last thirty years. A second is the growing importance of the economic and political changes associated with the phenomenon that is usually called globalization. This phenomenon includes the rise of gigantic multinational corporations that employ women at low wages throughout the globe as well as the massive international migration of people—probably half of them women—from poor countries to rich ones in search of better lives for themselves and their families. Finally, some of the hostility Baird encountered stemmed from innuendos that she was too ambitious and had foisted her child care responsibilities onto hired help. While this implicit antifeminism was a minor motif in the Baird fiasco, the backlash against feminism was a major theme of the late twentieth century and contributed significantly to the strength of the conservative "new right" in American politics. The success of that movement not only limited feminism's advance but also presented serious challenges to women's lives in general, especially their reproductive freedoms and economic opportunities.

FEMINISM AND THE NEW RIGHT

An ironic measure of feminism's radicalism and historical impact was the antifeminist movement that emerged in the late 1970s to advocate the defense and reinstitution of traditional womanhood. As of 1968, the obstacles faced by insurgent feminism stemmed mostly from traditional beliefs and long-established sexism. Within a decade, however, a much more determined and organized resistance began to surface, concentrated especially on stopping ratification of the Equal Rights Amendment (ERA) and reversing the 1973 Supreme Court decision in *Roe v. Wade*. The political gains of antifeminism were reinforced by a cultural and media backlash that questioned the desirability of feminist life choices. This antifeminism was part of a

1996	**Madeleine Albright becomes first woman secretary of state**
1996	Personal Responsibility and Work Opportunities Act passed
1998	Clinton impeached by U.S. House of Representatives
1999	Senate votes not to remove Clinton from office
2000	Highly contested presidential election resolved by Supreme Court in favor of George W. Bush
2000	**United Nations approves Resolution 1325**
2001	Terrorists destroy New York's World Trade Center and attack Pentagon on September 11
2002	**Code Pink founded**
2003	United States and allies invade Iraq
2003	**Jessica Lynch's capture and rescue in Iraq**
2004	**Cindy Sheehan establishes "peace camp" at Crawford, Texas**
2004	**March for Women's Lives draws 1 million pro-choice activists to Washington, D.C.**
2004	**Gay marriages begin in California and Massachusetts**
2004	George W. Bush reelected president
2005	**Condoleezza Rice is first African American woman to become secretary of state**
2005	John G. Roberts Jr. becomes chief justice of the Supreme Court
2006	Immigration rights protest marches in cities throughout the United States
2006	**Nancy Pelosi becomes first woman speaker of the House of Representatives**
2006	**Nobel Women's Initiative founded**

broader movement of religious and other conservatives against the social and cultural transformations fueled by the events of the 1960s and 1970s. Ultimately unable to reverse the changes in women's lives that feminism championed, antifeminism and the "New Right" nonetheless had a tremendous impact on mainstream American political life, all the way up to and including the presidency.

The STOP-ERA Campaign

Unlike the past labor-based criticisms of the ERA, opposition to the ERA in the 1970s and early 1980s came primarily from the far right of the Republican Party. Throughout the 1950s and 1960s, right-wing leaders had dedicated themselves to halting the spread of communism and resisting efforts to expand federal power and programs. Starting in the early 1970s, however, a self-proclaimed New Right (a kind of mirror image of the New Left of the 1960s) switched to new domestic issues and contested the dramatic gains of the civil rights and feminist movements (and later the gay rights movement). The New Right had many strands, but it included evangelical Christians, many of them women, determined to bring their religious values into the political arena. The Republican Party, eager to break out of its image as the party of the rich, found this focus on social issues extremely useful in attracting new adherents. They were important to the election of Republican Ronald Reagan (1980–1988) and continued to play a vital role in presidential politics through the presidency of George W. Bush (2001–2009).

Antifeminism was critical in the conservative offensive that marked American political life in the late twentieth century. The rank and file of the antifeminist movement were primarily women. Mostly white, devoutly Christian, and most often married with children, they rose in defense of traditional gender roles and what they called family values. Ironically, the antifeminist movement, like the feminist movement against which it was aligned, pushed concerns about women's social role and status to the forefront of American political life. Indeed, the prominence of women in the antifeminist and larger conservative movements is one of the most striking measures of the changing place of women in American life in the late twentieth century.

Activist Phyllis Schlafly almost single-handedly put New Right antifeminism on the political map. One of the most important female conservative leaders in U.S. history, she first made a name for herself when she wrote *A Choice Not an Echo* in support of Barry Goldwater's bid for the Republican presidential nomination in 1964. In her book Schlafly argued that eastern elite Republicans controlled the party and had abandoned its principles of limited government and strong national defense. The book sold 3 million copies and contributed to Goldwater's nomination and the temporary ascendancy of right-wing conservatives in the Republican Party. Goldwater was trounced by Lyndon B. Johnson in the 1964 election, and conservatives lost ground within their party, but grassroots efforts in the states, especially those in the South and Southwest—in the burgeoning Sunbelt—continued and were crucial to the election of Ronald Reagan in 1980.

Schlafly persisted in her political activism emphasizing the themes of anti-communism and limited government, but then in 1972 she discovered the ERA issue, which transformed her approach to galvanizing grassroots support on behalf of conservative goals. She formed a new organization, STOP (Stop Taking Our Privileges)-ERA, into which she recruited women who felt marginalized by the feminist upsurge and who were convinced that feminists threatened the moral and social order of the nation. Many of her followers were evangelical Christians who viewed the battle against the ERA as a fight against secular values that were undermining their notion of family values.

A lawyer, an author, and the mother of six, Schlafly maintained a highly public career that contradicted her message, which was that American society was best served and women happiest when they remained full-time housewives and mothers (see box, "What's Wrong with 'Equal Rights' for Women"). She claimed that ratification of the ERA would wreak social chaos by eroding fundamental gender distinctions. Her charge that the ERA would forbid separate men's and women's public toilets got much attention, but her claim that the ERA would extend the draft to women proved more troubling. She also insisted that instead of ending sex discrimination, the ERA would deprive women of crucial privileges such as the expectation of economic support from their husbands. Schlafly's statements put the pro-ERA forces on the defensive. Ironically, many of her concerns, such as women playing a more active role in the armed services (even though they still cannot be drafted), came to pass even with the defeat of the ERA. Despite Schlafly's fears, however, the erosion in the position and status of the housewife was the consequence not of a potential change in the constitution but of underlying economic and social developments.

By lobbying forcefully in crucial state legislatures, STOP-ERA slowed the pace of ratification to a crawl. The National Organization for Women (NOW) fought back by urging feminists to refuse to travel to or do business in states that refused to ratify the ERA, but to no avail. In 1977, Indiana was the thirty-fifth and last state to ratify the amendment. Congress extended the period for ratification by four years, but it made no difference. In 1982, the ERA went down to defeat, three states short of ratification, with both pro- and anti- forces exhausted but also battle-strengthened (see Map 12.1). The contest contributed to a growing sense of a cultural divide in American politics between those with conservative social values, especially concerning women and the family, and those who emphasized individual choice and the importance of federal government protection against discrimination.

From Anti-abortion to Pro-life

The campaign to undo *Roe v. Wade* was not as successful as STOP-ERA and failed to recriminalize abortion, but its impact on the larger political climate was, if anything, greater. To the anti-abortion movement, the legalization of abortion represented the triumph of untrammeled individualism over women's sacred vocation

PHYLLIS SCHLAFLY
What's Wrong with "Equal Rights" for Women

Phyllis Schlafly (b. 1924) began her conservative activism in the 1950s when she fervently embraced the anti-Communist campaign. In the 1970s, she took up the cause of antifeminism and founded the organization STOP-ERA. In this 1972 article published in her own newsletter, The Phyllis Schlafly Report, *Schlafly details her objections to the Equal Rights Amendment and feminism. What are her major reasons for opposing the amendment?*

In the last couple of years, a noisy movement has sprung up agitating for "women's rights." Suddenly, everywhere we are afflicted with aggressive females on television talk shows yapping about how mistreated American women are, suggesting that marriage has put us in some kind of "slavery," that housework is menial and degrading, and—perish the thought—that women are discriminated against. New "women's liberation" organizations are popping up, agitating and demonstrating, serving demands on public officials, getting wide press coverage always, and purporting to speak for some 100,000,000 American women.

It's time to set the record straight. The claim that American women are downtrodden and unfairly treated is the fraud of the century. The truth is that American women never had it so good. Why should we lower ourselves to "equal rights" when we already have the status of special privilege?

The proposed Equal Rights Amendment states: "Equality of rights under the law shall not be denied or abridged by the United States or by any state on account of sex." So what's wrong with that? Well, here are a few examples of what's wrong with it.

This Amendment will absolutely and positively make women subject to the draft. Why any woman would support such a ridiculous and un-American proposal as this is beyond comprehension. Why any Congressman who had any regard for his wife, sister, or daughter would support such a proposition is just as hard to understand. Foxholes are bad enough for men, but they certainly are *not* the place for women—and we should reject any proposal which would put them there in the name of "equal rights." . . .

of motherhood. Opponents staked their ground on the rights of the fetus, framing the women who sought abortions either as murderously selfish or victimized by abortion advocates. To indicate the larger issues at stake, the anti-abortion movement renamed itself "pro-life"—prompting the pro-abortion-rights forces to christen themselves, in equally expansive language, "pro-choice."

Another bad effect of the Equal Rights Amendment is that it will abolish a woman's right to child support and alimony, and substitute what the women's libbers think is a more "equal" policy, that "such decisions should be within the discretion of the Court and should be made on the economic situation and need of the parties in the case."

Under present American laws, the man is *always* required to support his wife and each child he caused to be brought into the world. Why should women abandon these good laws — by trading them for something so nebulous and uncertain as the "discretion of the Court"?

The law now requires a husband to support his wife as best as his financial situation permits, but a wife is not required to support her husband (unless he is about to become a public charge). A husband cannot demand that his wife go to work to help pay for family expenses. He has the duty of financial support under our laws and customs. Why should we abandon these mandatory wife-support and child-support laws so that a wife would have an "equal" obligation to take a job?

By law and custom in America, in case of divorce, the mother always is given custody of her children unless there is overwhelming evidence of mistreatment, neglect or bad character. This is our special privilege because of the high rank that is placed on motherhood in our society. Do women really want to give up this special privilege and lower themselves to "equal rights," so that the mother gets one child and the father gets the other? I think not. . . .

Many women are under the mistaken impression that "women's lib" means more job employment opportunities for women, equal pay for equal work, appointments of women to high positions, admitting more women to medical schools, and other desirable objectives which all women favor. We all support these purposes, as well as any necessary legislation which would bring them about.

But all this is only a sweet syrup which covers the deadly poison masquerading as "women's lib." The women's libbers are radicals who are waging a total assault on the family, on marriage, and on children.

SOURCE: William H. Chafe et al., *A History of Our Time: Readings on Postwar America*, 6th ed. (New York: Oxford University Press, 2003), 211–13. Original source: *The Phyllis Schlafly Report* 5, no. 7 (February 1972), noted as reprinted with permission of the author.

The anti-abortion movement has consistently been based in religious sentiment. It got its start in 1971 when the Catholic Church sponsored the formation of the National Right to Life Committee. A sophisticated media campaign, including films of late-term fetuses in utero and photographs of tiny fetal hands, built popular support. (Pro-choicers retaliated with the image of a wire coat

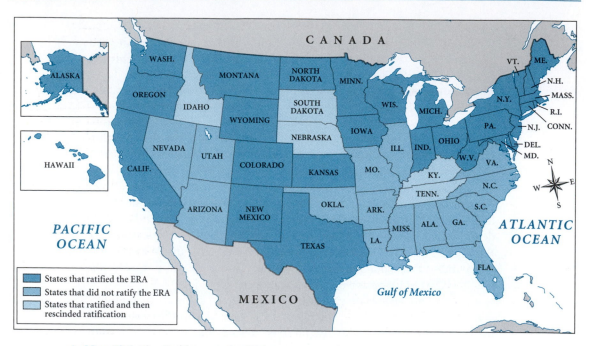

◆ **Map 12.1 The Battle over the ERA**

The ERA quickly won support in 1972 and 1973 but then stalled. ERAmerica, a coalition of women's groups formed in 1976, lobbied extensively, especially in North Carolina, Florida, and Illinois, but failed to sway the conservative legislatures in those states. After Indiana ratified it in 1977, the amendment still lacked three states' votes toward the three-fourths majority required for a constitutional amendment. Subsequent efforts to revive the ERA were unsuccessful.

hanger, to symbolize deaths from illegal abortions.) Starting in the late 1970s, leadership of the anti-abortion movement shifted to fundamentalist Protestants. Although many leaders of right-to-life organizations were male, women dominated the grass roots, with some estimates that they represented 80 percent of the membership. Activists marched in front of abortion clinics that had sprung up since *Roe v. Wade*. They intimidated so many physicians from providing abortions that, in 80 percent of the nation's counties, women lost access to abortion.[1] In 1995, the movement secured a tremendous public relations victory when Norma McCorvey, the Roe of *Roe v. Wade*, renounced her support for abortion (see p. 692). In cities across the country, pro-choicers and pro-lifers engaged in angry face-to-face encounters. Eventually, the heightened rhetoric of the pro-lifers, which characterized legalized abortion as a "holocaust" of unborn babies, spilled into physical violence, as clinics were bombed and abortion providers murdered from Boston to California. Between 1982 and 1997, there were 167 attacks on clinics.

Anti-abortion activists also exerted significant political muscle. In the late 1970s and 1980s, the U.S. Congress and state legislatures started to pass new legal limitations on who could get abortions, when, and under what conditions. These laws required underage girls to obtain parental permission for an abortion, denied public funds for abortion, and mandated waiting periods and elaborate counseling. As cases challenging these laws made their way through the court system, the fate of abortion rights seemed increasingly precarious. In the 1989 *Webster v. Reproductive Health Services* and the 1992 *Planned Parenthood v. Casey* cases, the Supreme Court ruled that many of the restrictions on abortion were constitutional; however, the Court stopped short of overturning *Roe v. Wade* altogether (see the Appendix, p. A-32). Further cases focused on local ordinances forbidding aggressive pro-life picketing at clinics, and a Nebraska law prohibited a late-term abortion procedure known as intact dilation and extraction (but called "partial-birth abortion" by opponents), intended to help pregnant women whose health was in danger and whose physicians were unable or unwilling to pursue the case-by-case exemption required for the procedure. A 5–4 Court majority struck down the Nebraska law in 2000 as placing an "undue burden" on women seeking abortions for health-related reasons.

In the following years, the balance in the Supreme Court shifted as a result of appointments made by President George W. Bush. Conservative John G. Roberts Jr. became chief justice in 2005, and when Sandra Day O'Connor, who consistently refused to overturn *Roe v. Wade*, resigned in 2006, President Bush replaced her with another conservative, Samuel Alito Jr. In 2007, by a mere 5–4 majority, the Supreme Court upheld a 2003 federal law banning intact dilation and extraction. Even more important, the language of the decision seems to invite further challenges to abortion access. Justice Anthony M. Kennedy, writing for the Court, commented that the "respect for human life finds an ultimate expression in the bond of love the mother has for her child," noting that "some women come to regret their choice to abort the infant life they once created and sustained."[2] The debate over abortion is thus likely to continue to be one of the most contentious in American life.

The Fate of Feminism

Simultaneous with the gains that conservatives were making in the late twentieth century against the ERA and abortion rights, a more diffuse antifeminism began to surface. In her best-selling book *Backlash: The Undeclared War on American Women* (1991), Susan Faludi explored claims that circulated widely in the 1980s about the unhappiness and disappointment that women who had chosen feminist lifestyles were allegedly suffering. One particularly inflammatory sociological study, reported in *Newsweek* magazine in 1986, stated that if a woman was over forty and single, her chances for marriage were less than her chances of being killed by a terrorist.[3] Frightening and often exaggerated statistics and news stories also appeared about an infertility "epidemic" among women who delayed childbearing, the economic costs to women of the rising divorce rate, and widespread

◆ **The Abortion Controversy**
Few issues in recent American political life have been more divisive than a woman's right to choose an abortion. Rallies for and against abortion often provoke heated confrontations. Here demonstrators face off in Washington, D.C., in 2005. *Win McNamee/Getty Images.*

psychological depression among unmarried career women. Not only were there no remaining tasks for feminism, according to the backlash mentality, but the movement's achievements had cost women dearly.

But what of organized feminism itself? Major organizations, including NOW, the National Abortion Rights Action League, the National Coalition for Women and Girls in Education, and the Association of American University Women continued to be important lobbying groups for women's causes. Working-class women in and out of unions persisted in the struggle for equity in employment. The feminist agenda was reinforced by policy think tanks, such as the National Council for Research on Women. Just as conservative groups put pressure on the Republican Party, NOW and other feminist lobbying organizations had significant influence among Democrats.

The smaller, more radical women's liberation groups that flourished in the late 1960s and early 1970s had largely disappeared by 1975, in part because of internal dissension. In the 1980s a key issue that provoked much debate among feminists was pornography. One group insisted that, in the words of Robin Morgan, "pornography is the theory, rape is the practice," and supported the drive for antipornography ordinances. Another faction claimed that antipornography activism assisted right-wing attacks on free speech and sexual nonconformity, arguing that images were never the same as acts. Critics such as Lisa Duggan, Nan D. Hunter, and Carole S. Vance maintained that antipornography activists failed to recognize that women "are agents, and not merely victims, who make decisions and act on them and who desire, seek out and enjoy sexuality."[4] Despite these and other passionate disagreements, veterans from the women's liberation movement took their feminism into new channels. Many became academics, teaching and writing about women's issues throughout universities and colleges in the United States. Others became public intellectuals, while many took their commitment to social change into a wide range of progressive causes such as labor activism, shelters and other services for abused women, and, most recently, the peace movement.

Some of the most vital feminist ideas emerged from a flowering in literature among women of color. Following the identity politics approach to women's oppression, the 1981 anthology *This Bridge Called My Back: Writings by Radical Women of Color* brought together the unabashedly feminist writings of Chicana, African American, Native American, and Asian American women. According to editors Cherríe Moraga and Gloria Anzaldúa, "What began as a reaction to the racism of white feminists soon became a positive affirmation of the commitment of women of color to our *own* feminism."[5] The anthology's contributors, many of them lesbians, were not intimidated by the disapproval of men of color, dedicating themselves to the strengthening of bonds between women. While they criticized white feminists for treating them as token symbols of women's universal victimization and for failing to recognize the power and resources that their home cultures provided them, they challenged the sexism and homophobia of their fathers, brothers, husbands, and political comrades. The challenge, according to Japanese American writer Mitsuye Yamada, was to "affirm our own culture while working within it to change it."[6] A further measure of the importance of the feminism of women of color was the tremendous efflorescence in their fiction. The writings of Toni Morrison, Sandra Cisneros, Amy Tan, and Louise Erdrich, among others, played a major role in bringing the feminist message and perspective to the masses of American women.

In the 1990s, a new generation of young women sought to revitalize feminism in the face of the backlash of their era by developing what is sometimes called the "third wave." (See Documents: Feminist Revival in the 1990s, pp. 766–77.) They had learned from the conflicts of the seventies to create much more racially diverse politics. They built on the previous generation's success at combating sexual violence and defending women's right to greater sexual pleasure, and they advanced a more consistently positive approach to female sexuality. All this was important as the controversies over the character and direction of modern women's lives were becoming central to national politics.

◆ **Gloria Anzaldúa**

Poet, writer, and cultural theorist Gloria Anzaldúa was one of the first openly lesbian Chicana writers. Coeditor with Cherríe Moraga of the now-classic multicultural anthology *This Bridge Called My Back*, and author of the pathbreaking *Borderlands/La Frontera: The New Mestiza* (see Documents: Feminist Revival in the 1990s, pp. 766–77), she was instrumental in revisioning feminism to embrace the concerns of lesbians and women of color. She died in 2004. *Photo copyright © by Annie Valva.*

WOMEN AND POLITICS

The backlash against feminism and the culture wars symbolized by the battles over the ERA and abortion put the women's movement on the defensive. Nevertheless, a wide variety of feminist groups have kept women's issues a vital part of national, especially presidential, politics over the last thirty years. Despite the expansion of the New Right's conservative power, women's political influence continued to grow and individual women achieved high visibility as national leaders in Congress, the presidential cabinet, and the Supreme Court. The dramatic impact of the terrorist attacks against the United States on September 11, 2001, as well as the subsequent American-led attacks against the Taliban in Afghanistan and the regime of Saddam Hussein in Iraq, have also had significant implications for women at home and abroad and have prompted some women's increased military service and others' antiwar activism.

The Reagan Era

Feminists were lukewarm to the presidency of Democrat Jimmy Carter (1977–1981). A social conservative, Carter was unsympathetic to the pro-choice movement and supported the law banning the use of federal funds for abortions. But Carter also appointed feminist Bella Abzug to head the planning commission for the 1977 International Women's Conference in Houston, Texas, and his wife, Rosalynn, a proponent of the ERA, attended. Even more important, his appointment of civil rights veteran Eleanor Holmes Norton (see pp. 686, 687) to head the Equal Employment Opportunity Commission led to a significant increase in the federal government's commitment to challenging the workplace discrimination faced by minority men and by women.

The election of Ronald Reagan in 1980, however, promised to throw more obstacles in the path of feminists' efforts to promote their agenda on the national stage. Reagan had campaigned with the promise "to get the government off our backs"—a reaction to the Great Society of Lyndon Johnson and its expansion of a welfare state and increased federal regulatory powers. In particular, his administration went on the offensive against government support for feminist programs. After an extensive battle in which feminist politicians fought back, the Reagan administration succeeded in marginalizing the Women's Education Action Project within the Department of Education, which had promoted programs that addressed discrimination in education. More significant was that Reagan filled leadership vacancies on the Commission on Civil Rights and the Equal Employment Opportunity Commission by appointing men who opposed the mandate of those agencies to address past discrimination on the grounds of race or sex. Reagan's budget cuts—he trimmed federal agencies' resources by 12 percent—also dismayed feminists as federal programs to assist poor women and children shrank during his presidency.

Catering to pressure from the New Right, Reagan endorsed an amendment to make abortion unconstitutional. Among his many friendly gestures to the pro-life movement was the 1988 announcement of an Emancipation Proclamation of Preborn Children declaring his support for the extension of "unalienable personhood" from the moment of conception. His administration also pursued continued cuts in public funding for abortions for poor women and blocked organizations that received federal funds from counseling women about abortion. During his administration, "pregnancy crisis centers"—which often misleadingly presented themselves as abortion clinics to deflect women away from real clinics while counseling them to carry their pregnancy to term—began to receive public funds. Today there are more of these centers in the United States than there are abortion providers.

Yet Reagan disappointed his New Right backers when he appointed the first woman justice to the Supreme Court, Sandra Day O'Connor, in 1981. To the growing consternation of many opponents of abortion, over the twenty-seven years of her term on the court, O'Connor often cast the swing vote in abortion cases, usually upholding the constitutionality of numerous restrictions but not voting against the essential holding in *Roe v. Wade*, that women's constitutionally protected right to privacy included the right to choose an abortion. From this point on, every major presidential candidate had to take a position on abortion, with Republicans generally favoring the pro-life side and Democrats the pro-choice.

Supreme Court nominations became key in the battle over abortion and other issues affecting American women. One of the most dramatic fights took place in 1991, when Reagan's vice president and successor, President George H. W. Bush, nominated Clarence Thomas to fill the seat vacated by the great civil rights leader Thurgood Marshall. Thomas had been Reagan's Equal Employment Opportunity Commission (EEOC) chairman and had already established his conservative credentials by his hostility to affirmative action. During the nomination process, Anita Hill—like Thomas, an African American lawyer—charged that Thomas had sexually harassed her when they worked together at the EEOC. Television audiences sat riveted while Hill told intimate and embarrassing details of Thomas's unwanted sexual advances before the entirely male Senate Judiciary Committee. Thomas angrily denied the charges and claimed that he was being subjected to a "high-tech lynching for uppity blacks." The senators, unwilling to appreciate the gravity of Hill's charges, voted in favor of Thomas, who went on to become one of the Court's most consistently conservative and anti-abortion justices.

The Thomas-Hill incident catapulted the issue of sexual harassment into public consciousness. In the wake of the hearings, national polls confirmed the widespread experience of sexual harassment on the job, with four of ten women saying that they had faced unwanted sexual advances from men at work. The Thomas-Hill incident also contributed to the growing power and assertiveness of women in electoral politics. In the 1992 elections, the number of women elected to the U.S. Senate increased from three to seven, and Carol Moseley Braun, an Illinois state legislator, became the first African American woman elected to the Senate. In the same election, female membership in the House of Representatives rose from thirty to forty-eight. The figures have been steadily rising ever since.

Building a Coalition of Women

While the Thomas-Hill hearings may have facilitated the 1992 election of more women to Congress, another crucial factor was the growing sophistication of women's political networking and fund-raising. In 1981, the Congresswomen's Caucus, hamstrung by the refusal of many Republican women to join after Reagan's election, re-formed as the Congressional Committee for Women's Issues and expanded its membership to men, one hundred of whom joined, helping to make it one of the largest caucuses in Congress. Outside of Congress, lobbying groups, such as the National Women's Political Caucus, continued to be important vehicles for promoting women's issues. The Women's Campaign Fund became especially active in the 1980s, not only providing funds and training candidates but also working on the "pipeline" approach to identify congressional seats where women had a good chance of being elected. Then, in 1984, African American women created the National Political Congress of Black Women to address political issues of specific concern to African Americans. The following year, Ellen

◆ Congresswomen on the March
The October 1991 Senate hearings to confirm Clarence Thomas to the Supreme Court highlighted not only the issue of sexual harassment but also the persistent under-representation of women in Congress. The Senate had only two women members, and the committee that heard Hill's testimony was entirely male. On October 9, seven female members of the House of Representatives, enraged by the treatment that Hill was receiving in the "men's club" atmosphere of the hearings, marched up the Capitol steps to demand that the Senate delay the hearings and investigate Hill's charges. The delegation was led by Barbara Boxer of California, who a year later became a U.S. senator. *Paul Hosefros/NYT Pictures.*

Malcolm founded Emily's List — "Emily" being an acronym for "Early Money Is Like Yeast" — to provide seed money for pro-choice women candidates. It claimed several notable successes, including the senatorial election of Barbara Mikulski (D-Maryland) in 1986. At the state and local levels, many organizations focused on women of color and campaigned in support of women's issues and women candidates. By the end of the decade, women held 15.5 percent of the seats in state legislatures, a fourfold increase since 1969. Following the election of 2006, women holding office in the United States included 16 senators (16 percent), 86 congressional representatives (16.1 percent), 9 governors (18 percent), and 1,681 state legislators (23 percent).

Women's political activism grew alongside a powerful new recognition of the importance of female voters. In the 1980s, more than sixty years after women won the right to vote, a female voting bloc had finally emerged, with women more likely to vote Democratic and men Republican.[7] "The gravitation of men and women to different political camps appears to be the outstanding demographic development in American politics over the past twenty years," claimed the *Atlantic Monthly* in 1996.[8] Men and women evidenced basic differences not only over feminist issues but over the general role of government, especially with respect to social services, with women favoring more and men favoring less.

In the 1992 election, women supported Democratic candidate Bill Clinton over Republican president George H. W. Bush, but only by a few percentage points. During his first administration, Clinton's strength among women voters grew. Betty Ford and Rosalynn Carter had supported the ERA when they were First Ladies, but Hillary Rodham Clinton was America's first First Lady to have worked full-time for a living. To supporters, but even more to opponents, the Clintons as individuals and as a couple embodied the massive changes that had taken place in America's gender and marital practices over the last quarter century. Among the women President Clinton appointed to prominent federal offices was Madeleine Albright, who as secretary of state became the highest-ranked female cabinet member to that point in history. For the Supreme Court's second female member, Clinton chose women's rights litigator Ruth Bader Ginsburg (see p. 687). In the 1996 presidential election, the female vote for a second Clinton administration was eleven points higher than the male vote.

Then, in 1998, President Clinton became embroiled in a scandal over a sexual affair with a twenty-two-year-old White House intern named Monica Lewinsky. On the grounds that he had publicly lied about the relationship, he became the second president in American history (after Andrew Johnson in 1868) to be tried on articles of impeachment. Feminism played a complicated, even ironic, role in this episode. Although many previous presidents had been notorious adulterers, thirty years of feminism had called into question the long-standing assumption that men in power could engage in extramarital sex with impunity, and the proponents of impeachment made ample use of this new revulsion at the double standard. Nonetheless, in striking contrast to the position most feminist groups had taken on the Thomas-Hill affair, they stood by Clinton, probably because of his consistent defense of abortion rights and other women's issues.

The first president of the twenty-first century, George W. Bush, pursued a mixed path with respect to women in politics. Far more than his Republican predecessors—Ronald Reagan and his father, George H. W. Bush—George W. Bush was closely allied with the religious right. An evangelical Protestant, he tailored his rhetoric to appeal to the "pro-family" lobby. During his administration, in small and large ways, he wore away at abortion rights, including the withdrawal of $34 million in congressionally authorized funds from United Nations family planning programs, claiming that the money would facilitate the availability of abortions to women around the world. His opposition to research involving stem cells derived from fetal tissue, a position strongly held by the pro-life movement, proved particularly controversial because of its interference with scientific breakthroughs in the treatment of diabetes, Alzheimer's, and other diseases. His appointments to the federal bench and the Supreme Court overwhelmingly included pro-life advocates. Yet Bush nominated a significant number of women for important government positions, including the courts. One of his closest aides was Condoleezza Rice, a black woman who held the role of national security adviser in his first administration and who in his second term became secretary of state, the second woman and first African American woman to hold that position.

A New Kind of War: 9/11 and Its Aftermath

National security issues moved to center stage on September 11, 2001, when extremists from a terrorist group calling itself al-Qaeda hijacked four commercial airliners. Two of the planes destroyed the World Trade Center in New York City, another seriously damaged the Pentagon, and a fourth crashed in a Pennsylvania field. Among the more than three thousand people who died were women such as CeeCee Lyles and Debby Welse, flight attendants who apparently joined passengers in bringing down the fourth plane before it could be flown into its probable target: the White House or the Capitol building. The United States went to war against Afghanistan in October 2001, justifying its decision primarily because the ruling group, the Taliban, had harbored al-Qaeda leaders. A side note to the decision was the Taliban's barbaric treatment of Afghan women, to which women's groups in the United States had been trying to draw attention for some time. Few permanent gains for Afghan women have emerged during the U.S. war against Afghanistan, and the Taliban has continued to be a major force both in that nation and in fueling terrorism abroad.

Less than two years after the opening attack on Afghanistan, President Bush announced the need for a preemptive strike on Iraq, a country he claimed (misleadingly, it turned out) had weapons of mass destruction and links to al-Qaeda. The war in Iraq, which began in March 2003, was condemned by U.S. allies abroad but widely supported in the United States. But although Bush proclaimed an end to major combat operations in May 2003, actual victory remained elusive. The war became a bloody battle between U.S. forces and insurgents, and helped fuel a continuing civil war among Iraqis. As with Afghanistan, the administration's promise that Iraqi women would have increased rights under a new U.S.-backed government has been disappointing. Many opponents have likened the Iraq war to the quagmire of Vietnam, and, after 2005, public opinion polls increasingly called for an end to U.S. involvement. As of March 2008, almost 4,000 Americans had been killed in Iraq; approximately 65 of them were women.

The war in Iraq has affected women in diverse ways. The instability of the country has created health and safety crises for all Iraqis; women in particular fear rape, kidnapping, and even murder at the hand of religious extremists. Although the new Iraqi constitution provides that women hold at least one-quarter of the seats of the national assembly, in other ways women's rights freedoms have contracted. Despite the repressive quality of the dictatorship of Saddam Hussein, the secular Iraqi government had permitted women access to education and professional jobs and allowed for their freedom of movement. The new regime is heavily influenced by radical Muslim fundamentalists, and there has been increased pressure on women to return to a subordinate position in the home. The new constitution permits local religious sects to oversee family courts, and the implications of this have alarmed many women's rights activists. Outside the home, women increasingly find it necessary to wear headscarves and long skirts and to avoid driving cars, attending schools, or speaking out for women's rights. Safia Taleb al-Suhail, who had been George and Laura Bush's guest at the president's State of the Union address in 2005 as a representative of the "new Iraq," later criticized the increased repression against women: "When we came back from exile, we thought we were going to improve rights and the position of women. . . . But look what has happened—we have lost all the gains we made over the last 30 years. It's a big disappointment."[9]

The Iraq war has affected American women in a number of ways, especially women in the military. Women first began to serve in large numbers in a military action in positions other than nurses during the U.S.–Iraq Desert Storm war of 1990–91, when the United States intervened after Iraq invaded Kuwait over access to an important oil-producing area. In that short war, women constituted 11 percent of the soldiers, serving as mechanics, transport pilots, and in other noncombat support positions. Although officially barred from combat, they undertook support work that routinely exposed them to danger: thirteen women died during Desert Storm.

Conservative critics of women's participation in the war zone tried to block women's full access to military training and careers. By 2007, regulations had

◆ Lori Piestewa

Despite regulations that strictly limit women's ability to participate in armed combat, American military women are fighting and dying in the nation's wars. Private Lori Piestewa, a Hopi woman, was in a maintenance unit of the U.S. Quartermaster Corps serving in Iraq when the truck she was driving was ambushed. Piestewa's friend, Private Jessica Lynch, became a national hero when she was captured by Iraqi forces and later rescued by the U.S. military (see Visual Sources: American Women in the World, pp. 778–93). Piestewa died in the attack, making her the first known Native American woman to die in combat on foreign soil. *El Paso Times.*

changed to allow women in combat aviation and on naval ships but still techni-cally excluded them from ground combat and the use of offensive weapons. Nonetheless, women made up a significant proportion of the troops in Iraq—roughly one in seven—and the nature of the fighting exposed them to consider-able danger. Ironically, considering the attention paid to military women's vulner-ability to the enemy, one of their most serious problems is sexual harassment, including rape, from their fellow soldiers.

Male colleagues are often verbally abusive as well, accusing women soldiers of being promiscuous, homosexual, or both. The lesbian label, freighted with meaning, is intended to devalue all women soldiers as deviant. And because the military bars open homosexuals from service through the "don't ask, don't tell" policy, the designation "lesbian" can be dangerous for a woman who wants to stay in the armed services. For lesbians, military service to their country requires for-going the relative freedom ushered in by the gay rights and feminist movements. As one graduate of the U.S. Military Academy expressed it, "I cannot understand why the institution would adopt a regulation that asks me to lie about myself, at the same time that it asks of me exacting standards of integrity and moral courage. There is nothing courageous about the closet."[10] Ironically, despite the significant political power of conservatives in contemporary America, many military leaders are calling for lifting the ban on gays in the armed services, in part because of the need for military personnel to serve in Iraq.

On the home front, some women, most notably Condoleezza Rice, have been active in supporting the war while others have been active in opposing it. The most publicized female critic has been Cindy Sheehan, whose son Casey died in Iraq in April 2004. Sheehan set up a "peace camp" on the outskirts of President Bush's Crawford, Texas, ranch and vowed to stay there until Bush agreed to meet with her. Given the moniker "peace mom," Sheehan emphasized the cost to Amer-ican families who had lost their sons and daughters in Iraq, but she also made spe-cific criticisms of Bush's war policy. After two years, she gave up her encampment without achieving her goal of meeting with the president, but she remains active in the antiwar movement. One women's activist group is Code Pink, which started on the eve of the Iraq invasion and calls itself a grassroots social justice movement of women. It has organized petitions, demonstrations, and humanitarian aid to Iraq. NOW came out against the war early as well and, like Code Pink, views its antiwar sentiment in the context of a sense of sisterhood with women all over the world. As one NOW document put it, "[W]omen bear additional personal costs in patriarchal wars that ruin their country's physical infrastructure, destabilize their economy, destroy their homes and kill and maim children and families."[11] (See Documents: Feminist Revival in the 1990s, pp. 766–77.)

In the presidential election of 2004, a majority of the American public still supported the goals of the Iraq war. Democratic Party candidate John Kerry largely agreed with President Bush on the need to protect the nation from terror-ism and to win the war in Iraq, but he argued for a more multilateral approach. The shadow of the sixties loomed over the election, owing to Kerry's role as a founder of the antiwar group Vietnam Veterans Against the War. Kerry's antiwar activities became tied to a perceived "culture war" between conservatives and liberals as the two candidates took opposing sides on a number of issues, including abortion. They also sparred over the legalization of gay marriage, with Bush supporting a constitutional amendment that would restrict marriage to two people of the opposite sex, and Kerry opposing such an amendment, with the argument that the matter should be left to the states to decide.

Public attention to gay marriage exploded in 2003 when the Massachusetts Supreme Court held that same-sex couples were entitled to the "protections, benefits, and obligations of civil marriage." Then, in early 2004, officials in a number of states, including New York, California, and Oregon, began performing highly publicized gay marriages. In August 2004, responding to a state law that restricted marriage to opposite-sex partnerships, the California Supreme Court voided the nearly four thousand marriages performed in San Francisco. In May 2008, the court declared the law unconstitutional. The gay-marriage issue galvanized conservatives throughout the United States. In the 2004 election, referenda banning the practice passed in eleven states, including Ohio, where the issue helped to bring out voters who voted for Bush. In 2008, California will vote for or against a state constitutional amendment banning same-sex marriage.

Pundits quickly assessed Bush's election as a reflection of the so-called culture wars in America and of the growing political clout of religious conservatives. Others have argued that concerns about terrorism and the need to prosecute the war in Iraq were the determinants in Bush's victory. Women political commentators, ranging from Barbara Ehrenreich on the left to Ann Coulter on the right, emerged as a new feature of the political scene. Two years later, however, in the 2006 elections, public sentiment had changed dramatically. Growing discontent over the war, domestic scandals involving White House officials, and the federal government's mishandling of the relief efforts of the devastating 2005 Hurricane Katrina led to an extraordinary victory for the Democratic Party, which succeeded in winning a majority in both houses in Congress. Ten of the new representatives and two of the senators were women. Perhaps more significant was that Californian Nancy Pelosi became the first woman majority leader and Speaker of the House of Representatives, which placed her second in line of presidential succession after the vice president.

Despite the significant successes of women in politics, the nation's top offices, the presidency and vice presidency, remained elusive. In 1972 Shirley Chisholm was the first African American to make a meaningful bid for her party's presidential nomination and in 1984 Geraldine Ferraro unsuccessfully ran for vice president, but until 2008 neither party had seriously considered nominating a woman candidate for president. In her campaign for the 2008 Democratic Party presidential nomination, New York Senator Hillary Clinton dramatically challenged the political "glass ceiling." Throughout the primary season, Clinton and Illinois Senator Barack Obama were locked in a tight and contentious race for the Democratic presidential nomination, with their delegate count so close that many observers thought that the nomination would not be decided until the national convention in August 2008. In June, however, Obama won a majority of delegates and

◆ The Most Powerful Women in American Government

One measure of the increased political influence of American women in recent decades is the growing number of women in powerful government positions. Condoleezza Rice, pictured at left, became President George W. Bush's national security adviser in 2001 and in 2005 became the second woman and second African American to be secretary of state. San Franciscan Nancy Pelosi, pictured at right, has served in the House of Representatives since 1987 and became Speaker of the House when the Democrats gained control of that body in 2007. In the center is Senator Hillary Rodham Clinton. Clinton, wife of former president Bill Clinton, played a highly visible role in her husband's presidency and went on to become a U.S. senator from New York in 2000. Clinton serves on the powerful Senate Armed Services Committee and a front-runner for the Democratic presidential nomination for 2008. *Left: Pool/epa/CORBIS. Center: Ted Soqui/CORBIS. Right: Congressional Quarterly/Getty Images.*

clinched the nomination. Meanwhile, Clinton won the popular vote in the primary contest, garnering over 18 million votes and precipitating a concentrated female presence in electoral politics which even she did not anticipate. The election will be historic, as Obama stands poised to be the nation's first African American president. The low approval rating of President George W. Bush and Americans' worries about the unpopular war in Iraq, national security, and a serious economic recession could seriously hamper the appeal of Republican candidate John McCain, and give the Democrats and Obama the edge.

The contest between Clinton and Obama raised troubling questions, with the Clinton and Obama campaigns trading charges of sexism and racism, in a conflict reminiscent of the Stanton/Douglass disagreements over the Fourteenth Amendment (see pp. 327–28). Despite Clinton's Senate experience, the active role she took in the presidency of husband Bill Clinton, and her forceful campaign style, pundits talked about her clothing and speculated about how she responded to key events — charging her with lack of emotion in some cases and too many tears in others. For both candidates, the issues were at times subsumed by questioning about whether the American people are ready to elect either a woman or an African American to the presidency.

WOMEN'S LIVES IN MODERN AMERICA AND THE WORLD

While feminism and the conservative backlash against it provide an essential framework for understanding the recent history of American women, indeed of American politics and culture in general, they have not been the only engines of change. The modern feminist movement was as much a response to deep social changes affecting women as it was a cause of those changes, especially the maturation of the female labor force and corresponding shifts in American family life. Further, developments in the market that had transformed women's lives within the United States reverberated globally by the end of the millennium. Within the United States, changing immigration patterns and increased globalization turned the dramatic changes in and shifting expectations about American women's lives into a significant worldwide phenomenon.

Women in the Labor Force

For almost two centuries, the numbers and percentages of women in the labor force have been rising steadily, but in the last third of the twentieth century, this steady quantitative change was accompanied by a dramatic qualitative change. This development took place in the context of broad economic transformations, beginning with the move abroad of much of America's manufacturing sector to be replaced by a labor force of service workers and a rapidly growing high-tech sector. Between 1970 and 2000, employment rates, stock market averages, and average incomes went up and down, while inequality of wealth increased. By 1996, the United States was the most economically stratified industrial nation in the world. It was in this context that the place of work in women's lives was undergoing major alterations. By 1990, women constituted almost half of paid labor, drawn into the workforce by economic pressures as well as by shifting attitudes and practices. The working mother was now the norm (see the Appendix, p. A-38).

From one perspective, women workers were moving in the direction of equality with men. The median wage for full-time women workers increased from 62 percent of men's average earnings in 1969 to 80 percent in 2006. The wage gap between white and black women also narrowed, although the combined impact of race, ethnicity, and gender left black women earning 68 percent and Hispanic women 58 percent of the average earnings of white men. Asian women, by contrast, earned the most income among women: the ratio of Asian women's earnings to white men's was 92 percent. In the professions, the infusion of women was stunning. The percentage of medical degrees awarded to women jumped from 7 percent in 1966 to 49 percent in 2006, and the percentage of law degrees increased from 4 percent to 49 percent in that same period. By the turn of the twenty-first century, women were the majority of graduates in veterinary medicine and pharmacy programs. Even in the corporate world, the substantial barrier against women in high positions, called the "glass ceiling" because it was invisible until hit, began to give way. The percentage of major corporations with female executives quintupled from 5 percent in 1970 to 25 percent in 2002. The narrowing of the gender gap in wages reflected both women's gains and men's losses as the number of high-paying jobs in the skilled manufacturing sector, in which men predominated, declined significantly.

Examined more closely, however, the experience of working women has been decidedly mixed. While barriers were falling in male-dominated occupations and professions, the vast majority of women continued to work in female-dominated jobs. These sectors of the labor force generally pay less and thus help increase the disparity between men's and women's earnings. In 2005, 75 percent of clerical and administrative support jobs, 90 percent of private household labor, and almost

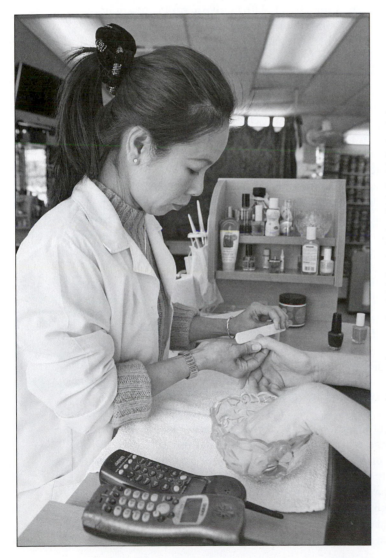

◆ **Los Angeles Manicurist**

As was the case in the nineteenth century, many immigrant women today cluster in specific occupations. Vietnamese women working as manicurists have helped to transform the personal service industry. Often working with family members and pooling resources, their innovation was the stand-alone manicure salon featuring low-cost manicures and pedicures, making these services affordable to a broad spectrum of American women (and some men). This photograph is of May Nguyen in her shop in Los Angeles, California. Sponsored by her sister who fled Vietnam in 1975, Nguyen came to California in 1995. A disciplined and ambitious woman who feels she is living the American dream, she works six days a week, nine hours a day, and attends classes to become a licensed esthetician. She was featured in a 2006 article published in the *International Herald Tribune* entitled "From L.A.'s Glitter, a Newcomer Seeks Gold." *Marissa Roth/IHT/Redux.*

90 percent of institutional health care service work continued to be performed by women. As one observer wrote, "[F]or women and men to be equally represented throughout all occupations in the economy today, 53 out of every 100 workers would have to change jobs."[12]

For women seeking to break into male-dominated fields, the agitation of feminists in NOW, the Women's Equity Action League, labor unions, and other organizations was crucial. In addition to focusing on legislation such as the 1964 Civil Rights Act to make their case for ending discrimination, women also seized on affirmative action programs, which had emerged as a major resource in 1971. Not only the federal government but also state and local governments, private corporations, and universities instituted affirmative action plans to qualify more women and minorities for professional employment. Affirmative action campaigns also opened up jobs in steel factories, construction trades, and police and fire departments (see pp. 686–88). A measure of the impact of these programs was the political and legal reaction against them. In 1978, the Supreme Court ruled in *University of California Regents v. Bakke* that race—and by implication gender—could be used as one of many criteria for admission to the University of California but that an affirmative action "quota" was unconstitutional (see the Appendix, p. A-33).

Dismantling affirmative action programs, which were recast as "reverse discrimination," became a major plank of the conservative Republican platform. In 2003, the Supreme Court continued to walk a narrow line, ruling that the University of Michigan Law School could consider race among other factors in admissions but that the undergraduate admission ranking, which awarded points to underrepresented racial groups, was unconstitutional. Three years later, Michigan voters passed a referendum that amended the state constitution to ban affirmative action programs "that give preferential treatment to groups or individuals based on their race, gender, color, ethnicity or national original for public employment, education or contracting purposes." Similar referenda had already passed in several other states, while still other states continued campaigns against affirmative action. As conservatives came to dominate the Supreme Court, affirmative action nationwide faced serious challenges in the twenty-first century, with widespread implications for women of all races and minority men.

Activists have also had mixed success in efforts to improve wages for women in female-dominated occupations. As late as the 1980s, jobs predominantly held by women were paid close to 30 percent less than those in which men were the majority. "Comparable worth" advocates proposed rectifying this inequity by systematically upgrading the pay rates of female-dominated job classifications. Despite repeated efforts in the late 1970s and throughout the 1980s by a vigorous coalition of feminist groups, labor groups such as the Coalition of Labor Union Women (see p. 667), and mainstream women's organizations, Congress failed to pass national legislation to promote pay equity for women. Some state and city governments instituted pay equity programs throughout the 1980s, but these advances stalled in the face of numerous court challenges. The pay gap between men and women, which had been narrowing in the last quarter of the twentieth century, started to widen again in the years of the George W. Bush presidency.

Labor unions, especially those in the clerical and service sectors, also became resources for women in female-dominated industries. Union membership in general declined sharply in this era, in part because of hostile Republican administrations and in part because of the shrinkage of jobs — mostly held by men — in heavy industry sectors that employed large numbers of union workers. Yet women's representation in organized labor rose from 19 percent in 1962 to 43 percent in 2006. Groups of female workers that were never before considered candidates for unionization formed militant labor organizations that took male labor leaders by surprise. The Association of Flight Attendants, formed in 1973 (see pp. 701–02) and accepted into the AFL-CIO in 1984, successfully fought demeaning aspects of the flight attendant's job such as age and weight requirements and the title of "airline hostess." Clerical workers also unionized, and nurses were a particularly militant group of new union members in this period.

In the 1980s and 1990s, unions in the service sector and public employment benefited by the growth in female unionization, especially among women of color, and saw a significant increase in female leadership. The Service Employees

◆ **Justice for Janitors**
The Service Employees International Union commissioned Los Angeles artist Irene Carranza to produce this image for the Houston, Texas, Justice for Janitors campaign that sought to organize over five thousand workers, mostly Latinas, in 2006. What aspects of these working women's lives does Carranza emphasize? *Courtesy of SEIU.*

International Union (SEIU) and the American Federation of State, County and Municipal Employees (AFSCME) played a particularly active role in promoting issues of concern to women, including bargaining for comparable worth. In 1983, a successful AFSCME strike against the City of San Jose, California, resulted in a $1.5 million payout to over eight hundred employees (70 percent of whom were women). In 1988, members of the Harvard Union of Clerical and Technical Workers, allied with AFSCME, won a seventeen-year battle to organize clerical workers at Harvard University. However, despite significant gains, especially for clerical workers, nurses, teachers, and other public employees, unions have faced significant challenges from employer intransigence and a hostile political climate. As one scholar has noted, "Labor feminists had increased their numbers and leadership in a class movement that was rapidly declining in power and prestige."[13] Today, perhaps the most vital area of union activity is among immigrant workers, many of whom are women, in local grassroots militancy in the low-wage sectors of food and cleaning service work (see Figure 12.3, p. 781).

Changes in Family and Personal Life

The tremendous growth in women's labor force participation led to profound changes in women's family and personal lives. Lifelong marriage became far less common as a goal and as an experience among women in the last third of the twentieth century than it had ever been. One historian refers to this as the "disestablishment" of the institution of marriage in favor of the "pluralization" of sexual and familial arrangements.[14] With women's increasing capacity for self-support and the widespread acceptability of cohabitation among unmarried couples, the rates of marriage declined. The divorce rate rose steeply to the point at which one out of every two marriages ended in divorce (although most divorced people remarried). By the late 1990s, only one out of four households in the United States included a married couple. The greatest shift was among those who had never married, with three times as many women unmarried in 1998 as in 1970.° The numbers of African American women who never married was fifteen to twenty percentage points higher than in the general population.

The increasing acceptability of lesbianism was an important element in the growing numbers of unmarried women. Formal statistics on numbers of lesbians are almost impossible to come by, but the 2000 census included approximately 5.5 million same-sex couples of both sexes. Particularly striking was the dramatic growth in visibility of gay families. Lesbians were mothers to children born during prior heterosexual marriages, to adopted children, to children fathered by male (often gay) friends, and to children conceived through artificial insemination.

Civil rights remain a pressing issue for lesbian activists, who share with gay men a concern about employment and health care. Lesbians particularly struggle

---

° The actual percentage varies depending on the age cohort. Thus, for women ages thirty to thirty-four, 21.6 percent have never married, while for women ages thirty-five to forty, the percentage goes down to 14.3 percent.

◆ **Lesbian Marriage Ceremony**
The battle over gay marriage and civil unions between same-sex couples has proved a divisive issue in American politics and society. Despite the legal conflicts, thousands of lesbian and gay couples have taken vows in states that allow gays marriage or civil unions. This photo depicts the ceremony performed in San Francisco on February 12, 2004, when Del Martin, eighty-three, and Phyllis Lyon, seventy-nine, two of the founders of the lesbian-advocacy group Daughters of Bilitis, were pronounced "spouses for life." This marriage was voided later that year by state high court ruling. On June 16, 2008, after the law against same-sex marriage in California was ruled unconstitutional, Martin and Lyon, now eighty-seven and eight-four, again married in San Francisco. *Courtesy of the* San Francisco Chronicle.

over family issues—the rights to keep custody of and to adopt children, to gain employment benefits routinely offered to married heterosexuals, and to enjoy the full privileges of marriage for their own committed relationships. Many large employers have begun to offer partner benefits such as health insurance, and over two hundred cities have enacted ordinances that prohibit discrimination based on sexual preference in employment and housing. While only two states (Massachusetts and California) acknowledge gay marriages as of this writing, other states permit civil unions or domestic partners. In addition, some states and localities have expanded their antidiscrimination ordinances to include the rights of transgendered persons. Nonetheless, the movement for an expansion of civil rights has been limited by the significant backlash against gays.

Marriage was changing not only among lesbians. There was also considerable change among heterosexual married couples, largely as a result of women's growing labor force participation. As young women concentrated on jobs and careers, the average age at which they married rose to 25.1 in 2002, the highest in American history. By the late 1990s, the majority of married couples included two wage earners, the wife as well as the husband. Increasingly the dual-income marriage was replacing the male-breadwinner structure as the most reliable way for a family to improve its standard of living.

The decline in marriage as a way of life pointed in two quite different directions for women, depending on economic status. At the upper end of the income ladder, single women were able to support themselves, engage in sexual relationships, become homeowners, and have children. As early feminist calls for publicly funded child care went unheeded, women in professional, corporate, and managerial jobs turned to low-wage women to care for their children, clean their homes, and tend to their aging parents. A century-long decline in the private domestic sector was dramatically reversed.

At the lower end, women supporting themselves and their children on a single female income found themselves much poorer. Female-headed families were six times as likely to be living below the poverty level as two-parent families. Observers disagreed on how to deal with this development, which sociologists labeled "the feminization of poverty." Conservatives mounted a national campaign to revive marriage and bring men's wages back into women's lives, while liberals called for higher wages for women and better access to social services.

Childbearing and childrearing also underwent significant change. Women had fewer children, had them later, had more of them outside of marriage, and were more likely never to have them at all. In 1998, one out of five women in their midforties was childless, twice the rate of two decades earlier. Increasingly, the functions of childbearing and childrearing were being separated from marriage, so that neither was a prerequisite for the other. Women were more likely to marry without having children and more likely to have children without marrying. In 2002 one out of three children in the United States was born to an unmarried mother. Although much attention was paid to pregnancies among unmarried teens, in fact their numbers were declining while the numbers of adult women who were having children outside of marriage were rising. Unmarried motherhood was still much more common among African American women, but the rate among white women was gaining.

The growth in single motherhood and female-headed households took place as funds for social services, on which the poorest of these women relied, were being reduced. The welfare rights movement of the late 1960s had encouraged poor women to regard federal welfare programs, especially Aid to Families with Dependent Children (AFDC), as entitlements. By the mid-1970s, 3.6 million families, or more than 5 percent of the American population, relied on AFDC. This program had been designed in the 1930s when stay-at-home motherhood was the standard, but American attitudes had changed dramatically, no longer assuming that mothers had to be kept at home with their children. As working mothers became the norm, AFDC became problematic and poor single mothers on welfare became political targets.

The attack on AFDC, begun in the Reagan years, culminated in 1996 when President Clinton signed the Personal Responsibility and Work Opportunities Act, claiming to "end welfare as we know it." The law limited to five years the time that poor women and children could receive federal welfare assistance. By 2000, the welfare rolls had been cut in half. Poor single mothers were now required to take any job available to them, no matter how low the pay; most of these jobs lacked any health benefits to replace the federal programs from which these families had been removed. Overall, more women were in the labor force but were not out of poverty. In 2003, census data indicated that one-fifth of all homes headed by working single mothers were below the poverty line of approximately $18,000 in annual income.

Poor women faced special challenges, but modern mothering was difficult for working women at all economic levels. The problem of balancing home and work life became the most persistent and difficult personal dilemma for many American women. As one historian writes, "Women remain caught between a world of work, which assumes that there is someone behind every worker who is available to take care of family needs, and the tenacious presumption that women have primary responsibility for children and household."[15] Only at the higher end of the economic scale did working mothers turn to paid nannies to care for their children in their own homes. The children of most working mothers were cared for by the children's fathers, their grandparents, formal or informal family day care providers, or day care centers. In contrast to the mothers of the 1950s, who were discontent because they spent too much time at home raising children, late twentieth-century mothers worried about their divided lives, about not having enough time with their children, and about falling behind at the workplace.

Women and the New Immigration

The last third of the twentieth century saw important changes in the racial and ethnic composition of American womanhood. In 1965 Congress passed the Immigration and Nationality Act. This law opened up the gates of immigration closed since 1924; it also shifted from quotas based on countries of origin to categories based on occupational skills, family ties, and political refugee status. For the first time in over forty years, large numbers of immigrants began to flow into the United States (see the Appendix, p. A-40). Many new immigrants lacked formal immigration papers, either because they overstayed temporary visas or because they crossed into the country without papers in the first place. One estimate is that in 2004 there were 10 million so-called undocumented immigrants in the United States.[16]

From a gendered perspective, post-1965 immigration differed dramatically from earlier waves, in particular the massive immigration between 1880 and 1920 (see pp. 403–10). By 1995, women were the majority of legal immigrants, drawn to the United States as immigrants have always been by the hope of greater individual opportunity but now within an international labor market of low-waged women. (See Visual Sources: American Women in the World, pp. 766–77.) Unlike earlier generations, immigrant women were more likely than native-born women to work outside the home. The new immigrants also differed dramatically in their lands of origin. Instead of eastern and southern Europe, half of the new immigrants came from Mexico and Central and Latin America, and a quarter from Asia.

The boom in immigration led to the revival of anti-immigrant sentiment, much of it focused on immigrants' reliance on publicly funded social services. Women and children were the special targets of these attacks because they made much greater use of educational, health, and welfare services than did men. In 1994, California passed a voter initiative barring immigrants and their children from public schools and hospitals, but the courts threw it out as unconstitutional. Two years later, the carefully titled federal Illegal Immigration Reform and Immigrant Responsibility Act barred immigrants, even those with legal status, from federal welfare programs for five years after their arrival. Such legislation did not actually reduce poor immigrants' dependence on public services but rather shifted it to other programs. Thus, immigrant women who were denied prenatal care turned to emergency rooms to have their babies and required costly neonatal intervention when their American-born (hence citizen) children were sickly or underweight. The debate over immigration continues to be one of the most contentious in American politics.

Despite the growing political hostility they faced, immigrant women made important and varied contributions to American society. At one end of the occupational ladder, immigrant women brought with them professional skills. Filipinas and Korean women became a major presence in the nursing profession. Chinese and Indian female immigrants also went into professional occupations. At the other end, immigrant women flowed into the lowest rungs of the female labor force ladder, where their low-paid labor made services and manufactured goods affordable for middle-class Americans. In the garment industry, the majority of workers were Latino and Asian women. Low pay, long hours, and dangerous working conditions recalled the immigrant sweatshops of a century before. Highly exploitative conditions have led immigrant women in the San Francisco, Los Angeles, and New York garment industries to work within community organizations and local unions for better pay and conditions. They face many obstacles, including their employers' use of undocumented laborers who fear retribution from the Immigration and Naturalization Service and whose desperation sometimes makes them more easily subjected to harsh hours and conditions.

Immigrant women also poured into the booming service sector. In institutional service work such as cooking and cleaning in hospitals and hotels, they usually did the dirtiest work and had the least desirable working shifts. Starting with the 1990 "Justice for Janitors" campaign in Los Angeles, immigrant women workers helped to spark a union revival in the service industry. Blanca Gallegos, spokeswoman for the Hotel and Restaurant Employees Union, explained, "If you're working hard, you shouldn't be living in poverty. . . . It presents a lot of difficulties for women, especially for single mothers."[17]

Immigrant women also constituted the overwhelming number of private domestic workers. The low cost of the labor of immigrant women was a crucial factor in the ability of middle-class women to take jobs outside the household. One of the many ironies of the predominance of immigrant women in private domestic labor, especially the thriving nanny sector, was that market forces drove native-born women to entrust the raising of their children to immigrant women unfamiliar with American culture who were not primarily English speakers. Thus the relationship between worker and employer was skewed toward cultural conflict and misunderstanding.

The immigrant women drawn to the United States were part of the larger phenomenon of "globalization," the process in which corporations have grown, in both size and power, to dominate separate national economies, exacerbating inequalities and eroding cultural differences among the peoples of the world. The end of the Cold War and the beginning of the collapse of the Soviet Empire in 1989 left international capitalism an unchallenged system, thus accelerating globalization. American corporations set up factories abroad, where they could evade U.S. government regulations and trade unions and thus lower their labor costs considerably. In this way, foreign women who work for American corporations — across the Mexican border making clothing, in China making children's toys, and in Vietnam making athletic shoes — can be considered part of the history of the United States through women's eyes.

Another side to globalization has encouraged American women to collaborate with women activists in the Middle East, Asia, and Africa to advance the legal, economic, and reproductive rights of women the world over. And, in the face of the devastation of the Iraq war, as well as wars elsewhere in Africa and Asia, women's groups have also come together to agitate for peace (see box, "The Nobel Women's Initiative"). The agenda and reach of feminism has thus been broadened far beyond what the founders of NOW or women's liberation could have imagined, giving greater reality to their initial vision of universal sisterhood.

CONCLUSION: Women Face a New Century

Just as the political and cultural upheavals of the 1960s profoundly influenced women's lives and gave rise to second wave feminism, women's experiences of the last thirty years need to be understood in the context of broad historical developments. Patterns of globalization have significantly shaped American women's economic opportunities and will continue to do so in the future. With high-skilled union jobs increasingly replaced by low-waged service sector employment and global outsourcing, many women find themselves limited to dead-end jobs with few or no benefits. Many of these women are part of an expansive immigration that has been one of the defining demographic developments of the last forty years. They symbolize the multifaceted way in which globalization has affected women in the United States and elsewhere.

Another aspect of globalization — the United States' enhanced military presence abroad, especially in Afghanistan and Iraq — is part of an ongoing process whose long-term implications for national development are unclear. As we noted in the first chapter of *Through Women's Eyes*, America in the twenty-first century is situated thoroughly in a global system of culture, economics, power relations, and human migration, and this system will continue to have a powerful impact on women at home and abroad.

The Nobel Women's Initiative

Women's international organizations are an important part of the contemporary peace movement, as they have been historically. American woman have been vital to that process—in 1931, Jane Addams was the first woman to win the Nobel Peace Prize—but today their prominence has given way to a much more diverse coalition from all over the world. The document below is a description of the Nobel Women's Initiative founded in 2006. Only one of the women—Jody Williams—is from the United States. What are the goals of this new movement, and how do those goals reflect a gendered understanding of war and peace?

The Nobel Women's Initiative was established in 2006 by sister Nobel Peace Laureates Jody Williams, Shirin Ebadi, Wangari Maathai, Rigoberta Menchú Tum, Betty Williams and Mairead Corrigan Maguire. We six women—representing North and South America, Europe, the Middle East and Africa—have decided to bring together our extraordinary experiences in a united effort for peace with justice and equality.

Only 12 women in its more than 100 year history have been recognized with the Nobel Peace Prize. The Nobel Peace Prize is a great honor, but it is also a great responsibility. It is this sense of responsibility that has compelled us to create the Nobel Women's Initiative to help strengthen work being done in support of women's rights around the world—work often carried out in the shadows with little recognition.

We believe that peace is much more than the absence of armed conflict. Peace is the commitment to equality and justice; a democratic world free of physical, economic, cultural, political, religious, sexual and environmental violence and the constant threat of these forms of violence against women—indeed against all of humanity.

It is the heartfelt mission the Nobel Women's Initiative to address and work to prevent the root causes of violence by spotlighting and pro-

In the United States one of the most important factors affecting women in recent years has been the power of right-wing conservatism in American politics. In part fueled by a backlash against feminism, it has eroded some of the advances forged by the women's movement, especially in the realm of reproductive freedom. Yet despite the culture wars and political conflicts that have so divided the nation, the conventional patterns by which women were subordinated in the family have continued to change. So, too, have the concrete gains made for women's political and economic equality. A not-quite-anticipated aspect of the 2008 election has been the excitement, involvement, and determination of many ordinary women about the possibility that the United States might elect its first woman

moting the efforts of women's rights activists, researchers and organizations working to advance peace, justice and equality. By sharing a platform with these women, the NWI will spotlight their tireless work to prevent violence against women. By helping to advance the cause of women, we believe we advance all of humanity.

United by our desire to combat all forms of violence against women in all circumstances, we also recognize that specific issues for women vary around the world. One element of our work will be to sponsor international meetings of women every two years—in a different region of the world—to highlight issues of concern to women there. The objective of these meetings is to underscore our commonalities and differences by providing inclusive and energizing forums that ensure meaningful dialogue and networking by women's rights activists around the world—but with a view to action.

It is our commitment to action that brings us together. Therefore, our meetings will be linked with concrete work in the target region leading up to the conference, along with post-conference plans of action to address the issues addressed at the conference. In this way, the Nobel Women's Initiative will support meaningful work on the ground.

We believe profoundly in the sharing of information and ideas. By networking and working together rather than in competition, we enhance the work of all. The Nobel Women's Initiative is committed to supplementing and enhancing existing work and is determined to avoid duplicating the work of others. We want to open new ground for discussion, debate and change.

We hope you share our excitement about the potential of the Nobel Women's Initiative to meaningfully contribute to building peace with justice and equality by working together with women around the world.

_____

SOURCE: Nobel Women's Initiative, http://www.nobelwomensinitiative.org/about.php.

president. Still, we cannot predict how much the twenty-first century will be one of "progress" for women or even what that progress might specifically entail. Yet, as noted in this book's introduction, our predecessor in the project of rethinking America "through women's eyes," Mary Ritter Beard, insisted in 1933 upon the need to understand women's role in "the development of American society—their activity, their thought about their labor, and their thought about the history they have helped to make or have observed in the making." This text, *Through Women's Eyes*, symbolizes how profound the changes have been over the last 75 years, changes not only in women's lives, but also in the way in which historians recognize the centrality of women's experiences for understanding the nation's past.

DOCUMENTS

Feminist Revival in the 1990s

T HE DEFEAT OF THE ERA in 1982 seems symbolic of the way in which the feminist movement itself stalled in the early 1980s. The antifeminism that Susan Faludi detailed in her 1991 best-seller *Backlash* (see p. 741) undermined a strong movement on behalf of women, but there were also problems within feminism. Membership in NOW declined, *Ms.* magazine struggled to stay afloat, and younger women seemed increasingly indifferent. But in the early years of the 1990s, a disparate group of young women started calling attention to a resurgent feminism. Many of these women adopted the term "third-wave feminism," drawing on the terms often used to describe nineteenth-century feminism (the first wave) and the movement of the 1960s and 1970s (the second wave). Others rejected the term, noting that it implied a sharp and misleading generational boundary and that it linked historical feminism too tightly to specific movements associated primarily with white women. While the term "third wave" may be problematic, feminism was definitely resurgent in the 1990s.

As older organizations like NOW began to see membership rise again, new organizations sprang into action, including the Third Wave Foundation, founded in 1992, its Web page proclaimed, "By empowering young women, Third Wave is building a lasting foundation for social activism around the country."[18] Anthologies of writings, most of them personal accounts that hark back in genre to the consciousness-raising essays of the 1970s, flourished. Women also pursued feminist agendas in popular culture, especially in the worlds of punk and hip-hop music. Unafraid to be outrageous, new feminist magazines like *Bitch* and *Bust* appeared, supplemented by inexpensively reproduced, small-run magazines ("zines") and Web pages self-published by young women and devoted to women's issues, reflecting how important Internet technologies have been to a renewed feminist movement.

Why and how did feminism renew itself? In part, the conservative political climate associated with the New Right startled many young women out of their complacent belief that the barriers to women's rights had been torn down. The Thomas-Hill hearings (see p. 746) and the *Webster* decision (see p. A-34) proved especially important in reviving feminism by highlighting sexual harassment on the job and new challenges to reproductive freedom. Third-wave feminism also grew out of critiques of the second wave. A major theme was that the movement's focus had been too narrowly constrained by the white women who dominated it and that it had a limited ability to speak to the concerns of women of color. These young women were also motivated to respond to what the popular press criticized as the feminist cult of victimhood, especially in the arena of sexuality, which undercut the goal of women's empowerment. Many commentators—especially those from an older feminist generation—note that the third-wave feminists often offered a simplistic sense of the complex contours of the second wave. But although their history may have been flawed at times, these new feminists redefined feminism in ways that made it more relevant to young women of their generation. Although it is not clear whether many young women today identify specifically with the third wave, the movement helped to generate new interest in feminist issues and to encourage young women to participate in a wide range of social justice issues, including environmental, anti-sweatshop, and reproductive rights campaigns, many of them pursued in the international arena.

A central characteristic of the third-wave redefinition of feminism was the insistence that feminism acknowledge the multiple identities of women. To focus exclusively on the analytic category of gender without also paying attention to such factors as race, ethnicity, age, class, and sexual orientation limits feminism's usefulness in interpreting women's lives or in becoming an agent for social change. The writings of U.S. women of color have been central to this reformulation of feminist ideology. Particularly important has been Gloria Anzaldúa, a prize-winning poet and writer who was coeditor of the pathbreaking 1981 collection *This Bridge Called My Back* (see pp. 743–44). In this passage from her book *Borderlands/La Frontera: The New Mestiza* (1987), Anzaldúa artfully integrates Spanish phrases to draw the reader into the experience of "the borderland" of her location as a Chicana. What multiple identities does Anzaldúa identify, and how are these crucial to the shaping of a new consciousness?

GLORIA ANAZALDÚA
La Conciencia de la Mestiza (1987)

Por la mujer de mi raza
Hablará el espíritu.°

Jose Vasconcelos, Mexican philosopher, envisaged *una raza mestiza, una mezcla de razas afines, una raza de color—la primera raza síntesis del globo*. He called it a cosmic race, *la raza cósmica*, a fifth race embracing the four major races of the world.

° Anzaldúa did not offer English translations for her Spanish phrases and sentences. We follow the same practice so as to preserve her intentions of intermixing American and Mexican cultures.

SOURCE: Dawn Keetley and John Pettegrew, eds., *Public Women, Public Words: A Documentary History of American Feminism, 1960 to the Present* (Madison, WI: Madison House, 2002), 3:347–49.

Opposite to the theory of the pure Aryan, and to the policy of racial purity that white America practices, his theory is one of inclusivity. At the confluence of two or more genetic streams, with chromosomes constantly "crossing over," this mixture of races, rather than resulting in an inferior being, provides hybrid progeny, a mutable, more malleable species with a rich gene pool. From this racial, ideological, cultural and biological cross-pollinization, an "alien" consciousness is presently in the making—a new *mestiza* consciousness, *una conciencia de mujer*. It is a consciousness of the Borderlands.

"Una Lucha de Fronteras" (A Struggle of Borders)

Because I, a *mestiza*,

Continually walk out of one
culture and into another,
because I am in all cultures at the same time,
alma entre dos mundos, tres, cuatro,
me zumba la cabeza con lo contradictorio.
Estoy norteada por todas las voces que me
  Haban
simultáneamente.

The ambivalence from the clash of voices results in mental and emotional states of perplexity. Internal strife results in insecurity and indecisiveness. The *mestiza*'s dual or multiple personality is plagued by psychic restlessness.

In a constant state of mental nepantilism, an Aztec word meaning torn between ways, *la mestiza* is a product of the transfer of the cultural and spiritual values of one group to another. Being tricultural, monolingual, bilingual, or multilingual, speaking a patois, and in a state of perpetual transition the *mestiza* faces the dilemma of the mixed breed: which collectivity does the daughter of a darkskinned mother listen to? . . .

The new *mestiza* copes by developing a tolerance for contradictions, a tolerance for ambiguity. She learns to be an Indian in Mexican culture, to be Mexican from an Anglo point of view. She learns to juggle cultures. She has a plural personality, she operates in a pluralistic mode — nothing is thrust out, the good the bad and the ugly,

nothing rejected, nothing abandoned. Not only does she sustain contradictions, she turns the ambivalence into something else.

She can be jarred out of ambivalence by an intense, and often painful, emotional event which inverts or resolves the ambivalence. I'm not sure exactly how. The work takes place underground — subconsciously. It is work that the soul performs. . . .

En unas pocas centurias, the future will belong to the mestiza. Because the future depends on the breaking down of paradigms, it depends on the straddling of two or more cultures. By creating a new mythos — that is, a change in the way we perceive reality, the way we see ourselves, and the ways we behave — *la mestiza* creates a new consciousness.

The work of *mestiza* consciousness is to break down the subject-object duality that keeps her a prisoner and to show in the flesh and through the images in her work how duality is transcended. The answer to the problem between the white race and the colored, between male and females, lies in healing the split that originates in the very foundation of our lives, our culture, our languages, our thoughts. A massive uprooting of dualistic thinking in the individual and collective consciousness is the beginning of a long struggle, but one that could, in our best hopes, bring us to the end of rape, of violence, of war.

IDEAS SIMILAR TO ANZALDÚA'S NOTIONS of the fluidity of identity appear repeatedly in the anthologies of self-described third-wave feminists. In the following contribution to the anthology *Listen Up: Voices from the Next Feminist Generation,* first published in 1995, Korean American writer JeeYeun Lee discusses the necessity and difficulties of creating a truly inclusive feminist movement. Why does Lee conclude that "no simplistic identity politics is ever possible"?

JeeYeun Lee
Beyond Bean Counting (1995)

I came out as a woman, an Asian American and a bisexual within a relatively short span of time, and ever since then I have been guilty of the crime of bean counting, as Bill Clinton oh-so-eloquently phrased it. Every time I am in a room of people gathered for any reason, I automatically count those whom I can identify as women, men, people of color, Asian Americans, mixed-race people, whites, gays, lesbians, bisexuals, heterosexuals, people with disabilities. . . .

Such is the nature of feminism today: an uneasy balancing act between the imperatives of outreach and inclusion on one hand, and the risk of tokenism and further marginalization on the other. This dynamic has indelibly shaped my personal experiences with feminism, starting from my very first encounter with organized feminism. This encounter happened to be, literally, Feminist Studies 101 at the university I attended. . . .

[Lee found the course "exhilarating" and "exciting" but also an "intensely uncomfortable experience." She was frustrated by the complete absence of material on Asian American women, "nothing anywhere." While grateful for the empowering insights the class gave her about feminism, she felt that she would have "been turned off from feminism altogether had it not been for later classes that dealt specifically with women of color."]

I want to emphasize that the feminism that I and other young women come to today is one that is at least sensitive to issues of exclusion. If perhaps twenty years ago charges of racism, classism and homophobia were not taken seriously, today they are the cause of extreme anguish and soul-searching. I am profoundly grateful to older feminists of color and their white allies who struggled to bring U.S. feminist movements to this point. At the same time, I think that this current sensitivity often breeds tokenism, guilt, suspicion and self-righteousness that have very material repercussions on women's groups. . . .

In this age when "political correctness" has been appropriated by conservative forces as a derogatory term, it is extremely difficult to honestly discuss and confront any ideas and practices that perpetuate dominant norms—and none of us is innocent of such collusion. . . .

Issues of exclusion are not the sole province of white feminists. I learned this very vividly at a 1993 retreat organized by the Asian Pacifica Lesbian Network. It has become somewhat common lately to speak of "Asian and Pacific Islanders" or "Asian/Pacific Americans" or, as in this case, "Asian Pacifica." This is meant to be inclusive, to recognize some issues held in common by people from Asia and people from the Pacific Islands. Two women of Native Hawaiian descent and some Asian American allies confronted the group at this retreat to ask for more than lip service in the organization's name: If the group was seriously committed to being an inclusive coalition, we needed to educate ourselves about and actively advocate Pacific Islander issues. And because I don't want to relegate them to a footnote, I will mention here a few of these issues: the demand for sovereignty for Native Hawaiians, whose government was illegally overthrown by the U.S. in 1893; fighting stereotypes of women and men that are different from those of Asian people; decrying U.S. imperialist possession and occupation of the islands of Guam, the Virgin Islands, American Samoa, the Marshall Islands, Micronesia, the Northern Mariana Islands and several others.

This was a retreat where one would suppose everyone had so much in common—after all, we were all queer API women, right? Any such myth

SOURCE: Barbara Findlen, ed., *Listen Up: Voices from the Next Feminist Generation* (Seattle: Seal Press, 2001), 67–73.

was effectively destroyed by the realities of our experiences and issues: We were women of different ethnic backgrounds, with very different issues among East Asians, South Asians, Southeast Asians and Pacific Islanders; women of mixed race and heritage; women who identified as lesbians and those who identified as bisexuals: women who were immigrants, refugees, illegal aliens or second generation or more; older women, physically challenged women, women adopted by white families, women from the Midwest. Such tangible differences brought home the fact that no simplistic identity politics is ever possible, that we had to conceive of ourselves as a coalition first and foremost: as one woman on a panel said, our identity as queer API women must be a *coalitional* identity. Initially, I thought that I had finally found a home where I could relax and let down my guard. This was true to a certain degree, but I discovered that this was the home where I would have to work the hardest because I cared the most. I would have to be committed to push myself and push others to deal with all of our differences, so that we could be safe for each other. . . .

All this is to say that I and other young women have found most feminist movements today to be at this point, where there is at least a stated emphasis on inclusion and outreach with the accompanying risk of tokenism. I firmly believe that it is always the margins that push us further in our politics. Women of color do not struggle in feminist movements simply to add cultural diversity, to add the viewpoints of different kinds of women. Women of color feminist theories challenge the fundamental premises of feminism, such as the very definition of "women," and call for recognition of the constructed racial nature of all experiences of gender. . . .

These days, whenever someone says the word "women" to me, my mind goes blank. What "women"? What is this "women" thing you're talking about? Does that mean me? Does that mean my mother, my roommates, the white woman next door, the checkout clerk at the supermarket, my aunts in Korea, half of the world's population? I ask people to specify and specify, until I can figure out exactly what they're talking about, and I try to remember to apply the same standards to myself, to deny myself the slightest possibility of romanticization. Sisterhood may be global, but who is in that sisterhood? None of us can afford to assume anything about anybody else. This thing called "feminism" takes a great deal of hard work, and I think this is one of the primary hallmarks of young feminists' activism today: We realize that coming together and working together are by no means natural or easy.

MULTIPLE IDENTITIES mean multiple concerns. The following selection is drawn from *Manifesta: Young Women, Feminism, and the Future* (2000), coedited by Jennifer Baumgardner and Amy Richards, two prominent white activists who founded the Third Wave Foundation. It celebrates the wide-ranging issues feminists embraced in the 1990s. What is the significance of their comments concerning the phrase, "I'm not a feminist, but . . ."?

JENNIFER BAUMGARDNER AND AMY RICHARDS
The Feminist Diaspora (1999)

Relationships, marriage, bisexuality, STDs, abortion, and having children were the topics our friends were thinking about on the night of our dinner party. Among the subjects with which our dinner companions have also grappled were immigration problems, access to education, racism as manifest by white women befriending black women to get over their white guilt, taking care of an aging relative, credit-card debt, depression, and body image. Every woman's life touches many issues, some of which demand urgent attention at different times.

On every Third Wave Foundation membership card, for example, there is a place that asks, "My issues are ?," and no two cards have ever listed the same answer. Among the responses provided, members list "Jewish progressive life," "war crimes," "student financial aid," "interracial dating," "issues of the South Asian Diaspora," "universal health care," "mothering as a teenager," "condom distribution," "chauvinistic fathers," "fat oppression," and "white and male supremacy." Those are just the tip of the iceberg of what young women are thinking about. And, when you scratch the surface of why someone cares about a certain issue, it's almost always because such issues have affected that person or someone he or she cares about. Whether it's a glance at the Third Wave Foundation's membership cards or at a plenary session of the Fourth World Conference on Women in Beijing, at an Honor the Earth board meeting or our dinner party, there is never one feminist issue that dwarfs all others. There will never be one platform for action that all women agree on. But that doesn't mean feminism is confused. What it does mean is that feminism is as various as the women it represents. What weaves a feminist movement together is consciousness of inequities and a commitment to changing them.

As two young women who believe in the importance of a political vision and have faith in our peers, we want to begin to articulate why a generation leading revolutionary lives is best known for saying, "I'm not a feminist, but . . ." Third Wave women have been seen as nonfeminist when they are actually living feminist lives. Some of this confusion is due to the fact that most young women don't get together to talk about "Feminism" with a capital F. We don't use terms like "the politics of housework" or "the gender gap" as much as we simply describe our lives and our expectations. To a degree, the lack of a Third Wave feminist terminology keeps us from building a potent movement, which is why we need to connect our prowoman ethics to a political vision. And yet, even without the rip-roaring political culture that characterized the sixties and the seventies, Third Wave women are laying the groundwork for a movement of our own.

SOURCE: Jennifer Baumgardner and Amy Richards, eds., *Manifesta: Young Women, Feminism, and the Future* (New York: Farrar, Straus and Giroux, 2000), 47–48.

A QUITE DIFFERENT VERSION of feminism emerged in popular music. When Madonna first burst on the scene in the mid-1980s, many labeled her as a new feminist icon. Her outrageous sexual style seemed to convey her control of her own sexuality rather than present her as a sex object. Other powerful female performers also convey what might be called feminist sensibilities. Many black female rap performers, including Queen Latifah, reject the label "feminist" but nonetheless appeal to young women because of their critique of racism and sexism. Queen Latifah's music video "Ladies First" (1989) includes historical references to African American women such as Sojourner Truth and Angela Davis. As Queen Latifah puts it, "I wanted to show the strength of black women in history—strong black women. Those were good examples. I wanted to show what we've done. We've done a lot, it's just that people don't know it. Sisters have been in the midst of these things for a long time, but we just don't get to see it that much."[19]

The most overtly feminist young women in music are the Riot Grrrls, a phenomenon that emerged in Washington, D.C., and Olympia, Washington, in 1991. There, young white women began to challenge the male domination of the punk rock scene with all-female bands such as Bikini Kill and Heavens to Betsy. Their lyrics often focus on themes of sexual abuse, an oppressive beauty culture, and patriarchal oppression. Enthusiasm for Grrrl power spread, leading to zines, Web sites, and even a national convention in Washington, D.C. As important as the music was to empowering the female artists, zines and other forms of interaction spread the enthusiasm well beyond the musicians themselves. As one young woman explains, "Zines are so important because so many girls feel isolated and don't have other girls to support them in their beliefs. Zines connect them to other girls who will listen and believe and care if they say they've been raped or molested and harassed. Zines provide an outlet for girls to get their feelings and lives out there and share them with others."[20]

Women associated with the Riot Grrrls reveal something of the complexity of third-wave feminism. They are not afraid of the concept of "girlishness"—both in their name and their penchant for little-girl clothing and images—but they reject the notions of powerlessness that mainstream culture associates with "girls." Older feminists had railed against using the word "girl" to describe an adult female because it infantilized women; Riot Grrrls transformed the term. As one young woman puts it, "'Grrrl' puts the growl back in our pussycat throats."[21]

The following declaration of Riot Grrrls' philosophy appeared originally in a Bikini Kill zine in 1991. How would you characterize their philosophy?

KATHLEEN HANNA

Riot Grrrl Manifesto (1991)

BECAUSE us girls crave records and books and fanzines that speak to US that WE feel included in and can understand in our own ways.

BECAUSE we wanna make it easier for girls to see/hear each other's work so that we can share strategies and criticize-applaud each other.

BECAUSE we must take over the means of production in order to create our own moanings.

BECAUSE viewing our work as being connected to our girlfriends-politics-real lives is essential if we are gonna figure out how [what] we are doing impacts, reflects, perpetuates, or DISRUPTS the status quo.

BECAUSE we recognize fantasies of Instant Macho Gun Revolution as impractical lies meant

SOURCE: Jessica Rosenberg and Gitana Garofalo, "Riot Grrrl: Revolutions from Within," *Signs* 23 (January 1998): 812–13.

to keep us simply dreaming instead of becoming our dreams AND THUS seek to create revolution in our own lives every single day by envisioning and creating alternatives to the bullshit christian capitalist way of doing things.

BECAUSE we want and need to encourage and be encouraged in the face of all our own insecurities, in the face of beergutboyrock that tells us we can't play our instruments, in the face of "authorities" who say our bands/zines/etc. are the worst in the U.S. and BECAUSE we don't wanna assimilate to someone else's (boy) standards of what is or isn't.

BECAUSE we are unwilling to falter under claims that we are reactionary "reverse sexists" AND NOT THE TRUEPUNKROCKSOUL CRUSADERS THAT WE KNOW we really are.

BECAUSE we know that life is much more than physical survival and are patently aware that the punk rock "you can do anything" idea is crucial to the coming angry grrrl rock revolution that seeks to save the psychic and cultural lives of girls and women everywhere, according to their own terms, not ours.

BECAUSE we are interested in creating nonhierarchical ways of being AND making music, friends, and scenes based on communication + understanding, instead of competition + good/bad categorizations.

BECAUSE doing/reading/seeing/hearing cool things that validate and challenge us can help us gain the strength and sense of community that we need in order to figure out how bullshit like racism, able-bodyism, ageism, speciesism, classism, thinism, sexism, antisemitism and heterosexism figures in our own lives.

BECAUSE we see fostering and supporting girl scenes and girl artists of all kinds as integral to this process.

BECAUSE we hate capitalism in all its forms and see our main goal as sharing information and staying alive, instead of making profits or being cool according to traditional standards. BECAUSE we are angry at a society that tells us Girl = Dumb, Girl = Bad, Girl = Weak.

BECAUSE we are unwilling to let our real and valid anger be diffused and/or turned against us via the internalization of sexism as witnessed in girl/girl jealousism and self-defeating girltype behaviors.

BECAUSE I believe with my wholeheartmindbody that girls constitute a revolutionary soul force that can, and will, change the world for real.

OTHER YOUNG FEMINISTS challenged the way in which the media and male-dominated culture had sexually objectified women and undermined their ability to embrace eroticism. They criticized their feminist foremothers, who, they argued, emphasized freeing women from their sexual oppression and their victimization by men and Madison Avenue to the exclusion of the joys and power of female sexuality. This critique was often based on a misleading stereotype of 1970s feminists that emphasized unshaven legs, Birkenstock sandals, and rigid rules for appropriate feminist behavior. Prominent black writer and activist Rebecca Walker, the daughter of well-known novelist Alice Walker, is one of the women most responsible for popularizing the term "third wave." She offers a far more sophisticated manifesto for reclaiming female sexuality in an essay published in the anthology *Listen Up* (1995). As she details her own sexual coming of age, she asks, "What do young women need to make sex a dynamic, affirming, safe and pleasurable part of our lives?" What answers does she suggest?

REBECCA WALKER
Lusting for Freedom (1995)

When I think back, it is that impulse I am most proud of. The impulse that told me that I deserve to live free of shame, that my body is not my enemy and that pleasure is my friend and my right. Without this core, not even fully jelled in my teenage mind but powerful nonetheless, how else would I have learned to follow and cultivate my own desire? How else would I have learned to listen to and develop the language of my own body? How else would I have learned to initiate, sustain and develop healthy intimacy, that most valuable of human essences? I am proud that I did not stay in relationships when I couldn't grow. I moved on when the rest of me would emerge physically or intellectually and say, Enough! There isn't enough room in this outfit for all of us. . . .

It is obvious that the suppression of sexual agency and exploration, from within or from without, is often used as a method of social control and domination. Witness widespread genital mutilation and the homophobia that dictatorially mandates heterosexuality; imagine the stolen power of the millions affected by just these two global murderers of self-authorization and determination. Without being able to respond to and honor the desires of our bodies and our selves, we become cut off from our instincts for pleasure, dissatisfied living under rules and thoughts that are not our own. When we deny ourselves safe and shameless exploration and access to reliable information, we damage our ability to even know what sexual pleasure feels or looks like.

Sex in silence and filled with shame is sex where our agency is denied. This is sex where we, young women, are powerless and at the mercy of our own desires. For giving our bodies what they want and crave, for exploring ourselves and others, we are punished like Eve reaching for more knowledge. We are called sluts and whores. We are considered impure or psychotic. Information about birth control is kept from us. Laws denying our right to control our bodies are enacted. We learn much of what we know from television, which debases sex and humiliates women.

We must decide that this is no longer acceptable, for sex is one of the places where we do our learning solo. Pried away from our parents and other authority figures, we look for answers about ourselves and how the world relates to us. We search for proper boundaries and create our very own slippery moral codes. We can begin to take control of this process and show responsibility only if we are encouraged to own our right to have a safe and self-created sexuality. The question is not whether young women are going to have sex, for this is far beyond any parental or societal control. The question is rather, what do young women need to make sex a dynamic, affirming, safe and pleasurable part of our lives? How do we build the bridge between sex and sexuality, between the isolated act and the powerful element that, when honed, can be an important tool for self-actualization?

Fortunately, there is no magic recipe for a healthy sexuality; each person comes into her or his own sexual power through a different route and at her or his own pace. There are, however, some basic requirements for sexual awareness and safe sexual practice. To begin with, young women need a safe space in which to explore our own bodies. A woman needs to be able to feel the soft smoothness of her belly, the exquisite softness of her inner thigh, the full roundness of her breasts. We need to learn that bodily pleasure belongs to us; it is our birthright.

Sex could also stand to be liberated from pussy and dick and fucking, as well as from marriage and procreation. It can be more: more sensual, more spiritual, more about communication and healing. Women and men both must learn to explore sexuality by making love in ways that are

SOURCE: Barbara Findlen, ed., *Listen Up: Voices from the Next Feminist Generation* (Seattle: Seal Press, 2001), 19–24.

different from what we see on television and in the movies. If sex is about communicating, let us think about what we want to say and how will we say it. We need more words, images, ideas.

Finally, young women are more than inexperienced minors, more than property of the state or of legal guardians. We are growing, thinking, inquisitive, self-possessed beings who need information about sex and access to birth control and abortion. We deserve to have our self-esteem nurtured and our personal agency encouraged. We need "protection" only from poverty and violence.

And even beyond all of the many things that will have to change in the outside world to help people in general and young women in particular grow more in touch with their sexual power, we also need to have the courage to look closely and lovingly at our sexual history and practice. Where is the meaning? What dynamics have we created or participated in? Why did we do that? How did we feel? How much of the way we think about ourselves is based in someone else's perception or label of our sexual experiences?

It has meant a lot to me to affirm and acknowledge my experiences and to integrate them into an empowering understanding of where I have been and where I am going. Hiding in shame or running fast to keep from looking is a waste of what is most precious about life: its infinite ability to expand and give us more knowledge, more insight and more complexity.

ONE OF THE MOST DISTINCTIVE aspects of third-wave feminism has been the attention to the international context of women's issues. As Rory Dicker and Alison Piepmeier put it in the introduction to the anthology *Catching a Wave: Reclaiming Feminism for the 21st Century*, "[T]hird wave feminism's political activism on behalf of women's rights is shaped by—and responds to—a world of global capitalism and information technology, postmodernism and postcolonialism, and environmental degradation."[22] One strand of this global thinking has led to a focus on finding common ground among women activists throughout the world. In this excerpt from the essay "Third World, Third Wave Feminism(s): The Evolution of Arab American Feminism," Arab American Susan Muaddi Darraj explores the differences between Arab and Western feminists. How does she characterize those differences, and how does she propose to overcome them?

SUSAN MUADDI DARRAJ
Third World, Third Wave Feminism(s): The Evolution of Arab American Feminism (2000)

But how is Arab feminism *different* from American and Western feminism? Are the goals and ideals of Arab feminism separate, and if so, why?

SOURCE: Rory Dicker and Alison Piepmeier, eds. *Catching a Wave: Reclaiming Feminism for the 21st Century* (Northeastern University Press, 2003), 188–207.

More important how can these differences be reconciled, and how can they be used positively to influence the "third wave" of feminism? . . .

Arab feminism is reluctant to prioritize the self and the individual above all. Palestinians, and Arabs in general, including Palestinian women, identify themselves strongly with family, both immediate and extended. Barbara Epstein writes that a focus on individualism and the pursuit of success has become prominent in American culture, and although most feminists would reject it, "most of us live according to these values anyway: we measure our value by our success at work, and we let little stand in the way of it."[23] Perhaps this is a direct result of capitalism and economic success, but Arab women and society generally do not measure their value by the factors. Owing to widespread poverty, neocolonialism, and the resistance to Israeli occupation, the goals of individual wealth and personal success have been generally replaced by nationalistic aims and attempts to ensure family survival and progress. Thus, Arab women generally have other priorities, including family, which perhaps a capitalist system does not reward, and they often feel that American feminism devalues them because of this.

While Western women asserted independence from Western men, Arab women, by and large, asserted independence from both Arab men and Western colonial forces: Palestinian women fought and still fight against British and Israeli colonizers; Algerian women waged war alongside their men against French imperialism; and Egyptian women struggled to oust British colonizers from their nation. Thus, the rise of Arab feminism is rooted in the context of nationalistic struggle at a time when men needed women to take on stronger social and political roles. . . .

As I grew up in the United States, reconciling Western and third world feminisms seemed impossible. Is it possible to be an Arab American feminist, especially when the two affiliations seem to oppose one another? Since second wave feminism seemed largely mired in the pit of East versus West and caught up in national and international politics, I often sought refuge in the words of Katha Pollitt, who writes, simply but powerfully, "For me, to be a feminist is to answer the question 'Are women human?' with a yes."[24] This is the spirit that should propel third wave feminism; the question is to find the mechanism. What is the best way to bring Arab and Western

women to the table to begin reconciling their feminists? . . .

Arab feminism and Western feminism should not be remote, "foreign" movements. Feminism should embrace the struggles of all women, but it currently does not. Increasingly, I have noticed that Western feminists, especially American feminists, consider and treat their Arab counterparts as "other," that is, as third world women who do not understand the struggles of women in the first world. Much of this is due to politics; in the current political climate, the United States and most of Europe (on one side) and the Middle East (on the other) are ideologically farther apart than ever before. I understand that Arab feminism is not totally innocent and often views American feminism as another agent of colonialism—a notion that is perpetuated by opponents of Arab feminism in the Arab world. Nonetheless, I contend that there needs to be a bridging and even a synchronization of Arab and Western feminisms if the term "feminism" is to maintain its integrity and address the experiences of all women. . . ."

. . . Arab feminism, which is susceptible to the postcolonial reaction of interpreting American feminism as a new form of imperialism, would also benefit immensely from such dialogue, which would rejuvenate the spirit of feminism and positively affect women catching the third wave by offering them a chance to deal with *real* women and not with misleading images of one another.

Furthermore, another important step will have been taken: real links will have been created between Arab feminists and other women of color. Here exists a fertile ground, waiting to be planted, and it can yield a rich harvest if Arab feminists form coalitions with other women of color, as well as with other branches of the feminist movement in the United States. Right now, women of color generally operate in small pockets, not as a collective whole. On a number of occasions I have been told by another woman of color—Latina, Asian, or Indian—that our conversations about the status of women in our respective parts of the globe helped her to envision more clearly what the next wave of feminism should look like. The third wave is a global wave, but it must sweep through and carry back messages from women all over the world—and those messages should, in their own words, articulate their visions, their concerns, and their histories.

QUESTIONS FOR ANALYSIS

1. What do the documents suggest are the most important characteristics of the feminist revival of the 1990s? How is it different from the movement of the 1960s and 1970s?

2. In what ways is the diversity emphasized by the third wave manifested?

3. Baumgardner and Richards claim that, despite the many faces of contemporary feminism, the movement is "not confused." Do you agree?

4. Do the documents offer compelling reasons for young women to identify with the term "feminism"?

American Women in the World

THROUGH WOMEN'S EYES FOCUSES on a single nation—the United States and its colonial antecedents. But the presence and the importance of the surrounding world have been implicit throughout this national saga, beginning in the sixteenth century with the interactions among indigenous peoples, European traders and settlers, and African slaves. Waves of immigration, international commerce in raw materials and finished goods, political and intellectual influences from abroad, and wars of defense, expansion, and international conflict have all been regular features of American history and are reflected in the experience and actions of women. For any period, it is possible—and useful—to re-vision American history so that this international context emerges from the background into the spotlight. The visual images in this final source essay are an exercise in just this change of focus.

The international context of American history has become increasingly obvious and important in the last decades of the twentieth century and the start of the twenty-first through the process known as globalization. Especially since the collapse of the Soviet Union and the consequent end of the of the Cold War in 1991, the United States has dominated an internationally integrated capitalist system in which financial investment, consumer goods, and workers all move from nation to nation with increasing fluidity. At the end of the nineteenth century, capitalist competition within the United States began to give way to corporate centralization. At the start of the twenty-first century, that process reached beyond national boundaries so that giant corporations, now termed "multinationals," have economic structures that exceed the capacity of any single nation to regulate or restrain. The benefits and human costs of these exchanges are distributed unevenly, both among nations and within them. Globalization has brought both greater wealth and more inequality for the U.S. economy: a flood of cheap consumer goods into the country, the export of many formerly U.S.-based manufacturing jobs to Asia and Latin America, and a burgeoning immigrant working class doing the most menial jobs within the United States.

Economic globalization has profoundly affected women both inside and outside America's borders. Manufacturing jobs, once highly unionized and (in the garment industry) filled by women workers, have been exported abroad, particularly in the wake of free trade policies such as the North American Free Trade Agreement (NAFTA), signed in 1994 by Canada, Mexico, and the United States. In foreign factories run by or subcontracted to companies with familiar brand names like Nike and Gap, garments are produced at a fraction of the wages paid to American workers and then shipped to the United States for sale. In Central

America these factories are known as *maquilas*; in Mexico, as *maquiladoras*. Such factories can also be found throughout Asia. In all, the workers are preponderantly female, many of them mothers whose earnings are crucial to their families' well-being.

Figure 12.1 depicts women in Tangerang, West Java, Indonesia, working at a Nike shoe factory. A 2006 Oxfam report concluded that "women producing brand-name sportswear in Indonesia need to work nearly four hours to earn enough to purchase 1.5 kilograms of raw chicken, which for some is all the meat they can afford for a month." What hints does the photograph offer as to the nature of their work?

Given the multinational character of the companies involved, unions and other activist groups in the United States have joined together with foreign workers to mount campaigns for improved wages and working conditions. In the

◆ **Figure 12.1 Nike Factory in Indonesia**
Crack Palinggi/Reuters/CORBIS.

tradition of the National Consumers' League of the Progressive era (see p. 463), groups like the United Students Against Sweatshops have organized buyers' boycotts of goods (such as clothing with official college logos) made abroad under exploitative conditions. A network of American women's antisweatshop activists called STITCH was formed in 1994.[25]

A U.S.-based consumer campaign was organized in 1996 against the Phillips–Van Heusen Corporation. The company initially agreed to the unionization of six hundred workers, 80 percent of whom were women, in one of its Guatemalan plants. But a year later it closed the plant and, following the pattern of the early twentieth-century American garment industry, subcontracted production to intermediaries, who paid sweatshop workers even lower wages. The poster in Figure 12.2 was designed to organize American support for the union campaign. In what ways might this poster appeal to the American consumer? How and why might it be effective (or ineffective)?

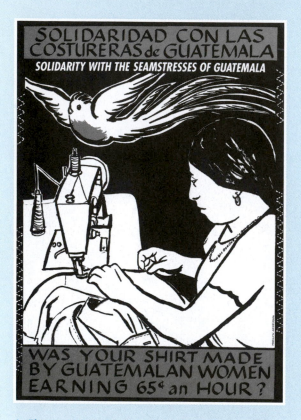

◆ **Figure 12.2 Antisweatshop Campaign Poster (1996)**
Marilyn Anderson.

The passage of NAFTA and the consequent loss of American manufacturing jobs were expected to discourage immigration into the United States, especially illegal immigration from Latin America. However, that did not happen. To cope with the post-NAFTA economic upheaval, many Mexicans and Central Americans sent family members to earn U.S. wages to send back home. Some U.S. manufacturers, searching to lower their labor costs to compete with *maquilas* and satisfy consumer demand for lower prices, turned to immigrant labor, especially to undocumented (illegal) immigrants who cannot use the courts or public agencies for protection against their extreme exploitation. In stark contrast to the waves of immigrants in the late nineteenth century, the majority of these and other international newcomers to the United States today are women.

Immigrant women have been central to community and labor organizing efforts to address poor wages and conditions, as well as anti-immigrant backlash. A related major national movement that addresses the concerns of poor workers is the Living Wage Campaign, begun in Baltimore in 1994, which brings together low-wage workers, many of them immigrant and African American women, with community organizers, labor unions, women's organizations, and religious groups to campaign for minimum wage ordinances in cities across the nation and to lobby for increases in state minimum wages. Estimates are that 61 percent of people receiving minimum wage are women. The campaign has met with success in five states and dozens of cities.

Immigrant women have also been central to the organizing activity of unions such as the Hotel and Restaurant Employees and Service Employees International Union (SEIU), which has spearheaded much of the union activism among service workers, including janitors and food servers. In 1985, SEIU created the Justice for Janitors Movement (see p. 762), designed to organize the cleaning personnel who work in office buildings and hotels in major cities. Using demonstrations and strikes, the movement has drawn attention to the issues of low wages, poor benefits, and difficult working conditions in cities all over the country. The campaign has had notable successes in Los Angeles, Houston, Miami, and Cincinnati. Figure 12.3 is from an October 2005 rally protesting California governor Arnold

◆ **Figure 12.3 Los Angeles Latinas Strike for Justice (2005)**
Photo by David McNew/Getty Images.

Schwarzenegger's anti-union initiatives. The majority of the protestors—firefighters, teachers, janitors, health care workers, and other labor union supporters—were Latino, and many of the speakers, including veteran farm labor activist Dolores Huerta (pp. 621–22), spoke in Spanish. The women chanting in the foreground are Janitors for Justice members Martina de Maroana, right, and Ana Castro, left. What do their expressions and body language suggest about how they view their labor activism?

Responses to the problems facing poor immigrants have been contradictory. From 1989 to 1994, the federal government granted legal amnesty to 2 million undocumented Mexican workers. At the same time, anti-immigrant attitudes have flourished, especially among working-class Americans who have suffered the most from the loss of U.S. manufacturing jobs. The 1996 federal law that denied public health and educational resources to immigrants, legal as well as illegal (see p. 762), also mandated the addition of new federal officers to patrol the borders, most of them posted in the Southwest. In Figure 12.4, one of these agents is taking a mug shot of an unnamed woman who was captured crossing into California. How does the photograph put a human face on these transnational border confrontations? What comparisons do you draw between this picture and the photographs taken by Jacob Riis of women immigrants a century before? (See Visual Sources: Jacob Riis's Photographs of Immigrant Girls and Women, pp. 434–40.)

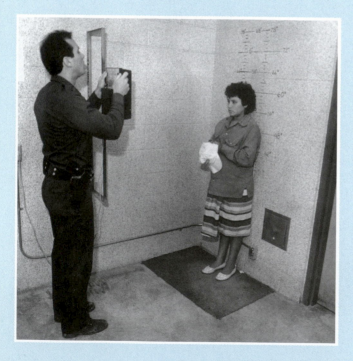

◆ **Figure 12.4 Mexican Woman Captured while Crossing the California Border (1988)**
Photo © Ken Light.

In recent years, tensions over immigration have continued to escalate. While calls for more stringent barriers to immigration and for restrictions on immigrants already in the country proliferated, immigrant communities began to mobilize in protest. On April 10, 2006, hundreds of thousands of marchers staged demonstrations in major cities across the nation, calling for amnesty for undocumented workers and a halt to the effort to restrict immigrant rights. Figure 12.5, a photograph from the demonstration in Seattle, shows Addie Ramirez, a high

◆ **Figure 12.5 Rally for Immigrant Rights, Seattle (2006)**
Jon Lok/Seattle Times.

school student in a suburb of Seattle. What is the significance of her sign? What does her expression suggest about why she is demonstrating? What effect might the presence of Americans flags at this demonstration have on people seeing this photo in the media?

Globalization has had cultural and intellectual as well as economic implications for women. Not only goods and labor but also information and images are transmitted around the globe. American movies, television, popular music, and the Internet reach an international audience, but influence goes the other way, too, facilitated by technology and corporate power. While some observers criticize the homogenization of diverse local cultures, others celebrate the ability of people from distant parts of the globe to share common understandings and a unifying culture.

The cultural impact of globalization has encouraged the internationalization of standards for gender equality, female independence, and women's rights. From the very beginning, international forces have influenced the American women's rights movement. The activists of the 1850s corresponded with women of similar sentiments in France and England, and immigrants from Germany and Poland joined in the movement. Many women of the Progressive era such as Jane Addams and Carrie Chapman Catt participated in international women's networks and drew inspiration from reform efforts initiated abroad. Nothing captures the historic links between American and international feminism better than the story of International Women's Day, which was first celebrated in 1908 by American Socialist women. The celebration was carried through the international Socialist and Communist movements until American women's liberationists rediscovered it when they visited Cuba and Vietnam in the 1960s. In 1981, the U.S. Congress declared Women's History Week (later Women's History Month) an official federal event. International Women's Day is still celebrated around the world and connects far-flung women's movements to one another.

In the late twentieth-century world, the United Nations became a major resource for the internationalization of feminism. When the UN was formed in 1946 in the immediate aftermath of World War II, it established the Commission on the Status of Women (UN-CSW). The twenty-fifth anniversary of the UN-CSW coincided with the upsurge in second-wave feminist energies in the United States and Europe, and in 1975 the UN sponsored the first International Women's Conference in Mexico City. Fifteen hundred delegates from 133 participating countries attended; for the first time in the history of UN conferences, the majority of official participants were women. The conference helped to advance what four years later became the UN's most comprehensive document on women's rights, the Convention° on the Elimination of All Forms of Discrimination Against Women (CEDAW), which the United States has refused to sign.

° A United Nations convention is a kind of international treaty that obligates signatory countries to certain actions, in this case regular reports on the status of women.

The Mexico City conference was followed by UN-sponsored international women's conferences in Copenhagen (1980) and Nairobi (1985). In 1995, the UN sponsored the Fourth International Women's Conference in Beijing to survey the gains of the international feminist movement over the previous two decades. While feminism had faded somewhat in the United States, it was flourishing in Asia, Africa, and parts of the Middle East. The growth in scope and self-confidence of global feminism could be measured in the size and enthusiasm of the official meeting, attended by fifteen thousand participants. As in Mexico City, the UN hosted a simultaneous conference of nongovernmental organizations, entitled "Looking at the World Through Women's Eyes," which was twice as large as the meeting of official delegates. Jo Freeman, a feminist activist and political scientist, was among the hundreds of American women who attended this extraordinary event. "In every country, even the smallest or least developed, there is a greater awareness of women, women's problems and women's importance than ever before," she wrote afterward. "In all but the most conservative of countries, the feminist message that women are people, not just wives and mothers, is taken seriously."[26]

Hillary Rodham Clinton also attended. Here, as at other times during her husband's presidency, she self-consciously modeled herself after Eleanor Roosevelt, who transformed the role of First Lady into a position of considerable political influence (see p. 624). Clinton made a major public speech at the UN conference. "By gathering in Beijing, we are focusing world attention on issues that matter most in the lives of women and their families," she declared, "access to education, health care, jobs and credit, the chance to enjoy basic legal and human rights and participate fully in the political life of their countries." She then added, "As an American, I want to speak up for women in my own country — women who are raising children on the minimum wage, women who can't afford health care or child care, women whose lives are threatened by violence, including violence in their own homes." The next year, Clinton published *It Takes a Village* (1996). Using her title to invoke traditional African childrearing structures, Clinton argued for greater collective involvement and public support for childrearing. Figure 12.6 pictures Clinton at a session at the Beijing conference to discuss greater economic support for the world's women. What does this image, as well as Clinton's words, suggest about the position of the United States toward and in the burgeoning global feminist movement?

The Beijing conference hammered out an extensive international platform for action that addressed diverse subjects, including poverty among the world's women; persistent educational, political, economic, and health inequality; the violation of the rights of girl children; media stereotyping; and gender inequality in environmental safeguards. The impact of armed conflict on women and the international scope of violence against women were particular areas of concern. At the 1993 World's Conference on Human Rights in Vienna, Austria, feminist activists successfully lobbied the UN and the international community to recognize the necessity of formally designating acts of violence against women, whether hidden in the family or condoned by governments, as full-fledged human rights abuses. The 1995 Beijing conference adopted the slogan that gained currency in Vienna and has since become the identifying statement of the international feminist movement: "Women's rights are human rights."

In 2000, the UN General Assembly approved Resolution 1325, which not only reinforced earlier criticisms of the specific hazards that war brings to women and girls but also called for an increased role for women in the peacemaking process. Although some progress has been made in bringing more women into the peace process and in drawing more attention to the specific problems — especially gender-specific violence — women face in war, critics argue that the resolution has fallen fall short in its implementation.

To increase women's role in promoting world peace, in 2006, six of the seven living women recipients of the Nobel Peace Prize (Jody Williams, Shirin Ebadi, Wangari Maathai, Rigoberta Menchú Tum, Betty Williams, and Mairead Corrigan Maguire) created the Nobel Women's Initiative (see box, "The Nobel Women's Initiative," p. 764). They are determined to use the influence and prestige associated with their Nobel status to expand women's roles in peacemaking and "to address and prevent the root causes of violence by spotlighting and promoting the efforts of women's rights activists, researchers and organizations working to advance peace, justice and equality."[27] Their work has drawn attention to women's issues in warfare in the Middle East, Darfur, the Sudan, and Oaxaca. They have also been active in attempting to mediate tensions between Iran and the United States and in calling for Iran to end the repression and discrimination against women there.

Only one of these Nobel laureates, Jody Williams, is an American, although two other American women—Jane Addams in 1931 and Emily Greene Balch in 1946—received the prize in the past. Addams and Carrie Chapman Catt (see pp. 481–82) helped found the Women's International League for Peace and Freedom in 1915, and the organization that continues its activism to this day. Contemporary women's emphasis on viewing peace in gendered terms has clear intellectual roots in women's early twentieth-century pacifism. Today, in a number of cities, women in the United States mount peace vigils as part of an international movement called Women in Black, a group started in 1988 in Israel when women there began protesting the Israeli occupation of the West Bank and Gaza. Today, the movement exists throughout the world and draws attention to specific military actions, including the current war in Iraq, from an explicitly feminist perspective: "We have a feminist understanding: that male violence against women in domestic life and in the community, in times of peace and in times of war, are interrelated. Violence is used as a means of controlling women."[28]

A similar ideology that views war through a gendered lens shapes an organization founded in the United States in 2002, Code Pink, which focuses primarily on ending the Iraq war. Vociferous in its criticism of the Bush administration, Code Pink explains that it based its name on a parody of "the Bush Administration's color-coded homeland security advisory system that signals terrorist threats. While Bush's color coded alerts are based on fear, the CODEPINK alert is based on compassion and is a feisty call for women and men to 'wage peace.'"[29] Figure 12.7 is from the organization's Web site. What do the images suggest about the organization's view of women's relationship to war? What characterizes its ideology and tactics? What does the Web site suggest about the importance of the Internet for mobilizing contemporary political movements of women? What do you think of the organization's decision to use the color pink?

The subject of peace brings us to the subject of war and the specific roles of American women in their country's far-flung military operations in recent decades. Overseas wars have traditionally exposed American men to foreign influences, but American women now enroll in the military for the same reasons as men— employment opportunities, education, and adventure. Thus, when America's armed service capacity is mobilized, as it has been with increasing frequency, the face of the American military that the country and the world see is often that of a woman deployed in difficult, dangerous, and controversial overseas campaigns.

In December 2003, as U.S. forces in Iraq struggled to subdue that country's insurgents, *Time* magazine named "The American Soldier" as its person of the year, with a cover photograph of three soldiers (Figure 12.8). One was female:

◆ **Figure 12.7 Code Pink Web Site (2007)**
By permission of CODEPINK.

Billie Grimes, a medic from Texas, the only woman in her unit. The cover story included an account of Grimes's platoon coming under fire and her work with several wounded men. *Time*'s decision to highlight Grimes reflected the realities of the American military. After the Vietnam War and the virtual elimination of the selective service system, or draft, the United States turned to an all-volunteer army. The need for personnel, coupled with feminist pressure to end the discrimination women faced in the armed forces, led to a decision to make women regular members of the armed forces instead of part of auxiliary groups such as the WACS (see pp. 546–47). And, after much resistance from the military, the U.S. military service academies were also opened to women by an act of Congress in 1976. In Figure 12.8, Billie Grimes is centered between two male comrades. What does Grimes's pose suggest about her relationship to these men? Why do you think *Time* chose to feature Grimes in this way? How does this image contrast with the one of Charity Adams on page 547?

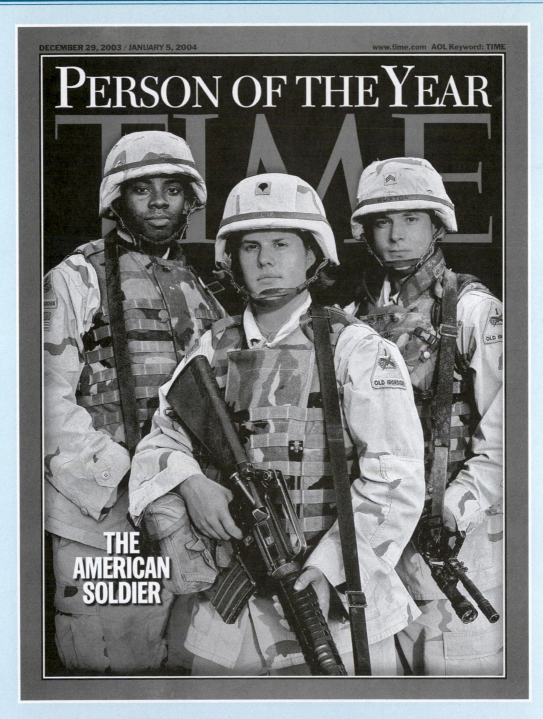

◆ **Figure 12.8 The American Soldier (2003)**
Time & Life Pictures/Getty Images.

Women first saw significant action in Operation Desert Storm (see p. 000) and have become increasingly important to military efforts abroad ever since. Despite the persistence of a no-combat rule, women in Afghanistan and Iraq, whether nurses, doctors, cooks, maintenance specialists, medics, or intelligence specialists, are routinely attached to units that bring them into the line of fire. Although some women receive training commensurate with the roles they actually undertake, most do not, leaving them in a vulnerable position.

Perhaps the most famous American woman to be exposed to the dangers of war is Private Jessica Lynch, who was taken prisoner in Iraq in March 2003. Lynch was part of a noncombat convoy that got lost and found itself in the midst of Iraqi forces, who attacked. Reports came out saying that Lynch fought valiantly before being captured. *Time* reported, "She was fighting to the death. . . . She did not want to be taken alive." Next came news of Lynch's dramatic rescue by U.S. forces from an Iraqi hospital. As it turned out, the reports about Lynch's capture and rescue were fabrications carefully calculated for public consumption. As Lynch later told it, her gun jammed and she crouched in the truck while the attack took place. The attack killed her best friend, Lori Ann Piestewa (p. 750), and Lynch's own injuries were the result of her truck crashing, not enemy fire. Although the government did not allow reporters to accompany the rescue mission and produced its own edited videotape of the event, there is much evidence to suggest that the dramatic raid was not necessary. There were no Iraqi forces at the hospital, and Lynch's doctors had tried to find a way to return her to U.S. forces without success. Lynch testified at a congressional hearing in 2007 regarding the "spin" that the government and the media put on her story. She denies having acted heroically and instead has worked to gain recognition for Lori Ann Piestewa.

One facet of the story depicting Lynch as the first woman heroine of the Iraq war was the emphasis on her role as a victim in need of saving. Critics have suggested that it is significant that Lynch is white, blond, and conventionally pretty. Neither Piestewa, a Native American woman, nor Shoshana Johnson, an African American woman wounded and taken prisoner at the same time, received the same government and media blitz. Figure 12.9 is of the official press briefing on her rescue, with a slide of Lynch in the background. What clues does it give as to how the government wanted to present Jessica Lynch? How do you account for the presence of the American flag placed on her body? Scholar Susan Jeffords has written, "This trend away from the war itself to the people who fought in it shifts the war from a national to a personal experience, making it possible for viewers to forget the specific historical and political forces that caused the war."[30] What connections can you make between Jeffords's comment and Jessica Lynch's story?

By enlarging the available pool of labor and talent, women have strengthened and modernized the American military. But the presence of women in military uniforms performing military service has also led to complications, especially in the recent series of Middle Eastern wars. In the first Gulf War against Iraq in 1991,

◆ **Figure 12.9** **The Saving of Private Jessica Lynch (2003)**
Reuters/CORBIS.

the United States was allied with Saudi Arabia and Kuwait, two of only five countries left in the world to deny voting rights to women. In deference to their orthodox Islamic practices, the U.S. military placed limits on its own female forces, forbidding them, for instance, to drive vehicles in violation of local custom. Ten years
later, when the United States went to war against Afghanistan in retaliation for
the Taliban regime's harboring of the terrorist forces responsible for the September 11, 2001, attack on the United States, the stark contrast between modern
American women and the drastic domestic confinement and abuse of Afghan
women made the liberation of Afghan women one of the rationales for the U.S.
decision to go to war, although that promise was not fulfilled (see p. 749).

◆ **Figure 12.10** **Two Women: An American Soldier and an Iraqi Civilian (2002)**
© *CORBIS.*

Figure 12.10 illustrates some of the complexities associated with women in the military in the context of the Iraq war. One of the reasons U.S. military women have been frequently exposed to combat conditions in Iraq is that they are crucial in house-to-house searches, where they are responsible for searching Muslim women. Their presence was intended to defuse tensions and protect the U.S. forces from the claims that Iraqi women have been violated. An army military police officer serving in Afghanistan gave the following explanation to an interviewer: "At first the Afghans thought I was a man. . . . The women would cry when I was going to search them, so I learned to take off my helmet and show them my hair and face."[31] This photograph was one of many shot during the Iraq war by Zohra Bensemra, an Algerian photographer. Although the American soldier's position and uniform make it difficult to see, the soldier, like the Iraqi civilian she is frisking, is a woman. Think about how the photograph emphasizes the contrast between the Iraqi civilian and the American soldier while playing on the fact that they are both women. What does the expression on the Iraqi woman's face suggest about her experience with being searched? What does the photograph reveal about the relationships that globalization establishes among women?

QUESTIONS FOR ANALYSIS

1. In what ways does increasing global integration bring American women closer to women around the world?

2. In what ways does globalization increase the distance and inequality among women?

3. In what ways does taking a gendered approach to immigration and war affect our understanding of international issues?

4. How can you re-vision American women's history in other periods in an international context?

NOTES

1. Flora Davis, *Moving the Mountain: The Women's Movement in America since 1960* (Urbana: University of Illinois Press, 1999), 163.

2. Quoted in "Supreme Court Upholds Federal Abortion Ban, Opens Door for Further Restrictions by States," *Guttmacher Policy Review* 10 (Spring 2007), http://www.guttmacher.org/pubs/gpr/10/2/gpr100219.html (accessed July 24, 2007).

3. Eloise Salholz, "The Marriage Crunch," *Newsweek*, June 2, 1986, 55.

4. Lisa Duggan, Nan D. Hunter, and Carole S. Vance, "False Promises: Feminist Antipornography Legislation" (1985), in Lisa Duggan and Nan D. Hunter, eds., *Sex Wars: Sexual Dissent and Political Culture* (New York: Routledge, 2006), 61.

5. Cherríe Moraga and Gloria Anzaldúa, eds., *This Bridge Called My Back: Writings by Radical Women of Color* (Watertown, MA: Persephone Press, 1981), iii.

6. Ibid., 73.

7. Anna Greenberg, "Deconstructing the Gender Gap," http://www.ksg.harvard.edu/prg/greenb/gengap.htm (accessed August 30, 2004).

8. Steven Stark, "Gap Politics," *Atlantic Monthly*, July 1996, 71–80.

9. *Independent* (London), August 28, 2005, LexisNexis, http://departments.oxy.edu/library/research/dbs/frame.asp?UID=LN (accessed August 4, 2007).

10. Virginia Solms, "Duty, Honor, Country: If You're Straight," in Judith Hicks Stiehm, ed., *It's Our Military, Too! Women and the U.S. Military* (Philadelphia: Temple University Press, 1996), 32.

11. "NOW Calls for End to War in Iraq," National Organization for Women, January 24, 2007, http://www.now.org/press/01-07/01-24a.html?printable (accessed July 29, 2007).

12. Nancy MacLean, "The Hidden History of Affirmative Action: Working Women's Struggles in the 1970s and the Gender of Class," *Feminist Studies* (Spring 1999): 50.

13. Dorothy Sue Cobble, *The Other Women's Movement: Workplace Justice and Social Rights in Modern America* (Princeton: Princeton University Press, 2004), 222.

14. Nancy Cott, *Public Vows: A History of Marriage and the Nation* (Cambridge: Harvard University Press, 2000), 212.

15. Sarah M. Evans, *Tidal Wave: How Women Changed America at Century's End* (New York: Free Press, 2003), 234.

16. Doreen Mattingly, "'Working Men' and 'Dependent Wives': Gender, 'Race,' and the Regulation of Migration from Mexico," in Cathy J. Cohen et al., eds., *Women Transforming Politics: An Alternative Reader* (New York: New York University Press, 1997), 51.

17. *The Daily Bruin*, March 9, 2000, http://www.dailybruin.ucla.edu/db/issues/00/03.09/news.janitors.html (accessed August 30, 2004).

18. Third Wave Foundation, http://www.thirdwavefoundation.org (accessed September 1, 2004).

19. Robin Roberts, "'Ladies First': Queen Latifah's Afrocentric Feminist Music Video," *African American Review* 28 (1994): 245–58.

20. Jessica Rosenberg and Gitana Garofalo, "Riot Grrrl: Revolutions from Within," *Signs* 23 (1998): 810.

21. Ednie Kaeh Garrison, "U.S. Feminism-Grrrl Style! Youth (Sub) Cultures and the Technologics of the Third Wave," *Feminist Studies* 26 (Spring 2000): 141.

22. Rory Dicker and Alison Piepmeier, eds., *Catching a Wave: Reclaiming Feminism for the 21st Century* (Lebanon, NY: Northeastern University Press, 2003), 10.

23. Barbara Epstein, "What Happened to the Women's Movement?" *Monthly Review* 53, no. 1 (May 2001), 13.

24. Katha Pollitt, *Reasonable Creatures: Essays on Women and Feminism* (New York: New York University Press, 1995), xxi.

25. STITCH, http://www.stitchonline.org.

26. Jo Freeman, "The Real Story of Beijing," *off our backs* 26, no. 3 (March 1996), 1, 8–11, 22–27; see http://www.jofreeman.com/womenyear/beijingreport.htm.

27. Nobel's Women's Initiative, http://www.nobelwomensinitiative.org/home.php (accessed August 5, 2007).

28. Women in Black, http://www.womeninblack.org/about.html (accessed August 7, 2007).

29. Code Pink: Women for Peace, http://www.codepink4peace.org/article.php ?list=type&type=3 (accessed August 7, 2007).

30. Susan Jeffords, "Telling the War Story," in Stiehm, ed., *It's Our Military, Too!*, 220.

31. Erin Solaro, *Women in the Line of Fire: What You Should Know About Women in the Military* (Emeryville, CA: Seal Press, 2006), 119.

SUGGESTED REFERENCES

General Works   Many of the titles in the Suggested References for Chapter 11 will prove useful for the material in this chapter. See especially Sarah M. Evans, *Tidal Wave: How Women Changed America at Century's End* (2003); Estelle B. Freedman, *No Turning Back: The History of Feminism and the Future of Women* (2002), which situates U.S. women's history in a global context; Ruth Rosen, *The World Split Open: How the Modern Women's Movement Changed America*, 2nd ed. (2007); and Myra Marx Ferree and Beth B. Hess, *Controversy and Coalition: The New Feminist Movement across Four Decades of Change*, 3rd ed. (2000). A useful reference book on contemporary issues is Cynthia B. Costello, et al., *The American Woman 2003–2004: Daughters of a Revolution — Young Women Today* (2003).

Feminism and the New Right in American Politics   On the general cultural atmosphere of the antifeminist reaction to women's liberation, see Susan Faludi's influential *Backlash: The Undeclared War against American Women* (1991). In *The Terror Dream: Fear and Fantasy in Post-9/11 America* (2007), Faludi has pursued the theme of backlash by analyzing the impact of the September 11 terrorist attacks on

American culture and in particular on gender values. In *Women of the New Right* (1987), Rebecca E. Klatch looks at the larger history of women in the conservative movement. Carol Felsenthal offers a biography of the movement's major figure in *The Sweetheart of the Silent Majority: The Biography of Phyllis Schlafly* (1981). Donald T. Critchlow, in *Phyllis Schlafly and Grassroots Conservatism: A Woman's Crusade* (2005), focuses on Schlafly's political career and ideology. For an overview of the conservative movement, see Jonathan M. Schoenwald, *A Time for Choosing: The Rise of Modern American Conservatism* (2001). On the battle over the ERA, see Mary Frances Berry, *Why ERA Failed: Politics, Women's Rights, and the Amending Process of the Constitution* (1986), and Jane J. Mansbridge, *Why We Lost the ERA* (1986). On the anti-abortion movement, see Dallas A. Blanchard, *The Anti-Abortion Movement and the Rise of the Religious Right: From Polite to Fiery Protest* (1994); Kristin Luker, *Abortion and the Politics of Motherhood* (1984); and Rickie Solinger, ed., *Abortion Wars: A Half Century of Struggle, 1950–2000* (1998). In *Contested Lives: The Abortion Debate in an American Community* (1998), Faye D. Ginsburg provides a fascinating study of women in both the pro-choice and anti-abortion movements in a single midwestern community. Donald Critchlow discusses federal abortion policy and politics in *Intended Consequences: Birth Control, Abortion, and the Federal Government in Modern America* (1999).

For a range of writings from all groups of women of color, see Cherríe Moraga and Gloria Anzaldúa, eds., *This Bridge Called My Back: Writings by Radical Women of Color* (1979), and the subsequent volume, edited by Gloria Anzaldúa and Ana Louise Keating, *This Bridge We Call Home: Radical Visions for Transformation* (2002). Third-wave feminism is well covered in Jennifer Baumgardner and Amy Richards, eds., *Manifesta: Young Women, Feminism, and the Future* (2000); Barbara Findlen, ed., *Listen Up: Voices from the Next Feminist Generation,* 2nd ed. (2001); Daisy Hernández and Bushra Rehman, eds., *Colonize This! Young Women of Color on Today's Feminism* (2002); Rory Dicker and Alison Piepmeier, eds., *Catching a Wave: Reclaiming Feminism for the 21st Century* (2003); and Vivien Labaton and Dawn Lundy Martin, eds., *The Fire This Time: Young Activists and the New Feminism* (2004). Two articles on the subject are Kimberly Springer, "Third Wave Black Feminism?" *Signs* 27 (2002): 1059–82, and Gayle Wald, "Just a Girl? Rock Music, Feminism, and the Cultural Construction of Female Youth," *Signs* 23 (1998): 585–610. On the pornography controversy, see antipornography activists Catharine A. McKinnon and Andrea Dworkin's edition of *In Harm's Way: The Pornography Civil Rights Hearings* (1998). For the counterargument, see Lisa Duggan and Nan D. Hunter, eds., *Sex Wars: Sexual Dissent and Political Culture* (2006).

On the Thomas–Hill hearings, see Toni Morrison, ed., *Race-ing Justice, Engendering Power: Essays on Anita Hill, Clarence Thomas, and the Construction of Social Reality* (1992). The sex and gender dimensions of the impeachment of President Clinton are analyzed in Lauren Berlant and Lisa Duggan, eds., *Our Monica, Ourselves: The Clinton Affair and the National Interest* (2001).

On women in the military, see the collection of essays edited by Judith Hicks Stiehm, *It's Our Military, Too! Women and the U.S. Military* (1996). In *Women in the Line of Fire: What You Should Know About Women in the Military* (2006), Erin Solaro is critical of both the military establishment and the pacifist feminists she calls "feministas." For theoretical insights about gender and the military, see Melissa S. Herbert, *Camouflage Isn't Only for Combat* (1998).

Arlie Russell Hochschild (with Anne Machung), *Second Shift: Working Parents and the Revolution at Home* (2003), examines the double responsibilities of working mothers. Barbara Ehrenreich, *Nickel and Dimed: On (Not) Getting By in America* (2001), offers a compelling portrait of women in low-wage jobs. For a study on contemporary women and poverty see Randy Albelda and Chris Tilly, *Glass Ceilings and Bottomless Pits: Women's Work, Women's Poverty* (1997). Studies on women and labor activism include John Hoerr, *We Can't Eat Prestige: The Women Who Organized Harvard* (1997); Vanessa Tait, *Poor Worker's Unions: Rebuilding Labor from Below* (2005); and the essays in Dorothy Sue Cobble, ed., *The Sex of Class: Women Transforming American Labor* (2007), as well as Dorothy Sue Cobble, *The Other Women's Movement: Workplace and Justice and Social Rights in Modern America* (2004). Nancy MacLean discusses the history of affirmative action in *Freedom Is Not Enough: The Opening of the American Workplace* (2003). Patricia Gurin et al., *Defending Diversity: Affirmative Action at the University of Michigan* (2004), and Barbara A. Perry, *The Michigan Affirmative Action Cases* (2007), provide insight to the affirmative action debate surrounding the Michigan case.

Sociologist Judith Stacey has written two books on the transformation of the family: *Brave New Families: Stories of Domestic Upheaval in Late Twentieth-Century America* (1998) and *In the Name of the Family: Rethinking Family Values in the Postmodern Age* (1996). For a study of the history of marriage, see Stephanie Coontz, *Marriage: A History* (2006).

On women and the new immigration, see Barbara Ehrenreich and Arlie Russell Hochschild, eds., *Global Woman: Nannies, Maids, and Sex Workers in the New Economy* (2003). On globalization, see Miriam Ching Yoon Louie, *Sweatshop Warriors: Immigrant Women Workers Take on the Global Factory* (2001), and Teri L. Caraway, *Assembling Women: The Feminization of Global Manufacturing* (2007).

For selected Web sites, please visit the *Through Women's Eyes* book companion site at bedfordstmartins.com/duboisdumenil.

The Declaration of Independence

IN CONGRESS, JULY 4, 1776,
THE UNANIMOUS DECLARATION OF THE
THIRTEEN UNITED STATES OF AMERICA

When in the Course of human events, it becomes necessary for one people to dissolve the political bands which have connected them with another, and to assume among the Powers of the earth, the separate and equal station to which the Laws of Nature and of Nature's God entitle them, a decent respect to the opinions of mankind requires that they should declare the causes which impel them to the separation.

We hold these truths to be self-evident, that all men are created equal, that they are endowed by their Creator with certain unalienable rights, that among these are Life, Liberty, and the pursuit of Happiness. That to secure these rights, Governments are instituted among Men, deriving their just powers from the consent of the governed. That whenever any Form of Government becomes destructive of these ends, it is the Right of the People to alter or to abolish it, and to institute new Government, laying its foundation on such principles and organizing its powers in such form, as to them shall seem most likely to effect their Safety and Happiness. Prudence, indeed, will dictate that Governments long established should not be changed for light and transient causes; and accordingly all experience hath shown, that mankind are more disposed to suffer, while evils are sufferable, than to right themselves by abolishing the forms to which they are accustomed. But when a long train of abuses and usurpations, pursuing invariably the same Object evinces a de-sign to reduce them under absolute Despotism, it is their right, it is their duty, to throw off such Government, and to provide new Guards for their future security.—Such has been the patient sufferance of these Colonies; and such is now the necessity which constrains them to alter their former Systems of Government. The history of the present King of Great Britain is a history of repeated injuries and usurpations, all having in direct object the establishment of an absolute Tyranny over these States. To prove this, let Facts be submitted to a candid world.

He has refused his Assent to Laws, the most wholesome and necessary for the public good.

He has forbidden his Governors to pass Laws of immediate and pressing importance, unless suspended in their operation till his Assent should be obtained; and, when so suspended, he has utterly neglected to attend to them.

He has refused to pass other Laws for the accommodation of large districts of people, unless those people would relinquish the right of Representation in the Legislature, a right inestimable to them and formidable to tyrants only.

He has called together legislative bodies at places unusual, uncomfortable, and distant from the depository of their public Records, for the sole purpose of fatiguing them into compliance with his measures.

He has dissolved Representative Houses repeatedly, for opposing with manly firmness his invasions on the rights of the people.

He has refused for a long time, after such dissolutions, to cause others to be elected; whereby the Legislative powers, incapable of Annihilation, have returned to the People at large for their exercise; the State remaining in the mean time exposed to all the dangers of invasion from without and convulsions within.

He has endeavoured to prevent the population of these States; for that purpose obstructing the Laws of Naturalization of Foreigners; refusing to pass others to encourage their migrations hither, and raising the conditions of new Appropriations of Lands.

He has obstructed the Administration of Justice, by refusing his Assent to Laws for establishing Judiciary powers.

He has made Judges dependent on his Will alone, for the tenure of their offices, and the amount and payment of their salaries.

He has erected a multitude of New Offices, and sent hither swarms of Officers to harass our People, and eat out their substance.

He has kept among us, in times of peace, Standing Armies without the Consent of our legislature.

He has combined with others to subject us to a jurisdiction foreign to our constitution, and unacknowledged by our laws; giving his Assent to their Acts of pretended Legislation:

For quartering large bodies of armed troops among us:

For protecting them, by a mock Trial, from Punishment for any Murders which they should commit on the Inhabitants of these States:

For cutting off our Trade with all parts of the world:

For imposing taxes on us without our Consent:

For depriving us, in many cases, of the benefits of Trial by jury:

For transporting us beyond Seas to be tried for pretended offences:

For abolishing the free System of English Laws in a neighbouring Province, establishing therein an Arbitrary government, and enlarging its Boundaries so as to render it at once an example and fit instrument for introducing the same absolute rule into these Colonies:

For taking away our Charters, abolishing our most valuable Laws, and altering fundamentally the Forms of our Governments:

For suspending our own Legislatures, and declaring themselves invested with Power to legislate for us in all cases whatsoever.

He has abdicated Government here, by declaring us out of his Protection and waging War against us.

He has plundered our seas, ravaged our Coasts, burnt our towns, and destroyed the lives of our people.

He is at this time transporting large armies of foreign mercenaries to compleat the works of death, desolation, and tyranny, already begun with circumstances of Cruelty & perfidy scarcely paralleled in the most barbarous ages, and totally unworthy the Head of a civilized nation.

He has constrained our fellow Citizens taken Captive on the high Seas to bear Arms against their Country, to become the executioners of their friends and Brethren, or to fall themselves by their Hands.

He has excited domestic insurrections amongst us, and has endeavoured to bring on the inhabitants of our frontiers, the merciless Indian Savages, whose known rule of warfare, is an undistinguished destruction of all ages, sexes, and conditions.

In every stage of these Oppressions We have Petitioned for Redress in the most humble terms: Our repeated Petitions have been answered only by repeated injury. A Prince, whose character is thus marked by every act which may define a Tyrant, is unfit to be the ruler of a free people.

Nor have We been wanting in attention to our British brethren. We have warned them from time to time of attempts by their legislature to extend an unwarrantable jurisdiction over us. We have reminded them of the circumstances of our emigration and settlement here. We have appealed to their native justice and magnanimity, and we have conjured them by the ties of our common kindred to disavow these usurpations, which, would inevitably interrupt our connections and correspondence. They too have been deaf to the voice of justice and of consanguinity. We must, therefore, acquiesce in the necessity, which denounces our Separation, and hold them, as we hold the rest of mankind, Enemies in War, in Peace Friends.

We, therefore, the Representatives of the United States of America, in General Congress, Assembled, appealing to the Supreme Judge of the world for the rectitude of our intentions, do, in the Name, and by Authority of the good People of these Colonies, solemnly publish and declare, That these United Colonies are, and of Right ought to be FREE AND INDEPENDENT STATES; that they are Absolved from all Allegiance to the British Crown, and that all political connection between them and the State of Great Britain, is and ought to be totally dissolved; and that as Free and Independent States, they have full Power to levy War, conclude Peace, contract Alliances, establish Commerce, and to do all other Acts and Things which Independent States may of right do. And for the support of this Declaration, with a firm reliance on the Protection of Divine Providence, we mutually pledge to each other our Lives, our Fortunes, and our sacred Honor.

John Hancock

Button Gwinnett
Lyman Hall
Geo. Walton
Wm. Hooper
Joseph Hewes
John Penn
Edward Rutledge
Thos. Heyward, Junr.
Thomas Lynch, Junr.
Arthur Middleton
Samuel Chase
Wm. Paca
Thos. Stone
Charles Carroll
    of Carrollton

George Wythe
Richard Henry Lee
Th. Jefferson
Benja. Harrison
Thos. Nelson, Jr.
Francis Lightfoot Lee
Carter Braxton
Robt. Morris
Benjamin Rush
Benja. Franklin
John Morton
Geo. Clymer
Jas. Smith
Geo. Taylor

James Wilson
Geo. Ross
Caesar Rodney
Geo. Read
Thos. M'Kean
Wm. Floyd
Phil. Livingston
Frans. Lewis
Lewis Morris
Richd. Stockton
John Witherspoon
Fras. Hopkinson
John Hart
Abra. Clark

Josiah Bartlett
Wm. Whipple
Matthew Thornton
Saml. Adams
John Adams
Robt. Treat Paine
Elbridge Gerry
Step. Hopkins
William Ellery
Roger Sherman
Sam'el Huntington
Wm. Williams
Oliver Wolcott

The Constitution of the United States of America

AGREED TO BY PHILADELPHIA
CONVENTION, SEPTEMBER 17, 1787
IMPLEMENTED MARCH 4, 1789

We the People of the United States, in Order to form a more perfect Union, establish Justice, insure domestic Tranquility, provide for the common defence, promote the general Welfare, and secure the Blessings of Liberty to ourselves and our Posterity, do ordain and establish this Constitution for the United States of America.

ARTICLE I

Section 1. All legislative Powers herein granted shall be vested in a Congress of the United States, which shall consist of a Senate and a House of Representatives.

Section 2. The House of Representatives shall be composed of Members chosen every second Year by the People of the several States, and the Electors in each State shall have the Qualifications requisite for Electors of the most numerous Branch of the State Legislature.

No Person shall be a Representative who shall not have attained to the Age of twenty-five Years, and been seven Years a Citizen of the United States, and who shall not, when elected, be an Inhabitant of that State in which he shall be chosen.

Representatives and direct Taxes shall be apportioned among the several States which may be included within this Union, according to their respective Numbers, *which shall be determined by adding to the whole Number of free Persons, including those bound to Service for a Term of Years, and excluding Indians not taxed, three fifths of all other Persons.*[1] The actual Enumeration shall be made within three Years after the first Meeting of the Congress of the United States, and within every subsequent Term of ten Years, in such Manner as they shall by Law direct. The Number of Representatives shall not exceed one for every thirty Thousand, but each State shall have at Least one Representative; and *until such enumeration shall be made, the State of New Hampshire shall be entitled to chuse three, Massachusetts eight, Rhode Island and Providence Plantations one, Connecticut five, New-York six, New Jersey four, Pennsylvania eight, Delaware one, Maryland six, Virginia ten, North Carolina five, South Carolina five, and Georgia three.*

When vacancies happen in the Representation from any State, the Executive Authority thereof shall issue Writs of Election to fill such Vacancies.

The House of Representatives shall chuse their Speaker and other Officers; and shall have the sole Power of Impeachment.

Section 3. The Senate of the United States shall be composed of two Senators from each State, *chosen by the Legislature thereof,*[2] for six Years; and each Senator shall have one Vote.

Note: The Constitution became effective March 4, 1789. Provisions in italics are no longer relevant or have been changed by constitutional amendment.

[1]Changed by Section 2 of the Fourteenth Amendment.
[2]Changed by Section 1 of the Seventeenth Amendment.

Immediately after they shall be assembled in Consequence of the first Election, they shall be divided as equally as may be into three Classes. The Seats of the Senators of the first Class shall be vacated at the Expiration of the second Year, of the second Class at the Expiration of the fourth Year, and of the third Class at the Expiration of the sixth Year, so that one-third may be chosen every second Year; and if Vacancies happen by Resignation, or otherwise, during the Recess of the Legislature of any State, the Executive thereof may make temporary Appointments until the next Meeting of the Legislature, which shall then fill such Vacancies.[3]

No person shall be a Senator who shall not have attained to the Age of thirty Years, and been nine Years a Citizen of the United States, and who shall not, when elected, be an Inhabitant of that State for which he shall be chosen.

The Vice President of the United States shall be President of the Senate, but shall have no Vote, unless they be equally divided.

The Senate shall chuse their other Officers, and also a President pro tempore, in the absence of the Vice President, or when he shall exercise the Office of President of the United States.

The Senate shall have the sole Power to try all Impeachments. When sitting for that Purpose, they shall be on Oath or Affirmation. When the President of the United States is tried, the Chief Justice shall preside: And no Person shall be convicted without the Concurrence of two thirds of the Members present.

Judgment in Cases of Impeachment shall not extend further than to removal from Office, and disqualification to hold and enjoy any Office of honor, Trust or Profit under the United States: but the Party convicted shall nevertheless be liable and subject to Indictment, Trial, Judgment and Punishment, according to Law.

Section 4. The Times, Places and Manner of holding Elections for Senators and Representatives, shall be prescribed in each State by the Legislature thereof; but the Congress may at any time by Law make or alter such Regulations, except as to the Places of Chusing Senators.

The Congress shall assemble at least once in every Year, and such Meeting *shall be on the first Monday in December, unless they shall by Law appoint a different Day.*[4]

Section 5. Each House shall be the Judge of the Elections, Returns and Qualifications of its own Members, and a Majority of each shall constitute a Quorum to do Business; but a smaller number may adjourn from day to day, and may be authorized to compel the Attendance of absent Members, in such Manner, and under such Penalties, as each House may provide.

Each House may determine the Rules of its Proceedings, punish its Members for disorderly Behavior, and, with the Concurrence of two thirds, expel a Member.

Each House shall keep a Journal of its Proceedings, and from time to time publish the same, excepting such Parts as may in their Judgment require Secrecy; and the Yeas and Nays of the Members of either House on any question shall, at the Desire of one-fifth of those Present, be entered on the Journal.

Neither House, during the Session of Congress, shall, without the Consent of the other, adjourn for more than three days, nor to any other Place than that in which the two Houses shall be sitting.

Section 6. The Senators and Representatives shall receive a Compensation for their Services, to be ascertained by Law, and paid out of the Treasury of the United States. They shall in all Cases, except Treason, Felony and Breach of the Peace, be privileged from Arrest during their Attendance at the Session of their respective Houses, and in going to and returning from the same; and for

---

[3]Changed by Clause 2 of the Seventeenth Amendment.

[4]Changed by Section 2 of the Twentieth Amendment.

any Speech or Debate in either House, they shall not be questioned in any other Place.

No Senator or Representative shall, during the Time for which he was elected, be appointed to any civil Office under the Authority of the United States, which shall have been created, or the Emoluments whereof shall have been increased, during such time; and no Person holding any Office under the United States, shall be a Member of either House during his Continuance in Office.

Section 7.   All Bills for raising Revenue shall originate in the House of Representatives; but the Senate may propose or concur with Amendments as on other Bills.

Every Bill which shall have passed the House of Representatives and the Senate, shall, before it becomes a Law, be presented to the President of the United States; If he approve he shall sign it, but if not he shall return it, with his Objections to that House in which it shall have originated, who shall enter the Objections at large on their Journal, and proceed to reconsider it. If after such Reconsideration two thirds of that House shall agree to pass the Bill, it shall be sent, together with the Objections, to the other House, by which it shall likewise be reconsidered, and if approved by two thirds of that House, it shall become a Law. But in all such Cases the Votes of both Houses shall be determined by Yeas and Nays, and the Names of the Persons voting for and against the Bill shall be entered on the Journal of each House respectively. If any Bill shall not be returned by the President within ten Days (Sundays excepted) after it shall have been presented to him, the Same shall be a Law, in like Manner as if he had signed it, unless the Congress by their Adjournment prevent its Return, in which Case it shall not be a Law.

Every Order, Resolution, or Vote to which the Concurrence of the Senate and the House of Representatives may be necessary (except on a question of Adjournment) shall be presented to the President of the United States; and before the Same shall take Effect, shall be approved by him, or being disapproved by him, shall be repassed by two thirds of the Senate and House of Representatives, according to the Rules and Limitations prescribed in the Case of a Bill.

Section 8.   The Congress shall have Power to lay and collect Taxes, Duties, Imposts and Excises, to pay the Debts and provide for the common Defence and general Welfare of the United States; but all Duties, Imposts and Excises shall be uniform throughout the United States;

To borrow money on the credit of the United States;

To regulate Commerce with foreign Nations, and among the several States, and with the Indian Tribes;

To establish an uniform Rule of Naturalization, and uniform Laws on the subject of Bankruptcies throughout the United States;

To coin Money, regulate the Value thereof, and of foreign Coin, and fix the Standard of Weights and Measures;

To provide for the Punishment of counterfeiting the Securities and current Coin of the United States;

To establish Post Offices and post Roads;

To promote the Progress of Science and useful Arts, by securing for limited Times to Authors and Inventors the exclusive Right to their respective Writings and Discoveries;

To constitute Tribunals inferior to the supreme Court;

To define and punish Piracies and Felonies committed on the high Seas, and Offenses against the Law of Nations;

To declare War, grant Letters of Marque and Reprisal, and make Rules concerning Captures on Land and Water;

To raise and support Armies, but no Appropriation of Money to that Use shall be for a longer Term than two Years;

To provide and maintain a Navy;

To make Rules for the Government and Regulation of the land and naval Forces;

To provide for calling forth the Militia to execute the Laws of the Union, suppress Insurrections and repel Invasions;

To provide for organizing, arming, and disciplining the Militia, and for governing such Part of them as may be employed in the Service of the United States, reserving to the States respectively, the Appointment of the Officers, and the Authority of training the Militia according to the discipline prescribed by Congress;

To exercise exclusive Legislation in all Cases whatsoever, over such District (not exceeding ten Miles square) as may, by Cession of particular States, and the acceptance of Congress, become the Seat of Government of the United States, and to exercise like Authority over all Places purchased by the Consent of the Legislature of the State in which the Same shall be, for the Erection of Forts, Magazines, Arsenals, dock-Yards, and other needful Buildings;—And

To make all Laws which shall be necessary and proper for carrying into Execution the foregoing Powers, and all other Powers vested by this Constitution in the Government of the United States, or in any Department or Officer thereof.

Section 9. The Migration or Importation of such Persons as any of the States now existing shall think proper to admit, shall not be prohibited by the Congress prior to the Year one thousand eight hundred and eight but a tax or duty may be imposed on such Importation, not exceeding ten dollars for each Person.

The privilege of the Writ of Habeas Corpus shall not be suspended, unless when in Cases of Rebellion or Invasion the public Safety may require it.

No Bill of Attainder or ex post facto Law shall be passed.

No capitation, or other direct, Tax shall be laid, unless in Proportion to the Census or Enumeration herein before directed to be taken.[5]

No Tax or Duty shall be laid on Articles exported from any State.

No Preference shall be given by any Regulation of Commerce or Revenue to the Ports of one State over those of another: nor shall Vessels bound to, or from, one State, be obliged to enter, clear, or pay Duties in another.

No Money shall be drawn from the Treasury, but in Consequence of Appropriations made by law; and a regular Statement and Account of the Receipts and Expenditures of all public Money shall be published from time to time.

No Title of Nobility shall be granted by the United States: And no Person holding any Office of Profit or Trust under them, shall, without the Consent of the Congress, accept of any present, Emolument, Office, or Title, of any kind whatever, from any King, Prince, or foreign State.

Section 10. No State shall enter into any Treaty, Alliance, or Confederation; grant Letters of Marque and Reprisal; coin Money; emit Bills of Credit; make any Thing but gold and silver Coin a Tender in Payment of Debts; pass any Bill of Attainder, ex post facto Law, or Law impairing the Obligation of Contracts, or grant any Title of Nobility.

No State shall, without the Consent of the Congress, lay any Imposts or Duties on Imports or Exports, except what may be absolutely necessary for executing its inspection Laws: and the net Produce of all Duties and Imposts, laid by any State on Imports or Exports, shall be for the Use of the Treasury of the United States; and all such Laws shall be subject to the Revision and Control of the Congress.

No State shall, without the Consent of the Congress, lay any duty of Tonnage, keep Troops, or Ships of War in time of Peace, enter into any Agreement or Compact with another State, or with a foreign Power, or engage in War, unless actually invaded, or in such imminent Danger as will not admit of delay.

ARTICLE II

Section 1. The executive Power shall be vested in a President of the United States of America. He

---

[5]Changed by the Sixteenth Amendment.

shall hold his Office during the Term of four Years, and, together with the Vice President, chosen for the same Term, be elected, as follows:

Each State shall appoint, in such Manner as the Legislature thereof may direct, a Number of Electors, equal to the whole Number of Senators and Representatives to which the State may be entitled in the Congress; but no Senator or Representative, or Person holding an Office of Trust or Profit under the United States, shall be appointed an Elector.

The Electors shall meet in their respective States, and vote by Ballot for two Persons, of whom one at least shall not be an Inhabitant of the same State with themselves. And they shall make a List of all the Persons voted for, and of the Number of Votes for each; which List they shall sign and certify, and transmit sealed to the Seat of the Government of the United States, directed to the President of the Senate. The President of the Senate shall, in the Presence of the Senate and House of Representatives, open all the Certificates, and the Votes shall then be counted. The Person having the greatest Number of Votes shall be the President, if such Number be a Majority of the whole Number of Electors appointed; and if there be more than one who have such Majority, and have an equal Number of Votes, then the House of Representatives shall immediately chuse by Ballot one of them for President; and if no Person have a Majority, then from the five highest on the List the said House shall in like Manner chuse the President. But in chusing the President, the Votes shall be taken by States, the Representation from each State having one Vote; a quorum for this Purpose shall consist of a Member or Members from two thirds of the States, and a Majority of all the States shall be necessary to a Choice. In every Case, after the Choice of the President, the Person having the greatest Number of Votes of the Electors shall be the Vice President. But if there should remain two or more who have equal Votes, the Senate shall chuse from them by Ballot the Vice President.[6]

The Congress may determine the Time of chusing the Electors, and the Day on which they shall give their Votes; which Day shall be the same throughout the United States.

No Person except a natural born Citizen, or a Citizen of the United States, at the time of the Adoption of this Constitution, shall be eligible to the Office of President; neither shall any Person be eligible to that Office who shall not have attained to the Age of thirty five Years, and been fourteen Years a Resident within the United States.

In Case of the Removal of the President from Office, or of his Death, Resignation, or Inability to discharge the Powers and Duties of the said Office, the same shall devolve on the Vice President, *and the Congress may by Law provide for the Case of Removal, Death, Resignation, or Inability, both of the President and Vice President, declaring what Officer shall then act as President, and such Officer shall act accordingly, until the Disability be removed, or a President shall be elected.*[7]

The President shall, at stated Times, receive for his Services a Compensation, which shall neither be increased nor diminished during the Period for which he shall have been elected, and he shall not receive within that Period any other Emolument from the United States, or any of them.

Before he enter on the Execution of his Office, he shall take the following Oath or Affirmation:—"I do solemnly swear (or affirm) that I will faithfully execute the Office of President of the United States, and will to the best of my Ability, preserve, protect and defend the Constitution of the United States."

Section 2.   The President shall be Commander in Chief of the Army and Navy of the United States, and of the Militia of the several States, when called into the actual Service of the United States; he may require the Opinion, in writing, of the principal Officer in each of the executive Departments, upon any Subject relating to the Duties of their respective Offices, and he shall have

---

[6]Superseded by the Twelfth Amendment.

[7]Modified by the Twenty-fifth Amendment.

Power to Grant Reprieves and Pardons for Offences against the United States, except in Cases of Impeachment.

He shall have Power, by and with the Advice and Consent of the Senate, to make Treaties, provided two thirds of the Senators present concur; and he shall nominate, and by and with the Advice and Consent of the Senate, shall appoint Ambassadors, other public Ministers and Consuls, Judges of the supreme Court, and all other Officers of the United States, whose Appointments are not herein otherwise provided for, and which shall be established by Law: but the Congress may by Law vest the Appointment of such inferior Officers, as they think proper, in the President alone, in the Courts of Law, or in the Heads of Departments.

The President shall have Power to fill up all Vacancies that may happen during the Recess of the Senate, by granting Commissions which shall expire at the End of their next Session.

Section 3. He shall from time to time give to the Congress Information of the State of the Union, and recommend to their Consideration such Measures as he shall judge necessary and expedient; he may, on extraordinary Occasions, convene both Houses, or either of them, and in Case of Disagreement between them, with Respect to the Time of Adjournment, he may adjourn them to such Time as he shall think proper; he shall receive Ambassadors and other public Ministers; he shall take Care that the Laws be faithfully executed, and shall Commission all the Officers of the United States.

Section 4. The President, Vice President and all civil Officers of the United States, shall be removed from Office on Impeachment for, and Conviction of, Treason, Bribery, or other high Crimes and Misdemeanors.

ARTICLE III

Section 1. The judicial Power of the United States, shall be vested in one supreme Court, and in such inferior Courts as the Congress may from time to time ordain and establish. The Judges, both of the supreme and inferior Courts, shall hold their Offices during good Behaviour, and shall, at stated Times, receive for their Services a Compensation, which shall not be diminished during their Continuance in Office.

Section 2. The judicial Power shall extend to all Cases, in Law and Equity, arising under this Constitution, the Laws of the United States, and Treaties made, or which shall be made, under their Authority;—to all Cases affecting Ambassadors, other public Ministers and Consuls;—to all Cases of admiralty and maritime Jurisdiction;—to Controversies to which the United States shall be a Party;—to Controversies between two or more States;—*between a State and Citizens of another State;*[8]—between Citizens of different States;—between Citizens of the same State claiming Lands under Grants of different States, and between a State, or the Citizens thereof, and foreign States, Citizens or Subjects.

In all Cases affecting Ambassadors, other public Ministers and Consuls, and those in which a State shall be Party, the supreme Court shall have original Jurisdiction. In all the other Cases before mentioned, the supreme Court shall have appellate Jurisdiction, both as to Law and Fact, with such Exceptions, and under such Regulations as the Congress shall make.

The trial of all Crimes, except in Cases of Impeachment, shall be by Jury; and such Trial shall be held in the State where said Crimes shall have been committed; but when not committed within any State, the Trial shall be at such Place or Places as the Congress may by Law have directed.

Section 3. Treason against the United States, shall consist only in levying War against them, or in adhering to their Enemies, giving them Aid and Comfort. No Person shall be convicted of Treason unless on the Testimony of two Witnesses to the same overt Act, or on Confession in open Court.

---

[8]Restricted by the Eleventh Amendment.

The Congress shall have Power to declare the Punishment of Treason, but no Attainder of Treason shall work Corruption of Blood, or Forefeiture except during the Life of the Person attainted.

ARTICLE IV

Section 1.   Full Faith and Credit shall be given in each State to the public Acts, Records, and judicial Proceedings of every other State. And the Congress may by general Laws prescribe the Manner in which such Acts, Records, and Proceedings shall be proved, and the Effect thereof.

Section 2.   The Citizens of each State shall be entitled to all Privileges and Immunities of Citizens in the several States.

A Person charged in any State with Treason, Felony, or other Crime, who shall flee from Justice, and be found in another State, shall on demand of the executive Authority of the State from which he fled, be delivered up, to be removed to the State having Jurisdiction of the Crime.

No Person held to Service or Labour in one State, under the Laws thereof, escaping into another, shall, in Consequence of any Law or Regulation therein, be discharged from such Service or Labour, but shall be delivered up on Claim of the Party to whom such Service or Labour may be due.[9]

Section 3.   New States may be admitted by the Congress into this Union; but no new State shall be formed or erected within the Jurisdiction of any other State; nor any State be formed by the Junction of two or more States, or parts of States, without the Consent of the Legislatures of the States concerned as well as of the Congress.

The Congress shall have Power to dispose of and make all needful Rules and Regulations respecting the Territory or other Property belonging to the United States; and nothing in this Constitution shall be so construed as to Prejudice any Claims of the United States, or of any particular State.

Section 4.   The United States shall guarantee to every State in this Union a Republican Form of Government, and shall protect each of them against Invasion; and on Application of the Legislature, or of the Executive (when the Legislature cannot be convened) against domestic Violence.

ARTICLE V

The Congress, whenever two thirds of both Houses shall deem it necessary, shall propose Amendments to this Constitution, or, on the Application of the Legislatures of two thirds of the several States, shall call a Convention for proposing Amendments, which, in either Case, shall be valid to all Intents and Purposes, as Part of this Constitution, when ratified by the Legislatures of three fourths of the several States, or by Conventions in three fourths thereof, as the one or the other Mode of Ratification may be proposed by the Congress; Provided that no Amendment which may be made prior to the Year One thousand eight hundred and eight shall in any Manner affect the first and fourth Clauses in the Ninth Section of the first Article; and that no State, without its Consent, shall be deprived of its equal Suffrage in the Senate.

ARTICLE VI

All Debts contracted and Engagements entered into, before the Adoption of this Constitution, shall be as valid against the United States under this Constitution, as under the Confederation.

This Constitution, and the Laws of the United States which shall be made in Pursuance thereof; and all Treaties made, or which shall be made, under the Authority of the United States, shall be the supreme Law of the Land; and the Judges in every State shall be bound thereby, any Thing in the Constitution or Laws of any State to the Contrary notwithstanding.

The Senators and Representatives before mentioned, and the Members of the several State Legislatures, and all executive and judicial Officers, both of the United States and of the several

---

[9]Superseded by the Thirteenth Amendment.

States, shall be bound by Oath or Affirmation, to support this Constitution; but no religious Test shall ever be required as a Qualification to any Office or public Trust under the United States.

Article VII

The Ratification of the Conventions of nine States shall be sufficient for the Establishment of this Constitution between the States so ratifying the Same.

Done in Convention by the Unanimous Consent of the States present the Seventeenth Day of September in the Year of our Lord one thousand seven hundred and Eighty seven and of the Independence of the United States of America the Twelfth. In Witness whereof We have hereunto subscribed our Names.

Go. Washington
President and deputy from Virginia

New Hampshire
John Langdon
Nicholas Gilman

Massachusetts
Nathaniel Gorham
Rufus King

Connecticut
Wm. Saml. Johnson
Roger Sherman

New York
Alexander Hamilton

New Jersey
Wil. Livingston
David Brearley
Wm. Paterson
Jona. Dayton

Pennsylvania
B. Franklin
Thomas Mifflin
Robt. Morris
Geo. Clymer
Thos. FitzSimons
Jared Ingersoll
James Wilson
Gouv. Morris

Delaware
Geo. Read
Gunning Bedford jun
John Dickinson
Richard Bassett
Jaco. Broom

Maryland
James McHenry
Dan. of St. Thos.
   Jenifer
Danl. Carroll

Virginia
John Blair
James Madison, Jr.

North Carolina
Wm. Blount
Richd. Dobbs
   Spaight
Hu Williamson

South Carolina
J. Rutledge
Charles Cotesworth
   Pinckney
Pierce Butler

Georgia
William Few
Abr. Baldwin

Amendments to the Constitution

AMENDMENT I [1791][1]

Congress shall make no law respecting an establishment of religion, or prohibiting the free exercise thereof; or abridging the freedom of speech, or of the press; or the right of the people peaceably to assemble, and to petition the government for a redress of grievances.

AMENDMENT II [1791]

A well-regulated militia being necessary to the security of a free State, the right of the people to keep and bear arms shall not be infringed.

AMENDMENT III [1791]

No soldier shall, in time of peace, be quartered in any house without the consent of the owner, nor in time of war, but in a manner to be prescribed by law.

AMENDMENT IV [1791]

The right of the people to be secure in their persons, houses, papers, and effects, against unreasonable searches and seizures, shall not be violated, and no warrants shall issue but upon probable cause, supported by oath or affirmation, and particularly describing the place to be searched, and the persons or things to be seized.

---

[1] The dates in brackets indicate when the amendment was ratified.

AMENDMENT V [1791]

No person shall be held to answer for a capital, or otherwise infamous crime, unless on a presentment or indictment of a grand jury, except in cases arising in the land or naval forces, or in the militia, when in actual service in time of war or public danger; nor shall any person be subject for the same offence to be twice put in jeopardy of life or limb; nor shall be compelled in any criminal case to be a witness against himself, nor be deprived of life, liberty, or property, without due process of law; nor shall private property be taken for public use without just compensation.

AMENDMENT VI [1791]

In all criminal prosecutions, the accused shall enjoy the right to a speedy and public trial, by an impartial jury of the State and district wherein the crime shall have been committed, which district shall have been previously ascertained by law, and to be informed of the nature and cause of the accusation; to be confronted with the witnesses against him; to have compulsory process for obtaining witnesses in his favor, and to have the assistance of counsel for his defence.

AMENDMENT VII [1791]

In suits at common law, where the value in controversy shall exceed twenty dollars, the right of trial by jury shall be preserved, and no fact tried by a jury shall be otherwise reexamined in any court of the United States, than according to the rules of the common law.

AMENDMENT VIII [1791]

Excessive bail shall not be required, nor excessive fines imposed, nor cruel and unusual punishments inflicted.

AMENDMENT IX [1791]

The enumeration in the Constitution, of certain rights, shall not be construed to deny or disparage others retained by the people.

AMENDMENT X [1791]

The powers not delegated to the United States by the Constitution, nor prohibited by it to the States, are reserved to the States respectively, or to the people.

AMENDMENT XI [1798]

The judicial power of the United States shall not be construed to extend to any suit in law or equity, commenced or prosecuted against one of the United States by citizens of another State, or by citizens or subjects of any foreign state.

AMENDMENT XII [1804]

The electors shall meet in their respective States, and vote by ballot for President and Vice-President, one of whom, at least, shall not be an inhabitant of the same State with themselves; they shall name in their ballots the person voted for as President, and in distinct ballots the person voted for as Vice-President, and they shall make distinct lists of all persons voted for as President, and of all persons voted for as Vice-President, and of the number of votes for each, which lists they shall sign and certify, and transmit sealed to the seat of government of the United States, directed to the President of the Senate;—the President of the Senate shall, in the presence of the Senate and House of Representatives, open all the certificates and the votes shall then be counted;—the person having the greatest number of votes for President shall be the President, if such number be a majority of the whole number of electors appointed; and if no person have such majority, then from the persons having the highest numbers not exceeding three on the list of those voted for as President, the House of Representatives shall choose immediately, by ballot, the President. But in choosing the President, the votes shall be taken by States, the representation from each State having one vote; a quorum for this purpose shall consist of a member or members from two-thirds of the States, and a majority of all the States shall be necessary to a choice. And if the House of Representatives shall not choose a President whenever the right of choice shall devolve upon them, before *the fourth day of March* next following, then the Vice-President shall act as President, as in the case of the death or other constitutional disability of the President.[2]

The person having the greatest number of votes as Vice-President shall be the Vice-President, if such number be a majority of the whole number of electors appointed; and if no person have a majority, then from the two highest numbers on the list the Senate shall choose the Vice-President; a quorum for the purpose shall consist of two-thirds of the whole number of Senators, and a majority of the whole number shall be necessary to a choice. But no person constitutionally ineligible to the office of President shall be eligible to that of Vice-President of the United States.

AMENDMENT XIII [1865]

Section 1. Neither slavery nor involuntary servitude, except as a punishment for crime whereof the party shall have been duly convicted, shall exist within the United States, or any place subject to their jurisdiction.

---

[2]Superseded by Section 3 of the Twentieth Amendment.

Section 2. Congress shall have power to enforce this article by appropriate legislation.

AMENDMENT XIV [1868]

Section 1. All persons born or naturalized in the United States, and subject to the jurisdiction thereof, are citizens of the United States and of the State wherein they reside. No State shall make or enforce any law which shall abridge the privileges or immunities of citizens of the United States; nor shall any State deprive any person of life, liberty, or property, without due process of law; nor deny to any person within its jurisdiction the equal protection of the laws.

Section 2. Representatives shall be appointed among the several States according to their respective numbers, counting the whole number of persons in each State, excluding Indians not taxed. But when the right to vote at any election for the choice of electors for President and Vice-President of the United States, Representatives in Congress, the executive and judicial officers of a State, or the members of the legislature thereof, is denied to any of the male inhabitants of such State, being twenty-one years of age and citizens of the United States, or in any way abridged, except for participation in rebellion, or other crime, the basis of representation therein shall be reduced in the proportion which the number of such male citizens shall bear to the whole number of male citizens twenty-one years of age in such State.

Section 3. No person shall be a Senator or Representative in Congress, or Elector of President and Vice-President, or hold any office, civil or military, under the United States, or under any State, who, having previously taken an oath, as a member of Congress, or as an officer of the United States, or as a member of any State legislature, or as an executive or judicial officer of any State, to support the Constitution of the United States, shall have engaged in insurrection or rebellion against the same, or given aid or comfort to the enemies thereof. Congress may, by a vote of two-thirds of each house, remove such disability.

Section 4. The validity of the public debt of the United States, authorized by law, including debts incurred for payment of pensions and bounties for services in suppressing insurrection or rebellion, shall not be questioned. But neither the United States nor any State shall assume or pay any debt or obligation incurred in aid of insurrection or rebellion against the United States, or any claim for the loss or emancipation of any slave; but all such debts, obligations, and claims shall be held illegal and void.

Section 5. The Congress shall have power to enforce, by appropriate legislation, the provisions of this article.

AMENDMENT XV [1870]

Section 1. The right of citizens of the United States to vote shall not be denied or abridged by the United States or by any State on account of race, color, or previous condition of servitude.

Section 2. The Congress shall have power to enforce this article by appropriate legislation.

AMENDMENT XVI [1913]

The Congress shall have power to lay and collect taxes on incomes, from whatever source derived, without apportionment among the several States, and without regard to any census or enumeration.

AMENDMENT XVII [1913]

Section 1. The Senate of the United States shall be composed of two Senators from each State, elected by the people thereof, for six years; and each Senator shall have one vote. The electors in each State shall have the qualifications requisite for electors of [voters for] the most numerous branch of the State legislatures.

Section 2. When vacancies happen in the representation of any State in the Senate, the executive authority of such State shall issue writs of election to fill such vacancies: Provided, that the Legislature of any State may empower the executive thereof to make temporary appointments until the people fill the vacancies by election as the Legislature may direct.

Section 3. This amendment shall not be so construed as to affect the election or term of any Senator chosen before it becomes valid as part of the Constitution.

AMENDMENT XVIII
[1919; REPEALED 1933 BY AMENDMENT XXI]

Section 1. After one year from the ratification of this article the manufacture, sale, or transportation of intoxicating liquors within, the importation thereof into, or the exportation thereof from the United States and all territory subject to the jurisdiction thereof, for beverage purposes, is hereby prohibited.

Section 2. The Congress and the several States shall have concurrent power to enforce this article by appropriate legislation.

Section 3. This article shall be inoperative unless it shall have been ratified as an amendment to the Constitution by the legislatures of the several States, as provided by the Constitution, within seven years from the date of the submission thereof to the States by the Congress.

AMENDMENT XIX [1920]

Section 1. The right of citizens of the United States to vote shall not be denied or abridged by the United States or by any State on account of sex.

Section 2. Congress shall have the power to enforce this article by appropriate legislation.

AMENDMENT XX [1933]

Section 1. The terms of the President and Vice-President shall end at noon on the twentieth day of January, and the terms of Senators and Representatives at noon on the third day of January, of the years in which such terms would have ended if this article had not been ratified; and the terms of their successors shall then began.

Section 2. The Congress shall assemble at least once in every year, and such meeting shall begin at noon on the third day of January, unless they shall by law appoint a different day.

Section 3. If, at the time fixed for the beginning of the term of the President, the President-elect shall have died, the Vice-President-elect shall become President. If a President shall not have been chosen before the time fixed for the beginning of his term, or if the President-elect shall have failed to qualify, then the Vice-President-elect shall act as President until a President shall have qualified; and the Congress may by law provide for the case wherein neither a President-elect nor a Vice-President-elect shall have qualified, declaring who shall then act as President, or the manner in which one who is to act shall be selected, and such person shall act accordingly until a President or Vice-President shall have qualified.

Section 4. The Congress may by law provide for the case of the death of any of the persons from whom the House of Representatives may choose a President whenever the right of choice shall have devolved upon them, and for the case of the death of any of the persons from whom the Senate may choose a Vice-President whenever the right of choice shall have devolved upon them.

Section 5. Sections 1 and 2 shall take effect on the 15th day of October following the ratification of this article.

Section 6. This article shall be inoperative unless it shall have been ratified as an amendment to the Constitution by the Legislatures of three-fourths of the several States within seven years from the date of its submission.

AMENDMENT XXI [1933]

Section 1. The eighteenth article of amendment to the Constitution of the United States is hereby repealed.

Section 2. The transportation or importation into any State, Territory, or Possession of the United States for delivery or use therein of intoxicating liquors, in violation of the laws thereof, is hereby prohibited.

Section 3. This article shall be inoperative unless it shall have been ratified as an amendment to the Constitution by conventions in the several States, as provided in the Constitution, within seven years from the date of the submission thereof to the States by the Congress.

AMENDMENT XXII [1951]

Section 1. No person shall be elected to the office of the President more than twice, and no person who has held the office of President, or acted as President, for more than two years of a term to which some other person was elected President shall be elected to the office of President more than once. But this article shall not apply to any person holding the office of President when this Article was proposed by the Congress, and shall not prevent any person who may be holding the office of President, or acting as President, during the term within which this Article becomes operative from holding the office of President or acting as President during the remainder of such term.

Section 2. This article shall be inoperative unless it shall have been ratified as an amendment to the Constitution by the legislatures of three-fourths of the several States within seven years

from the date of its submission to the States by the Congress.

AMENDMENT XXIII [1961]

Section 1. The District constituting the seat of Government of the United States shall appoint in such manner as the Congress may direct: A number of electors of President and Vice-President equal to the whole number of Senators and Representatives in Congress to which the District would be entitled if it were a State, but in no event more than the least populous State; they shall be in addition to those appointed by the States, but they shall be considered for the purposes of the election of President and Vice-President, to be electors appointed by a State; and they shall meet in the District and perform such duties as provided by the twelfth article of amendment.

Section 2. The Congress shall have the power to enforce this article by appropriate legislation.

AMENDMENT XXIV [1964]

Section 1. The right of citizens of the United States to vote in any primary or other election for President or Vice-President, for electors for President or Vice-President, or for Senator or Representative in Congress, shall not be denied or abridged by the United States or any State by reason of failure to pay any poll tax or other tax.

Section 2. The Congress shall have the power to enforce this article by appropriate legislation.

AMENDMENT XXV [1967]

Section 1. In case of the removal of the President from office or of his death or resignation, the Vice-President shall become President.

Section 2. Whenever there is a vacancy in the office of the Vice-President, the President shall nominate a Vice-President who shall take office upon confirmation by a majority vote of both Houses of Congress.

Section 3. Whenever the President transmits to the President pro tempore of the Senate and the Speaker of the House of Representatives his written declaration that he is unable to discharge the powers and duties of his office, and until he transmits to them a written declaration to the contrary, such powers and duties shall be discharged by the Vice-President as Acting President.

Section 4. Whenever the Vice-President and a majority of either the principal officers of the executive departments or of such other body as Congress may by law provide, transmit to the President pro tempore of the Senate and the Speaker of the House of Representatives their written declaration that the President is unable to discharge the powers and duties of his office, the Vice-President shall immediately assume the powers and duties of the office as Acting President.

Thereafter, when the President transmits to the President pro tempore of the Senate and the Speaker of the House of Representatives his written declaration that no inability exists, he shall resume the powers and duties of his office unless the Vice-President and a majority of either the principal officers of the executive department[s] or of such other body as Congress may by law provide, transmit within four days to the President pro tempore of the Senate and the Speaker

of the House of Representatives their written declaration that the President is unable to discharge the powers and duties of his office. Thereupon Congress shall decide the issue, assembling within forty-eight hours for that purpose if not in session. If the Congress, within twenty-one days after receipt of the latter written declaration, or, if Congress is not in session, within twenty-one days after Congress is required to assemble, determines by two-thirds vote of both Houses that the President is unable to discharge the powers and duties of his office, the Vice-President shall continue to discharge the same as Acting President; otherwise, the President shall resume the powers and duties of his office.

AMENDMENT XXVI [1971]

Section 1. The right of citizens of the United States, who are eighteen years of age or older, to vote shall not be denied or abridged by the United States or by any State on account of age.

Section 2. The Congress shall have power to enforce this article by appropriate legislation.

AMENDMENT XXVII [1992]

No law, varying the compensation for the services of the Senators and Representatives, shall take effect, until an election of Representatives shall have intervened.

Seneca Falls Declaration of Sentiments and Resolutions

I‌N 1848, E‌LIZABETH C‌ADY S‌TANTON, Lucretia Mott, and Martha Coffin Wright, among others, called a meeting in Stanton's hometown of Seneca Falls, New York, to discuss "the social, civil and religious condition of Woman." Over three hundred men and women attended, and one hundred signed a comprehensive document that detailed the discriminations women endured and demanded women's rights, most controversially the vote. "The Declaration of Sentiments" was forthrightly modeled on the Declaration of Independence (see p. A-1), which is telling evidence of the Seneca Falls signers' understanding that the liberties and rights promised by the American Revolution had not been extended to the female half of the population.

D‌ECLARATION OF S‌ENTIMENTS

When, in the course of human events, it becomes necessary for one portion of the family of man to assume among the people of the earth a position different from that which they have hitherto occupied, but one to which the laws of nature and of nature's God entitle them, a decent respect to the opinions of mankind requires that they should declare the causes that impel them to such a course.

We hold these truths to be self-evident: that all men and women are created equal; that they are endowed by their Creator with certain inalienable rights; that among these are life, liberty, and the pursuit of happiness; that to secure these rights governments are instituted, deriving their just powers from the consent of the governed.

Whenever any form of government becomes destructive of these ends, it is the right of those who suffer from it to refuse allegiance to it, and to insist upon the institution of a new government, laying its foundations on such principles, and organizing its powers in such form, as to them shall seem most likely to effect their safety and happiness. Prudence, indeed, will dictate that governments long established should not be changed for light and transient causes; and accordingly all experience hath shown that mankind are more disposed to suffer, while evils are sufferable, than to right themselves by abolishing the forms to which they were accustomed. But when a long train of abuses and usurpations, pursuing invariably the same object evinces a design to reduce them under absolute despotism, it is their duty to throw off such government, and to provide new guards for their future security. Such has been the patient sufferance of the women under this government, and such is now the necessity which constrains them to demand the equal station to which they are entitled.

S‌OURCE: Susan B. Anthony, Elizabeth Cady Stanton, and Matilda Joslyn Gage, eds., *History of Woman Suffrage* (Rochester, NY: S. B. Anthony, 1889).

The history of mankind is a history of repeated injuries and usurpations on the part of man toward woman, having in direct object the establishment of an absolute tyranny over her. To prove this, let facts be submitted to a candid world.

He has never permitted her to exercise her inalienable right to the elective franchise. He has compelled her to submit to laws, in the formation of which she had no voice. He has withheld from her rights which are given to the most ignorant and degraded men—both natives and foreigners.

Having deprived her of this first right of a citizen, the elective franchise, thereby leaving her without representation in the halls of legislation, he has oppressed her on all sides.

He has made her, if married, in the eye of the law, civilly dead.

He has taken from her all right in property, even to the wages she earns.

He has made her, morally, an irresponsible being, as she can commit many crimes with impunity, provided they be done in the presence of her husband. In the covenant of marriage, she is compelled to promise obedience to her husband, he becoming, to all intents and purposes, her master—the law giving him power to deprive her of her liberty, and to administer chastisement.

He has so framed the laws of divorce, as to what shall be the proper causes, and in case of separation, to whom the guardianship of the children shall be given, as to be wholly regardless of the happiness of women—the law, in all cases, going upon a false supposition of the supremacy of man, and giving all power into his hands.

After depriving her of all rights as a married woman, if single, and the owner of property, he has taxed her to support a government which recognizes her only when her property can be made profitable to it.

He has monopolized nearly all the profitable employments, and from those she is permitted to follow, she receives but a scanty remuneration. He closes against her all the avenues to wealth and distinction which he considers most honorable to himself. As a teacher of theology, medicine, or law, she is not known.

He has denied her the facilities for obtaining a thorough education, all colleges being closed against her.

He allows her in Church, as well as State, but in a subordinate position, claiming Apostolic authority for her exclusion from the ministry, and, with some exceptions, from any public participation in the affairs of the Church.

He has created a false public sentiment by giving to the world a different code of morals for men and women, by which moral delinquencies which exclude women from society, are not only tolerated, but deemed of little account in man.

He has usurped the prerogative of Jehovah himself, claiming it as his right to assign for her a sphere of action, when that belongs to her conscience and to her God.

He has endeavored, in every way that he could, to destroy her confidence in her own powers, to lessen her self-respect, and to make her willing to lead a dependent and abject life.

Now, in view of this entire disfranchisement of one-half the people of this country, their social and religious degradation—in view of the unjust laws above mentioned, and because women do feel themselves aggrieved, oppressed, and fraudulently deprived of their most sacred rights, we insist that they have immediate admission to all the rights and privileges which belong to them as citizens of the United States.

In entering upon the great work before us, we anticipate no small amount of misconception, misrepresentation, and ridicule; but we shall use every instrumentality within our power to effect our object. We shall employ agents, circulate tracts, petition the State and National legislatures, and endeavor to enlist the pulpit and the press in our behalf. We hope this Convention will be followed by a series of Conventions embracing every part of the country.

RESOLUTIONS

WHEREAS, The great precept of nature is conceded to be, that "man shall pursue his own true and substantial happiness." [William] Blackstone in his *Commentaries* remarks, that this law of Nature being coequal with mankind, and dictated by God himself, is of course superior in obligation to any other. It is binding over all the globe, in all countries and at all times; no human laws are of any validity if contrary to this, and such of them as are valid, derive all their force, and all their validity, and all their authority, mediately and immediately, from this original; therefore,

Resolved, That such laws as conflict, in any way, with the true and substantial happiness of woman, are contrary to the great precept of nature and of no validity, for this is "superior in obligation to any other."

Resolved, That all laws which prevent woman from occupying such a station in society as her conscience shall dictate, or which place her in a position inferior to that of man, are contrary to the great precept of nature, and therefore of no force or authority.

Resolved, That woman is man's equal—was intended to be so by the Creator, and the highest good of the race demands that she should be recognized as such.

Resolved, That the women of this country ought to be enlightened in regard to the laws under which they live, that they may no longer publish their degradation by declaring themselves satisfied with their present position, nor their ignorance, by asserting that they have all the rights they want.

Resolved, That inasmuch as man, while claiming for himself intellectual superiority, does accord to woman moral superiority, it is preeminently his duty to encourage her to speak and teach, as she has an opportunity, in all religious assemblies.

Resolved, That the same amount of virtue, delicacy, and refinement of behavior that is required of woman in the social state, should also be required of man, and the same transgressions should be visited with equal severity on both man and woman.

Resolved, That the objection of indelicacy and impropriety, which is so often brought against woman when she addresses a public audience, comes with a very ill-grace from those who encourage, by their attendance, her appearance on the stage, in the concert, or in feats of the circus.

Resolved, That woman has too long rested satisfied in the circumscribed limits which corrupt customs and a perverted application of the Scriptures have marked out for her, and that it is time she should move in the enlarged sphere which her great Creator has assigned her.

Resolved, That it is the duty of the women of this country to secure to themselves their sacred right to the elective franchise.

Resolved, That the equality of human rights results necessarily from the fact of the identity of the race in capabilities and responsibilities.

Resolved, therefore, That, being invested by the Creator with the same capabilities, and the same consciousness of responsibility for their exercise, it is demonstrably the right and duty of woman, equally with man, to promote every righteous cause by every righteous means; and especially in regard to the great subjects of morals and religion, it is self-evidently her right to participate with her brother in teaching them, both in private and in public, by writing and by speaking, by any instrumentalities proper to be used, and in any assemblies proper to be held; and this being a self-evident truth growing out of the divinely implanted principles of human nature, any custom or authority adverse to it, whether modern or wearing the hoary sanction of antiquity, is to be regarded as a self-evident falsehood, and at war with mankind.

[Signers, in alphabetical order]

Caroline Barker
Eunice Barker
William G. Barker
Rachel D. Bonnel
  (Mitchell)
Joel D. Bunker
William Burroughs
E. W. Capron
Jacob P. Chamberlain
Elizabeth Conklin
Mary Conklin
P. A. Culvert
Cynthia Davis
Thomas Dell
William S. Dell
Elias J. Doty
Susan R. Doty
Frederick Douglass
Julia Ann Drake
Harriet Cady Eaton
Elisha Foote
Eunice Newton Foote
Mary Ann Frink
Cynthia Fuller
Experience Gibbs
Mary Gilbert

Lydia Gild
Sarah Hallowell
Mary H. Hallowell
Henry Hatley
Sarah Hoffman
Charles L. Hoskins
Jane C. Hunt
Richard P. Hunt
Margaret Jenkins
John Jones
Lucy Jones
Phebe King
Hannah J. Latham
Lovina Latham
Elizabeth Leslie
Eliza Martin
Mary Martin
Delia Mathews
Dorothy Mathews
Jacob Mathews
Elizabeth W. M'Clintock
Mary M'Clintock
Mary Ann M'Clintock
Thomas M'Clintock
Jonathan Metcalf
Nathan J. Milliken

Mary S. Mirror
Pheobe Mosher
Sarah A. Mosher
James Mott
Lucretia Mott
Lydia Mount
Catharine C. Paine
Rhoda Palmer
Saron Phillips
Sally Pitcher
Hannah Plant
Ann Porter
Amy Post
George W. Pryor
Margaret Pryor
Susan Quinn
Rebecca Race
Martha Ridley
Azaliah Schooley
Margaret Schooley
Deborah Scott
Antoinette E. Segur
Henry Seymour
Henry W. Seymour
Malvina Seymour
Catharine Shaw

Stephen Shear
Sarah Sisson
Robert Smallbridge
Elizabeth D. Smith
Sarah Smith
David Spalding
Lucy Spalding
Elizabeth Cady Stanton
Catharine F. Stebbins
Sophronia Taylor
Betsey Tewksbury
Samuel D. Tillman
Edward F. Underhill
Martha Underhill
Mary E. Vail
Isaac Van Tassel
Sarah Whitney
Maria E. Wilbur
Justin Williams
Sarah R. Woods
Charlotte Woodward
S. E. Woodworth
Martha C. Wright

Presidents of the United States

Years in Office	President	Party
1789–1797	George Washington	No party designation
1797–1801	John Adams	Federalist
1801–1809	Thomas Jefferson	Democratic-Republican
1809–1817	James Madison	Democratic-Republican
1817–1825	James Monroe	Democratic-Republican
1825–1829	John Quincy Adams	Democratic-Republican
1829–1837	Andrew Jackson	Democratic
1837–1841	Martin Van Buren	Democratic
1841	William H. Harrison	Whig
1841–1845	John Tyler	Whig
1845–1849	James K. Polk	Democratic
1849–1850	Zachary Taylor	Whig
1850–1853	Millard Fillmore	Whig
1853–1857	Franklin Pierce	Democratic
1857–1861	James Buchanan	Democratic
1861–1865	Abraham Lincoln	Republican
1865–1869	Andrew Johnson	Republican
1869–1877	Ulysses S. Grant	Republican
1877–1881	Rutherford B. Hayes	Republican
1881	James A. Garfield	Republican
1881–1885	Chester A. Arthur	Republican
1885–1889	Grover Cleveland	Democratic
1889–1893	Benjamin Harrison	Republican
1893–1897	Grover Cleveland	Democratic
1897–1901	William McKinley	Republican
1901–1909	Theodore Roosevelt	Republican
1909–1913	William H. Taft	Republican

1913–1921	Woodrow Wilson	Democratic
1921–1923	Warren G. Harding	Republican
1923–1929	Calvin Coolidge	Republican
1929–1933	Herbert C. Hoover	Republican
1933–1945	Franklin D. Roosevelt	Democratic
1945–1953	Harry S. Truman	Democratic
1953–1961	Dwight D. Eisenhower	Republican
1961–1963	John F. Kennedy	Democratic
1963–1969	Lyndon B. Johnson	Democratic
1969–1974	Richard M. Nixon	Republican
1974–1977	Gerald R. Ford	Republican
1977–1981	Jimmy Carter	Democratic
1981–1989	Ronald W. Reagan	Republican
1989–1993	George H. W. Bush	Republican
1993–2001	William Jefferson Clinton	Democratic
2001–2009	George W. Bush	Republican

Major U.S. Supreme Court Decisions Through Women's Eyes

Tʜᴇ ꜰᴏʟʟᴏᴡɪɴɢ ʙʀɪᴇꜰ ᴇxᴄᴇʀᴘᴛꜱ of Supreme Court decisions, carefully abridged from the full opinions delivered by the Court, have been selected for their particular importance to the history of women in the United States. Not all of them deal solely or primarily with gender discrimination. Those decisions concerning racism and the legacy of slavery, beginning with the 1856 *Dred Scott* case, have profound implications for women. Read one after another, these decisions give evidence of both the continuity of judicial reasoning and the dramatic shifts in judicial conclusions that have characterized the nation's highest court.

Dred Scott v. Sandford involved a slave couple who claimed they had gained freedom by virtue of residence for many years on free soil. The case took almost ten years to arrive before the Court, where a seven-to-two majority ruled that the Scotts remained slaves. In his last major opinion, Chief Justice Roger Taney not only dismissed the Scotts' claims, but he sought to intervene in the raging national political debate over slavery by declaring that any federal intervention in slavery, including the 1820 Missouri Compromise (which had banned slavery from the territories in which the Scotts had lived), was unconstitutional.

Dred Scott v. Sandford (1856)

It is difficult at this day to realize the state of public opinion in relation to that unfortunate race, which prevailed in the civilized and enlightened portions of the world at the time of the Declaration of Independence, and when the Constitution of the United States was framed and adopted. . . .

They had for more than a century before been regarded as beings of an inferior order, and altogether unfit to associate with the white race, either in social or political relations; and so far inferior, that they had no rights which the white man was bound to respect; and that the negro might justly and lawfully be reduced to slavery for his benefit. . . . We refer to these historical facts for the purpose of showing the fixed opinions concerning that race, upon which the statesmen of that day spoke and acted. It is necessary to do this, in order to determine whether the general terms used in the Constitution of the United States, as to the rights of man and the rights of the people, was intended to include them, or to give to them or their posterity the benefit of any of its provisions.

[T]he right of property in a slave is distinctly and expressly affirmed in the Constitution. . . . This is done in plain words—too plain to be misunderstood. And no word can be found in the Constitution which gives Congress a greater power over slave property, or which entitles property of that kind to less protection than property of any other description. . . .

Upon these considerations, it is the opinion of the court that the act of Congress which prohibited a citizen from holding and owning property of this kind in the territory of the United States north of the line therein mentioned, is not warranted by the Constitution, and is therefore void; and that neither Dred Scott himself, nor any of his family, were made free by being carried into this territory.

THE FOURTEENTH AMENDMENT, which was designed to overturn the *Dred Scott* decision by defining national citizenship broadly enough to include the ex-slaves, became the constitutional basis for challenging both race and gender discrimination. Soon after its ratification in 1868, woman suffragists saw the amendment as a potential resource. The National Woman Suffrage Association contended that, inasmuch as women were citizens, their rights as voters were automatically secured. Accordingly, Virginia Minor tried to vote in her hometown of St. Louis, Missouri, and then sued the local election official who refused her ballot. Chief Justice Morrison Waite delivered the Court's unanimous opinion that although the Fourteenth Amendment did indeed grant women equal citizenship with men, it did not make them voters. His contention, that suffrage was not a civil right but a political privilege outside the amendment's intended scope, was underscored by the passage of the Fifteenth Amendment in 1870, which was addressed explicitly to voting. Waite's reasoning applied to all citizens, not just women. After the *Minor* decision, suffragists realized they needed a separate constitutional amendment to secure women's political rights.

Minor v. Happersett (1874)

The argument is, that as a woman, born or naturalized in the United States and subject to the jurisdiction thereof, is a citizen of the United States and of the State in which she resides, she has the right of suffrage as one of the privileges and immunities of her citizenship, which the State cannot by its laws or constitution abridge.

There is no doubt that women may be citizens. They are persons, and by the fourteenth amendment "all persons born or naturalized in the United States and subject to the jurisdiction thereof" are expressly declared to be "citizens of the United States and of the State wherein they reside." . . .

If the right of suffrage is one of the necessary privileges of a citizen of the United States, then the constitution and laws of Missouri confining it to men are in violation of the Constitution of the United States, as amended, and consequently void. . . . It is clear, . . . we think, that the Constitution has not added the right of suffrage to the privileges and immunities of citizenship as they existed at the time it was adopted.

It is true that the United States guarantees to every State a republican form of government. . . . No particular government is designated as republican, neither is the exact form to be guaranteed, in any manner especially designated. . . .

[I]t is certainly now too late to contend that a government is not republican, within the meaning of this guaranty in the Constitution, because women are not made voters.

INVOKING THE FOURTEENTH AMENDMENT three decades later, Homer Plessy argued that he had been denied equal protection of the law when a Louisiana statute forced him to travel in a separate all-black railroad car. By a vote of eight to one, the Court ruled against his claims and found the emerging system of state-sponsored racial segregation that was settling on the postslavery South to be fully constitutional. Writing for the majority, Justice Henry Brown argued that because a system of segregation affected both black and white, it was not discriminatory. The famous phrase by which this argument has come to be known — "separate but equal" — appears in the brave, dissenting opinion of Justice John Harlan. Note how the Court's ruling treats racial distinction and black inferiority as facts of nature that any legal decision must recognize.

Plessy v. Ferguson (1896)

A statute which implies merely a legal distinction between the white and colored races — a distinction which is founded in the color of the two races, and which must always exist so long as white men are distinguished from the other race by color — has no tendency to destroy the legal equality of the two races. . . .

The object of the [fourteenth] amendment was undoubtedly to enforce the absolute equality of the two races before the law, but, in the nature of things, it could not have been intended to abolish distinctions based upon color, or to enforce social, as distinguished from political, equality, or a commingling of the two races upon terms unsatisfactory to either. Laws permitting, and even requiring, their separation, in places where they are liable to be brought into contact, do not necessarily imply the inferiority of either race to the other. . . .

We consider the underlying fallacy of the plaintiff's argument to consist in the assumption that the enforced separation of the two races stamps the colored race with a badge of inferiority. If this be so, it is not by reason of anything found in the act, but solely because the colored race chooses to put that construction upon it. The argument necessarily assumes that if, as has been more than once the case, and is not unlikely to be so again, the colored race should become the dominant power in the state legislature, and should enact a law in precisely similar terms, it would thereby relegate the white race to an inferior position. We imagine that the white race, at least, would not acquiesce in this assumption. The argument also assumes that social prejudices may be overcome by legislation, and that equal rights cannot be secured to the negro except by an enforced commingling of the two races. We cannot accept this proposition. . . . Legislation is powerless to eradicate racial instincts, or to abolish distinctions based upon physical differences, and the attempt to do so can only result in accentuating the difficulties of the present situation.

IN *MULLER V. OREGON*, Curt Muller challenged the constitutionality of an Oregon law setting a maximum ten-hour working day for women employees. Starting in the 1880s, the Court had turned away from the Fourteenth Amendment's original purposes to emphasize its guarantee of the individual's right of contract in the workplace, free from state regulation. This reading made most laws setting limits on the working day unconstitutional. Arguing on behalf of Oregon, Louis Brandeis, lead counsel for the National Consumers' League, successfully pressed an argument for the law's constitutionality on the ground that it was directed only at women. Brandeis's argument circumvented the Fourteenth Amendment by contending that the federal government's constitutionally authorized police power, which permitted special regulations for the national good, allowed legislation to protect motherhood and through it "the [human] race." The Court ruled unanimously to uphold the Oregon law, with Justice David Brewer delivering the opinion. As in the *Plessy* decision, the Court held that physical difference and even inferiority are facts of nature that the law may accommodate and that are compatible with formal legal equality. Yet the decision here was hailed by many women reformers as a great victory. Brandeis was appointed to the Supreme Court in 1916, the first Jewish member of the Court.

Muller v. Oregon (1908)

We held in *Lochner v. New York* [1903] that a law providing that no laborer shall be required or permitted to work in bakeries more than sixty hours in a week or ten hours in a day was not as to men a legitimate exercise of the police power of the state, but an unreasonable, unnecessary, and arbitrary interference with the right and liberty of the individual to contract in relation to his labor, and as such was in conflict with, and void under, the Federal Constitution. That decision is invoked by plaintiff in error as decisive of the question before us. But this assumes that the difference between the sexes does not justify a different rule respecting a restriction of the hours of labor. . . .

That woman's physical structure and the performance of maternal functions place her at a disadvantage in the struggle for subsistence is obvious. This is especially true when the burdens of motherhood are upon her. Even when they are not, . . . continuance for a long time on her feet at work, repeating this from day to day, tends to in-

jurious effects upon the body, and, as healthy mothers are essential to vigorous offspring, the physical well-being of woman becomes an object of public interest and care in order to preserve the strength and vigor of the race. . . .

Even though all restrictions on political, personal, and contractual rights were taken away, and [woman] stood, so far as statutes are concerned, upon an absolutely equal plane with [man], it would still be true that she is so constituted that she will rest upon and look to him for protection; that her physical structure and a proper discharge of her maternal functions—having in view not merely her own health, but the well-being of the race—justify legislation to protect her from the greed as well as the passion of man. The limitations which this statute places upon her contractual powers, upon her right to agree with her employer as to the time she shall labor, are not imposed solely for her benefit, but also largely for the benefit of all.

THE IRONY OF THE *MULLER* DECISION in favor of maximum hours laws to benefit women workers on the basis of their maternal dependency is underlined by the *Adkins* case, decided fifteen years later. *Adkins v. Children's Hospital* involved a congressionally authorized procedure for setting minimum wages for women workers in the District of Columbia. Writing for a five-to-three majority (Justice Brandeis had recused himself from the case), Justice George Sutherland found the maximum hours law unconstitutional on two major grounds. First, while minimum hours laws were constitutionally sanctioned public health measures, maximum wage laws were unacceptable restraints on free trade. Second, the ratification of the Nineteenth Amendment granting woman suffrage in the years since the *Muller* decision made protections of women on the basis of their need to be sheltered by men outdated. Thus, whereas in the earlier case the Court used an appeal to nature to sustain special labor laws that benefited women, in *Adkins,* the Court relied on an evolutionary approach to overturn such regulations.

Adkins v. Children's Hospital (1923)

In the *Muller* case, the validity of an Oregon statute, forbidding the employment of any female in certain industries more than ten hours during anyone day was upheld. . . . But the ancient inequality of the sexes, otherwise than physical, as suggested in the *Muller* case has continued "with diminishing intensity." In view of the great—not to say revolutionary—changes which have taken place since that utterance, in the contractual, political and civil status of women, culminating in the Nineteenth Amendment, it is not unreasonable to say that these differences have now come almost, if not quite, to the vanishing point. . . .

[W]e cannot accept the doctrine that women of mature age, *sui juris* [able to act on their own behalf legally], require or may be subjected to restrictions upon their liberty of contract which could not lawfully be imposed in the case of men under similar circumstances. To do so would be to ignore all the implications to be drawn from the present day trend of legislation, as well as that of common thought and usage, by which woman is accorded emancipation from the old doctrine that she must be given special protection or be subjected to special restraint in her contractual and civil relationships.

I N THE WATERSHED CASE of *Brown v. Board of Education of Topeka,* the Supreme Court reversed its 1896 *Plessy v. Ferguson* decision to find state-sponsored racial segregation a violation of the Fourteenth Amendment guarantee of equal protection of the laws. The unanimous ruling was written by Earl Warren, newly appointed chief justice. Linda Brown was the plaintiff in one of several cases that the court consolidated, all of which challenged the constitutionality of racially segregated public schools. The case bears certain similarities to *Muller v. Oregon.* Both made use of sociological evidence, with *Brown* relying on research into the negative impact of segregation on young black children. Also as in *Muller,* the successful lead counsel in the *Brown* decision, NAACP lawyer Thurgood Marshall, ultimately was appointed to the Supreme Court, where he became the first African American justice.

Brown v. Board of Education of Topeka (1954)

The plaintiffs contend that segregated public schools are not "equal" and cannot be made "equal," and that hence they are deprived of the equal protection of the laws. . . .

Does segregation of children in public schools solely on the basis of race, even though the physical facilities and other "tangible" factors may be equal, deprive the children of the minority group of equal educational opportunities? We believe that it does. . . .

To separate them from others of similar age and qualifications solely because of their race generates a feeling of inferiority as to their status in the community that may affect their hearts and minds in a way unlikely ever to be undone. . . .

We conclude that, in the field of public education, the doctrine of "separate but equal" has no place. Separate educational facilities are inherently unequal. . . .

Because these are class actions, because of the wide applicability of this decision, and because of the great variety of local conditions, the formulation of decrees in these cases presents problems of considerable complexity.

E STELLE GRISWOLD, executive director of the Planned Parenthood Federation of Connecticut, was arrested for providing a married couple with birth control instruction in violation of an 1879 state law forbidding any aid given "for the purpose of preventing conception." Writing for a seven-to-two majority, Justice William O. Douglas held the law unconstitutional, developing an innovative argument for the existence of a "zone of privacy" not specifically enumerated in the Constitution but found in the surrounding "penumbra" of specified rights. Note Douglas's lofty language about the nature of marriage.

Griswold v. Connecticut (1965)

This law . . . operates directly on an intimate relation of husband and wife and their physician's role in one aspect of that relation. . . .

[S]pecific guarantees in the Bill of Rights have penumbras, formed by emanations from those guarantees that help give them life and substance. . . . Various guarantees create zones of privacy. The right of association contained in the penumbra of the First Amendment is one, as we have seen. . . . The Ninth Amendment provides: "The enumeration in the Constitution, of certain rights, shall not be construed to deny or disparage others retained by the people." . . .

The present case, then, concerns a relationship lying within the zone of privacy created by several fundamental constitutional guarantees. And it concerns a law which, in forbidding the use of contraceptives rather than regulating their manufacture or sale, seeks to achieve its goals by means having a maximum destructive impact upon that relationship. Such a law cannot stand in light of the familiar principle, so often applied by this Court, that a "governmental purpose to control or prevent activities constitutionally subject to state regulation may not be achieved by means which sweep unnecessarily broadly and thereby invade the area of protected freedoms." . . .

We deal with a right of privacy older than the Bill of Rights—older than our political parties, older than our school system. Marriage is a coming together for better or for worse, hopefully enduring, and intimate to the degree of being sacred. It is an association that promotes a way of life, not causes; a harmony in living, not political faiths; a bilateral loyalty, not commercial or social projects.

LIKE THE *GRISWOLD* CASE two years earlier, *Loving v. Virginia* concerns the marriage relationship and government intrusion into it. Richard Loving was a white man who married Mildred Jeter, a black woman, in 1958 in Washington, D.C. When they moved to Virginia a year later, they were found guilty in state court of violating a 1924 Virginia law forbidding white people from marrying outside of their race, a crime known as "miscegenation." They appealed their conviction to the U.S. Supreme Court. Speaking for a unanimous Court, Chief Justice Earl Warren found this and similar laws in fifteen other states unconstitutional under the Fourteenth Amendment. The court's rejection of the argument that antimiscegenation laws were constitutionally acceptable because they rested equally on all races echoes the logic of its ruling in *Brown v. Board of Education,* in which intent to discriminate is crucial despite the superficially neutral language of the law.

Loving v. Virginia (1967)

This case presents a constitutional question never addressed by this Court: whether a statutory scheme adopted by the State of Virginia to prevent marriages between persons solely on the basis of racial classifications violates the Equal Protection and Due Process Clauses of the Fourteenth Amendment. . . .

In upholding the constitutionality of these provisions, . . . the state court concluded that the State's legitimate purposes were "to preserve the racial integrity of its citizens," and to prevent "the corruption of blood," "a mongrel breed of citizens," and "the obliteration of racial pride," obviously an endorsement of the doctrine of White Supremacy. . . . [T]he fact of equal application does not immunize the statute from the very heavy burden of justification which the Fourteenth Amendment has traditionally required of state statutes drawn according to race. . . .

Over the years, this Court has consistently repudiated "distinctions between citizens solely because of their ancestry" as being "odious to a free people whose institutions are founded upon the doctrine of equality." At the very least, the Equal Protection Clause demands that racial classifications, especially suspect in criminal statutes, be subjected to the "most rigid scrutiny." . . .

Marriage is one of the "basic civil rights of man," fundamental to our very existence and survival. . . . Under our Constitution, the freedom to marry, or not marry, a person of another race resides with the individual and cannot be infringed by the State.

THE *REED V. REED* CASE involved the mother of a deceased child contesting an Idaho law mandating that preference be given to the father in designating an executor for a dead child's estate. Sally Reed's case was argued by then American Civil Liberties Union lawyer Ruth Bader Ginsburg. Ginsburg revived elements of the argument made in the 1874 *Minor* case, that the Fourteenth Amendment's guarantees of equal protection before the law applied in cases of discrimination against women. This time the Court accepted the argument. The unanimous opinion was written by Chief Justice Warren Burger. Like Brandeis and Marshall, Ginsburg was later a pathbreaking appointee to the Supreme Court, the second woman (after Sandra Day O'Connor) to serve.

Reed v. Reed (1971)

[W]e have concluded that the arbitrary preference established in favor of males by . . . the Idaho Code cannot stand in the face of the Fourteenth Amendment's command that no State deny the equal protection of the laws to any person within its jurisdiction.

In applying that clause, this Court has consistently recognized that the Fourteenth Amendment does not deny to States the power to treat different classes of persons in different ways. . . . The Equal Protection Clause of that amendment does, however, deny to States the power to legislate that different treatment be accorded to persons placed by a statute into different classes on the basis of criteria wholly unrelated to the objective of that statute. A classification must be reasonable, not arbitrary, and must rest upon some ground of difference having a fair and substantial relation to the object of the legislation, so that all persons similarly circumstanced shall be treated alike.

JANE ROE WAS THE PSEUDONYM of Norma McCorvey, an unmarried pregnant woman whose name headed up a class action suit challenging an 1879 Texas law criminalizing abortion. In *Roe v. Wade,* the Court ruled seven to two in Roe's favor. Justice Harry Blackmun wrote the lead opinion, relying on the concept of privacy developed in the *Griswold* case. His opinion included a detailed history of laws prohibiting abortion to show that these were of relatively recent vintage, an approach that contrasted with the antihistorical arguments of nineteenth-century cases such as *Dred Scott* and *Minor v. Happersett.* The *Roe* decision very carefully avoids declaring that a woman's right to abortion is absolute. The limits placed on women's choice—consultation with a physician, government interest in fetal life in the third trimester—opened the way for attempts to reinstitute limits on abortion.

Roe v. Wade (1973)

We forthwith acknowledge our awareness of the sensitive and emotional nature of the abortion controversy. . . . One's philosophy, one's experiences, one's exposure to the raw edges of human existence, one's religious training, one's attitudes toward life and family and their values, and the moral standards one establishes and seeks to observe, are all likely to influence and to color one's thinking and conclusions about abortion.

In addition, population growth, pollution, poverty, and racial overtones tend to complicate and not to simplify the problem. . . .

The Constitution does not explicitly mention any right of privacy. In a line of decisions, however, . . . the Court has recognized that a right of personal privacy, or a guarantee of certain areas or zones of privacy, does exist under the Constitution. . . .

This right of privacy . . . is broad enough to encompass a woman's decision whether or not to terminate her pregnancy. The detriment that the State would impose upon the pregnant woman by denying this choice altogether is apparent. Specific and direct harm medically diagnosable even in early pregnancy may be involved. Maternity, or additional offspring, may force upon the woman a distressful life and future.

Psychological harm may be imminent. Mental and physical health may be taxed by child care. There is also the distress, for all concerned, associated with the unwanted child, and there is the problem of bringing a child into a family already unable, psychologically and otherwise, to care for it. In other cases, as in this one, the additional difficulties and continuing stigma of unwed motherhood may be involved.

[A]ppellant [in this case Jane Roe] . . . [argues] that the woman's right is absolute and that she is entitled to terminate her pregnancy at whatever time, in whatever way, and for whatever reason she alone chooses. With this we do not agree. . . . [A] State may properly assert important interests in safeguarding health, in maintaining medical standards, and in protecting potential life. At some point in pregnancy, these respective interests become sufficiently compelling to sustain regulation of the factors that govern the abortion decision. The privacy right involved, therefore, cannot be said to be absolute. . . .

The appellee . . . argue[s] that the fetus is a "person" within the language and meaning of the Fourteenth Amendment. . . . If this suggestion of personhood is established, the appellant's case, of course, collapses, for the fetus' right to life would then be guaranteed specifically by the Amendment. . . .

The Constitution does not define "person" in so many words. . . . [T]he word "person," as used in the Fourteenth Amendment, does not include the unborn.

In view of all this, we do not agree that, by adopting one theory of life, Texas may override the rights of the pregnant woman that are at stake. We repeat, however, that the State does have an important and legitimate interest in preserving and protecting the health of the pregnant woman, . . . and that it has still *another* important and legitimate interest in protecting the potentiality of human life. . . .

With respect to the State's important and legitimate interest in the health of the mother, the "compelling" point, in the light of present medical knowledge, is at . . . the end of the first trimester. . . . [F]rom and after this point, a State may regulate the abortion procedure to the extent that the regulation reasonably relates to the preservation and protection of maternal health. Examples of permissible state regulation in this area are requirements as to the qualifications of the person who is to perform the abortion; as to the licensure of that person; as to the facility in which the procedure is to be performed. . . .

[T]he attending physician, in consultation with his patient, is free to determine, without regulation by the State, that, in his medical judgment, the patient's pregnancy should be terminated. If that decision is reached, the judgment may be effectuated by an abortion free of interference by the State.

With respect to the State's important and legitimate interest in potential life, the "compelling"

point is at viability. This is so because the fetus then presumably has the capability of meaningful life outside the mother's womb. State regulation protective of fetal life after viability thus has both logical and biological justifications.

AFFIRMATIVE ACTION PROGRAMS were initially developed in the 1960s to aid African Americans to achieve greater educational and economic opportunity. President Richard Nixon urged them as a moderate response to the demands of militant civil rights activists. Nonetheless, these programs came under fire. In 1976, Allan Bakke, a white man, filed suit when his application for admission was rejected by the University of California at Davis Medical School. He argued that affirmative was the problem. His claim, based on the Fourteenth Amendment, became known as the "reverse discrimination" argument. The Court was sharply divided, four justices believing that Bakke was the victim of reverse discrimination, four justices believing that the Davis Medical School's affirmative action policy offered a reasonable approach to eradicating the effects of a long history of racial injustice. Justice Lewis Powell forged a five-to-four majority by writing an opinion that took both positions into account. An educational affirmative action plan premised on the goal of racial diversity could be constitutional if the system used was less rigid, less "quota"-like, than that of the Davis Medical School. The Court ordered Bakke admitted to the university's medical school.

University of California Regents v. Bakke (1978)

The Medical School of the University of California at Davis (hereinafter Davis) had two admissions programs for the entering class of 100 students—the regular admissions program and the special admissions program.... A separate committee, a majority of whom were members of minority groups, operated the special admissions program. The 1973 and 1974 application forms, respectively, asked candidates whether they wished to be considered as "economically and/or educationally disadvantaged" applicants and members of a "minority group" (blacks, Chicanos, Asians, American Indians).... Special candidates, however, did not have to meet the 2.5 grade point cutoff and were not ranked against candidates in the general

admissions process.... Without passing on the state constitutional or federal statutory grounds the [lower] court held that petitioner's special admissions program violated the [Fourteenth Amendment] Equal Protection Clause.... Racial and ethnic classifications of any sort are inherently suspect and call for the most exacting judicial scrutiny. While the goal of achieving a diverse student body is sufficiently compelling to justify consideration of race in admissions decisions under some circumstances, petitioner's special admissions program, which forecloses consideration to persons like respondent, is unnecessary to the achievement of this compelling goal and therefore invalid under the Equal Protection Clause.

A SERIES OF CASES followed *Roe v. Wade* that both upheld and limited a woman's right to seek an abortion. The plaintiff in *Webster v. Reproductive Health Services* was attorney general for the State of Missouri, appealing a lower court ruling that found restrictions on a woman's right to abortion unconstitutional, including the requirement that a woman seeking a second- or third-trimester abortion must have a test to make sure that the fetus was not viable (could not live outside the womb). The lower court ruled that the law violated the Supreme Court's *Roe v. Wade* decision. The Supreme Court overturned this ruling. Chief Justice William Rehnquist wrote for the five-to-three majority that, while the *Roe* decision had recognized the state's obligation to protect potential life, it had been too rigid in establishing the point at which this became paramount. From Rehnquist's perspective, it was permissible for the state to act to favor childbirth even while preserving the woman's formal right to abortion.

Webster v. Reproductive Health Services (1989)

In *Roe v. Wade,* the Court recognized that the State has "important and legitimate" interests in protecting maternal health and in the potentiality of human life. During the second trimester, the State "may, if it chooses, regulate the abortion procedure in ways that are reasonably related to maternal health." ...

[But] the rigid trimester analysis of the course of a pregnancy enunciated in *Roe* has resulted in ... making constitutional law in this area a virtual Procrustean bed. ... [T]he rigid *Roe* framework is hardly consistent with the notion of a Constitution cast in general terms, as ours is, and usually speaking in general principles, as ours does. ...

[W]e do not see why the State's interest in protecting potential human life should come into existence only at the point of viability, and that there should therefore be a rigid line allowing state regulation after viability but prohibiting it before viability. ... [W]e are satisfied that the requirement of these tests permissibly furthers the State's interest in protecting potential human life, and we therefore believe [the article] to be constitutional.

Both appellants and the United States as *amicus curiae* [filing a brief sympathetic to the parties that appealed the decision] have urged that we overrule our decision in *Roe v. Wade.* The facts of the present case, however, differ from those at issue in *Roe.* Here, Missouri has determined that viability is the point at which its interest in potential human life must be safeguarded. ... This case therefore affords us no occasion to revisit the holding of *Roe.*

Table 1
Female Population of the United States by Race, 1790–2000

	Number of Women				Percent Distribution		
Year	Total	White	Black	Other Races	White	Black	Other Races
1790	n/a	1,556,572	n/a	n/a	n/a	n/a	n/a
1800	–	2,111,141	—	—	—	—	—
1810	–	2,873,943	—	—	—	—	—
1820	4,741,848	3,870,988	870,860	—	81.6	18.4	—
1830	6,333,531	5,171,165	1,162,366	—	81.6	18.4	—
1840	8,380,921	6,940,261	1,440,660	—	82.8	17.2	—
1850	11,354,216	9,526,666	1,827,550	—	83.9	16.1	—
1860	15,358,117	13,111,150	2,225,086	21,881	85.4	14.5	0.1
1870	19,064,806	16,560,289	2,486,746	17,771	86.9	13.0	0.1
1880	24,636,963	21,272,070	3,327,678	37,215	86.3	13.5	0.2
1890	30,710,613	26,830,879	3,753,073	126,661	87.4	12.2	0.4
1900	37,243,479	32,622,949	4,447,539	172,991	87.6	11.9	0.5
1910	44,727,298	39,579,044	4,942,228	206,026	88.5	11.0	0.5
1920	51,935,452	46,421,794	5,253,890	259,768	89.4	10.1	0.5
1930	60,807,176	54,404,615	6,035,789	366,772	89.5	9.9	0.6
1940	65,815,399	58,819,215	6,596,652	399,532	89.4	10.0	0.6
1950	76,139,192	67,894,638	7,744,182	500,372	89.2	10.2	0.7
1960	90,991,681	80,464,583	9,758,423	768,675	88.4	10.7	0.8
1970	104,299,734	91,027,988	11,831,973	1,439,773	87.3	11.3	1.4
1980	116,492,644	96,686,289	13,975,836	5,830,519	83.0	12.0	5.0
1990	127,470,455	102,210,190	15,815,909	9,444,356	80.2	12.4	7.4
2000	143,368,343	107,676,508	18,077,075	17,614,460	75.1	12.6	12.3

Source: Sandra Opdycke, *The Routledge Historical Atlas of Women in America* (New York: Routledge, 2000), p. 130; U.S. Census Bureau, *Statistical Abstract of the United States, 2001* (Washington: GPO, 2001).

Chart 1
U.S. Birthrate, 1820–2000

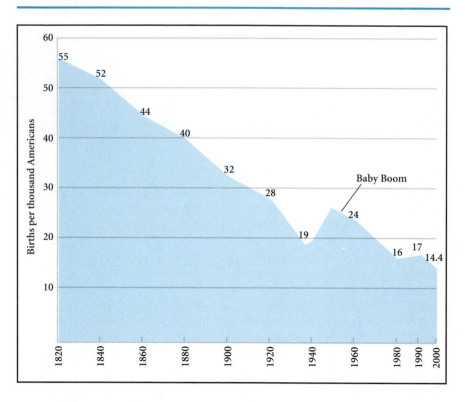

Source: Data from *Historical Statistics of the United States, Colonial Times to 1970* (1975); U.S. Census Bureau, *Statistical Abstract of the United States, 2001* (Washington: GPO, 2001).

Table 2
U.S. Women and Work, 1820–2000

Year	Percentage of Women in Paid Employment	Percentage of Paid Workers Who Are Women
1820	6.2	7.3
1830	6.4	7.4
1840	8.4	9.6
1850	10.1	10.8
1860	9.7	10.2
1870	13.7	14.8
1880	14.7	15.2
1890	18.2	17.0
1900	21.2	18.1
1910	24.8	20.0
1920	23.9	20.4
1930	24.4	21.9
1940	25.4	24.6
1950	29.1	27.8
1960	34.8	32.3
1970	43.3	38.0
1980	51.5	42.6
1990	57.4	45.2
2000	60.2	46.5

Source: U.S. Census Bureau, *Historical Statistics of the United States, Colonial Times to 1970* (Washington: GPO, 1975); *Statistical Abstract of the United States, 2002* (Washington: GPO, 2002).

Table 3
Percentage of Women in the U.S. Labor Force, by Family Status, 1890–2000

	Total Female Labor Force				Participation Rate in the Female Labor Force			
Year	Single	Widowed/ Divorced	Married	Mothers*	Single	Widowed/ Divorced	Married	Mothers*
1890	68	18	14	—	41	30	5	—
1900	67	18	15	—	41	33	6	—
1910	61	15	24	—	48	35	11	—
1920	77[†]	—[†]	23	—	44[†]	—[†]	9	—
1930	54	17	29	—	46	34	12	—
1940	49	15	36	11	48	32	17	28
1950	32	16	52	26	51	36	25	33
1960	23	6	61	27	44	13	32	37
1970	22	14	63	38	53	46	41	43
1980	26	19	55	40	64	44	50	56
1990	26	20	54	39	67	47	58	67
2000	27	20	53	39	69	61	49	73

*Mothers of children under age eighteen.

[†]Single women counted with widows and divorced women.

Sources: Lynn Weiner, *From Working Girl to Working Mother: The Female Labor Force in the United States, 1820–1980* (Chapel Hill: University of North Carolina, 1985), 6; Bureau of Labor Statistics, "Labor Force Participation Rates of Women by Presence and Age of Children, March 1980–2000," http://www.bls.gov/opub/rtaw/pdf/table06.pdf (accessed August 13, 2004).

Table 4
Occupational Distribution (in Percentages) of Working Women Ages Fourteen Years and Older, 1900–2000

	1900	1910	1920	1930	1940	1950	1960	1970	1980	1990	2000
Professional, Technical, and Kindred Workers	8.2	9.6	11.7	13.8	12.8	12.2	12.5	15.2	13.6	18.5	21.8
Managers, Officials, and Proprietors	1.4	2.0	2.2	0.7	3.3	4.3	0.6	3.5	7.2	11.1	14.3
Clerical and Kindred Workers	4.0	9.2	18.7	20.9	21.5	27.4	29.1	34.2	33.6	27.8	23.5
Sales Workers	4.3	5.1	6.3	6.8	7.4	8.6	7.8	7.3	11.3	13.1	13.0
Craftsmen, Foremen, and Kindred Workers	1.4	1.4	1.2	1.0	1.1	0.5	1.2	1.8	2.4	2.2	2.2
Operatives and Kindred Workers	23.8	22.9	20.2	17.4	19.5	20.0	16.2	14.9	10.1	8.0	6.4
Laborers	2.6	1.4	2.3	1.5	1.1	0.9	0.6	1.0	2.0	0.5	0.4
Private Household Workers	28.7	24.0	15.7	17.8	18.1	8.9	7.9	3.8	1.3	1.0	1.3
Service Workers (Not Household)	6.7	8.4	8.1	9.7	11.3	12.6	13.5	16.5	17.8	16.8	16.4
Farmers and Farm Managers	5.8	3.7	3.2	0.4	1.2	0.7	0.5	0.2	0.3	0.3	0.3
Farm Laborers	13.1	12.0	10.3	6.0	2.8	2.9	1.2	0.6	0.6	0.7	0.4

Source: U.S. Census Bureau, *Historical Statistics of the United States,* Part 1, table D, 182–232; *Statistical Abstract of the United States, 1985* (Washington, D.C.: GPO, 1984), table 673; 1991 (Washington, D.C.: GPO, 1991), table 652; 2000 (Washington, D.C.: GPO, 2001), table 593; "Employed Persons by Major Occupation, Sex, Race, and Hispanic Origin, Annual Averages, 1983–2002," Current Population Survey, Bureau of Labor Statistics.
Note: Data beginning in 1990 are not directly comparable with data for earlier years because of the introduction of a new occupational classification system.

Table 5
Immigration to the United States, 1900–2006

Years	Female Immigrants to the United States	Total Immigrants to the United States
1900–1909	2,492,336	8,202,388
1910–1919	2,215,582	6,347,156
1920–1929	1,881,923	4,295,510
1930–1939	386,659	699,375
1940–1949	454,291	856,608
1950–1959	1,341,404	2,499,286
1960–1969	1,786,441	3,213,749
1970–1979	2,299,713	4,366,001
1980–1989	3,224,661	6,332,218
1990–1999	4,740,896	9,782,093
2000–2006	3,857,135	7,018,463

Source: U.S. Census Bureau, *Historical Statistics of the United States, Colonial Times to 1970* (Washington: GPO, 1975), Series C 102–114; U.S. Department of Justice, *1978 Statistical Yearbook of the Immigration and Naturalization Service* (Washington: GPO, 1978), table 10; *1984 Statistical Yearbook of the Immigration and Naturalization Service* (Washington: GPO, 1987), table I M M 4.1; *1988 Statistical Yearbook of the Immigration and Naturalization Service* (Washington: GPO, 1989), table 11; *1994 Statistical Yearbook of the Immigration and Naturalization Service* (Washington: GPO, 2002), table 1; *2003 Statistical Yearbook of the Immigration and Naturalizaton Service* (Washington: GPO, 2004), table 6; *2004 Statistical Yearbook of the Immigration and Naturalization Service* (Washington: GPO, 2005), table 7; *2005 Statistical Yearbook of the Immigration and Naturalization Service* (Washington: GPO, 2006), table 8; and *2006 Statistical Yearbook of the Immigration and Naturalization Service* (Washington: GPO, 2007), table 9.

Table 6
Women in the U.S. Congress, 1918–2008

| Year | Number of Women | | | Percentage of Full Membership |
	Senate	House	Total	
1918	0	1	1	0.2
1922	1	3	4	0.8
1926	0	3	3	0.6
1930	0	9	9	1.7
1934	1	7	8	1.5
1938	2	6	8	1.5
1942	1	9	10	1.9
1946	0	11	11	2.1
1950	1	9	10	1.9
1954	2	11	13	2.4
1958	1	15	16	3.0
1962	2	18	20	3.8
1966	2	11	13	2.4
1970	1	10	11	2.1
1974	0	16	16	3.0
1978	2	18	20	3.7
1982	2	21	23	4.3
1986	2	23	25	4.7
1990	2	29	31	5.8
1994	7	47	54	10.1
1998	9	54	63	11.8
2000	9	57	66	13.0
2002	14	62	76	14.2
2004	14	60	74	13.8
2006	14	68	82	15.3
2008	16	71	87	16.3

Source: Sandra Opdycke, *The Routledge Historical Atlas of Women in America* (New York: Routledge, 2000), 133; Center for American Women and Politics, Rutgers University, http://www.rci.rutgers.edu/~cawp/Facts2.html (accessed on November 30, 2007).

Acknowledgments

Chapter 9

From *All for One* by Rose Schneiderman with Lucy Goldthwaite. Copyright © Paul S. Eriksson. Reprinted with permission of Paul Eriksson.

Chapter 10

"The Problem That Has No Name," from *The Feminine Mystique* by Betty Friedan. Copyright © 1983, 1974, 1973, 1963 by Betty Friedan. Used by permission of W. W. Norton & Company, Inc.

"Women in the Civil Rights Movement: Autobiographical Account" by Septima Clark, from *Ready from Within: Septima Clark and the Civil Rights Movement*, edited by Cynthia Stokes Brown. Copyright © by Africa World Press. Reprinted with permission of the publisher.

"Women in the Movement" by Casey Hayden and Mary King, from *Takin' It to the Streets: A Sixties Reader*. Copyright © 1995 Oxford University Press. Reprinted with permission of the authors.

"Fields of Blue" by Casey Hayden, from *Deep in Our Hearts: Nine White Women in the Freedom Movement*, by Constance Curry et al. Reprinted with permission of Casey Hayden.

Diane Nash Bevel, excerpt from *Voices of Freedom: An Oral History of the Civil Rights Movement from the 1950s through the 1980s*, by Henry Hampton and Steve Fayer. Copyright © 1990 by Henry Hampton. Used by permission of Bantam Books, a division of Random House, Inc.

"Mary Dora Jones" from *My Soul Is Rested* by Howell Raines. Copyright © 1977 Howell Raines. Used by permission of G. P. Putnam's Sons, a division of Penguin Group (USA) Inc.

Chapter 11

"Statement of Purpose," National Organization for Women. From *It Changed My Life: Writings on the Women's Movement* by Betty Friedan. Used with permission of Curtis Brown, Ltd., as agents for the author.

Chart, "Degrees Granted to Women, 1950–1980." From Sandra Opdycke, Mark C. Carnes, series editor, *The Routledge Historical Atlas of Women in America*. Copyright © 2000, Routledge Publishers. Used with permission.

"Letter to the Left," 1969, Ellen Willis, unpublished letter to *The Guardian*, author's personal collection. Reprinted with permission of Nona Willis Aronowitz.

"Statement, 1968," Third World Women's Alliance. Reprinted with permission of Duke University Library, Special Collections.

"New Voice of La Raza: Chicanas Speak Out" by Mirta Vidal. Originally published in *International Socialist Review*, October 1971. Reprinted with permission of Duke University Library, Special Collections.

"Who Is Saying Men Are the Enemy?" by Dana Densmore. Originally published in *No More Fun and Games: A Journal of Female Liberation* 4 (April 1970). Used with permission of Dana Densmore.

"The Woman Identified Woman," copyright © 1970 by Radicalesbians. Reprinted with permission of the Sallie Bingham Center for Women's History and Culture, Duke University.

"The Myth of the Vaginal Orgasm," by Anne Koedt. Reprinted with permission of the Sallie Bingham Center for Women's History and Culture, Duke University.

Chapter 12

"What's Wrong with 'Equal Rights' for Women." Published in *The Phyllis Schafly Report* 5, no. 7 (February 1972). Reprinted with permission of the author.

Susan Muaddi Darraj, excerpt from *Third World, Third Wave Feminism(s): The Evolution of Arab American Feminism* 2003. Reprinted with permission of the author.

INDEX

Gadol, Joan Kelly, 690
Gallegos, Blanca, 762
Garment industry. *See also* Textile
    industry
    globalization of, 778–79
    immigrants in, 409, 762
    labor laws and, 416–17
    Mexican American women in, 581,
        582(*v*)
    Puerto Rican women in, 599, 599(*i*)
    sewing machine and, 339
    strikes in, 460, 490–92(*v*)
    sweatshops in, 336, 339, 416, 436–37,
        436(*v*), 780, 780(*i*)
Garret, Mary, 376–77
Gault, Charlayne Hunter, 612
Gay marriage, 697, 752
Gay rights movement, 677, 697, 720, 736
Gender discrimination. *See also* Sex
        discrimination
    in civil rights movement, 616–17,
        619–20, 620–21(*b*)
    in employment, 528–31, 456–57,
        540–45, 548–59, 551, 601, 626
    in higher education, 690
    in military, 546–48, 547(*i*)
    New Deal and, 540–41, 542–45
    U.S. Constitution and, 326, 327,
        A-31(*d*)
    wages and, 754–55
Gender roles. *See also* Labor, sexual
        division of
    conservatives views of, 736
    double standard in, 734
    feminine mystique reinforcing, 597
    feminism on, 477, 678
    Gilded Age stereotypes of, 443–45,
        444(*v*)
    housework and, 724, 725–27(*d*)
    images of women on World War I
        posters and, 498–99, 499(*v*)
    immigrants and, 408, 441, 442(*v*), 761
    Native Americans and, 392
    in 1920s, 534
    in 1950s, 631-34(*v*)
    race and, 326, 327, 335–36
    sexual revolution in the 1960s and,
        671
    western expansion and, 392, 401–02

General Motors, 541
Gentlemen's Agreement, 406
Geronimo, 392
"Get Thee Behind Me, (Mrs.) Satan!"
        (cartoon), 350(*i*)
Ghost Dance, 393
GI Bill, 589
Gibson, Charles Dana, 445
Gibson girl, 445–46, 445(*v*)
Gibson, Mayme, 531
Gil, Dinora, 681
Gilded Age, 343–56, 379–84(*v*), 478
Gilman, Charlotte Perkins, 356, 478, 459
Ginsburg, Ruth Bader, 686, 687(*i*), 748
Glass ceiling, in women's employment,
        686–88, 754
Globalization, 735
    cultural implications of, 784
    labor and economic development
        and, 778–82, 779(*v*), 780(*v*),
        781(*v*)
    immigration and, 763, 782–84,
        782(*v*), 783(*v*)
    United Nations programs and,
        784–86
    world peace and, 786–87
Going to the Bath (McEnery), 479(*i*)
Goins, Irene, 487
Goldbergs, The (TV show), 637–38,
        638(*v*)
Goldman, Emma, 404, 415, 480, 483–84
    Living My Life, 405(*b*)
Gold rush, 401
Goldwater, Barry, 607, 736
Gompers, Samuel, 343, 460
Gordon, Kate, 472
Grange, 335, 400, 411
Great Depression, 535–45
    migrant mother image in, 520,
        535–37, 536(*i*)
    New Deal and, 539–45
    relief programs during, 542–44
    unemployment during, 535, 538–39
    women's reform network, 544,
        563–69(*d*)
    working women during, 538–39
Great Migration, 487–88, 509–11
Great Plains, settlers of, 397–400, 399(*i*)
Great Society, 694, 745

Green, Hetty Robinson, 346
Gregory, Samuel, 376
Griffiths, Martha, 666
Grimes, Billie, 788, 789(v)
Griswold v. Connecticut, A-29–A-30(d)
Groves, Ernest, 530
Guam, 419
Gulf War, First (1991), 790–91. *See* also
    Iraq; Operation Desert Storm

Haener, Dorothy, 667
Haley, Mary, 457
Hallock, Mary, 414(i)
Hamer, Fannie Lou, 616, 618, 617(i), 619,
    695
Hampton Institute, 373–75, 374(v)
Hanna, Kathleen, 772
    "Riot Grrrl Manifesto," 772–73(d)
Harlem Renaissance, 534–35
Harvard University, 758
Hawaii, 420–21
Hayden, Sandra ("Casey"), 617, 618, 620,
    651–52
    "Fields of Blue," excerpt, 641–52(d)
    "Women in the Movement,"
        620–21(b)
Hayden, Sophia, 355(i)
Hayes, Rutherford B., 342
Haymarket Square protest, 342–43
Health. *See* also Medicine
    feminist movement and, 691–94
Hearst, Phoebe Appleton, 402
Hernandez, Aileen, 667
Hester Street, Egg Stand (Austen), 384(v)
Heterodoxy (club), 503
Heterosexuality, 593
Higher education. *See* Colleges and
    universities
Highgate, Edmonia, 333
Hijas de Cuauhtémoc, 680
Hill, Anita, 746, 766
Hitler, Adolf, 545, 606
Hobby, Oveta Culp, 546
Homeownership, 589–90
Homestead Act (1862), 397, 399(i)
Homesteaders
    African American, 332
    immigrants and, 399(i)
    women as, 399–400

Homophobia, 743
Homosexuality, 546, 592–93, 721(d),
    751. *See* also Lesbianism
Homosocial relationships, 348–49,
    534
Honeymooners, The (TV show), 638,
    639(v)
Hospitals. *See* Medicine; Nursing
Household labor. *See* also Domestic
    workers
    feminism and equal responsibilities
        in, 697
Housekeeping, role of women in, 724,
    725–27(d)
Housewives
    advertising aimed at, 570–71, 571(v),
        631(v), 641–42(v)
    conservative views of, 737
    during Great Depression, 537–38
    immigrant women as, 408, 409–10
    leisure class and, 346
    in 1950s, 595–97
    sexual changes in 1920s and,
        531–34
    television and, 628–42(v)
    women's role as, 631(v), 641–42(v)
    working women and, 505–06(d)
    during World War II, 553–55
Howard University, 333, 372
Howe, Julia Ward, 350–51
Howe, Marie Jenney, 503
How the Other Half Lives (Riis), 434–35,
    438
Huerta, Dolores, 622(i), 622, 782
Hull House, 415–17, 427, 429
Human rights, 786
Humphrey, Hubert, 618
Hunter, Nan D., 743
Hunton, Addie, 525
Hurston, Zora Neale, 535
Hutchinson, Anne, 708

Ichikawa, Fusae, 429
Identity politics, 685, 743
ILGWU. *See* International Ladies
    Garment Workers Union
Illegal (undocumented) immigrants,
    762, 780, 783–84, 783(v)
I Love Lucy (TV show), 638–41, 640(v)

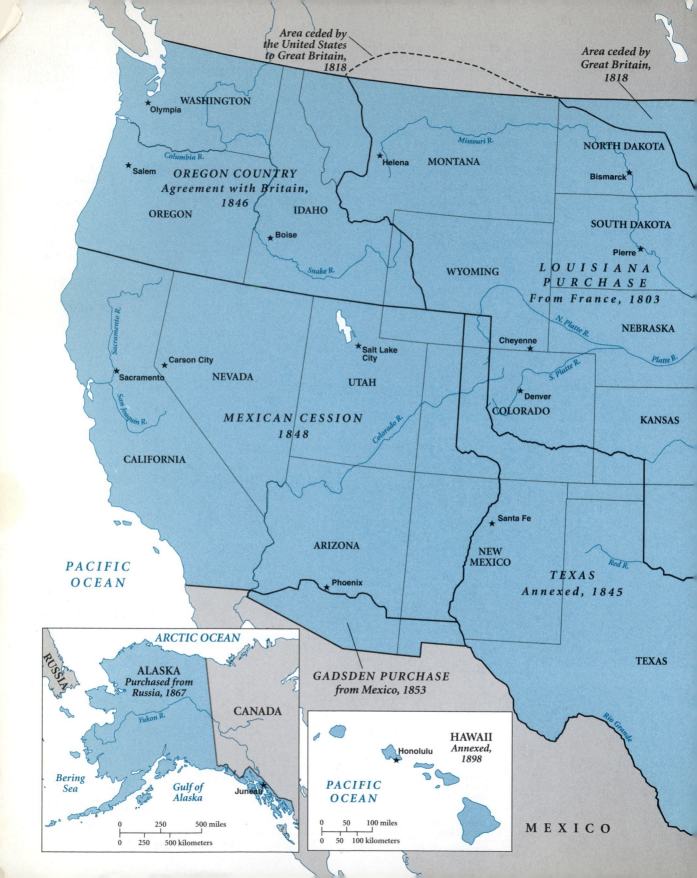

Area ceded by the United States to Great Britain, 1818

Area ceded by Great Britain, 1818

WASHINGTON
★ Olympia

Columbia R.

★ Salem
OREGON COUNTRY
Agreement with Britain, 1846
OREGON

IDAHO

★ Boise

Snake R.

★ Helena
MONTANA

Missouri R.

NORTH DAKOTA
Bismarck ★

SOUTH DAKOTA

Pierre ★

WYOMING

LOUISIANA
PURCHASE
From France, 1803

N. Platte R.

NEBRASKA

Sacramento R.

★ Carson City
★ Sacramento
NEVADA

San Joaquin R.

★ Salt Lake City

UTAH

Colorado R.

Cheyenne ★

S. Platte R.

★ Denver
COLORADO

Platte R.

KANSAS

MEXICAN CESSION
1848

CALIFORNIA

ARIZONA

★ Phoenix

★ Santa Fe

NEW
MEXICO

TEXAS
Annexed, 1845

Red R.

PACIFIC
OCEAN

GADSDEN PURCHASE
from Mexico, 1853

TEXAS

Rio Grande

MEXICO

ARCTIC OCEAN

RUSSIA

ALASKA
Purchased from Russia, 1867

CANADA

Yukon R.

Bering
Sea

Gulf of
Alaska

Juneau

| 0 | 250 | 500 miles |
| 0 | 250 | 500 kilometers |

HAWAII
Annexed, 1898

Honolulu ★

PACIFIC
OCEAN

| 0 | 50 | 100 miles |
| 0 | 50 | 100 kilometers |

Areas ceded by Britain, 1842
(Webster-Ashburton Treaty)

C A N A D A

Lake Superior

St. Lawrence R.

MAINE

★ Augusta

VERMONT

Montpelier ★

Lake Huron

Lake Ontario

NEW YORK

Connecticut R.

Concord ★ ——— N.H.

★ Boston

Albany ★

MASS.

Hudson R.

Providence

Hartford ★ ——— RHODE
ISLAND

CONNECTICUT

MINNESOTA

St. Paul ★

WISCONSIN

Lake Michigan

MICHIGAN

Lansing ★

Lake Erie

PENN.

★ Trenton ——— NEW JERSEY

Harrisburg ★

Susquehanna R.

Delaware R.

★ Dover ——— DELAWARE

IOWA

★ Madison

INDIANA

OHIO

★ Columbus

Indianapolis ★

WEST
VIRGINIA

Potomac R.

☆ Annapolis ——— MARYLAND
WASHINGTON, D.C.

*Chesapeake
Bay*

ILLINOIS

Springfield ★

Missouri R.

Des
Moines ★

Lincoln ★

Ohio R.

Frankfort ★

★ Charleston

★ Richmond

James R.

VIRGINIA

THE ORIGINAL THIRTEEN COLONIES

Proclamation Line of 1763

Topeka ★

Jefferson
City ★

MISSOURI

KENTUCKY

*Gained by treaty
with Britain, 1783*

Cumberland R.

NORTH
CAROLINA

Raleigh ★

Cape Fear R.

ATLANTIC
OCEAN

Oklahoma
City ★

ARKANSAS

TENNESSEE

Nashville ★

Tennessee R.

SOUTH
CAROLINA

Arkansas R.

OKLAHOMA

Little
Rock ★

Mississippi R.

Columbia ★

0   150   300 miles
0   150   300 kilometers

Austin ★

LOUISIANA

MISSISSIPPI

Jackson ★

ALABAMA

Montgomery ★

Atlanta ★

GEORGIA

Savannah R.

Baton
Rouge ★

Tallahassee ★

FLORIDA

*Areas taken
from Spain
in 1810, 1813*

*FLORIDA
Treaty with Spain,
1819*

Gulf of Mexico

U.S. Territories

*ATLANTIC
OCEAN*

San
Juan ★

*VIRGIN
ISLANDS
Acquired from
Denmark,
1916–1917*

*PUERTO RICO
Acquired from
Spain, 1898*

Caribbean Sea

0   50   100 miles
0   50   100 kilometers

BAHAMAS

CUBA

Book Companion Site for *Through Women's Eyes* at bedfordstmartins.com/duboisdumenil

The book companion site provides instructors and students with many resources for teaching and learning U.S. women's history.

A **new** Online Instructor's Resource Manual features teaching tips and lecture suggestions, TV/film suggestions, ideas for term papers and other assignments, tips on working with visual sources, revised multiple-choice quizzes as well as exam questions, questions focused on in-text documents and visuals, and PowerPoint chapter outlines. Also available is a set of questions for use with i>clicker, a classroom response system.

A **revised** Online Study Guide for students includes annotated chapter outlines, note-taking outlines, identification terms, and chapter focus questions.

Make History contains a wealth of relevant chapter-by-chapter resources for classroom use or further research, including maps, images, primary documents, and links to historical Web sites.

Online Research and Reference Aids

- Jules R. Benjamin's *A Student's Online Guide to History Reference Sources*
- *The Bedford Bibliographer*
- *The Bedford Research Room*
- Diana Hacker's *Research and Documentation Online*
- *The St. Martin's Tutorial on Avoiding Plagiarism* by Margaret Price

For more information, please visit **bedfordstmartins.com/duboisdumenil**